Mastering the Nil

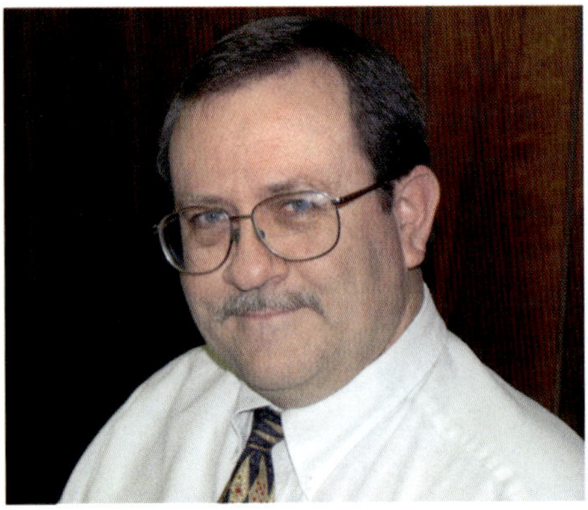

Darrell Young - Author

Darrell Young (*DigitalDarrell*) is an information technology engineer by trade and has been an avid photographer for over 35 years. He has a rather large family, with his wife and five children, so he has a constantly interesting flow of photographic opportunities. In fact, his entire family uses Nikon cameras to pursue what has become a cohesive family hobby.

Darrell delights in using Nikon's newest digital cameras but if pressed, he will admit to being a "closet" film user too. Living next to the Great Smoky Mountains National Park has given him a real concern for, and interest in, nature photography. Darrell loves to write, as you can see in the Resources area of the Nikonians.org community. He joined the community in the year 2000, and his literary contributions led to his invitation to become a Founding Member of the Nikonians Writers Guild.

Mastering the Nikon D5000

Darrell Young

rockynook
NikoniansPress

Darrell Young (aka Digital Darrell)

Editor (Rocky Nook): Gerhard Rossbach
Editor (Nikonians): Tom Bone´
Production editor: Joan Dixon
Copyeditor: Judy Flynn
Proof reader: Mark Hall
Layout and type: Jan Martí, Command Z
Cover design: Helmut Kraus, www.exclam.de
Printer: Lifetouch, Inc. through Four Colour Print Group, Louisville, Kentucky
Printed in USA

Cover photo: Nikon USA
Back cover photo: Gratien Jonxis

1st Edition

Rocky Nook Inc.
26 West Mission Street Ste 3
Santa Barbara, CA 93101-2432

Library of Congress Cataloging-in-Publication Data

Young, Darrell, 1958-
Mastering the Nikon D5000 / Darrell Young (aka Digital Darrell). -- 1st ed.
p. cm.
ISBN 978-1-933952-52-9 (alk. paper)
1. Nikon digital cameras--Handbooks, manuals, etc. 2. Single-lens reflex cameras--Handbooks, manuals, etc. 3. Photography--Digital techniques--Handbooks, manuals, etc. I. Title.
TR263.N5Y686 2009
771.3'2--dc22

2009041045

Distributed by O'Reilly Media
1005 Gravenstein Highway North
Sebastopol, CA 95472

This book is printed on acid-free paper.

This book is dedicated to:

My mother, Barbara, who birthed me ...

My father, Joe, who guided my early life ...

My wife, Brenda, who puts up with my grouchiness,
and feeds me while I'm at the keyboard ...

My kids, Autumn, David, Emily, Hannah, and Ethan
who see the back of Daddy's head often ...

My Nikonians editor, Tom Boné,
without whose assistance I could not possibly write books ...

My friends, J. Ramon Palacios and Bo Stahlbrandt,
who make it possible to belong to Nikonians.org,
the world's best Nikon User's Community ...

And, finally, to Nikon, who makes the world's best cameras and lenses.

Table of Contents

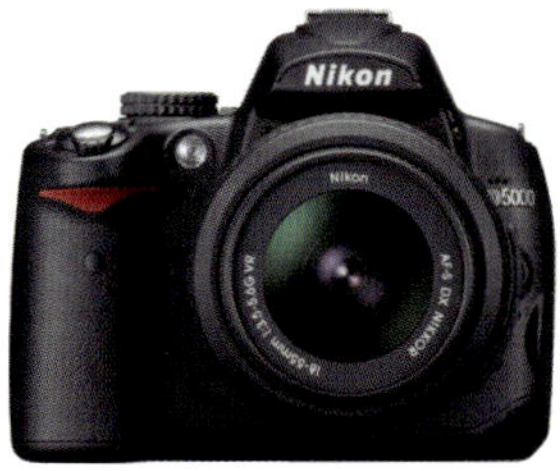

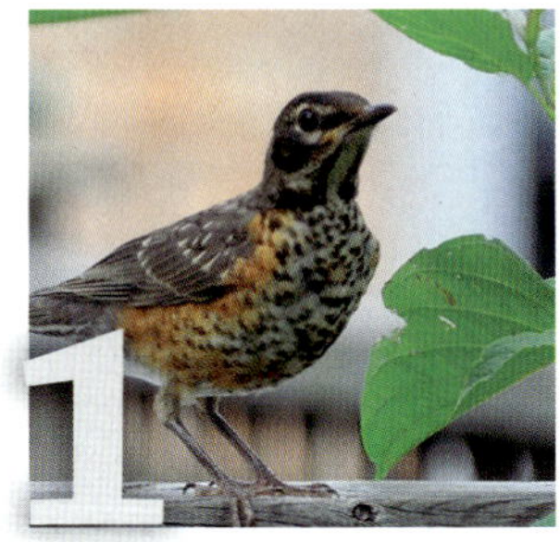

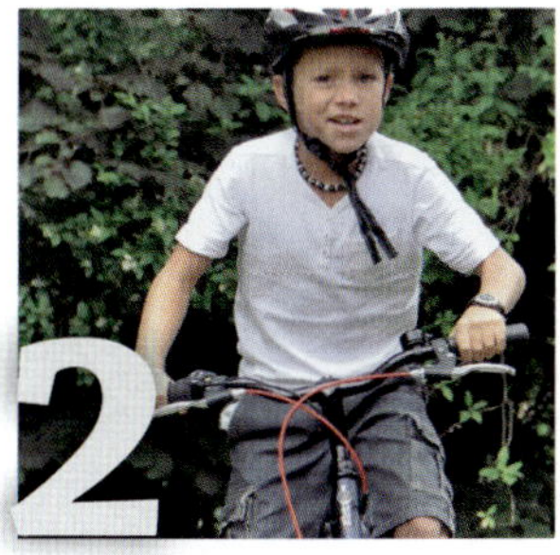

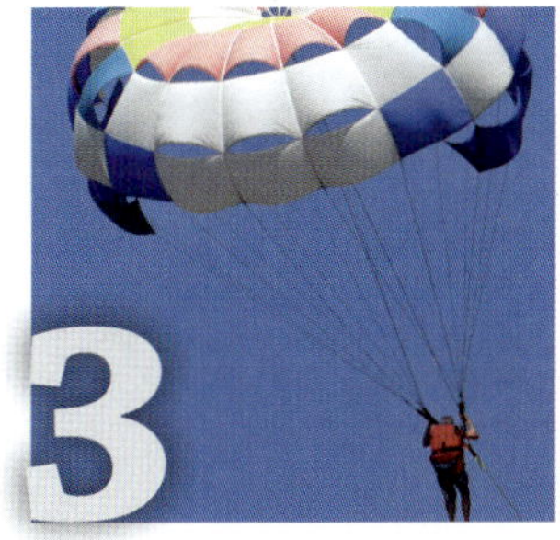

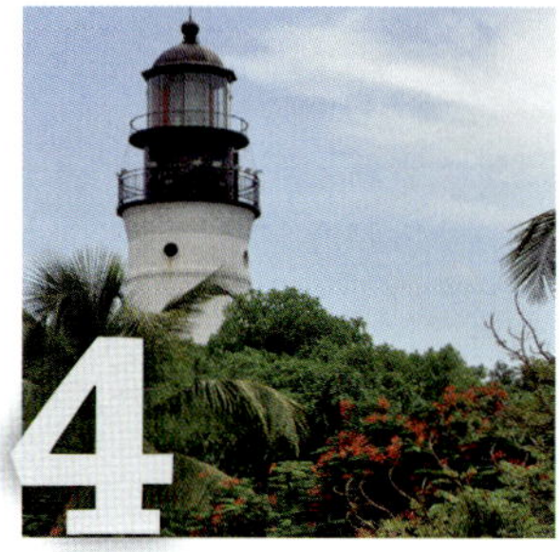
4

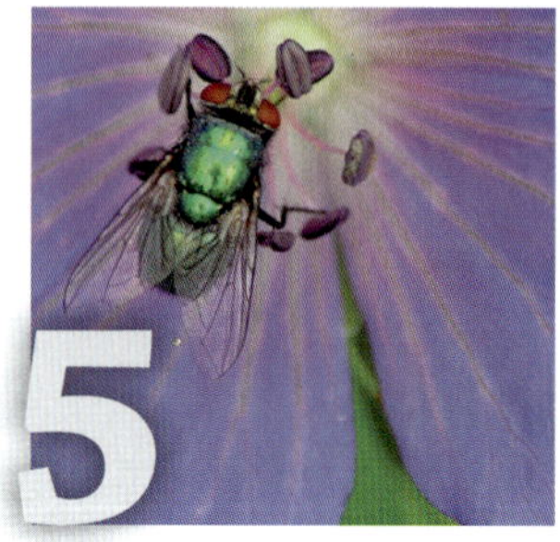
5

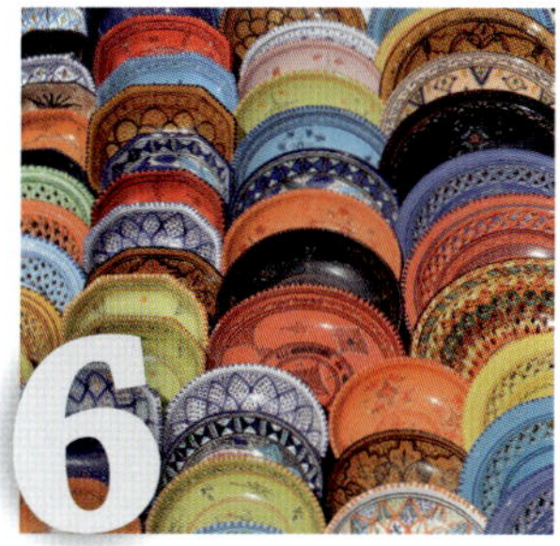

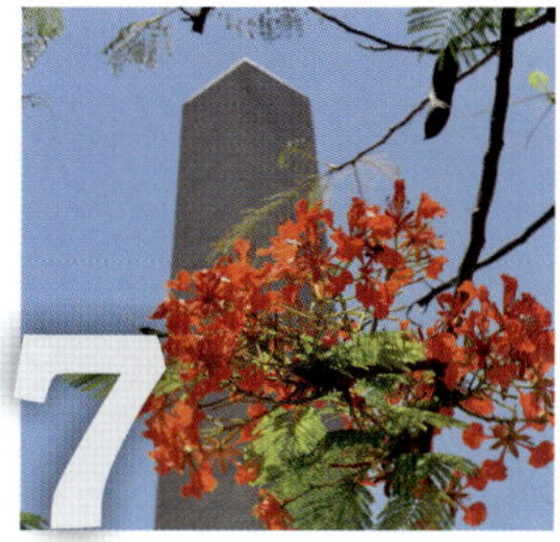

252 Setup Menu

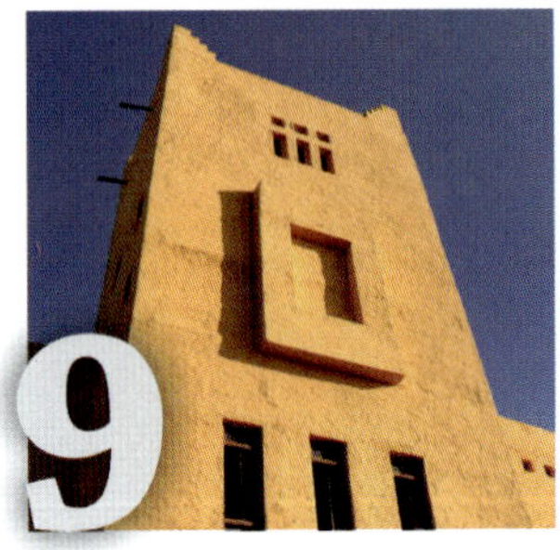

282 Retouch Menu, Recent Settings/My Menu

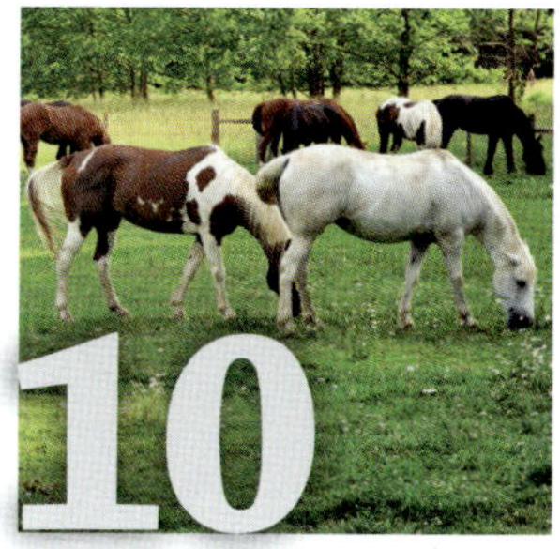

324 Multi-CAM 1000 Autofocus

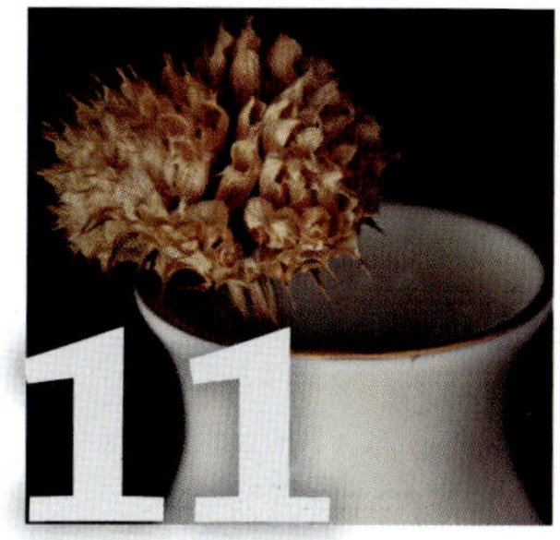

346 Speedlight Flash Photography

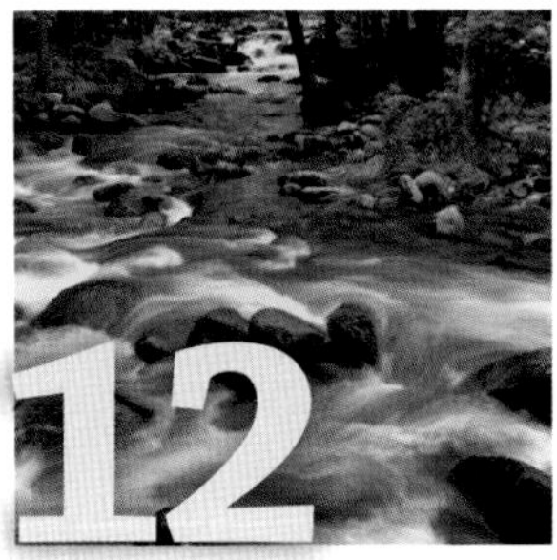

Foreword

nikonians.org

Nikonian Darrell Young, known to us for many years as Digital Darrell, has consistently been a source of instructional wisdom delivered with a touch of friendly humor. His extensive collection of informative articles has been a valuable resource in the articles knowledge base, Resources at Nikonians.

This work represents yet another progression in the rapid growth of our international community of photographers from all walks of life, recently exceeding 200,000 members from nearly 150 countries, and is a way to further confirm our Nikonians vocation in education, reopening an additional communication channel—books—to our more than 80 existing interactive forums including The Nikonian eZine, Nikonians Academy Workshops, Nikonians News Blog, Nikonians podcasts, etc.

Nikonians has earned a reputation as a friendly, reliable, informative, and passionate Nikon user's community thanks in great measure to members like our own Digital Darrell, who have taken the time to share the results of their experiences with Nikon imaging equipment, despite the pressures of their day jobs.

The Nikonians community has long been known as a welcoming, worldwide home for Nikon users, and Darrell's specialty in his writing is the ability to share his knowledge in the spirit of a friendly uncle in the comfort of your own living room.

Darrell's easy and friendly approach is appreciated by the increasing number of our community members who have been fortunate enough to acquire the Nikon D5000 DSLR. This camera represents a new step in bridging the gap between "prosumer" and professional DSLRs, and Darrell helps to explain some of the complex engineering that makes this all possible. As with his previous books on Nikon DSLRs, his goal is always to help readers understand not only the camera, but also the wealth of photographic advantages it can deliver thanks to the ingenuity of Nikon engineering.

We would like to congratulate Darrell for his work on this project, and special thanks goes to Tom Boné, Nikonians Chief Editor who has helped in streamlining the publication process in this, the fifth in the series of the NikoniansPress books, in association with Rocky Nook.

Bo Stahlbrandt (bgs) and J. Ramón Palacios (jrp)
Nikonians Founders
www.nikonians.org

Preface

I grew up looking at pictures.

Ever since I was a baby my mother took hundreds of photographs of our family life, capturing small pieces of time frozen in little negative squares. Today, I can still look back at those images and they awaken memories that would otherwise be forgotten.

In 1968, my dear Mom gave me my first Brownie Hawkeye camera, and that little camera ignited a fire in me for taking pictures. I remember my mother's words of instruction, "Load the film in a dark place, never open the film door until after you rewind, and keep the sun behind you when you shoot".

From that day forward I often carried a camera with me. I took the fuzzy pictures of a 13-year-old as I hiked up the Roosevelt Mountain in Rockwood, Tennessee, USA, with my brother Steven and my friend named Scott. Every major event of my life has a few frames attached.

As an adult, I began photographing my own family, and to this day I've been documenting the growth of my five children. From my earliest memories, photography has been a part of my life, and I'll keep on shooting as long as I am able.

The year 1980 was a milestone for me; that's when I got my first Nikon camera. It was a nearly new Nikon FM, and I reveled in its incredible build, and the unbelievable images it produced. Before then, I had been shooting with Kodak 110 and 126 cameras, and although those images have priceless personal value, they would win no contests. I graduated from negatives to transparencies in 1981, as I realized that even sharper and less grainy images could be created in those delightful little two-inch squares. I loved film, and shot a lot of it. I wanted to shoot even more, but the cost of raising kids took precedence over the cost of film and processing.

The year 2002 changed everything for me photographically. I had been playing around with a Kodak point-and-shoot digital camera, and I finally got a Nikon Coolpix 990. While the pictures were fun and easy to make, they did not equal the quality of my 35mm images, so I viewed digital photography only as a toy. Then Nikon released the 6 MP D100, and Digital Darrell was born. Never before had I shot so many images. With the "free" use of the camera, I took thousands of photographs that I would never have considered taking with expensive film, and thus I moved to a new level of photography in the process. Digital cameras can offer an educational course in photography within themselves.

My love of digital photography grew, as did my relationship with the world's premier Nikon User Community, www.Nikonians.org. I came on board as a charter member in late 2000, and after my D100 arrived I really become involved as a member. I wrote a camera review that J. Ramón Palacios liked, (JRP is one of the co-owners of the Nikonians.org website, along with Bo Stahlbrandt) and he asked me if I'd like to write a few articles for Nikonians.org. At that time, I didn't even know I was a writer! Thank you, JRP!

I practically lived on Nikonians.org, spending hours there each day, first as a moderator, and then as founding member of the Nikonian Writer's Guild. JRP asked me to write as often as I could, and he posted my articles for others to read. Wow, did my ego swell! Now, I am privileged to write instructional books for Nikon users. This book is my fourth in the Mastering the Nikon DSLR series. These books are a joint effort between Nikonians Press, Rocky Nook, and myself.

Since 2002, I've used nearly all of Nikon's DSLR cameras. All of them were excellent and gave me great images. Now, in 2009, I have the new Nikon D5000. Since I carry a camera with me everywhere, I love the smaller size. The swivel screen allows me to shoot from odd angles, and I can take "street" pictures because it just looks like I am adjusting my camera's controls. I can take macro shots without lying on the ground. This swivel screen is a very useful idea and isn't found on any other Nikon DSLR (yet). I love having a video mode so that I can shoot beautiful nature images, and then take some video too. I can later make wonderful computer presentations, combining music, stills, and video. The image quality from the camera is simply outstanding—one of the best I've seen in the DX sensor line.

The D5000 is a truly impressive camera, with many pro-level features in a small portable body. And since it is a rather complex camera, this book should help you to understand it well.

Additional help is available to you at the world's premier Nikon User's Community, Nikonians.org. This truly is an International Community of over 200,000 Nikon users. Talk about a Nikon resource! As a Nikon user, you are probably already a member, but if you're not, please log on to www.Nikonians.org and become at least a Silver member. Nikonians.org is a goldmine of photographic knowledge for Nikon users and is unmatched by any other resource available.

Mastering the Nikon D5000 has a coupon in the back for 50% off a Gold Membership at Nikonians.org. The Gold level gives you a lot of benefits, such as a personal blog, a large gallery, access to private forums, personal business cards, photographer's ID, membership certificate, and your own Nikonians.org email address. If you use the coupon, it will basically pay for the price of this book, making it free!

I feel greatly privileged to be a Nikonian, to have such knowledgeable and friendly associates, and to help provide yet another, much requested resource in the form of a printed book. I hope you enjoy this book and that you greatly benefit from it, and most of all that you find joy in using your chosen photographic tool ... the Nikon D5000.

Keep on capturing time ...

Digital Darrell
(Darrell Young)

1

Nikon D5000 Initial Configuration

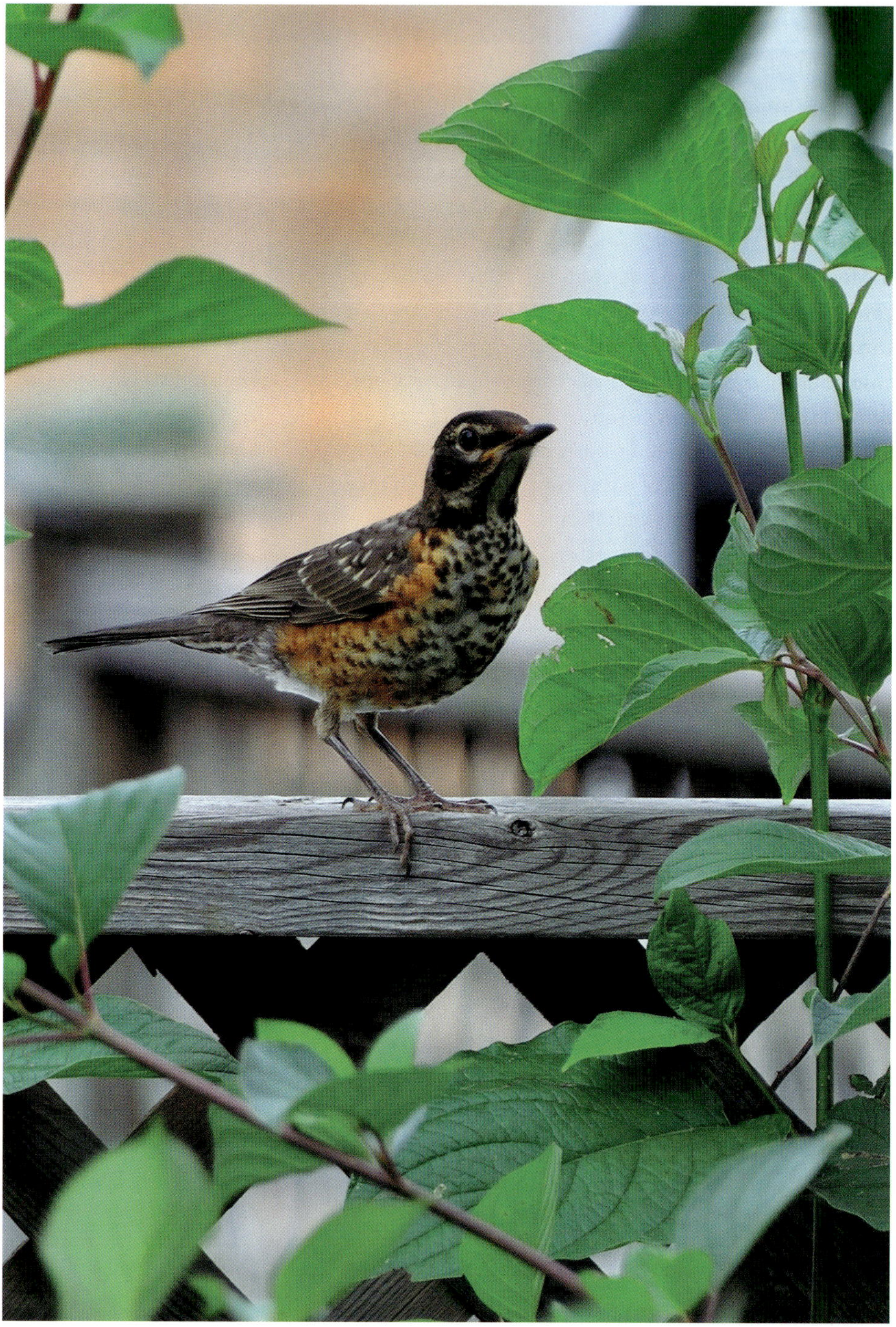

The new Nikon D5000 is simply an incredible little camera! It has most of the features found in its predecessor, the advanced Nikon D90, yet in a smaller, more portable body. Its small size belies its flexibility and image quality. Compared to the similarly sized Nikon D60, the D5000 is strikingly more powerful and feature rich.

It shares a 12.2-megapixel sensor with the Nikon D90 and pro-level Nikon D300. You'll take some of the best pictures of your life with this powerful little camera. In fact, using it, you can create images with the quality and size needed for things like stock photography (micro and traditional) and print sales. You may not be interested in earning money with your camera, but it feels good to know you could if you wanted to.

If you simply want to make beautiful images, the D5000 will give you enough control to create fine art photographs. If you're at a party and just want to take great pictures without thinking about camera settings, the D5000's green AUTO mode will take control so you can just point and shoot. If you know nothing about cameras, the D5000 offers 19 scene modes that give you creative control under different shooting conditions without making other camera adjustments.

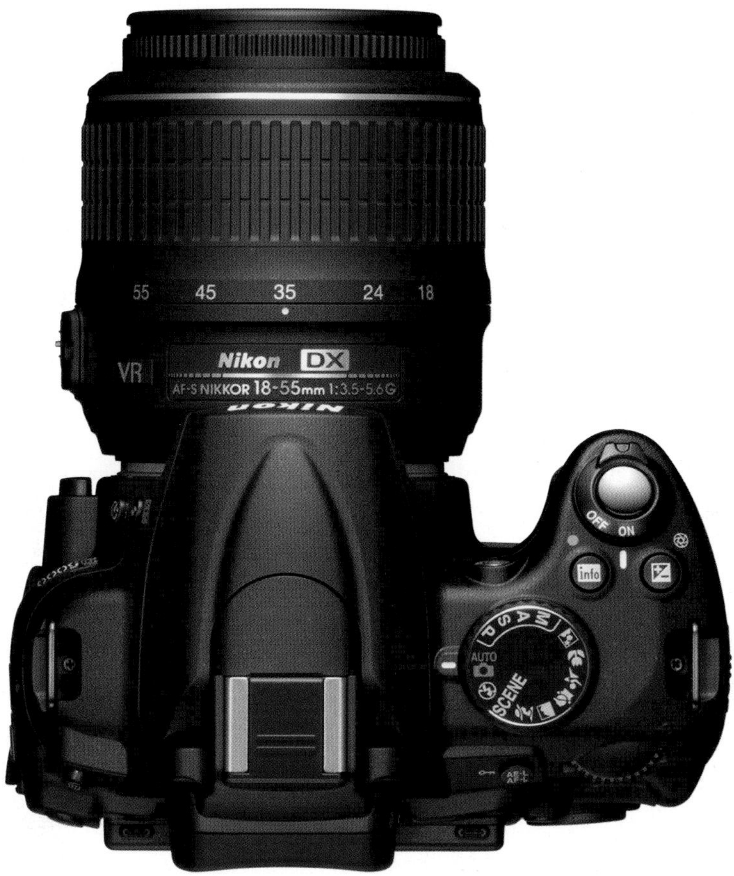

Can you see why I say this camera is incredible? It will take full automatic control of the picture process when you ask it to or give you complete manual control when you need it. If you want to control only some of the camera's functions while you learn other functions, it will allow you to do that too. In short, you now have amazing flexibility in a small and easy-to-carry package.

The Nikon D5000 may be the first digital single-lens reflex (DSLR) camera you've purchased. You may have been using a point-and-shoot (P&S) camera but found that your passion for photography exceeded its capability. With a DSLR, you can change lenses for greater image control. You look through the viewfinder or use Live View with the rear LCD and actually view through the lens your camera uses to take the picture. You can configure the camera to work in different ways, using different color styles, image formats, and exposure types. You have different types of exposure meters and a powerful feature called the histogram. Using a DSLR gives you much more control over how an image is created.

Digital Sensor Basics, or Why Does a DSLR Make Better Images?

The sensor size in your D5000 provides potential image quality unobtainable by even the best of the P&S cameras. Many do not realize why a DSLR can make such high-quality images in comparison. Let me explain.

All digital cameras have an imaging sensor that uses very tiny light-gathering points called pixels—an abbreviation of picture elements. Your D5000 has almost 12.3 million pixels on its sensor in an array 4,288 pixels wide and 2,848 pixels tall (4,288 x 2,848 = 12,212,224 pixels, or just over 12.2 megapixels). To be accurate, I'll refer to the megapixel rating of the D5000 as 12.2 usable megapixels.

A point-and-shoot camera has a digital imaging sensor about the size of your little fingernail. Imagine cramming millions of pixels into a space the size of your little fingernail, like the P&S cameras have done. Those pixels are so small that they're not very light sensitive. For a P&S camera to make a good picture, especially in lower light levels, the power gain must be turned up on the pixels. That boosts the signal but also increases noise, thereby degrading the image.

On the other hand, the Nikon D5000 has an imaging sensor about the size of a postage stamp—15.8 x 23.6 mm in size. That's a big difference! Its pixels are much larger than a P&S's and can gather light much more efficiently. The image quality from your new DSLR is sharper and has better color, contrast, and dynamic range and its photos can be enlarged more effectively and with higher quality. You'll be amazed at the difference and so will your friends and family.

So you can get the best use out of your much more complex DSLR camera, let's examine some of the most important settings to confirm and configure for first use of the camera.

First Use of the Nikon D5000

In this section, I'll help you set up your camera for first-time use. There are important functions scattered all through the various menus of the camera that you'll need to examine and set. Even if you've been using your D5000 for a while, please read this section because you might have overlooked some things that will benefit your use of the camera.

Some of the settings we'll look at in this chapter are already preconfigured the way I suggest you set them. Nikon uses many of these settings as factory defaults. However, I wanted to cover these areas for two reasons:

- You may have purchased a preowned D5000, and some of these items may have been changed from the default settings and may not be configured for your style of shooting.
- I want you to become familiar with where these settings are. They are important, and you may decide to change them as you shoot different types of images.

We'll look at two methods to configure the initial settings. First we'll consider how to use the regular menu system to modify settings. Then, for several commonly changed settings, we'll look at how to use the *Information edit* screen for quick reconfiguration. But first, let's take care of the most important starting point... you need power for this electronic device.

Charging the Battery

If you're like me, you'll open the box, put the lens on your camera, insert a battery, and take your first picture. Wouldn't it be a better idea to wait an hour to charge the battery and only then take the first picture? Sure it would, but I've never done that, and I bet you haven't either. Nikon knows this and they don't send out new cameras with dead batteries.

Most of the time the battery is not fully charged, but it has enough charge to set the time and date and then to take and review a few pictures. Think about it. How do you test a brand-new battery? You charge it and see if it will hold a charge. Nikon doesn't send batteries that are untested, so most of the time, you can play with your camera for at least a few minutes before charging the battery. I've purchased nearly every DSLR Nikon has made since 2002, and not one of them has come in with a dead battery.

When my D5000 arrived, the battery was about 65 percent charged. I played with the camera for an hour or two before I charged the battery. However, let me mention one important thing. If you plug in the battery and it is very low, such as below 25 percent, it might be a good idea to go ahead and charge it before shooting and reviewing too many pictures. Maybe you can get the time and date set and test the camera a time or two, but go no further with a seriously low battery.

The D5000 uses a lithium-ion (Li-ion) battery pack. While this type of battery doesn't develop the memory effects of the old nickel-cadmium (NiCd) batteries from years past, there can be a problem if you let them get too low. *A li-ion battery should never be used to complete exhaustion.* The battery can develop metal shunts internally if you run it completely down, and that will cause it to short out and stop working. *When your camera's li-ion battery gets down to the 25 percent level, please recharge it.* I don't let mine go below 50 percent for any extended use.

That said, the optimum situation would be to restrain yourself from turning on the camera until after the battery is charged. That'll give you some time to read the section of this book on initial camera setup and check out the Nikon D5000 User's Manual.

Initial Camera Setup

Let's look at the most important functions for initial configuration. In this chapter I'll just point you to the critical and most-used functions. Use the other chapters in the book to read about the advanced configuration of these and many other items.

I'll start with the absolutely necessary items and then advance through the various menus, touching on features that, in my opinion, you should learn for the best initial imaging experience with the D5000.

There are seven menus systems in the D5000 that you'll have to deal with over time. *Figure 1* shows a view of the four menus that affect initial camera setup: the *Playback Menu*, *Shooting Menu*, *Custom Setting Menu*, and *Setup Menu*.

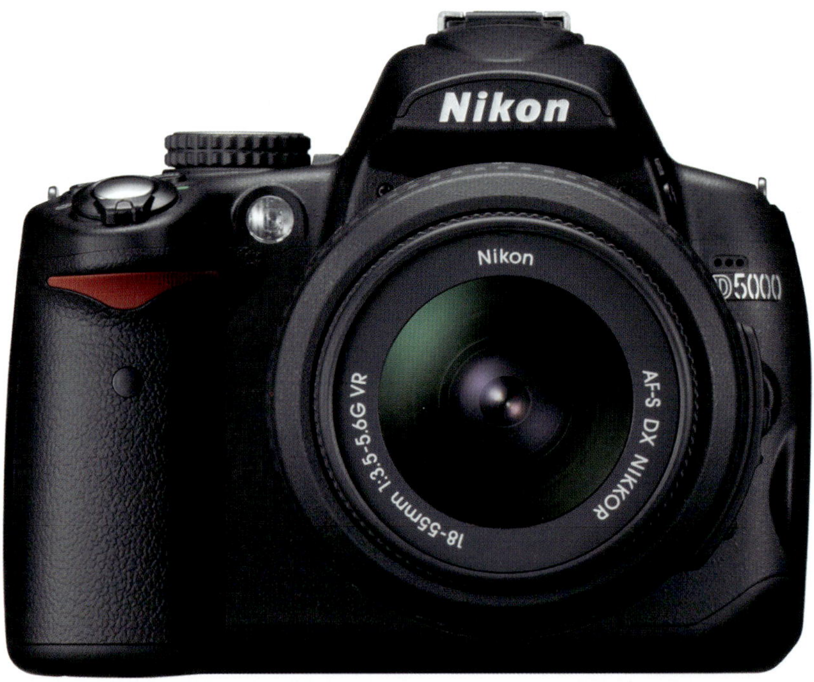

Nikon D5000 front view

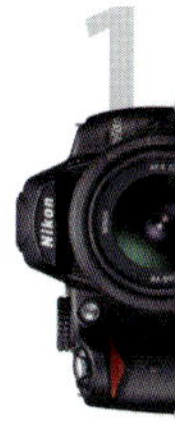

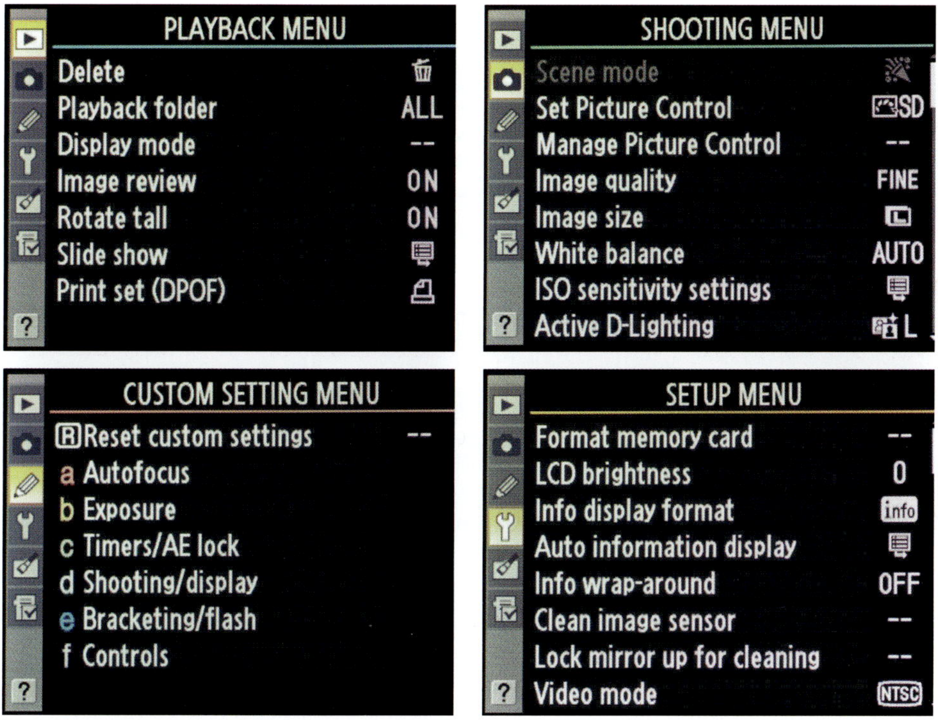

Figure 1 – The four critical camera configuration menus

As we go through the chapters of this book, we'll be peering deeply into these four menus for camera configuration and three other menus for in-camera image configuration and convenience items.

First, we'll consider the two bottom-line *Setup Menu* items that must be configured even before any pictures are taken.

Setup Menu – World time

When you open the box with a new D5000, insert the battery and turn it on, you will be prompted to set the time zone and date before you do anything else with the camera. Let's look at this in detail.

There are several functions to set under the *Time zone* and the *Date and time* sections of the *Setup Menu*:

- Time zone
- Date and time
- Date format
- Daylight saving time

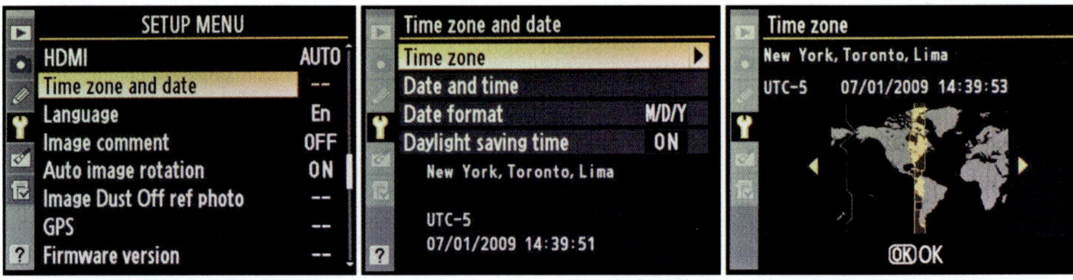

Figure 2 – *Time zone* screens

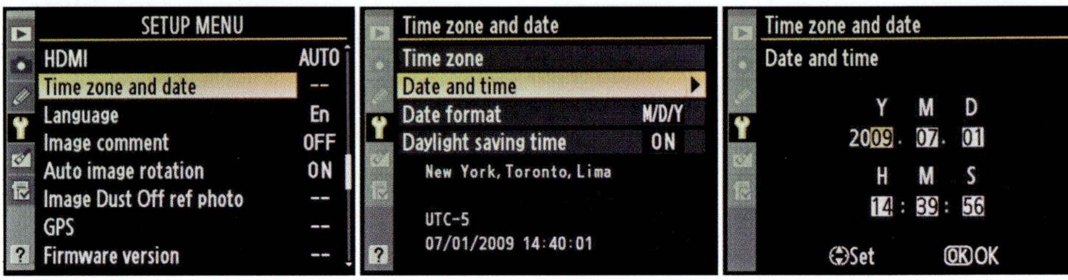

Figure 2A – *Date and time* screens

Time zone – *Figure 2* shows the *Time zone* configuration screens. The screen used to set the zone uses a world map interface to select the area of the world in which you are using the camera. To set the time zone, follow these steps:

1. Press the MENU button and scroll to the Setup Menu.
2. Select *Time zone and date*, and then scroll to the right.
3. Select *Time zone*, and then scroll to the right.
4. Use the Multi Selector to scroll left or right until your time zone is under the yellow vertical bar in the center of the world map screen (see *figure 2*).
5. Once your time zone is selected, press the *OK* button to save the setting.

Date and time – *Figure 2A* shows the three *Date and time* configuration screens. The final screen in the series allows you to select the year, month, and day (Y, M, D) and the hour, minute, and second (H, M, S):

1. Press the MENU button and scroll to the *Setup Menu*.
2. Select *Time zone and date*, and then scroll to the right.
3. Select *Date and time*, and then scroll to the right.
4. Using the Multi Selector, scroll left or right until you have selected the value you want to change. Then scroll up or down to actually change the value.
5. First set the year (*Y*) by scrolling up or down to the correct year, and then scroll to the right.

6. Next set the month (*M*) and scroll to the right.
7. Now set the day (*D*) and scroll to the right. The yellow box will drop down to the next line. The date showing in figure 2A is July 1, 2009.
8. Now scroll up or down to select the correct 24-hour time. If you are not familiar with a 24-hour military-style clock, see the 24-Hour Time Equivalents chart. As an example, if it is 2:39 p.m. where you are, the 24-hour equivalent time is 14:39. You should set the hour to 14, scroll to the right, and set the minute (*M*) to 39. I usually just scroll on past the seconds (*S*) setting, but you can set it too if you want to synchronize your camera's time with an external source for accuracy. *Figure 2A* shows 56 seconds in the second field.
9. When you have set the correct date and time, press the *OK* button to save the settings.

24 Hour Time Equivalents

For your convenience, here is a listing of the 24-hour time equivalents:

A.M. Settings:

12:00 a.m. = 00:00 (midnight)
01:00 a.m. = 01:00
02:00 a.m. = 02:00
03:00 a.m. = 03:00
04:00 a.m. = 04:00
05:00 a.m. = 05:00
06:00 a.m. = 06:00
07:00 a.m. = 07:00
08:00 a.m. = 08:00
09:00 a.m. = 09:00
10:00 a.m. = 10:00
11:00 a.m. = 11:00

P.M. Settings:

12:00 p.m. = 12:00 (noon)
01:00 p.m. = 13:00
02:00 p.m. = 14:00
03:00 p.m. = 15:00
04:00 p.m. = 16:00
05:00 p.m. = 17:00
06:00 p.m. = 18:00
07:00 p.m. = 19:00
08:00 p.m. = 20:00
09:00 p.m. = 21:00
10:00 p.m. = 22:00
11:00 p.m. = 23:00

Interestingly, there is no 24:00 time (midnight). After 23:59 comes 00:00.

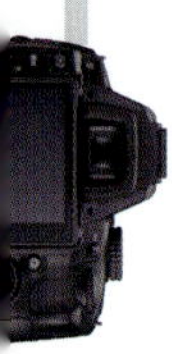

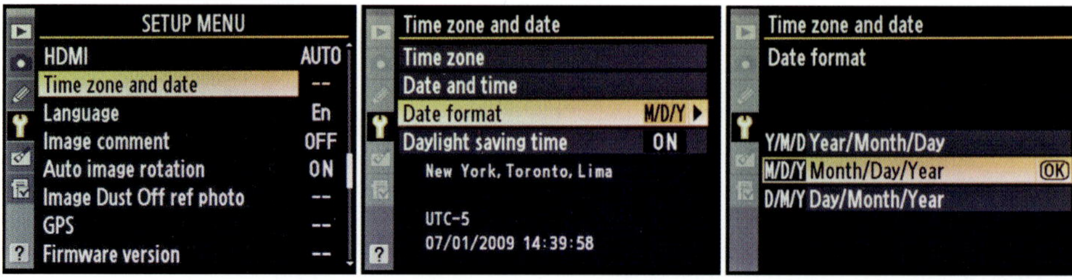

Figure 2B – *Date format* screens

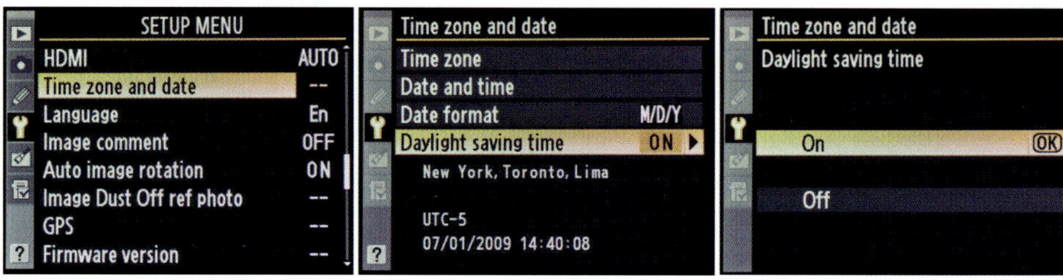

Figure 2C – *Daylight saving time* screens

Date format – The D5000 gives you three ways to format the date (see *figure 2B*):

- Y/M/D = Year/Month/Day (2010/12/31)
- M/D/Y = Month/Day/Year (12/31/2010)
- D/M/Y = Day/Month/Year (31/12/2010)

D5000 owners in the United States will probably use the second setting, which matches the Month/Day/Year format so familiar to Americans (for example, 12/31/2010). People in other areas of the world can select their favorite date format.

To select the date format of your choice, do the following:

- Press the MENU button and scroll to the *Setup Menu*.
- Select *Time zone and date*, and then scroll to the right.
- Select *Date format*, and then scroll to the right.
- Choose the format you like best from the three available formats by scrolling up or down.
- Press the *OK* button.

Daylight saving time – Many areas of the United States observe daylight saving time. In the springtime, many American residents set their clocks forward by one hour on a specified day each year. Then in the fall they set it back, leading to the clever saying, "spring forward or fall back."

To enable automatic *Daylight saving time*, follow these steps (see *figure 2C*):

1. Press the MENU button and scroll to the *Setup Menu*.
2. Select *Time zone and date*, and then scroll to the right.
3. Select *Daylight saving time*, and then scroll to the right.

4. Select *On* or *Off* from the menu by scrolling up or down.
5. Press the *OK* button.

If you turned daylight saving time to *On*, your D5000 will now automatically "spring forward and fall back," adjusting your time forward by one hour in the spring and back one hour in the fall of the year.

Recommendation

If you live in an area that observes daylight saving time, it's a good idea to set your camera to make this adjustment automatically. I always leave my camera set to *On*. Why not let the camera remember to change this value twice per year?

Next, you'll learn how to format an SD memory card in your camera so that it's ready to take pictures. It's important that you format the card in your new camera before using it so it's customized to your particular camera.

Setup Menu – Format Memory Card

While you're in the *Setup Menu*, please notice the location of the memory card formatter. As mentioned previously, when you insert a card into a new camera for the first time, it's a good idea to format the card with that camera. This will match the card to the camera and give you greater image storage reliability in the long run.

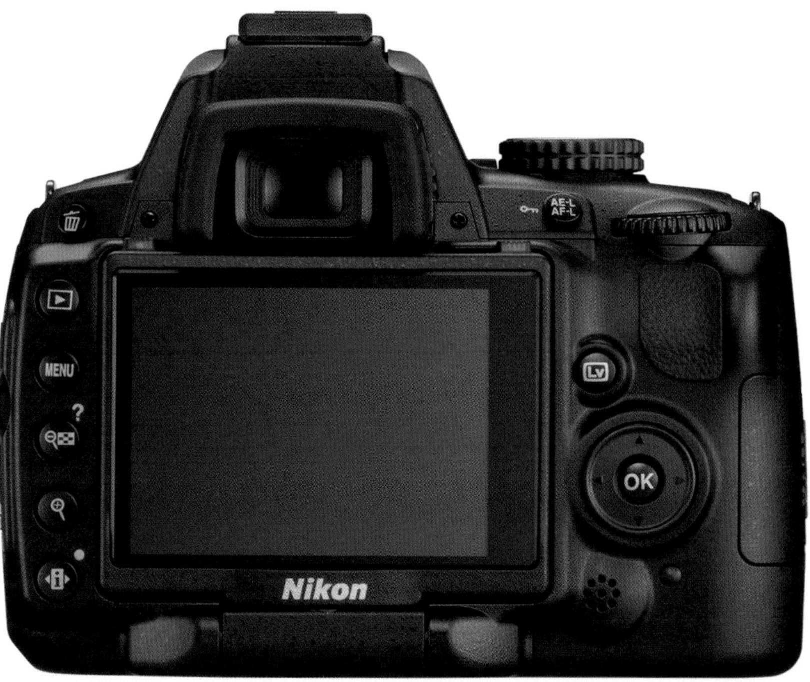

Nikon D5000 back view

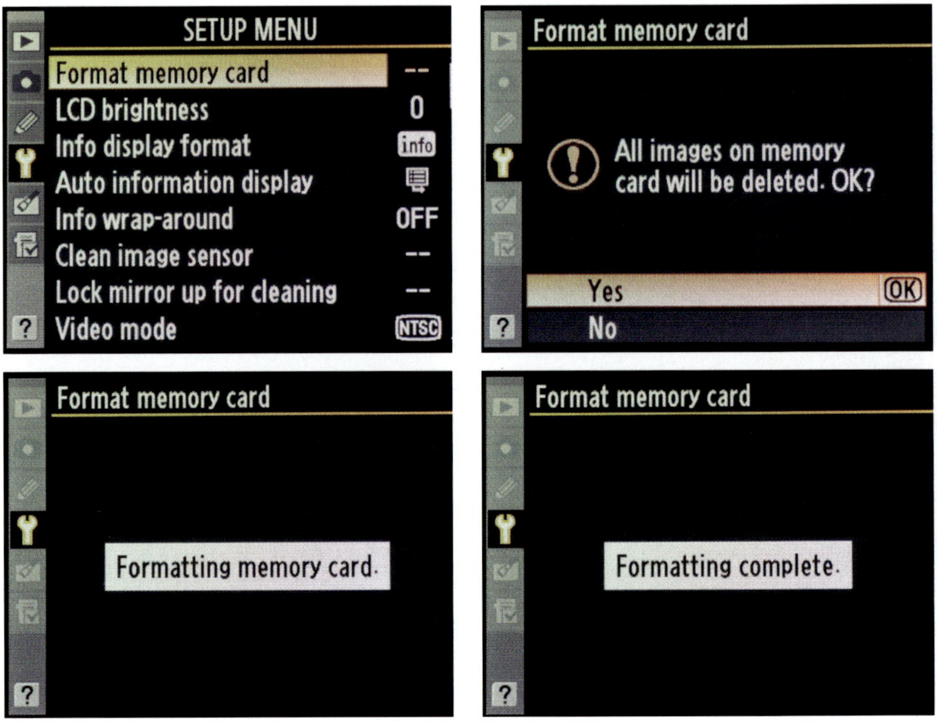

Figure 3 – *Format memory card* screens

Here are the four steps to format a memory card using the menus (see *figure 3*):

1. Press the MENU button and scroll to the *Setup Menu*.
2. Select *Format memory card*, and then scroll to the right.
3. Select *Yes* from the screen with the big red exclamation mark and the words *All images on memory card will be deleted. OK?*
4. Press the *OK* button.

Once you press the *OK* button, you'll see two screens in quick succession. One says *Formatting memory card*, and the next says *Formatting complete*. Then the camera switches back to the *Setup Menu*'s first screen. The card is formatted, and you can take lots of pictures.

Where to Format the Memory Card

It is always a good idea to format the memory card in your camera and not with your computer (*and ONLY when it has no images on it!*). I once had an expensive 16 GB memory card fail after I formatted it in my computer. The camera would not recognize it afterward, nor would it format it. I had to send the card back to the manufacturer, who replaced it for me, fortunately. Since then, I have always formatted the card in the camera *after* I've transferred all the images to my computer. Better safe than sorry.

Now, let's move to the *Shooting Menu* for several important configuration changes.

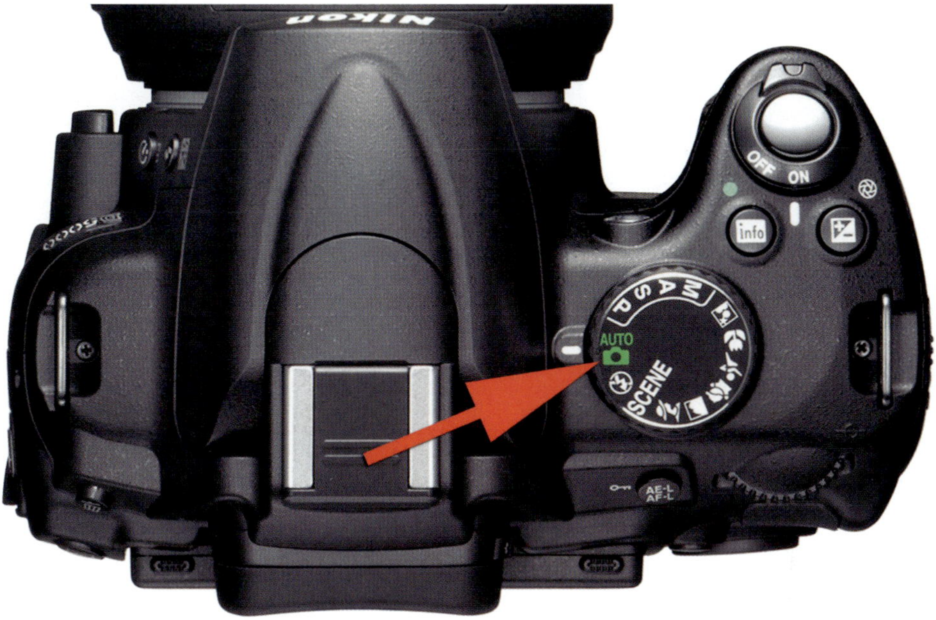

Figure 3A – Using AUTO mode – Shoot now!

Wait… I Want to Take Pictures Now! (Using Full Auto Mode)

If you're the impatient type, or you just want to experiment with your camera before configuring it, you can do that now. Once you've set the time and date on the camera and formatted a memory card, you can take pictures immediately. (Hopefully the battery has enough charge!)

As shown in *figure 3A*, simply turn the dial on top of the camera until the green AUTO lines up with the white line. This puts the camera into completely automatic mode, and it becomes a like a big COOLPIX P&S camera. It's rather intelligent in this mode and knows when you need flash, what ISO sensitivity to use for current conditions, and which white balance, autofocus mode, D-Lighting level, and Picture Control will give you the best image under the circumstances.

All you have to worry about in AUTO mode is how you compose the image. The D5000 will get the picture at all costs. What I mean is that the camera will automatically adjust the settings mentioned in the preceding paragraph to get an image, even if it has to turn the ISO sensitivity up to very high levels or adjust other settings to the edge of their capabilities. However, while in normal light, the AUTO mode will give you excellent images.

If you just want to play with the camera for a while, before you read the rest of this chapter on initial configuration, go right ahead. Have some fun, and then return for deeper configuration.

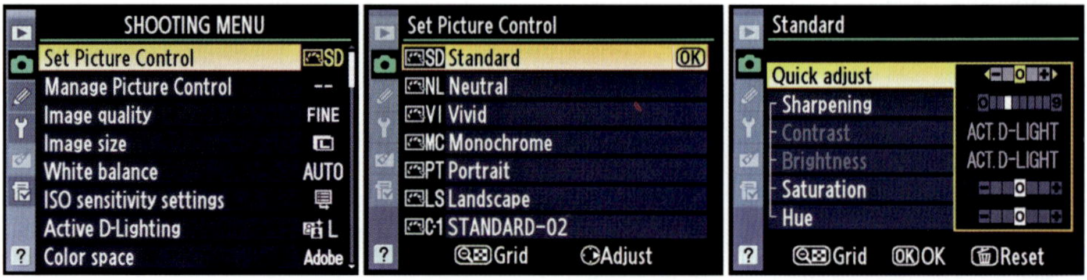

Figure 4 – Selecting the Standard (SD) Picture Control

Getting Down to Basics – Shooting Menu Settings

Now that you've had an opportunity to play with your camera for a while in AUTO mode, it's time to do some important basic camera configuration. This allows you—the more creative photographer type — to take greater control of your camera.

Let's begin by looking at some of the most important settings in the camera; you'll learn where they are located, both in the menus, and on the *Information edit* screen. First, let's look into the various menus.

Shooting Menu – Set Picture Control

Later, in chapter 6 "Shooting Menu," we'll cover Picture Controls in detail, even discussing how to use the included Nikon Picture Controls to create new custom Picture Controls that you can use and share with others. For now, until you get a good understanding of Picture Controls, let's select one for initial use.

Using the menu screens shown in *figure 4*, here is how to select the Standard (SD) Picture Control:

1. Press the MENU button and scroll to the *Shooting Menu*.
2. Select *Set Picture Control*, and then scroll to the right.
3. Select *SD Standard* from the menu, and then press the *OK* button.

The *SD Standard* Picture Control sets your camera up for medium contrast and color saturation for a look sort of like Fuji Provia 100F slide film or Kodak Gold 100. It's a good starting point for how your camera captures contrast and color, with enough contrast for rich blacks and sufficient color saturation for a realistic look in skin tones and foliage. Later, you can experiment with the other controls and make more informed choices. This is a safe setting for Picture Control until you understand them more fully.

SD Picture Control Recommendation

I use the SD Picture Control most of the time on my D5000. I like the way it maintains contrast so that the images have nice "snap." And, it helps control color saturation without going too far.

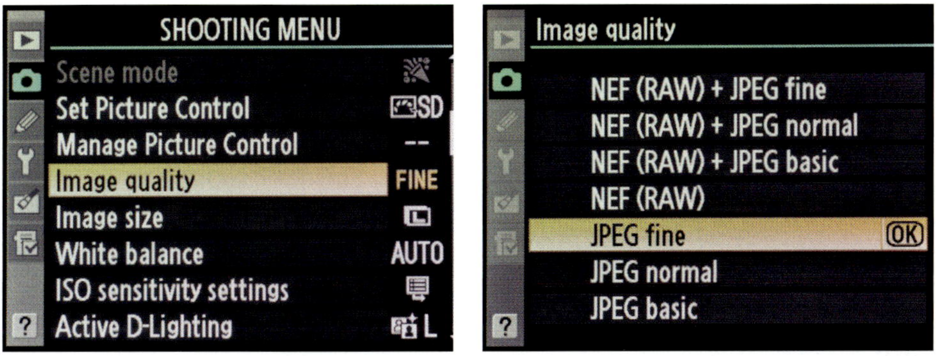

Figure 5 – Selecting the *JPEG fine Image Quality* setting

Shooting Menu – Image Quality

If you're new to digital photography and inexperienced with post-processing images later in the computer, or if you have no interest in working on images after the fact, you'll need to select the *Image quality – JPEG fine* setting. This setting allows your camera to create excellent, immediate-use images that are compatible with virtually everything for printing or displaying your images. The JPEG format is the standard basic final format for almost everything done in photography today.

With the menus in *figure* 5, select *JPEG fine* and press the *OK* button. Later in chapter 6, we'll consider all the formats available in the D5000, and I'll even point out which is best to use for various types of photography. The *JPEG fine* format is the factory default for the D5000, but I want you to know where it is located when you decide to change it. Here's how:

1. Press the MENU button and scroll to the *Shooting Menu*.
2. Select *Image quality*, and then scroll to the right.
3. Select *JPEG fine* from the menu, and then press the *OK* button.

The JPEG image format is great to use if you have little experience with modifying images on a computer. If you intend to use your computer like a digital darkroom, then it would be good to learn about and use the NEF (RAW) format too. We'll examine how in chapter 6.

Use *JPEG Fine* to Preserve Data

When I'm not shooting in NEF (RAW) mode, I'll be using *JPEG fine*. Anytime you increase image compression, as you do by using *JPEG normal* or *JPEG basic*, you're telling the camera to throw away more of your image data. Since I want the best images I can make, I want to keep as much image data as possible. *JPEG fine* gives me top-quality images; therefore I never use *JPEG normal* or *JPEG Basic*.

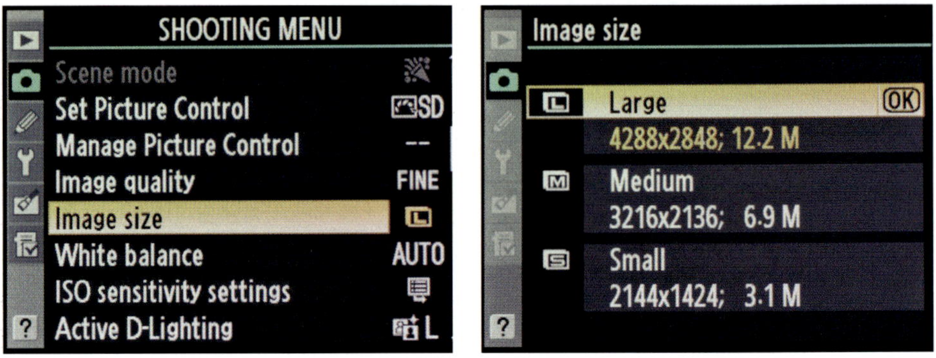

Figure 5B – Selecting the large image size

Shooting Menu – Image Size

The Nikon D5000 can shoot in three image sizes. I have never taken mine off of the *L-Large* setting because I have no need for smaller pictures. Here are the three sizes under *Image size*:

- *Large* – 4288 x 2848 – 12.2 megapixels
- *Medium* – 3216 x 2136 – 6.9 megapixels
- *Small* – 2144 x 1424 – 3.1 megapixels

Here are the steps to select the large size (see *figure 5B*):

1. Press the MENU button and select *Shooting Menu*.
2. Choose *Image size*, and then scroll right.
3. Choose the size of the image by scrolling up or down. For this example, choose *Large*.
4. Press the *OK* button.

Large Setting for Maximum Image Quality

I want maximum quality out of every image I create. In shooting digitally for several years, I've found no reason to ever take my camera off of the *Large* setting. It's easy to resize the image later if you want to, for example, email it to friends or family. Many software programs, such as Nikon's free Nikon ViewNX, will automatically convert an image to a smaller size and email it for you. (Search for "Nikon ViewNX download" to find the free program on Nikon's website.)

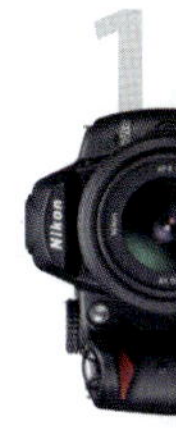

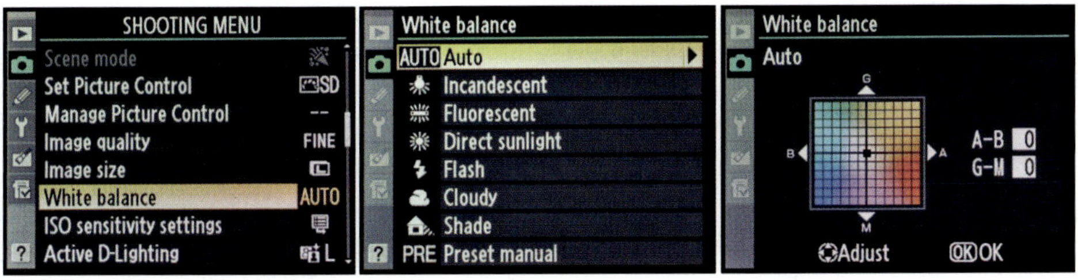

Figure 6 – Selecting *White* balance – *Auto* with menus

Shooting Menu – White Balance

White balance is a subject that many digital photographers do not fully understand. In chapter 6, I'll discuss the basic configuration of white balance. Also, an entire chapter of this book, chapter 4, "White Balance", is devoted to thorough coverage of this very important subject.

For now, just remember that the default setting for *White balance* is *Auto*. This will allow your camera to make decisions about the ambient color of the light in which it finds itself. That way, you'll initially get reasonable color balance in your images without unintended tints. Please take the time later to fully understand how white balance works. It'll make you a better digital photographer.

Using the menus in *figure 6*, here's how to select the *White balance – Auto* setting:

1. Press the MENU button and scroll to the *Shooting Menu*.
2. Select *White balance*, and then scroll to the right.
3. Select *Auto* from the menu, and then scroll to the right.
4. Press the *OK* button.

When you get to the third screen with the color *Adjust* box, which lets you fine-tune the white balance, just press *OK*. (Leave the little black square directly in the center of the *Adjust* box.) This is a fine-tuning screen, and at this time, you may not have sufficient need or experience to use it. If you accidentally moved the little black square in the color adjust box, just put it back in the center and press *OK*.

The factory default is *A* (*Auto*), but I want you to know where this important control is located for later use.

True Colors With *Auto* White Balance

Auto white balance works very well on the Nikon D5000. There may be some minor variation in white balance between images because *Auto* white balance reads the ambient light for each and every picture. However, I have rarely seen the D5000 make a mistake. My whites are white, my blues are blue, and my greens are green. When you have time to read chapter 4, "White Balance", you'll have a much better understanding of white balance issues and can make more informed decisions.

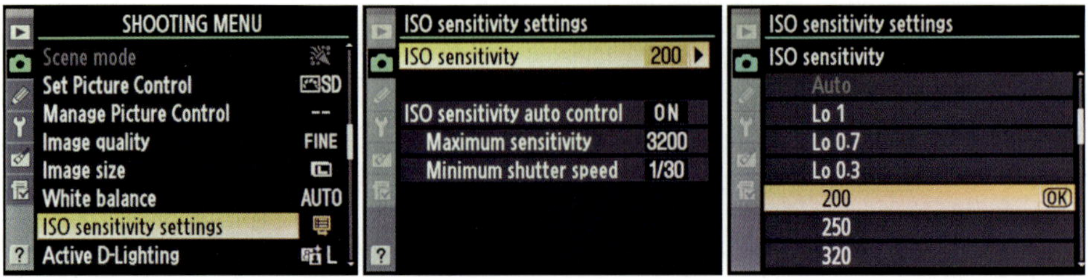

Figure 7 – The *ISO sensitivity* settings

Shooting Menu – ISO Sensitivity Settings

An International Organization for Standardization (ISO) sensitivity number, such as 200, 800, or 1600, is an agreed-upon sensitivity setting for the image capturing sensor. Virtually everywhere you go, all camera ISO sensitivity numbers will mean the same thing. Using that common denominator, camera bodies and lenses can be designed to take advantage of the ISO sensitivity ranges they will use.

In the D5000, the ISO numbers are sensitivity equivalents. To put it simply, ISO "sensitivity" is the digital equivalent of film speed. The higher the ISO sensitivity, the less light is needed for the exposure. A high ISO setting allows faster shutter speeds and smaller apertures. A low ISO setting requires slower shutter speeds and larger apertures.

The default value of your D5000's ISO sensitivity setting is 200. This will work for normal, bright images, but at night or in darker areas, you might want to increase the ISO sensitivity to get sharp pictures from slow shutter speeds. Be careful when using high ISO settings because somewhere above 800 ISO, noise (graininess) will start appearing in the images. Above 1600 ISO, the noise is not very pretty.

To select an ISO setting, do the following (*see figure 7*):

1. Press the MENU button and select *Shooting Menu*.
2. Choose *ISO sensitivity*, and then scroll right.
3. Choose an ISO number and press the *OK* button.

Which ISO Setting Do I Use?

I leave *ISO sensitivity* set to 200 most of the time on my D5000. This gives me virtually noiseless, high-quality images as long as I carefully control my exposures. If there is less light, I may increase the sensitivity just enough to get the picture. I rarely use settings above 400 ISO, but this is just a personal preference.

Shooting Menu – Color Space

Color space is another thing that newer digital photographers often don't fully understand. It is also discussed well in chapter 6. The industry-standard color space for conversion to CYMK offset printing (the four-color printing process used in most magazines and newspapers) is Adobe RGB. The *RGB* stands for red, green, blue). The D5000 defaults to sRGB color space because it is the default color

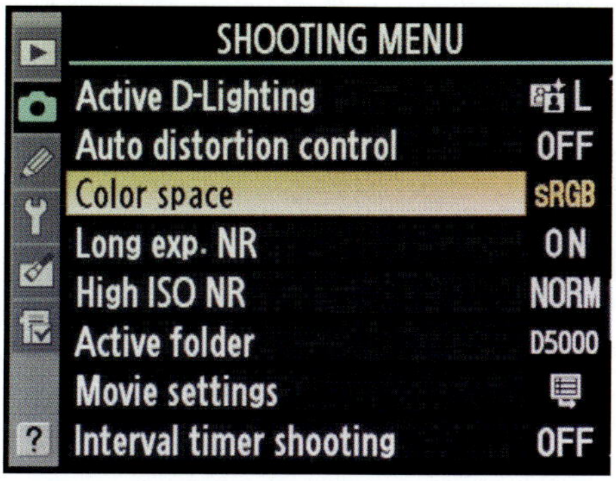

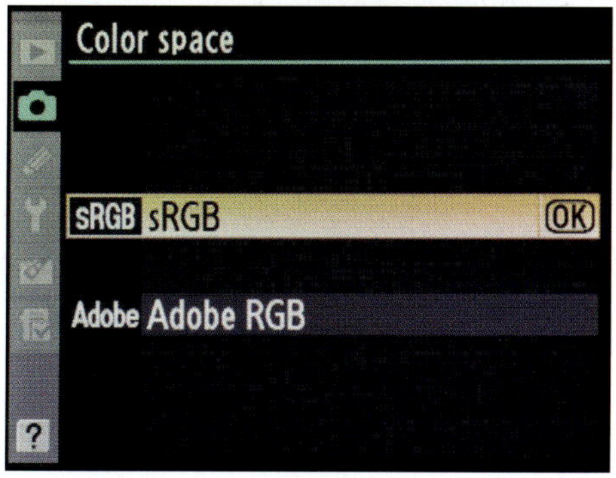

Figure 8 – Selecting a color space

space for most in-home printing and for the many retail places where you can get prints made.

Let me give you a basic understanding of why color space is important. There is a big color space called LAB CIE that basically represents the range of human color vision. The Adobe RGB color space allows your camera to capture about 50 percent of that color range. The sRGB color space allows the D5000 to capture only about 35 percent of that color range.

The standard defined color spaces are basically an agreement between manufacturers of all sorts of equipment. If you take a picture using the *sRGB* or *Adobe RGB* color space setting built into your D5000, it helps your picture's color match the output of a device such as an inkjet printer, an offset press, a computer monitor, or an HDTV. All these devices have color space standards. Your Nikon D5000 must fit within the standards or your images may print or display with inaccurate colors.

Which color space should you use? This depends on what you intend to do with your images. Roughly, if you intend to sell your images in some format, it is usually best to use the Adobe RGB color space, which is the industry-standard starting place for color printing on most commercial devices. If you intend to print your own images on an inkjet printer or send them off to the superstore lab, then sRGB is usually sufficient. This is not a hard-and-fast rule. However, this is a good place to start off your voyage into digital imaging.

Here are the steps to select a color space setting on your D5000 (see *figure 8*):

1. Press the MENU button and select *Shooting Menu*.
2. Choose *Color space*, and then scroll to the right.
3. Choose *sRGB* or *Adobe RGB*.
4. Press the *OK* button.

Set it to sRGB… and Forget It!

If you are still unsure what to do about the *Color space* setting, just select *sRGB* and don't worry about it. You'll be selecting a color space that does a great job with JPEG image shooting and printing. Later, you can take time to study this book and other resources in more depth to learn about the very important issue of color space.

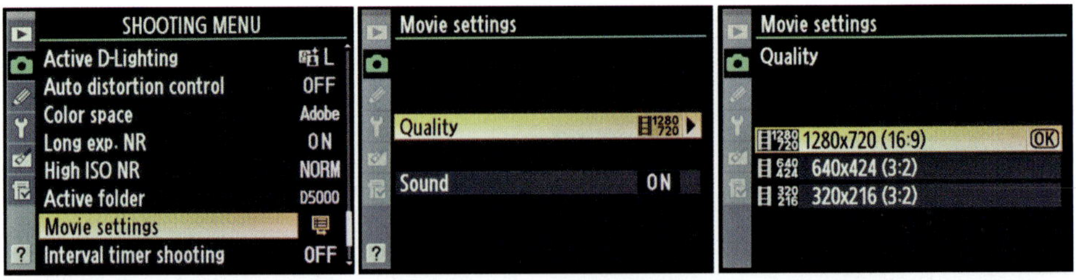

Figure 9 – D5000 *Movie settings - Quality*

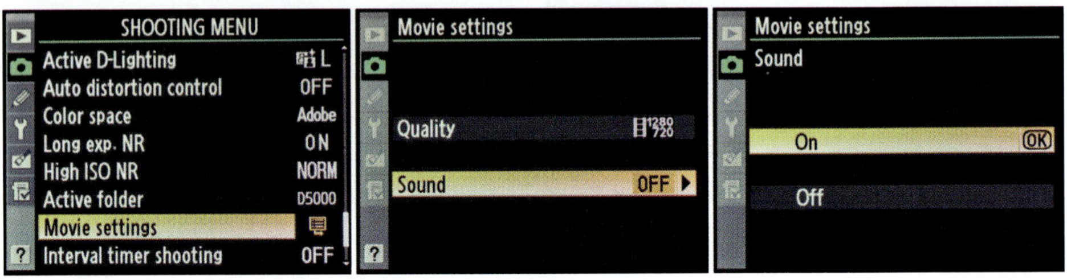

Figure 9A – D5000 *Movie settings - Sound*

Shooting Menu – D-Movie Settings

Since the D5000 is also a movie camera (imagine that!), you should select an initial format for your movies. Plan on shooting short video segments of 5 minutes each. The 5-minute limitation applies only to the highest-resolution mode. You can record for longer periods in lower resolutions, up to 20 minutes.

Before shooting, you can turn mono sound on or off, and you can select the video quality (size) from the following (see *figure 9*):

- 1280 x 720
- 640 x 424 (default)
- 320 x 216

Since autofocus doesn't work in movie mode, you'll need to prefocus in Live View mode before starting the movie and then manually refocus if you significantly change the distance from your subject.

Your video is saved in the familiar AVI format, which will play on most computers since it's compatible with Windows Media Player and Apple QuickTime, among other computer applications. You can even connect the D5000 to an HDTV, with an optional HDMI cable, and show your videos to friends and family.

Using the menus shown in *figure 9* and *figure 9A*, select one of the *Quality* and *Sound* settings:

1. Press the MENU button and select *Shooting Menu*.
2. Choose *Movie settings*, and then scroll to the right.
3. Choose a *Quality* level, and then press the *OK* button.
4. Select the *Sound* menu item, and scroll to the right.
5. Choose *On* or *Off* and then press the *OK* button.

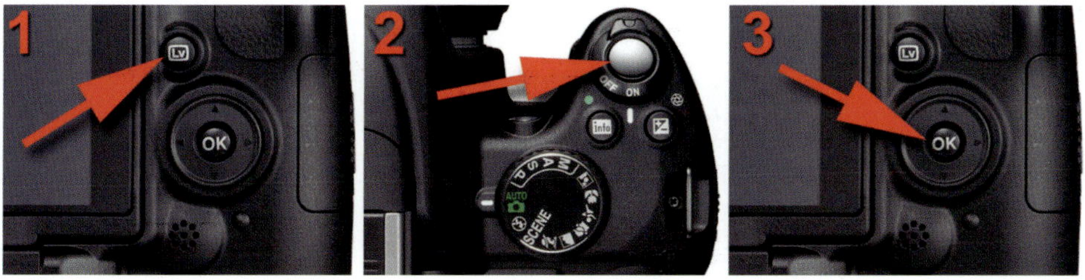

Figure 9B – Recording a D5000 movie

Now, simply follow these steps to start recording a D-Movie:

1. Turn the camera on, and remove the lens cap.
2. Press the LV (Live View) button on the D5000's back (*figure 9B*, image 1).
3. Prefocus the camera on your subject by pressing the shutter release button halfway down until the little green square stops flashing (*figure 9B*, image 2).
4. Press the *OK* button to start the video recording (*figure 9B*, image 3).
5. When you are finished, press the *OK* button again to stop recording.

Video Quality Size Recommendation

I often shoot "fun" movies at the 640 x 424 video quality size so that I can record longer than 5 minutes. If I am serious about a movie, I'll increase the quality size to 1280 x 720 and live with the 5-minute limitation.

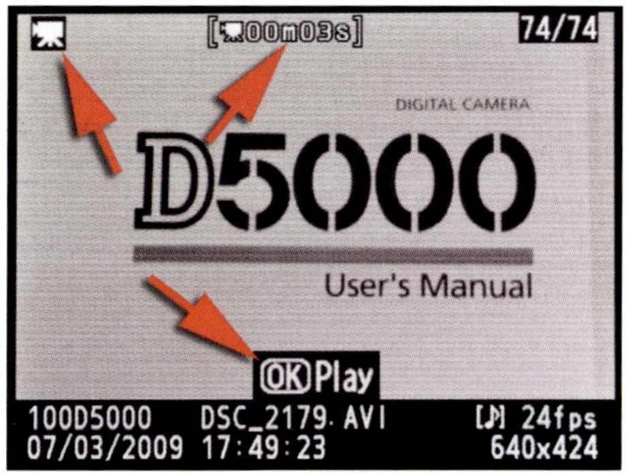

Figure 9C – Identifying a movie on the playback screen

After you have recorded your video, press the Playback button and you'll see the first frame of your movie. Press *OK* to play the movie. (Be sure to have some popcorn ready!)

Look at *figure* 9C— in the camera display, you can tell it's a movie instead of a still image when you see a little movie camera icon in the upper-left corner along with a minutes and seconds counter at the top in the middle. *OK Play* will show in the middle at the bottom of the display.

Please see chapter 12, "D-Movie Mode," for detailed information on using the video capability of your D5000.

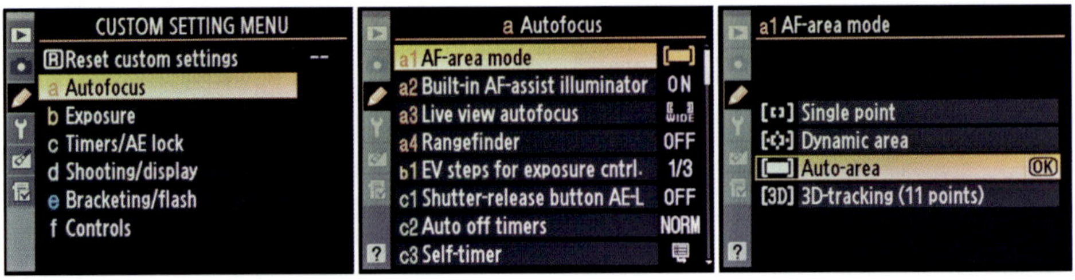

Figure 10 – Setting *Auto-area* autofocus mode

Custom Settings Menu Basics

The D5000 has 23 separate Custom Settings that are designed to allow personalized configuration of the camera. For now, we'll just touch on the basic Custom Settings to help you get started with you new camera.

Custom Setting Menu – Autofocus Area Mode

Until you've had an opportunity to study the configuration of the autofocus system, let's select a safe setting so that you can get excellent in-focus images. Autofocus is another of those confusing systems that many people have problems with. Chapter 10, "Multi-CAM 1000 Autofocus," is devoted to teaching you the entire autofocus system in great detail, along with related functionality like area and release modes.

We really should set an *Autofocus* area mode. Later, when you are more familiar with what these modes do, you can experiment with different ones. In the meantime, we'll set *Auto-area AF* so that your camera can use its face recognition technology to take clear portraits and assist you with the autofocus process for all your other subjects. *Figure 10* shows the menu screens to set the autofocus area modes.

Notice that there are four *AF-area mode* settings shown in *Custom Setting a1*:

- *Single-point*
- *Dynamic-area*
- *Auto-area*
- *3D-tracking (11 points)*

Auto-area lets the camera select a combination of AF focus points that will automatically achieve the best autofocus. It works quite well.

Here are the steps to set the *Auto-area* mode:

1. Press the MENU button and select the *Custom Setting Menu*.
2. Choose *Autofocus*, and then scroll right.
3. Choose *a1 AF-area mode,* and then scroll to the right.
4. Select *Auto-area*, and press the *OK* button.

Use the *Auto-area* Setting… for Now

For now, use the *Auto-area* setting. This will let the camera decide how to best use autofocus for the current subject. After you read chapter 10, you'll be ready to take control of this functionality.

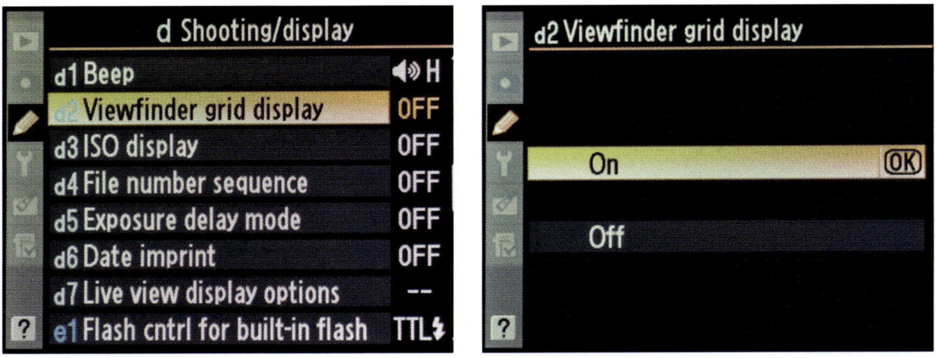

Figure 11 – Enabling viewfinder gridlines

Custom Setting Menu – Viewfinder Grid Display

The *Viewfinder grid display* is not absolutely necessary for daily shooting, but it sure does make a difference in helping you to keep images level. Most of us tend to tilt the camera in one direction or another. In our excitement to capture a great image, we might be tilting the camera a few degrees. Having gridlines on the viewfinder makes it much easier to keep your images level.

- *On* – On-demand gridlines are displayed in the viewfinder.
- *Off* (default) – No gridlines are displayed.

Here are the steps to configure on-demand gridlines (see *figure 11*):

1. Press the MENU button and scroll to the *Custom Setting Menu*
2. Select *d Shooting/display,* and then scroll to the right.
3. Select *d2 Viewfinder grid display*, and then scroll to the right.
4. Select *On*.
5. Press the *OK* button.

I Love These Gridlines!

If you enable on-demand gridlines, I doubt you'll ever turn them back off. You *can* turn them on and off at will using *Custom Setting d2*. This will be discussed in more detail in chapter 7, "Custom Setting Menu." I leave mine turned on at all times!

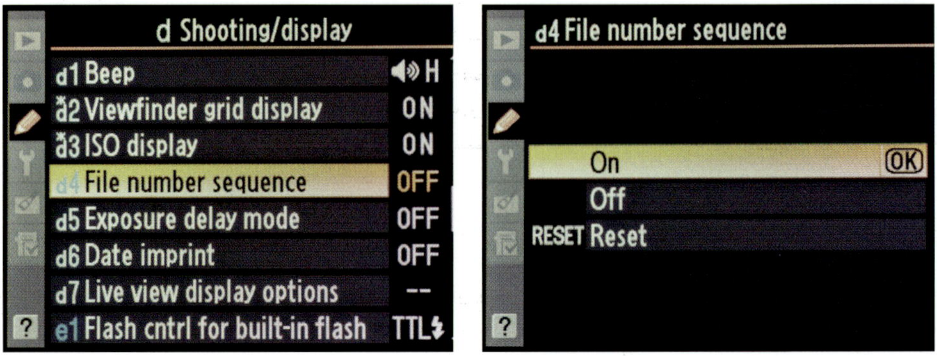

Figure 12 – Enabling *File number sequence*

Custom Setting Menu – File Number Sequence

Wouldn't you like to know how many images you've shot with the D5000 and make sure each image has its own unique image number? With *File number sequence* set to *On*, your camera will keep count of the image numbers in a running sequence from 0001 to 9999 (after 9999, it rolls back over to 0001).

Otherwise, anytime you format the memory card or insert a different card, the D5000 will start over at 0001. You could later accidentally copy a set of images right over the top of another set with the same image numbers. At least with *File number sequence* set to *On*, you don't have to worry about accidentally overwriting other images except when you've taken 9,999 images.

Here's how to enable File number sequence under Custom Setting d4 (see *figure 12*):

1. Press the MENU button and scroll to the *Custom Setting Menu*
2. Select *d Shooting/display,* and then scroll to the right.
3. Select *d4 File number sequence* from the menu, and then scroll to the right.
4. Select *On*.
5. Press the *OK* button.

Set the File Number Sequence to *On*

I like knowing how many images I've shot. I also like having a running file number sequence. I choose *On*. Customizing your file numbering will be discussed in more detail in chapter 7.

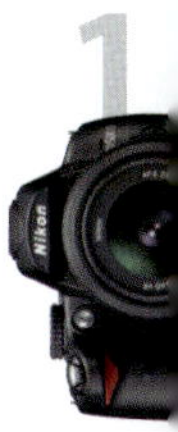

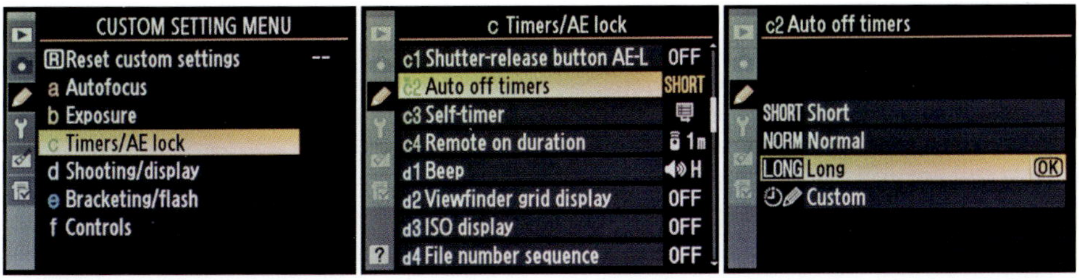

Figure 13 – Setting LCD monitor time-out to 20 seconds

Custom Setting Menu – *Auto off timers*

One of the cool things about digital photography is your ability to immediately view images on the LCD monitor after you take the shot. Unfortunately, the factory default is to display the image for only a few seconds. Often, I like to view the image for a longer time while showing it off to friends and family.

Also, I find myself playing around with the menus and settings on a regular basis. It bugs me to have a menu shut off while I am thinking about a setting.

The reason Nikon set the defaults for these display times to be short is to save battery life. However, I've found that the lithium-ion battery in my D5000 lasts a long time. I don't worry about using the LCD monitor frequently because I rarely run the battery down, even after a full day of shooting.

For that reason I want you to know where to find the settings that control how long the LCD monitor stays on for picture and menu displaying. I like mine to stay on for at least 20 seconds.

I had a little trouble finding this setting at first because, in my opinion, it's not labeled in an intuitive way. I was looking for something like *image display time* in the menus but didn't easily find it. Finally, I located it in the *Custom Setting* section of the menus under *Custom Setting c2 – Auto off timers*.

We will look into all the things that this setting affects in a detailed way in chapter 7, but for now let's just use the setting that provides a longer display time for the pictures and menus.

Figure 13 shows the menu screens to select the *Long* setting, which give you 20 seconds for image and menu display.

Use the following steps to configure the LCD monitor time-out:

1. Press the MENU button, and scroll to the *Custom Setting Menu*.
2. Select *c Timers/AE lock*, and then scroll to the right.
3. Select *c2 Auto off timers* from the menu, and then scroll to the right.
4. Select *Long*.
5. Press the *OK* button.

LCD Monitor Time-Out Recommendation

Using the *Long* setting, you'll have a full 20 seconds before the monitor shuts off from inactivity. This will allow you more time to enjoy your own photography on the large monitor screen, and you'll even have some time to show pictures to others. This will also allow for enough time to adjust various settings in the menu system while referring to this book and the User's Manual, without the screen shutting off prematurely.

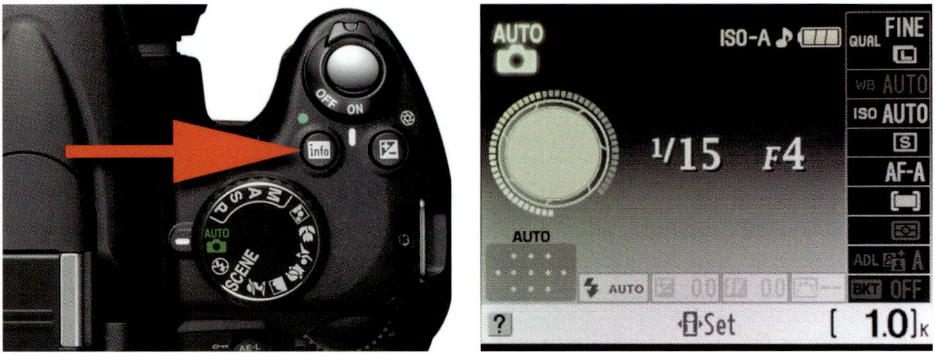

Figure 14 – The info (information) button and screen

Information Edit Screen

The Nikon D5000 has a shortcut method to allow you to set various critical settings. Some of them are available only on the *Information edit* screen.

There are two screens that we'll consider in this section. One is the information screen, and the other is the *Information edit* screen. The information screen shows you the camera's current settings. The *Information edit* screen allows you to change many of those settings.

There are a total of 14 configurable settings on the *Information edit* screen. We'll initially configure 10 of them. Later, in various parts of this book, we'll consider the other 4 settings. For now, the factory defaults on those settings should suffice.

Let's look at the two informational screens — the information screen and the *Information edit* screen.

You will see some terms that may not be familiar to you, so here is a quick overview:

- RAW = unprocessed digital image (like raw food that has yet to be cooked).
- NEF RAW = Nikon's version of RAW NEF stands for Nikon electronic file.
- JPEG = Joint Photographic Experts Group image compression standard

Accessing and editing the information screen can be a little confusing at first. *Figure 14* shows the information screen, which displays when you first turn the camera on or press the info button on top of the camera. The info button is like a light switch—it toggles the information screen on and off. You can also get to the information screen by pressing the <**i**> information edit button once (see *figure 15*) whenever the information screen is not showing. The information edit button is found on the lower-left rear of the camera.

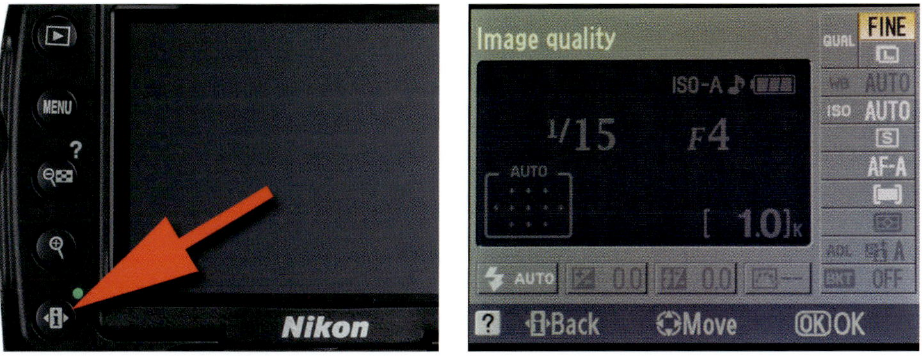

Figure 15 – The information edit button and screen

Using the Information Edit Screens

To use the *Information edit* screen, just turn the camera on, and when you see the normal information display appear (see *figure 14*), press the <**i**> information edit button on the back of the camera in the lower-left corner. If the camera is already on, you may have to press the information edit button twice.

To make this process less confusing, just keep pressing the information edit button until you see the *Information edit* screen, shown in *figure 15*. You'll be using that screen to reconfigure some of the settings you set earlier using the normal camera menus. I think you'll like using the *Information edit* screen to configure the critical items it contains because you won't have to remember what menu the item normally lives under.

Let's just start at the top of the *Information edit* screen and look at what can be adjusted. Once again, we have already adjusted some of these settings using the menu screens earlier in the chapter. However, I want you to learn this shortcut method to setting those same functions, and also have you use the menus to learn where things live. The D5000 has hundreds of settings in its menus (many more than could be contained on the *Information edit* screen), therefore, it's important that you learn to use the menus for other settings you'll need to adjust as your proficiency with the camera increases.

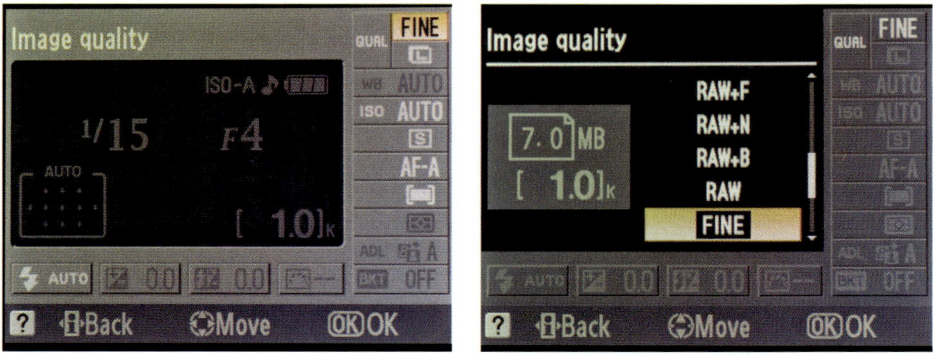

Figure 16 – Information edit screens – *Image quality*

<i> Image Quality Settings

The first settings we'll examine are the *Image quality* selections (see *figure 16*).

You'll notice the words *Image quality* in the upper-left portion of the screen and the word *QUAL* next to *FINE* and *L* (unless your camera has been set to different settings). There are seven settings available to you for *Image quality*:

- *RAW+F* (NEF RAW + JPEG Fine)
- *RAW+N* (NEF RAW + JPEG Normal)
- *RAW+B* (NEF RAW + JPEG Basic)
- *RAW* (NEF RAW)
- *FINE* (JPEG Fine) (Here's the one we want to use!)
- *NORM* (JPEG Normal)
- *BASIC* (JPEG Basic)

To use the *Information edit* screen to adjust the image quality to one of the seven available settings, follow these steps:

1. Press the <**i**> information edit button until you see the *Information edit* screen (see *figure 16*, image at left).
2. Make sure the yellow highlighted rectangle is positioned in the *Image quality* field, as shown in the image on the left in *figure 16* (where is says *FINE*).
3. Press the *OK* button.
4. You'll be presented with the second *Image quality* screen (the image on the right in *figure 16*). Here you'll see the *Image quality* selections mentioned previously. Using the Multi Selector, scroll up or down the list and choose *FINE* (JPEG Fine) for now. You'll also notice that the camera gives you a couple of useful pieces of information. Just to the left of the *Image quality* selections, you'll see information on the approximate image file size (MB) and the number of images your camera's memory card can hold for the current *Image quality* selection.
5. Once you've made your selection, press the *OK* button. The camera will return to the main *Information edit* screen with *FINE* showing in the *Image quality* field.

This is a shortcut to using the *Shooting Menu* to set the image quality. We'll discuss this setting, and what the various selections mean in more detail in chapter 6, "Shooting Menu". Now let's look at the next setting, *Image size*.

Use JPEG Mode for Now... RAW Mode for Experienced Shooters

Until you are familiar with using a DSLR camera and have learned to adjust images on your computer (called post-processing), I suggest you use JPEG mode. Shooting in RAW mode has significant benefits but forces you to use your computer to decide the image's final format (i.e., JPEG, TIFF, and so on). You can convert the image in-camera from RAW to JPEG if you'd like, but it's simply easier to work on an image in the computer. Later, when we look into the *Retouch Menu*, you'll see lots of ways you can work on images in-camera. We'll examine the various image formats and their pros and cons in chapter 6, "Shooting Menu".

<i> Image Size Settings

If you want to reduce your D5000's image size so that it's no longer a 12.2-megapixel camera, you can do it with this setting. You can make the camera shoot a 6.9- or 3.1-megapixel image instead. This is basically what *Image size* is all about.

Why would someone want to reduce the megapixel rating of their camera? I've scratched my head over this issue. The only thing I can come up with is that the smaller file size saves card space.

I suppose it would be good to use this setting if you were in the wilds of Africa on safari and realized that you forgot to bring spare memory cards. Or maybe you only shoot images for websites and don't need the normal file size. Other than those reasons, I can't see why anyone would want to reduce their megapixel rating. To me, this is like driving an eight-cylinder car and pulling the spark plug wires on four cylinders. Limited usefulness! Of course, you may have good reasons for shooting smaller images besides the ones I mentioned.

The *Image size* settings are found in the *Information edit* screens as shown in *figure 17*.

Here are the selections for the *Image size* setting:

- *L* (Large – 4288 x 2848 pixels – 12.2 megapixels)
- *M* (Medium – 3216 x 2136 pixels – 6.9 megapixels)
- *S* (Small – 2144 x 1424 pixels – 3.1 megapixels)

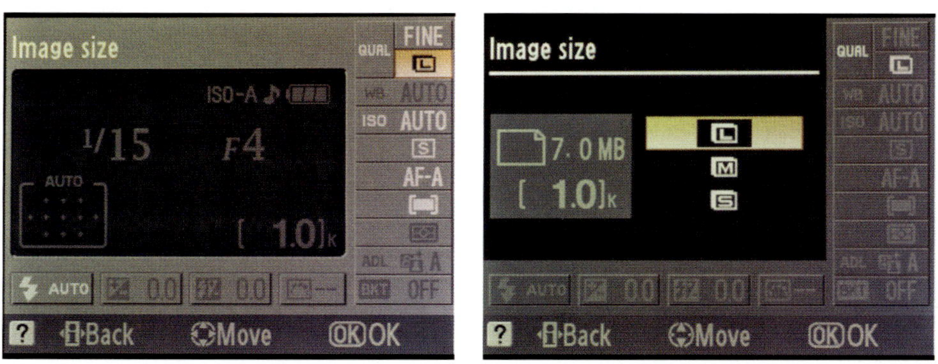

Figure 17 – Information edit screens – *Image size*

The following steps will help you set or validate *Image size*:

1. Press the <**i**> information edit button until you see the *Information edit* screen.
2. Make sure the yellow highlighted rectangle is positioned in the *Image size* field (see *figure 17*, on left).
3. Press the *OK* button.
4. You'll be presented with the second *Image size* screen (on the right in *figure 17*). It has the list of image size selections mentioned previously. Using the Multi Selector, scroll up or down the list and choose *L* (Large). You'll also notice that the camera gives you a couple of useful pieces of information. Just to the left of the list of *Image size* selections, you'll see information on the approximate image file size (MB) and number of images your camera's memory card can hold for the current *Image size* selection.
5. Once you've made your selection, press the *OK* button. The camera will return to the main *Information edit* screen with *L* showing in the *Image size* field.

Image size applies to shooting only in the JPEG modes. If you shoot exclusively in RAW mode, you won't be able to select *Image size*. When you select RAW, the size section "grays out," or becomes unavailable.

JPEG *Image Size* Setting

I always use the large image size when I shoot in JPEG.

<i> White Balance (WB) Settings

White balance is very important for getting correct colors in your pictures. This book has an entire chapter devoted to the subject. For now, we'll just select the setting that most people use most of the time: *AUTO*. This setting instructs your camera to read the "color temperature" of the light when you press the shutter release button down to take each picture. It allows your camera to calculate how to balance the colors in the picture according to how "warm" or "cool" the light source is. It does a good job; so don't worry about it for now. We'll discuss WB, and its various settings, in great detail in chapter 4, "White Balance".

Figure 18 shows the screens used to select the *AUTO WB* setting.

Follow these steps to configure *White balance* to *AUTO*:

1. Press the <**i**> information edit button until you see the *Information edit* screen (on the left in *figure 18*).
2. Make sure the yellow highlighted rectangle is positioned in the *WB* (white balance) field.
3. Press the *OK* button.
4. You'll be presented with the second *White balance* screen (on the right in *figure 18*). It has a list of WB selections. The selection we are concerned with is the AUTO setting at the top of the list. If *AUTO* is not currently selected, use the Multi Selector to select it.
5. Press the *OK* button. The camera will return to the main *Information edit* screen with *AUTO* showing in the *WB* field.

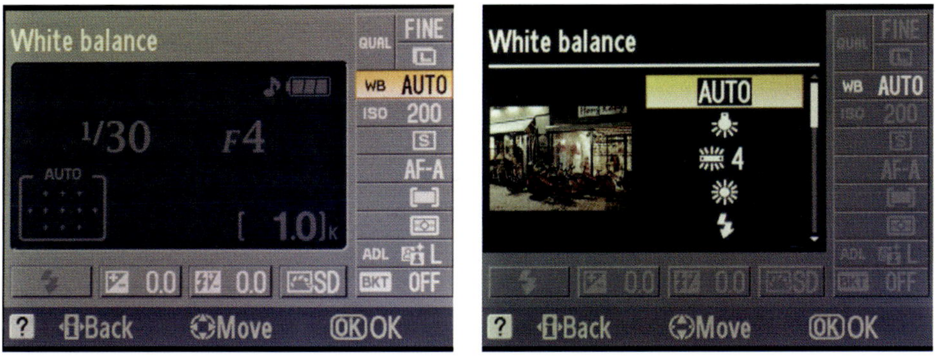

Figure 18 – Selecting AUTO white balance

AUTO White Balance Recommendation

Until you've read chapter 4 on white balance, the *AUTO* setting will give you excellent color balance in your images. Why would you ever want to change it from AUTO then? Many won't! However, there can be some variance in the color balance of each shot in *AUTO* mode since the camera makes a separate WB decision for *each* picture. If you are concerned with image color consistency, you'll need to learn to use the WB settings. Plus, there are other reasons to control white balance carefully, as you'll discover in chapter 4.

<i> ISO Sensitivity Settings

Normally, the lower the *ISO sensitivity* you use for current light conditions, the better. For now, just leave the camera set to ISO 200, which is three menu positions down from its absolute lowest setting (Lo 1, or ISO 100). The camera defaults to ISO 200, so you may not have to change this. However, eventually, you *will* want to change it, and often, so learn how to use this setting now.

Figure 19 shows the *Information edit* screens to select 200 ISO.

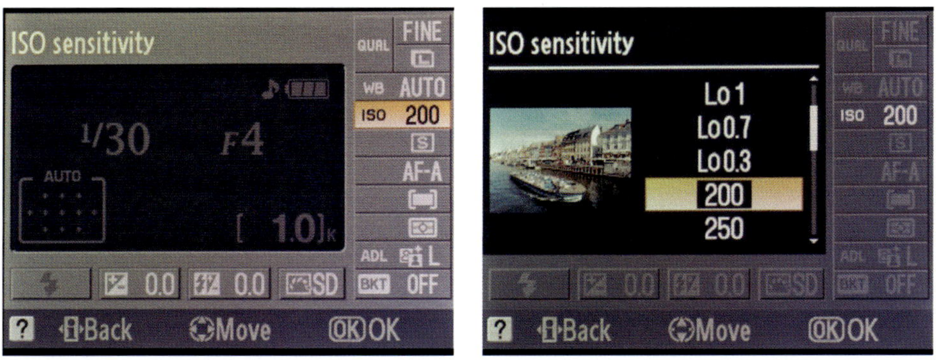

Figure 19 – Selecting ISO sensitivity level 200

Follow these steps to make the ISO sensitivity selection:

1. Press the <**i**> information edit button until you see the *Information edit* screen (on the left in *figure 19*).
2. Make sure the yellow highlighted rectangle is positioned in the *ISO* field.
3. Press the *OK* button.
4. You'll be presented with the second *ISO sensitivity* screen (on the right in *figure 19*). It has a list of ISO selections. The selection we're concerned with is the ISO 200 setting, fourth position down from the top of the list. If 200 is not currently selected, use the Multi Selector to select it.
5. Press the *OK* button. The camera will return to the main *Information edit* screen with 200 showing after the ISO setting.

ISO Sensitivity Recommendation

I use ISO 200 most often for handheld shots and 100 ISO (*Lo 1*) when I'm shooting nature shots from a tripod. Remember, ISO sensitivity is how sensitive the camera's image sensor is to light. The higher the ISO (more sensitive), the lower the light can be while you take pictures. However, when you raise the ISO, you also raise the potential for grainy-looking digital noise in your images. Keep the ISO as low as possible. You may want to change this to between 400 and 800 for indoor photography, especially if you aren't using the pop-up flash. You can select from ISO 100 to 6400. Everything lower than ISO 200 is represented by *Lo*, and everything higher than ISO 3200 is represented by *HI*. In other words, the "normal" ISO range for this camera is 200 to 3200. If you want, you can select one exposure value (EV) step lower (half the sensitivity) than ISO 200 (*Lo 1* = ISO 100) and one EV step higher (twice the sensitivity) than ISO 1600 (HI 1 = 6400 ISO).

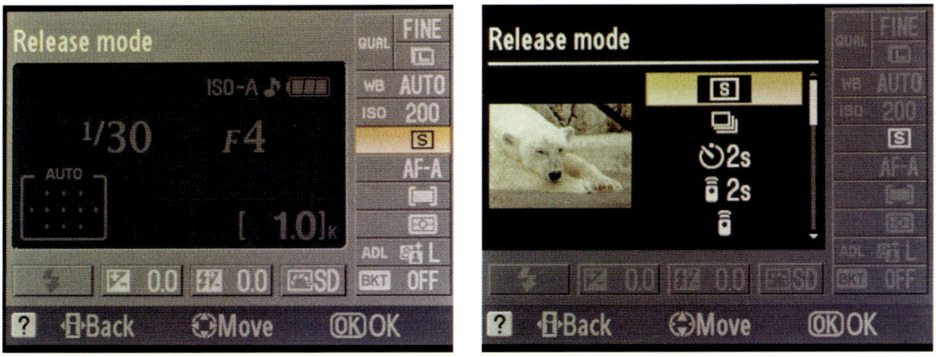

Figure 20 – Setting the release mode to *S*, single frame

<i> Release Mode Settings

The D5000 has several release modes that control how many images per second you can shoot. Until you've learned to use the release modes, covered in chapter 10, "Multi-CAM 1000 Autofocus", use *S*, or single frame release mode. This mode takes only one picture each time you press the shutter release button.

Figure 20 shows the series of *Information edit* screens to select single frame release mode.

Here are the steps to make sure your camera is set to *S* mode:

1. Press the <**i**> information edit button until you see the *Information edit* screen (on the left in *figure 20*).
2. Make sure the yellow highlight rectangle is positioned in the *Release mode* field.
3. Press the *OK* button.
4. You'll be presented with the second *Release mode* screen (on the right in *figure 20*). It has a list of mode selections. The selection we're concerned with is the *S* setting at the top of the list. If *S* isn't currently selected, use the Multi Selector to select it.
5. Press the *OK* button. The camera will return to the main *Information edit* screen with *S* showing in the *Release mode* field.

There are several other modes in the list, such as self-timer, infrared remote, and quiet shutter-release. Let's discuss quiet shutter-release briefly. You can find the directions for selecting this mode in your User's Manual (page 68).

Quiet shutter-release mode: This mode mutes the sound of the shutter by slowing its operations and separating the raising and lowering of the internal camera "reflex" mirror in two steps. The reflex mirror is used to pass light from the camera's lens through the viewfinder and to your eye.

Have you noticed how a DSLR's viewfinder very briefly goes black when you take a picture? That's the mirror being raised so the shutter can open and allow light to pass onto the camera's image capturing sensor. The mirror and shutter both make a clicking noise as they raise and lower. That's the sound you hear when you take a picture, and it is somewhat loud.

When the camera is *not* in quiet shutter-release mode and you press the shutter release button, the mirror raises, the shutter opens and closes, and then the mirror lowers so that you can see through the lens for the next picture. What quiet shutter-release mode does is slow the entire process down, separating the individual functions. Here are the steps the camera takes in normal mode, and then in quiet mode.

Normal shutter-release:

1. You press the shutter release button.
2. The camera raises the mirror, opens and closes the shutter, then lowers the mirror.
3. The sound could be described as "ker-chunk"—A loud double-click.

Quiet shutter-release:

1. You press the shutter release button.
2. The camera raises the mirror, delays very slightly, then opens and closes the shutter.
3. The camera does nothing else until you release the shutter button. When you let go of the button, only then does the camera lower the mirror.
4. The sound could be described as "Click click...delay until you release button... click."

The whole quiet shutter-release process seems slower and muted. It *is* quieter than a normal release and could make a difference when taking a picture of a skittish creature like a bird, a huge grizzly bear, or a bride during a wedding ceremony.

Continuous Release Mode Recommendation

If you want to experiment with shooting a large number of images in a continuous sequence, select the release mode that looks like a series of small rectangles. It's just below the *S* in the screen on the right in *figure 20* and is called the continuous release mode. Now when you hold the shutter release down, the camera will shoot at up to four frames per second until you release the button or it runs out of internal camera memory buffer space (up to 100 images). When you don't need the rapid fire of continuous mode, just use single frame instead. By the way, you can't use continuous release mode with the pop-up flash raised. The flash can't recycle fast enough to fire continuously, so the camera reverts to single frame release mode.

<i> Focus Mode Settings

Now, let's consider the focus mode (*figure 21*). First, we'll set the D5000 to use *AF-A* mode. This is the best mode for a less-experienced user or for someone who doesn't want to be bothered with selecting autofocus (AF) modes. There are two other modes (*AF-S* and *AF-C*), but *AF-A* mode will automatically imitate one of the other two based on what your subject is doing.

Here's how it works when you set your camera to *AF-A* mode:

- ***Subject is not moving:*** The camera sees a static subject so it uses *Single-servo AF* (*AF-S*) mode automatically. Focus becomes static on the subject and does not continue updating unless the subject starts moving.

- ***Subject is, or starts, moving:*** The D5000 uses *Continuous-servo AF* (*AF-C*), and as long as the subject is moving, the camera keeps seeking the best focus.

Until you are experienced with the autofocus system, I suggest you leave the camera set to *AF-A*. Later, after you've read chapter 10, "Multi-CAM 1000 Autofocus", you'll have a much better understanding of how to use these modes.

Here are the steps to make sure your camera is set to *AF-A* (see (*figure 21*):

1. Press the <**i**> information edit button until you see the *Information edit* screen (on the left in *figure 21*).
2. Make sure the yellow highlighted rectangle is positioned in the *Focus mode* field.
3. Press the *OK* button.
4. You'll be presented with the second *Focus mode* screen (on the right in *figure 21*). It has a list of mode selections. The selection we're concerned with is the *AF-A* setting at the top of the list. If it isn't currently selected, use the Multi Selector to select it.
5. Press the *OK* button. The camera will return to the main *Information edit* screen with *S* showing in the *Release mode* field.

AF-A Mode Recommendation

Don't tell anyone, but I leave my D5000 set to *AF-A* mode most of the time. It works really well. If I'm shooting critical images, I may change it to one of the other two settings, but only in rare cases. *AF-A* gives us the best of both worlds—with *AF-S* or *AF-C* on call and as needed without thinking about it.

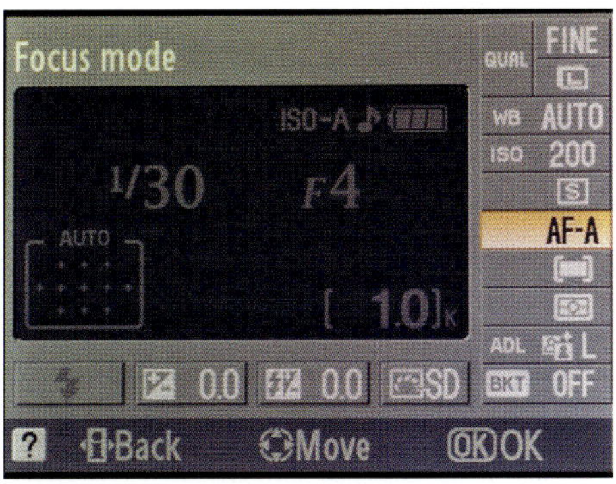

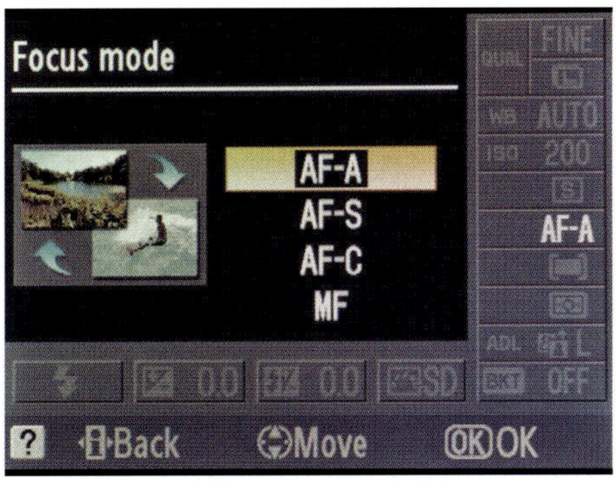

Figure 21 – Autofocus set to *AF-A*

<i> *AF-Area* Mode Settings

This setting is designed to let you select how many of the 11 autofocus sensor points are active at any moment. We will discuss these modes in great detail in chapter 10, "Multi-CAM 1000 Autofocus", but for now let's use a mode that will protect you while you learn to use the camera.

The D5000 has excellent face recognition technology and will automatically recognize people that are facing the camera. It will focus on faces as its highest priority. By using the auto-area mode, you let the camera decide where your subject is located and focus on it automatically. I tested this by having my wife stand next to various objects while I tested focus. Even with her face positioned next to high-contrast objects, the camera invariably focused on her face instead of the object. It always seemed to focus on the edge of her eyes and the corners of her mouth. Clearly, the face recognition is based on the eye, nose, and mouth relationship. When she turned her face away from the camera so that both eyes were not in view, the D5000 had a much harder time focusing exclusively on her face.

You'll be able to see which *AF* points are in use by how they show on the viewfinder as you look through it and press the shutter button halfway down. You'll see various *AF* points pop up in the viewfinder as the camera explores the subject. If there are no faces in view, it will look for the closest and brightest (highest-contrast) subject and focus on that.

Figure 22 shows the *Information edit* screens used to set the *AF-area mode*.

These steps will help you set auto-area *AF*:

1. Press the <**i**> information edit button until you see the *Information edit* screen (on the left in *figure 22*).
2. Make sure the yellow highlighted rectangle is positioned in the *AF-area mode* field.
3. Press the *OK* button.
4. You'll be presented with the second *AF-area mode* screen (on the right in *figure 22*). It has a list of mode selections. The selection we're concerned with is the auto-area setting, third down from the top of the list. It looks like a white rectangle inside of square brackets. If it isn't currently selected, use the Multi Selector to select it.

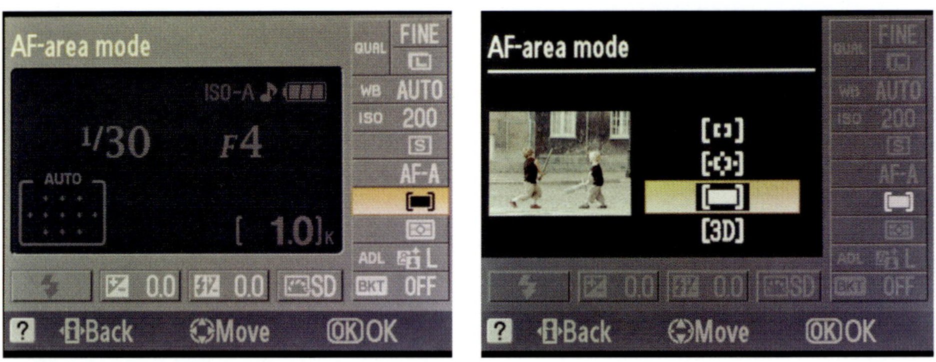

Figure 22 – Autofocus set to *AF-area* mode

5. Press the *OK* button. The camera will return to the main *Information edit* screen with [■] showing in the *AF-area mode* field.

Single Point Mode Recommendation

If you want to use a single AF point and move it around the viewfinder with the Multi Selector, select the single point mode instead. This mode looks like a couple of small brackets side-by-side, like this: **[ ]**. *Single point mode* let's you control where you want to focus the camera. If you feel uncomfortable using it, at least wait until you've read chapter 10 "Multi-CAM 1000 Autofocus", and use *AF-area mode* as described earlier. I use *Single point* a lot, but it requires me to make sure the AF point is over my subject when I get ready to take a picture. Don't be afraid to experiment; you can always change it back.

<i> Metering Settings

The D5000 has three exposure meter settings: 3D Color Matrix Metering II (or matrix), center-weighted, and spot metering. For our initial configuration purposes, we'll use the matrix meter. This metering mode uses a database of thousands of professionally shot images to help decide the best exposure. It uses tone distribution, subject color, and your chosen composition to evaluate the scene. It is amazingly accurate and provides great exposures most of the time. When used with the histogram, which we'll discuss in chapter 3 "White Balance", you can have the high number of well exposed images you've ever taken.

Figure 23 shows the screens to select matrix metering mode.

The following steps will allow you to select matrix mode from the *Metering* menu:

1. Press the <**i**> information edit button until you see the *Information edit* screen (on the left in *figure* 23).
2. Make sure the yellow highlighted rectangle is positioned in the *Metering* field.
3. Press the *OK* button.
4. You'll be presented with the second *Metering* screen. It has a list of meter-type selections. The selection we're concerned with is the matrix setting at the top of the list (see the image on the right in *figure* 23). If it isn't currently selected, use the Multi Selector to select it.

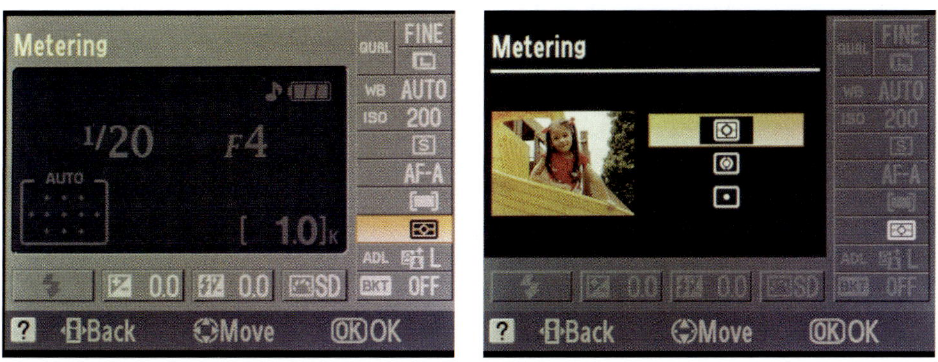

Figure 23 – Selecting the matrix metering mode

5. Press the *OK* button. The camera will return to the main *Information edit* screen showing the matrix metering symbol in the *AF-area mode* field.

Matrix Metering for General Shooting

I use matrix metering for general shooting. When I get very critical about my images, I'll often switch to spot metering. However, using the spot meter tends to emphasize the correct exposure of one very small section of the image, so use it carefully. Matrix, on the other hand, analyzes the entire image before making an exposure decision. My best suggestion to you is to learn to use the histogram as discussed in chapter 3 "Exposure Metering System, Exposure Modes, and Histogram." Then your choice of meter types will not be as critical. In the meantime, use matrix and enjoy your camera.

<i> Active D-Lighting Settings

Image sensors can capture only a limited range of light. In a scene with a broad range of brightness levels (i.e., a wide dynamic range), as on a bright sunny day, it is not possible to completely capture all the detail in the highlights and shadows at the same time.

The D5000 has a neat feature that helps extend the light range of an image so that detail that is normally lost in the darkest darks and lightest lights can be salvaged to a degree. It is called *Active D-Lighting*. This mode allows the camera to pull detail out of the darker areas of the image while trying to protect the highlights from blowout, without you having to do anything with the image on your computer.

Active D-Lighting has the effect of lowering contrast in an image. If overused, it can make the image look weird

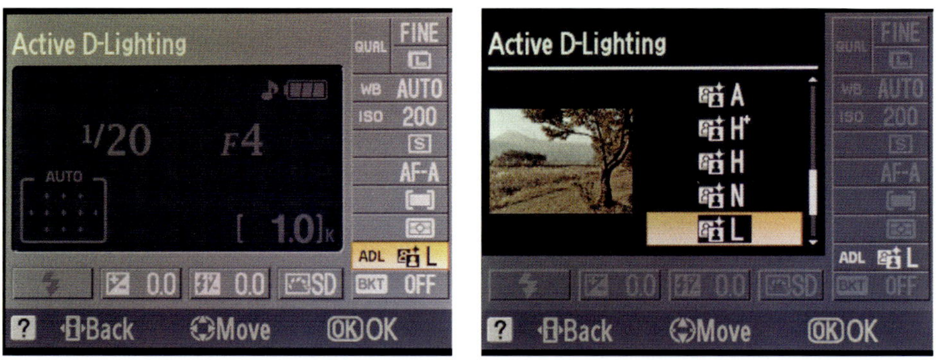

Figure 24 – Setting *Active D-Lighting* to Low

My Conclusions

In this chapter we went through some of the most important initial configuration items in the camera. As you read through this book, you'll find plenty of other things to think about and configure. For instance, the *Custom Setting Menu* has 23 separate items to consider. Each item is composed of multiple selections that you'll need to understand.

In chapter 3, "Exposure Metering System, Exposure Modes, and Histogram", we'll examine all the different scene modes found in the D5000. Those are the six scene modes available on the mode dial on top the camera. Plus, the D5000 gives you 13 more scene modes you can access only by setting the mode dial to SCENE, and using the *Shooting Menu* or *Information* screen to select them.

When you consider the fact that the D5000 has seven separate menu systems, you may realize that this chapter has only barely scratched the surface of the configurations you can do. The Nikon D5000 is a very complex camera, with functions designed to appeal to a large number of people shooting all sorts of image styles. If you just want the camera to be a more powerful point-and-shoot camera, like a heavy, very advanced Nikon Coolpix, it is happy to comply. If you want to take control of the camera and learn to use all its many features, you can become, as Nikon often says, "a passionate photographer" with it.

Fortunately, you don't have to configure all the settings in the camera immediately. You can safely get by with just the settings we've covered in this chapter—for a while anyway. As your skills in photography grow and you discover ways to use the more esoteric features of the D5000, you'll have a resource in this book to help you in your mastery of the camera. It certainly is a powerful and flexible digital imaging system.

Enjoy your new D5000!

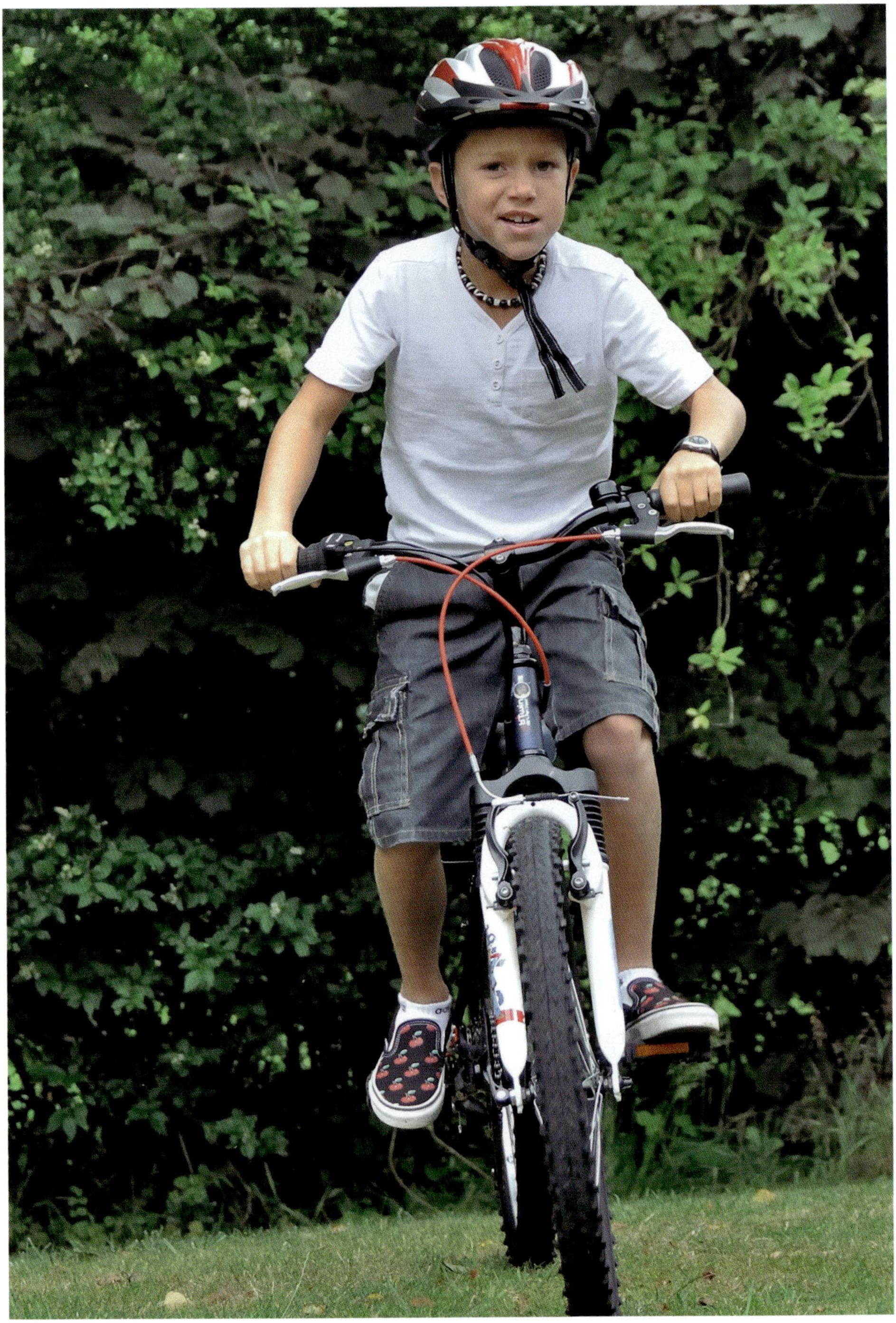

The Nikon D5000 allows you to take excellent pictures without understanding how the aperture and shutter speed works or what a focal length is. You can simply select either Aperture-priority Auto mode and/or Shutter–priority Auto mode, or you can just go fully automatic and the camera has you covered. So why have I included a chapter devoted to aperture and shutter speed?

Many D5000 owners are interested in going beyond basic photography. They may have been using a camera with fewer features or even a point-and-shoot model. The D5000 is an advanced camera in that it provides a fine degree of control over the final look of an image.

Since beginners may need just a little help with how these most basic of camera and lens functions work, I decided to include this chapter. Even if you feel that you understand the concepts well enough, why not do a quick review? Maybe you'll learn something helpful.

The relationship between the aperture and shutter speed seems to be a difficult thing to understand for quite a few photographers. Yet it is one of the most important concepts to understand since it significantly affects how an image looks.

In this chapter, we'll look at the aperture and shutter speed settings in a comprehensive way. Then, we'll explore how the relationship between the two settings changes the appearance of an image. Finally, we'll consider how the various focal lengths of your lenses will affect your choice of lens.

Understanding the Camera's Aperture

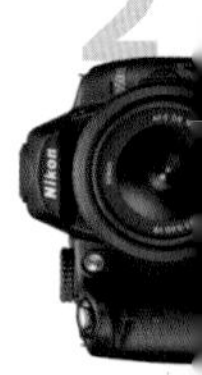

You've probably read about or seen what's called a pinhole camera. A few years back many people liked to experiment with them for fun and education. All you needed was a box or tube, a piece of film, and a pinhole to use instead of a lens.

The concept involves fastening a piece of film on an inside wall of a light-tight box and pricking a tiny pinhole in the opposite wall of the box. This will later allow light to shine through the pinhole onto the film on the opposite side. To use the pinhole camera, you temporarily cover the pinhole, take the box out into the sunlight, place it in front of an interesting scene, uncover the pinhole, and leave for while.

When you return, you cover the pinhole, go into a darkroom, cut the box open, and develop the film. If your pinhole was the right size for the amount of time the light was shining on the film through the pinhole, you'll have a nice image taken in a very basic way. If you guessed wrong about the amount of time you allowed the light to shine through the pinhole and onto the film, the image will be either overexposed or underexposed.

It seems a lot easier to use your D5000 instead of a pinhole camera, doesn't it? While it might be fun to use a pinhole camera a few times, it certainly wouldn't allow you to take the wide range of beautiful images you've been getting from your complex digital camera.

The D5000 works in a similar way to the basic pinhole camera. The difference is variability. You can vary the size of the "pinhole" with the D5000.

With the pinhole camera, if you wanted to leave the box out in the sun for a longer period, you'd make a very small pinhole so only a little light shines on the film. If you wanted to leave the box out in the sun for a shorter period, you'd make the pinhole bigger so that more light would hit the film.

That's the concept of an aperture. It is basically a variably-sized pinhole, and you (or the camera) can choose that size. Instead of a hole in a box with film taped to one wall, you have a light-tight camera "box" with a lens that has aperture blades that allow you to vary the size of the pinhole. Instead of shining light on a piece film, you have a digital sensor.

Figure 1 shows a sample of lenses with the aperture blades set to various aperture sizes. We are looking at the outer end of the lens, which would normally be pointed at the subject.

If you look at the front of your lens with the lens cap off, you'll see the actual maximum aperture of your camera. Hold your D5000 so that you can look from the front of your lens from about half an arm's length away. Make sure something bright is behind the eyepiece on the back of the camera. You can actually see through the front of your lens, right through the rear eyepiece of the camera. It's sort of like the time you looked through a pair of binoculars backwards when you were a child. Everything appeared small and distant, but you could see things.

The hole you see behind the glass of the lens is the biggest aperture (or largest pinhole) your D5000 can use with the particular lens mounted on the camera. Basically, the opening in the lens is your camera's "aperture."

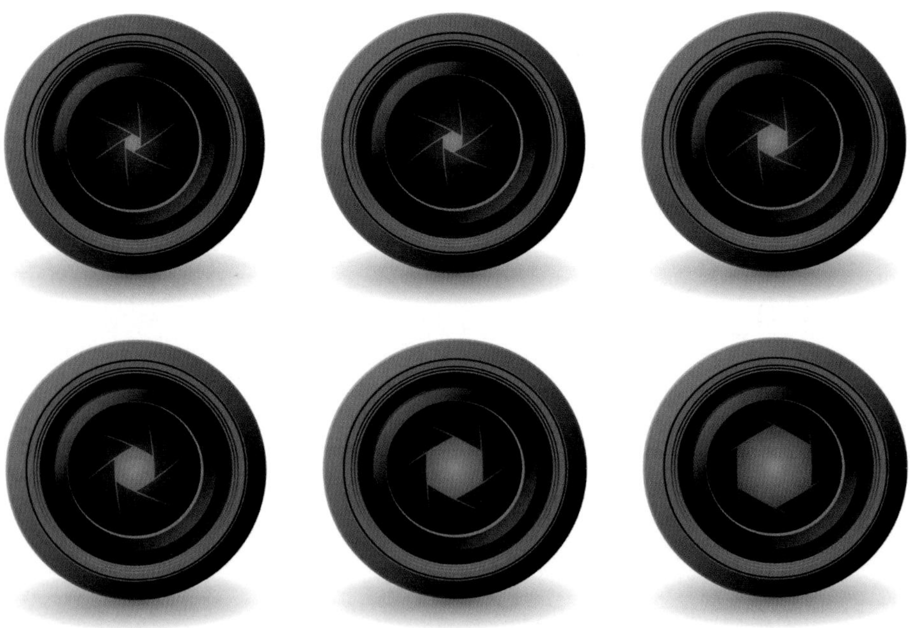

Figure 1 – Aperture variability

How Does the Aperture Work? – An Experiment

Now, go to an area bright enough that your D5000 will *not* need to use the popup Speedlight flash. It's best, for this experiment, if you go outside so that there's a lot of light. Now, I want you to take a picture of your face from an arm's length away. You can keep the picture as an example of how you look while concentrating.

While you take the picture, pay careful attention to the aperture opening you saw earlier. If the light is bright enough, you will see the D5000 do something quite interesting. At the moment the picture is taken, the camera meters the light and adjusts the aperture size by moving a series of blades around the aperture opening (see *figure 1*). You will see the aperture size change very briefly as the picture is being taken. If there is bright light outside, the opening will very briefly appear to get darker and smaller.

This aperture opening can be changed from large to small so that the amount of light getting into the camera can be accurately adjusted for a correct exposure. The size of that opening—chosen either by you in a manual mode or by the camera in the automatic mode—is referred to as an aperture number.

What Is an Aperture Number?

If you look through the eyepiece of your D5000, you can see the shutter speed and aperture shown on the lower-left side of the viewfinder screen. You'll see something like *125 F4* or *30 F5.6* displayed. The number on the left is the shutter speed, and on the right is the aperture size. You'll also see these same characters displayed in the middle of the information screen.

In *figure 1A*, you'll see the two settings from both the viewfinder and information screen LCD.

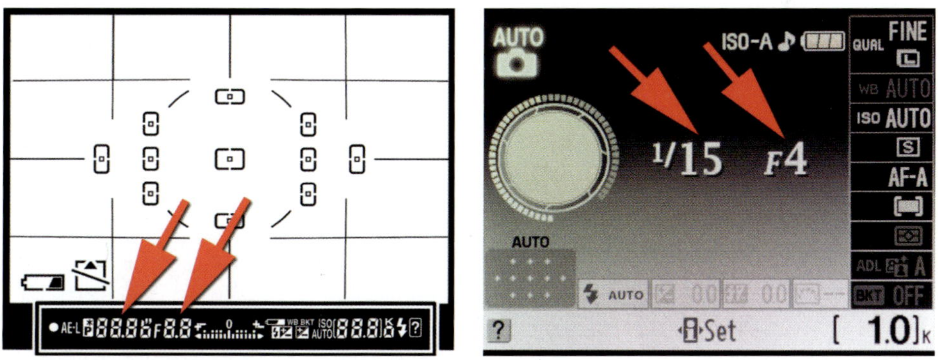

Figure 1A – Shutter speed and aperture settings

We'll look at the shutter speed in the next major section of this chapter. For now, let's examine the aperture numbering system. This system has evolved through many generations to standardize on what we now commonly refer to as f-stops or f-numbers. The *f* comes from terms such as *focal length* and *focal ratio*. The usual method for referring to a specific aperture setting like the one in *figure 1A* is f/4.

If you bought the "kit" version of the Nikon D5000, you will have received the AF-S Nikkor 18-55mm f/3.5-5.6G VR zoom lens with your camera body. You may have chosen a different lens or already owned some lenses when you bought your D5000. However, for this chapter we'll assume that the 18-55mm is the lens on your camera. Let's talk about aperture numbers for this and other lenses.

I am going to discuss only lenses for normal use on a Nikon D5000. There are all sorts of specialty lenses out there with aperture numbers outside the normal range you'll likely use. Many of us will have lenses that run from about f/1.4 to f/32. The AF-S Nikkor 18-55mm f/3.5-5.6G has a range of aperture openings varying between f/3.5 to f/22, although it can actually go all the way down to f/36 when fully zoomed out. What does this mean?

Since it is easier to see, let's look at some aperture openings. In *figure 1B*, you'll see a 50 mm f/1.8 lens set to a large aperture of f/3.5, a medium aperture of f/5.6, and a small aperture of f/11.

The aperture number works the opposite from what many expect. A high number means a small aperture opening. A low number means a big aperture opening. In *figure 1B*, notice how f/3.5 is a big hole compared to f/11's small hole? The big aperture opening of f/3.5 allows more light into the camera, while the small aperture opening of f/11 allows less light to pass through.

Moving from a large aperture opening to a smaller aperture opening is called "stopping down." The word *stop* comes from the time when we had aperture rings on virtually all our lenses instead of only a few. As you turned the aperture ring, you would feel a click, or a stopping

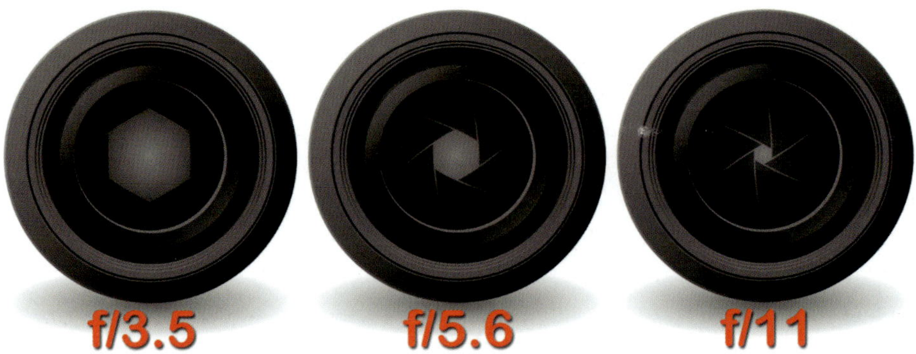

Figure 1B – Aperture settings f/3.5, f/5.6, and f/11

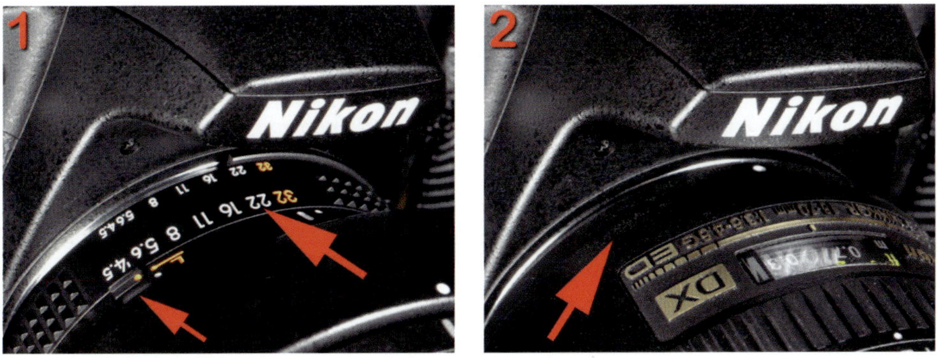

Figure 1C – Manual aperture ring with lock and G lens with no aperture ring

point, for each aperture. Moving the ring one stop meant moving between these click points by one click. In older lenses, each click stop is equal to 1 EV of light transmission—either half or double the brightness according to the direction you turned the ring. Newer manual-use lenses generally have 1/2 and 1 exposure value (EV) click stops also.

In *figure 1C,* on the left, you can see the aperture adjustment ring on my AF Nikkor 80-400mm f/4-5.6 lens, which is designed for use on older and newer cameras. The large arrow points to the ring, while the small arrow points to the ring lock.

Figure 1C, the right side shows a G Nikkor lens (like your 18-55mm kit lens), which has no external aperture ring. Most lenses produced today are G-type lenses with no aperture adjustment rings since we use the command dial to adjust aperture.

If you have an older lens with an aperture ring, you need to set it (and lock it) to its smallest aperture, like f/22, if you want to adjust the aperture using normal camera controls. If you don't lock it to the smallest aperture setting on the lens, your D5000 will show an error message on the camera's LCD screen and will disable the shutter. The error will say, *Lock lens aperture ring at minimum aperture (largest f/-number).*

Look at your lens, and if it doesn't have an aperture adjustment ring, as shown on the left of *figure 1C*, you don't have to worry about locking it. Yours probably does *not* have an external aperture adjustment ring. Now, let's get back to aperture information.

An aperture opening of f/8 is one stop down from aperture opening f/5.6. F/8 lets in one stop less light than f/5.6, which simply means that f/8 transmits one half as much light as f/5.6.

The amount of light entering the camera is measure in stops, or EV steps. You could express this by saying f/5.6 allows 1 EV step more light into the camera than f/8, which is a fancy way of saying that f/5.6 allows twice as much light into the camera as f/8 does.

So, 1 EV step, or one stop, is simply a value with one-half or twice as much light as the previous step, depending on which direction you are changing the aperture opening. One stop up allows in twice as much light. For example, opening the aperture from f/8 to f/5.6 allows the camera to receive twice as much light. One stop down reduces the light by one-half. Closing the aperture from f/5.6 to f/8 allows only one-half the amount of light into the camera.

Figure 1B shows the lens "stopping down" from f/3.5 to f/5.6, then to f/11. When you stop down from a large aperture to a smaller aperture, you do so in EV steps, or stops. Following this paragraph is a list of f/stops for the AF-S Nikkor 18-55mm f/3.5-5.6 in 1/3 or 1/2 EV steps. You can modify this step value by changing *Custom Setting b1(EV steps for exposure cntrl.)* to either 1/3 or 1/2. The default is 1/3. We'll consider the various custom controls in detail in chapter 7, "Custom Settings." Here are the apertures available with your 18-55mm f/3.5-5.6 lens:

Custom Setting b1 set to 1/3 EV step (1/3 of a full stop):

Moving from big aperture (large opening) to small aperture (small opening)

- f/3.5, f/4, f/4.5, f/5, f/5.6, f/6.3, f/7.1, f/8, f/9, f/10, f/11, f/13, f/14, f/16, f/18, f/20, f/22

Custom setting b1 set to 1/2 EV step (1/2 of a full stop):

Moving from big aperture (large opening) to small aperture (small opening)

- f/3.5, f/4, f/4.8, f/5.6, f/6.7, f/8, f/9.5, f/11, f/13, f/16, f/19, f/22

Each step in the preceding lists lets in either more or less light; depending on which direction you are moving in the list. When you are using aperture-priority or manual exposure mode, as will be discussed in chapter 3, "Exposure Metering System, Exposure Modes, and Histogram," you'll be able to control the aperture with the command dial on your camera.

Remember that you can buy other lenses that will have a larger maximum aperture, such as Nikon's professional-level AF-S Nikkor 17-55mm f/2.8 lens. These types of lenses cost more than the D5000 itself, sometimes significantly more. What do you get for your money? You get a lens with a larger maximum aperture that can let in more light for low-light shooting along with premium lens glass and a more robust lens build (less plastic).

The basic concept to learn and remember about the aperture on the Nikon D5000 is that the aperture controls the *amount* of light (how much) entering the lens during an exposure. Later in this chapter, we'll discuss the shutter speed, which allows you to control the other side of the issue—*how long* the light is allowed to enter the camera.

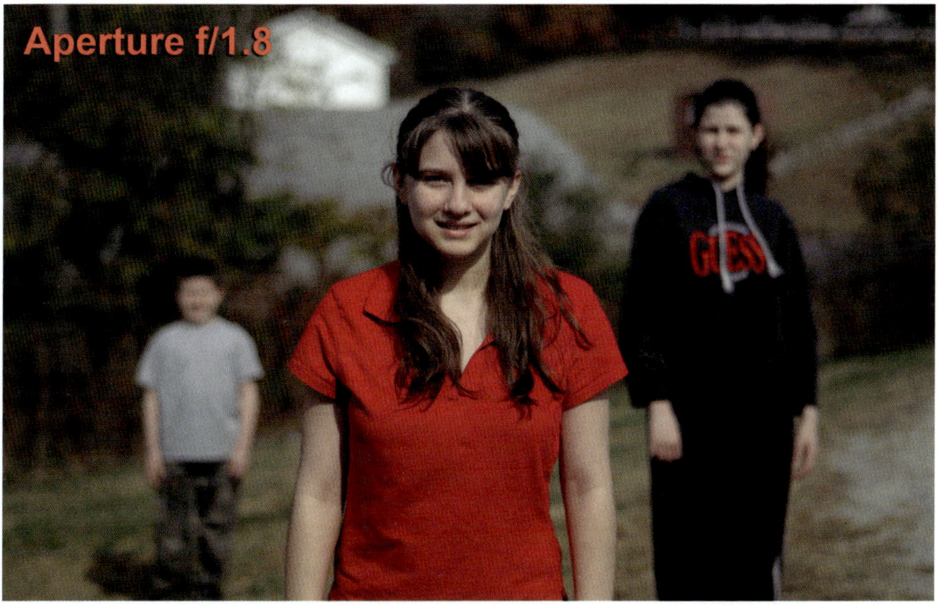

Figure 2 – Three kids at f/1.8 aperture—shallow depth of field

Understanding Depth of Field

Depth of field (DOF) is one of those things that confuse many new DSLR users, yet it is very important. The aperture opening controls the depth of field, or range of sharp focus, in your images. I'm going to attempt to explain this concept with pictures.

Let's say you are taking a picture of a friend who is standing 6 feet (2m) away from you. About 6 feet behind your friend is another person. There is also a third person standing about 6 feet behind the second person. Imagine three people total, each about 6 feet apart, with the friend in front (see *Figure 2*).

You are shooting with a 50mm f/1.8 lens. You focus on your friend's face, the young lady in red, and take a picture. It looks like the image in *figure 2*.

Notice in the *figure 2* that your friend (in red) is in good focus since the focus is on her face. The girl standing behind her, to the right, is not in focus, nor is the young lad even farther away to the left. This is the result of shooting with a big aperture. F/1.8 is a big opening in the aperture blades of your lens. A large aperture opening causes the depth of field, or zone of sharp focus, to be shallow. Only the girl in front is in focus at f/1.8. Not much else is in focus, so there is very little depth of field, probably something like 1.5 feet (.45m). The zone of sharp focus, or depth of field, is only about 1.5 feet deep.

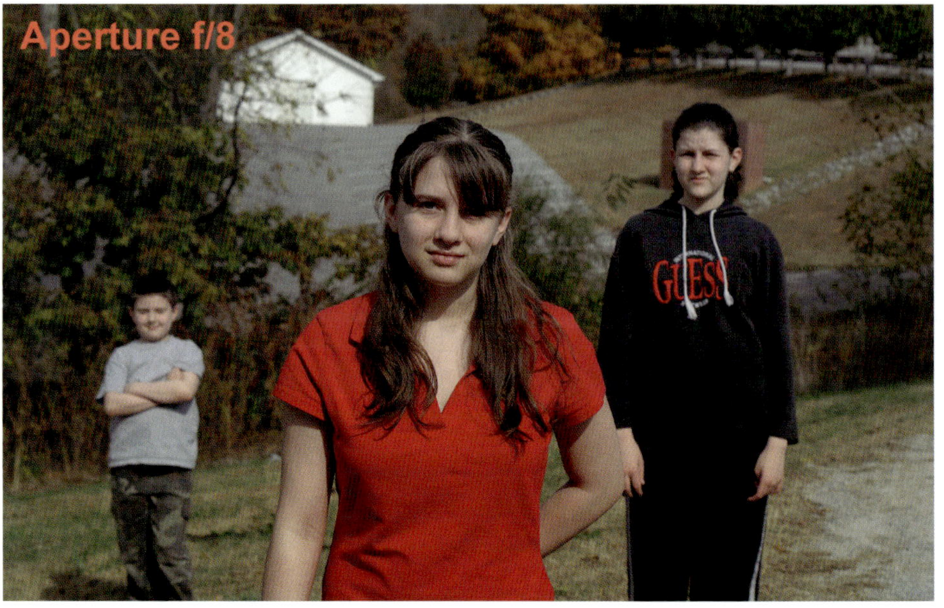

Figure 2A – Three kids at f/8 aperture—medium depth of field

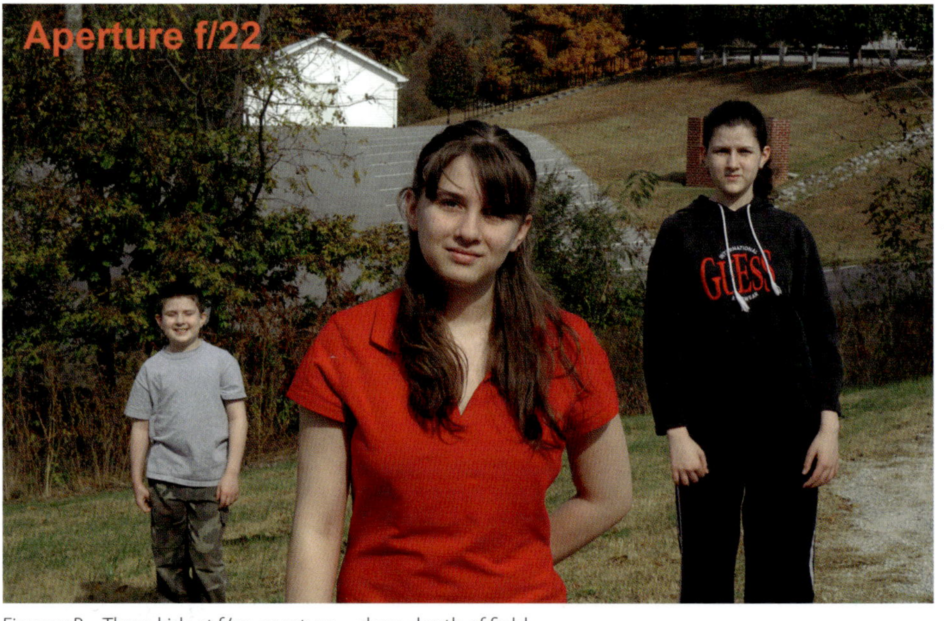

Figure 2B – Three kids at f/22 aperture—deep depth of field

So what would happen if we made the aperture opening smaller, or stopped down, to a medium aperture like f/8? The picture in *figure 2A* shows the resulting depth of field.

In the previous example, *figure 2*, the camera is focused on the young lady in front, and at the large aperture opening of f/1.8, the other subjects in the image were out of focus. In *figure 2A*, without changing the focus in any way, you adjusted your aperture (stopped down) to f/8. Something changed!

Notice in *figure 2A* how the girl in front still looks sharp, but now the girl to the right looks sharp too. You focused your camera on the girl in front, but now the girl to the right is in the zone of sharp focus, even though you didn't change your focus point on the first girl's face. The depth of field, or zone of sharp focus, now extends past the girl in front and covers the girl in back. The zone got deeper.

However, also notice that the boy to the left is still not in focus. The background is not in focus either. The depth of field is deeper, but it's still not deep enough to cover all your subjects.

The image in *figure 2A* is the result of a medium aperture opening (f/8), not large (f/1.8) and not small (f/22). Now, let's consider what happens if we "stop down," or close the aperture to a small opening like f/22.

Aha! Now everything in the picture is sharp. In *figure 2B*, we see that an aperture as slow and small as f/22 makes it easy to get sharp focus. Remember, you focused on the girl in front in all these pictures. At first only she was in focus (f/1.8), and as the aperture got smaller, more and more of the surroundings came into sharp focus (f/8 and f/22).

So, *depth of field is simply the zone of sharp focus*. It extends in front of and behind your focused subject and gets deeper in both directions, toward the camera and away from it, as you "stop down" your lens. If you set your camera to aperture-priority (or manual mode), you can adjust this powerful functionality to control what is in focus in your pictures (see chapter 3).

Here's a basic exposure rule:

- Aperture = How *much* light comes in
- Shutter speed = How *long* the light comes in

Apertures In Review

F/1.8 is an aperture number. An aperture is simply an opening in your lens controlled by blades. It lets light come in through the lens to expose your D5000's sensor. You normally can't see the aperture when you look in the front of your lens because your D5000 allows you to focus with the aperture blades wide open and out of the way. The aperture closes down to its selected setting when you press the shutter release fully to take your picture.

Effect of Focal Length on Depth of Field

One other issue to consider is how the focal length of a lens affects depth of field. When you use a wide-angle lens on your D5000, such as an 18 mm lens, you have significantly more depth of field available. A wide-angle lens is considered a "short" focal length. The shorter the focal length, the greater the potential depth of field. If you are using a "longer" lens, such as a telephoto of 105 mm, which reaches out and pulls a subject in closer, the depth of field that's available will be considerably more shallow. Longer lenses, because they compress perspective, have a smaller zone of sharp focus. So, if you are interested in maximum depth of field, use the shortest focal length that will cover the subject.

Now, let's move on to a detailed discussion of the shutter speed and how it works.

"Fast" Lenses and "Slow" Lenses Explained

You may have heard of a certain lens being a "fast lens" or another lens disparagingly called a "slow lens." Fast or slow means how large the maximum aperture size is. A fast lens will have a large maximum aperture, like f/1.4, f/1.8, or f/2.8, while a slower lens might have a maximum aperture of f/3.5, f/4, or f/5.6. In the lens world, the larger the maximum aperture, the "faster" the lens and greater the cost. The 18-55mm f/3.5-5.6G kit lens included with the D5000 is a medium speed lens.

Understanding the Camera's Shutter Speed

While the camera's aperture is concerned with *how much* light gets to the image sensor, the shutter speed is concerned with *how long* the light shines on the sensor.

Here is a list of many of the shutter speeds available in your D5000 with *Custom Setting b1* set to either 1/3 step or 1/2 step EV (fastest speed is 1/4000 of a second, slowest speed is 30 seconds):

Custom Setting b1 set to 1/3 EV step (1/3 of a full stop):

Moving from fast shutter speed to a slow shutter speed (s = second)

- 1/4000s, 1/3000s, 1/2000s, 1/1500s, 1/1000s, 1/750s, 1/500s, 1/350s, 1/250s, 1/180s, 1/125s, 1/90s, 1/60s, 1/45s, 1/30s, 1/20s, 1/15s, 1/10s, 1/8s, 1/6s, 1/4s, etc. to 30s

Custom Setting b1 set to 1/2 EV step (1/2 of a full stop):

Moving from fast shutter speed to a slow shutter speed (s = second)

- 1/4000s, 1/3200s, 1/2500s, 1/2000s, 1/1600s, 1/1250s, 1/1000s, 1/800s, 1/640s, 1/500s, 1/400s, 1/320s, 1/250s, 1/200s, 1/160s, 1/125s, 1/100s, 1/80s, 1/60s, 1/50s, etc. to 30s

What does shutter speed do to for an image? It allows you to control movement. A fast shutter speed stops action, while a slow shutter speed blurs movement.

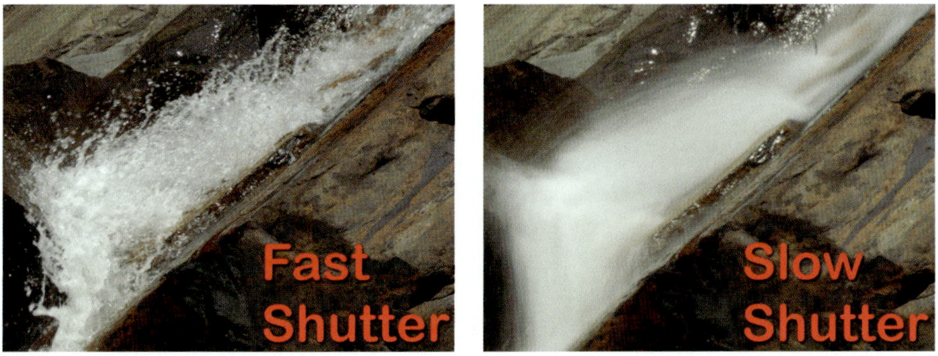

Figure 3 – Fast and slow shutter speeds compared

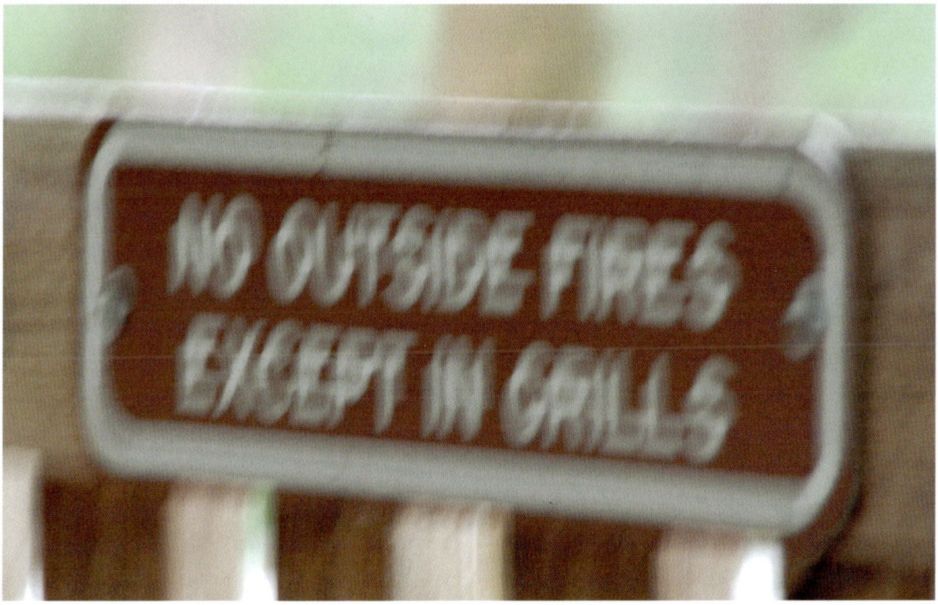

Figure 3A – Handheld at 1/10 of a second. Use a tripod instead!

In *figure 3*, you see a small waterfall. The water in the "Fast Shutter" image looks agitated and frozen. It was taken using a shutter speed of 1/250 of a second. Now look at the "Slow Shutter" picture. The water seems to be flowing and has a smooth, more natural appearance. It was taken using a 1/2 second shutter speed. I was shooting from a tripod when I took this picture, so the rocks look about the same in both images. The slower shutter speed is more appropriate for taking this type of image, making the water apear more natural and flowing.

Primarily, we use shutter speed to control movement, including camera shake. If you try to handhold your camera at shutter speeds below 1/60 of a second, you may get images that look like the one in *figure 3A*, taken with a shutter speed of 1/10 of a second.

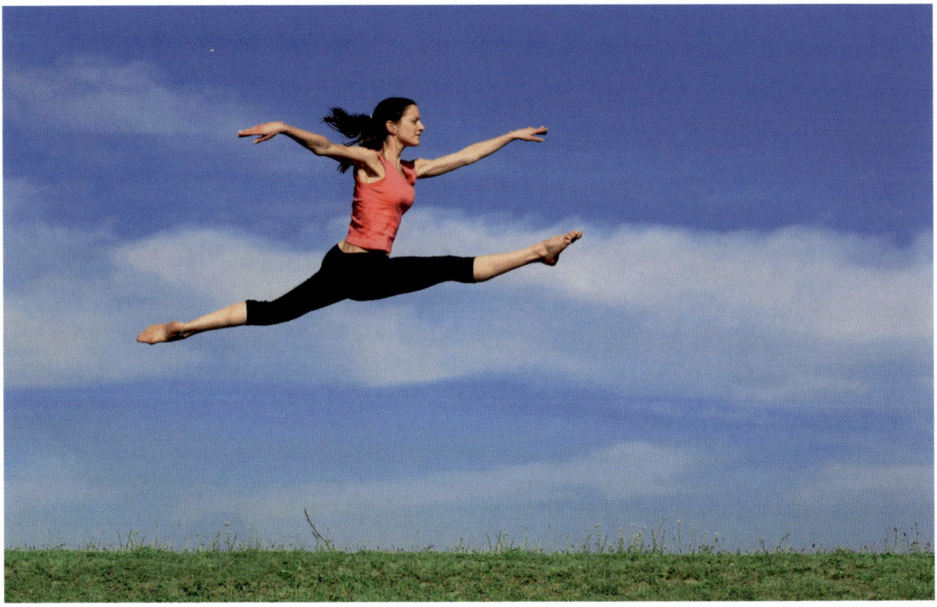

Figure 3B – Fast shutter speed stops action! (© Kristian Sekulic)

If you want sharp pictures when you are handholding a camera, you must keep your shutter speed above a minimum number that varies with the steadiness of the photographer. Most people can handhold a camera and create a relatively sharp image at 1/60 of a second. Some can't! You'll have to try it yourself to see what your limit is. Below those speeds, you must do one of the following:

1. Hold your elbows against your chest with your camera at your eye, and stand with one foot slightly in front of the other and several inches apart. (You are steadying yourself.)
2. Brace yourself against something like a tree or post.
3. Use a tripod or monopod.

Using a tripod is the preferred method of dealing with slow shutter speed camera shake, especially when using long telephoto lenses, which magnify camera shake greatly when pulling in distance subjects.

If you are taking pictures of cars racing, birds flying, or people moving quickly, you'll need to use a faster shutter speed to stop the action. In *figure 3B*, a young woman is leaping gracefully into the air. There is no blur or apparent movement in the woman's image. This was accomplished by using a fast shutter speed of at least 1/1000 of a second.

If you plan to shoot sports or anything with quickly moving subjects, you'll need to control the shutter speed. If you set your camera to shutter-priority (or manual mode), you can adjust this powerful functionality to control movement in your pictures. When you are using shutter-priority or manual exposure mode, you'll control the shutter speed by turning the command dial.

Shutter speed is controlled by turning the command dial alone, while aperture is controlled by turning the command dial while holding down the exposure compensation button. These issues are discussed more fully in chapter 3. In this chapter, you're just learning about how aperture and shutter speed relate to each other. Later we'll talk about how to use the camera controls in greater detail.

Sutter Speed In Review

A camera's shutter speed is primarily used to keep a moving subject sharp (jumping woman) or to allow it to show motion blur (flowing water). Handholding a camera at slow shutter speeds can lead to blurry pictures. Use a tripod for the sharpest images!

Using the Aperture and Shutter Speed Together for Great Pictures

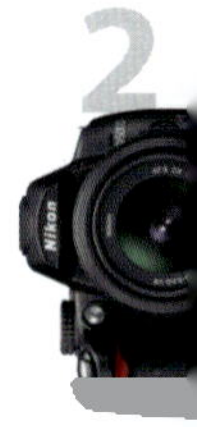

While the camera's aperture is concerned with *how much* light gets to the image sensor, the shutter speed is concerned with *how long* the light shines on the sensor.

In *figure 4*, you see a test image with three exposures of the same subject. The first exposure is underexposed (too dark), the second exposure is just right, and the third exposure is overexposed (too light).

You must understand how to control both depth of field (aperture) and subject movement (shutter speed) in your pictures. Which is most important? That varies with the type of subject you are shooting.

Let's say you are taking a picture of a bird flying through the air. Of course, you want the bird to be in sharp focus including its eye, body, and both wings, if possible. You need enough depth of field to be able to focus on the bird's eye and still get the rest of him in the zone of sharp focus. You could set a small aperture, which you know will give you a sufficient deep depth of field so that the bird is entirely in focus. However, when you use a small aperture for deep depth of field, the opening the aperture blades form is rather small and not much light gets into the camera. So to compensate, you'll need to let the light come in for a longer time period, which means using a slower shutter speed. Unfortunately, a slow shutter speed means the bird will appear blurred in the image. You've got yourself into a real quandary!

How can you balance your need for stopping action (a fast shutter speed) with your need to keep all parts of your subject in focus (small aperture)? Great question! Let's find an answer.

Now, let's say you are taking a picture of a beautiful scenic view of the mountains. You need deep depth of field focus to cover the distance out past the mountain ridges to infinity, which means a small aperture. You also want to compensate for the wind blowing the tree limbs and blurring them, so you want a faster shutter speed.

This quandary is what makes photography a learned skill. We are always balancing our need for depth of field with our need to stop motion. When there's a lot of light, as on a bright sunny day, there may be enough light to have a small aperture *and* a fast shutter speed, which gives us deep depth of field and stop motion capability. However, if there is less light on our subject, we can't have both.

You can artificially make your camera more sensitive to light by raising the ISO sensitivity of the sensor. In the old days, we called it "film speed." That can be helpful, but when you take your camera much above the native ISO (200), you start introducing digital artifacts called noise into your picture. We had the same results with very high speed films, and we called it "grain." High ISO sensitivity can create so much noise that your image is no longer very nice. So, higher ISO sensitivity is used only in an emergency when the shot *must* be acquired at all costs.

What you have to learn to do is to balance your shutter speed and aperture according to the most important goal you are trying to accomplish. What do you think is more important in our flying bird example? Should every part of the bird be in critical focus, or do we want to stop the motion of the bird flying through the air? Clearly, if the bird is blurry from movement, it doesn't matter if you have good focus and depth of field, does it? So, in the bird example, the most important thing is a fast shutter speed. You have to use whatever shutter speed will stop the bird's movement, even if you have to sacrifice some of your depth of field. In other words, you'll need to open the aperture to let enough light in so that you can limit the time the light comes in. We need a fast shutter speed, since that limits the time and can stop action.

In our mountain scene example, the mountain is not moving very fast, is it? So, the most important thing in that picture is that you have as much depth of field as possible. You want everything from the foreground all the way out to the far distance to be in good focus. You have to use a small aperture for depth of field (letting in less light), which means your shutter speed must be slower to let the light in longer. You still want to have a shutter speed fast enough to keep the limbs from blowing, but that's not as important overall as the deep depth of field.

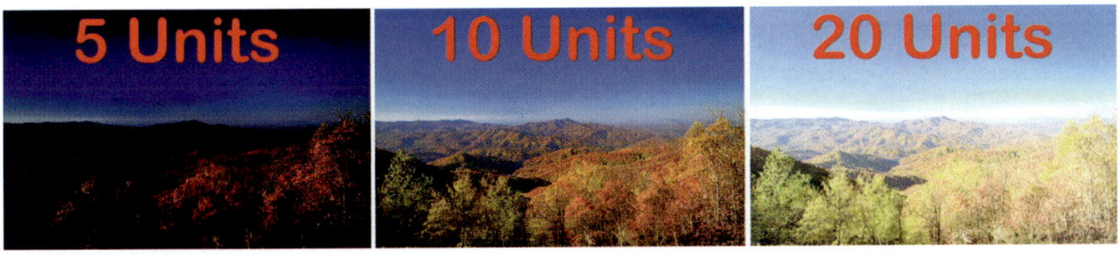

Figure 4 – Imaginary units of light

To enjoy your pictures, they must be exposed properly in the first place. So, you'll have to learn how to balance aperture and shutter speed to get a proper exposure while still capturing the image in the best way for the subject.

Let's discuss how a correct exposure is made using a combination of aperture and shutter speed. We'll use an *imaginary* amount of light called "units." In *figure 4*, you see a picture that takes 10 units of light to properly expose the subject. The picture with 10 units is correctly exposed, while the other two are not. How can you get a good "10 unit" exposure and make sure you have good depth of focus and movement control?

We put the camera in *manual* exposure mode, and focus on the scene. The light meter reports that to get 10 units of light, we need a shutter speed of 1/500s at an aperture of f/2. Now think about this for a minute. At f/2, a big aperture, we will have very little depth of field. Surely, the limbs blowing in the wind will be stopped since the shutter speed is so fast at 1/500s, but the depth of field will be so shallow that the mountains in the distance will not be in focus.

Let me show you a series of exposure amounts that all give us exactly 10 of our imaginary "units of light":

- Exposure amount 1: 1/500s at f/2
- Exposure amount 2: 1/125s at f/4
- Exposure amount 3: 1/30s at f/8
- Exposure amount 4: 1/8s at f/16

Our light meter tells us that at our current setting (1/500s at f2) gives us an acceptable exposure, but we want more depth of field for a good distant focus. What can we do? We can select one of the other exposure amounts in the list with a better aperture for our needs. Which is best? Well, Exposure amount 1 (aperture f/2) will not work because the aperture is so large we have little depth of field. Exposure amount 2 (aperture f/4) is better but only marginally so. Exposure amount 3 (aperture f/8) is getting much better, but since our distance is so great, it still may not provide deep enough depth of field to reach all the way out to infinity while keeping the foreground sharp too. It looks like our solution is to use Exposure amount 4 (aperture f/16), which gives us a good aperture for deep depth of field and should cover our scene well. However, the shutter speed is so slow at 1/8 of a second that we will blur the image from camera movement if we try to hand hold the camera while taking the picture.

What's our solution? Do either one of the following:

- Go ahead and use Exposure amount 3 (aperture f/8), since it provides good depth of field. However, at 1/30 of a second it's hard to get a sharp image due to camera shake, so you'll have to be very careful and brace yourself.
- Put your camera on a tripod and use the best value—Exposure amount 4, (aperture f/16)—to keep the image sharp from foreground to distant mountains. It is nearly impossible to get a sharp image at a shutter speed of 1/8 of a second, so we *must* use a tripod at speeds this slow!

The whole point of inventing this imaginary "10 units of light" exposure system is to show you that you can arrive at a correct exposure using combinations of different aperture and shutter speed settings. In the real world, there are no "units" of light, just a correct or incorrect exposure. Our imaginary "10 units of light" simply represents a correct exposure.

In summary, 1/30s at f/8 gives the image a correct exposure. 1/8s at f/16 provides exactly the same amount of light for a great exposure. 1/8s at f/16 is best for the mountain scene because the f/16 aperture gives so much depth of field and deep focus from foreground to infinity.

A Little More Exposure Detail

Let's play with our exposure amounts for a bit until this makes sense. I'll explain why 1/30s at f/8 and 1/8s at f/16 are exactly the same amount of exposure, and why either one will give a "10 unit" well-exposed picture, like in *figure 4*. The reason I used the imaginary units of light was to represent the way in which light (or exposure) is cut in half or doubled by either the aperture or shutter speed.

If 1/125s at f/8 lets in 10 units of light, how many units would 1/125s at f/11 let in? Remember, when the aperture number gets bigger, the aperture opening gets smaller. Since f/11 is one-half the aperture size of f/8, it will let in only one-half as much light. Consequently, 1/125s at f/11 would then give us only 5 units of light (or half of what is needed), and our exposure would be dark, as in *figure 4's* underexposed "5 unit" picture.

Let's examine the following two examples:

- 1/125 at f/8 = 10 units
- 1/125 at f/11 = 5 units (aperture is half the size, so lets in half as much light)

The two exposures above use the same shutter speed, but the second exposure has an aperture of half the size, and only lets in 5 units, or half as much light. How can we compensate so that we get back to 10 units of light, without changing the aperture? We'll have to change the shutter speed! Since we've cut our light in half by using a smaller aperture opening, what would happen if we held the smaller aperture open for twice as long?

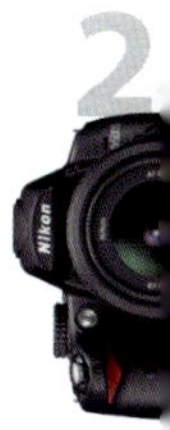

Aha! Holding the half-sized f/11 aperture open for twice as long—1/60 of a second—gives us exactly the same amount of light as an aperture opening of f/8 at 1/125 of a second. 1/60 of a second is twice as much time as 1/125 of a second. Therefore, 1/60s at f/11 is half the light for double the time, resulting in an equivalent exposure, as shown below:

- 1/125s at f/8 = 10 Units
- 1/60s at f/11 = 10 Units (aperture half-sized, shutter speed twice the time)

In other words—we've changed it so that our shutter speed is twice as long. Why? Since, the aperture is half the size, we must allow more time for the light to enter into the camera by increasing the length of time the shutter is open. We double the time the shutter stays open, allowing light through the half-sized f/11 aperture for twice as long. This gives us our imaginary 10 units of light, for a correct exposure.

General Shutter Speed/Aperture Exposure Rule

To arrive at a similar exposure, you have to first use the light meter to get a correct exposure reading. Then you think about what

Shutter Speed/Aperture Exposure General Rule

1. Get a good meter reading.
2. Decide whether you need a different aperture or shutter speed than what the meter recommends.
3. Let's say the camera suggested 1/125s at f/8 for a good exposure but you want a *faster shutter speed* to stop action. If you select a shutter speed one step faster, or 1/250s, which cuts the exposure to the sensor by one-half, you must open the aperture to let in more light. If you set the shutter speed one step higher (restricting light), you'll need to open the aperture one step larger too (adds light). So if your original exposure was 1/125s at f/8 and you select 1/250s instead, simply open the aperture to f/5.6 and you get the same amount of exposure. By increasing your shutter speed by one step, you cut the time the light comes into the camera by one-half, so there is only one-half as much light reaching the sensor. To compensate, you open the aperture to twice the previous size so that *twice as much* light reaches the sensor. You have the exact same exposure with a different combination of aperture/shutter speed: 1/125s at f/8 = 1/250s at f/5.6.
4. Likewise, if you wanted more *depth of field* than the metered amount of 1/125s at f/8 would allow, you could close the aperture to the smaller size (stop down) of f/11. The aperture f/11 lets in exactly one-half the light of f/8. So your exposure is exactly one-half of the suggested good exposure. To compensate, you could use the slower shutter speed of 1/60s, which lets light in *twice as long*. Now you are giving the camera exactly the amount of light it needs to make a good exposure. If you close the aperture by one step (restricting light), you'll need to slow the shutter speed by one step (adding light): f/11 at 1/60s equals f/8 at 1/125s.

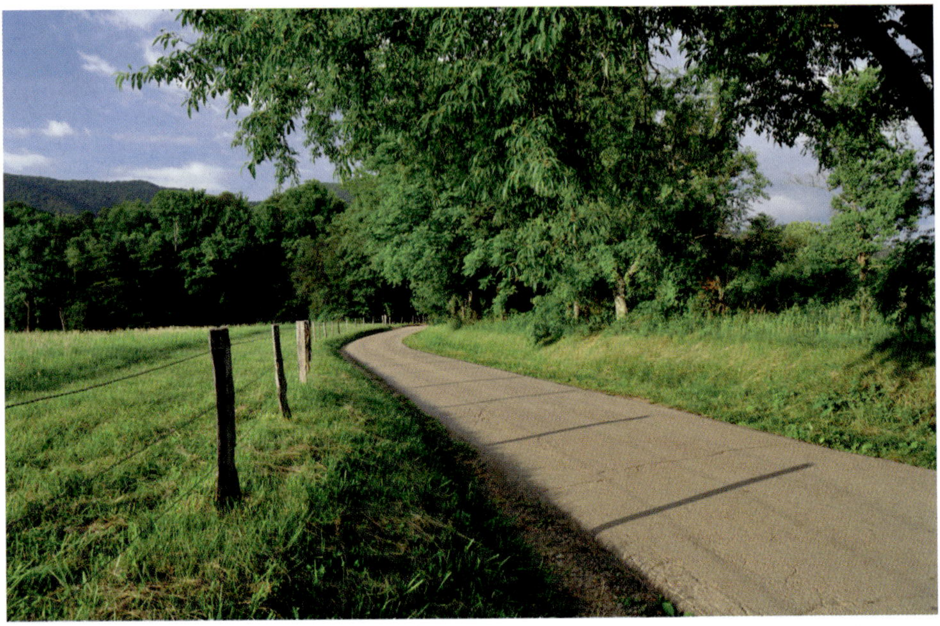

Figure 5 – Shooting at 18mm—Wide-angle focal length

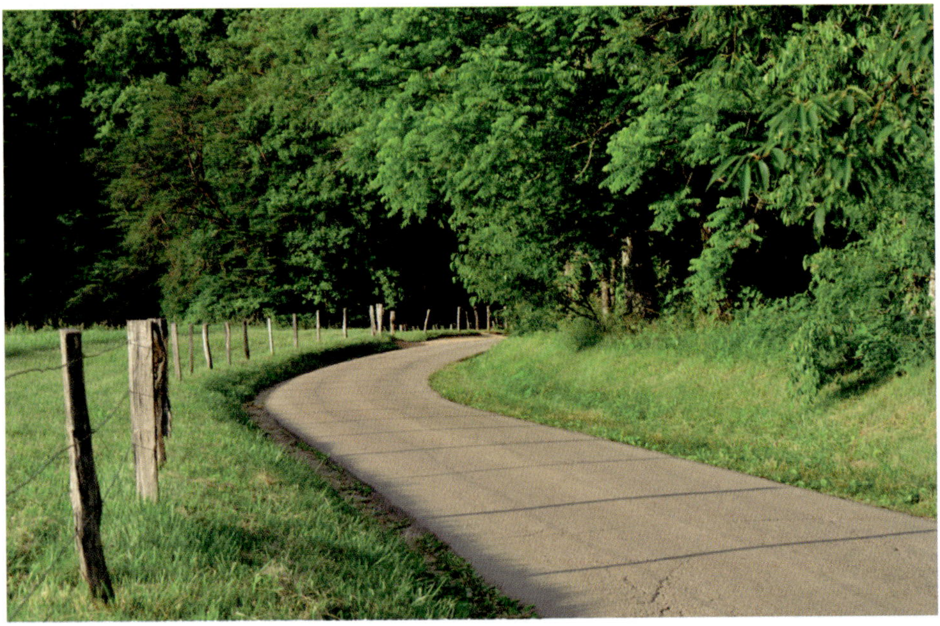

Figure 5A – Shooting at 55mm—Short telephoto focal length

the aperture/shutter speed combination will give you. Do you need a faster shutter speed to control motion? Do you need a smaller aperture to have more depth of field? Only you can make those decisions. The camera just suggests a combination that will give you a correct exposure, nothing more (unless you are using one of the "scene" modes—see chapter 3).

The two most important considerations are how much, and how long. Use your aperture to control *how much* light gets on to the sensor. Use your shutter speed to control *how long* the light gets to the sensor. Balance the two for a correct exposure!

Focal Length

Your camera was most likely shipped with an 18-55mm kit lens. This small zoom lens is quite sharp and easy to use. It is considered a wide-angle-to-short telephoto lens length. What I mean by that is that its range of focal lengths is from wide-angle (18 mm) to short telephoto (55 mm).

Let's look at a few pictures to see the effects of focal length on the image:

In *figure* 5, you see an image taken with the kit lens at 18mm. This wide-angle setting has lots of depth of field, so the scenic image is in good focus from near to far. You'll use this 18 mm focal length often when you are taking pictures of beautiful landscapes and groups of people.

Now, in *figure 5A*, you see an image taken at the opposite end of the 18-55 mm lens's focal length. This "longer" 55 mm lens setting narrows down the amount your lens can see. The image in *figure 5A* is at the same spot as the image in *figure* 5, but look at how much less of the scene is captured with 55 mm setting in *figure 5A*. It pulls the view in closer to you, or magnifies it.

The width and height of the area the lens can see is called *field of view*. In other words, a wide-angle lens has a wide field of view, while a telephoto lens has a narrow field of view. *Figure* 5 shows a wide-angle field of view, and *figure 5A* shows a short telephoto's narrower field of view.

You can purchase lenses for your D5000 that vary from as (super) wide as 6 mm to as long as 1200 mm. The wider and/or longer lenses cost a *lot* more money. You can even buy lenses that are so wide-angled that see slightly behind themselves. I'm not kidding!

If you want to take a picture of a skittish deer in a field without getting too close, you may want to get a longer telephoto lens. Nikon makes an inexpensive lens that matches the next step up in focal length from your kit lens. It's the Nikkor 55-200mm f/4-5.6 ED lens. This will let you reach out and pull in more distant subjects, like shooting sports from the bleachers or taking a picture of the moon.

Vibration Reduction (VR) Lenses

Your 18-55mm VR kit lens should have what's called VR, or vibration reduction. If so, there is a switch on the side of the lens with VR On/Off above it. Leave this turned on when you're handholding your camera because it will cut down on vibrations and make your pictures significantly sharper. You don't need VR when you are using a tripod, so it's best to turn it off, unless your tripod is old and wobbly.

VR lenses are a delight to use because they allow you to handhold your camera at lower shutter speeds than normal. Many new lenses in the Nikkor lineup are now equipped with VR. Buy one of those if you can; you'll get better images as a result.

Focus Motor in the Lens

Since the Nikon D5000 does not have a motor in the body that will cause a lens to autofocus, like some older and larger Nikons, you'll need to be sure any new lenses you buy have the AF-S Nikkor name. The AF-S stands for *autofocus–silent wave* motor, and it means that the lens is equipped with an internal autofocus motor, so your camera doesn't have to have one itself. Sigma calls its in-lens focus motor lenses hypersonic motor (HSM) lenses.

Nikon Acquisition Syndrome - A Friendly Warning

Besides the desire for much better image quality, owning new and exciting lenses is one of the major reasons we purchase a Nikon DSLR camera. Sometimes I just go online and look at (i.e., desire intensely) lenses just for the fun of it.

Owning a Nikon DSLR may cause you to develop a certain, uh, "sickness" from which few recover. In fact, the condition is quite pleasurable due to the sensations it causes in the human brain, so few ever really seek a way to cure themselves. What is this malady? It's called Nikon Acquisition Syndrome, or NAS. If you ever experience the persistent desire to own every lens ever made by Nikon, you'll realize (too late of course) that you've come down with NAS. You may never recover! The only real treatment for it is buying new Nikon equipment.

My Conclusions

The relationship between aperture and shutter speed—and how each changes the picture—is rather difficult to understand. If you don't quite get it yet, put your camera in manual mode and reread the information in this chapter while adjusting your camera's aperture and shutter speed. Focus on something that has a consistent level of ambient light and see if you can get a correct exposure with various aperture and shutter speed combinations.

This is sort of like learning to ride a bicycle. You cannot understand it until suddenly you do. Keep studying this subject because it will make you a better photographer who is able to control your camera for the best image results. Obviously, I can only give an overview of this subject here, since this book is not designed to be a tutorial on exposure.

I'd like to see you use your D5000 effectively and enjoyably. You have an advanced camera, and you are a passionate photographer. Learning to effectively use the aperture, shutter speed, and focal length in combination will only increase your enjoyment.

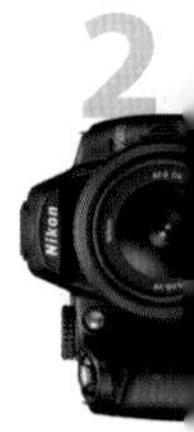

3

Exposure Metering System, Exposure Modes, and Histogram

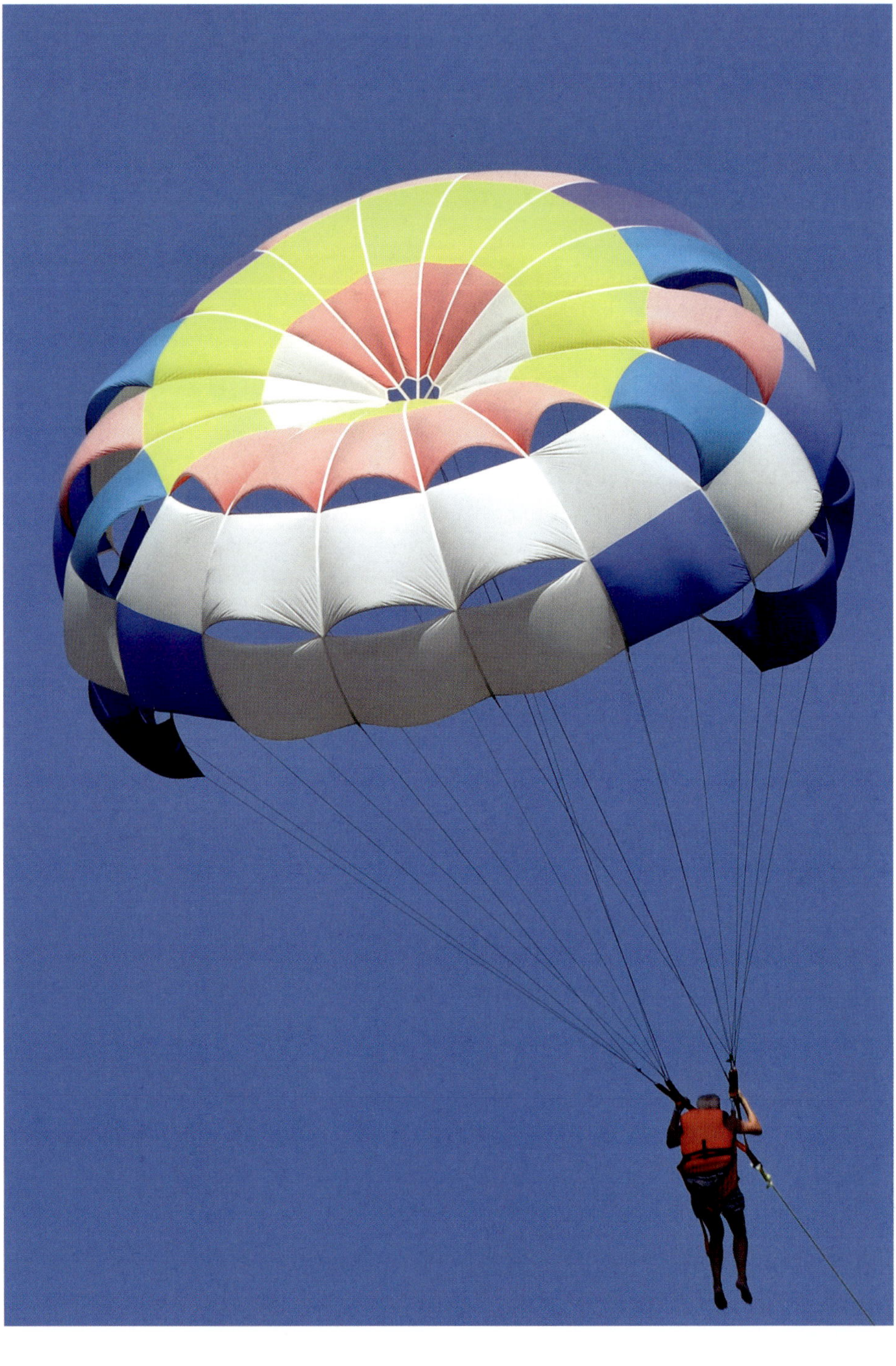

I've been using Nikon cameras for about 30 years. It seems that each camera Nikon has released has had improvements in its light metering modes. The Nikon D5000 is no exception.

With this new camera, Nikon has designed metering to work not only with still images but also with moving pictures and video.

In this chapter, you'll learn how the exposure metering system and modes work. We'll look at how each of three different light meter types is best used. We'll examine the various modes you can use when using your camera, including several presets for when you want the camera to do most of the work while you enjoy shooting. And finally, we'll look in detail at how the histogram works on the Nikon D5000.

The histogram is a new feature to those who are coming over from film photography. This little readout gives you great control over metering and will help you make the most accurate exposures you've ever made. It is very important that you understand the histogram, so we'll look at it in detail.

This chapter is divided into three parts:

- **Metering systems** – The exposure metering systems: matrix, spot, and center-weighted.
- **Exposure Modes** – Programmed auto, shutter-priority, aperture-priority, and manual. In addition, there are 19 scene modes that give a "new" user command of certain styles of shooting.
- **Histogram** – How to read it and better control your exposures.

In this chapter we'll discuss six controls to change values and move through screen settings (see *figure 1*):

- Mode dial
- Info button
- Information edit button
- Multi Selector
- +/- Exposure compensation button
- Command dial

Remember the locations of these controls. You'll be using them a lot as you learn to use the camera's features.

Let's get started by looking into the three exposure metering systems.

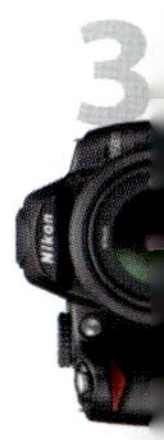

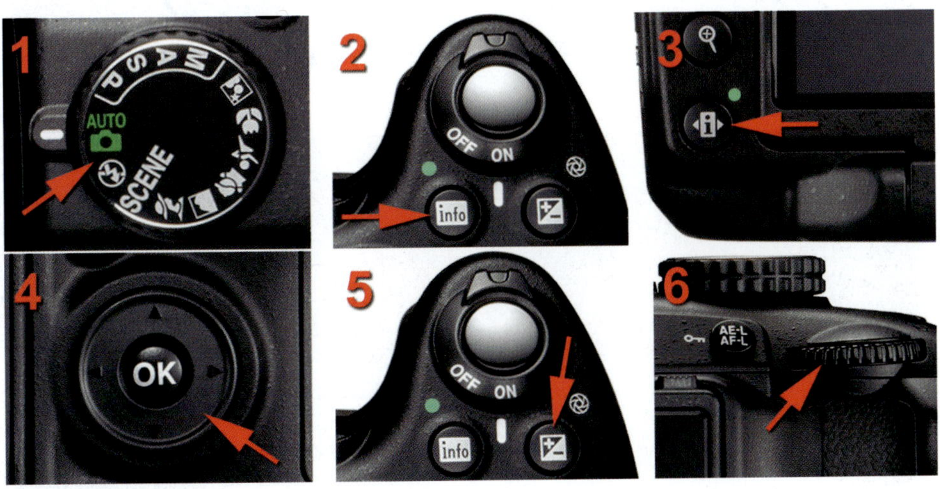

Figure 1 – Important external camera controls

Section 1 – Metering Systems

(User's Manual pages 88–93)

The basis for the Nikon D5000's exposure meter is a 420-segment red, green, and blue (RGB) sensor that meters a wide area of the frame. When used with a G or D Nikkor lens containing a CPU (central processing unit), the camera can set exposure based on the distribution of brightness, color, distance, and composition. Most people leave their camera set to matrix metering and enjoy excellent results. Let's look more closely at each of the Nikon D5000's exposure metering systems.

You'll need to use the *Information edit* screen to change between the three exposure metering types on the D5000. To access the *Information edit* screen, press the <**i**> information edit button twice (see the red arrow in the screen on the left in *figure 1A*) until you see the screen shown on the right in *figure 1A*.

Then, using the camera's Multi Selector (see *figure 1*) scroll down until you get to the *Metering* settings. The metering mode controls on the Nikon D5000 are shown in *figure 2*.

You are provided with three types of exposure metering: matrix metering, spot metering, and center-weighted metering. Let's examine each of these in detail.

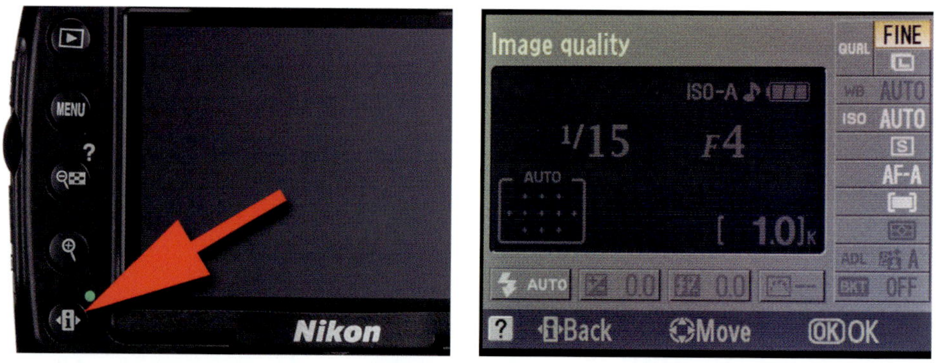

Figure 1A – Accessing the information edit screen

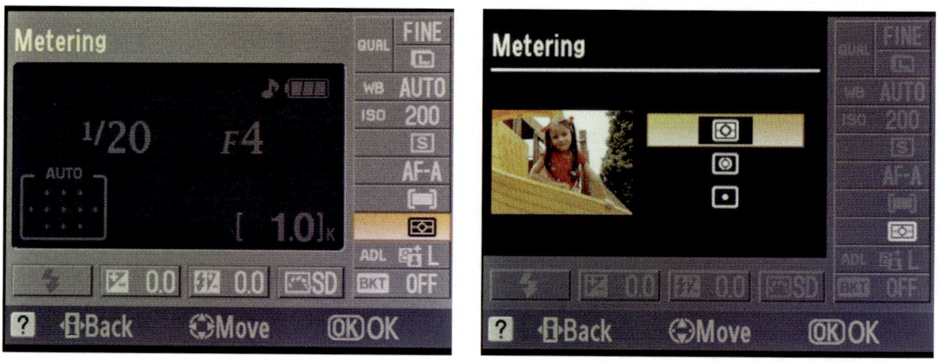

Figure 2 – Metering mode set to matrix metering

3D Color Matrix II Metering

(User's Manual page 88)

The Nikon D5000 contains a 3D Color Matrix Metering II system that's one of the most powerful and accurate automatic exposure meters in any camera today. In the screen on the right in *figure 2*, you'll notice that the top selection in the menu has been chosen. This is the matrix metering symbol.

Here are the steps to choose the matrix metering system:

1. Press the <**i**> information edit button twice, and you'll see the *Information edit* screen appear (see figure 1, image 3).
2. Scroll down with the camera's Multi Selector until you have the Metering selection highlighted (see the left screen in figure 2).
3. Press the OK button and you'll see the Metering screen with its three selections (on the right in figure 2).
4. Choose the top menu item, which is matrix metering.
5. Press the OK button to select it, and the camera will return to the main *Information edit* screen. You are now ready to take pictures with matrix metering active.

How does matrix metering work? Through complex mathematical formulas, characteristics from many thousands of images have been stored in the camera. These characteristics are used, along with proprietary Nikon software and complex algorithms, to analyze the image that appears in your viewfinder. The meter is then set to provide very accurate exposures for the majority of your images.

A simple example of this might be when the horizon runs through the middle of an image. The sky above is bright and the earth below is much dimmer. The metering system evaluates the image, compares it to hundreds of similar images in the camera's database, and then automatically selects and inputs a meter setting for you.

The meter examines four critical areas of each picture. It compares the levels of *brightness* in various parts of the scene to determine the total range of EV values. It then notices the *color* of the subject and surroundings. If you are using a G or D lens with a microprocessor, it also determines how far away your lens is focused so that it can determine the *distance* to your subject. Finally, it looks at the *compositional* elements of the subject.

After it has all this information, it compares your image to tens of thousands of image characteristics in its image database, makes complex evaluations, and comes up with an exposure value that is usually right on the money, even in complex lighting situations.

Try It—You Just Might Like It!

Most people primarily use the matrix meter. I know that it does a great job for me, and I use it most of the time. If you are just interested in getting great pictures from your camera, why not try shooting with this meter setting for a while? I think you'll see what I mean. It's truly world class!

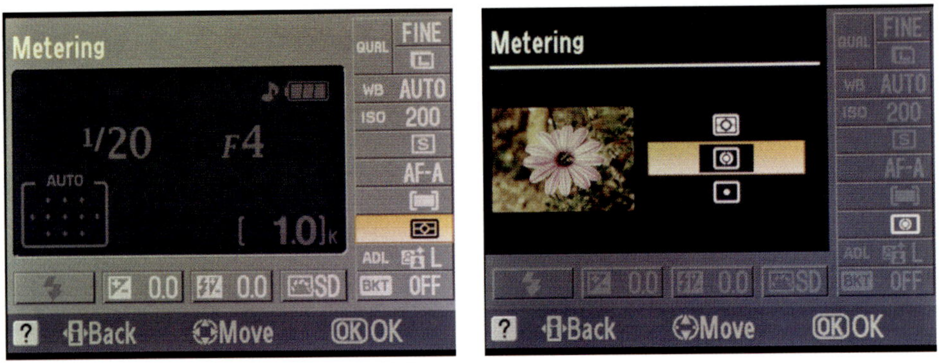

Figure 3 – Metering mode set to center-weighted metering

Center-Weighted Metering

(User's Manual page 88)
If you're a bit old-fashioned, having been raised on a classic center-weighted meter and still prefer that type, the D5000's exposure meter can be transformed into a center-weighted meter.

Figure 3 shows how to select the center-weighted meter. Here are the steps:

1. Press the <**i**> information edit button twice, and you'll see the *Information edit* screen appear (see *figure 1*, image 3).
2. Scroll down with the camera's Multi Selector until you have the Metering selection highlighted (see the left screen in *figure 3*).
3. Press the OK button, and you'll see the Metering screen with its three selections (on the right in *figure 3*).
4. Choose the second menu item down from the top, which is the selection for the center-weighted meter.
5. Press the OK button to select center-weighted metering, and the camera will return to the main *Information edit* screen. You are now ready to take pictures with center-weighed metering active.

How does it work? The center-weighted meter in the D5000 meters the entire frame but concentrates 75 percent of the metering into an 8 mm circle in the middle of the frame. The other 25 percent of the frame, outside the circle, provides the rest of the metering. You can see an approximation of the primary metering area within a partially drawn circle in your camera's viewfinder. In *figure 3A*, shown in red is the approximate area where the camera looks for 75 percent of its metering choice.

Just keep your subject in the center of your viewfinder for accurate metering.

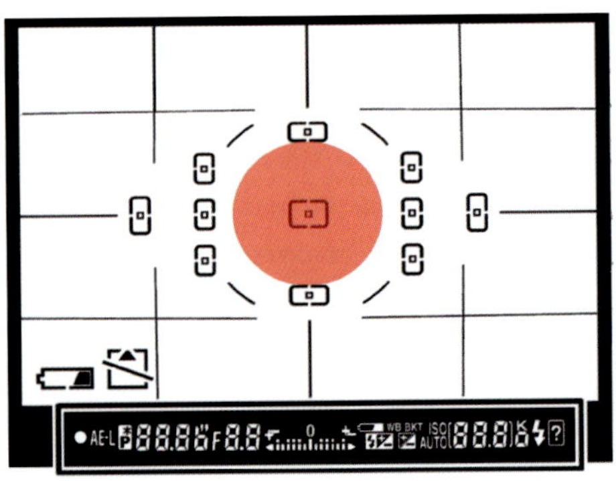

Figure 3A – Approximate center-weighted 75 percent metering area

This, of course, violates the rule of thirds principle of composition. The rule of thirds basically says that images are more interesting if your main subject is not centered directly in the frame, but about one-third of the way into the frame instead. Imagine your camera's viewfinder divided into three parts (both horizontally and vertically), and place your subject at one of the imaginary one-third boundaries. If the viewfinder grid display (*Custom Setting d2*) is turned on, the viewfinder is divided into four parts: left and right and top and bottom. You can use that reference to place your subject between one-quarter and one-half of the way into the frame for a quick one-third positioning.

You may need to meter the subject with the center circle, press the auto exposure lock (AE-L) button, and then recompose the picture using the rule of thirds. The rule of thirds is not a hard-and-fast rule, but with appropriate subjects, it does tend to make an image have a more powerful effect on viewers.

Center-Weighted vs. Matrix or Spot Metering

I rarely use the center-weighted meter these days. Most of the time, I use matrix or spot metering. Some people will state vigorously that they prefer the center-weighted meter. For them, it seems more accurate. Why not shoot for a few hours in center-weighted mode and see what you think. Or shoot some images in matrix and then shoot the same images in center-weighted and compare them. Center-weighted worked well in the "good old days," so it ought to work well enough today.

Tip on When to Use Center-Weighted Metering

If you are using really dark filters (filter factor over 1x), it might be a good idea to temporarily switch to center-weighted or spot metering mode. Also, if you use auto exposure lock (AE-L), you may want to switch to center-weighted or spot metering mode. Matrix may not give you the "desired results"—according to Nikon—when used under these circumstances. Personally, I have not experienced a problem when using matrix metering with darker filters or AE-L. However, I wanted to warn you, just in case.

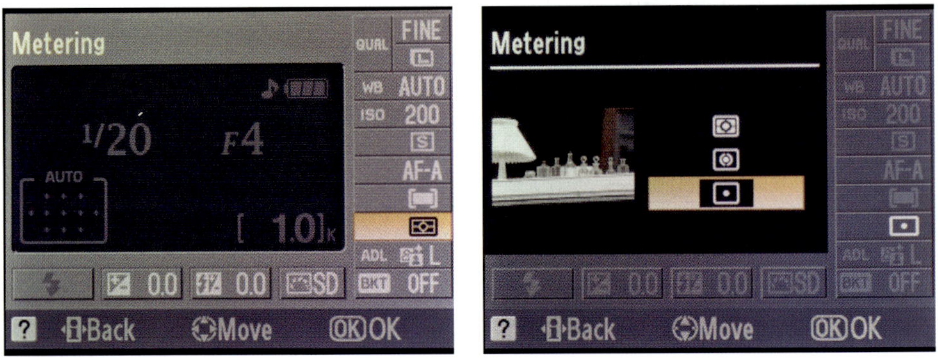

Figure 4 – Metering mode set to spot metering

Spot Metering

(User's Manual page 88)

Often no other meter but a spot meter will do. In situations in which you must get an accurate exposure for a very small section of the frame, or you must get several meter readings from various small areas, the D5000 can, once again, be adjusted to fit your needs.

Figure 4 shows how to select the spot meter. Here are the steps:

1. Press the <**i**> information edit button twice, and you'll see the *Information edit* screen appear.
2. Scroll down with the camera's Multi Selector until you have the *Metering* selection highlighted (see the left screen in *figure 4*).
3. Press the *OK* button, and you'll see the *Metering* screen with its three selections (on the right in *figure 4*).
4. Choose the third menu item down from the top, which is the spot meter selection.
5. Press the *OK* button to select it, and the camera will return to the main *Information edit* screen. You are now ready to take pictures with spot metering active.

How does spot metering work? The D5000's spot meter consists of a 3.5 mm circle (0.14 inch) surrounding the currently active auto focus (AF) point, if you are using single or continuous AF modes (*AF-S* or *AF-C*). In *AF auto-servo* mode (*AF-A*), the spot meter is metering from the center AF sensor only and does not move when other AF sensors are automatically selected. *If you are going to use the spot meter effectively, you should set your D5000 to AF-S or AF-C mode.*

The spot meter evaluates only 2.5 percent of the frame, so it is indeed a "spot" meter. Since the spot is surrounding the currently active AF sensor, you

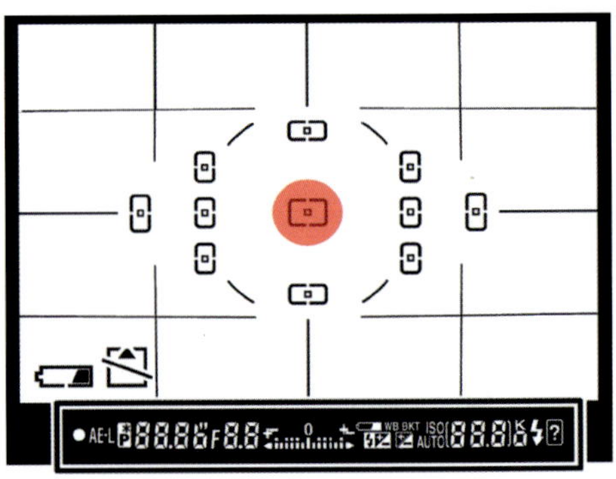

Figure 4A – Viewfinder view of the 3.5 mm spot

can move the spot meter around the viewfinder within the 11 AF points.

How big is the 3.5 mm spot? Well, the spot meter barely surrounds the little AF point square in your viewfinder. It is fairly close to the size of the little brackets that appear around the active AF sensor when you slightly press the shutter release button.

When your D5000 is in spot meter mode and you move the selected AF point to some small section of your subject, you can rest assured that you're getting a true spot reading.

In fact, you can use your spot meter to determine an approximate EV range of light values in the entire image. You can do this by metering the lightest and darkest spots in the frame. If this value exceeds a 5 or 6 stop difference, you've got to decide which part of your subject is most important to you and meter only for it.

On an overcast day, you can usually get by with no worries since the range of light values is often within the recording capability of the sensor. On a bright sunny day, the range of light exceeds what your sensor can record by as much as two times, which can often be as much as 12 stops total, while your sensor can record a maximum of only 6 or 7 stops.

Don't let the numbers make you nervous. Just remember that spot metering is often a trade-off. You trade the highly specific ability to ensure that a certain portion of an image is "spot-on" for the camera's multiple "averaging" skills to generally get the correct exposure throughout the frame. The choice is yours, depending on the shooting situation.

If you spot-meter a person's face while they are standing in the sun, the shadows around that person will contain little or no data. The shadows will be underexposed and look like solid black. Then, if you spot-meter for the shadows instead, the person's face is likely to "blow out" to solid white. We'll discuss this in more detail in section 3 of this chapter, about the histogram.

Use your spot meter to get specific meter readings of small areas on and around your subject; then make some exposure decisions yourself, and your subject should be well exposed. Just remember that the spot meter evaluates only for the small area that it sees, so it cannot adjust the camera for anything except that one tiny area. Some practice is required to learn how to use spot metering well, but it is a very professional way to compose images.

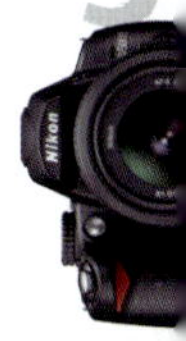

Which Metering Mode Would I Use?

Most of the time, I'll leave my camera set to matrix metering. I only use the spot metering mode when I am using flash to get the best reading from my subject or when I need to meter a difficult subject with a range of light that is wider than my sensor can contain. I haven't used center-weighted metering since back in the film days and look at it as an old-fashioned system. However, there are those who love the old-style center-weighted meter. It's there if you want it.

Section 2 – Exposure Modes

(User's Manual pages 28–38 and 80–87)

My first Nikon was an FM back in 1980, which I remember with fondness because that was when I got really serious about photography. It's hard for me to imagine that it has already been nearly 30 years since I last used my FM! Things were simpler back then. When I say simple, I mean that the FM had a basic center-weighted light meter, a manual exposure dial, and manual aperture settings. I had to decide how to create the image in all aspects. It was a camera with only one mode—M, or manual.

Later on, I bought a Nikon FE and was amazed to use its A mode, or aperture priority. I could set the aperture manually and the camera would adjust the shutter speed for me. Luxury! The FE had two modes, M-manual, and A-aperture-priority.

A few more years went by and I bought a Nikon F4 that was loaded with features and was much more complex. It had four modes, including the two I was used to, M and A, and two new modes, S-shutter-priority, and P-programmed auto. I had to learn even more stuff! The F4 was my first P,S,A,M camera.

Does this sound anything like your progression? If you are over 40, maybe so; if not, you may be just getting into the digital photography realm with your D5000 (and I ought to stop reminiscing and get to the point).

The point is that today's cameras are amazingly complex compared to cameras only a few years ago. Let's examine how we can use that complexity for our benefit. The D5000 is also a P,S,A,M camera. That's the abbreviated progression of primary modes that allow you to control the camera's shutter speed and aperture. In addition, the D5000 has 19 scene modes and a fully auto mode for when you just want to take good pictures without thinking about exposure. Let's examine each in detail.

There is just one control on the D5000 to set the auto, scene, and P,S,A,M modes. It is a convenient dial called the mode dial (see *figure 5*).

In the next few sections, we'll discuss the various modes that deal with exposure, and will mention aperture and shutter speed. If you aren't sure about your D5000's aperture and shutter speed, don't despair. We covered those concepts extensively in chapter 2.

Now, let's discuss each exposure mode in detail.

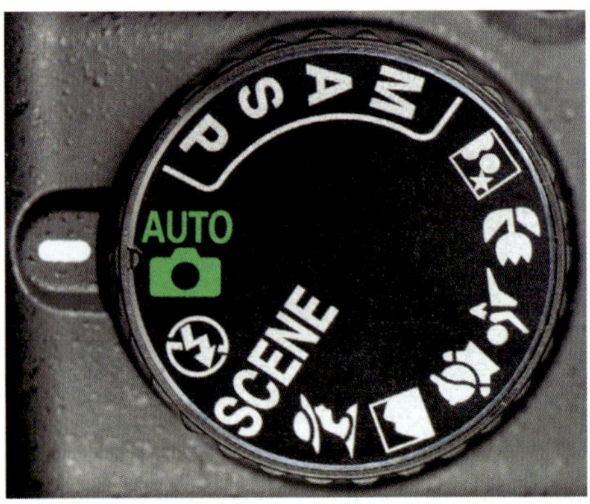

Figure 5 – Mode dial for exposure modes

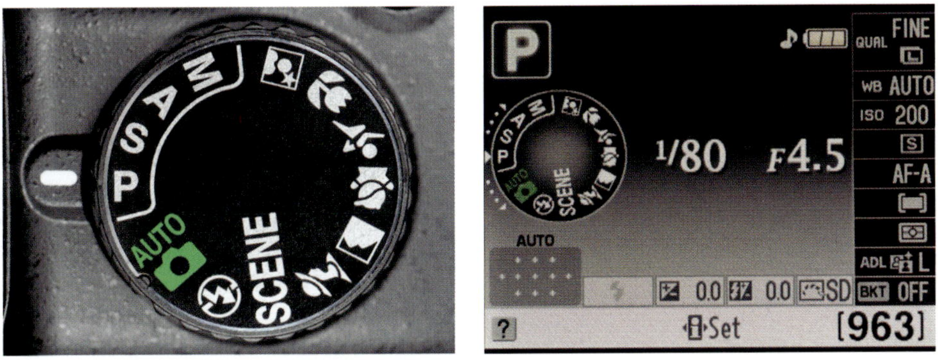

Figure 6 – Mode dial set to programmed auto mode, or P mode

P – Programmed Auto Mode

(User's Manual page 81)
Programmed auto *(P)* mode is designed for those times that you just want to shoot pictures and not think much about camera settings, but you still want emergency control when needed. The camera takes care of the shutter speed and aperture for you and uses your selected exposure meter type to create the best pictures it can without human intervention. *Figure 6* shows the mode dial set to *P*–programmed auto mode.

It is called programmed auto because it uses an internal software program built into the camera. It tries its best to create optimal images in most situations. However, even the User Manual (on page 81) calls this a "snapshot" mode. P mode can handle a wide variety of situations well, but I personally wouldn't depend on it for my important shooting. It can be great at a party, for example, where I want some nice snapshots but I don't want to think too much about the camera—I just want to enjoy the party. P mode to me is *P* for *Party*.

P mode actually comes in two parts: *programmed auto* and *flexible program*. *Flexible program* works similarly to *A-aperture-priority* mode. Why do I say that? Let me explain.

Get Down, Daddy-O!

You're shooting at a family party and suddenly you see a perfect shot of Dad dancing on the dinner table and Mom standing on the floor behind him with her hand over her mouth. You (being a well-trained D5000 photographer) press the info (or <**i**>) button, glance down at your camera's information screen, and realize that the current f/4 aperture won't give you enough depth of field to focus on Dad and still have a sharp picture of Mom, who by this time is tugging at Dad's pant leg. With only seconds to spare, you turn your camera's command dial to the left. The D5000 realizes that it is being called upon to leave snapshot mode and give you some control. It displays a small P with an asterisk next to it on the information screen to let you know it realizes that you are taking over control of the aperture. Since you are turning the dial to the left, it obligingly starts cranking down the aperture. A few clicks to the left and your aperture is now at f/8. As soon as the D5000 detected that you were turning the command dial, it started adjusting the shutter speed to match the new aperture. With only milliseconds before Mom starts dragging Dad off the dinner table, you get the camera to your eye, compose the shot, press the shutter release button, and the D5000 starts grabbing frames. You get several frames off in the few seconds it takes Mom to get Dad down from the table.

What you did in my imaginary scenario was invoke the flexible program mode in your D5000. How? As soon as you turned the command dial, the D5000 left normal *P* mode and switched to flexible program. Before you turned the command dial, the D5000 was happily controlling both shutter speed and aperture for you. When you turned the dial, the D5000 immediately switched to flexible program mode and let you have control of the aperture. It then controlled only the shutter speed. In effect, the D5000 allowed you to exercise your

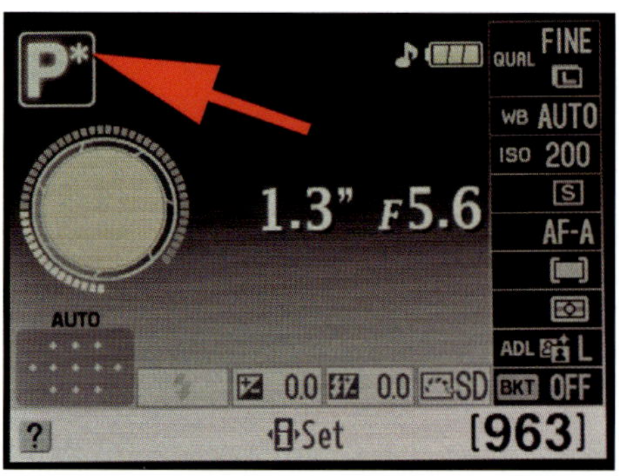

Figure 6A – *Flexible program* mode *P** showing on information screen

knowledge of photography very quickly and only assisted you from that point.

As mentioned previously, when the camera enters flexible program mode,

From *P* to *P** and Back Again

Once you've entered *flexible program* mode, you have to turn the command dial back the same number of clicks to get back into normal *P* mode. This is a little weird and has a strange side effect. If you have your D5000 in *P* mode and turn the main command dial to the right, the D5000 goes into *P** mode (or flexible program mode) and starts counting clicks to the right. To get back into normal P mode (or *programmed auto* mode), you have to turn the command dial back to the left that same number of clicks, up to 15 clicks.

The reason I know that the D5000 is actually counting clicks is that I counted it counting clicks. Here's what I did: I set my D5000 to P mode and got into a darker area where it was at maximum aperture. I then started cranking the main command dial to the right, which should increase the aperture. Since I was already at maximum aperture, the D5000 could not increase the aperture size, so it just sat there counting clicks instead. In order for me to get back into normal P mode, and out of flexible program, I had to turn back to the left the exact number of clicks I turned to the right, up to 15 clicks.

I am telling you this just in case you do what I did. Then you'll already know that the D5000 will let you out of *P**- flexible program mode only when you return to the original position on the dial. You can also turn the camera off or turn the mode dial to another setting to get out of the flexible program mode.

it displays a small asterisk after the *P* in the upper-left corner of the information screen (see *figure 6A*). It also shows a small *P* with an asterisk above it in the viewfinder, just to the left of the shutter speed readout.

When you enter *P**-flexible program mode, you control only the aperture and the D5000 controls the shutter speed. If you turn the command dial to the left, the aperture gets smaller. Turn it to the right and the aperture gets larger. Nikon gave you control of only the aperture in flexible program mode. Can you see why I say that flexible program mode acts like *A*-aperture-priority mode?

S – Shutter-Priority Auto Mode

(User's Manual page 82)
Shutter-priority auto mode is for those who need to control their camera's shutter speed while allowing the camera to maintain the correct aperture for the available light. *Figure 7* shows the mode dial set to S for shutter-priority auto mode.

If you find yourself shooting action scenes, you'll want to keep the shutter speed high enough to capture an image without excessive blurring. Shooting sports, air shows, auto races, or any quickly moving subject requires careful control of the shutter. Sometimes you might want to set your shutter speed to slower settings for special effects or time exposures. For instance, if you shoot a helicopter in flight, you may want to use a shutter speed that perfectly allows for just a tiny bit of motion blur on the helicopter blades.

If the light changes drastically and the D5000 cannot maintain a correct exposure, it will inform you by replacing the normal aperture reading with either *Hi* or *Lo* where the shutter speed or aperture is shown on the information screen. They mean what they imply. *Hi* means there is too much light for a good exposure. *Lo* means there is not enough light for a good exposure. The D5000 will also display a message on the top of the information screen that says, *Subject is too dark* (or *too light*). It will also display *Hi* or *Lo* in the viewfinder where the aperture or shutter speed is normally listed.

To change the shutter speed, simply rotate the command dial to any value between 30 seconds and 1/4000 of a second. Turn the wheel to the right for

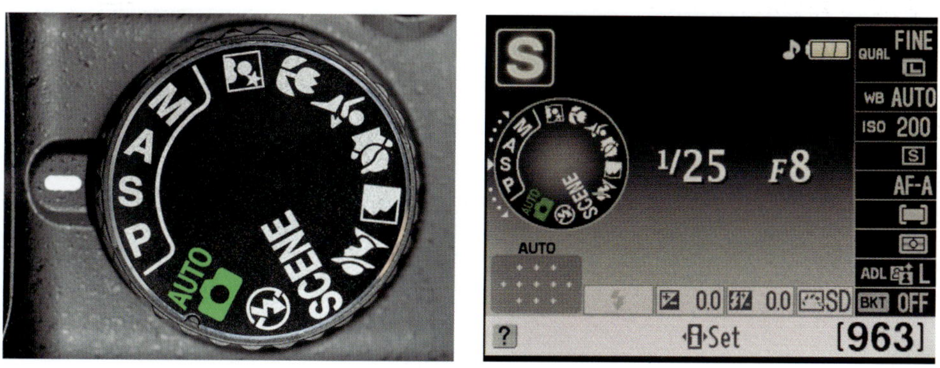

Figure 7 – Mode dial set to shutter-priority auto mode, or S mode

faster shutter speeds and to the left for slower speeds. The camera will adjust your aperture to maintain a correct exposure and will warn you when it can't with *Hi* or *Lo* and an information screen message.

A – Aperture-Priority Auto Mode

(User's Manual page 83)
Nature and macro shooters, and anyone concerned with carefully controlling depth of field, will often leave their D5000 set to aperture-priority mode, or A mode. Figure 8 shows the mode dial set to aperture-priority auto mode.

A-aperture-priority mode lets you control the aperture while the camera takes care of the shutter speed for optimal exposures. To select an aperture, you'll use the command dial. Turn the wheel to the right for smaller apertures and to the left for larger.

The minimum and maximum aperture setting is limited by the minimum and maximum aperture available on the lens you've mounted on the camera. Most consumer lenses run from f/3.5 to f/22. More pricey pro-style lenses may have apertures as large as f/1.4, but they generally start at f/2.8 and end at f/22.

The aperture directly controls the amount of depth of field (DOF) in an image. DOF is an extremely important concept for photographers to understand. Simply put, it allows you to control the range or depth of sharp focus in your images. If you are focused on a person's face, will a person standing behind also be in focus? DOF controls that! See chapter 2, "Aperture and Shutter Speed," for more detailed information on DOF.

M – Manual Mode

(User's Manual pages 84-85)
Manual mode takes a big step backward to days of old. It gives you complete control of your camera's shutter and aperture so that you can make all the exposure decisions, with suggestions from the exposure meter. The image on the left in *figure 9* shows the mode dial set to Manual mode. In figure 9 notice, too, the M in the upper-left corner of the image on the right. This information screen shows that the camera is in Manual mode.

Also, in the screen on the right in *figure 9*, notice the electronic analog exposure display. This display, found when you press the info button on top of

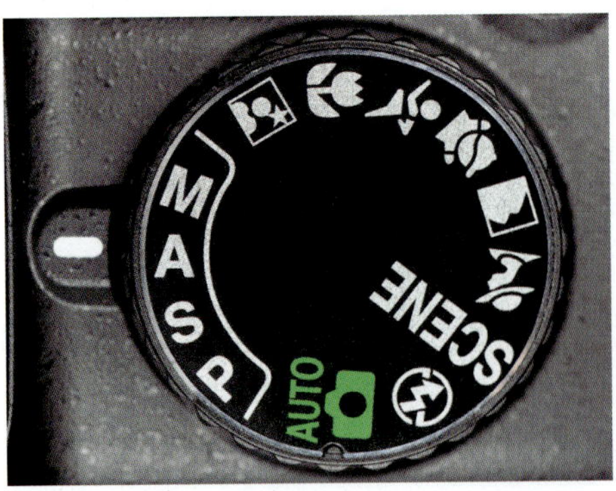

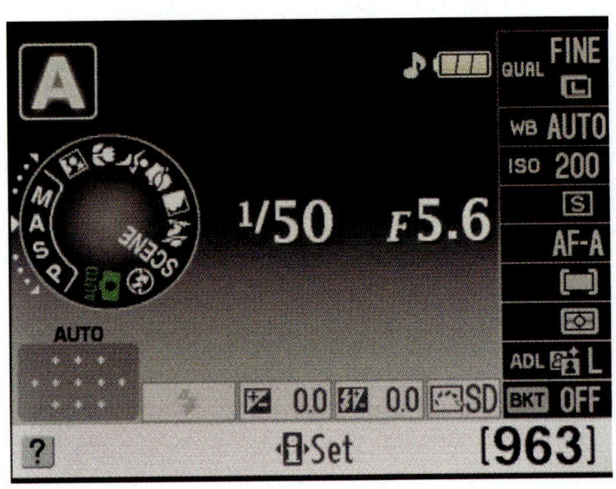

Figure 8 – Mode dial set to aperture-priority auto, or A mode

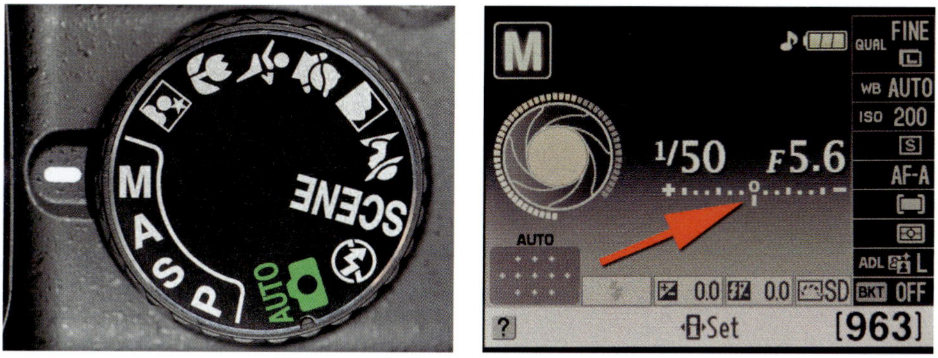

Figure 9 – Mode dial set to Manual (M) mode and the info exposure display

the camera, has a plus sign (+) on the left and a minus sign (-) on the right. Each dot on the scale represents 1/3 EV step and each line represents 1 EV step. You'll see a miniature version of the same scale at the bottom of the viewfinder when you look through the eyepiece.

You can control how sensitive this scale is by changing *Custom Setting b1* – EV steps for exposure control. (See chapter 7 or the User's Manual pages 85 and 156.) You can set b1 to 1/3 or 1/2 EV steps.

When you are metering your subject, a bar will extend from the zero in the center toward the plus side to indicate overexposure, or toward the minus side to indicate underexposure (see *figure 9A*). You can gauge the amount of over- or underexposure by the number of dots and lines the bar passes as it heads toward one side or the other. The goal in Manual mode is to make the bar disappear. In *figure 9A*, the bar is indicating 1 1/3 or 1.3 EV steps (stops) overexposure.

You'll adjust the aperture by holding down the +/- exposure compensation button and rotating the command dial (see *figure 1*). The shutter speed is

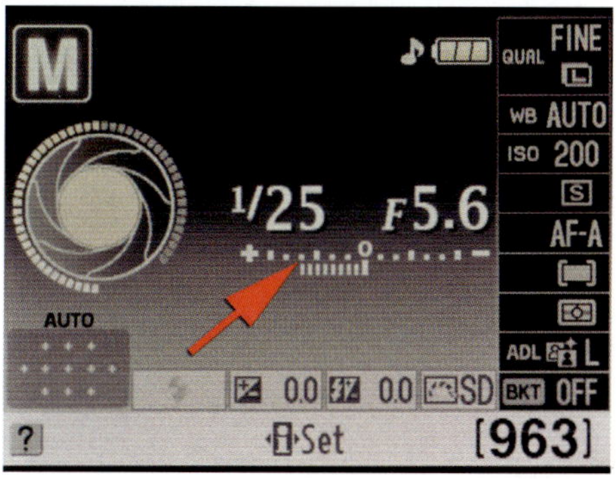

Figure 9A – Info exposure display with 1.3 EV steps of overexposure

adjusted with the command dial alone. When the camera is in Manual mode, you have control over the aperture for depth of field and the shutter speed for motion control. If your subject needs a little more depth of field, just make the aperture smaller, but be sure to slow down the shutter speed too or your image may be underexposed. If you suddenly need a faster shutter speed, then set it faster, but be sure to open the aperture to compensate.

The point is, you are in complete control of the camera and must make decisions for both the shutter speed and aperture. The camera makes suggestions with its meter, but you make the final decision about how the exposure will look. Manual mode is for taking your time and enjoying your photography. It gives you the most control of how the image looks, but you must also have a higher level of knowledge to get correct exposures.

My Recommendations on Exposure Mode selection

As a nature photographer, I am mostly concerned with getting a nice sharp image with deep depth of field. My camera is set to *A*-aperture-priority and f/8 about 90 percent of the time. I started using this mode back in about 1986 when I bought my Nikon FE and have stayed with it since.

However, if I were shooting sports or action, I would have my camera set to S-shutter-priority most often, which would allow me to control the speed of the shutter and capture those fast-moving people and objects without a lot of blur. The camera will control the aperture so that I only have to concentrate on which shutter speed best fits my subject's movement.

I only use the other two modes, *P*-programmed auto and *M*-manual, for special occasions.

M-manual mode is for those times when I want to just enjoy my photography. When I want to control the camera absolutely, I'll go to Manual. I've even been known to carry a small blanket with me so that when I'm shooting in Manual mode, I can toss it over the back of the camera and my head. That way, I can feel like Ansel Adams, or another view camera artist. With my blanket, I might even look like an artist to the tourists with their tiny point-and-shoot cameras, right? I've heard kids say, "Mom, look at that man with a blanket over his head!" (I just grin.)

I probably use *P*-programmed auto mode least of all. I might use it when I am at a party and just want to take nice pictures for my own use. I'll let the camera make most of the decisions by using P mode while still having the ability to quickly jump into *P**-flexible program mode when events call for a little more aperture control.

Full Auto and Scene Modes

(User's Manual pages 28–38)

Some people have recently switched from using a point-and-shoot (P&S) camera to a more powerful DSLR like the Nikon D5000. Most P&S cameras have a completely auto mode and some scene modes representing common photographic opportunities.

The Nikon D5000 is (in my opinion) a "bridging" camera. It is like a bridge between a P&S camera and a professional-level camera such as the D300 and D3x. The D5000 is an excellent camera for advanced amateurs and will even serve as a nice backup for a professional camera. This versatility in features allows you to choose how you want the camera to support you while you are taking your pictures.

If you have just come over from the P&S world, you might enjoy using the *Auto* and *Scene* modes while learning the more advanced uses of the P, S, A, and M modes. Let's look into how these extra modes work.

Auto Exposure Mode

(User's Manual pages 28–31)

The *Auto* exposure mode is for those times you want to get the picture with no thought as to how the camera works (see *figure 9B*).

About all you need to be concerned about when in *Auto* mode is how well the image is composed and whether the battery is fully charged.

The D5000 becomes a big point-and-shoot camera, like a heavy COOLPIX. Many of its internal modes go to auto too. For instance, here is a list of important camera features that become automatic (mostly under the *Shooting Menu*):

- White balance
- Active D-Lighting
- ISO sensitivity
- Picture Controls
- Pop-up flash control
- Auto bracketing

In effect, you relinquish control of some of the camera's functions for a "guarantee" that some sort of picture will be provided. In most cases, the D5000 will provide its normal excellent images when you've selected auto. However, in difficult circumstances, the camera is free to turn up the ISO sensitivity and extend the D-Lighting range to get a picture even at the expense of image quality. If I had no experience shooting weddings but was suddenly called on to shoot one, I might be convinced to use *Auto* since I am going to get a picture no matter what. I don't have to think about anything except framing the subject and pressing the shutter release.

If you want to loan your camera to your grandmother and she has no interest in how cameras work, the D5000 will happily make nice images for her in *Auto* mode. While you are learning to use the more advanced functions of the camera, you too might benefit from using this mode for a while. You'll usually get better pictures when you control the camera, but the D5000 has some awfully efficient software for when you don't want to take control yet.

Now, let's consider the 19 scene modes found in your D5000.

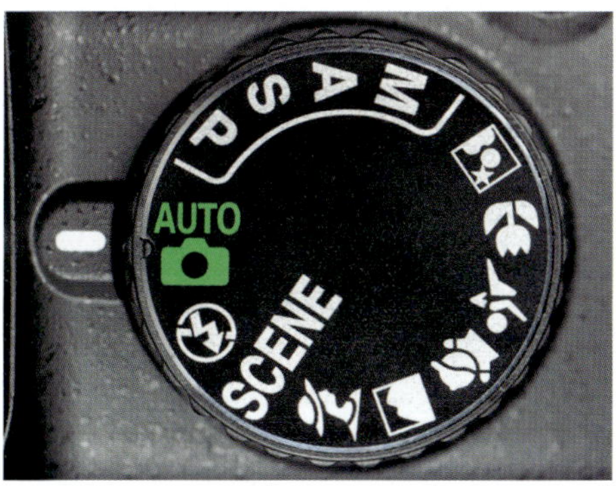

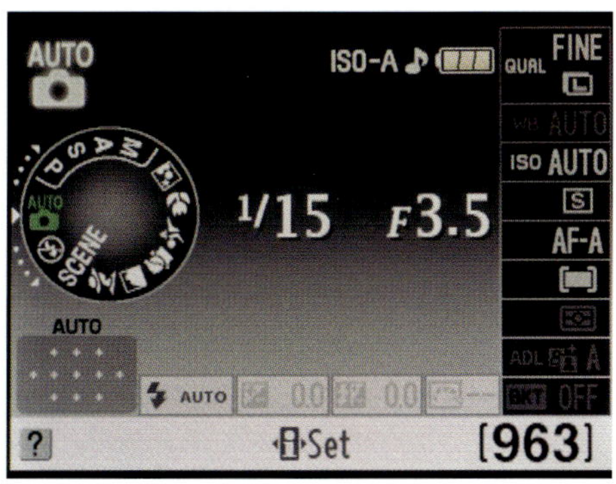

Figure 9B – Full *Auto* exposure mode

Why Have Scene Modes?

The SCENE modes are considered "creative photography" modes by Nikon. In fact, they allow average, beginning photographers to emulate the camera settings they would be inclined to use if they had more experience. They give you access to a level of photographic experience built into the camera that will help you make consistently good images. Later, as your experience grows, you can use the P, S, A, and M modes to get more creative control over your images.

Since the Nikon D5000 has about 30,000 image styles stored in its matrix metering system database, I wouldn't be surprised if each of these modes used a subset of stored image types more closely matching the scene mode. This might hold true in matrix metering mode. I have no way to prove this, so don't quote me!

If you choose to use SCENE modes, do so with the understanding that you can eventually learn to control an image to a finer degree with the P, S, A, and M modes if you'd like. Don't be afraid to experiment with the more powerful features of the D5000. You can always fall back on the scene modes if you feel uncomfortable. With the P, S, A, and M, Auto, and SCENE modes, Nikon has given us the best of both worlds in one camera: Full or partial automation or complete manual control. What flexibility!

Six External Scene Modes Found on the Mode Dial

The camera offers the six most-used SCENE modes right on the mode dial. There are an additional 13 scene modes found by setting the mode dial to SCENE and then selecting a scene mode on the information screen or under the *Shooting Menu*. We'll look at the extra scene modes in the next section. For now, let's look at the most-used modes found on the external mode dial.

Portrait Scene Mode

Portrait Scene mode is best used when you are taking pictures of people or static subjects. The icon looks like a lady wearing a fancy hat (see *figure 9C*). The camera tends to emphasize shallow depth of field (large apertures) so that only your subject is in sharp focus. That is a more flattering way to focus attention on your subject while trying to blur out the background as much as possible. If you are taking pictures of friends (alone or in small groups), use this mode. Nikon says that this mode tries to take pictures with "soft, natural-looking skin tones."

Portrait Scene mode uses the PT (Portrait) Picture Control and auto white balance.

Landscape Scene Mode

If you are spending a day in the mountains, you'll want to use *Landscape Scene* mode a lot. Its icon looks like a couple of mountain peaks with a square around them (see *figure 9D*). Landscapes are usually best photographed on a tripod at small apertures so that the entire scenic view is nice and sharp. The *Landscape Scene* mode will emphasize smaller apertures for more depth of field. It also tends toward making the colors deep and vivid. This is sort of like using the *A-aperture-priority* mode but much with less control over the aperture. The camera disables the pop-up flash and focus assist light in this mode. You can't light up a mountain with a pop-up flash!

Landscape Scene mode uses the LS (Landscape) Picture Control and auto white balance.

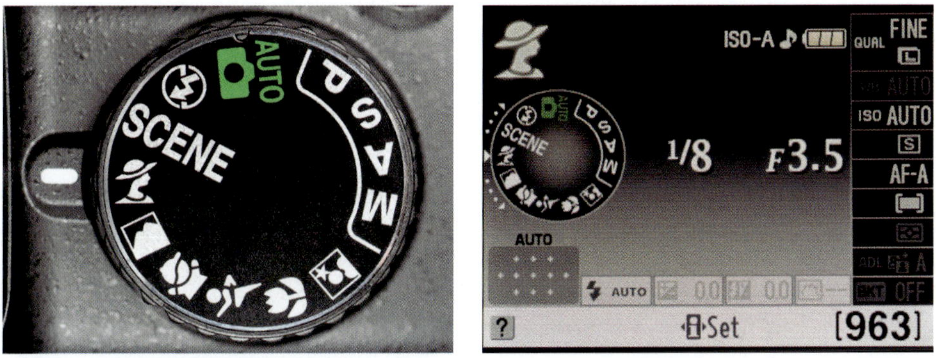

Figure 9C – *Portrait Scene* mode

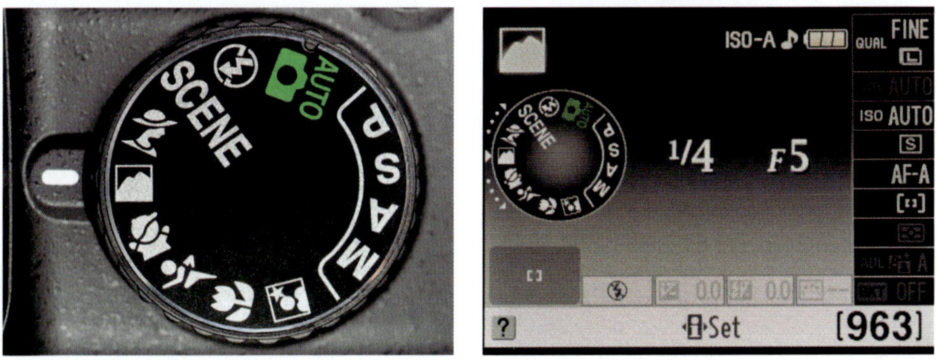

Figure 9D – *Landscape Scene* mode

Child Scene Mode

The *Child Scene* mode tries to balance the need for saturated colors in a child's clothes and any colorful background elements while not overly saturating skin tones. Its icon looks like a child wearing a cap with his arms raised (see *figure 9E*). The primary emphasis of this mode seems to be making skin tones look good while giving you a fast enough shutter speed to capture a moving child and with a large enough aperture to have some depth of field. It seems to be a balanced mode when it comes to shutter and aperture.

Child Scene mode uses the SD (Standard) Picture Control and auto white balance.

Sports Scene Mode

Since sports usually involve people and other subjects moving at a rapid pace, the *Sports Scene* mode emphasizes faster shutter speeds. Its icon is a person in full running motion (see *figure 9F*). Since you certainly don't want slow shutter speeds at a car race or air show, the camera will attempt to use the fastest shutter speed that the light will allow and will open up the aperture to keep the exposure reasonable. Expect shallow depth of field in *Sports* mode. This mode is similar to using *S-shutter-priority* mode but with less control over specific shutter speeds.

The pop-up flash is too weak to light up a sports scene, so the camera disables it

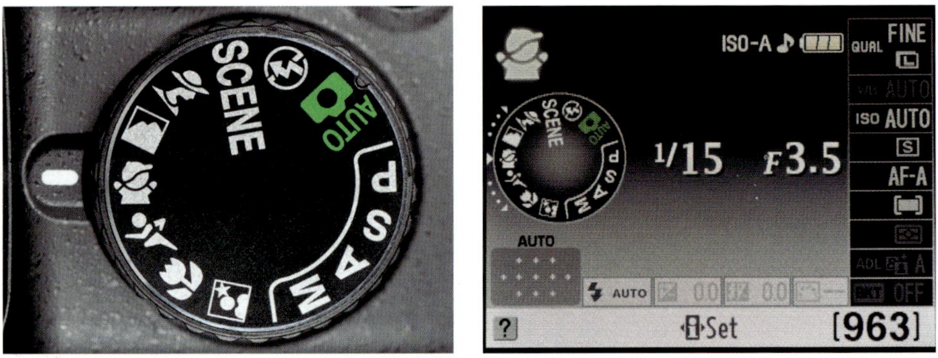

Figure 9E – *Child Scene* mode

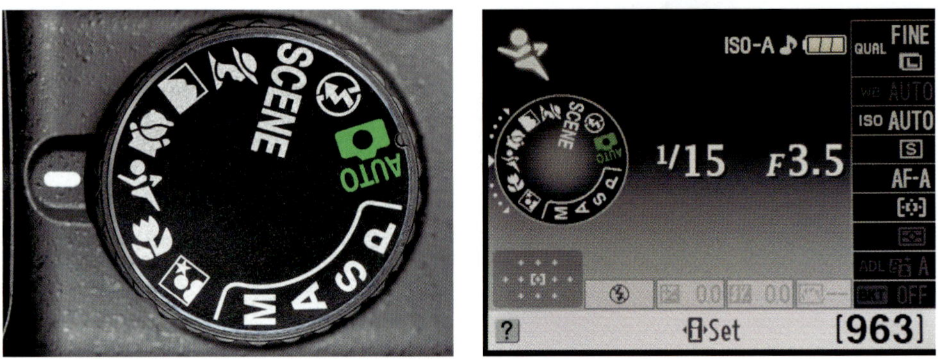

Figure 9F – *Sports Scene* Mode

and the focus assist light. It will still fire a more powerful accessory-shoe-mounted (hotshoe- mounted) Speedlight flash like the Nikon SB-400, SB-600, SB-800, and SB-900. A powerful flash unit is often needed to stop action for indoor sports shots.

Sports Scene mode uses the SD (Standard) Picture Control and auto white balance.

Close Up Scene Mode

Another name for the *Close Up Scene* mode might be "flower mode," or even "macro mode." Its icon is a flower (see *figure 9G*). It's designed to let you to take closeup pictures of flowers, insects, and other small items. It uses small apertures to provide enough depth of field for the subject. Nikon suggests that you use a tripod when you are shooting in this mode (when you can) so that you won't have blurry images from camera shake. This is because the emphasis on small apertures may make the shutter speed drop so low that you can't handhold the camera without shaking it. If there is enough light, you may not have to worry and can handhold the camera, but in darker settings, it is advisable to use a tripod.

Close Up Scene mode uses the SD (Standard) Picture Control and auto white balance.

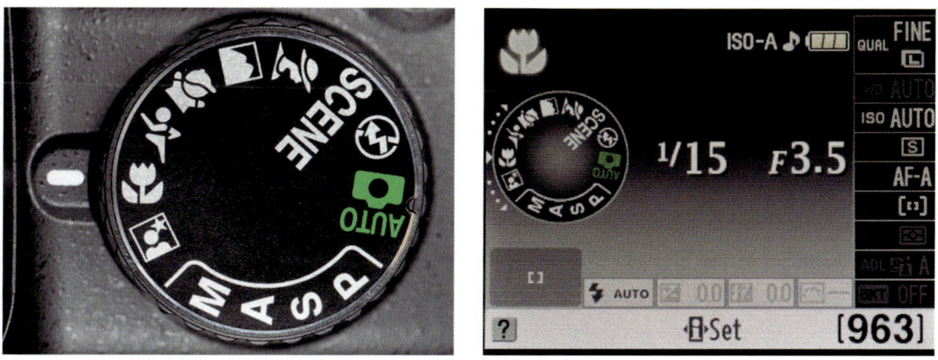

Figure 9G – *Close Up Scene* mode

Night Portrait Scene Mode

If a person is shooting handheld at night, it is best to try to balance the shutter speed and aperture so that the shutter stays fast enough to handhold the shot while the aperture is open as much as possible to let in dim light. *Night Portrait Scene* mode appears to do that. It seems to emphasize large apertures more than faster shutter speeds. Its icon looks like a person with a star above the head (see *figure 9H*).

Night Portrait Scene mode uses the PT (Portrait) Picture Control and auto white balance.

Thirteen Internal Scene Modes

With these scene modes, you'll need to set the mode dial to SCENE and use the information screen to see what mode is selected. You can scroll through the various *Scene* modes by rotating the command dial.

Night Landscape Scene Mode

The *Night Landscape Scene* mode is designed to use with a tripod. Since it's dark outside, the camera uses longer exposures, higher ISO sensitivity, and noise reduction to keep noise from being a big problem. Various light sources have different colors, so the camera tries to "reduce ... unnatural colors," according to Nikon. The pop-up flash and the focus

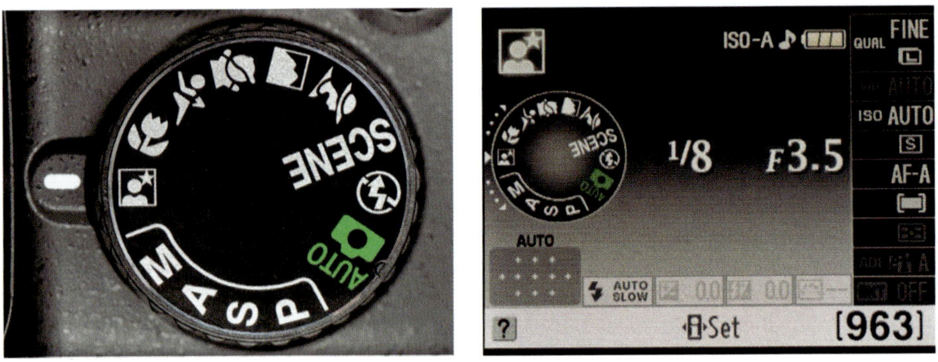

Figure 9H – *Night Portrait Scene* mode

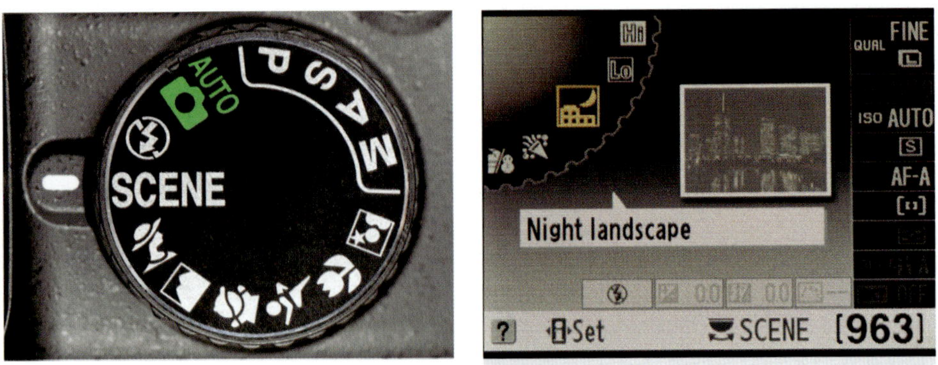

Figure 9I – *Night Landscape Scene* mode

assist light are disabled. It will still fire an accessory-shoe-mounted flash in case you want to use flash for special effects or fill. (See *figure 9I.*)

Night Landscape Scene mode uses the SD (Standard) Picture Control and auto white balance.

Party/Indoor Scene Mode

The *Party/Indoor Scene* mode balances the use of your fill flash and ambient background lighting. It tries to overcome the look of bright people and dark backgrounds by allowing more background light to register on the sensor. (See *figure 9J.*)

Party/Indoor Scene mode uses the SD (Standard) Picture Control and auto white balance.

Beach/Snow Scene Mode

The *Beach/Snow Scene* mode is designed to work well with the commonly bright expanses of water, sand, or snow. This is a landscape mode, so it will intensify colors, if present, and will also sharpen the image a little. The pop-up flash and focus assist light are disabled. (See *figure 9K.*)

Beach/Snow Scene mode uses the LS (Landscape) Picture Control and auto white balance. It also raises *sharpening* by +3.

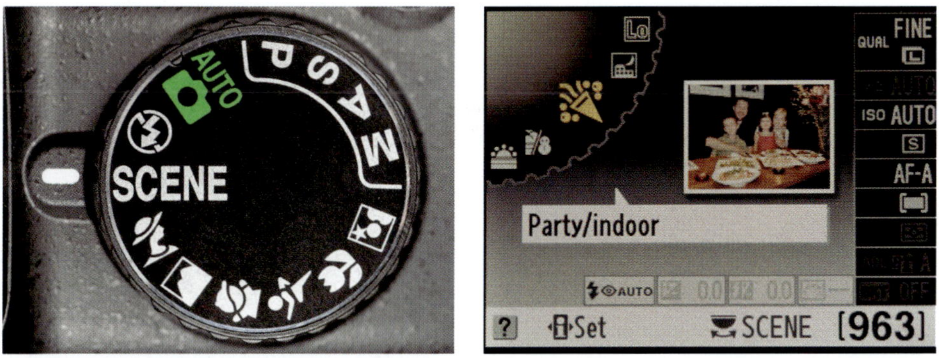

Figure 9J – *Party/Indoor Scene* mode

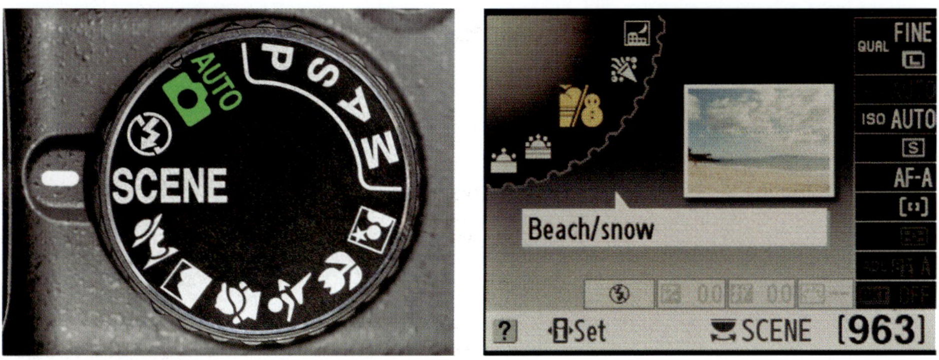

Figure 9K – *Beach/Snow Scene* mode

Sunset Scene Mode

Sunsets often provide deep colors, so *Sunset Scene* mode is designed to emphasize them. It uses small apertures and slow shutter speeds, so it may be best to use a tripod to keep from blurring the image from handheld camera shake. The pop-up flash and focus assist light are disabled. To provide nice contrast, it raises image sharpening. (See *figure 9L*.)

Sunset Scene mode uses the LS (Landscape) picture Control and direct sunlight white balance. It also raises *sharpening* by +3.

Dusk/Dawn Scene Mode

At dusk and dawn, there is often nice color in the sky and muted color elsewhere due to darkness, so the *Dusk/Dawn Scene* mode saturates the color a bit. It works like the *Sunset* mode, except that it uses a specific "cooler" white balance setting of 4450K. Since light is so low at dusk and dawn, you may want to use a tripod. The pop-up flash and focus assist light are disabled. (See *figure 9M*.)

Dusk/Dawn Scene mode uses the LS (Landscape) Picture Control and a white balance of 4450K. It also raises *sharpening* by +3.

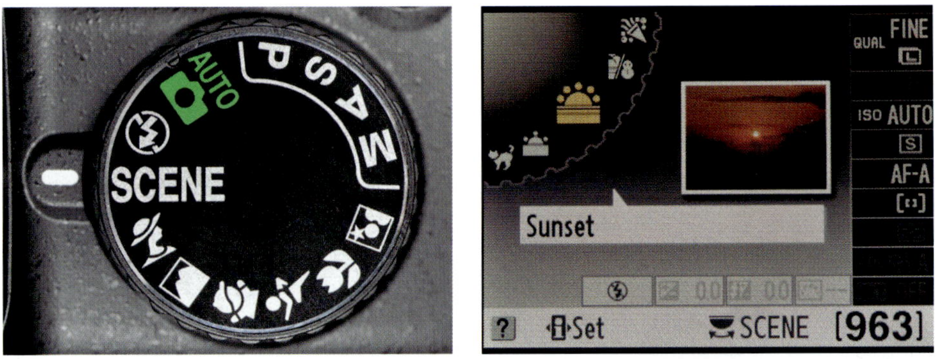

Figure 9L – *Sunset Scene* mode

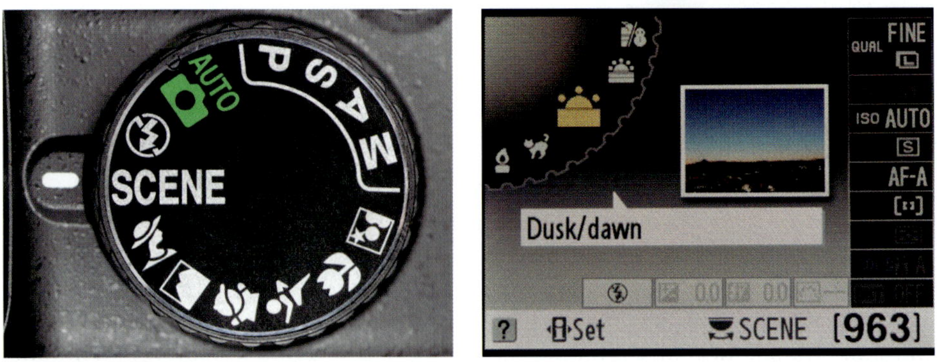

Figure 9M – *Dusk/Dawn Scene* mode

Pet Portrait Scene Mode

Pet Portrait Scene mode emphasizes faster shutter speeds in order to capture that wiggling Fluffy and Spot. The depth of field is shallow to better draw your attention to your pet. Color saturation and contrast is set to medium so your pet won't have abnormally strong colors. (See *figure 9N*.)

Pet Portrait Scene mode uses the SD (Standard) Picture Control and auto white balance.

Candlelight Scene Mode

Candlelight Scene mode is designed to get those delightful candlelight pictures at parties and for special-effect shots. If you can, use a tripod since shutter speeds will be low by candlelight. The camera uses a medium white balance of 4350K to better match the specific color of candlelight. A little extra sharpening is provided to help the image look sharper. The pop-up flash is disabled but the focus assist light still works. (See *figure 9O*.)

Candlelight Scene mode uses the SD (Standard) Picture Control and 4350K white balance. It also raises *sharpening* by +2.

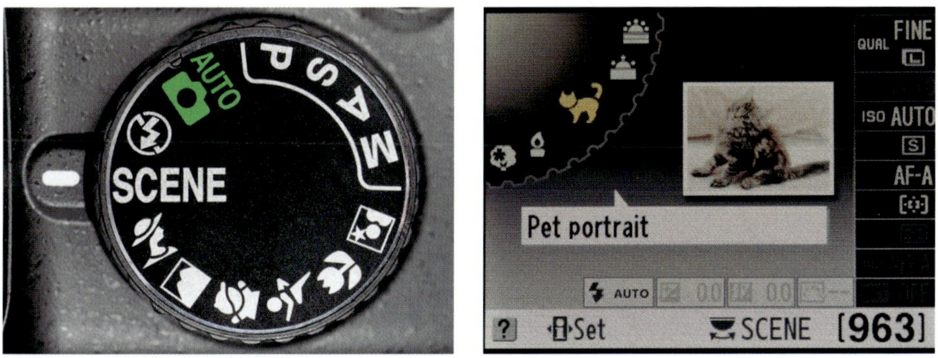

Figure 9N – *Pet Portrait Scene* mode

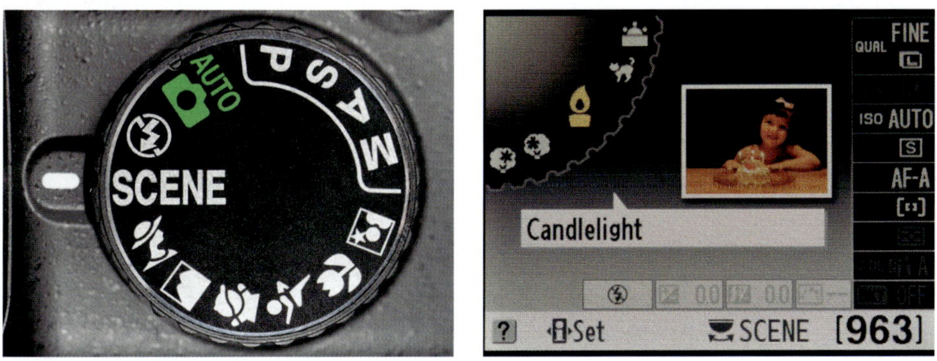

Figure 9O – *Candlelight Scene* mode

Blossom Scene Mode

If you are a gardener or visit places with lots of flowers, you'll enjoy the *Blossom Scene* mode. It tends to emphasize color saturation. Since you need deep depth of field when taking pictures of landscapes or close-up shots of flower blossoms, the camera uses small apertures. Use a tripod if the ambient light is low. The pop-up flash is disabled but the focus assist light still works. (See *figure 9P*.)

Blossom Scene mode uses the LS (Landscape) Picture Control and auto white balance. It also raises *sharpening* by +3 and moves *hue* by -1.

Autumn Colors Scene Mode

Who doesn't love the beautiful reds, yellows, and oranges of autumn? The *Autumn Colors Scene* mode really saturates the deep color and raises the image contrast significantly for lots of "snap." It also uses smaller apertures to get lots of deep focus for those colorful landscape shots. If the light gets low, please use a tripod because shutter speeds will be slow. The pop-up flash is disabled but the focus assist light still works when needed. (See *figure 9Q*.)

Autumn Colors Scene mode uses the VI (Vivid) Picture Control and auto white balance.

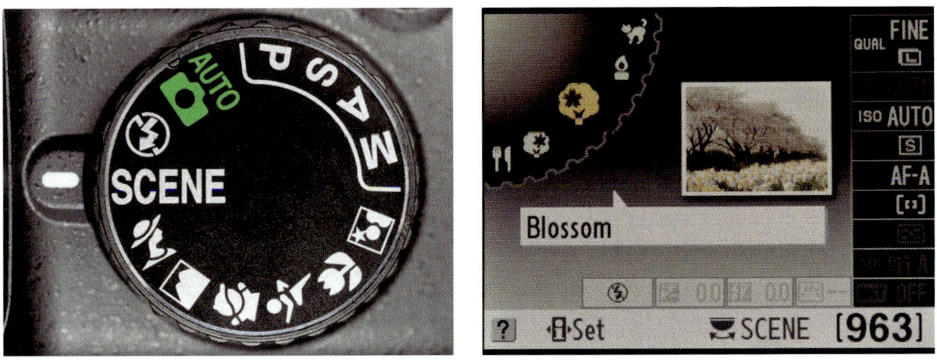

Figure 9P – *Blossom Scene* mode

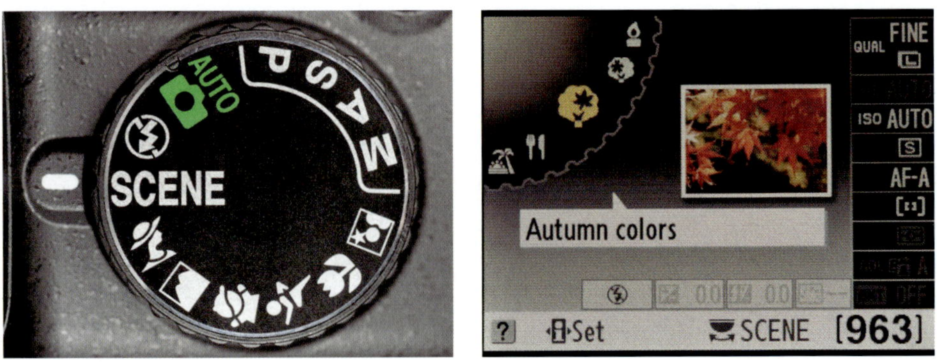

Figure 9Q – *Autumn Colors Scene* mode

Food Scene Mode

Food images should have nice color but should not be overly saturated. The *Food Scene* mode uses medium color saturation and contrast to provide a natural look to food images. It also emphasizes smaller apertures to provide enough depth of field to get most of the food in focus. You'll need to use a tripod if you are shooting food images in low light. Pop-up flash and the focus assist light are available. (See *figure 9R*.)

Food Scene mode uses the SD (Standard) Picture Control and auto white balance. It also raises Saturation by +1.

Silhouette Scene Mode

When you take a picture by silhouette, your subject is dark and the background is well lit. *Silhouette Scene* mode is not for taking pictures of someone standing in front of a window because the camera disables the pop-up flash. Instead, use it to take pictures of interestingly shaped foreground objects—like trees—silhouetted against a beautiful sunset or sky. The pop-up flash is disabled but the focus assist light still works. (See *figure 9S*.)

It uses the LS (Landscape) Picture Control and auto white balance. It also raises contrast by +3.

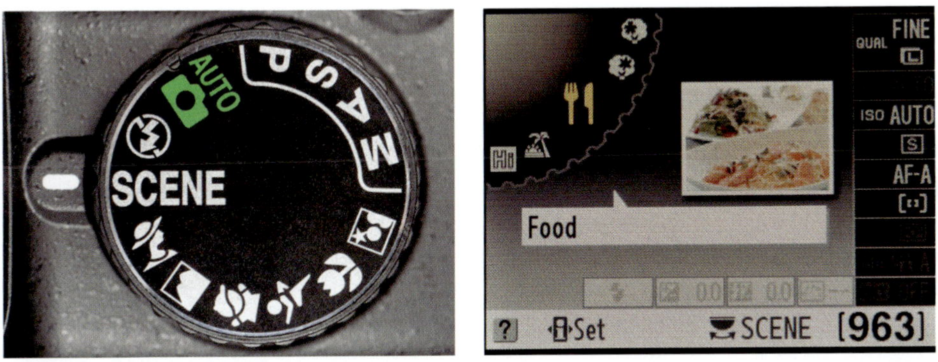

Figure 9R – *Food Scene* mode

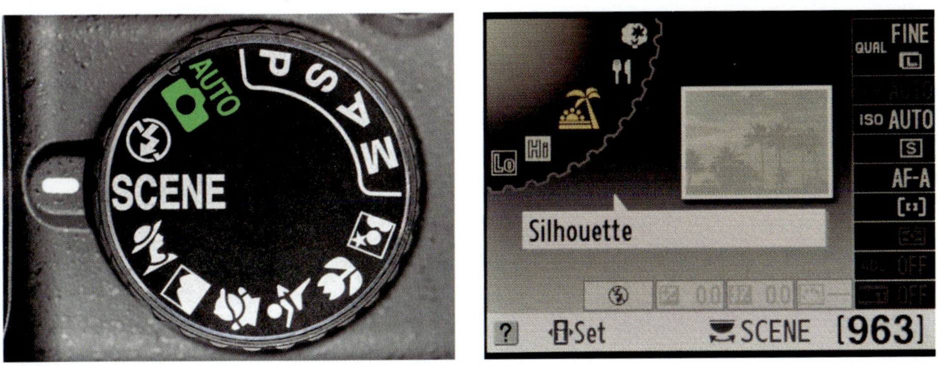

Figure 9S – *Silhouette Scene* mode

High Key Scene Mode

High-key imagery is deliberately slightly overexposed to give a very bright look to the image. The image almost seems to shine with extra light, to the point that some highlight detail is lost. High-key is often used with white subjects on white backgrounds. With *High Key Scene* mode, contrast is slightly lowered to save some highlights, and brightness is raised automatically. The pop-up flash is disabled but the focus assist light is still available, even though you won't need it. (See *figure 9T*.)

High Key Scene mode uses the SD (Standard) Picture Control and auto white balance. It also lowers contrast by -1 and raises brightness by +1.

Low Key Scene Mode

Low-key photography is all about the highlights. Reflections from shiny subjects do well as low-key subjects. Most of the subject is dark and somber looking, with highlights preserved. With *Low Key Scene* mode, the camera raises contrast to deepen the shadows and automatically lowers the brightness more than normal. Since light is low, it's a good idea to use a tripod when shooting in this mode. Color saturation is set to medium because dark images often do not emphasize color. The pop-up flash is disabled but the focus assist light is still available. (See *figure 9U*.)

Low Key Scene mode uses the SD (Standard) Picture Control and auto white balance. It also raises contrast by +1 and lowers brightness by -1.

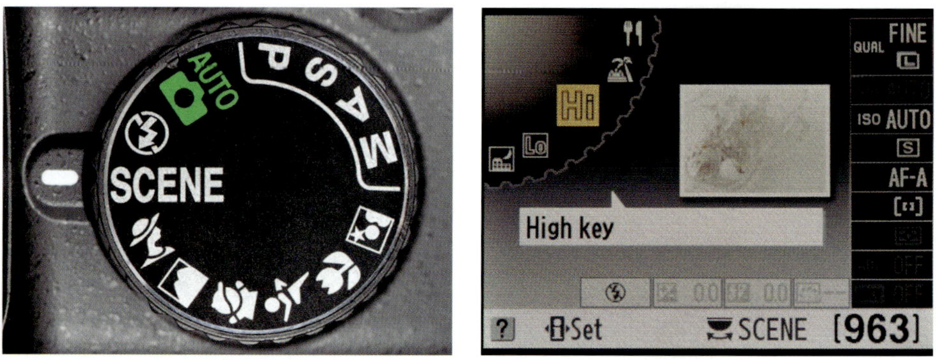

Figure 9T – *High Key Scene* mode

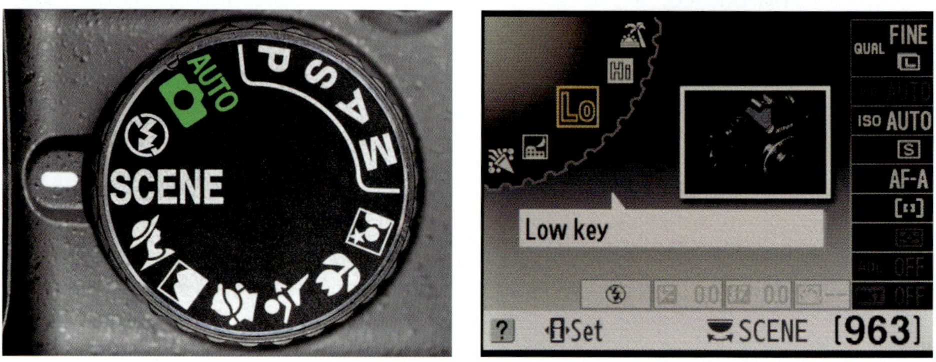

Figure 9U – *Low Key Scene* mode

Section 3 – Histogram

(User's Manual page 118)

Back in the "good old" film days, we had no histogram, so we had to depend on our experience and light meter to get a good exposure. Since we couldn't see the exposure until after we had left the scene, we measured our success by the number of usable images we were able to create. With the exposure meter/histogram combination found in the D5000, and the ability to zoom into our images with the high-resolution monitor on the back of our cameras, the success rate we can experience is very much higher than ever before.

The histogram can be as important, or even more so, than the exposure meter. The meter sets the camera up for the exposure, and the histogram visually verifies that the exposure is properly balanced.

If your exposure meter stopped working, you could still get perfect exposures using only the histogram. In fact, I gauge my efforts more by how the histogram looks than anything else. The exposure meter and histogram work together to make sure you get excellent results from your photographic efforts.

In *figure 10* is a picture of the D5000's histogram screens. The screen on the left is a basic informational screen with only a luminance histogram shown in white. You can always access it by scrolling up or down with the Multi Selector during image review.

The second histogram screen in *figure 10*, is actually a series of histograms. On the upper right is a white-colored luminance histogram. Next is the red channel, then the green channel, and at the bottom is the blue channel (RGB = red, green, blue).

When you look closely at the top white luminance histogram, notice how it looks very similar to the green channel. That's because the human eye is more sensitive to green light than red or blue. Doesn't it make sense to give us a histogram that helps us accurately meter the light that our eyes perceive best?

Let's discuss the use of a histogram in detail.

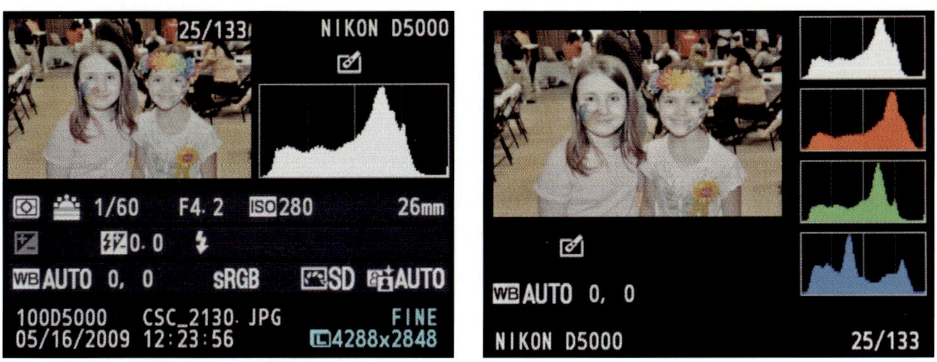

Figure 10 – Two D5000 histogram screens

Understanding the Histogram (An Overview)

Using the histogram screens on your D5000's image viewing LCD will guarantee you a much higher percentage of well-exposed images. Learning to understand the histogram is well worth the effort, and it's not overly complicated.

I'll try to cover this feature with enough detail to give you a working knowledge of how to use the histogram to make better pictures. If you are deeply interested in the histogram, there is much research material available on the Internet. This section covers only a small amount of the information that is actually available, but it will give you enough knowledge to improve your technique immediately.

Light Range

The D5000's sensor can record only a certain range of light values. It seems able to record about 5 to 7 usable EV steps. Unfortunately, many of the higher-contrast subjects we shoot can contain over 12 stops of light values. This is quite a bit more than it is possible to capture in a single exposure. It's important to understand how your camera records light so that you can better control how an image is captured.

Look at *figure 11* closely. The gray rectangular area is a representation of an in-camera histogram.

The histogram is basically a graph that represents the maximum range of light values your camera can capture, in 256 steps (0 = pure black and 255 = pure white). In the middle of the histogram are the mid-range values that represent middle colors like grays, light browns, and greens. The values from just above 0 and just below 255 contain detail.

The actual histogram graph looks like a mountain peak or a series of peaks, and the more of a particular color in an image, the taller the peak. In some cases the graph will be rounded or flattened on top.

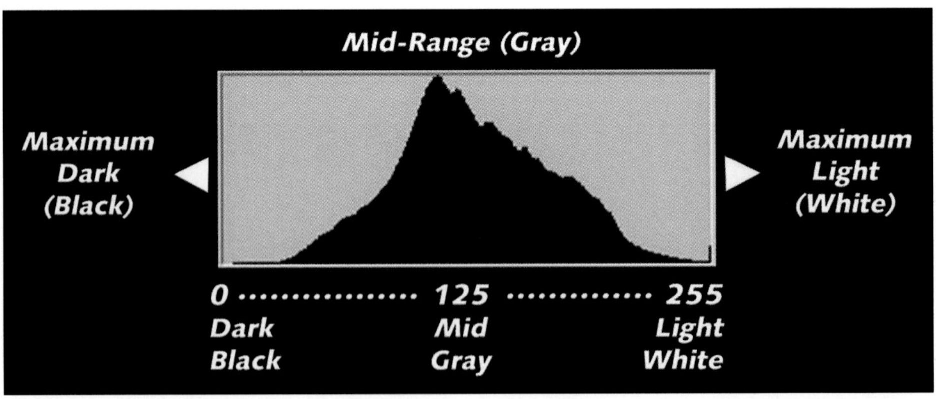

Figure 11 – Basic histogram

The left side of the histogram represents the maximum dark values that your camera can record. The right side represents the maximum white values your camera can capture. On either end of the histogram the light values contain no detail. They are either completely black or completely white.

The top of the histogram (top of the mountain peaks) represents the amount of individual colors, a value you cannot control in-camera, so it is for your information only.

We are mostly concerned with the left- and right-side values of the histogram because we do have control over those (dark vs. light). So basically, the histogram's left-to right directions are related to the darkness and lightness of an image, while the up and down directions of the histogram (valleys and peaks) have to do with color information. I repeated this for emphasis!

The left (dark) to right (light) directions are very important for your picture taking. If the image is too dark, the histogram will show this by clipping off the light values on the left, and if it's too light, by clipping on the right. This will become easier to understand as we look at properly exposed and poorly exposed images. Check out the histogram basic tutorial in *figure 12*, and then we'll look at things in more detail.

When you see the three histograms next to each other, does it make more sense? You can see that the histogram for the underexposed photo of the black Nikon camera shows nearly all the graphic information sitting on the left side of the histogram window, and it is clipped mid-peak. Then look at the histogram for the properly exposed landscape image in the middle and notice how both edges of the histogram just touch the edges of the histogram window. Finally, notice how the overexposed image's histogram is crammed and clipped on the right. I hope this helps somewhat. Now let's look at some histogram detail.

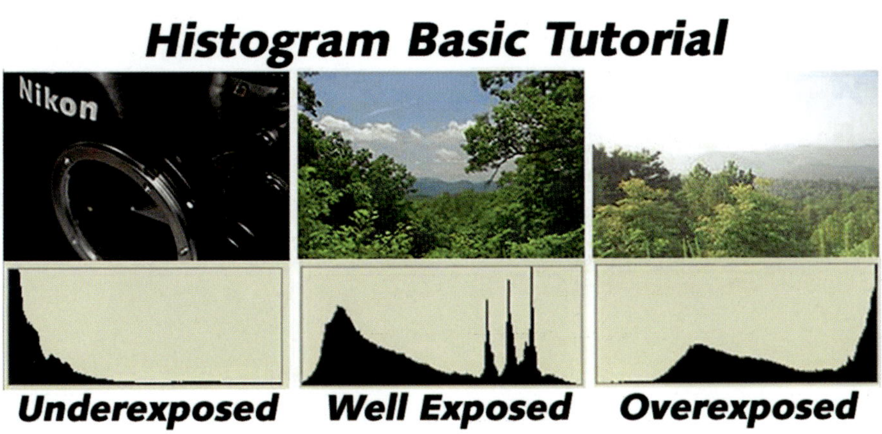

Figure 12 – Three histograms: underexposed, correct, overexposed

Image and Histogram Shape

Look at the image in *figure 13*. It is well exposed, with no serious problems. The entire light range of this particular image fits within the histogram window, which means that it is neither too light nor too dark, and it will take very little or no adjustment to view or print. It contains no more than 4 or 5 stops of light range.

Look at the left side of the histogram graph in *figure 12*. See how it does not cram itself against the dark value side? In other words, the dark values are not clipped off on the left. This means that the camera recorded all the dark values in this image, with no loss of detail in the shadows.

Then look at the right side of the histogram and note that it is not completely against the right side, although quite close. The image contains all the light values available, and everything in between is exposed quite well, with full detail. A histogram does not have to cover the entire window for the exposure to be fine. When there is a limited range of light, the histogram may be rather narrow.

The image in *figure 13* is a relatively low-contrast image with smooth graduations of tone, so it makes a nice smooth mountain peak histogram graph. This will not occur every time because most images contain quite a bit more color information. Each prominent color will be represented with its own peak on the histogram graph. The most prominent colors will have higher peaks, while the

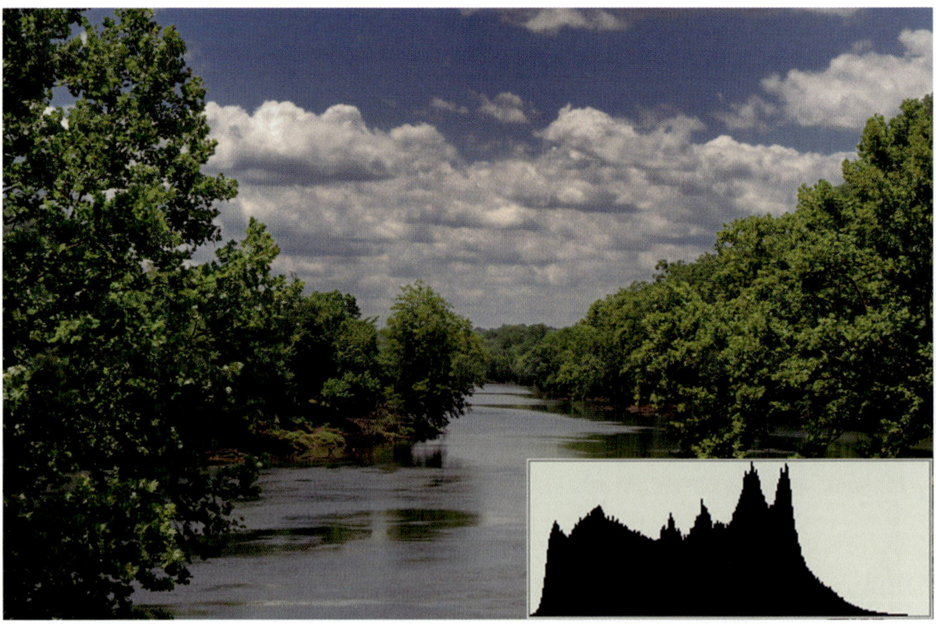

Figure 13 – Normal histogram mountain peak shape

less prominent colors will have lower or no peaks.

As we progress into images with more color or light information, you'll see that the histogram looks quite different. Look at the image in *figure 14*. This is an image that exceeds the range of the D5000's digital sensor.

Notice that, overall, this image is dark and underexposed looking. The histogram in *figure 14* is crammed to the left, effectively being clipped off there. There are no gradual climbs as on a mountain range, from valley to peak and back to valley. Instead, the image shows up on the left side in mid-peak. It is "clipped." This is an underexposed image and the histogram reflects this well.

The most important thing to understand when you see a histogram like the one in *figure 14* (with part of the peak and valley clipped off on the left) is that some or all of the image is underexposed.

Now look at a similar image in *figure 15*. In this image, a larger aperture was used and more light was allowed in. We can now see much more detail. However, once again, the range of light is too wide for the sensor, so it is now clipped off on the highlight side (right). The dark-side graph value is not clipped; instead the graph extends to the left dark-side edge but stops there.

The image in *figure 15* shows more detail, but it's not professional looking and will win no awards. The range of light is simply too wide to be recorded fully.

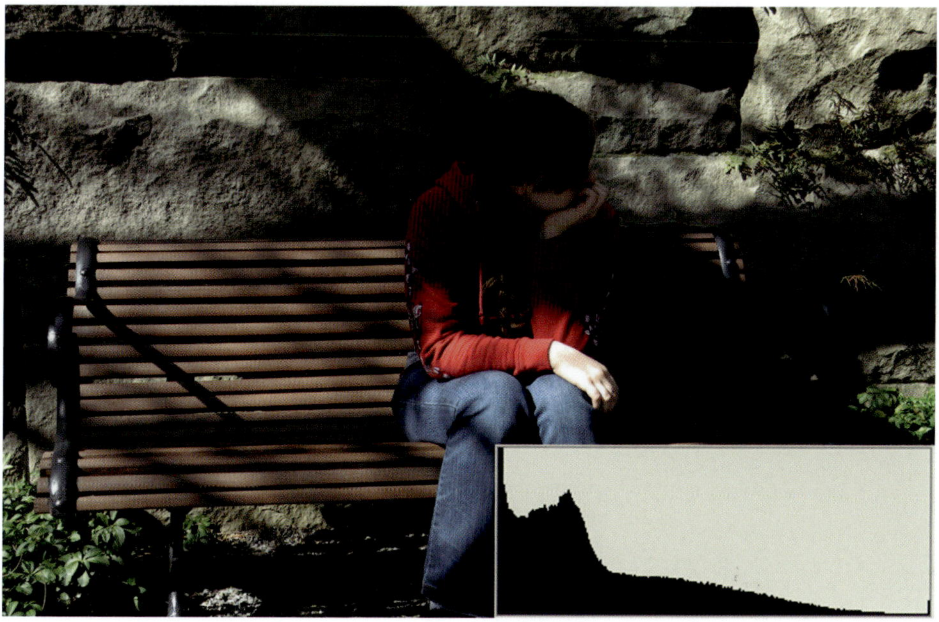

Figure 14 – Underexposed histogram

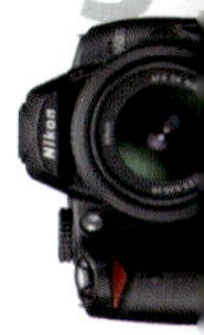

Many of the details are overly light, which can be seen by the histogram's clipping on the right side. The most important thing to remember with this image is that when you see a histogram that is crammed all the way to the right and is clipped, some or all of the image is too light. A portion of the image in *figure 15* is recorded as pure white and is permanently lost. In other words, it is "blown out."

It's important is that you try to center the histogram without either edge being clipped off. This is not always possible because there is often too wide a light range and the sensor or histogram window can't contain it. If you center the histogram, your images will be better exposed. If you take a picture and the histogram is shifted far left or right, you can then retake it, exposing in the direction of the opposite light value.

If there is too much light to allow centering the histogram, you must decide which part of the image is more important, the light or dark values. Does that make sense? You must expose for the highlights or you will lose detail in the light areas. Which is more important, the dark areas, or the light areas?

Capturing a Wider Dynamic Range

You can take several pictures of the same scene with varying exposure settings to capture a larger range of light, and then later combine them in your computer using high dynamic range (HDR) techniques. You can also use your D5000's Retouch Menu and the image overlay system to combine two images, one exposed brightly and the other exposed darkly; and then combine them for a wider dynamic range.

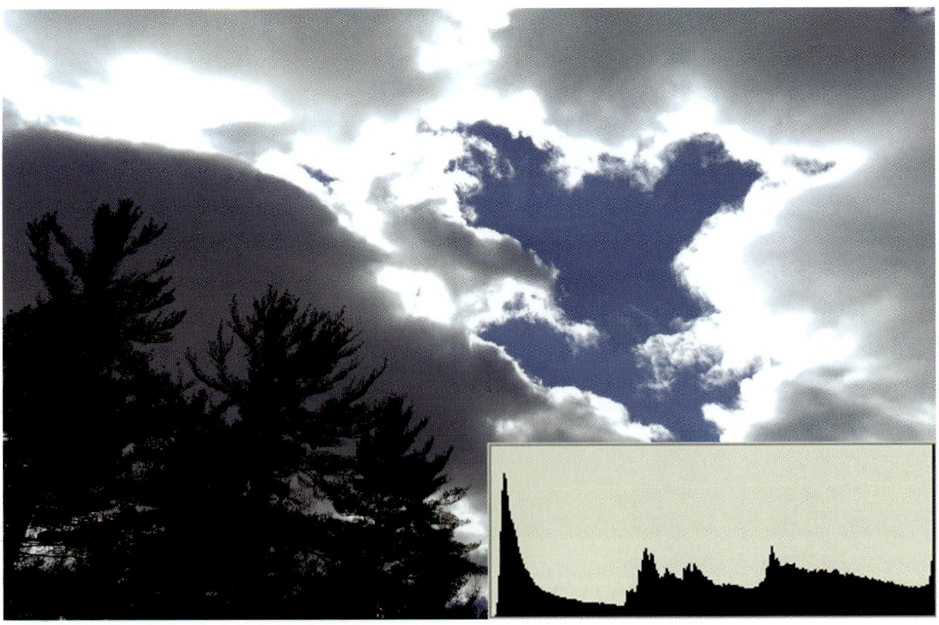

Figure 15 – Overexposed histogram

How Does the Eye React to Light Values?

The D5000 camera with its imaging sensor and glass lenses is only a weak imitation of our marvelously designed eye and brain combination. There are very few situations in which our eyes cannot adjust to the available light range. So, as photographers we are always seeking ways to record even a small portion of what our eye and mind can perceive.

Since our eyes and brains know that shadows are black, and we expect that, it is usually better to expose for the highlights. If you see dark shadows, that seems normal. We're simply not used to seeing light that's so bright that all detail is lost. An image exposed for the dark values will look very weird because most highlight detail will be burned out.

Your eyes can see a *huge* range of light in comparison to your digital sensor. The only time you will ever see light values that are so bright that detail is lost is when you are looking directly at an overwhelmingly bright light, like the sun. So, in a worst-case scenario, expose an image so that the right side of the histogram just touches the right side of the histogram window and the image will look more normal.

Since photography's beginning, we have always fought with being able to record only a limited range of light. But with the digital camera and its histogram, we can now see a visual representation of the light values and immediately approve of the image, reshoot it with emphasis on lighter or darker values, or see that we must use a filter or multiple-exposure high dynamic range (HDR) imaging to capture it at all.

An Alternate Method to Modify Exposure

You can also use the +/- exposure compensation button (see figure 1) and command dial to add or subtract exposure by overriding the light meter. This allows you to manually push the histogram to one side of the window or the other. Try it—it isn't difficult. Just be sure to set the exposure compensation back to 0.0 when you are done.

Computer Adjustment of Images

Looking at the image in *figure16*, taken in mid-day overhead sunshine, you can see an example of a range of light that is too great to be captured by a digital sensor but is exposed in such a way that we can get a usable photo later.

Notice in *figure16* how the dark values are clipped off and dark detail is lost. But look to the right side of the histogram and notice how the light values are not clipped off. So the camera recorded all the light values but lost some dark values. Since our eye sees this as normal, this image looks okay. In this image I "exposed for the highlights," letting the dark values go black.

If we were standing there looking at the cabin ourselves, our eyes would be able to see much more detail in the front porch area. But the camera just can't record that large of a light range. If we want to get a bit more detail in the shadows than this image seems to contain, we can do it using the D5000's *Retouch Menu* and the D-Lighting function. D-Lighting allows us to raise detail out of the shadows and extend the dynamic range of the image. It is somewhat limited because there are only three levels available; high, normal, and low. However, it works for images that don't have extreme dynamic range values.

Since your computer screen is much larger and computer "post-processing" software, like Nikon Capture NX2 and Photoshop, allows much finer control, many choose to use their computers for image adjustment. In this case, it is good to use the histogram to get the best possible exposure and then adjust the image later in the computer. Primarily, we need a way to take all this light and compress it into a more usable range.

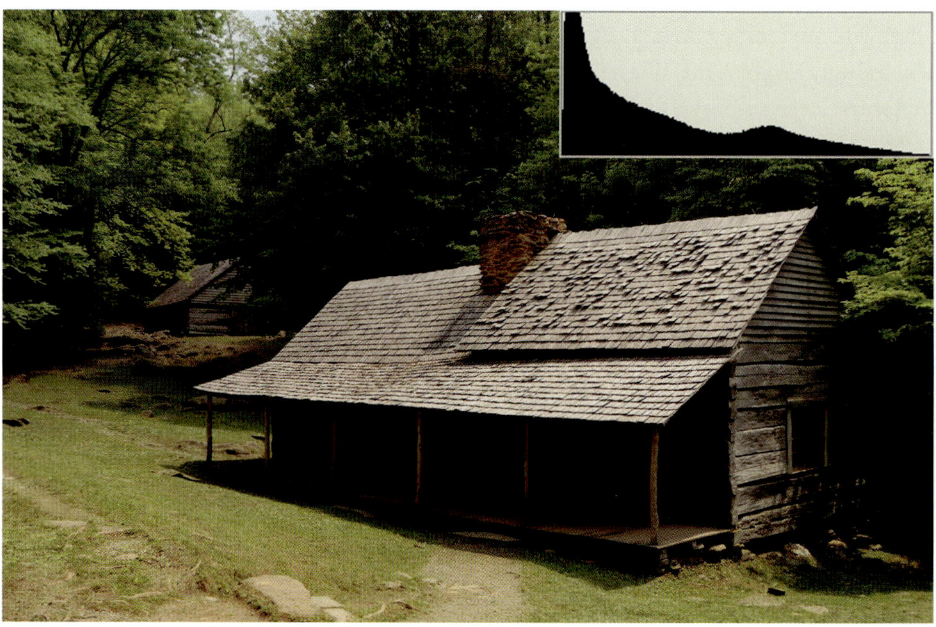

Figure 16 – Cabin picture with correct exposure but dark shadows

We are now entering the realm of post-processing, or in-computer image manipulation. Look at the image in *figure 17*. This is the exact same image as the one in *figure 16*, but it has been adjusted in Photoshop to cram more image detail into the histogram by compressing the mid-range values. Notice that the entire histogram seems to be farther right toward the light side. Also notice that the mid-range peaks are basically gone. We removed a good bit of the mid-range, but since there was already a lot of mid-range there, our image did not suffer greatly.

How this computer post-processing was done is outside the scope of this book, but it is not very difficult with a graphics program like Nikon Capture NX2, Photoshop, Photoshop Elements, or Lightroom or another fine graphics program designed for photographers. Your digital camera and your computer are a powerful imaging combination—a digital darkroom where you are in control from start to finish, from clicking the shutter to printing the image. But, retreating from philosophy, let's continue with histogram exploration.

Notice in *figure 17* how the histogram edge is just touching the highlight side of the histogram window. A small amount of clipping is taking place, and you can see the slightly blown-out area on the peak of the cabin's roof. Sometimes a very small amount of clipping does not seriously harm the image. The photographer must be the judge.

The greater apparent detail in this image is the result of compressing the mid-range of the light values a bit in the computer. If you compress the mid-range light values, or make them smaller, that will tend to pull the dark values toward the light side and the light values toward

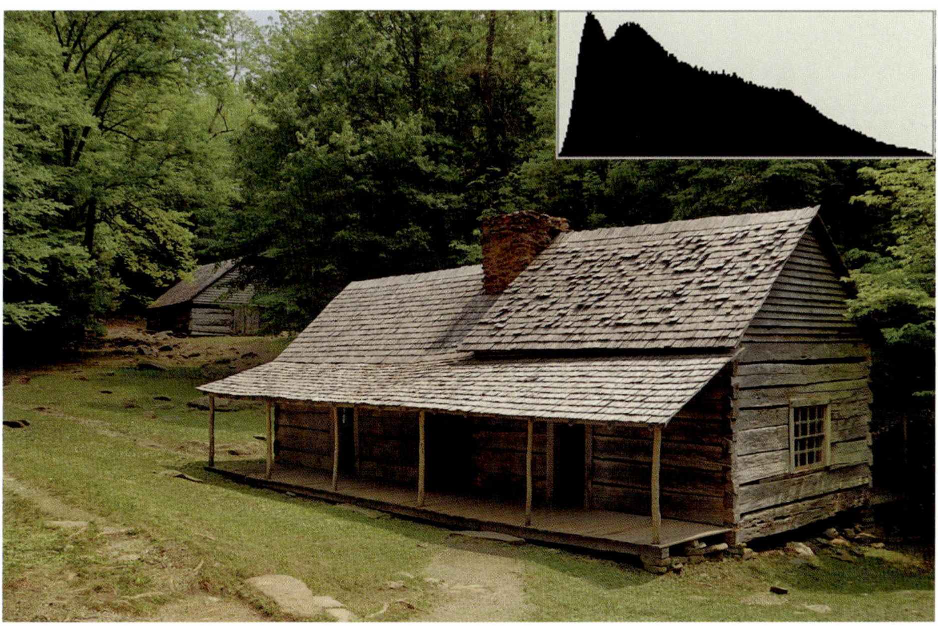

Figure 17 – Post-processed cabin picture with correct exposure and lightened shadows

the dark side. You will have more apparent detail in your image. It's like cutting a section out of the middle of a garden hose. If you pull both of the cut ends together, the other two ends of the hose will move toward the middle and the hose will be shorter overall. If you compress or remove the mid-range of the histogram, both ends of the graph will move toward the middle. If one of the ends of the graph is beyond the edge of the histogram window, or is clipped off, it will be less so when the mid-range is compressed.

We are simply trying to make the histogram fit into the frame of its window. If we have to cut out some of the middle (to bring both ends into the window), there is usually plenty in the middle to cut out, so the image rarely suffers. Remember, this is being done outside of the camera on a computer. You can't really control the in-camera histogram to compress values, other than with *Retouch Menu D-Lighting* option, but you need to be aware that it can be done in the computer so that you can expose accordingly with your camera's histogram. Then you will be prepared for later post-processing of the image on your computer.

In fact, now that we have compressed the mid-range values, the image more closely resembles what our eyes are used to seeing; therefore it looks more normal to us.

You have even more flexibility by choosing to shoot in the NEF/RAW mode. (See the discussion of the *Shooting Menu > Image quality* setting in chapter 6, "Shooting Menu," or check pages 62 and 63 of the User's Manual for more details on shooting both RAW and JPEG images in a single shot.)

A RAW digital image contains an adjustable range of light. You can use controls in Capture NX2, Photoshop, or even the basic Nikon Picture Project software included with the D5000 to select from the range of light within the big RAW image file. It's like moving the histogram window to the left or right over all that wide range of RAW image data. You select a final resting place for the histogram window, capture the underlying RAW data, and then your image is ready for use.

This is a serious oversimplification of the process, but I hope it makes the process more understandable. In reality, the digital sensor records a wider range of light than you can use in one image. While you might be able to use about 5 stops of light range in a normal image, the digital sensor is probably recording about 7 stops of light range. You just can't get all of that range into the final image. It is there in the RAW file as a selectable range. I prefer to think of it as a built-in bracket since it works the same way.

This bracketed light range within the image is present to a very limited degree in JPEG files, but it's the most pronounced in pure RAW images. That is why many choose to shoot in RAW mode instead of JPEG.

My Conclusions

The Nikon D5000 has a Multi Selector that can be pressed right or left to scroll through the images you have already taken. You can also press the multi selector switch up or down to scroll through the various informational modes, such as the histogram screens. When you take a picture of an important subject, find the histogram view of your image. If you can't find the screen with multiple histograms, as shown in *figure 10*, see the *Playback Menu> Display mode* and enable *RGB histogram*. (For more information, see chapter 5, "Playback Menu.")

Your camera meter should be used to get the initial exposure only. Then you can look at the histogram and see if the image's light range is contained within the limited range of the sensor. If it is clipped off to the right or the left, you may want to add or subtract light with your +/- exposure compensation button (see *figure 1*) or use your camera's manual mode. Expose for the light range with your histogram. Let your light meter get you close, and then fine-tune with the histogram.

There are also other LCD viewing modes that you can use along with the histogram, such as the *Highlights* (blinky blinky) mode for blown-out highlights. (In the *Playback Menu*, select *Display mode* and then *Highlights*. This is fully discussed in chapter 5). This causes your image on your LCD to blink from light to dark in the blown-out highlight areas. This blinking is a rough representation of a highlight-value clipped histogram and is useful for quick shooting. Using your camera's light meter, histogram and the highlight burnout blinky mode together is a very powerful method to control your exposures.

If you master this method, you will have a very fine degree of control over where you place your images' light ranges. This is sort of like using the famous black and white Ansel Adams Zone System, but it is represented visually on the LCD of your D5000.

The manipulation of the histogram "levels" in-computer is a detailed study in itself. It's part of having a digital darkroom and an image workflow. Learn to use your computer to tweak your images and you'll be able to produce superior results most of the time. More importantly, learn to use your histogram to capture a nice image in the first place!

Your histogram is simply a graph that allows you to see at a glance how well (or how poorly) your image's light values were captured by your camera. Too far left and the image is too dark—too far right and the image is too light. Learn to use the histogram well and your images are bound to improve.

White Balance

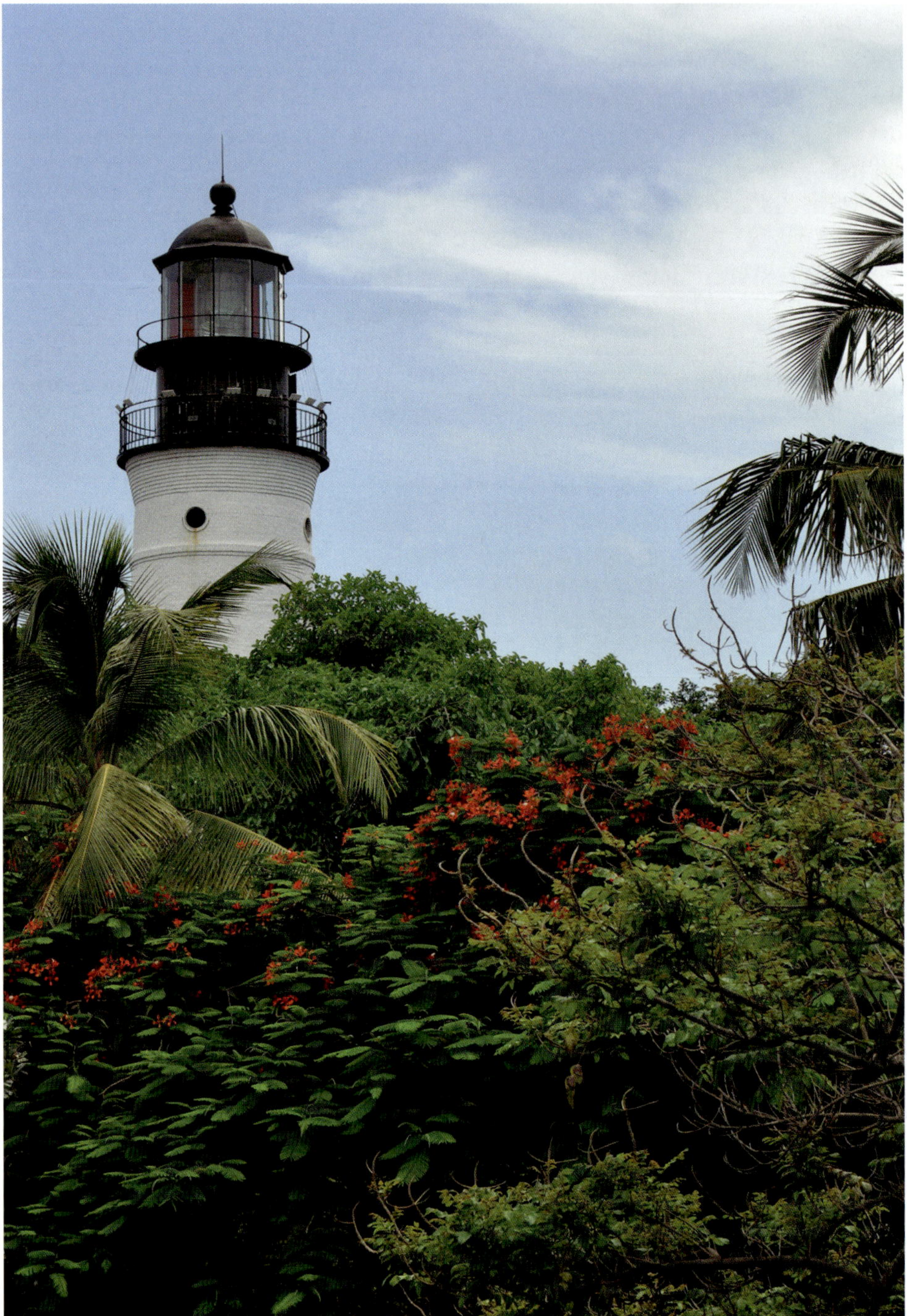

The human eye and brain can adjust to virtually any lighting situation.

Let's say you're reading a book with an old-fashioned incandescent light bulb in your lamp. You probably won't notice that the normally white pages of your book have a warm orange tint. Your brain adjusts your color perception so that the pages of the book look white to your eye. If you take your book outside and sit under a tree in the shade, the color of the light is now a cool bluish, yet your eyes keep on perceiving the pages as white.

Every light source has a different color. If you're taking pictures in direct sunlight, and suddenly a cloud's shadow covers your subject, there is a difference in the color of the light. This is referred to as the color temperature of the light. Your brain adjusts automatically to different color temperatures and you perceive everything with normal colors, no matter what the light source.

Unfortunately, a camera does not have the power of your brain. The Nikon D5000 has an auto white balance setting that does its best to adjust to the current lighting color temperature, and most of the time it does a good job. However, sometimes it needs a little help, especially when you want very consistent results.

It will significantly benefit your photography to understand how the white balance features of your camera operate. Let's consider them in detail.

How Does White Balance (WB) Work?

Normally, the WB settings are used to adjust the camera so that whites are truly white and other colors are accurate under whatever light source you are shooting. You can also use the white balance controls to deliberately introduce color casts into your image for interesting special effects.

Camera WB color temperatures are exactly backwards from the Kelvin (K) scale we learned in school for star temperatures. Remember that a red giant star is "cool" while a blue/white star is "hot." The WB color temperatures are backwards because the camera's WB system is adding color to make up for a deficit of color in the original light of the subject.

For instance, under a fluorescent light there is a deficit of blue, which makes the image appear greenish-yellow. When blue is added, the image is balanced to a more normal appearance. Normal camera WB under fluorescent light may be about 4200 K.

Another example might be shooting on a cloudy overcast day. The ambient light could cause the image to look bluish if left unadjusted. The WB control in your camera sees the "cool" color temperature and adds some red to "warm" the colors a bit. Normal camera WB on a cloudy overcast day might be about 6000 K.

Just remember that we use the real Kelvin temperature range in reverse and that warm colors are considered reddish while blue colors are cool. Even though this is backwards from what we were taught in school, it fits our situation better. Blue seems cool while red seems warm to photographers. Just don't let your astronomer friends convince you otherwise.

> **Main Point**
> Understanding WB in a simplified way is simply realizing that light has a range of colors that go from cool to warm. We can adjust our cameras to use the available light in an accurate, neutral, "balanced" way that matches the actual light source, or we can allow a color cast to enter the image by unbalancing the settings.
>
> We will discuss these options from the standpoint of the Nikon D5000's camera controls and how they deal with WB.

Color Temperature

The WB range (User's Manual page 97) can vary from a very cool 2700 K to a very warm 8000 K by using various preset White Balance settings. We'll examine how shortly.

Figure 1 shows the same picture adjusted in Photoshop to three WB settings manually; 2500 K, 5000 K, and 10,000 K. Notice how the 2500 K image is much bluer or cooler than the 10,000 K image. The 5000 K image is about right for the picture's actual daylight. The 10,000 K image is much too warm.

In the good old days of film, many of us used daylight-balanced film and an 81A filter to warm up our subjects. Or maybe we added a filter to put some blue in on a foggy day to make the image feel cold and foreboding. You can get the same results with the hard-coded white balance settings built in to the D5000.

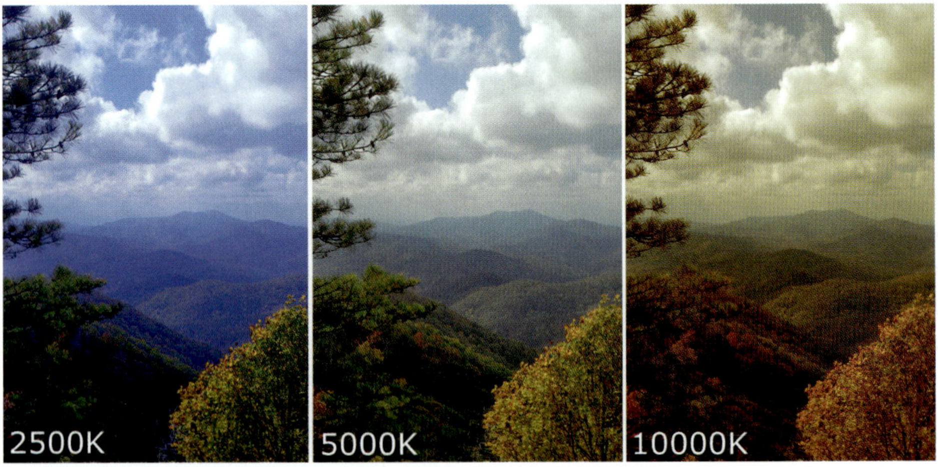

Figure 1 – Same image with different WB settings

These settings are presented with generic names to put you in the ballpark. Just because you have a choice of *Cloudy* (represented by the "cloud" symbol on on the right screen in *figure 2*) does not necessarily mean that if you see clouds, it's the exact setting you need to choose.

To achieve the same effect as daylight film and a warming filter, simply select the *Cloudy* white balance setting while shooting in normal daylight. This sets the D5000 to balance at about 6000 K and make nice warm-looking images. If you want to really warm the image up, set the controls to *Shade*, which sets the camera to 8000 K.

On the other hand, if you want to make an image appear cool or bluish, try using the symbols for *Fluorescent* (4200 K) or *Incandescent* (3000 K) settings in normal daylight.

Remember, the color temperature shifts from "cool" values to "warm" values. The D5000 can record your images with any color temperature from 2500 K (very cool or bluish) to 10,000 K (very warm or reddish) and any major value in between. There's no need to carry various film emulsions or filters to deal with light color range. The D5000 has very easy-to-use color temperature controls and a full range of color temperature selections available.

There are two methods of setting the WB on the D5000 (User's Manual pages 96–102):

1. Manually setting a WB preset by selecting options from the *Information edit /White Balance* (Method 1) or *Shooting menu/White Balance* (Method 2) screens.
2. Manually setting WB using the *PRE* function and measuring the actual white balance with a gray or white card under the light source for your subject.

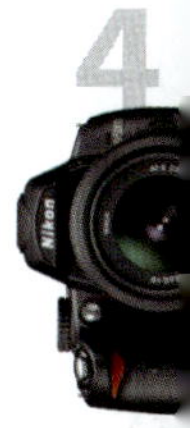

We'll consider each of these methods in the following sections since you may prefer to use different methods according to the time you have to shoot and the color accuracy you want. Most critical photographers will use method number 2, the PRE measurement method. We'll discuss the PRE function in an upcoming section called "Measuring Ambient Light and Using PRE".

Manual White Balance With P,S,A,M Modes

You can manually choose or adjust the white balance values only if you are using one of the P, S, A, M modes on the mode dial. These stand for Programmed Auto, Shutter-priority, Aperture-priority, and Manual (see chapter 3). Since you take full or partial control over the camera when you use these modes, it makes sense that they would allow you to control WB also. The other modes allow the camera to take control, so it decides what white balance the image needs—which works fine most of the time.

Method 1: Setting White Balance with the Information Edit Screens

(User's Manual page 96)
Sometimes you might want to manually choose WB settings. The D5000 allows you to change the WB by using either the *Information edit* screens or internal *Shooting Menu*. The *Shooting Menu* gives you more control over things like fine-tuning the white balance. We'll look at both methods in this chapter. First, let's examine the *Information edit* screen method, which is very easy.

You'll need to think about the type of light source in which you are shooting images. You'll also want to recognize the individual symbols and what they mean. The symbols are fairly self-explanatory.

Seven Choices for Flourescent WB

You'll notice in the screen on the right in *figure 2* that the fluorescent symbol has a 4 after it. This is because I had previously selected the fourth type of fluorescent lighting available within the WB preset settings when I was using the *Shooting Menu* WB screens. There are actually seven different fluorescent WB presets available, but you can't access them from the *Information edit* screens. For now, just realize that the WB presets you can choose from the *Information edit* screens must be configured using the shooting menu screens. We'll discuss this in the next section.

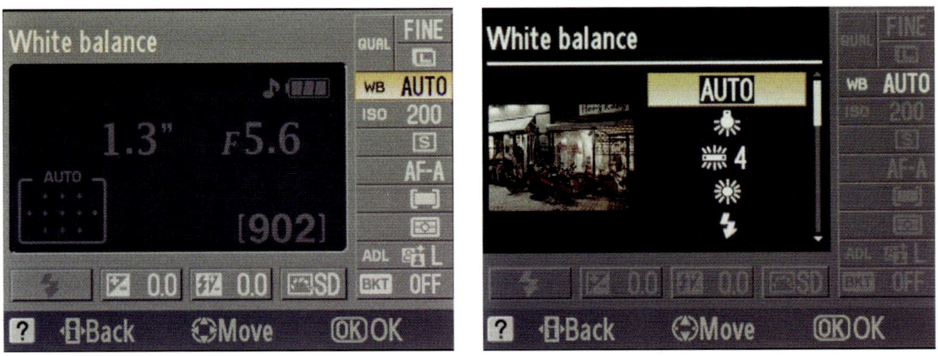

Figure 2 – The WB information edit screens

Information Edit Screens

Here is how to set the White Balance using the *Information edit* screens:

1. Press the <i> information edit button until you see the *Information edit* screen (see *figure 2*).
2. Make sure the yellow highlighted rectangle is positioned in the *White balance* (*WB*) field.
3. Press the *OK* button.
4. You'll be presented with the second *White balance* screen. It has a list of WB selections, as shown here:

AUTO Auto White Balance, 3500-8000K.

Incandescent, 3000K.

Fluorescent, 4200K.

Direct Sunlight, 5200K.

Flash, 5400K.

Cloudy, 6000K.

Shade, 8000K.

PRE PRE, Use to measure WB for the actual ambient light. If no measurement is taken, the camera uses the last value stored in camera WB memory.

5. Choose one of the white balance settings from the list.
6. Press the *OK* button. The camera will return to the main *Information edit* screen with your selection showing after the WB setting.

Recommendation

Why not just leave the camera in Auto WB mode? Well, if you want a certain consistent color balance in your images, you can select one of the preset WB settings. For instance, let's say that you are shooting on a cloudy day and you want to make the images have the same color. You could select the *Cloudy* WB setting and all your images will have 6000 K as the base color temperature. Or, you might be shooting in bright sunlight and want to use the *Direct sunlight* WB setting. If you're shooting lots of images under a certain type of light and use the corresponding WB setting, you'll later have excellent consistency when they are viewed side-by side. Otherwise, each image may have a slightly different color balance, and you'll be forced to do a lot of extra work later to rebalance the images. This is especially important when you are shooting a series of images that must be viewed together. It's not so important when the images are viewed individually. If an image is a stand-alone image—with no strong relationship to its mates— then Auto WB may work just fine.

4

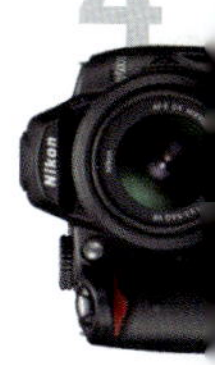

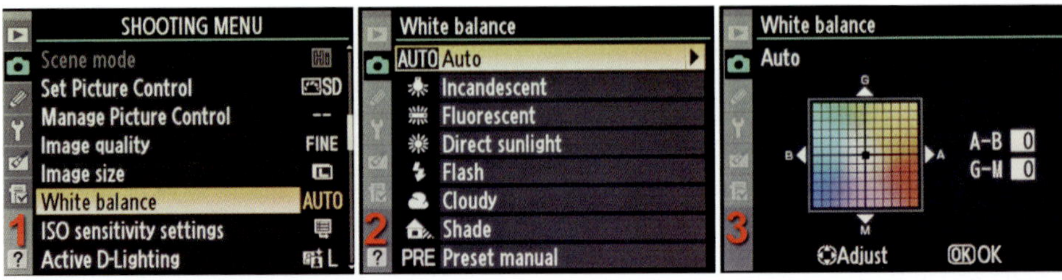

Figure 3 –Setting the WB via the *Shooting Menu*

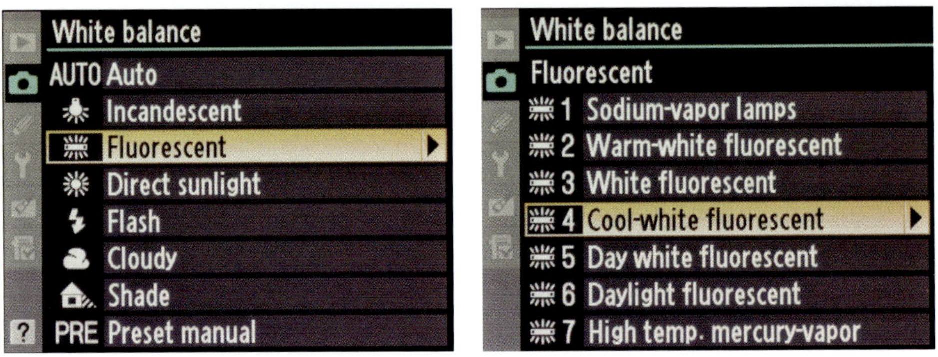

Figure 3A – Fluorescent white balance choices

Method 2:

Setting White Balance with the Menus and Selecting Options

(User's Manual pages 97–102)

This method is similar to method 1, but you use the camera's *Shooting Menu* screens to select the WB range. Instead of using the *Information edit* screens and command dial, you'll open the Shooting Menu and set the WB by selecting from it. In figure 3 are the screens used to set the WB selection in your D5000's *Shooting Menu*.

Normally, you'll use only the first two screens to set one of the preset WB values such as *Cloudy*, *Shade*, or *Direct Sunlight*; then you'll just press the *OK* button on the final screen, without changing anything. Here are the steps used to select a WB setting:

1. Press the MENU button and select the *Shooting Menu*.
2. Select *White balance* and then scroll to the right.
3. Select one of the preset values, such as *Direct Sunlight*, *Flash*, or *Cloudy*, and then scroll to the right.

Special note on the Fluorescent WB settings: Since fluorescent light comes in all sorts of color temperatures, from sodium-vapor to mercury-vapor, you see an additional screen just before the fine-tuning screen. This will appear between the two screens in *figure 3*. It is a screen giving you seven types of fluorescent lighting to choose from. In *figure 3A* are your fluorescent choices.

The fluorescent choices are as follows:

1 – Sodium-vapor lamps
2 – Warm-white fluorescent
3 – White fluorescent
4 – Cool-white fluorescent
5 – Day white fluorescent
6 – Daylight fluorescent
7 – High temp. mercury-vapor

Once you've chosen a fluorescent type, just scroll to the right and the fine-tuning screen will appear. If you don't know your fluorescent types, you may have to experiment a bit. I recommend just doing a *PRE* ambient light measurement under *Fluorescent*. We'll discuss how shortly.

4. The fine-tuning screen will now appear (the screen on the right in *figure 3*). Unless you want to fine-tune the preset, just press *OK* immediately without moving the little square from its center position.

That's all there is to selecting a preset WB from within the *Shooting Menu* system. The only difference in doing it this way is that you can fine-tune the color temperature values in the third screen (on the right in *figure 3*). If you decide to fine-tune a WB preset, then an asterisk will appear next to the *Shooting Menu*'s WB symbol for that preset. You'll see this symbol on the main *Shooting Menu* screen to the right of the symbol for that WB preset. (Refer to method 1 for a listing of what each symbol means.)

Once you have configured the various WB presets, you can select from them with the *Information edit* screens to save time.

Mired WB Fine-Tuning Values

(User's Manual pages 97–98)
One of methods used in measuring color temperatures is to use micro reciprocal degrees, commonly referred to by the abbreviation mired. You may enjoy studying this color temperature measurement. Why? Simply because Nikon makes the WB fine-tuning adjustment in mired values. Mired is merely a way of expressing a very fine color temperature measurement. The manual doesn't directly mention it on page 98, and you are not required to understand mired values to use the D500, but does help to understand the adjustment method.

If you choose to fine tune any of the color temperature settings after you have selected one of the preset WB values, the last menu screen (see *figure 3*) allows you to do so by mired clicks. Each press of the Multi Selector is equal to five mired values each in the four color directions. Up is green (G), down is magenta (M), left is blue (B), and right is amber (A).

If you aren't familiar with fine-tuning the preset's default color temperature, or if you don't want to change it (most won't), then simply press the *OK* button without moving the little square from the center (see the third screen in *figure 3*). If you've accidentally moved it, simply move it back with the Multi Selector until it's in the middle again, then press *OK*, which will select the preset WB value you wanted to use without modifying its default value (the example default value is Flash at 5400 K).

However, if you feel that one of the D5000's preset WB values is not exactly what you would like it to be, you can experimentally fine tune the color temperature in mired values for that preset by adjusting it along the horizontal or vertical color directions.

Recommendation

I normally use method 1 because it allows me to select a preset WB value without accidentally modifying the settings of its default color temperature and doesn't require that I use the menus. I find that method 1 is much faster than using the *Shooting Menu*. Since I am using the *Information edit* screens, it only takes seconds to set the values. I can't do a *PRE* measurement of the ambient light with method 1, but I can select a previously set *PRE* setting. Let's consider how a *PRE* measurement is done since it gives you very accurate WB under the current source of light.

A Brief Technical Foray

Color temperature is a characteristic of visible light and is determined by comparing the subject's color with that of an ideal "black-body radiator." The color temperature, measured in K (Kelvin) or mired (micro-reciprocal degrees Kelvin), is the temperature at which a heated black-body radiator matches the color of the light source of the subject. In depth information is available by looking up Planck's Law and Wien's Displacement Law. Now back to easy-to-understand stuff!

Measuring Ambient Light and Using *PRE*

This method allows you to measure ambient light values and set the camera's WB accordingly. It's not hard to learn and is very accurate since it's an actual through-the-lens measurement of the Kelvin temperature of the source light. You'll need a white or neutral gray card to accomplish this measurement.

Figure 3B shows the *Shooting Menu* screens used to take a *PRE* ambient WB reading.

Here's how to use the *PRE* white balance measurement method (see *figure 3B* and page 99 in the D5000 user's manual):

1. Press the MENU button and select the *Shooting Menu*.
2. Select *White balance* from the *Shooting Menu* and then scroll to the right.
3. Scroll to the bottom of the list with the multi selector button until *PRE – Preset manual* is selected, then scroll to the right.
4. Select *Measure* from the list, and scroll to the right.
5. Select *Yes* from the choices on the *Overwrite existing preset data?* screen.
6. Press the *OK* button, and you'll be presented with a screen that says *Take photo of a white or gray object filling viewfinder under lighting for shooting.*
7. The screen will switch to an information screen with *PRE* flashing in the lower-right corner (see *figure 3B*, image 6, red arrow).
8. Point the camera lens at a white or neutral gray card and take a picture. The object is not to focus on this card,

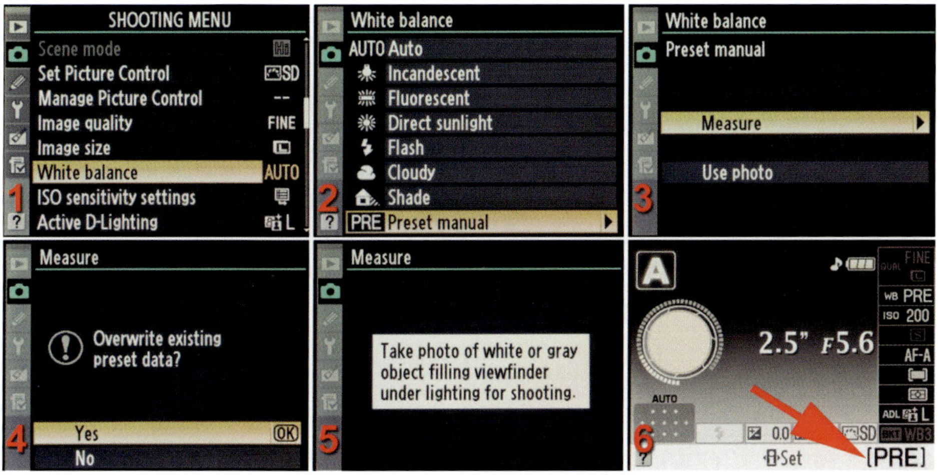

Figure 3B – *PRE* ambient Light WB Reading

so get to within four inches (10 cm) when you take the picture. Make sure a shadow from the lens does not show in the picture or it may change the reading slightly.

9. The information screen will appear again with a small line at the top saying, *Data acquired* (see *figure 3C*). The *PRE* in the lower-right corner will stop flashing, and your new measurement is in place.

The camera will continue to use this measurement until you change it. If you forget—which I often do—you'll later find yourself getting strangely colored pictures when shooting under a different light source. Just remember to change back to Auto WB for general shooting.

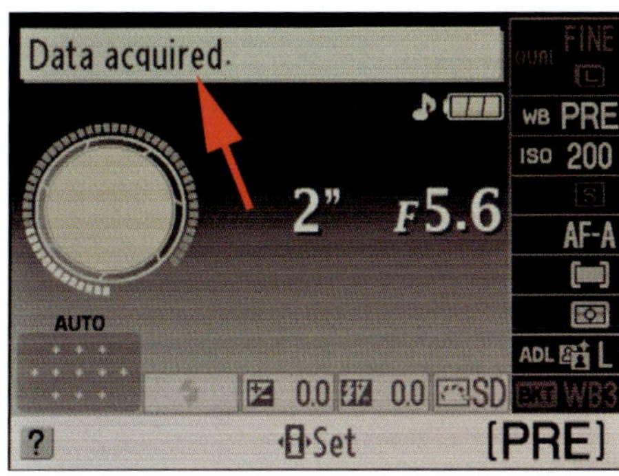

Figure 3C – *PRE* ambient light WB reading acquired

Recommendation

The *PRE* measurement is very sensitive because it's using the light coming through the lens to set the WB. Unless you're measuring in an extremely low light level, it will virtually always be successful. In fact, I have never yet had the camera tell me that it wasn't successful. Be sure that you're using a correct white or gray card (or something comparable) to take the reading or you may have some weird color casts as a result. When I am shooting under most indoor forms of light, I will often use the *PRE* method and take a measurement. I don't want to be bothered with trying to figure out what type of lighting is used where I'm taking pictures. A *PRE* reading solves that completely!

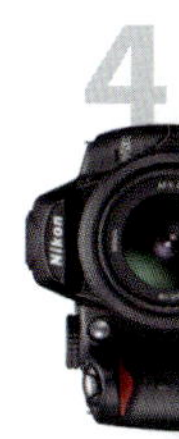

Selecting the White Balance from a Previously Taken Image

It's easy to select a white balance value from an image you've already taken. A previous image's value can be applied to the new image you are about to take. This may come in handy when you are shooting in the same place frequently and can use an image shot the day before as a reference.

Figure 4 shows the eight screens used to recall the white balance from an image already taken and stored on your camera's memory card.

Follow these steps to get the white balance from an image:

1. Press the MENU button and select the *Shooting Menu.*
2. Select *White balance* and scroll to the right.
3. Scroll to the bottom of the list with the multi selector button until *PRE – Preset manual* is selected; then scroll to the right (*figure 4, image 2*).
4. Select *Use photo* from the list, and scroll to the right (*figure 4, image 3*).
5. If a current image shows and is the correct image, select *This image* and press *OK*. Skip the next steps. Otherwise, choose *Select image* and scroll to the right (*figure 4, image 4*).
6. Select a folder that contains the image you want to use. Most of the time it will simply be D5000, unless you've created different folder names (*figure 4, image 5*). Scroll to the right. You'll now be presented with a list of images

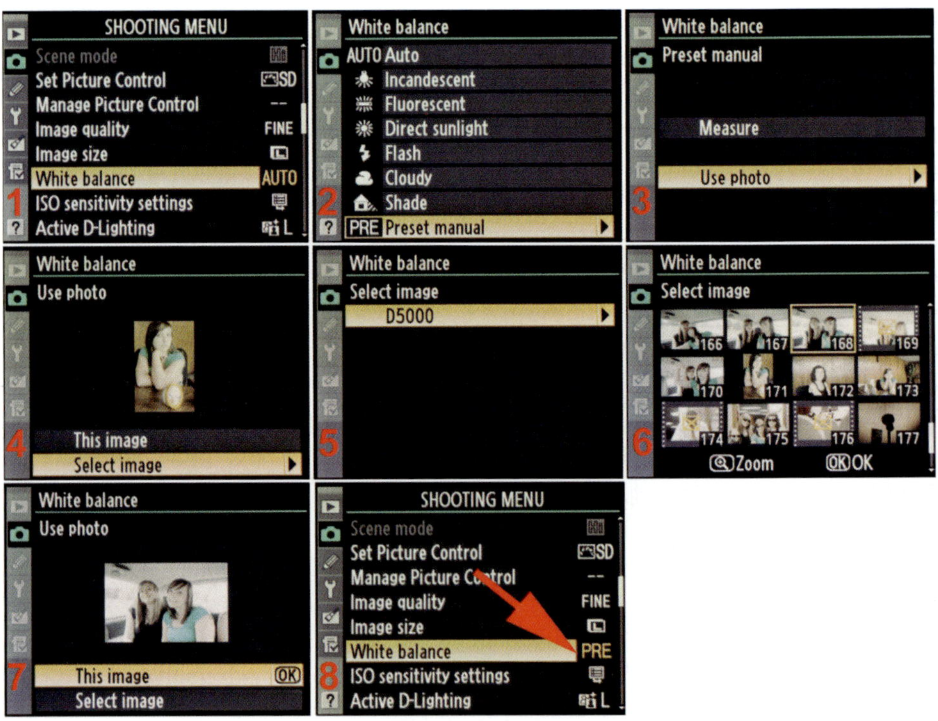

Figure 4 – Screens used to recover a white balance setting from an image from which to choose (*figure 4, image 6*). If you see an image that has a small box with an *X* in it, you'll not be able to select it for WB information. These are movie files, not images, and cannot be used to select a WB color temperature.

7. Highlight one of the images by scrolling to it and pressing the *OK* button.
8. The *Use photo* screen will return with *This image* highlighted (*figure 4, image 7*).
9. Press the *OK* button with *This image* highlighted and the camera will return to the main *Shooting Menu* screen with *PRE* after the *White balance* setting (*figure 4, image 8*). You are now ready to take new images using the WB from an existing image.

Recommendation

We've considered two ways to use the *PRE* method to select a WB setting. If you'll experiment with these methods a time or two, it will become easy for you. It is especially important to learn how to make *PRE* ambient light measurements. Buy yourself a small card from a photo shop or online that's white on one side and gray on the other. They don't cost much and will allow you to make professional images with no colors casts unless you deliberately introduce one.

White Balance Bracketing

WB bracketing allows you to take a series of three JPEG (only) images that vary in color temperature by an increment set with the *Information edit* screens. WB bracketing does not work when your camera is in RAW mode! It may appear to be working because you could enable WB bracketing when the camera is in RAW mode. However, the camera does not take the bracketed three-image series.

WB bracketing is similar to flash or exposure bracketing. If you want to use it, you must select *WB bracketing* from *Custom Setting e2 (Auto bracketing set)*. This means that flash or exposure *bracketing* will not work during the time that *e2* is set to *WB bracketing*. It works similarly to exposure bracketing (User's Manual pages 103–105).

Figure 5 shows the *Custom Setting Menu* and *figure 5A* shows the *Information edit* screens used to set WB bracketing.

Here are the steps to set up WB bracketing:

1. Press the MENU button and select the *Custom Setting Menu*.
2. Select *e Bracketing/flash* and scroll to the right.
3. Select *e2 Auto bracketing set* and scroll to the right.
4. Select *WB bracketing* from the list, and press the *OK* button to select it.

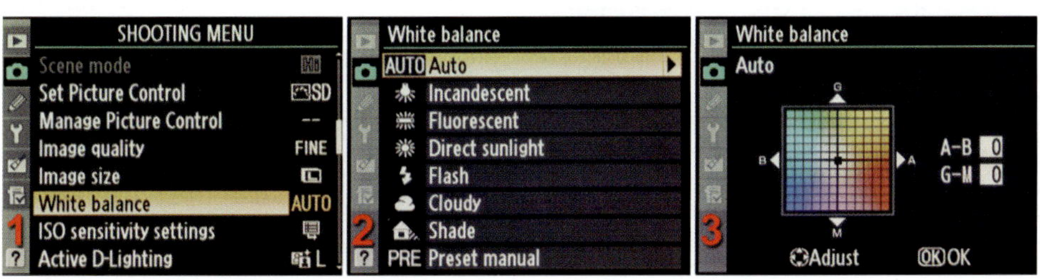

Figure 5 – Use *Custom Setting e2* to set WB bracketing

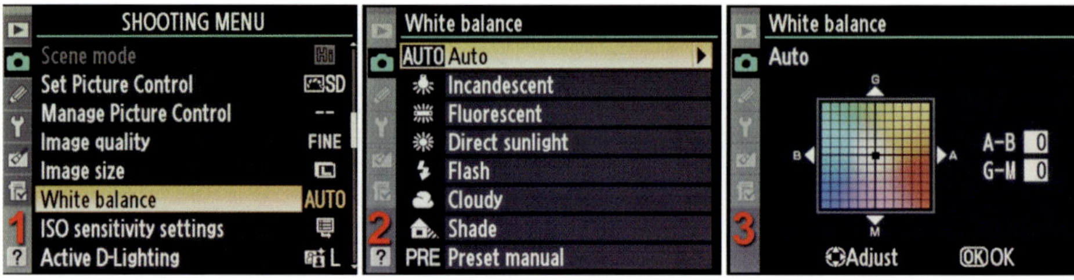

Figure 5A – Information edit screens to set WB bracketing

5. Press the <**i**> information edit button (usually twice) until you see the *Information edit* screen, as in *figure 5A*.
6. Make sure the yellow highlight rectangle is positioned in the WB bracketing (*BKT*) field at the lower right in the list of *Information edit* selections.
7. Press the *OK* button, and you'll be presented with the second *WB bracketing* screen.
8. Select one of the WB bracket increments from the list, A1–A3.
9. Press the *OK* button and the *Information edit* screen will switch back to the first screen with your selection next to the *BKT* field (see *figure 5A, image 3*). You are now ready to go take your three-image WB brackets.

Bracket Sequences and Memory Use

Be careful that your bracket sequence does not fill up your memory card. If there are WB brackets with each bracket's three pictures and you have room on your card for only two pictures, the D5000 will disable the shutter release and flash *FUL* in the viewfinder. If this happens, simply insert a new memory card and shoot the sequence again.

The User's Manual describes how to turn bracketing on and off and how to set the bracket increments, but it doesn't do a good job of explaining what the A1, A2, and A3 increments mean. I took a bunch of bracketed WB pictures and finally noticed the slight differences in the depth of color temperature change in the various bracket series. Only then did I realize what the bracket "increments" stand for. Here is an explanation of the three bracket increment levels:

- A1: 5 mired difference in each image. First is normal, second is 5 additional mired of amber, third is 5 additional mired of blue.
- A2: 10 mired difference in each image. First is normal, second is 10 additional mired of amber, third is 10 additional mired of blue.
- A3: 15 mired difference in each image. First is normal, second is 15 additional mired of amber, third is 15 additional mired of blue.

In effect, the three (A1, A2, A3) WB bracket increments give you three levels of WB bracketing that varies from as low as 5 mired to a maximum of 15 mired of amber and blue.

There is no need to press the shutter more than once to get the bracketed sequence of images. The D5000 is programmed to take three images in succession. It takes them all with one normal press of the shutter button—you don't have to hold it down. The camera actually takes only a single picture and then saves it to the memory card into three separate pictures, each with a different white balance and sequential file name/number. If you already had 20 pictures on your card and then press the shutter button once, you will then have 23 pictures on the card. Three pictures in one shutter press!

Recommendation

Personally, I prefer to shoot in RAW mode (NEF files) and make minor or major WB adjustments in the computer post-processing stage of the image's preparation. However, since some people want to shoot JPEGs and use WB bracketing, Nikon has given us this option. Just remember that WB bracketing applies only to shooting JPEG images. You cannot use WB bracketing with any of the Image quality modes that include the word *RAW*.

Auto White Balance

Auto WB works pretty well in the D5000. As the camera's RGB meter senses colors, it does its best to balance to any whites or mid-range grays it can find in the image. However, the color may vary a little on each shot. If you shoot only in Auto WB mode, your camera considers each image a new WB problem and solves it without reference to the last image taken. Therefore, there may be variance in the color balance of each image with Auto WB.

Figure 6 shows the *Information edit* screens to set Auto WB.

These are the steps used to set the camera to Auto WB:

1. Press the <**i**> information edit button until you see the *Information edit* screen.
2. Make sure the yellow highlight rectangle is positioned in the *White balance (WB AUTO)* field.
3. Press the *OK* button.
4. You'll be presented with the second *White balance* screen. It has a list of WB selections. The selection we are concerned with is the *AUTO* setting at the top of the list. If *AUTO* is not currently selected, use the multi selector thumb switch to select it.

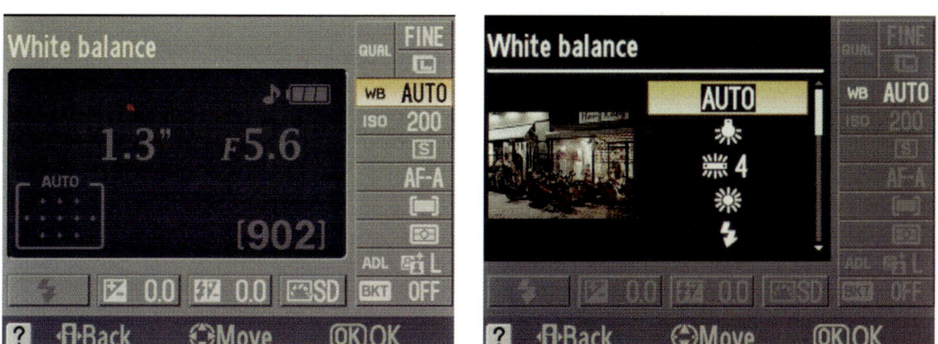

Figure 6 – Selecting auto white balance

5. Press the *OK* button. The camera will return to the main *Information edit* screen with *AUTO* showing after the *WB* setting.

In this chapter, you've come to understand how white balance works, when you might want to use preset WB values like *Flash* and *Cloudy*, and how to *PRE* measure ambient light settings. You've even learned how to create white balance brackets. Now that you have this knowledge, you can make decisions about when it's best to use *Auto WB* and when it's better to use a preset, or *PRE* readings. Don't fail to use these features often so that you'll remember how to use them.

Should I Worry About White Balance If I Shoot in RAW Mode?

The quick answer is no, but that may not be the best answer. When you take a picture using RAW mode (creating NEF files), the sensor image data has no WB, sharpening, or color saturation information applied. Instead, the information about your camera settings is stored as "markers" along with the raw black and white sensor data. Color information is applied permanently to the image only when you post-process and save the image in another format, like JPEG, TIFF, or EPS.

When you open an image in Nikon Capture NX2 or another raw conversion program, the camera settings are applied to the sensor data in a temporary way so that you can view the image on your computer screen. If you don't like the color balance or any other setting you used in-camera, you simply change it in the conversion software and the image looks as if you used the new settings when you took the picture.

Does that mean I am not concerned about my WB settings since I shoot RAW most of the time? No. As mentioned at the beginning of this chapter, the human brain can quickly adjust to an image's colors and perceive them as normal, even when they are not, which is one of the dangers of not using correct WB. Since an unbalanced image on-screen is not compared to another correctly balanced image side-by-side, there is a danger that your brain may accept the slightly incorrect camera settings as normal and your image will be saved with a color cast.

Use your WB correctly at all times and you'll make better images. You'll do less post camera work if the WB is correct in the first place. As RAW shooters, we already have a lot of post-processing work to do on our images. Why add WB corrections to the workflow?

Additionally, you might decide to switch to JPEG mode in the middle of a shoot, and if you are not accustomed to using your WB controls, you'll be in trouble. When you shoot JPEGs, your camera will apply the WB information directly to the image and save it on your card—permanently. Be safe and always use good WB technique.

White Balance Tips

Tips for using a white/neutral-gray card: When measuring WB with a gray or white card, keep in mind that your camera does not need to focus on the card. In *PRE* mode, it will not focus anyway because it is only trying to read light values, not take a picture. The important thing is to put your lens close enough to the card to prevent it from seeing anything other than the card. Three or four inches (about 10 cm) away from the card is about right for most lenses.

Also, be careful that the source light is not casting a shadow from the lens onto the card in a way that lets your lens see some of the shadow. This will make the measurement less accurate. Being sure that your source light does not make a glare on the card is a little harder to do since the card has a matte surface, but it still can be done. You may want to hold the card at a slight angle to the source light if it is particularly bright and might cause glare.

Finally, when the light is dim, use the white side of the card since it has more reflectivity. This may prevent a bad reading in low light. The gray card may be more accurate for color balancing, but it might be a little dark for a good measurement in dim light. If you are shooting in normal light, the gray card is best for balancing. I doubt it makes a lot of difference, however; you might want to experiment in normal light with your camera and see which you prefer.

My Conclusions

Pages 96 to 102 and 103 to 105 of your D5000's User's Manual have extensive WB information. With the simple tips in the preceding section and a little study of the manual, you can become a D5000 WB expert. Learn to use the color temperature features of your camera to make superior images.

You'll be able to capture accurate colors or make pictures with intentional color casts reflecting how you feel about the image. Practice a bit and you'll find it easy to remember how to set your WB in the field.

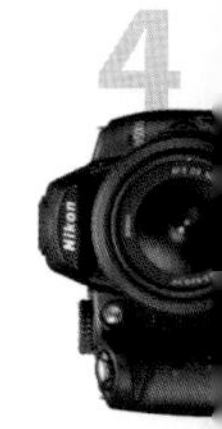

Playback Menu

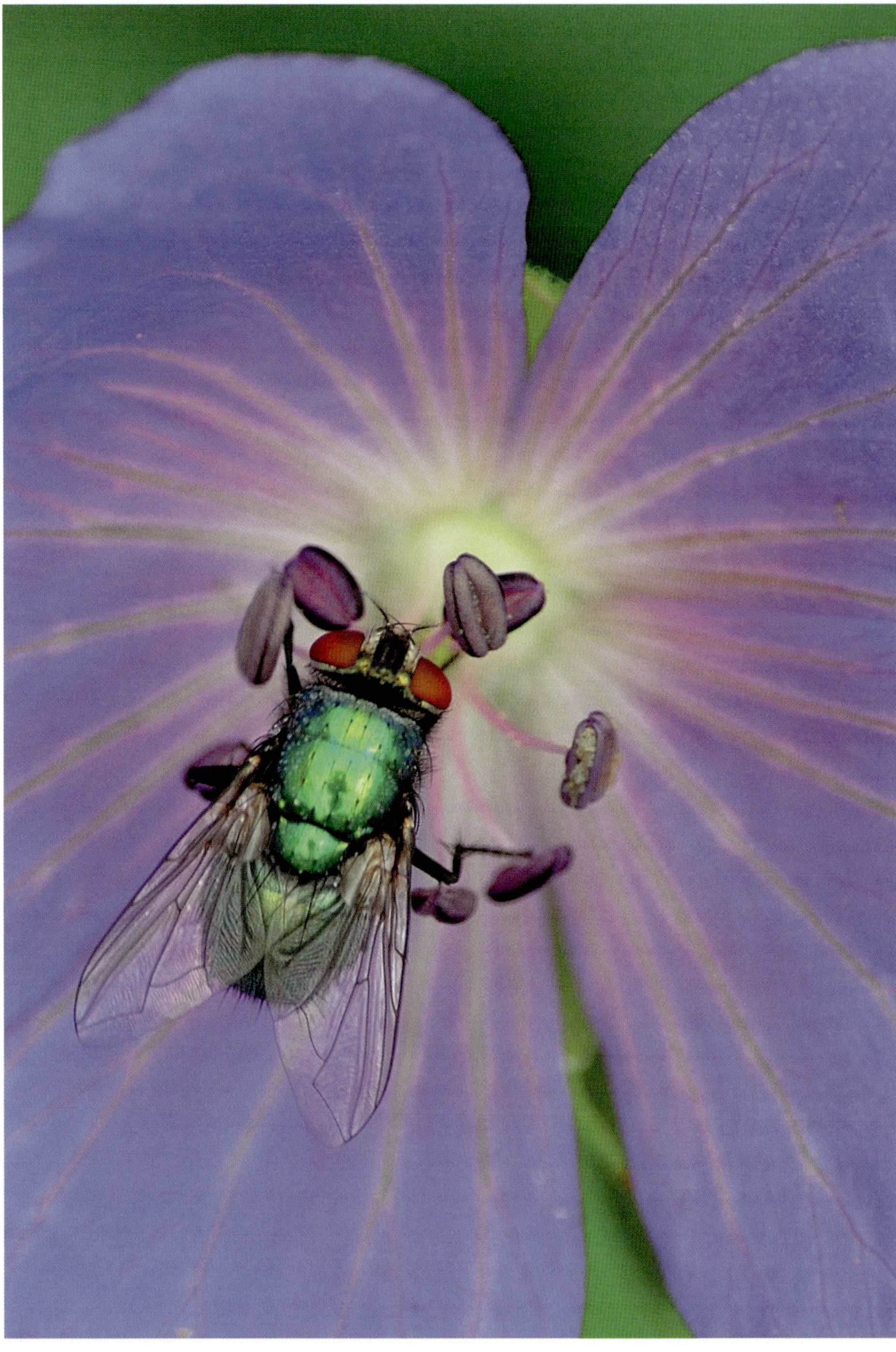

The Nikon D5000 has an excellent 2.7-inch (6.9 cm) monitor with 230,000 dots of resolution. It allows you to view your images with much detail—and even zoom in past the 100 percent "pixel peeping" level (up to 27x) to check your focus and image detail.

It has a really cool new feature that allows you to easily examine faces in your images at high magnification. You don't even have to scroll around with the Multi Selector to find them. Instead, once you've zoomed in to whatever level you want to view the detail in an image, you can press the <**i**> information edit button while turning the command dial and the camera uses its face recognition technology to find a face. Then, if you keep turning the command dial, the D5000 will jump to each face it can find in the image automatically.

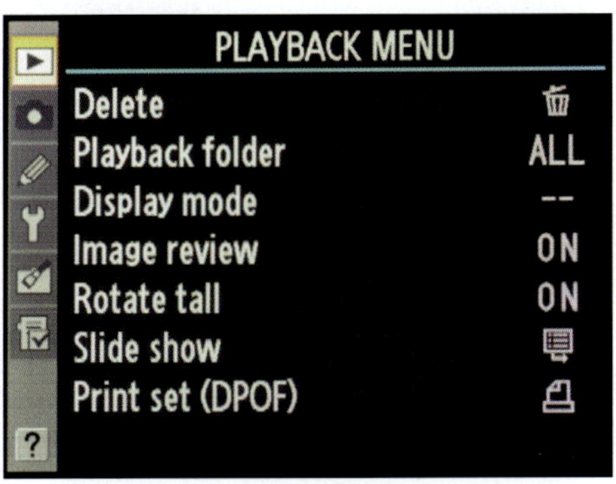

Figure 1 – The *Playback Menu* main screen

Everything you need to control your D5000's image playback is concentrated in a series of menu selections. They're found under the first menu in the camera, called the *Playback Menu* (see *figure 1*).

We'll examine the seven selections of the *Playback Menu* in the following sections. (User's Manual pages 115–129)

Delete Function

The *Delete* function allows you to selectively delete individual images from a group of images in either single or multiple folders on your camera's memory card. It also allows you to clear all folders of images without deleting the folders. This is sort of like a card format that affects only images. However, note that if you have protected images, this function will not delete them.

Delete Menu and Playback Folder Configuration

The *Delete* menu selection has a close relationship with the next selection, *Playback folder*. Please understand that the deletion of images is affected by how you have *Playback folder* configured. In other words, be sure you understand that the D5000 might delete more images than you expect if you have the *Playback folder* set to *All*.

There are three parts to the *Delete* menus (User's Manual pages 126–127):

- *Selected*
- *Selected date*
- *All*

Selected – This option allows you to delete only selected images.
Figure 1A shows the menu screens you'll use to control the *Delete* function for *Selected* images.
Here are the steps to delete *Selected* images:

1. Press the MENU button and select the *Playback Menu* (top menu).
2. Select *Delete* from the *Playback Menu*, and scroll to the right.
3. Choose *Selected* from the *Delete* menu, and scroll to the right.
4. Use the checkered thumbnail/playback zoom out button (User's Manual page 4, selection 7) to select each image you want to delete. A trash can symbol will appear in the upper-right corner of each image marked for deletion (see the red arrow in the lower-left screen in *figure 1A*).
5. Press the *OK* button. The *Delete?* warning screen appears (see the lower-right screen in *figure 1A*). It lists the number of images you have selected for deletion like this: *Delete? NN images. Yes/No*.
6. Scroll up to *Yes* and press the *OK* button. An hourglass briefly appears, and then *Done* flashes on the monitor. Then the camera returns to the main *Playback Menu*.

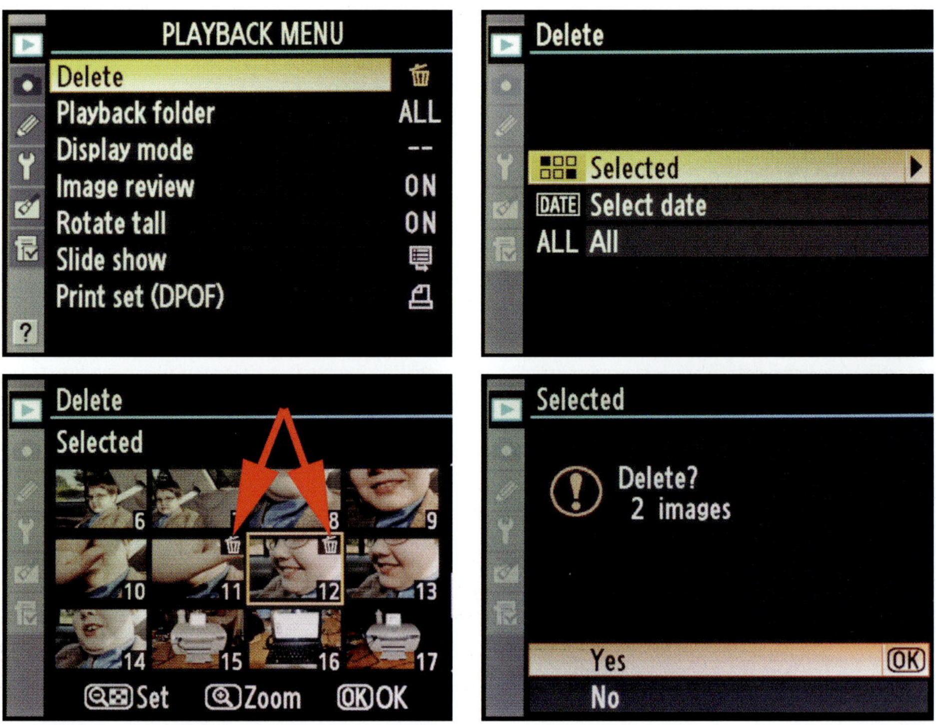

Figure 1A – *Delete* menu screens for selected images

Notice in the lower-left screen in *figure 1A* that there is a display of tiny images, each with a numbers in its lower-right corner. These numbers run in a sequence from 1 to whatever number of images you have in your current image folder, or on the entire memory card. The number of images shown will vary according to how you have the *Playback folder* settings configured. (See the next section of this chapter.)

If you have *Playback folder* set to *Current* (factory default), the camera will show you only the images found in your current playback folder. If you have *Playback folder* set to *All* instead, the D5000 will display all the images it can find in all the folders on your camera's memory card. I leave mine set to *All*.

The camera will delete only images that you've selected with the trash can symbol. Another way to delete images is by choosing a date or dates. All images dated within your chosen date range will be deleted. (Be careful with this function!) Here's how it works.

Selected date – With this option, you can choose to delete images taken on a specific date.

Using the *Selected date* method is simple. When you preview your images for deletion you won't be shown a list of all the images as with the *Delete* option. Instead, the *Select date* screen (the bottom-left screen in *figure 1B*) will give you a list of dates with a single representative image following each date. Notice how there's a check box to the left of each

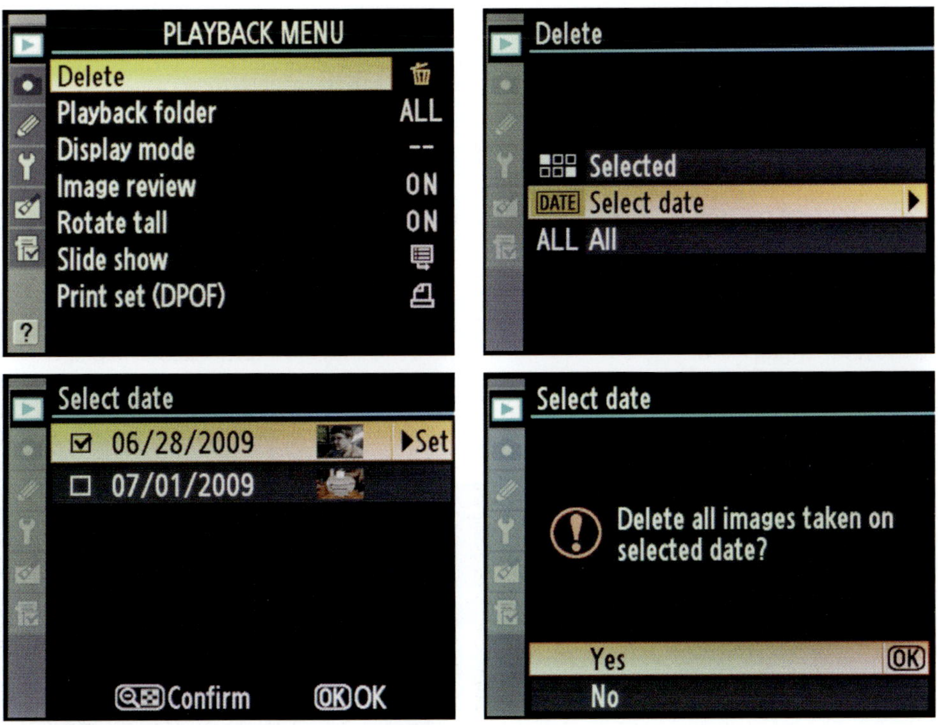

Figure 1B – *Delete* menu screens for the *Selected date* option

date? You'll check this box by scrolling up or down to the date of your choice with the Multi Selector, and then scrolling to the right where you'll see a tiny black arrow and the word *Set*. This "sets" the check box to give the camera permission to delete all images it finds with the date you've checked. This selection ability also serves as a reminder that one of the first things you should do when you get your brand-new camera is to set the date and time.

Figure 1B shows the menu screens used to delete all images under various dates.

If the single tiny representative image next to the date is insufficient to help you remember which images you took on that date, you can confirm the images you want to delete by viewing them. Press the checkered thumbnail/playback zoom out button and the D5000 will show you the images under that date. If you want to examine an image more closely, you can use the checkered playback zoom in button to temporarily zoom in on individual images. (User's Manual page 4, selections 7 and 8.)

Here are the steps to delete all images under a single or multiple dates:

1. Press the MENU button and select the *Playback Menu*.
2. Select *Delete* from the *Playback Menu*, and scroll to the right.
3. Choose *Selected date*, and scroll to the right.
4. Scroll right with the Multi Selector on each date you want to delete. A check mark will appear in the box next to each date you select. *Remember that all images under the dates you select will be deleted permanently!*
5. Press the *OK* button. The warning *Delete all images taken on selected date?* appears on the screen will appear (see the screen on the lower right in *figure 1B*).
6. Scroll up to *Yes* and press the *OK* button. An hourglass appears briefly, and then *Done* will flash on the monitor. Then the camera returns to the main *Playback Menu*.

Next, we'll look at how to delete all images, either in the current folder or every image on the memory card. Read this carefully because you might end up deleting more images than you wanted to!

All – This is like formatting a memory card, except that it will not delete folders. It will only delete images. And as mentioned previously, it will not delete protected files. This is a quick way to "format" your card while maintaining a favorite Playback folder structure.

Figure 1C shows the *Playback Menu* screens used to delete all images.

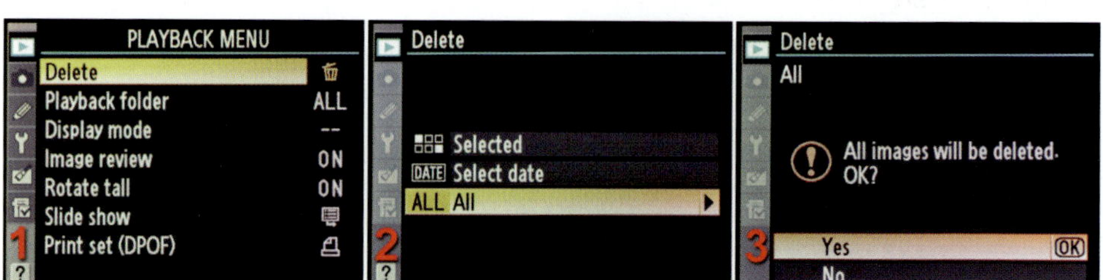

Figure 1C – *Delete* menu screens for the *All* option

Here are the steps to delete all images. Did I mention that you must be *very careful* with this function? Please understand that this deletion function works differently according to how you have *Playback folder* set. *Please read the next section in this chapter before using this function!*

1. Press the MENU button and select the *Playback Menu*.
2. Select *Delete* from the *Playback Menu*, and scroll to the right.
3. Choose *All*, and scroll to the right.
4. If you have *Playback folder* set to *Current*, the camera will delete only images in the current folder, and the following warning appears on the screen: *All images will be deleted. OK?* (See the image on the right in *figure 1C*.) However, if you have *Playback folder* set to *All*, you'll see *All images in all folders will be deleted. OK?* (See the next section for information on the *Playback folder* option.)
5. Scroll up to *Yes* and press the *OK* button. An hourglass appears briefly, and then *Done* will flash on the monitor. Then the camera returns to the main *Playback Menu*.

Being the paranoid type, I tested this extensively and found that the D5000 really *will not* delete protected images. Plus, it will keep any folders you have created. However, if you're a worrier, you should transfer your data before deleting any images.

Quick image deletion – You can also delete a single image by displaying it on the monitor with the playback button and then pressing the delete button (trash can icon) to the left of the viewfinder eyepiece. A red exclamation point with the question *Delete?* pops up over the image. Press the delete button again to delete the image. A fast way to do this is to simply display the image and press the delete button twice quickly (User's Manual pages 40 and 126).

Protecting an image from deletion – This is an easy process and will prevent an image from being accidentally deleted—*except by formatting the memory card.* Here's how to prevent an image from being deleted: (1) Display the image in the normal way, by pressing the playback button. (2) Press the AE-L/AF-L (protect) button and the image will be marked for protection. The AE-L/AF-L button to the right of the viewfinder eyepiece doubles as an image protect button, as signified by a small key symbol to the left of the button. You'll see a small key symbol surrounded by a rectangle appear on the top-left of the protected image on the LCD monitor. Now this image cannot be deleted by normal camera functions. *It will be deleted if you format the memory card.*

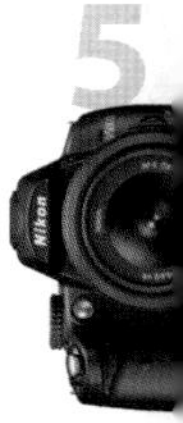

Recovering Deleted Images

If you accidentally delete an image or a group of images, or even format the entire memory card and then realize with great pain that you didn't really mean to, all is not lost. Simply remove the memory card from your camera *immediately* and *do not use it until you can run image recovery software on the card.*

Deleting or formatting doesn't permanently remove the images from the card. It merely marks them as deleted and removes the references to them in the memory card's File Allocation Table (FAT). The images are still there and can usually be recovered as long as you don't write any new data to the card before you try to recover them.

As a digital photographer, it's wise to have a good image recovery program on your computer at all times. Sooner or later you'll make a mistake or have problems with a card and will need to recover images. Many of the better brands of memory cards include recovery software either on the card itself or on a separate CD that comes packaged with the card. (Make sure you install the software on your computer before formatting the new memory card!) Recovery software is often available for download from the card manufacturer's website.

Playback Folder

The *Playback folder* setting specifies the folder from which your camera displays images for you during preview and slide shows. You can have the D5000 show you images only in the current image folder (usually D5000) or in all the folders on the memory card.

If you regularly use your memory card in multiple cameras as I do, and sometimes forget to transfer images, adjusting the playback folder is a good idea. I use a D5000, D90, and D40x on a fairly regular basis. Often, I'll grab a 4-gigabyte card out of one camera and pop it in another for a few shots. If I'm not careful, later I'll transfer the images from one camera and forget that I have more folders on the memory card created by the other camera. It's usually only after I have pressed the format buttons that I remember the other folders and images on my D5000's memory card. The D5000 comes to my rescue with its *Playback folder – All* function.

Let's look at how the *Playback folder* function works by first looking at the menus screens in *Figure 2*.

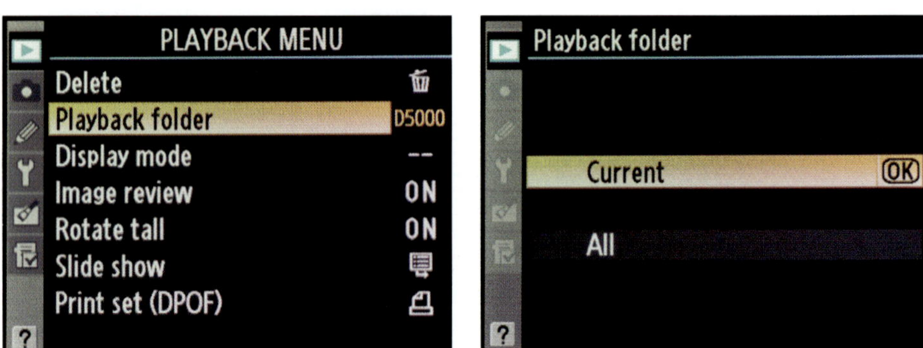

Figure 2 – *Playback folder* menu screens

Here are the two selections you can choose from (User's Manual page 146):

- *Current* (default)
- *All*

Current – This is the most limited playback mode available. Whatever playback folder your camera is currently using will be displayed during playback. No other images or folders will be displayed.

All – When you select *All*, your D5000 will obligingly show you every image it can find in all the folders on the memory card. This maximum flexibility setting has saved my buns several times when I thought to check my camera for images *before* I formatted the card and found that I had other images on the card besides D5000 images. During playback, or before deletion, the D5000 will display images from other Nikon cameras you've used with the current memory card. Each camera usually creates its own unique folders, and normally the other cameras do not report that they are there except by showing a reduced image capacity. The D5000 intelligently displays its own images along with any other Nikon images on the card.

Here are the steps used to select *Current* or *All*:

1. Press the MENU button and select the *Playback Menu*.
2. Select *Playback folder* from the *Playback Menu*, and scroll to the right.
3. Choose *Current* or *All*.
4. Press the *OK* button.

The camera will switch back to the main *Playback Menu* with the current folder name displayed after *Playback folder* if *Current* is selected or with *ALL* displayed if *All* is selected.

Recommendation

I leave my D5000 set to the *All* playback folder mode since I want to be sure I can see every image on the memory card. This helps me avoid being worried about losing images as a result of my own mistakes. One day it may get to the point that memory cards might be big enough to store images from months of picture-taking in various folders as another form of image backup. I'd like to be able to see all those images without switching folders.

Display Mode

The *Display mode* selection allows you to customize how the D5000 displays all the histogram and data screens for each image. If you want to see a lot of information on each image, you can specify it here. Or, if you would rather take a minimalist approach to image information, you can turn off some of the screens.

If you turn off certain screens, the camera still records the information for each image, such as lens used, shutter speed, and aperture. However, with no data screens selected, you'll see only two screens. One is the main image view, and the other is a summary screen with a luminance histogram and basic shooting information. I haven't found a way to turn this summary screen off. You get to

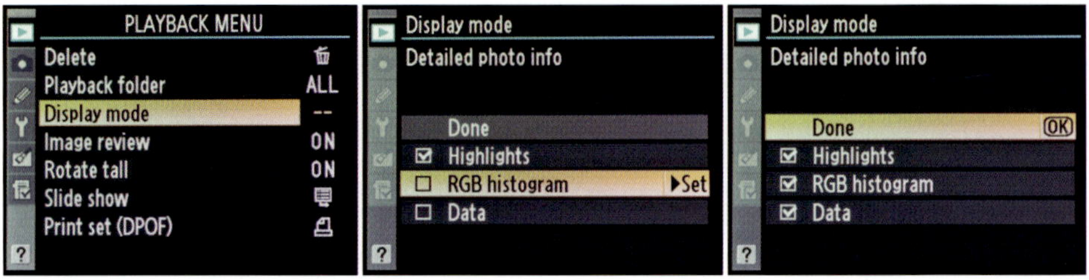

Figure 3 – *Display mode* menu screens

the screens by scrolling with your Multi Selector in the direction opposite from the direction you would scroll when viewing images. For example, if you scroll through your images by pressing left or right on the Multi Selector, you can move through the data screens by scrolling up or down.

Here are the steps to select the *Detailed photo info* screens (see *figure 3*):

1. Press the MENU button and select the *Playback Menu*.
2. Select *Display mode* from the *Playback menu*, and scroll to the right.
3. Select your combination of screens from the list on the *Detailed photo info* screen. You'll highlight a line such as *RGB histogram* and place a check mark in the little box by scrolling right. Check as many as you'd like.
4. Scroll back up to *Done* at the top of the list.
5. Press the *OK* button to make the selected photo info screens active.

Here are the selections found in *Display mode* and a description of what each does (User's Manual page 146):

Detailed Photo Information

- *Highlights*
- *RGB histogram*
- *Data*

When you make changes to these selections, just be sure to scroll up to the word *Done* and press the *OK* button to save your setting. I keep forgetting to do this when I make changes (see the screen on the right in *figure 3*).

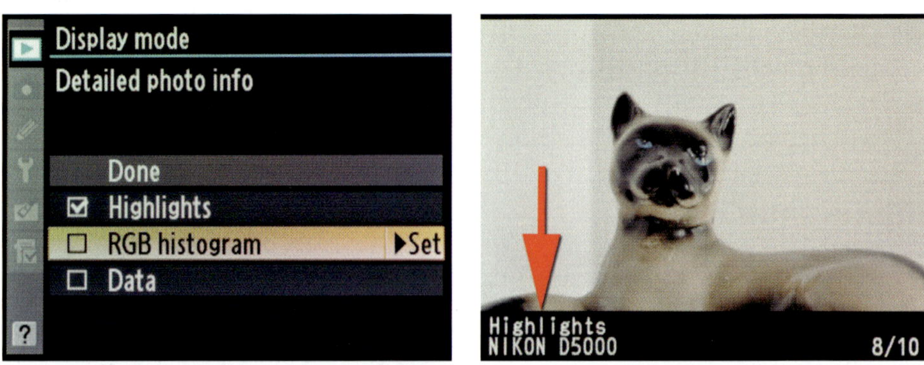

Figure 3B – *Display mode* menu screens – *Highlights*

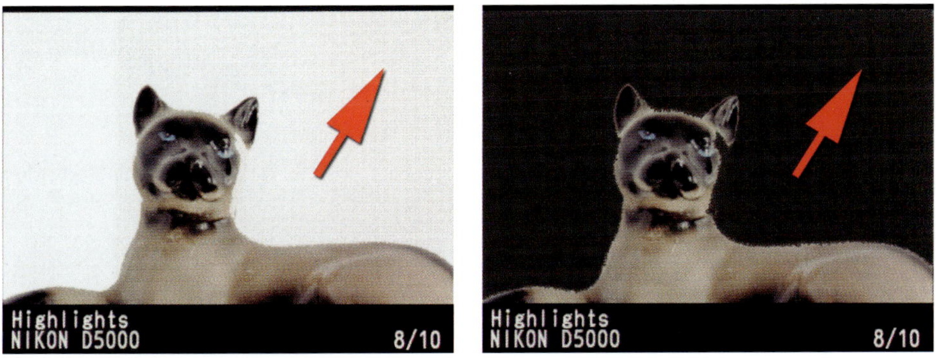

Figure 3C – *Highlights* blinky mode in action

Highlights – If you put a check mark next to the *Highlights* selection, as shown in *figure 3B*, you will turn on what I call the "blinky" mode of the camera. The D5000 adds a new *Highlights* screen so that you can view the image with special emphasis on areas that might be overexposed. It looks very similar to the normal viewing screen except that there is only information about highlights on the new screen. You'll see the word *Highlights* on the bottom left of the camera monitor, just above the words *NIKON D5000* (in *figure 3B*, where the red arrow is pointing). If you want, you can leave this screen selected as your normal viewing screen. If you turn the camera off and back on when this screen is selected, it will remember and return to this screen instead of the regular image-viewing screen. You can get to the normal viewing screen, or the image summary screen, by scrolling up or down with the Multi Selector.

What does the *Highlights* screen do? When *Highlights* is enabled, if any part of the image is overexposed, that section will blink an alternating white and black. This is a warning that certain areas of the image are overexposed and have lost detail. You will need to use exposure compensation or manually control the camera to contain the exposure within the dynamic range of the camera's sensor.

Figure 3C shows how an image looks when an area has been overexposed and is blinking on your LDC. The image on the left is showing the white blink, and the one on the right is showing the black blink.

Where you see the blinking white to black to white, that section of the image has lost all detail, or has "blown out." If you examine the histogram for the image, you'll see that it's cut off, or "clipped" on the right side. Current software cannot usually recover any image detail from the blown-out areas. The exposure has exceeded the range of the sensor and the image has become completely overexposed in the blinking area. All previous detail in the image has gone to pure white. (See the section about the histogram in chapter 3.)

Highlights mode allows your camera to warn you when you have surpassed what its sensor can capture and you are losing image data.

5

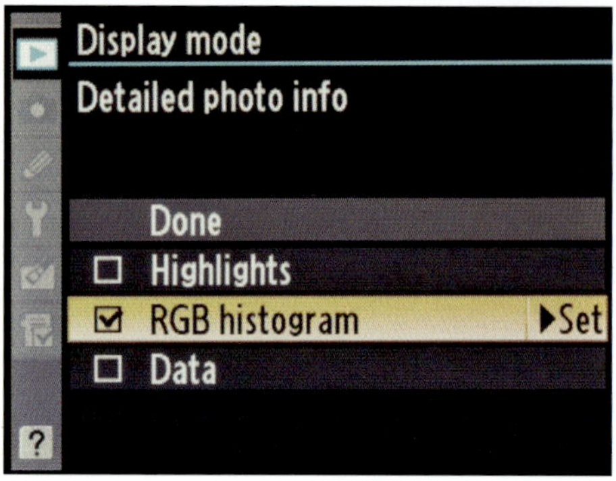

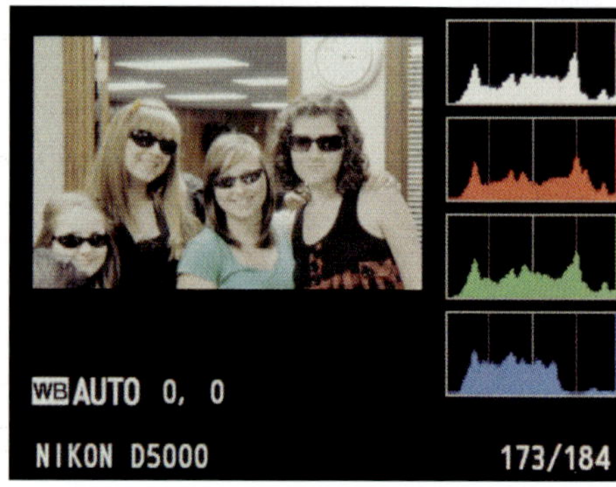

Figure 3D *Display mode* menu screens – *RGB histogram*

RGB histogram – I like this feature! It allows me to view not just a basic luminance histogram, which is a combination of all three color channels, but it displays all three color histograms and a luminance histogram in one screen (see *figure 3D*).

Each color channel, red, green, and blue (or RGB), is displayed with its own small histogram. This is quite useful because it is possible to overexpose, or "blow out," only one color channel, which often happens with the red channel in my case.

You can view the luminance histogram on top in white, and the three RGB color histograms below it. When you examine the *Histogram* screen, you'll see that each of the RGB color channel histograms is different. R=red will look different from B=blue, for instance. The luminance histogram on top always seems to closely resemble the G=green channel histogram. It makes me wonder if the white luminance histogram is basically just a copy of the green channel histogram with a bit of minor influence from the other two channels. The luminance and green histograms are not absolutely identical, but they are very close, so it appears that green colors influence the luminance histogram more than the other two (red and blue).

Data – Checking this setting will give you three additional image data screens to scroll though. The data found on these screens is quite detailed and includes the following information:

Image Data Screen 1:

- **Light meter in use**
  (Matrix, Spot, or Center-weighted)
- **Shutter speed and aperture**
  (e.g., 1/60, F8)
- **Exposure mode**
  (P,S,A,M) and ISO (e.g., 200 or Lo 1)
- **Exposure compensation**
  (+/- EV)
- **Lens focal length**
  (e.g., 18mm)
- **Lens overview**
  (e.g., 18-55mm f/3.5-5.6)
- **AF/VR**
  (e.g., AF / VR-On)
- **Flash mode and compensation**
  (e.g., built-in, TTL, +0.7)

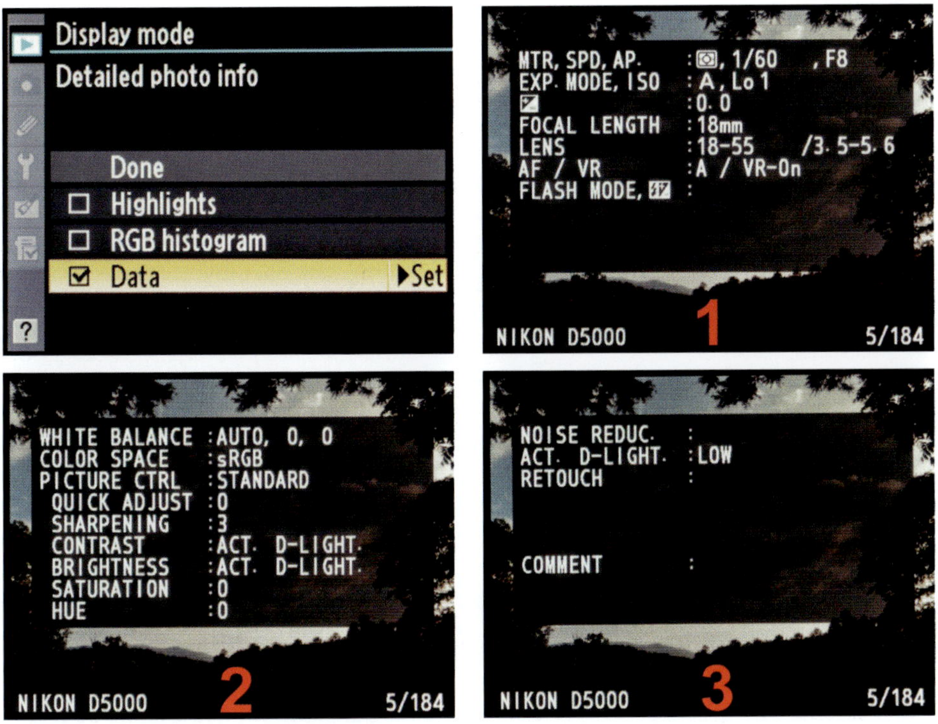

Figure 3E – *Display mode* menu screens – *Data*

Image Data Screen 2:

- **White balance**
  (Auto, 0, 0)
- **Color space**
  (sRGB, AdobeRGB)
- **Picture Control detail**
  (Standard, Neutral, Vivid, Monochrome, Portrait, Landscape)
- **Picture Control fine-tuning**
  (Quick Adjust, Sharpening, Contrast, Brightness, Saturation, Hue)

Image Data Screen 3:

- **Noise reduction**
  (e.g., Long exp., High ISO, Norm)
- **Active D-Lighting**
  (Auto, Extra high, High, Normal, Low, Off)

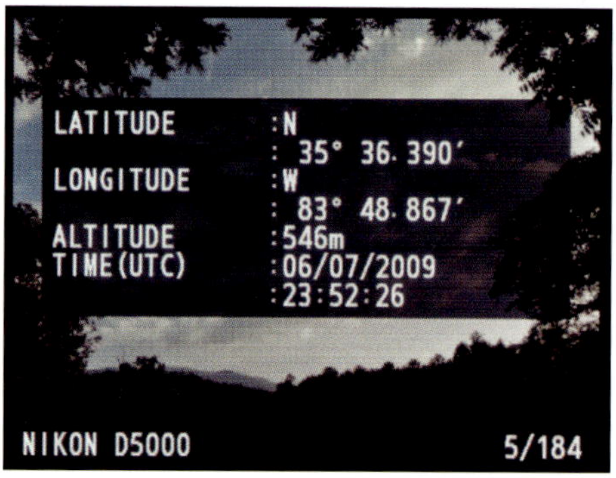

Figure 3F – GPS information display screen

Retouching – (D-Lighting, red-eye correction, trim, monochrome, filter effects, color balance, small picture)

Comment – (Up to 36 characters attached to each image)

GPS screen – The GPS information screen (figure 3F) displays only if you've recorded GPS location data to the image. I have a Nikon GP-1 unit that works very well with my D5000, and I usually have it mounted when shooting nature and landscapes.

If you have a compatible GPS and use it to record GPS data to your images, the screen will display latitude, longitude, altitude, and UTC time. The GPS screen shows between image data screens 2 and 3 (the *luminance histogram and basic data summary screen* and *image data screen)*. If GPS data is missing from the image, the screen will not display.

There is no setting to turn the GPS screen on or off. If the image has GPS data, this screen will display in the series of data screens. If not, it doesn't display—no choice.

Although there are many screens to scroll through, they provide a great deal of information on an image. Look how far we've come from the old film days of writing some date information on the lower-right corner of an image, permanently marking it, or between the frames on the pro-level cameras.

In fact, there are seven screens just brimming with data if you enable all the *Display mode* settings (eight, if you used a GPS). Or, you can get by with the main image display and one summary display. Complex control at your fingertips!

My Personal Settings

I always leave the *Highlights* and *RGB histogram* settings turned on. I want to be sure I don't accidentally "blow out" important areas of my images. The *Highlights* "blinky mode" always warns me when my images have overexposed areas, thereby allowing me to quickly adjust my exposure.

The *RGB histogram* setting is also very important to me. It allows me to see all the color channels, just in case one of them is being clipped off on the light or dark sides. It also allows me to see how well I am keeping my exposure balanced for light and dark. (See chapter 3 for more information on histogram usage.)

The *Data* screens are not terribly important to me since the D5000 has a summary screen with the most important exposure information displayed. Also, if the *Data* screens are enabled, I have to scroll through three more screens to get to my *RGB histogram* screen. So my recommendation is to enable only the *Highlights* and *RGB histogram* screens. If you really feel the need to examine a large amount of extra image data, then enable the *Data* screens too.

Image Review

The factory default for the D5000 is to display a just-taken image on the monitor for several seconds. (You can adjust this value from 4 seconds to 10 minutes using *Custom Setting c2 (Auto off timers) > Custom > Image review*.) *Figure 4* shows how to turn *Image review* on and off.

Here are the *Image review* settings (User's Manual page 147):

- *On* – Shows a picture on the monitor after each shutter release (default).
- *Off* – Monitor stays off when you take pictures.

Here are the steps to select whether *Image review* is on or off (see *figure 4*):

- Press the MENU button and select the *Playback Menu*.
- Select *Image review* from the *Playback Menu*, and scroll to the right.
- Select *On* or *Off* from the list.
- Press the *OK* button.

Most of us will leave this function set to *On*; otherwise, the only way to view an image after taking it is to press the playback button. The battery life will be affected if you constantly review images and for longer periods of time than the default 4 seconds. However, with the overall low power consumption of the camera, you will find that your battery lasts long enough for a full day of shooting in most instances. I carry one extra battery, just in case, because I am a world-class image "chimper."

Chimping Defined

"Chimping" refers to reviewing images on the camera's LCD after each shot. It's derived from the words ***ch**eck **im**age **p**review*. I guess people think you look like a monkey if you review your images while making all those "Ooh, ooh" and "Aah, aah" sounds. Well, I do it anyway!

Recommendation

I don't want to waste hard drive space by storing lots of almost good images, so I delete many images right after I take them. I have to review them to know whether I want to keep them, or not, so I leave my *Image review* selection set to *On*. In fact, I set my *Image review* time to 1 minute in *Custom Setting c2*. That way, I can look at my images for extended periods of time and even show them to others. The battery lasts a long time on the D5000, and I carry a spare, so I am ready to "chimp" with the best of them.

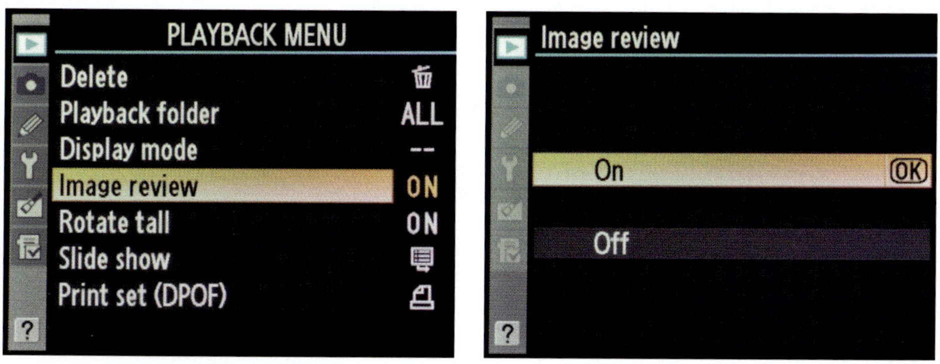

Figure 4 – *Image review* menu screens

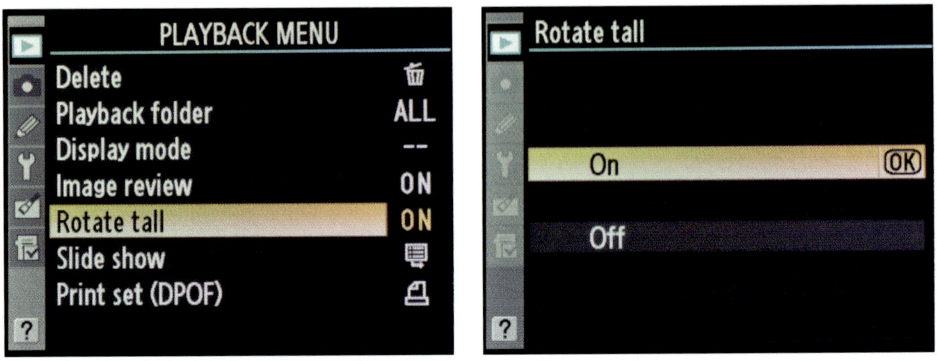

Figure 5 – *Rotate tall* menu screens

Rotate Tall

When you turn your camera sideways to shoot an image as a vertical or portrait image, the image is recorded to the card as a horizontal image lying on its side. If you chimp the image—view it immediately after taking it—Nikon assumes that you'll still be holding the camera in the rotated position, so the image is left lying on its side in portrait mode. Later, when you're reviewing the images as a group and using the D5000's *Playback* function, the image will be displayed as an upright vertical image that is quite a bit smaller in size so it will fit on the horizontal monitor.

If you would rather that the camera leave the image in a horizontal view, forcing you to turn the camera sideways to view it, you'll need to turn the *Rotate tall* setting *Off*. The default is *On*.

Here are the two available settings: (see *figure 5* and the User's Manual page 147):

- ***On*** (default) – When you take a vertical image, the D5000 will rotate it so you don't have to turn your camera to view it naturally in later playback. This sizes the image so that a vertical fits in the normal horizontal frame of the monitor. The image will be a bit smaller than normal to view. When you first view (chimp) the image after taking it, the camera does not rotate it because it assumes you are still holding the camera in a vertical orientation.
- ***Off*** – Vertical images are left in a horizontal direction so that you'll need to turn the camera to view it as it was taken. This provides a slightly larger view of the image.

Here are the steps to select whether *Rotate tall* is on or off (see *figure 5*):

1. Press the MENU button and select the *Playback Menu*.
2. Select *Rotate tall* from the *Playback menu*, and scroll to the right.
3. Select *On* or *Off*.
4. Press the *OK* button.

Recommendation

I leave *Rotate tall* set to *On* since I can zoom in if I want more detail. This allows me to view a vertical image in its natural vertical orientation without rotating my camera during playback. Some would prefer not to display the vertical image in a horizontal direction because it is so much smaller. You'll need to turn this on and off to see which you prefer.

Slide Show

I used to do slide shows back in the old film days. I'd set up my screen, warm up my projector, load my slides, and watch everyone fall asleep by the 100th slide. For that reason, I hadn't been using the slide show function of my camera. However, all that has changed recently.

Now, instead of hauling out a slide projector and a box of slides, you can just plug your D5000 into the closest high definition (HD) device, such as a television. The camera has a cool High-Definition Multimedia Interface (HDMI) port on the left side under a rubber cover. (We'll talk more about HDMI in a later chapter.)

Or, if you prefer, you can just set your camera on a table and have a few friends gather around for a quick slide show. It's fast and simple to start one.

As shown in *figure 6*, it's easy to simply select the *Playback Menu*'s *Slide show* setting, scroll right, and select *Start*. The slide show will commence immediately with a default display time of 2 seconds per image (User's Manual page 129).

Here are the steps to set up a slide show:

1. Press the MENU button and select the *Playback Menu*.
2. Select *Slide show* from the *Playback Menu*, and scroll to the right.
3. Select *Start* or *Frame interval* from the list. If you select *Frame interval*, you'll have additional choices, as shown in *Figure 6A*.
4. Press the *OK* button.

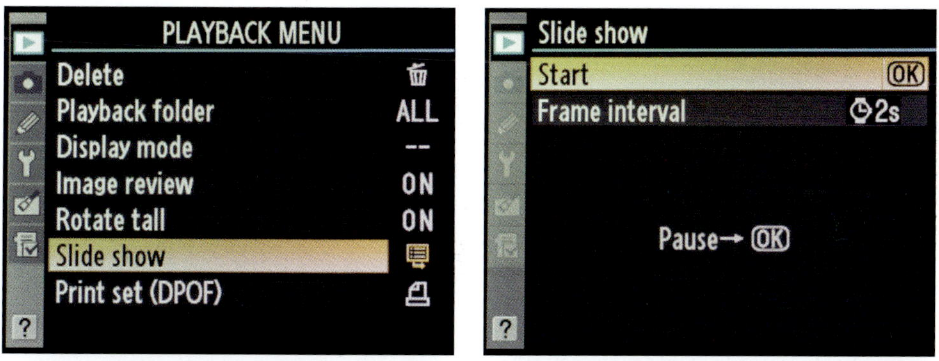

Figure 6 – *Slide show* menu screens

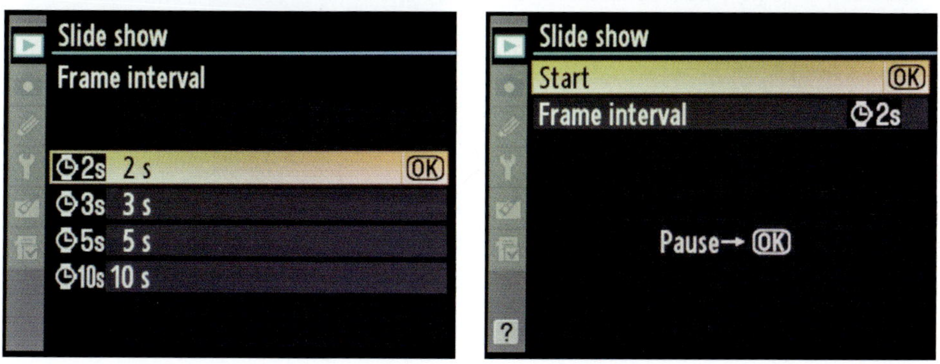

Figure 6A – The *Frame interval* menu screens for the *Slide show* option

There are two settings available under *Slide show*:

- *Start*
- *Frame interval*

Start – This does what it says and starts the slide show.

Frame interval – This setting controls the amount of time each image displays, in seconds. You'll need to change the display time to a value from 2 to 10 seconds. The default value is *2s*, or 2 seconds.

As shown in *figure 6A*, you can select from the following options:

- **2s** – 2 seconds (default)
- **3s** – 3 seconds
- **5s** – 5 seconds
- **10s** – 10 seconds

To start the slide show, repeat the steps shown in *figure 6*, but this time the show will run at your newly chosen speed.

Recommendation

I usually set my slide *Frame interval* setting to 3 seconds. If the images are especially beautiful, I might set it to 5 seconds. I've found that 2 seconds is not quite long enough, and 5 or 10 seconds may be too long. I wish there were a 4-second setting, but 3 seconds seems to be sufficient most of the time.

There are several key things that will affect how the images display during the slide show:

Skip back/skip ahead – During the slide show, you can go back to the previous image for another 2 seconds by simply pressing left on the Multi Selector. You can also see the next image with no delay by pressing right on the Multi Selector. This is just a quick way to skip images or review previous images without stopping the slide show.

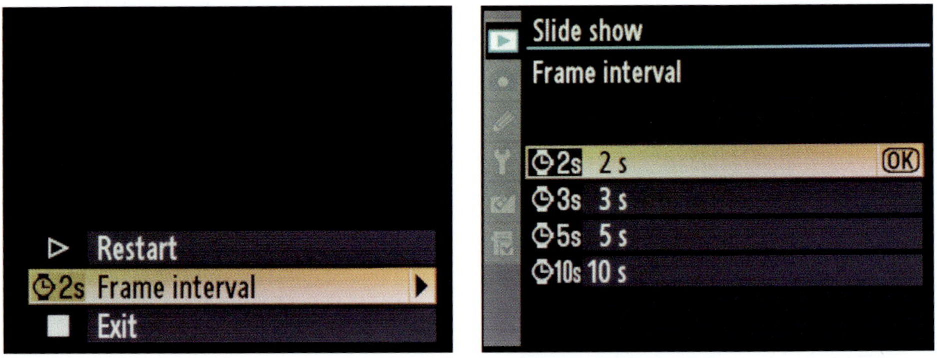

Figure 6B – The pause menu screens for slide shows

View additional photo info – While the slide show is running, you can press up or down on the Multi Selector to view the additional data screens. This is dependant on how you have your D5000's display mode configured (see the section on the *Display mode* section earlier in this chapter) for *Highlights*, *Histogram*, and *Data*. If any of these screens are available, they can be used during the slide show.

Pause slide show – During the slide show, you may need to pause, change the image display time, or even exit. When you press the *OK* button, the slide show pauses and you are presented with the menu in *figure 6B*).

Using this menu screen, you can select from the following options:

- ***Restart*** - Pressing OK or scrolling to the right on the Multi Selector continues the slide show from the image following the one last viewed.
- ***Frame interval*** – Scrolling to the right with the Multi Selector takes you to the screen that allows you to change the display time to one of four values. You can choose 2, 3, 5, or 10 seconds. After choosing the new frame interval, you'll have to select *Restart* to continue where you left off in the slide show.
- ***Exit*** – This does what it says—exits the slide show.

Exit to Playback Menu – If you want to quickly exit the slide show, simply press the MENU button and you'll jump directly back to the *Playback Menu*, with no items selected.

Exit to Playback mode – By pressing the playback button (the right arrow key, with a rectangle around it, on the top rear left of the D5000), you'll stop the slide show and change to normal full-frame or thumbnail image view of the last image seen in the show.

Exit to shooting mode – Pressing the shutter button halfway down stops the slide show. The camera is now in shooting mode, meaning that it is ready to take some pictures.

Using any of these buttons affects the slide show in the ways listed.

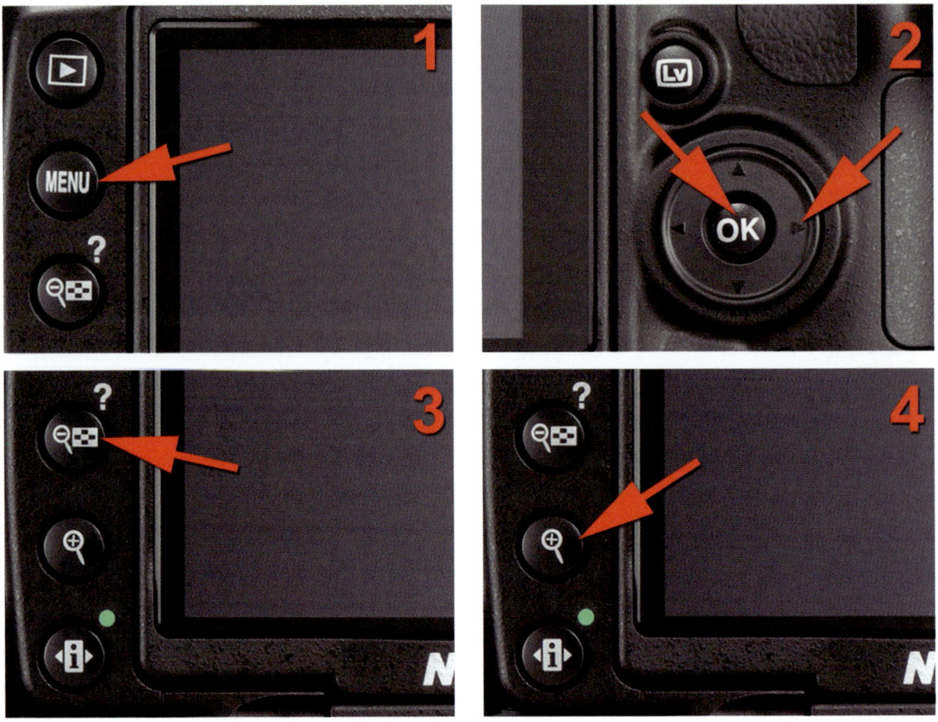

Figure 6C – Camera controls for PictBridge/DPOF Printing

Print Set

(User's Manual pages 136-144)
At first I thought it odd that Nikon chose to put printing functions in the *Playback Menu*. Then I thought about it and realized that printing is a *permanent* form of image playback. You play (print) the images to your printer and then "chimp" (view) them without battery power!

Before we get further into this section, let's take a look at the external camera controls we'll be using to set various features (see *figure 6C*).

Here is a list of controls with list numbers matching the screen numbers in *figure 6C*:

- MENU button
- Multi Selector and OK button (in the middle of the Multi Selector)
- Thumbnail/playback zoom out button
- Playback zoom in button

Now, let talk about how this non-computer printing system works.

PictBridge Printing

PictBridge allows you to connect your camera directly to a compatible printer and then print any or all the images on the memory card, without having to involve a computer in any way. Your D5000 comes with a special USB cable with a very small end that fits the D5000 (see *figure* 7) and a normal big USB end that plugs into the compatible printer's PictBridge port. This is the same cable that you use to transfer images from the camera to a computer.

Another way you can print images that involve the D5000 and a compatible printer is by using the Digital Print Order Format (DPOF). You can print to any device that supports DPOF. You'll create a "print order," right on the D5000, that saves out to the memory card. This print order allows a DPOF-compatible printer or service to print the images you have selected on your memory card via the PictBridge menu of the D5000. All you have to do is insert the memory card, select Print on the printer, and wait for your pictures to print out. This is not a difficult process, and it's quite fun and satisfying.

In researching printers that will support all the Nikon D5000's features, like borders, cropping, multiple prints, and DPOF compatibility, I spent considerable time reading about printers on the Internet. Some mentioned being PictBridge compatible. Some mentioned DPOF and others didn't. Few manufacturers had much information on their websites to let me know how many features they support in my camera.

After a couple hours of frustration, I decided to call some printer manufacturers and simply ask them some questions. Since I've been using an Epson R2200 for several years and always loved its output, I decided to call Epson first. I didn't have to call anyone else. I got a technical person that had real knowledge of cameras and printers. He was kind enough to talk with me about the various features in the Nikon D5000 and which Epson printer I could buy to use all of them. I wanted a portable 4 x 6-inch (10 x 15 cm) printer that supported my camera. He suggested the Epson PictureMate Dash Personal Photo Lab. I had already read about this printer in several ratings and reviews, and it had one of the highest print quality ratings out there. I spent about 30 minutes on the phone with Epson's tech and ordered the printer immediately.

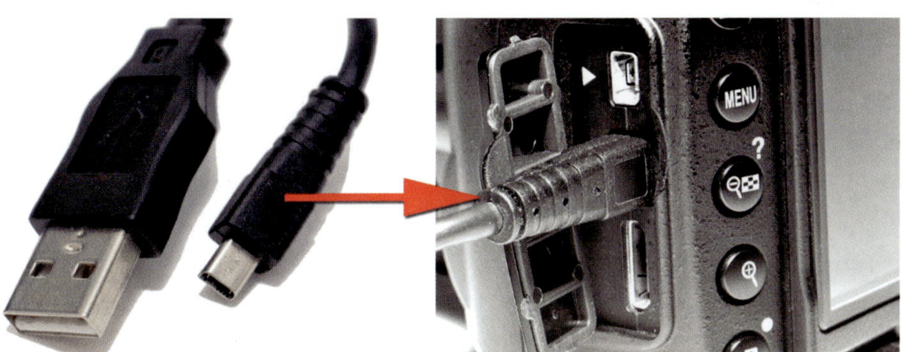

Figure 7 – USB port on D5000 and included cable

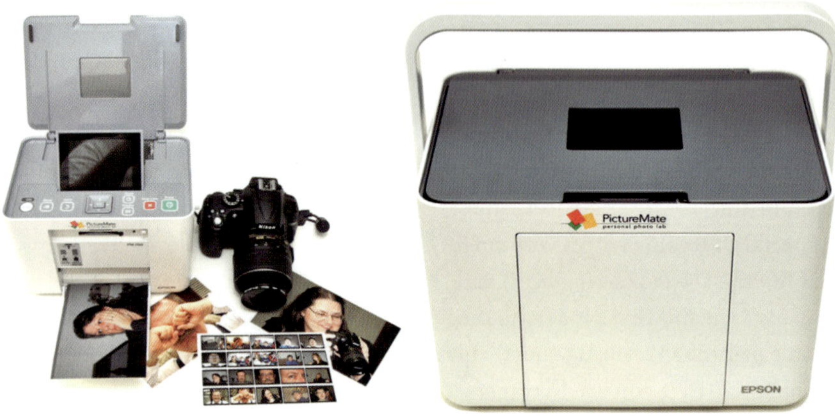

Figure 7A – Epson PictureMate Dash and my D5000

In *figure 7A* is a picture of my D5000 plugged into this tiny 4 x 6 printer. When closed, the little thing looks like a lunch box, but it opens up to reveal a printer that indeed gives me images that look just like the ones I've been getting from my local labs. With this printer I don't even need a computer to print. I can even get a battery for the printer if I want to go out on safari and print on the spot. They make another version of this printer called the Epson PictureMate Zoom that includes a CD-ROM burner. With this model you wouldn't need a computer to print 4x6 size prints or even to back up your images to CD.

Note

If you are a RAW shooter, the PictBridge process won't benefit you. Not all printers can handle printing from RAW files, so Nikon chose to limit PictBridge and DPOF printing to JPEG files in the D5000. Also, you won't be able to use the PictBridge screens unless your D5000 is plugged into a compatible PictBridge printer.

Now, let's look at how I used my Nikon D5000 and new Epson PictureMate Dash to print without a computer. We'll examine both PictBridge and DPOF printing.

Basic Single-Image PictBridge Printing

Let's just jump right in to printing pictures directly from your camera to a compatible PictBridge printer. All you have to do is go out and shoot some images and then come in and plug your camera into the printer. Make sure the printer is turned on! Nikon says to turn the D5000 off before you plug the transfer cable into the camera. When you first turn the camera on, you'll see a series of screens.

As shown in the screen on the left in *figure 7B*, the first screen you'll see is the PictBridge logo that looks like a couple of stretched water droplets. Next you'll be presented with the PictBridge playback screen and a JPEG image found on your memory card. You'll notice on the left in *figure 7B*, how the PictBridge playback screen has the droplet logo in the upper-left corner, letting you know that the screen is not a normal playback screen.

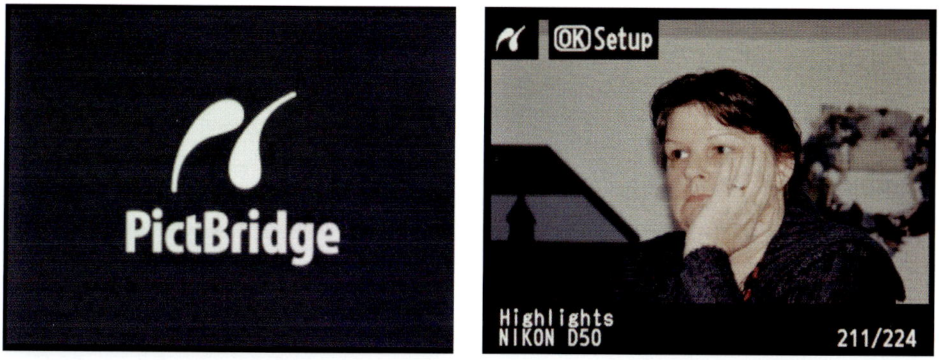

Figure 7B – Initial D5000 PictBridge screens

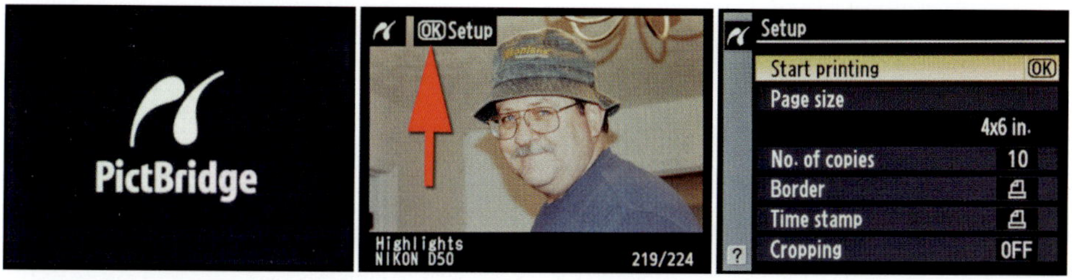

Figure 7C – Press *OK* to enter Setup

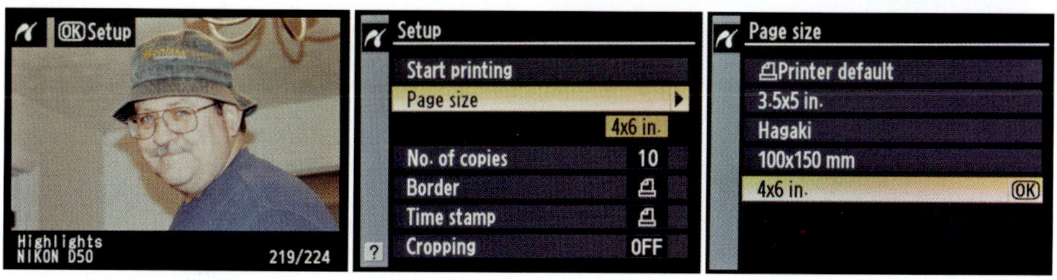

Figure 7D – Select a page size for the print

Now, we'll consider how to get a picture or pictures printed once you've gotten to this point. In *figure 7C* you'll find a series of screens used to select pictures and send them to the printer for printing.

Here are the steps you'll use to print out your pictures:

1. Turn your camera off.
2. Connect the USB cable to the already turned-on PictBridge printer and then to the camera.
3. Turn the camera on.
4. You'll be presented with the PictBridge logo screen and the first image in the PictBridge playback menu (see the leftmost screen in *figure 7C*). Scroll through your pictures with the Multi Selector until you find an image you'd like to print.
5. Press the *OK* button (*figure 7C*, middle screen) and you'll be taken to the printing *Setup* screen (rightmost screen in *figure 7C*).
6. Select *Page size* from the list and match it to the printer paper in your printer. (Mine is only a 4x6 printer, so I included a screen that shows other file sizes. See *Figure 7D*.)

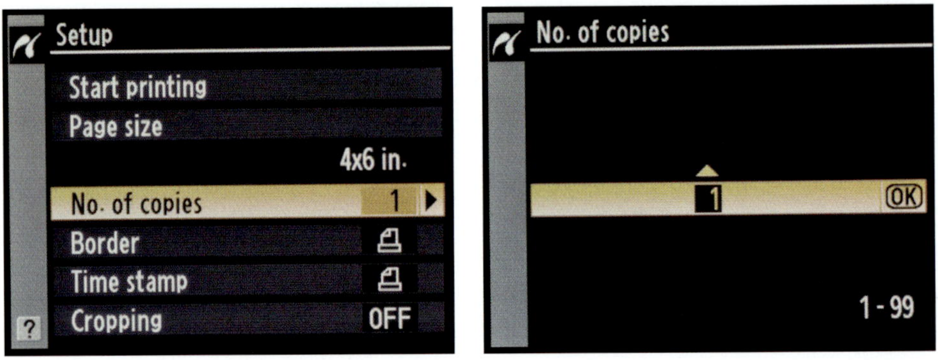

Figure 7E – Select the number of copies for the print

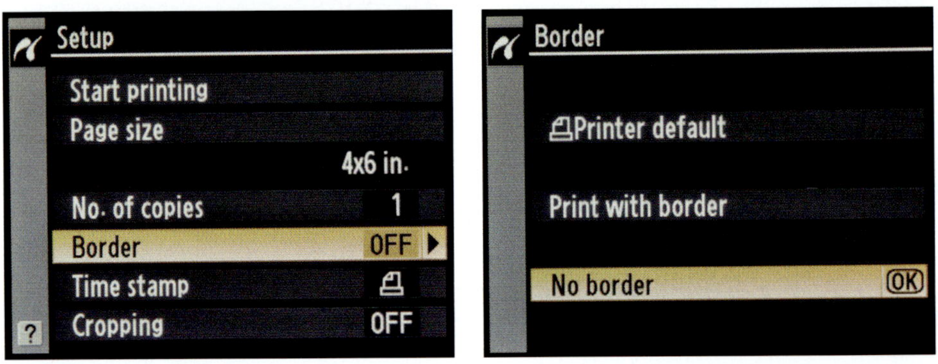

Figure 7F – Choose a bordered or borderless print

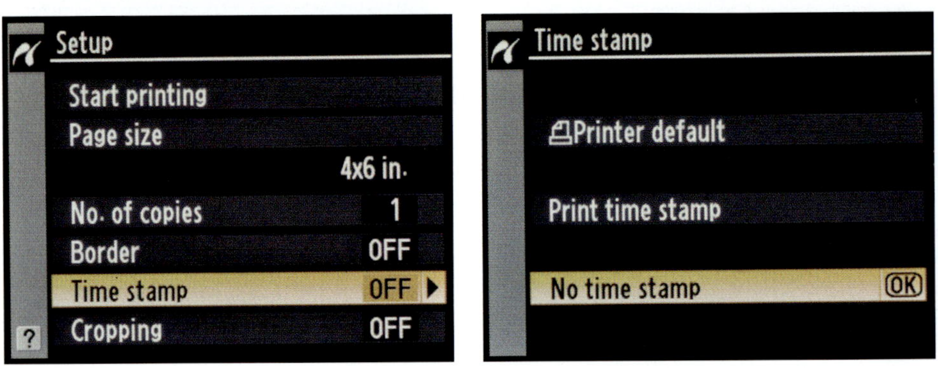

Figure 7G – Select the time stamp for the print

7. Now, select the number of copies you'd like to have of this print (see *figure 7E*). You can select between 1 and 99 prints.

8. Choose either *Print with border* and *No border* (see *figure 7F*). If your printer does not support printing with borders, the *Print with border* option will be grayed out. You can also select *Printer default* if you want to leave it up to the printer to decide.

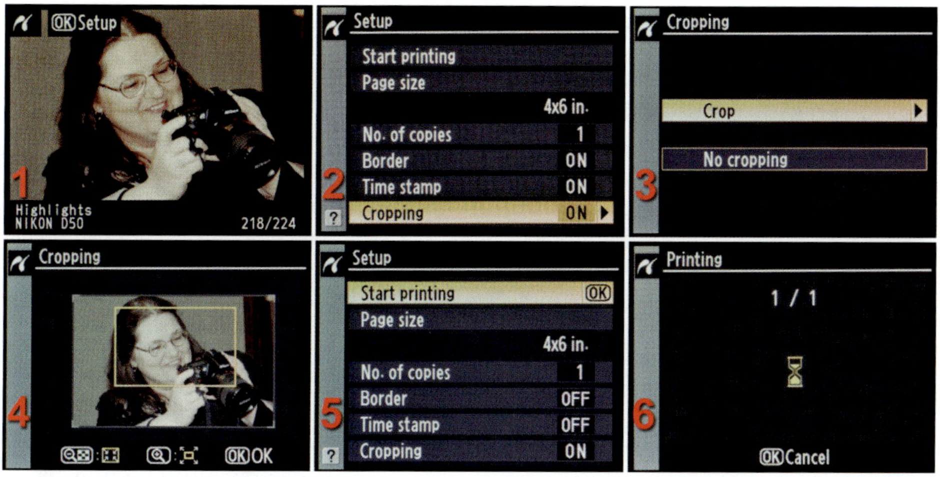

Figure 7H – Select cropping for the print

9. Next, select whether you want a time stamp on the lower-right corner of the picture. Select *Print time stamp* or *No time stamp* (see *figure 7G*).
10. Finally, you must choose whether or not you want to crop the print:
    - ***Crop***: If you select *Crop*, you'll use the thumbnail/playback zoom out button to select the area of the crop (see *figure 6C* for button locations). You can move the yellow crop frame around with the Multi Selector. If you need to zoom back out, you'll use the playback zoom in/out button (see *figure 7H*, image 4).
    - ***No cropping***: If you don't want to crop, just select *No cropping*, and press the *OK* button.
11. Once you've made all your selections, scroll back up to the *Start printing* line and press the *OK* button (see *figure 7H, image 5*). Your printer will now print your picture. *Figure 7H, image 6*, shows the D5000 screen you'll see while the print is flowing to the printer. Immediately thereafter, the printing starts.

Hint

If you want to check for a firmware update on any Nikon digital camera, you can go to this web page on the NikonTech website. It lists virtually all the camera firmware updates that are available from Nikon:

http://support.nikontech.com/app/answers/detail/a_id/13783

If by the time this book is published, that Internet address has changed, you can always go to the Nikon website in your part of the globe and search under technical support for "firmware updates".

A Little Bug Explained

I've noticed a tiny firmware label bug in the PictBridge playback screen. In *figure 7B,* image 2, look at the lower-left corner under the *Highlights* label and see if you notice it. Yes, it says *Nikon D50* instead of *Nikon D5000*. My D5000 was one of the first units to be sold in the United States. If you have newer firmware, you may not see this bug at all, and it does not affect camera functionality.

Since so much of this camera was directly inherited from the more expensive Nikon D90, I suspect that a programmer somewhere didn't allow enough room in the label to contain the new longer name. I expect this will be fixed in the next firmware update, but I thought I should mention it in case you've purchased a new or used D5000 with firmware version A: 1.00, B: 1.00, or L: 1.001. You can look at the bottom of the *Setup Menu* under *Firmware version* to see what firmware your camera is using.

Check the Nikon D5000 forum on www.Nikonians.org for announcements, instructions, and discussion about when a new firmware version is available for download. Nikon usually releases a firmware update within a few months of a new camera coming on the market. It's not possible for programmers to find every little bug in firmware this complex. We help by noticing little things like this—and then Nikon hears about it. A firmware update comes out shortly thereafter.

Multiple Print PictBridge Printing

The "basic" method mentioned in the preceding section is for when you want to select a single image and print one or more copies. There are alternate PictBridge methods available, but you won't be able to see these screens unless your camera is plugged into a PictBridge printer:

- *Print select*
- *Select date*
- *Print (DPOF)*
- *Index print*

Let's discuss each of these in detail.

Print select – This method is for when you want to print more than one image at a time. You can choose from many images, set the number of prints for each, and then choose borders and time stamp information.

Here are the steps to configure *Print select*:

1. Turn your camera off.
2. Connect the transfer USB cable to the already turned-on PictBridge printer and then to the camera.
3. Turn the camera on.
4. As shown in *figure 8*, you'll see a JPEG image after the PictBridge logo finishes displaying. Since we're interested in printing more than one picture, we'll *not* press the *OK-Setup* button at this time, as the PictBridge playback screen suggests. Instead, we'll press the *MENU* button. That will display the PictBridge menu with *Print select* as the top choice. Choose *Print select* and scroll to the right.
5. The *Print select* screen appears (see *figure 8A*). It contains the JPEG files available on your camera's memory

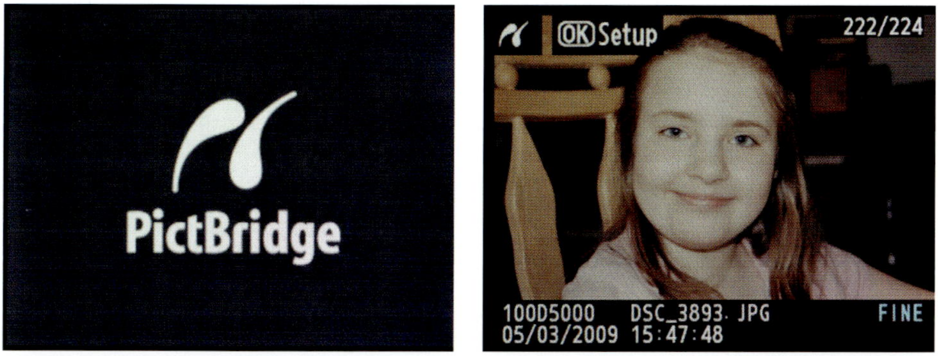

Figure 8 – The PictBridge opening screens

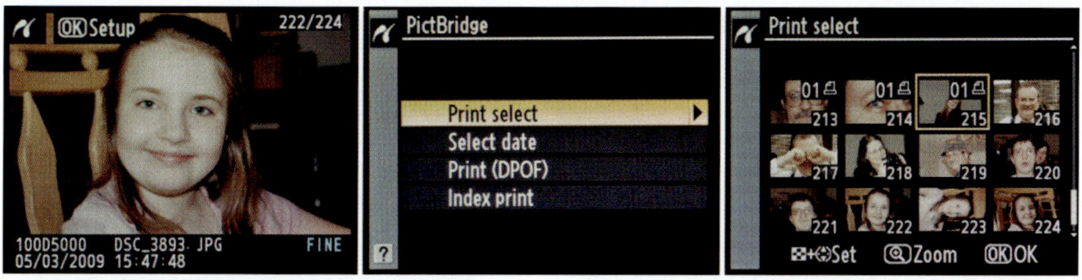

Figure 8A – *Print select* screens

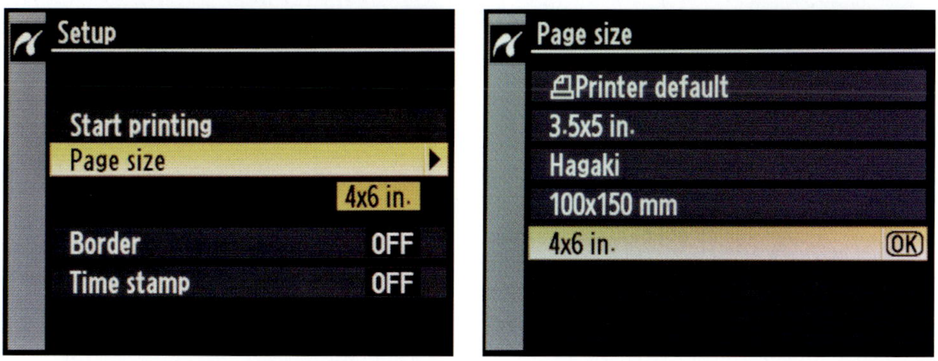

Figure 8B – Printing Setup screen – Select a page size

card. Scroll around with the Multi Selector. To select images for printing, follow these steps:

a. Highlight an image.
b. Hold down the thumbnail/playback zoom out button and scroll up with the Multi Selector to increase the number of prints for this image, up to 99 prints per picture. Notice in the screen on the right in *figure 8A* how the first three thumbnails have a 01 and a small printer symbol? That means print 1 picture for each.
c. Repeat steps a and b for each additional image you want to print.
d. Press the *OK* button when all images are prepared.

6. The camera will now switch to the printing *Setup* screen. You'll need to choose a page size that fits your desired image (see *figure 8B*). Mine is 4 x 6 inches.

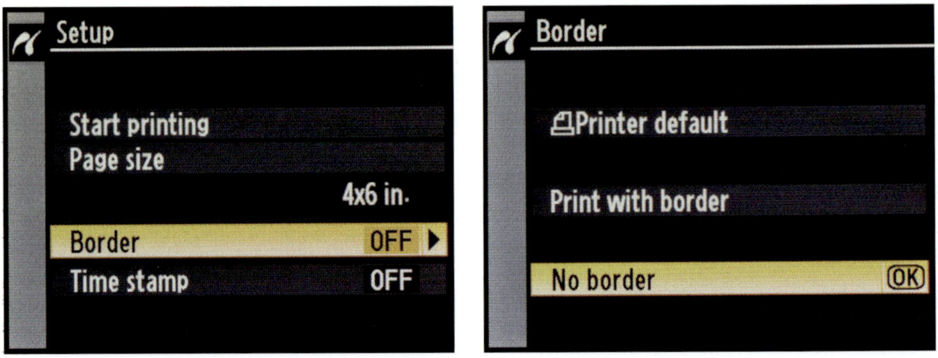

Figure 8C – Choose a border style

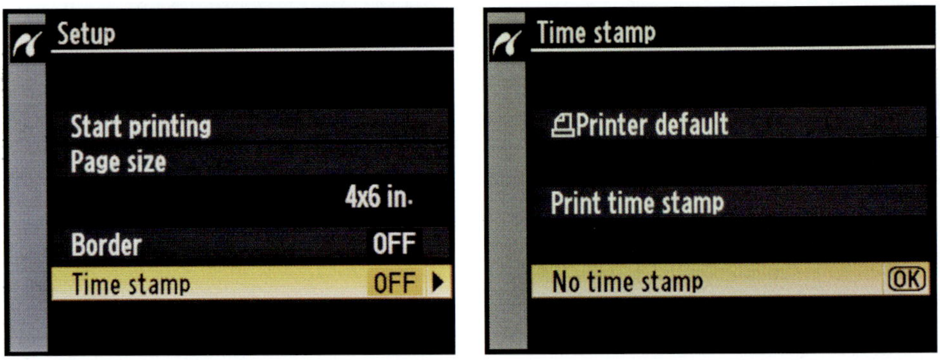

Figure 8D – Choose whether to print a time stamp

7. Do you want a border on this image? If so, scroll down and select *Border* and then scroll to the right (see *figure 8C*). Select *Print with border*. Press *OK* to return to the *Setup* screen.
8. Now, choose whether to print a time stamp. This will add the date to the printed picture in the lower-right corner. Select either *Print time stamp* or *No time stamp* (see *figure 8D*). Press the *OK* button to return to the print *Setup* screen.
9. To print the pictures, scroll up to *Start printing*, and press the *OK* button. Your images will now print with a variable number of copies of each picture per your selections.

Select date – You can select a single or multiple dates and print all images within those dates. *Figure 9* shows the opening screens for printing by date.

Here are the steps to print all images by a specific date:

1. Turn your camera off.
2. Connect the transfer USB cable to the already turned-on PictBridge printer and then to the camera.
3. Turn the camera on.
4. As shown in *figure 9*, you'll see a JPEG image after the PictBridge logo finishes displaying. Since we're interested in printing more than one picture, we'll *not* press the *OK-Setup* button at this time, as the PictBridge playback screen suggests. Instead, we'll press

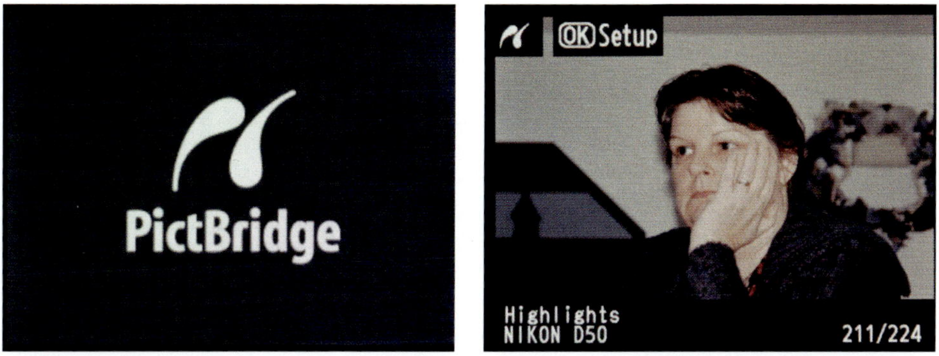

Figure 9 – PictBridge opening screens

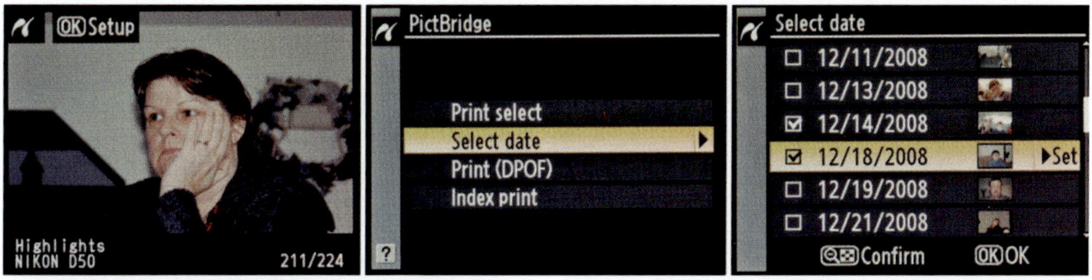

Figure 9A – Choose a date or dates to print

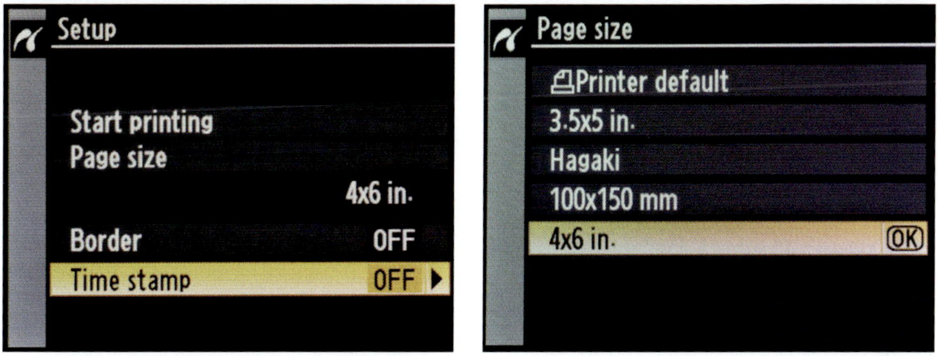

Figure 9B – Printing *Setup* screen – *Page size*

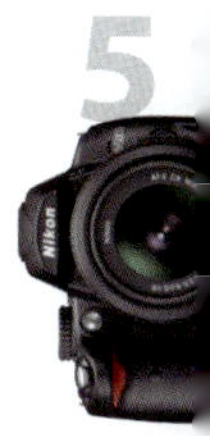

the MENU button. That will display the PictBridge menu with *Select date* as the second choice from the top. Choose *Select date* and scroll to the right.

5. To choose dates, simply scroll down through the list and put a check mark in each date you want to print (see *figure 9A*). You set the check mark in the little box by scrolling to the right on each line. If you want to select a date to see what's in it, you can use the checkered thumbnail/playback zoom out button to toggle a view of the images under a certain date. It's a toggle, so pressing it opens and closes a detailed image display. Press the *OK* button when you have finished selecting the image dates.
6. The camera will now switch to the printing *Setup* screen. You'll need to choose a page size that fits your desired image (see *figure 9B*).

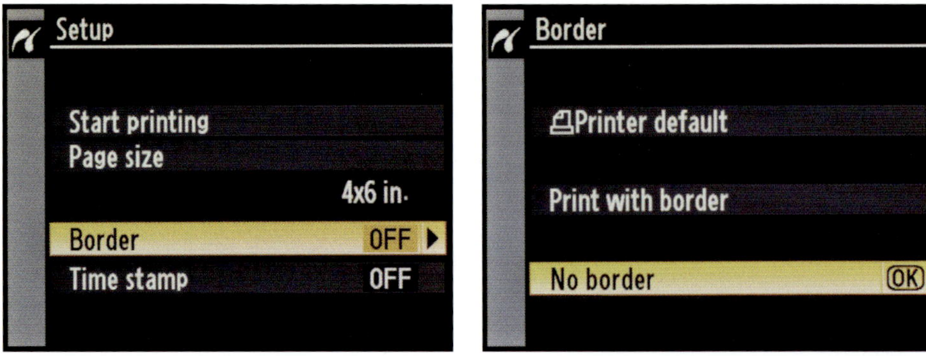

Figure 9C – Choose a border style

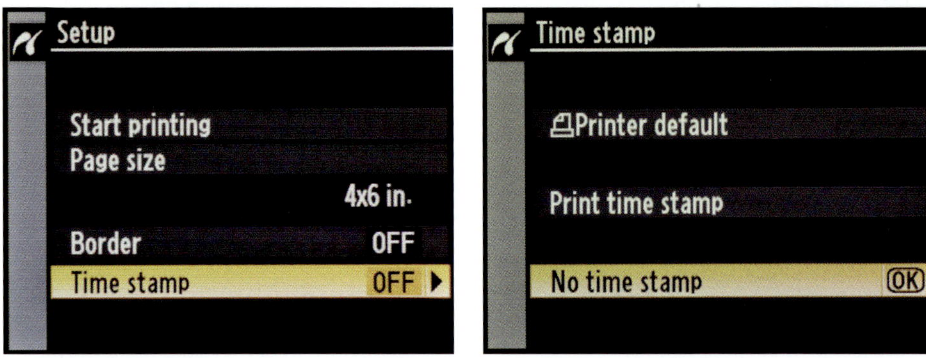

Figure 9D – Choose whether to print a time stamp

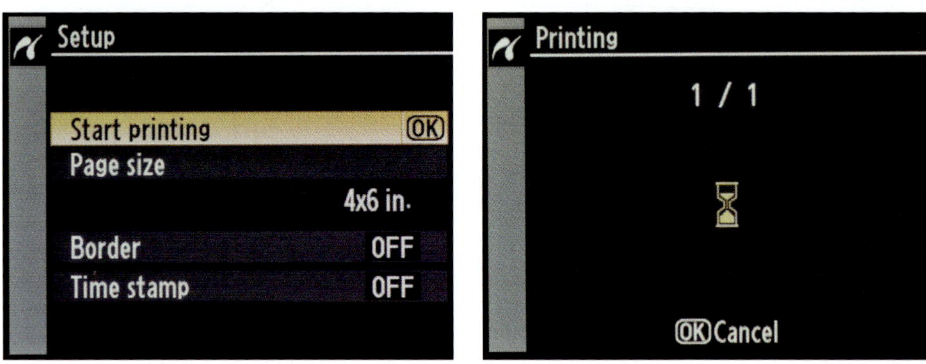

Figure 9E – Printing the picture

7. Do you want a border on this image? If so, scroll down and select *Border* and then scroll to the right (see *figure 9C*). Select *Print with border*. Press *OK* to return to the *Setup* screen.
8. Now, choose whether to print a time stamp. This will add the date to the printed picture in the lower-right corner. Select from *Print time stamp* or *No time stamp* (see *figure 9D*). Press the *OK* button to return to the print Setup screen
9. To print the pictures, scroll up to *Start printing* and press the *OK* button. Your images will now print with a variable number of copies of each picture per your selections. The screen on the right in *figure 9E* shows the D5000 screen you'll see while the print is flowing to the printer. Immediately thereafter, the printing starts.

Print Order (DPOF)

If you have created a print order and saved it to your camera's memory card, this function will give you the option of printing the existing digital print order. I haven't found a way to make more than one print order at a time with the D5000. To learn more about creating a print order, see the section "DPOF Printing" later in this chapter.

If there is no print order already created, this method acts like the *Print select* function we discussed previously.

Here are the steps to create a print order for images by a specific date:

1. Turn your camera off.
2. Connect the transfer USB cable to the already turned-on PictBridge printer.
3. Turn the camera on.
4. As shown in *figure 10*, you'll see a JPEG image after the PictBridge logo finishes displaying. Since we're interested in printing more than one picture, we *will not* press the *OK-Setup* button at this time, as the PictBridge playback screen suggests. Instead, we'll press the MENU button. That will display the PictBridge menu with *Print (DPOF)* as the third choice from the top. Choose *Print (DPOF)* and scroll to the right.

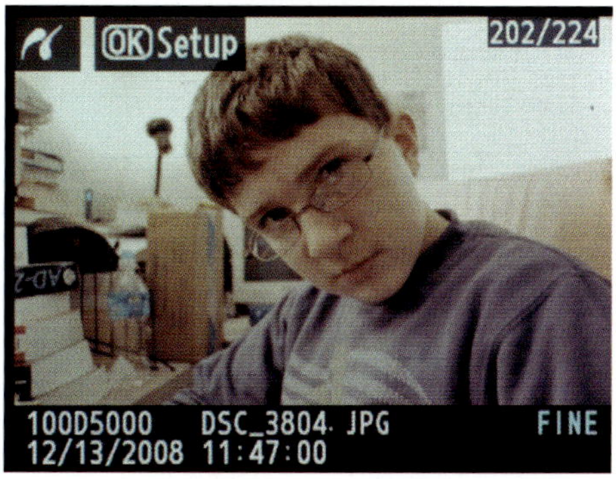

Figure 10 – PictBridge opening screen

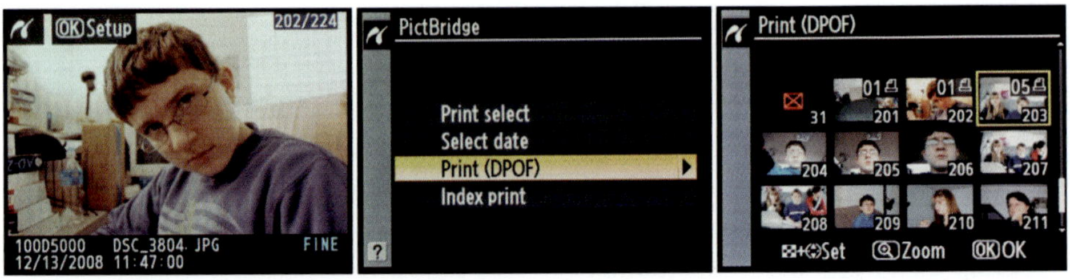

Figure 10A – Validate or change the existing print order

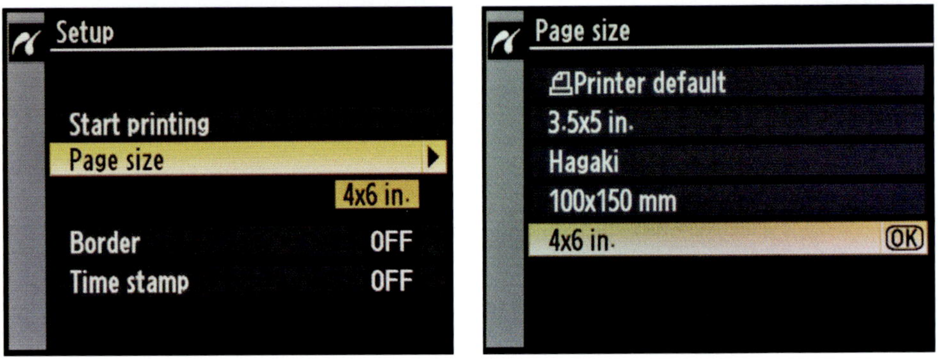

Figure 10B –Choose a page size

5. The screen will now present an existing print order from your memory card (see *figure 10A*). If there are no existing print orders, the images will have no quantity numbers in their upper-right corners and you can proceed to add some. You can change the quantity on any image by selecting it, holding down the checkered thumbnail/playback zoom out button, and then pressing up on the Multi Selector. You can increase or decrease the number of prints for the selected image by toggling up or down on the Multi Selector. Press the *OK* button when you have examined, modified, or approved the print order.
6. The camera will now switch to the printing *Setup* screen. You'll need to choose a page size that fits your desired image (see *figure 10B*).
7. If you want a border on this image, scroll down and select *Border* and then scroll to the right (see *figure 10C*). Select *Print with border*. Press *OK* to return to the Setup screen.
8. Now, choose whether to print a time stamp. This will add the date to the printed picture in the lower-right corner (see *figure 10D*). Select from *Print time stamp* or *No time stamp*. Press the *OK* button to return to the print *Setup* screen
9. To print the pictures, scroll up to *Start printing* and press the *OK* button. Your images will now print with a variable number of copies of each picture per your selections. The right screen in *figure 10E* is the D5000 screen you'll see while the print is flowing to the printer. Immediately thereafter, the printing starts.

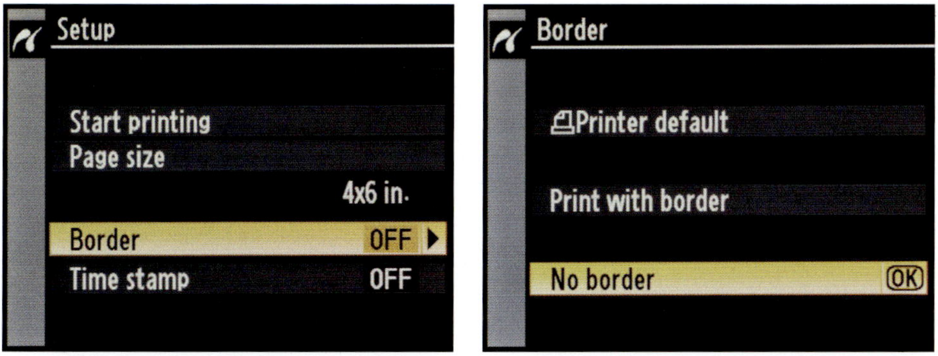

Figure 10C – Choose a border style

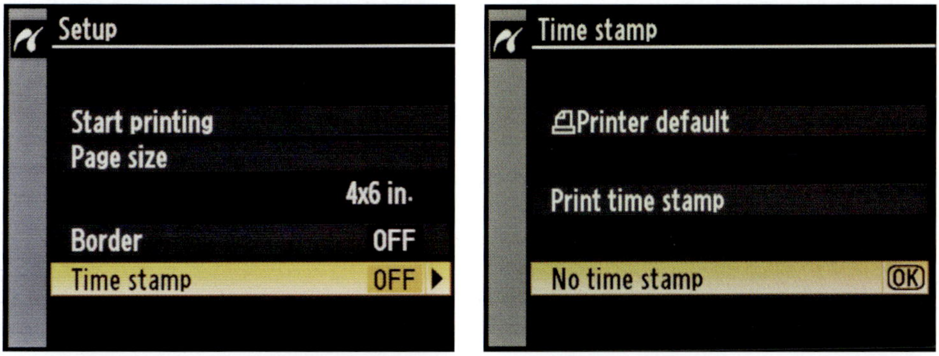

Figure 10D – Choose whether to print a time stamp

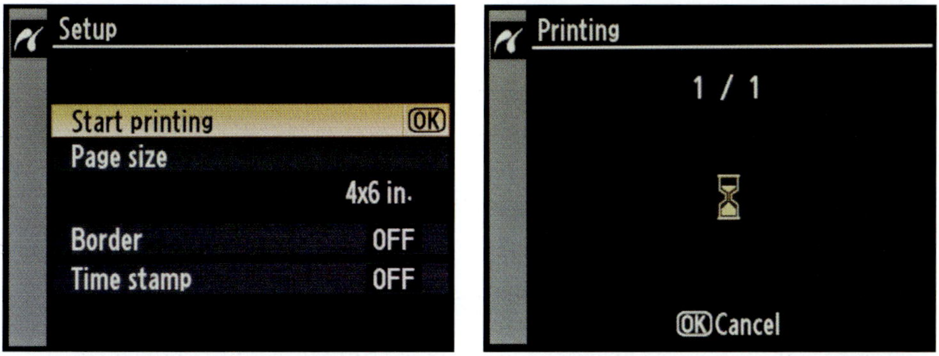

Figure 10E – Printing the picture

Index Print

When you select *Index print*, the camera will find up to the first 256 JPEG images on your memory card and make an index print containing thumbnails of each of them. If the paper size will not contain all the thumbnails, the printer will print multiple pages. This is basically the same as the old contact sheet of yesteryear.

Here are the steps to create an index print for your JPEG images:

1. Turn your camera off.
2. Connect the transfer USB cable to the already turned-on PictBridge printer and then to the camera.
3. Turn the camera on.
4. As shown in *figure 11*, you'll see a JPEG image after the PictBridge logo finishes displaying. Since we're interested in printing an *Index print*, we'll *not* press the *OK-Setup* button at this time, as the PictBridge playback screen suggests. Instead, we'll press the MENU button. That will display the PictBridge menu with *Index print* as the last choice on the list. Choose *Index print* and scroll to the right (see *figure 11A*).
5. You'll now be presented with the first 256 JPEG images found on your camera's memory card. You can't do anything with the images except scroll through them. Press the *OK* button when you are ready to print.
6. The camera will now switch to the printing *Setup* screen. You'll need to choose a page size that fits your desired image (see *figure 11B*).

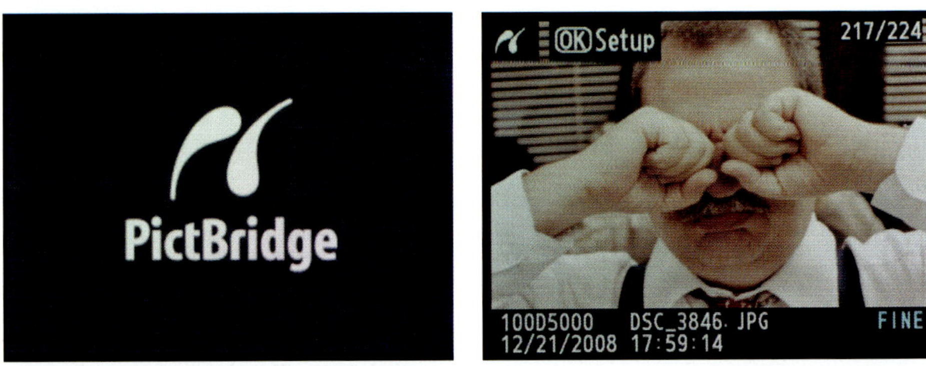

Figure 11 – The PictBridge opening screen

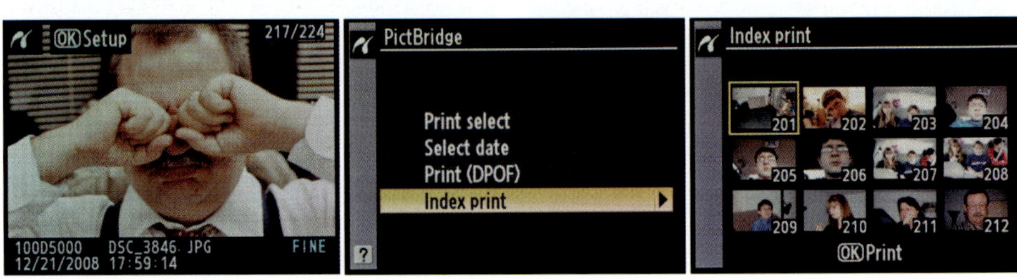

Figure 11A – *Index print* screens

7. If you want a border on this image, scroll down and select *Border* and then scroll to the right (see *figure 11C*). Select *Print with border*. Press *OK* to return to the *Setup* screen.

8. Now, choose whether to print a time stamp (see *figure 11D*). This will add the date to the printed picture in the lower-right corner. Select from *Print time stamp*. Press the *OK* button to return to the print *Setup* screen.

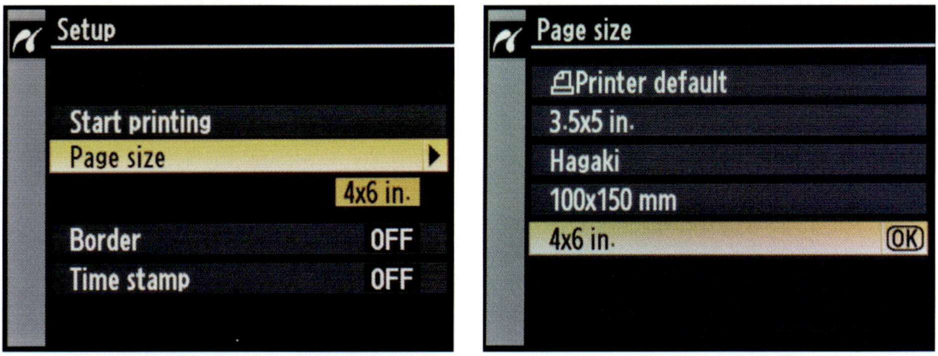

Figure 11B –Select a page size

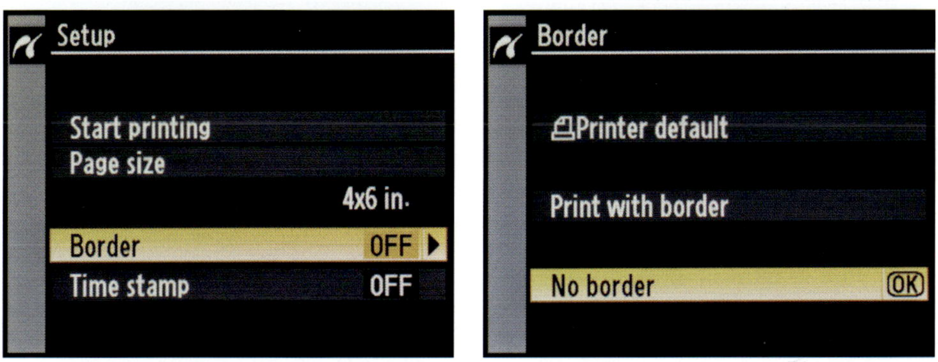

Figure 11C – Choose a border style

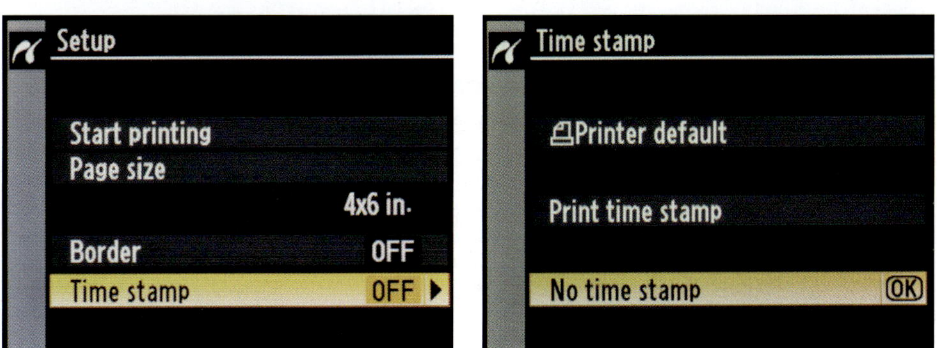

Figure 11D – Choose whether to print a time stamp

9. To print the index print(s), scroll up to *Start printing* and press the *OK* button. The printer will now output one or more index print pages containing small-sized images in a grid pattern like a contact sheet (see *figure 11F*).

In *figure 11F*, you can see a 4 x 6 (10 x 15cm) index print printed on my little Epson PictureMate Dash. Even a print this small can contain 20 thumbnail images. I took a picture of a picture to capture this index print for the book. These are snapshots of family and friends. The D5000 gets passed around my family quite a bit. As a matter of fact, I don't think I took one of the images on the index print. Everyone loves to use the D5000—especially the kids—since they can set a scene mode and shoot lots of images without thinking about camera settings. My 12-year-old son once took 200 images of his own face. It's a good thing the D5000 doesn't use film!

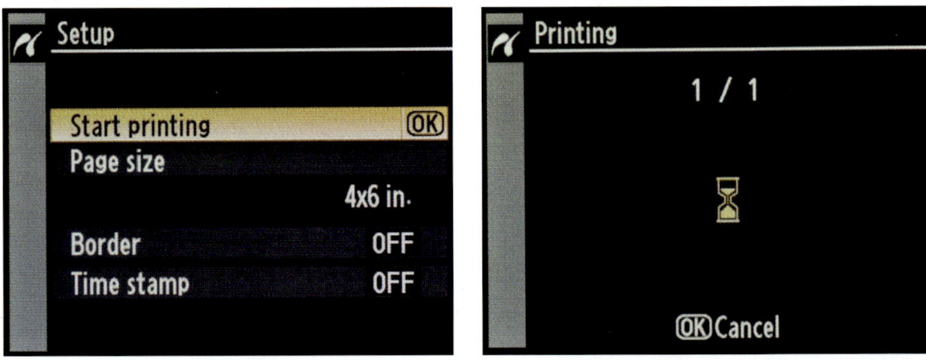

Figure 11E – Printing the picture

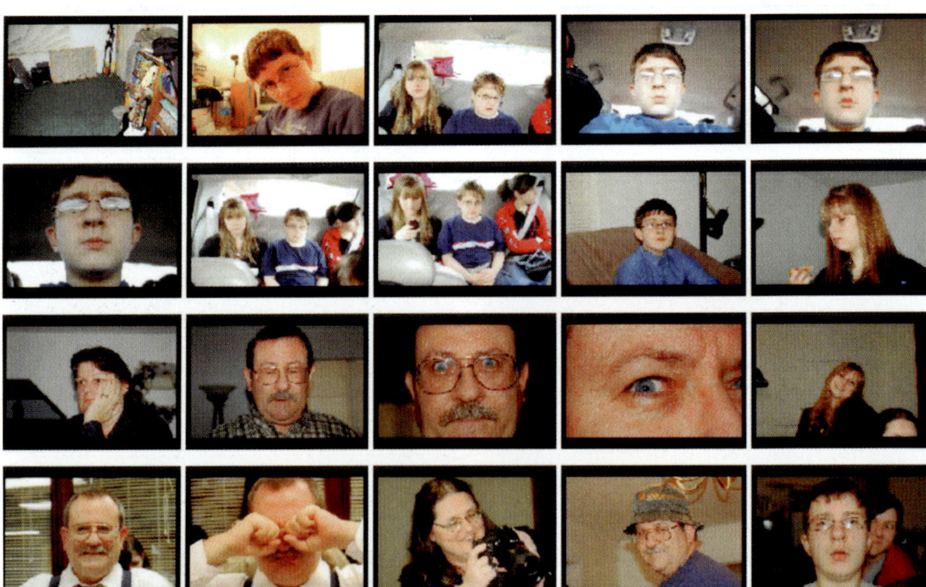

Figure 11F – Sample 4x6 inch (10x15cm) index print

That's about all there is to PictBridge printing directly from camera to printer. Now let's see how you can use the D5000 to create a "print order," store it on the camera's memory card, and print directly from the memory card without attaching the camera or computer to the printer.

Digital Print Order Format (DPOF) Printing

As mentioned, using Digital Print Order format (DPOF) you do not have to connect the printer to any other device. All you have to do is insert a memory card that contains a digital print order on it and the printer will detect the order and offer to fill it.

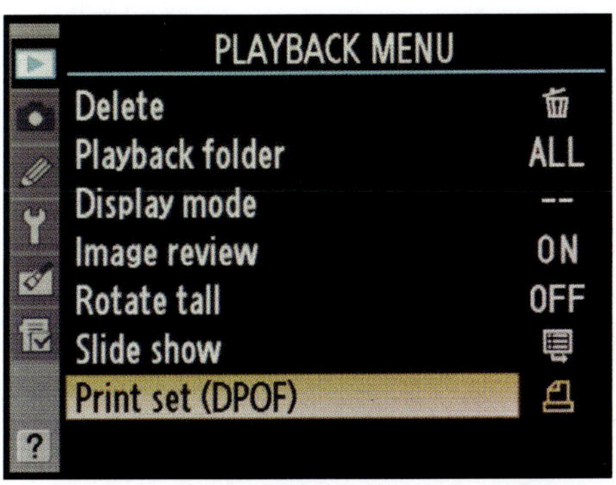

Figure 12 – *Print set (DPOF)* option on the *Playback Menu*

Since my printer is an Epson PictureMate Dash, I'll have to use its screens to do the final DPOF print. Your printer's screens and methods may vary, but I doubt they'll be much different than the Epson's.

These steps will allow you to print your order on your DPOF compatible printer:

1. On your D5000, press the MENU button and select the first menu on the list, the *Playback Menu*.
2. Scroll down and select *Print set (DPOF)* (*figure 12*) and then scroll to the right.
3. If you don't have any existing print orders on the memory card, please skip this step and go directly to step 4. Otherwise, if you have an existing print order that you no longer want, you'll need to choose *Deselect all?* from the list and then scroll to the right (see the first screen in *figure 12A*). The next screen will ask you, *Remove print marking from all images? Yes/No*. Choose *Yes* and press *OK*. If there are previously marked images, a brief message saying, *Markings removed from all images* will flash in the screen, and it will return to the *Playback Menu*. Otherwise, no message will appear and it will just return to the menu.

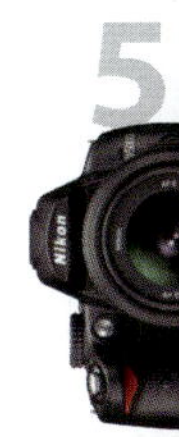

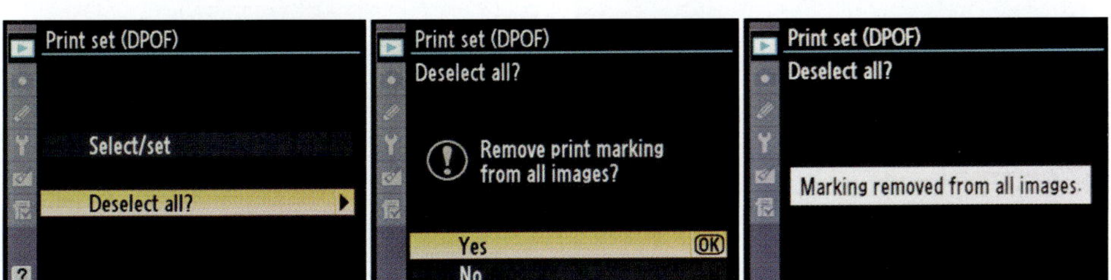

Figure 12A – Deselecting an existing print order

4. Since you're going to create a new print order and save it to the memory card, you'll choose *Select/set* from the *Print set (DPOF)* screen, then scroll to the right (see *figure 12B, image 1*).
5. Now you'll see the *Select/set* screen with all the JPEG images on your memory card (see *figure 12A, image 2*). You'll need to choose images with the multi selector. Once you have an image highlighted, hold down the checkered thumbnail/playback zoom out button and scroll up with the multi selector (see *figure 6C* earlier in this chapter for button location). This changes the number of prints ordered for that particular image (see *figure 12B, image 2*, red arrow). You can select from 1 to 99 prints for each image you highlight. Each print you choose will be marked with a tiny printer icon and a number of prints value. Once you scrolled through your images—highlighting and incrementing print amounts—just press the *OK* button.
6. The next screen allows you to add data imprints to each of the images in the print order (see *figure 12B, image 3*). You can choose from the following:
   a. *Data imprint*: This prints the shutter speed and aperture on each print in the order.
   b. *Imprint date*: This causes a date to be added to each print in the order.

You put check marks in the tiny boxes by highlighting the line and scrolling right on the word *Set*. When you have completed your choices, scroll up to *Done*

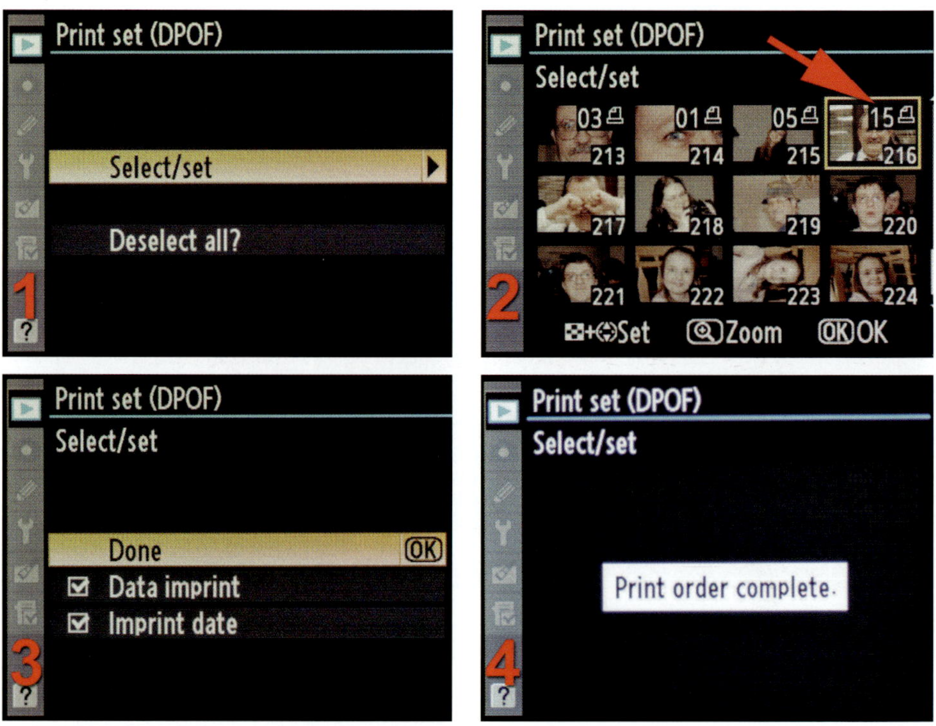

Figure 12B – Choosing images and print amounts

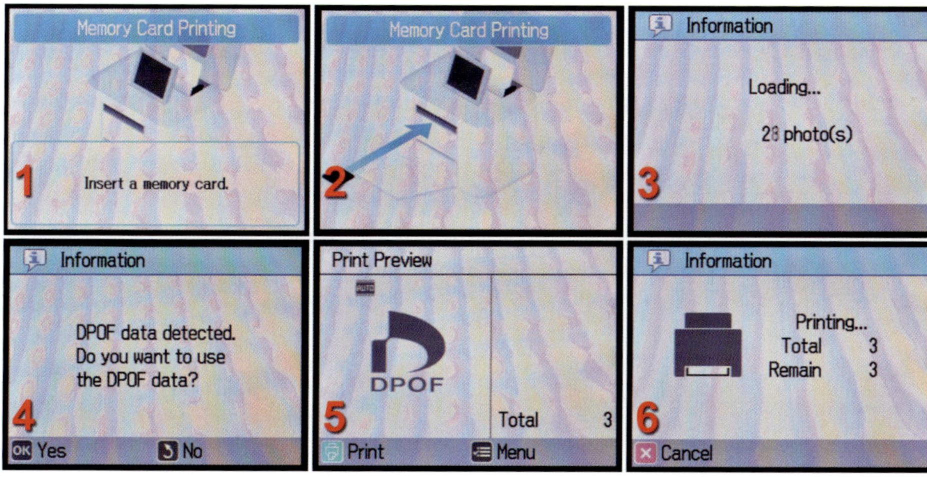

Figure 12C – Print order fulfillment

and press the *OK* button (see *figure 12B, image 3*).

7. You'll be presented with a screen telling you that the print order is complete (*figure 12B, image 4*).

At this point, your print order has been saved to the memory card, and you'll need to insert the card into the printer's memory card slot. *Figure 12C* shows the screens I see at this point on my Epson PictureMate Dash printer. Your printer's screens may be different, but since your printer is PictBridge/DPOF compatible, you'll find something very similar.

As these screens appeared, I followed the prompts and ended up with my selected four prints within a few minutes.

Recommendation

I had absolutely no interest in printing directly from my camera to a PictBridge printer until I wrote this chapter and saw how fun and easy it is. Printer costs are reasonable, so you might want to pick up a PictBridge-compatible printer. Just look for the PictBridge logo on the printer's packaging or body. Thank you, Nikon, for giving us this easy method for making nice prints!

My Conclusions

I remember the old days when to "play back" some images, you'd have to find the old shoebox full of pictures or open an album and flip pages. Sometimes I miss photo albums. I'm going to run down to the superstore right now and buy several albums. Then I'll use PictBridge to print some actual images to put into those albums.

In the meantime, though, I'll use the Playback features of my D5000 to impress my friends with my images and my really cool camera.

Shooting Menu

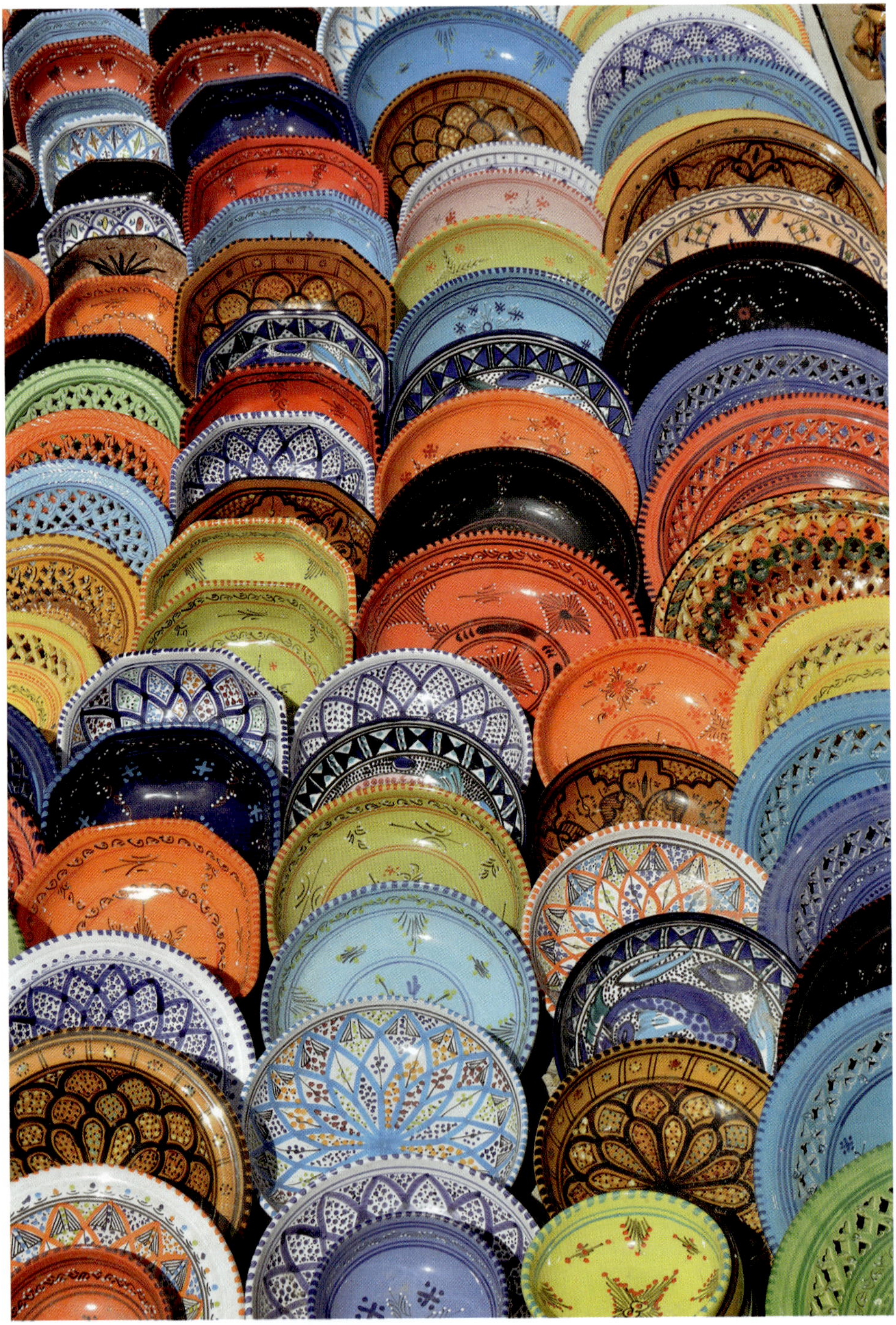

One of the hallmarks of the Nikon D5000 camera is the way in which its many functions are configurable. Between the *Shooting Menu* and the *Custom Settings Menu* (detailed in the next chapter), you can configure the camera for distinct shooting styles. These settings give you control over how the camera works. It's easy to change styles with just a few button presses.

Or, if you're a new user of DSLR cameras and want the D5000 to "hold your hand" for a while as you learn about advanced camera techniques, it's happy to oblige with 19 scene modes. As described in chapter 3, the scene modes allow an inexperienced photographer to make great pictures by setting the camera for specific types of shooting (or "scenes"). As a newer user advances in knowledge, the camera makes it easy to gradually take control.

The *Shooting Menu* allows you to configure functions such as picture control style, image quality modes (RAW, JPEG, etc.), white balance, ISO sensitivity, sharpening, D-Lighting, and color space. In fact, there are total of 15 separate menu items to configure within the *Shooting Menu*.

There are several external camera controls we'll be using to set various functions in the *Shooting Menus*. *Figure 1* shows the control locations and their names.

Referring to the numbers on the images in *figure 1*, here is a list of control names:

- Mode dial
- Command dial
- Multi Selector switch and *OK* button
- Delete and MENU buttons
- Playback zoom in button
- Information edit button

As we proceed through this chapter, you'll use these controls frequently. Place a bookmark at this page so that you can refer back to *figure 1*. Now, let's look into each menu item and discover the best settings for your style of photography.

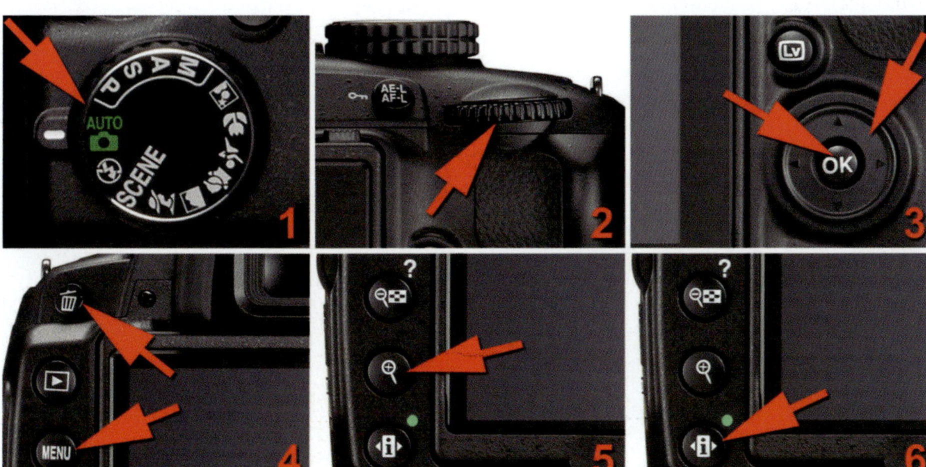

Figure 1 – Controls used to configure the *Shooting Menus*

Setting Up the Shooting Menu

Press the MENU button on the back of your D5000 and use the Multi Selector to scroll to the left, and then up or down until you find the *Shooting Menu*. The icon looks like a small green camera on the left side of the screen, second from the top.

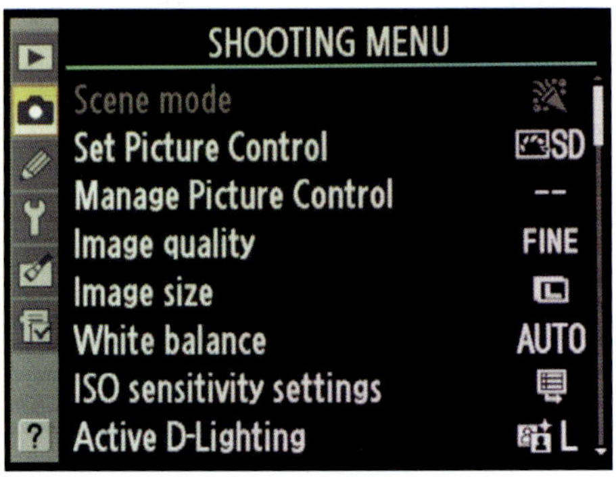

Figure 1A – *Shooting Menu* screen

Figure 1A shows what the screen looks like after you select the *Shooting Menu*. Let's examine each of the 15 configurable items on the *Shooting Menu* (User's Manual pages 148–152).

Scene Modes

The D5000 is designed so that you can decide whether to manually control certain functions or let the camera assist you in a general, more automatic way. With the scene modes, you can "dial in" specific styles of shooting with the mode dial. If you are new to all the functions of the camera, using the scene modes is a great starting point. The information screen displays a useful picture that shows the style of shooting selected. *Figure 1B*

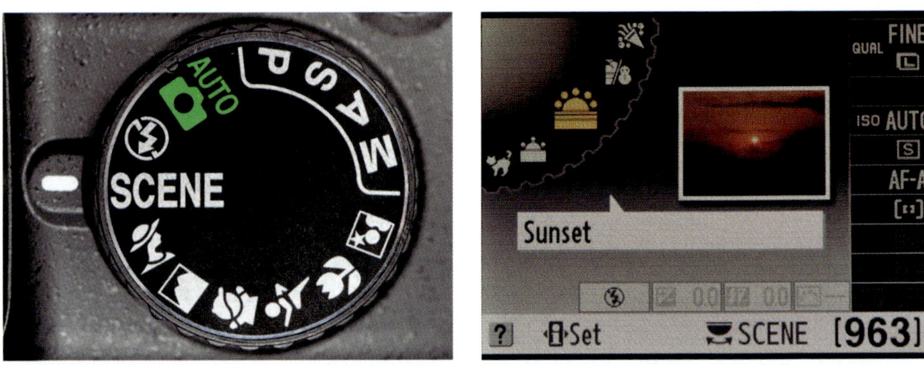

Figure 1B – Sunset scene mode

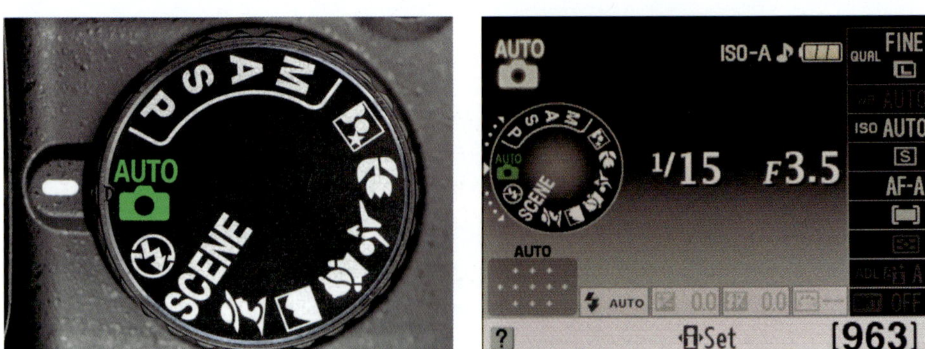

Figure 1C – Scene modes on the mode dial and information screen shows the camera set to sunset Scene mode.

We won't consider each scene mode in detail since they were already covered in chapter 3 - "Exposure Metering System, Exposure Modes, and Histogram" (User's Manual page 33).

You can access six scene modes directly on the mode dial (see *figure 1C*):

- Portrait
- Landscape
- Child
- Sports
- Close up
- Night portrait

To choose a scene mode with the mode dial, follow these steps:

1. Choose one of the scene modes on the mode dial.
2. Examine the information screen to make sure *Lo* or *Hi* is not showing in the shutter speed or aperture readouts.
3. Verify that *Subject is too dark* is not showing on the top left of the information screen.
4. Take your pictures.

There are 13 additional scene modes on the *Shooting Menu* (see *figure 1D*):

- *Night landscape*
- *Party/indoor*
- *Beach/snow*
- *Sunset*
- *Dusk/dawn*
- *Pet portrait*
- *Candlelight*
- *Blossom*
- *Autumn color*
- *Food*
- *Silhouette*
- *Low key*

In chapter 3 we looked at the scene modes from the perspective of setting them on the LCD monitor's information screen display. In this chapter, we'll examine how to set these same modes from the *Shooting Menu*.

Here are the steps to choose a scene mode not on the mode dial:

1. Set the mode dial to SCENE.
2. Press the MENU button and scroll to the *Shooting Menu* (second from top).
3. Choose *Scene mode*. If it is grayed out, you have not set the mode dial to SCENE; do so now. Next, scroll to the right.

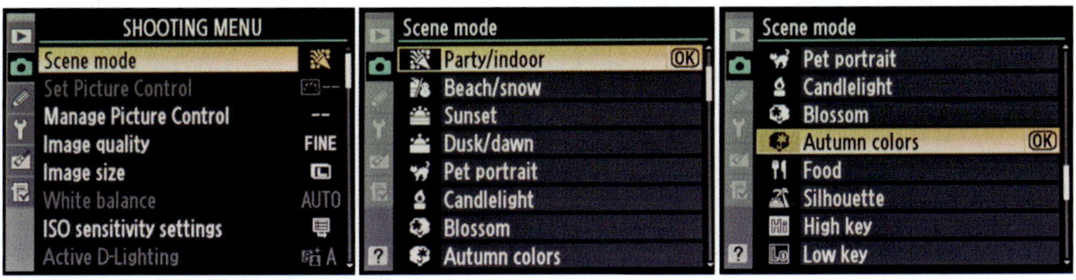

Figure 1D – Scene modes on the *Shooting Menu*

4. Choose one of the scene modes from the list. Notice the symbol or icon connected to the particular scene mode.
5. Press the *OK* button, and the camera will return to the *Shooting Menu*. You should see the symbol for your selected mode at the end of the *Scene mode* menu line. For this example, I chose *Party/indoor*, and you can see the symbol at the end of the *Scene mode* line in the screen on the left in *figure 1D*.
6. Press the info button on top or the information edit button on the bottom left of the camera. The symbol for your selected scene should now show on the top left of the information screen.
7. Take your pictures.

Chapter 3 in this book, and pages 33 to 38 in the User's Manual cover each scene mode in detail. Read this information carefully and enjoy the scene modes while you learn to use the more advanced modes of the camera.

Note on Scene Modes

If you have the camera set to SCENE on the mode dial, many of the *Shooting Menu* options will be grayed out, and you won't be able to access them. Remember, the scene modes are designed to let the camera make decisions for you until you've gained enough knowledge to use the more advanced features of a DSLR. Since it has to make choices for you, it turns off the menus that you would normally use to set things yourself.

Picture Controls

Next, we'll investigate the Picture Control system built into the Nikon D5000. This flexible image control system was designed by Nikon to allow you to customize how you create images. There are six different Nikon Picture Controls in the camera. If you are a former film user, this is sort of like having six different film types available at all times.

The scene modes we discussed in the preceding section all use one of these Picture Controls to give your images a certain look. You can use them for a similar look while controlling other features of the camera yourself.

Each control makes the image look different, with different levels of color saturation, contrast, brightness, hue, and sharpening. You can modify any of the Nikon-supplied controls to make your own custom Picture Controls. Your custom Picture Controls can be saved in-camera with unique names or to your memory card for sharing with other cameras, devices, and software that support the Picture Control system.

Downloadable Picture Controls have been around for a while, but the Nikon D5000 has made it easier to use them than ever before. The Nikon Picture Control specification provides for compatibility between different cameras. You can download your D5000 Picture Controls to other Nikon cameras and your images will look the same as they do in the D5000. That's one of the reasons for the existence of Picture Controls—to allow, as Nikon says, "nearly the same results on all cameras that support the Nikon Picture Control system."

So, if you own other newer Nikon cameras, why not develop some Picture Controls and share them with your other cameras, and friends' cameras too. You'll become known as the Picture Control guru!

Now let's look at how to use the six supplied Nikon Picture Controls.

Set Picture Control

(User's Manual pages 106–107)

There are two ways to set a Picture Control, but only one method allows you to fine-tune it. You can choose a Picture Control from the *Information edit* screen, or you can choose and tweak a picture control from the *Shooting Menu*. We'll look at both ways in this section.

First, let's look at the *Shooting Menu* method. The screens are shown in *figure 2*.

To select a particular Picture Control, simply follow these steps:

1. Press the MENU button and select the *Shooting Menu*.
2. Scroll to *Set Picture Control,* and then scroll to the right. If it is grayed out, set your mode dial to P, S, A, or M. You can't adjust Picture Controls when using the scene modes.
3. Select one of the Nikon Picture Controls from the menu. As you can see in *figure 2*, I selected *Vivid* for this example. If you want to modify the control to have different sharpening, contrast, brightness, saturation, or hue, scroll to the right for the fine-tuning screen (the screen on the right in *figure 2*). Otherwise, go directly to step 4.
4. Press the *OK* button (without scrolling right) to make the selected control active. The two-letter abbreviation for the control will show on the *Shooting Menu*. For example, in the screen on the left in *figure 2*, you can see *VI* next to *Set Picture Control*.

Note

At the very bottom of the center image in *figure 2*, you may notice a Picture Control called *STANDARD-03*. This is a custom Picture Control that I created. We'll talk about how you can create custom controls in the next section, "Manage Picture Control."

Now, let's briefly look at choosing a Picture Control from the *Information edit* screen.

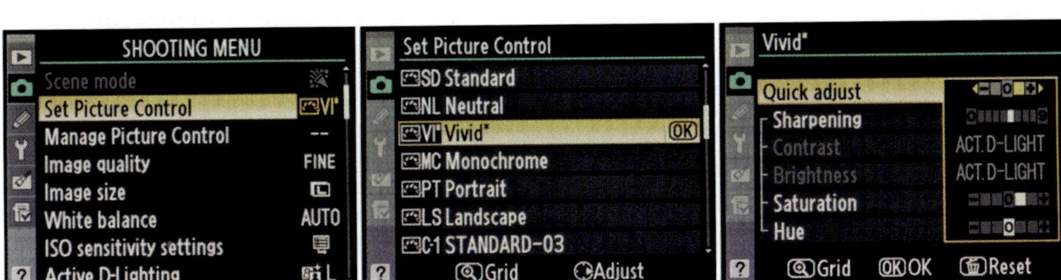

Figure 2 – *Set Picture Control* menu screens

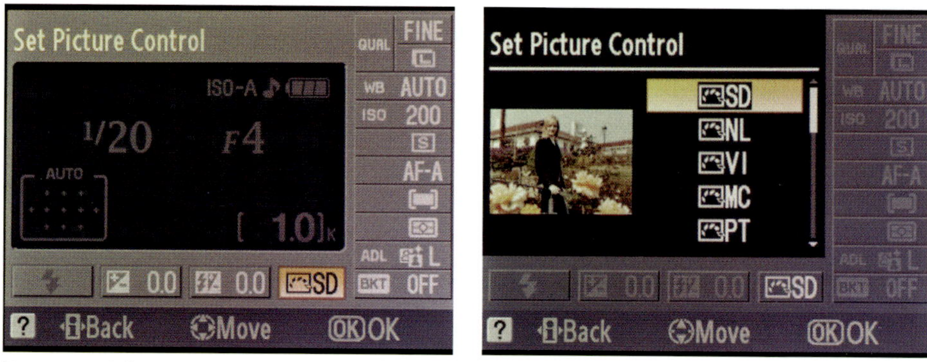

Figure 2A – Selecting a Picture Control from the information edit screen

Here are the steps to choose a Picture Control using the *Information edit* screen instead of the *Shooting Menu* (see *figure 2A*):

1. Press the <**i**> information edit button until you see the *Information edit* screen.
2. Make sure the yellow highlighted rectangle is positioned in the *Set Picture Control* field.
3. Press the *OK* button. You'll be presented with the second *Set Picture Control* screen. It has a list of Picture Control selections. Choose your favorite control with the Multi Selector.
4. Press the *OK* button to select the Picture Control. The camera will return to the main *Information edit* screen showing your choice in the *Set Picture Control* field.

Now, let's consider the purpose behind each control so that you can make good choices about which you'll use regularly.

Here is a list of the six Nikon Picture Controls and detail on each of them (User's Manual page 107):

- *SD - Standard*
- *NL - Neutral*
- *VI - Vivid*
- *MC - Monochrome*
- *PT - Portrait*
- *LS - Landscape*

Standard – This is the most balanced Picture Control. It does not try to make your image too colorful or too "contrasty", but it does provide a great look. If I were to compare this control to a certain film, I would say it looks most like Fuji Provia. It has medium contrast and saturation. I wouldn't consider this a portrait film but would tend to use it when I wanted natural and realistic colors in nature or indoor settings.

Neutral – This is for individuals wanting an image that will be easier to post-process later in the computer. It has a somewhat extended dynamic range, so it can capture more shadow and highlight detail. If you used Fuji NPS in the past, you'll find that this has a somewhat similar look. It can be used for portraits or nature and has lower contrast for ease of working on the image in-computer. If you are forced to shoot in extremely bright conditions with high contrast—such as on a bright sunny day—this control works well to tame some of that deep contrast.

Vivid – Are you a hard-core nature shooter who loved Fuji Velvia? Do you regularly add a little saturation to your colors? Do you boost contrast to get that "snap" needed for great nature images? If so, here's your Picture Control! This mode is an "in your face" deep saturation, high-contrast, "make it green, blue, and beautiful" Picture Control. Are the colors accurate? Well, were they accurate with Fuji Velvia? No! However, if you want beautiful nature shots, this will do it. Be careful using *Vivid* on a sunny day because it tends to increase contrast to higher levels. You will get deep, dark blacks and very saturated greens, reds, and blues with this control. If you are shooting on a low-contrast overcast day, this mode will add contrast for you.

Monochrome – Have you wanted to experiment with black & white (B&W) pictures? This Picture Control makes pretty decent straight B&W images, with rich blacks and clean whites. In addition, you can tone the images with different tints. The old style sepia (warm reddish) and cyanotype (cool bluish) are available. Nikon also provides other tints for your experimentation, including red, yellow, green, blue green, blue, purple, and red purple. The normal B&W mode looks like Kodak Plus-X film to me but has slightly less black. It is hard to fully imitate the effect of silver-based film with a digital sensor. However, this control gives you a good starting point for deepening the blacks and brightening the whites so that your picture can look the way you want it to look.

Portrait – Nikon's User Manual (page 107) claims that this control is "...for skin with natural texture and a rounded feel". I've taken numerous images with this *Portrait* control and shot the same images with the *Neutral* control. The results are very similar. I'm sure that Nikon has included some software enhancements specifically for skin tones in this control, so I recommend this for shooting portraits. The results from this control look a bit like smooth Kodak Portra film to me.

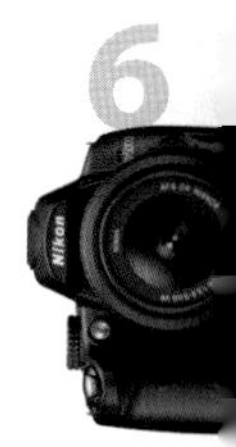

Landscape – This control "produces vibrant landscape and cityscapes", according to Nikon. That sounds like the *Vivid* control to me. I shot a series of images using both the *Landscape* and *Vivid* controls and got similar results. Compared to the *Vivid* control, the *Landscape* control seemed to have very slightly less saturation in the reds and a tiny bit more saturation in the greens while blues stayed about the same. It could be that Nikon has created the *Landscape* control to be similar but not quite as drastic as the *Vivid* control. There is so little difference between the two that you would have to compare them side-by-side to notice. Maybe this control is meant to be slightly more natural than the supersaturated *Vivid* control. It will certainly improve the looks of your landscape images. I'd say the look of this control is somewhere between Fuji Velvia and Provia, providing great saturation and contrast with emphasis on the greens of natural settings.

Each of these controls is fully configurable. You can fine-tune them and the camera will remember your changes. In the middle image in *figure 2*, notice how *Vivid* has an asterisk after it. It looks like this: *VI* Vivid**.

I added a couple of levels of sharpening to *Vivid* as an experiment, therefore it displays the asterisk to remind me that the default values of the control have been changed. Any control that you've fine-tuned stays the way you set it until you change it back to the normal factory settings. You can't save the Nikon Picture Controls from this menu. Instead, you'll need to use the *Manage Picture Control* menus, which are detailed in the next section. However, your values will stay with the control until you change them again.

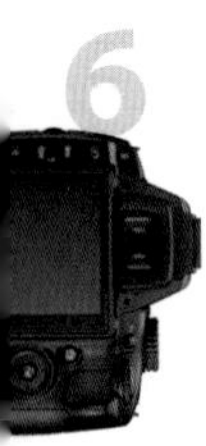

Which Picture Control should you use? Good question. It really boils down to whether you are a person who likes to shoot in RAW mode and later post-process the images into their final form or you simply enjoy taking great pictures in JPEG mode and will use them immediately.

Personally, I am a post-processing kind of guy. I use the *Neutral* control most of the time since I'm shooting in RAW mode and want to get extra dynamic range from lower contrast for later computer enhancement. I realize that by shooting in *Neutral* I'm not going to create images with immediate "snap" or deep color saturation. However, I've found that when I use *Neutral* I can make superior images later in Nikon Capture NX2. I boost the color until it matches what I remember and I raise the contrast until it is just right to my eyes. It's extra work of course, but it's deeply satisfying when I create a great looking image. For me, digital imaging is a two-part process.

First, shoot the RAW picture, and second, finish it in Capture NX2. *Since I'm shooting in RAW mode, it really makes no difference what Picture Control I'm using since the RAW file is completely adjustable after the fact.* I find that when I've shot in *Neutral*, Capture NX2 displays it as a low-contrast, low-saturation image so that I can easily see the effects I am trying to achieve when I make modifications.

If you are allergic to computers or have no interest in post-processing, then you should carefully match the Picture Control to the type of images you are shooting. If you're shooting portraits of people, you may want to use *Neutral*, *Standard*, or *Portrait*. For scenics, landscapes, and indoor events, you might want to use *Landscape*, *Vivid*, *Standard*, or even *Neutral* if you are conservative. This is especially important if you are shooting in JPEG mode because you can modify a JPEG only a small amount later without causing problems from image recompression losses.

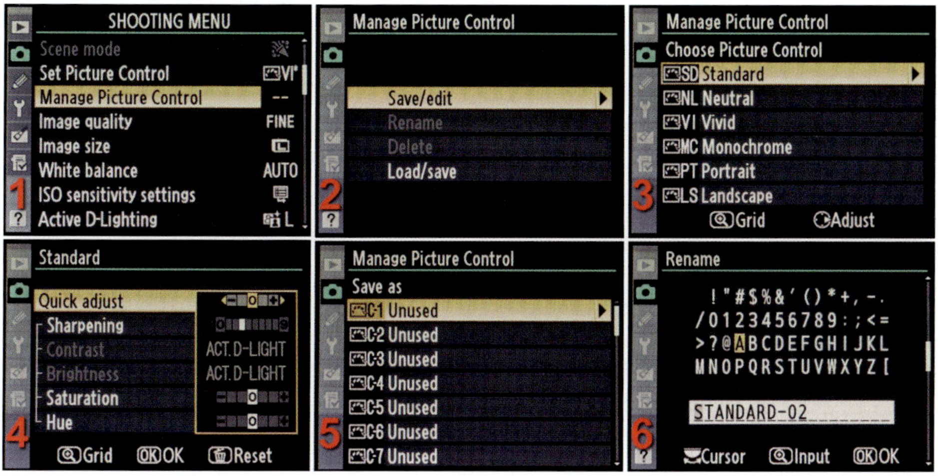

Figure 3 – Creating custom Picture Controls

Ask yourself, "When I shot film, what type was it?" Did you shoot Kodak Gold negative film? Then you will probably like using the *Standard* control. Did you shoot Velvia slide film? Then go for *Vivid* or *Landscape*. Was your imaging mostly pictures of people—using negative film? In that case, *Portrait*, *Standard*, or even *Neutral* might work best.

Nikon has given us a wide selection of Picture Controls as a base. Now let's discuss how we can modify them to suit our own styles and then save the results into our own custom Picture Controls.

Manage Picture Control

(User's Manual pages 111–113)
"Managing" a Picture Control refers to modifying and saving a base Nikon Picture Control as a newly named custom Picture Control. It can also mean deleting, renaming, and copying those controls. We'll look at each of those processes in this section.

Creating Custom Picture Controls

Let's visually examine the steps and screens used to change a base Nikon Picture Control into your own custom Picture Control.

Here is a detailed look at the steps to set up a custom Picture Control (see *figure 3*):

1. Press the MENU button and select the *Shooting Menu*.
2. Scroll down to *Manage Picture Control* and scroll to the right.
3. Select *Save/edit* from the menu and scroll to the right.
4. Select one of the base Nikon Picture Controls and scroll to the right. (If there is an asterisk after the control name, you have already modified the control.)
5. On the *Quick adjust* screen, make your favorite modifications to *Sharpening*, *Contrast*, *Brightness*, *Saturation*, and *Hue*. (Note that if you have Active D-Lighting turned on, you will not be able to modify the *Contrast* and

Brightness settings. They will be grayed out. When Active D-Lighting is on, it handles those two settings automatically. After the *Contrast* and *Brightness* settings, you'll see the words *ACT.D-LIGHT*. We'll talk about Active D-Lighting later in this chapter.)

6. Click the *OK* button to let the camera know that you're done modifying the settings. It will switch to the *Save as* screen (*figure 3, image 5*).
7. Select one of the nine unused save locations, *C-1* through *C-9*, and then scroll to the right. The camera will put words reflecting the type of control you're working with in the *Rename* screen for you. If you're modifying a *Standard* Picture Control, you'll see the words *STANDARD-01*. For a Vivid Picture Control, you'll see *VIVID-01*. You can leave these words the way they are and press *OK* to save the control. The words will become the new name of your custom control and will show up under the *Set Picture Control* list. You also have the option of creating a more descriptive name of your choice, up to 19 characters long (User's Manual page 152).

   To create a new name, use the command dial to scroll back and forth within the old name. When you have the small gray cursor positioned over a character, you can delete it with the trash can delete button. To insert a new character, position the yellow cursor in the character list above and press the playback zoom in button. Whatever character is under the yellow cursor will appear on the name line below, at the position of the gray cursor. If a character is already under the gray cursor, it will be pushed to the right. Make sure you limit the name to a maximum of 19 characters. Press the *OK* button when you have completed the new name. (See *figure 1* for the locations of the camera controls.)
8. Click the *OK* button to save the new custom Picture Control name. It will now be available in the *Set Picture Control* list.

If you've previously fine-tuned a Nikon Picture Control, it will be there for you to save as a custom Picture Control, using the preceding steps. Once you have created and saved your own custom Picture Control, it will show up in the *Set Picture Control* selection list, which normally includes only the base Nikon Picture Controls. (See section "Set Picture Control" earlier in this chapter.) Your new custom controls will stay in the list with the Nikon controls until you remove them. You can also rename them, delete them, and save them out to your memory card for later use or to trade with friends. Let's see how.

Sharing Custom Picture Controls

You can share any of the custom Picture Controls you create by copying them to your memory card and transferring them to your computer (User's Manual page 113).

Here's a description of how to save a custom Picture Control to your camera's memory card (see *figure 4*):

1. Press the MENU button and select the *Shooting Menu*.
2. Scroll down to *Manage Picture Control* and scroll to the right.
3. Select *Load/save* from the menu and scroll to the right.
4. Select *Copy to card* and scroll to the right.
5. Select one of your previously created custom Picture Controls from the list and scroll to the right.
6. Your camera now displays a *Choose destination* screen. These "destinations" simply represent an index on your memory card. You can have up to 99 custom Picture Controls on any one memory card. If there are already custom controls on the memory card, you'll see them in the *Choose destination* list. Choose one of the "Unused" destination lines by using the *Multi selector* to scroll to its position. If you choose the position of an existing *Custom Picture Control*, instead, it will be overwritten.
7. Press *OK* and you'll see a brief pop-up screen saying *Data saved to memory card*.

Once you've saved a custom Picture Control to your memory card, you can transfer it to your computer for use in software or other cameras. If one of your friends makes a new control you'd like to try, or if you find one on the Internet and download it, you can transfer it into your D5000.

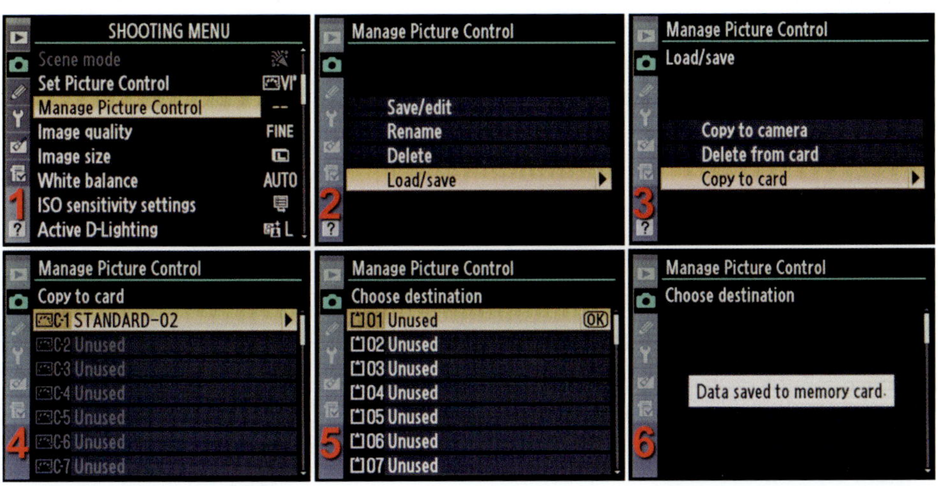

Figure 4 – Sharing custom Picture Controls

Copying Custom Picture Controls to Your D5000

To transfer a custom Picture Control from your camera's memory card to your *Set Picture Control* list, do the following (see *figure* 5 and the User's Manual page 113):

1. Press the MENU button and select the *Shooting Menu*.
2. Scroll down to *Manage Picture Control* and scroll to the right.
3. Select *Load/save* from the menu and scroll to the right.
4. Select *Copy to camera* and scroll to the right.
5. You'll be presented with a *Copy to camera* list. This list shows the total number of custom Picture Controls that are currently on the memory card in your camera. Select one of them and click the *OK* button. (If you scroll to the right instead, you will be able to examine and adjust the control before saving it to your camera. If you don't want to modify it, simply press *OK*.)
6. The *Save as* screen appears and shows any custom Picture Controls already on your camera. There are nine memory locations, labeled *C-1* through *C-9*. Select one of the memory locations labeled *Unused* and press the *OK* button.
7. The *Rename* screen appears, just in case you want to change the name of the custom control. If you don't want to change the name, simply press the *OK* button and the custom control will be added to your *Set Picture Control* list.

   To create a different name, use the command dial to scroll back and forth within the old name. When you have the small gray cursor positioned over a character, you can delete it with the trash can delete button. To insert a new character, position the yellow cursor in the character list above and press the playback zoom in button. Whatever character is under the yellow cursor will appear on the name line below, at the position of the gray cursor. If a character is already under the gray cursor, it will be pushed to the right. Make sure you limit the name to a

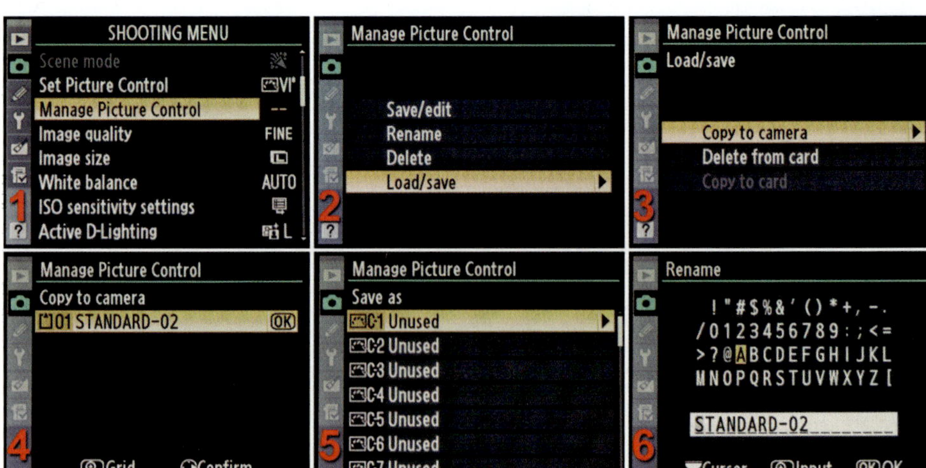

Figure 5 – Copying custom Picture Controls to your D5000

maximum of 19 characters. Press the *OK* button when you have completed the new name. (See *figure 1* for the locations of the camera controls.)

When you save a custom Picture Control that has the same name as an existing one, the camera merely saves the control in the list of nine locations with the same name (*C1* to *C9*). In other words, you will then see two custom Picture Controls, with the same name, in the list of nine. If you do not rename it, you may be confused later since there will be two controls with the same name. The D5000 won't overwrite a control with the same name when copying from the memory card to the camera.

You can also create custom Picture Controls in programs like Nikon Capture NX2 and later load them into your camera using the previous steps.

What if you decide to rename an already existing custom Picture Control? You can do it by following the next set of steps.

Renaming a Custom Picture Control

If you decide to rename a custom Picture Control, do the following (see *figure 6*):

1. Press the MENU button and select the *Shooting Menu*.
2. Scroll down to *Manage Picture Control* and scroll to the right.
3. Select *Rename* from the menu and scroll to the right.

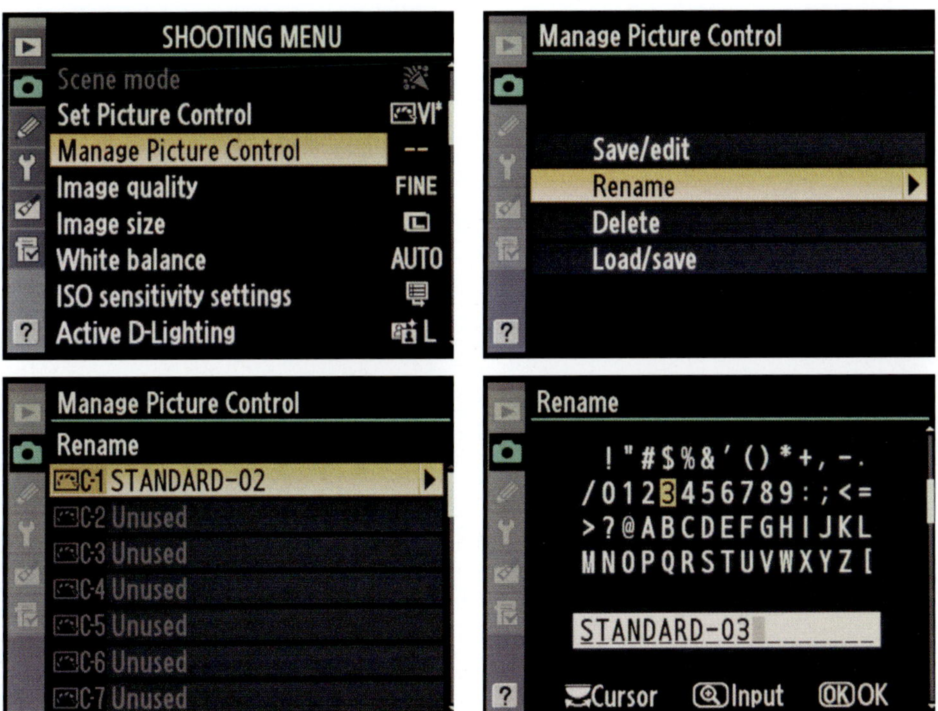

Figure 6 – Renaming custom Picture Controls

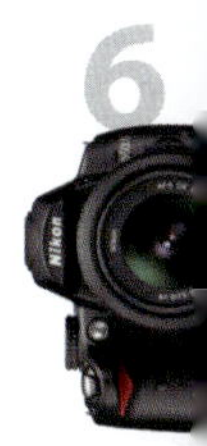

4. Select one of your custom Picture Controls from the list (*C-1* to *C-9*), and scroll to the right.
5. You'll now be presented with the *Rename* screen. To create a different name, use the command dial to scroll back and forth within the old name. When you have the small gray cursor positioned over a character, you can delete it with the trash can delete button. To insert a new character, position the yellow cursor in the character list above and press the playback zoom in button. Whatever character is under the yellow cursor will appear on the name line below, at the position of the gray cursor. If a character is already under the gray cursor, it will be pushed to the right. Make sure you limit the name to a maximum of 19 characters. Press the *OK* button when you have completed the new name. I renamed the control in *figure 6* to *STANDARD-03*. (See *figure 1* for the locations of the camera controls.)

When a custom Picture Control is no longer needed, you can easily delete it.

Deleting Custom Picture Controls from the Camera

When you are ready to delete custom Picture Controls from within your Nikon D5000, removing them permanently from the *Set Picture Control* list, just follow these steps (see *figure 7*):

1. Press the MENU button and select the *Shooting Menu*.

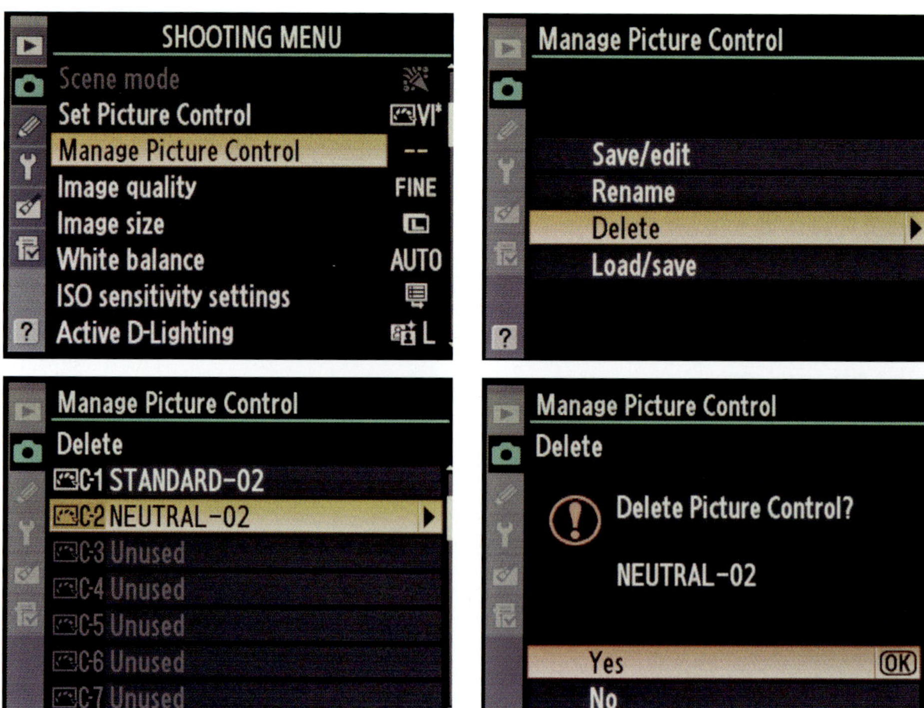

Figure 7 – Deleting custom Picture Controls from the D5000

2. Scroll down to *Manage Picture Control* and scroll to the right.
3. Select *Delete* from the menu and scroll to the right.
4. Select one of your custom Picture Controls from the list (*C-1* to *C-9*), and scroll to the right. I chose the *Neutral-02* in *figure 7* (see the lower-left image). It's in position *C-2*.
5. The *Delete* screen appears showing the question *Delete Picture Control?* with the name of the control and *Yes/No*.
6. Scroll up to *Yes* and press the *OK* button.
7. You'll see *Done* briefly pop up on your screen, and the custom control is no more.

What if you have some controls on the memory card and want to use the D5000 to remove them? You can do that by following the next set of steps.

Deleting Custom Picture Controls from an Inserted Memory Card

Previously, we looked at how to remove a custom Picture Control from within the Nikon D5000's *Set Picture Control* list. If you have old custom Picture Controls on your inserted memory card, you can remove them by doing the following (see *figure 8*):

1. Press the MENU button and select the *Shooting Menu*.
2. Scroll down to *Manage Picture Control* and scroll to the right.
3. Select *Load/save* from the menu and scroll to the right.
4. Select *Delete from card* from the list and scroll to the right.
5. The first *Delete from card* screen appears. It shows a list of all the custom Picture Controls it can find on the memory card, numbered from 01 to 99. (I had only one control, named *STANDARD-02*, on the card.)

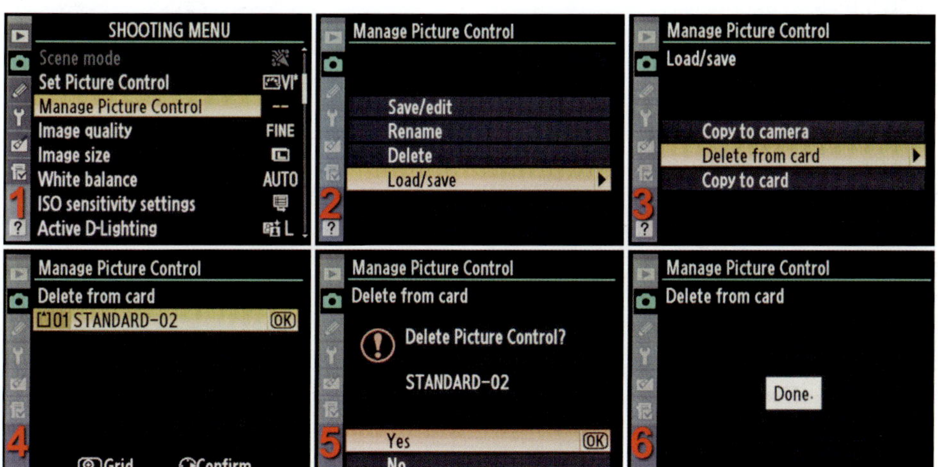

Figure 8 – Deleting custom Picture Controls from a memory card

6. Now you'll see the final *Delete from card* screen and the question "*Delete Picture Control?*"
7. Scroll up to *Yes* and press the *OK* button.
8. You'll see *Done* briefly pop up on your screen, and the custom control is now deleted from the memory card.

Custom Picture Controls give you the ability to make your camera take pictures the way you want them to look. Don't be afraid to experiment with different looks since you can always delete or adjust a control you don't like. You can't delete the base Nikon Picture Controls from which your custom controls are derived, so don't let that worry you. Enjoy the flexibility your D5000 gives you, and use it to the fullest!

Image Quality

(User's Manual pages 62–63)

There are two ways to select *Image quality*. One is by using the *Shooting Menu*, and the other via the *Information edit* screen. We'll examine both. First let's see how we can set the image quality from the *Shooting Menu* (see *figure* 9).

The "quality" of your image is directly related to what image format or type you use. The Nikon D5000 has two specific image types that can be used alone or together.

It supports the following image types:

- NEF (RAW). The *NEF* stands for Nikon Electronic Format.
- JPEG Fine, Normal, and Basic
- Combination of NEF and JPEG at the same time. (Same image stored twice, one as a NEF, the other as a JPEG.)

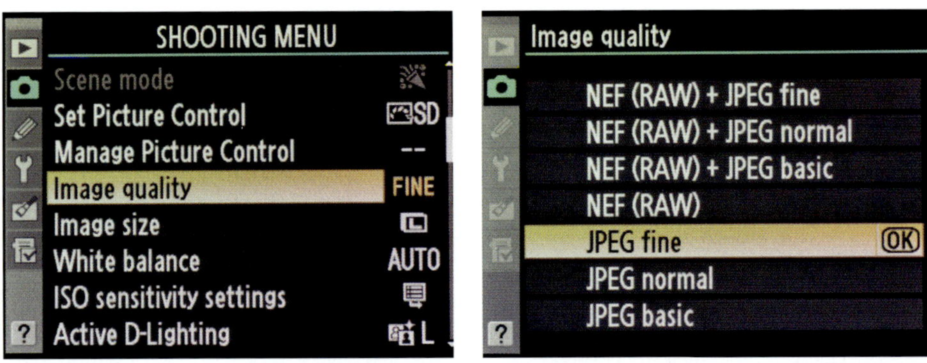

Figure 9 – *Image Quality* screens on the *Shooting Menu*

Also, you can select *Image quality* from the *Information edit* screen (see *figure 9A*).

Follow these steps to make the selection:

1. Press the <**i**> information edit button until you see the *Information edit* screen (the screen on the left in *figure 9A*).
2. Make sure that the yellow highlight rectangle is positioned in the *Image quality* field (as shown in the screen on the right in *figure 9A*, where is says *FINE*).
3. Press the *OK* button.
4. You'll be presented with the second *Image quality* screen. It has the list of selections mentioned previously. Select your favorite *Image quality* level. You'll also notice that the camera gives you a couple of useful pieces of information. Just to the left of the list of *Image quality* selections, you'll see information on the approximate image file size (MB) and number of images your camera's memory card can hold for the current selection.
5. Once you've made your selection, press the *OK* button. The camera will return to the main *Information edit* screen with your choice showing in the *Image quality* field.

Since this chapter is about the *Shooting menus*, we won't go into detail on the *Information edit* screen method. That method is very simple, and once you've used it, it will seem like second nature. For quick changes, I always use the *Information edit* screens. For more deliberate changes, I use the *Shooting Menu*. It's cool that Nikon gives us a choice. To me, it reflects the dual nature of the D5000. It's designed to work well for both new and advanced DSLR users.

Let's look at each of the *Shooting Menu* image quality formats and see which you might want to use regularly.

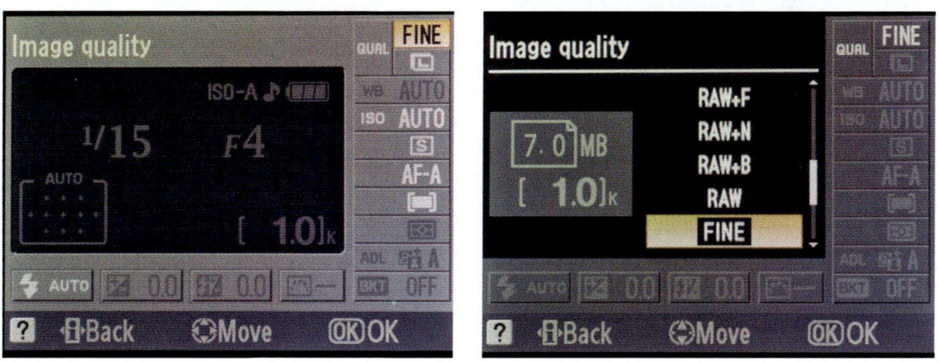

Figure 9A – Information edit screens – *Image quality*

Understanding Image Formats

In this special section, I will go beyond just how to turn the various formats on and off and will discuss why you might want to use a particular format over another. I will cover details you should know as a digital photographer.

NEF (RAW) Format

This Nikon proprietary format (*figure 10*) stores RAW image data directly to the camera's memory card in files and can easily be recognized because the filename ends with .nef, which stands for **N**ikon **E**lectronic **F**ormat. This is not an image format used in day-to-day graphical work (like JPEG), and an NEF image is not yet really even an image. Instead, NEF is a base storage format used to store images for conversion to another format like JPEG, TIFF, or EPS. Other than initial compression, it stores all available image data and can be easily manipulated later.

You must use conversion software, such as the Nikon Software Suite (included with the camera), Nikon ViewNX, Nikon Capture NX2, Adobe Lightroom, or Adobe Photoshop, to later change your NEF format RAW file into a format like TIFF or JPEG. There are also several aftermarket RAW conversion applications available, such as Bibble, Capture One, and PhaseOne.

Before you go out shooting in the NEF RAW format, why not install your conversion software of choice so that you'll be able to view, adjust, and save the images to another format when you return?

You may not be able to view NEF files directly on your computer unless you have RAW conversion software installed. Some operating systems provide a

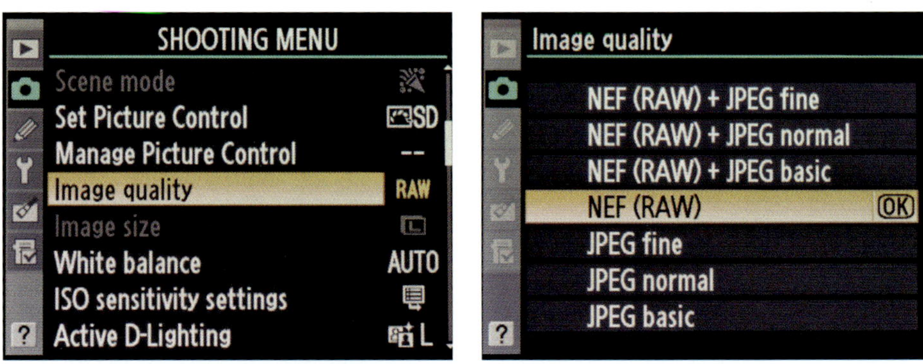

Figure 10 – *NEF (RAW) Image quality* selection

downloadable patch or codec that lets you at least see NEF files as small thumbnails. Do a Google search on these specific words, and you'll find a Microsoft Windows XP patch for NEF files: "microsoft raw thumbnail viewer download." You'll be able to download a file called RAWViewerSetup.exe (about 5.8 MB), which allows XP to display small NEF file "thumbnails" when you view a folder containing them. Windows Vista users can also get the patch/codec if they have a genuine copy of Vista. You'll have to pass the Windows Genuine Advantage (WGA) program barrier to obtain it.

Nikon provides a CD with the D5000 that includes the Nikon Software Suite for both Macintosh and Windows computers. It provides Nikon ViewNX, which can be used to examine your NEF (RAW) files in detail, and convert them to other formats. It also has Nikon Transfer, a program that helps you download your images from your camera and onto your computer.

NEF (RAW) mode uses an image data compression type known as *visually lossless*. Compression is applied to the image, and reduces its size by 40 to 55 percent (which varies according to the amount of detail in the image). There is a small amount of data loss involved in this compression method because the file size is reduced by a considerable degree. Most people won't be able to see the loss because it doesn't affect the image visually. I have never really seen any loss in my RAW images. However, I've read that some have noticed slightly less highlight detail, so there may be a small amount of dynamic range loss toward the highlights.

Nikon says that this is a "non-reversible" compression, so once you've taken an NEF image, it is permanently compressed and any small amount of compression data loss is permanent. Not to worry though—the compression type used in NEF (RAW) images throws away far less data than any form of JPEG image. Maximum quality will always come from a RAW image.

The image storage capacity reported by my D5000 for RAW (NEF) format is 539 images on an 8 GB SanDisk Extreme III SDHC memory card. See the user's manual on page 215 for a capacity list using a 4 GB SanDisk Extreme III SDHC memory card.

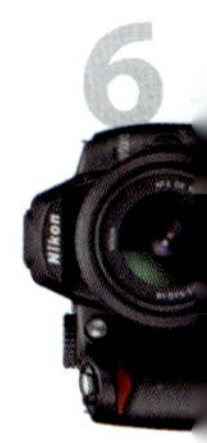

My Personal Software Choices

Nikon ViewNX RAW conversion software is supplied free with the D5000, while Nikon Capture NX2 requires a separate purchase. Capture NX2 has become my favorite conversion software, along with Adobe Photoshop. I use ViewNX to look at my images because it has an excellent browser-type interface and then push them to Capture NX2 for final post-processing. If I need to remove an ugly tree branch from the edge of an otherwise spotless image or a blemish from a person's face, I'll use Photoshop's Clone and Healing tools.

JPEG (Joint Photographic Experts Group) Format

As shown in *figure 11*, the D5000 has three JPEG modes. Each one affects the final quality of the image. Let's look at each mode in detail:

- *JPEG fine* (compression approximately 1:4)
- *JPEG normal* (compression approximately 1:8)
- *JPEG basic* (compression approximately 1:16)

Each of the JPEG modes provides a certain level of *lossy* image compression. The human eye compensates for small color changes quite well, so the JPEG compression algorithm works effectively for viewing by humans. A useful feature of JPEG is that one can vary the file size of the image (via compression) without greatly affecting quality.

JPEG fine (or fine quality JPEG) uses a 1:4 compression ratio, so there is a significant difference in the file size that can be as small as 25 percent of the original size. In this mode, an image can be compressed down to as little as 4 or 5 megabytes without significant loss of image quality. If you decide to shoot in JPEG, this mode will give you the best quality JPEG your camera can produce. Where a *RAW* setting allows only 539 images on an 8-gigabyte memory card, the *JPEG fine* setting raises that to about 1,100 files.

JPEG normal (or normal quality JPEG) uses a 1:8 compression ratio. This makes the D5000 image file as small as 2.5 megabytes. The image quality is still very acceptable in this mode, so if you are just shooting at a party for an average 4x6 printed image size, this mode will allow you to capture a large quantity of images. An 8-gigabyte card will hold about 2,100 JPEG normal image files.

JPEG basic (or basic quality JPEG) uses a 1:16 compression ratio, so the D5000's image file size drops to a 1.25 megabyte JPEG file. Remember, these are full-size files, so you can surely take a lot of pictures. If you are shooting for the Web, or you just want to document an area well, this mode has sufficient quality. My D5000 tells me it can store a whopping 4,200 JPEG basic files on my 8-gigabyte memory card.

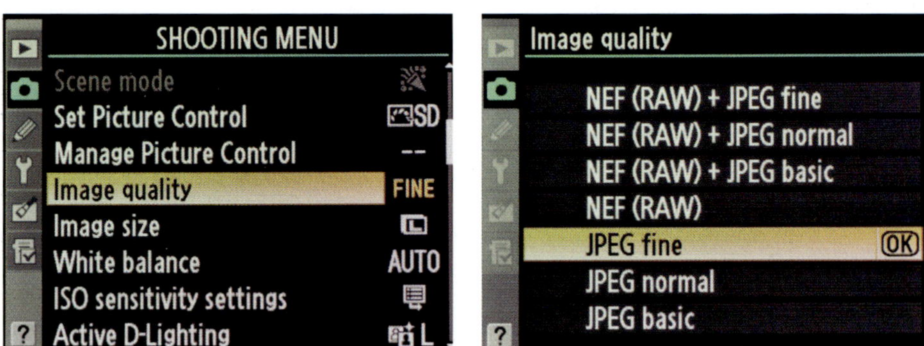

Figure 11 – JPEG *Image quality* selection

Combined NEF and JPEG Shooting (Two Images at Once)

Some shooters use a clever option of storage modes whereby the D5000 takes two images at the same time. NEF (RAW) + JPEG is what it's called. This option gives you the best of both worlds in that you shoot a nice RAW file and a JPEG file each time you press the shutter button. In NEF (RAW) + JPEG fine, my camera's storage drops to about 361 images since it is storing an NEF and a JPEG file at the same time for each picture taken.

You can use the RAW file to store all the image data and later to post-process it into a masterpiece, or you can just use the JPEG file immediately with no adjustment. Many people use one of these three modes quite often. You can have a JPEG to give others immediately and later work on the RAW file for special purposes. Here are the three modes:

- *NEF (RAW) + JPEG fine*
- *NEF (RAW) + JPEG normal*
- *NEF (RAW) + JPEG basic*

There is no need to go into any amount of detail about these modes other than what I have already discussed. The NEF + JPEG modes have the same features as the modes they consist of. In other words, the NEF (RAW) file works in a NEF + JPEG works just like an NEF (RAW) file if you were using the stand-alone NEF (RAW) mode. The JPEG taken in NEF + JPEG mode works just like a stand-alone JPEG shot without a NEF (RAW) file.

Now, let's consider the benefits each of these formats might bring to your photography and which might become your favorite.

Examining the Pros and Cons of NEF and JPEG Formats

There are many discussions on Internet camera forums on the question "Which is the best image format?" To decide which format you may frequently use, why not examine the pros and cons of each? This special section is designed to do just that. We'll examine the two formats available in the D5000: NEF (RAW) and JPEG.

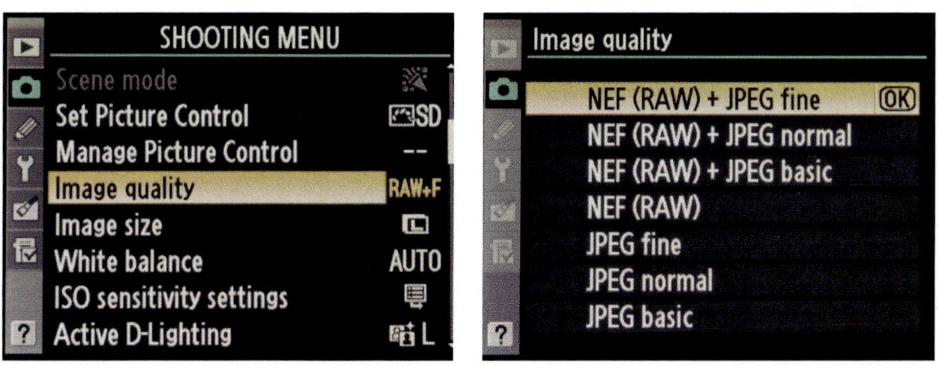

Figure 12 – *NEF (RAW) + JPEG fine Image quality* selection

Nikon Electronic Format — NEF (RAW)

I am an NEF (RAW) photographer about 98 percent of the time. I think of a RAW file as I thought of my slides and negatives a few years ago. It's my original file that must be saved and protected. There are only a couple of problems I can think of with the RAW format:

- You must post-process and convert every image you shoot into a TIFF or JPEG (or another viewable format).
- There is no industry-standard RAW image format, and Nikon has the option of changing the internals of the NEF (RAW) format each time it comes out with a new camera.

Other than those drawbacks, many photographers, myself included, shoot NEF (RAW) for maximum image quality.

It is important that you understand something very different about NEF (RAW) files. They are not really images... yet. Basically, all a RAW file is composed of is black and white sensor data and camera setting information markers. The RAW file is saved in a form that must be converted to another image type to be used in print or on the Web.

When you take a picture in RAW, the camera records the sensor data and markers for how the camera's color, sharpening, and so on are set, but it *does not apply the camera setting information to the image*. In your computer's post-processing software, the image will appear on-screen using the settings you initially set in your

The Pros and Cons of NEF (RAW) Format

NEF (RAW) Pros

- It allows the manipulation of image data to achieve the *highest quality image available* from the camera.
- All original detail stays in the image for future processing needs.
- No conversions, sharpening, sizing, or color rebalancing will be performed by the camera. Your images are untouched and pure!
- You can convert to any of the other image formats by using your computer's much more powerful processor instead of the camera processor.
- You have *much* more control over the final look of the image because *you*, not the camera, are making the decisions.
- It is a 12-bit format for maximum image data.

NEF (RAW) Cons

- It's not often compatible with the publishing industry, except by conversion to another format.
- It requires post-processing by special proprietary software as provided by the camera manufacturer or third-party software programmers.
- The file sizes are larger (so you must have large storage media).
- There is no accepted industry-standard RAW mode. Each camera manufacturer has its own proprietary format. Adobe has a RAW format called DNG (Digital Negative) that might become an industry standard. We'll see!
- The 12-bit format is not really in use; 8-bit is the industry standard.

D5000. However, they are only applied in a temporary manner.

If you do not like the white balance you had selected at the time you took the picture, simply apply a new white balance and the image will be just as if you had used the new white balance setting when you took the picture. If you had low sharpening set in-camera and change it to normal sharpening in-computer, then the image will look just like it would have looked if you had used normal in-camera sharpening when you took the image. You can change sharpening levels in the Picture Control you have selected.

This is quite powerful. Virtually no camera settings are applied to a RAW file in a permanent way. That means you can change the image to completely different settings and the image will be as if you had used the new settings when you first took the picture. This allows for significant flexibility later. If you shot the image initially with the *Standard* Picture Control and now want to use *Vivid*, all you have to do is change the image to *Vivid* and it will be as if you used the *Vivid* Picture Control when you first took the picture. Complete flexibility!

NEF (RAW) is generally used by individuals concerned with maximum image quality and who have time to convert the image in the computer after taking it with the camera.

JPEG Notes

JPEG (.jpg) is the format used by individuals who want excellent image quality but have little time or interest in later post-processing or converting images to another format. They want to use the image immediately when it comes out of the camera, with no major adjustments.

The JPEG format applies whatever camera settings you have chosen to the image when it is taken. It comes out of

The Pros and Cons of JPEG Mode

JPEG Pros

- Maximum number of images on camera card and later on computer hard drive storage.
- Fastest writes from camera memory buffer to memory card storage.
- Absolute compatibility with everything and everybody in imaging.
- Uses the industry standard 8 bits.
- High-quality first-use images.
- No special software needed to use the image right out of the camera (no post-processing).
- Immediate use on websites with minimal processing.
- Easy transfer across I nternet and as e-mail attachments.

JPEG Cons

- JPEG is a lossy format, which means that it permanently throws away image data from compression algorithm losses as you select higher levels of compression (fine, normal, basic).
- You cannot use JPEG to manipulate an image more than once or twice before it degrades to an unusable state. Every time you modify and resave a JPEG image, it loses more data.

the camera ready to use, as long as you have exposed it properly and have all the other settings set in the best way for the image.

Since JPEG is a lossy format, you cannot modify and save an image more than a time or two before ruining it from compression losses. However, since there is no post-processing required later, this format allows much quicker usage of the image. A person shooting a large quantity of images, or someone who does not have the time to convert RAW images, will usually use JPEG. That encompasses a lot of photographers!

While a nature photographer might want to use RAW because they have more time for processing images and wringing the last drop of quality out of them, an event or journalist photographer may not have the time or interest in processing images, so they'll use JPEG.

Final Image Format Ramblings

Which format do I prefer? Why, RAW, of course! But, it does require a bit of a commitment to shoot in this format. The D5000 is simply an image-capturing device, and *you* are the image manipulator. You decide the final format, compression ratios, sizes, color balances, picture controls, and so on. In RAW mode, you have the absolute best image your camera can produce. Your RAW image is not modified by the D5000 and is ready for your personal touch. No in-camera processing allowed!

If you get nothing else from this section of the chapter, remember this: *by letting your camera process the images in any way, it is modifying or throwing away image data*. There is only a finite amount of data for each image that can be stored on your camera and later on the computer. With JPEG mode, your camera is optimizing the image in-camera, according to the assumptions recorded in its memory. Data is being thrown away permanently, in varying amounts.

If you want to keep virtually all the image data that was recorded in the image, you must store your originals in RAW format. Otherwise, you'll never again be able to access that original data to change how it looks. RAW format is the closest thing to a film negative or a transparency that your digital camera can make. And, maintaining all that data is important if you would like to use the image later for modification. If you are a photographer that is concerned with maximum quality, you should probably shoot and store your images in RAW format. Later, when you have the urge to make another masterpiece out of the original RAW image file, you will have *all* of your original data intact for the highest quality.

If you are concerned that the RAW format may change too much over time to be readable by future generations, then you might want to convert your images into TIFF, DNG, or JPEG files. TIFF is best if you want to modify them later. I often save a TIFF version of my best files in addition to the RAW version, just in case RAW changes too much in the future. Why not do a little more research on this subject and decide which you like best.

Image Size

(User's Manual page 64)

Again, there are two methods for selecting the image size: by using the *Shooting Menu* and via the *Information edit* screens. First, I'll cover the *Shooting Menu* method (see *figure 13*).

This menu selection applies only to images captured in the JPEG modes. If you are shooting with your D5000 in an NEF + JPEG mode, it applies only to the JPEG image in the pair. Here's how to select the size of the image:

1. Press the MENU button and select the *Shooting Menu*.
2. Choose *Image size*, and then scroll right.
3. Choose the size of the image.
4. Press the *OK* button.

The *Image size* settings are also found in the *Information edit* screens (see *figure 13A*).

The following steps will help you set or verity the image size using the *Information edit* screens:

1. Press the <**i**> information edit button until you see the *Information edit* screen (on the left in *figure 13A*).
2. Make sure the yellow highlight rectangle is positioned in the *Image size* field.
3. Press the *OK* button.
4. You'll be presented with the second *Image size* screen. It has the list of image size selections mentioned previously. Using the Multi Selector, scroll up or down in the list and make your choice. You'll also notice that the camera gives

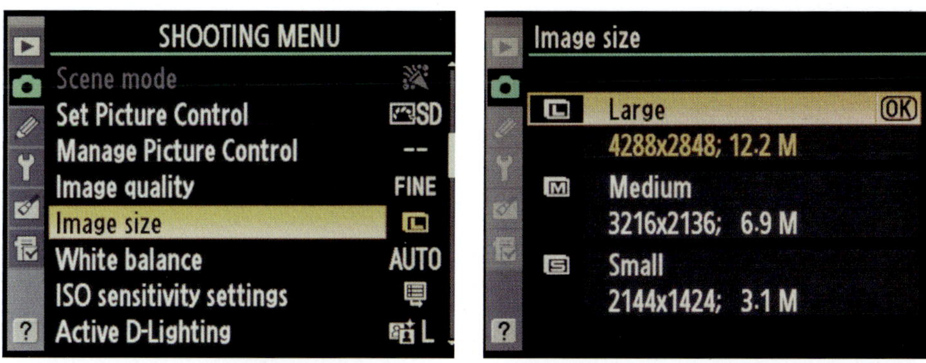

Figure 13 – *Image size* selection

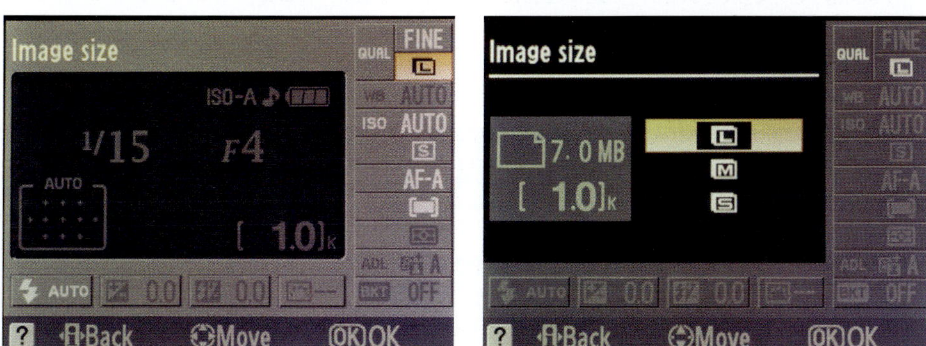

Figure 13A – screens – *Image size*

you a couple of useful pieces of information. Just to the left of the list of image size selections, you'll see information on the approximate image file size (MB) and the number of images your camera's memory card can hold for the current selection. (on the left in *figure 13A*).

5. Once you've made your selection, press the *OK* button. The camera returns to the main *Information edit* screen with your choice showing in the *Image size* field.

The image size affects the megapixel (MP) size of the image. Here are the three settings under *Image size*:

- **L** *(Large) – 4288 x 2848 – 12.2 megapixels*
- **M** *(Medium) – 3216 x 2136 – 6.9 megapixels*
- **S** *(Small) – 2144 x 1424 – 3.1 megapixels*

I've been playing around with these settings for the fun of it. I'm certainly not interested in using my 12.2 MP D5000 as a 6.9 MP or 3.1 MP camera. I suppose there may be some reasons to reduce the MP rating of the camera, but not for me.

If I set the image quality to *JPEG basic* and image size to *Small,* my D5000 will capture 15,500 images on an 8-gigabyte card. The images are 3.1 MP in size (2144 x 1424 = 3,053,056, or 3.1MP) and compressed to the maximum the D5000 will create, but there are a large number of them.

If I were to set off today to walk completely around the earth and I had only one 8-gigabyte memory card to take with me, well, my D5000 will give me over 15,000 images on the one card, so I could at least document my trip very well.

White Balance

(User's Manual pages 96–102)

An entire chapter of this book has been devoted to the subject of white balance. Please turn to chapter 4 for detailed information on this very important subject.

White balance is so important because it makes sure your colors are accurate: whites are white, greens are green, and so on. These are the white balance modes:

In *figure 14*, you will see three screens. The middle screen allows you to select one of the white balance modes according to the type of light in which you are shooting. For general shooting, auto is generally sufficient. However, if you want the images to match each other in color response, it is important to use a preset white balance mode like Sunlight or

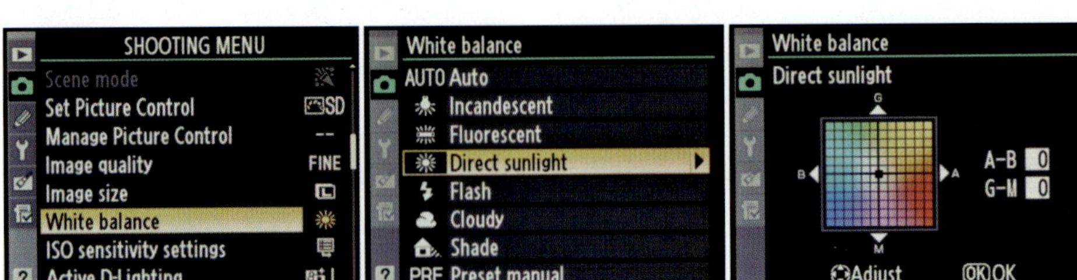

Figure 14 – *White balance* selection and fine-tuning screens

Flash. If you are really critical about your images, the *PRE* ambient light measurement method is best.

You can also use the *Information edit* screens to set the white balance. *Figure 14A* shows the screens used to select the *Auto WB* setting.

Use these steps to configure the white balance to *Auto*:

1. Press the <**i**> information edit button until you see the *Information edit* screen (on the left in *figure 14A*).
2. Make sure that the yellow highlighted rectangle is positioned in the *White balance (WB)* field.
3. Press the *OK* button.
4. You'll be presented with the second *White balance* screen. It has a list of WB selections. Choose the WB setting you want to use for the current ambient light and use the Multi Selector to select it.
5. Press the *OK* button. The camera returns to the main *Information edit* screen with your choice showing after the WB setting.

You can select from a total of eight white balance settings with the camera controls. Remember, this subject is so important that an entire chapter has been devoted to it. I've given you only the basics here, so please be sure to read chapter 3 for more detailed information.

White Balance Modes

AUTO Auto White Balance, 3500-8000K.

Incandescent, 3000K.

Fluorescent, 4200K.

Direct Sunlight, 5200K.

Flash, 5400K.

Cloudy, 6000K.

Shade, 8000K.

PRE PRE (Preset Manual), used to measure WB for the actual ambient light. If no measurement is taken, the value used is whatever was last stored in camera WB memory location d-0.

6

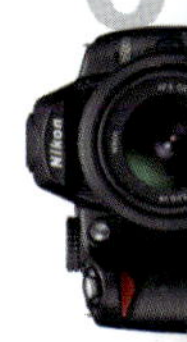

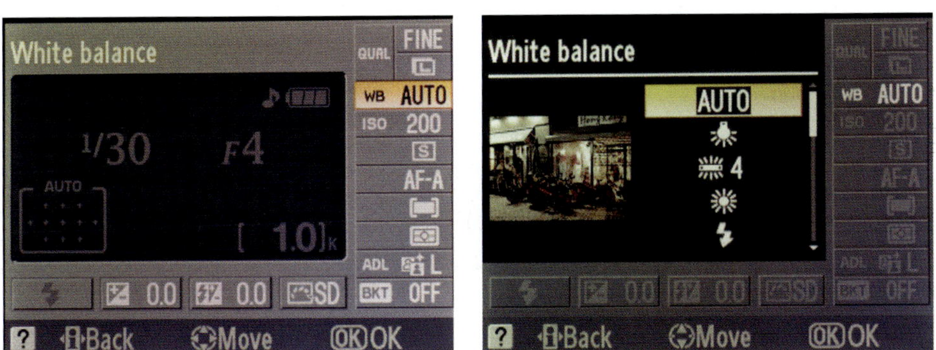

Figure 14A – Selecting auto white balance

ISO Sensitivity Settings

(User's Manual pages 74–75 and 149)
After this section on how to set the ISO sensitivity settings, you'll find a section called "When and Why Should I Use ISO-AUTO?" It goes beyond just how to set ISO-AUTO and explains the reasons you may or may not want to use it with your style of photography. Now, let's get to the configuration information.

An ISO number, such as 200 or 3200, is an agreed-upon sensitivity for the image-capturing sensor. Virtually everywhere one goes in the world, all camera ISO numbers will mean the same thing. With that fact established, camera bodies and lenses can be designed to take advantage of the ISO sensitivity ranges they will have to deal with. Standards are good!

In the D5000, the ISO numbers are sensitivity equivalents. To make it very simple, ISO "sensitivity" is the digital equivalent of film speed. *The higher the ISO sensitivity, the less light needed for the exposure.* A high ISO setting allows faster shutter speeds and smaller apertures.

First, let's look at the *Shooting Menu* screens for setting ISO sensitivity and then we'll consider the *Information edit* screens too.

Figure 15 shows the three *Shooting Menu* screens used to change the camera's ISO.

Notice in the screen on the right that you have a scrollable list of ISO values; although they can't all be seen in the figure, they range from LO 1.0 (100 ISO) to HI 1.0 (6400 ISO). The "normal" ISO range for the D5000 is 200 to 3200 ISO. Here's how to select your ISO from the list of available ISO numbers:

1. Press the MENU button and select the *Shooting Menu*.
2. Choose *ISO sensitivity settings*, and then scroll right.
3. Choose *ISO sensitivity*, and then scroll right.
4. Choose an ISO number.
5. Press the *OK* button.

The standard minimum ISO sensitivity setting for the D5000 is 200 ISO. You can adjust the camera in its 100 to 6400 ISO range, in 1/3 steps.

Figure 15A shows the *Information edit* screens to select and ISO.

Follow these steps to make the selection:

1. Press the <**i**> information edit button until you see the *Information edit* screen (on the left in *figure 15A*).

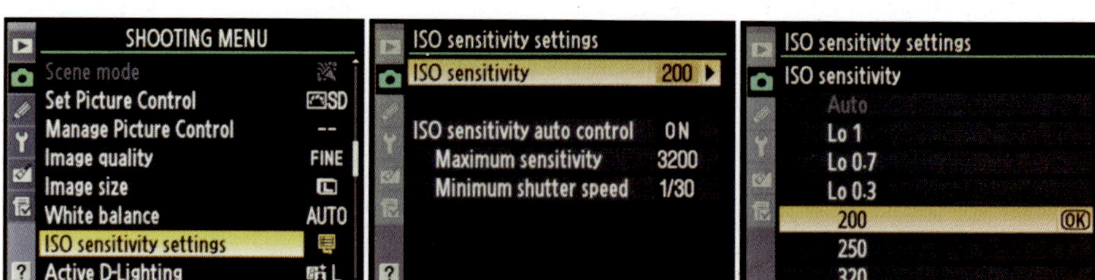

Figure 15 – *Shooting Menu* screens to set ISO

2. Make sure the yellow highlight rectangle is positioned in the *ISO* field.
3. Press the *OK* button.
4. You'll be presented with the second *ISO sensitivity* screen. It has a list of ISO selections. Choose the ISO you want to use and scroll with the Multi Selector to select it.
5. Press the *OK* button. The camera returns to the main *Information edit* screen with your choice showing in the *ISO* field.

Select your favorite ISO setting either with the *Information edit* screens or with the *Shooting Menu*'s *ISO sensitivity* settings.

If you would like, you can also simply let your camera decide which ISO it would like to use. Let's consider this often-misunderstood feature in detail.

Which ISO Setting Do I Use?

I often use *ISO Lo 1.0* (100 ISO equivalent) because I appreciate the smoothness and lack of noise that setting provides. As a stock shooter, I want to avoide noise in all of my images, so I go with the lowest ISO my camera allows if the light is bright enough. In thousands of shots, I have never seen a problem with shooting at that "nonstandard" setting. I have read that some feel there is less dynamic range in the image if the nonstandard settings are used. However, I have not found that to be true. ISO 200 is a stop faster, so it provides a little more speed for handholding the camera. My most critical work is always done on a tripod, so I do not worry about slow shutter speeds as often as a "handholder" would. I can just detect the smallest amounts of noise showing up in images at ISO 200 when I underexpose by as little as 1/3 stop. You'll have to test your images and discover your noise tolerance level. I am an anti-noise fanatic. You may not be.

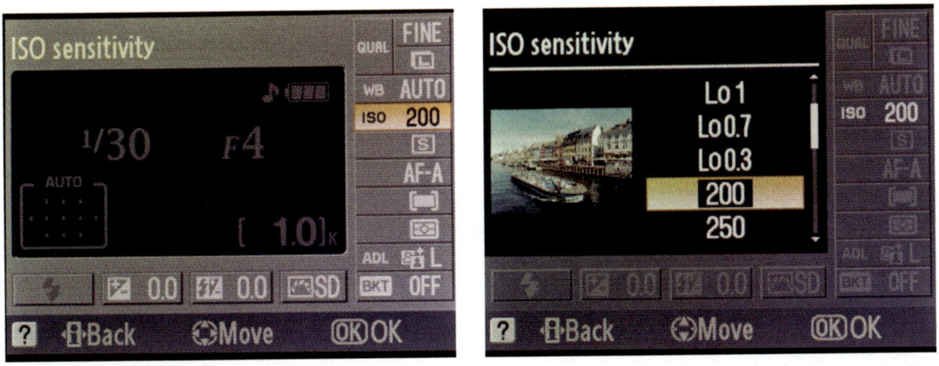

Figure 15A – Selecting ISO sensitivity level 200

ISO Sensitivity Auto Control (ISO-AUTO)

You may have noticed in the middle screen *figure 15* that there is another setting available, *ISO sensitivity auto control*, which defaults to off. This was known on earlier Nikon cameras as ISO-AUTO.

This setting is used to allow the camera to control the ISO according to the light levels sensed by the camera meter. *Figure 16* shows the *Shooting Menu* screens used to enable ISO-AUTO. I can find no *Information edit* screens to set ISO-AUTO.

To enable ISO-Auto, do the following:

1. Press the MENU button and select the *Shooting Menu*.
2. Choose *ISO sensitivity settings*, and then scroll right.
3. Choose *ISO sensitivity auto control*, and then scroll right.
4. Select *On*.
5. Press the *OK* button.

Once you've turned ISO-AUTO on, you should set two values, according to how you shoot:

- *Maximum sensitivity*
- *Minimum shutter speed*

Maximum sensitivity – This setting is a safeguard for you because it allows you to control how high the ISO will go when you shoot. If you would prefer that ISO-AUTO not exceed a certain ISO number, simply select from the list shown in the screen on the right in *figure 16A*.

To select the maximum ISO sensitivity that your camera can use while in ISO-AUTO, simply follow these steps:

1. Press the MENU button and select the *Shooting Menu*.
2. Choose *ISO sensitivity settings*, and then scroll right.
3. Choose *Maximum sensitivity,* and then scroll right.
4. Select the ISO maximum sensitivity that you want the camera to use.
5. Press the *OK* button.

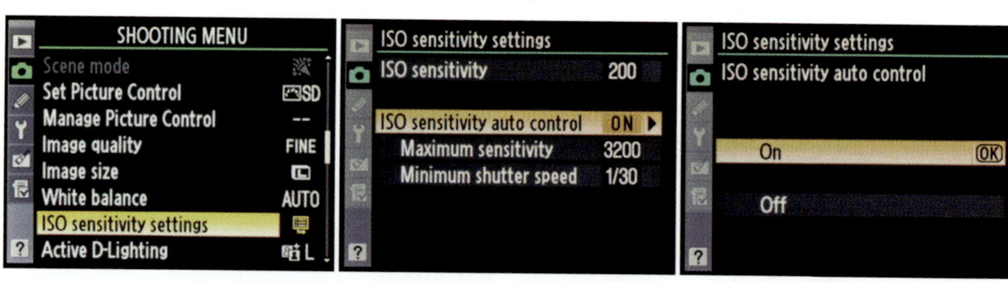

Figure 16 – *Shooting Menu* screens to set ISO-AUTO ranges

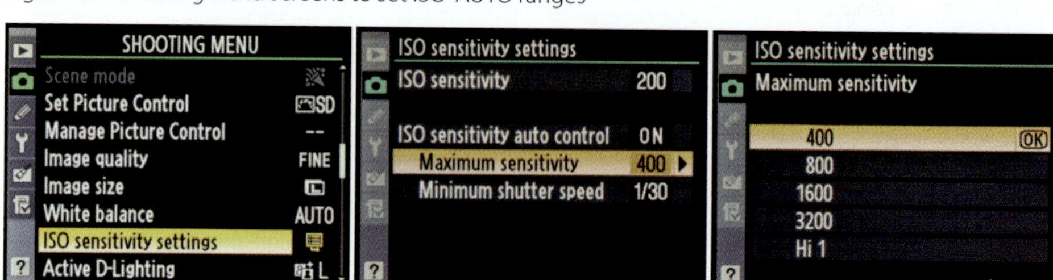

Figure 16A – ISO-AUTO *Maximum sensitivity* settings

You'll note that there are only five available settings:

- *400*
- *800*
- *1600*
- *3200*
- *HI 1*

Whichever one of these settings you choose will be the maximum ISO the camera will use to get a good exposure when the light drops. To protect the image from excessive noise, it won't exceed this ISO level. Once again, you'll have to determine your personal noise-level tolerance to select one of these settings. *The higher the ISO, the higher the potential noise level.*

ISO Settings and Noise

In testing the Nikon D5000 for noise, I find that it makes entirely usable images, with low noise, all the way up to ISO 1600. However, being noise sensitive, I do not often set *ISO-AUTO Maximum sensitivity* higher than ISO 800. I will leave it set to ISO 400 most of the time. If you are an event shooter who must get the image no matter what, then open the ISO maximum up to its highest levels. The camera will use them only when it can't get the shot otherwise.

Minimum shutter speed – Since shutter speed controls how sharp an image can be, due to camera shake and subject movement, you'll need some control over the minimum shutter speed allowed while ISO-AUTO is turned on. See *figure 16B* for a list of shutter speeds.

You can select a shutter speed from the list to set the minimum shutter speed the camera will allow when the light diminishes. The available shutter speeds run from 1 second to 1/2000 second. Here are the steps:

1. Press the MENU button and select the *Shooting Menu*.
2. Choose *ISO sensitivity settings*, and then scroll right.
3. Choose *Minimum shutter speed*, and then scroll right.
4. Select a *Minimum shutter speed,* keeping in mind that most people have problems handholding a camera below 1/30 second.
5. Click the *OK* button.

When you have enabled ISO-AUTO, the top *Information edit* screen will show *ISO-A* next to the battery symbol, and the viewfinder will show *ISO-AUTO*. When you first activate the meter, the ISO-AUTO notifications will often blink once per second until the meter goes off.

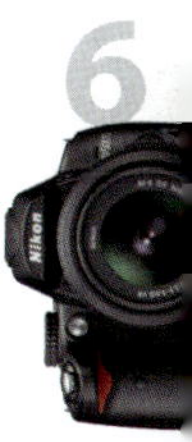

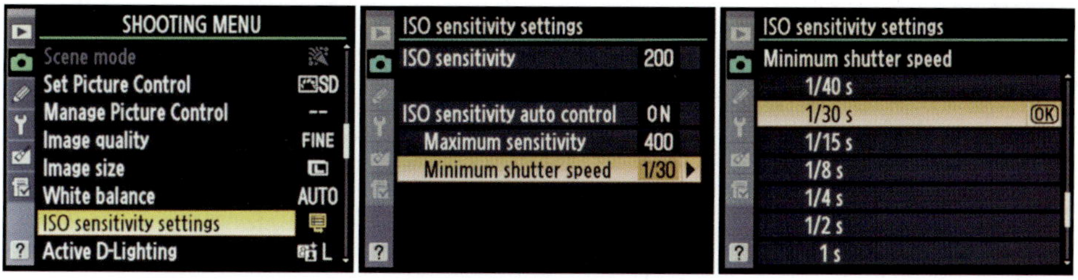

Figure 16B – ISO-AUTO *Minimum shutter speed*

The blinking seems to stop sometimes or become intermittent. When I first activate the meter, the camera will sometimes start blinking the reminder immediately, while at other times it seems to wait a few seconds before it starts. The blinking is a reminder to turn ISO-AUTO off when not needed so that you don't get unnecessarily noisy images.

Note on ISO-AUTO

When you enable ISO-AUTO, it might be a good idea to also enable *High ISO Noise Reduction*. This is especially true if you leave the camera set to the higher ISO values above 800. Otherwise, you may have excessive noise when the light drops. *High ISO Noise Reduction* will be discussed later in this chapter.

When and Why Should I Use ISO-AUTO?

How much automation do you need to produce consistently excellent images? Let's explore how and when automatic self-adjusting ISO might improve or degrade your images. What is this feature all about? When and why should you use it? Are there any compromises in image quality in this mode?

Normally, you will set your camera to a particular ISO number, such as 200 or 400, and shoot your images. As the light diminishes (or in the deep shade) you might increase the ISO number to allow the handheld camera to continue making images.

If you are in circumstances in which you absolutely *must* get the shot, ISO-AUTO will work nicely. Here are a few scenarios:

Scenario #1: Let's say you are a photojournalist and you're shooting flash pictures of a famous politician or celebrity as he quickly disembarks from his airplane, walks into the terminal, and departs in a limousine. Under those circumstances, you will have little time to check your ISO settings or shutter speeds and will be shooting in widely varying light conditions.

Scenario #2: You are a wedding photographer in a church that does not allow the use of flash. As you follow the bride and groom from the dark inner rooms of the church out into the lobby and finally up to the altar, your light conditions will be varying constantly. You have no time to deal with the fluctuations in light by changing your ISO since things are moving too quickly.

Scenario #3: You are at a party, and you want some pictures. You want to use flash, but the built-in pop-up flash may not be powerful enough to reach across the room at low ISO settings. You really don't want to be bothered with camera configuration at this time, but you still want some well-exposed images. Light will vary as you move around the room, talking, laughing, and snapping pictures.

These scenarios represent excellent environments for ISO-AUTO. The camera will use your normal settings (such as your normal ISO), shutter speed, and aperture *until* the light will not allow those settings to provide an accurate exposure. Only then will the camera raise or lower the ISO value to keep functioning within the shutter/aperture parameters you have set.

Look at ISO-AUTO as a fail-safe for times when you must get the shot but have little time to deal with camera settings, or when you don't want to vary the shutter/aperture settings but still want to be assured of a well-exposed image.

Of course, if, due to lack of experience, you are unsure of how to use the "correct" ISO for the light level, don't be afraid to experiment with this mode. At the very worst, all you might get are noisier than normal images. However, it may not be a good idea to depend on this mode over the long term because noisy images are not very desirable.

Note

ISO-AUTO is available only when you have the mode dial set to P, S, A, or M mode. It grays out when you're using the scene modes because the camera then controls the ISO sensitivity.

Use ISO-AUTO Only When Needed

Unless you are a private detective shooting handheld telephoto images from your car or a photojournalist or sports photographer who must get the shot every time regardless of maximum quality, I personally would not recommend leaving your camera set to ISO-AUTO. Use it only when you really need to get the shot under any circumstances.

The Drawbacks to ISO-AUTO

Are there any drawbacks to using ISO-AUTO? Maybe. It really depends on how widely varying the light conditions will be when you are shooting. Most of the time your camera will maintain normal ISO range settings in ISO-AUTO, so your images will be their normal low-noise, sharp masterpieces.

Just be aware that ISO-AUTO can and will push your ISO into a range that causes noisier images when light levels drop if you've set the ISO *Maximum sensitivity* to high levels. Use it with this understanding and you'll do fine. The maximum ISO-AUTO setting is 6400 ISO (*Hi 1*), unless you have set the maximum to a lower number. Make sure you understand this or you might get some noisy images.

ISO-AUTO is yet another feature in our powerful Nikon cameras. Maybe not everyone needs this "failsafe" feature, but for those who do, it must be there. I will use it myself in circumstances where getting the shot is the most important thing and where light levels may get too low for normal ISO image making.

Even if you think you might only use it from time to time, do learn how to use it for those times. Experiment with ISO-AUTO. It's fun and can be useful.

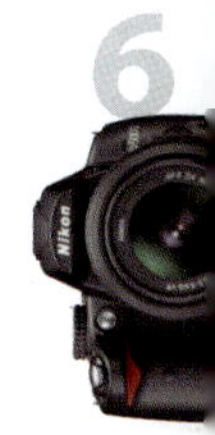

Active D-Lighting

(User's Manual pages 94 and 95)

Often the range of light around our image's subject is broader than our D5000's sensor can capture. Where the D5000 might be able to capture 4 to 7 stops of light, the light out in the world on a bright summer day might equal 12 stops in range. The contrast can be too high.

Since the D5000 cannot grab the full range of light, and many people use the histogram to expose for the highlights, some of the image detail will be lost in shadow. The D5000 allows you to "D-Light" the image and bring out additional shadow detail to lower the image contrast.

As usual, there are two ways to select *Active D-Lighting*: using the *Shooting Menu* and the *Information edit* menu. Let's examine them.

Here's how to select a level of *Active D-Lighting* using the *Shooting Menu* (see *figure 17*):

1. Press the MENU button and select the *Shooting Menu*.
2. Select *Active D-Lighting*, and then scroll right.
3. Select the level that you want to use, keeping in mind that the higher the D-Lighting setting, the lower the image contrast.
4. Press the *OK* button.

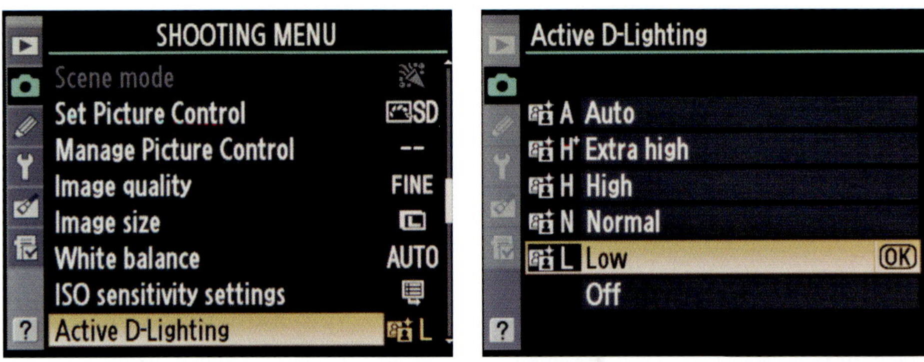

Figure 17 – *Active D-Lighting* screens

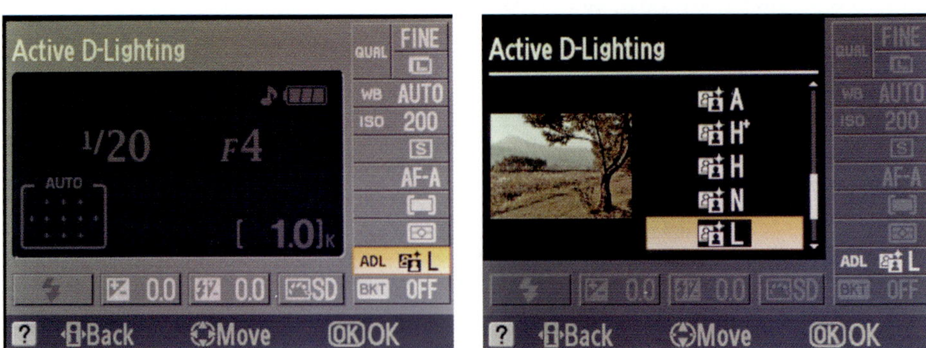

Figure 17A – Setting *Active D-Lighting* to low

Use these steps to configure *Active D-Lighting* via the *Information edit* screens (see *figure 17A*):

1. Press the <**i**> information edit button until you see the *Information edit* screen (on the left in *figure 17A*).
2. Make sure the yellow highlight rectangle is positioned in the *Active D-Lighting* field.
3. Press the *OK* button.
4. You'll be presented with the second *Active D-Lighting* screen. It has a list of D-Lighting selections. Choose your favorite D-Lighting level and then use the Multi Selector to select it.
5. Press the *OK* button. The camera returns to the main *Information edit* screen showing your choice at the end of the *Active D-Lighting* field.

Active D-Lighting has these settings:

- AUTO *Auto*
- *H* Extra high*
- *H High*
- *N Normal*
- *L Low*
- *Off (no Active D-Lighting)*

If you are familiar with Nikon Capture NX2, you may know how D-Lighting works because it's a function of that software. You can use it to bring up "lost" shadow detail, at the expense of adding noise in the darker areas recovered.

Active D-Lighting will bring out detail in areas of your image that are hidden in shadow due to excessive image contrast. *Figure 17B* shows a series of four images with D-Lighting set to various levels.

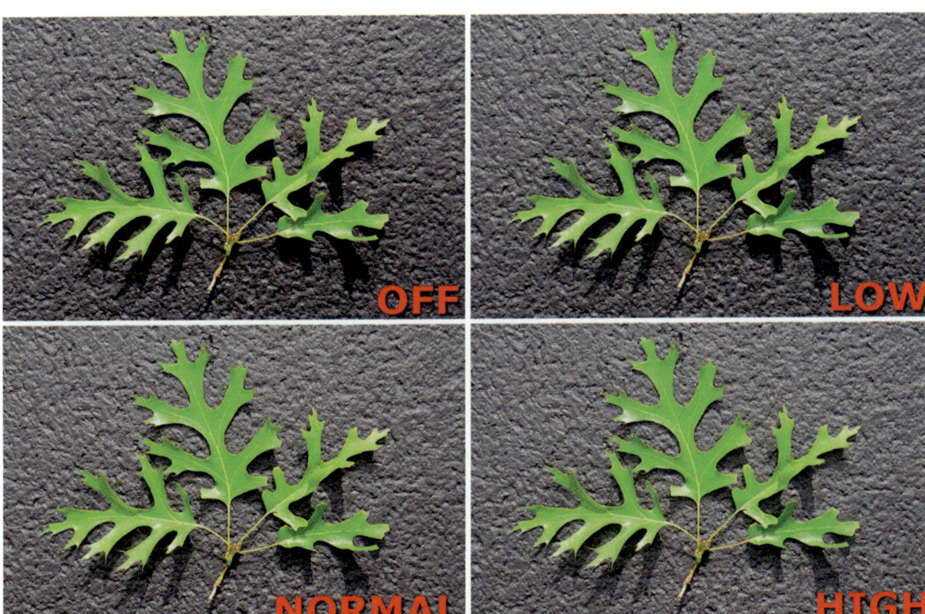

Figure 17B – Four example *Active D-Lighting* images: Off, Low, Normal, High

In addition to the four levels shown in *figure 17B*, the D5000 has *Extra high* and *Auto* available. *Extra high* simply goes a step farther in reducing shadows. *Auto* makes a decision based on the detected range of light in the image. *Auto* may cause the amount of D-Lighting to vary with each image, per the camera's decision. Use *Auto* only if you fully understand what is happening with D-Lighting. Otherwise, you may get unexpected results.

How I Use *Active D-Lighting*

I like D-Lighting, however, I only use it on *Low* unless there is a special need. D-Lighting tends to expand the dynamic range of the image. It not only opens up the shadow details, it also seems to protect the highlights, so they don't blow out as quickly. If you are shooting on a bright sunny day, using *Active D-Lighting* will improve your images because there is so much contrast. However, I have noticed that using D-Lighting at higher levels will start to make an image look unnatural. The human eye expects that there will be little detail in shadows. If you see a picture that normally would have dark shadows and yet the shadows have detail, your brain might just do a double take. It can look weird. Also, I find that skin tones tend to get very pink looking at higher *Active D-Lighting* levels.

You'll need to experiment with the *Active D-Lighting* settings to see which you like best. These options have the effect of lowering contrast, and many people do not like low-contrast images. Also, anytime you recover lost detail from shadows, there will be extra noise in the areas recovered. So watch the noise!

Active D-Lighting and Scene Modes

Active D-Lighting is not available when you are using the scene modes. The camera takes over that functionality when the mode dial is not in P, S, A, or M mode.

Auto Distortion Control

Lenses sometimes can slightly distort an image at different zoom settings. The two main types of distortion are pincushion and barrel.

Barrel distortion causes lines in the image to bulge outward like the curves on the side of a barrel. This is normally caused by wide-angle settings. Pincushion is the opposite. Imagine an hourglass shape, with the sides curving in. That is an extreme version of pincushion distortion. Zooming all the way out on a lens—making it a telephoto—can cause pincushion distortion. Of course, lenses don't normally have large amounts of either of these types of distortion or people wouldn't buy them. However, many lenses have visible amounts at extreme ends of their zoom ranges, especially low-cost lenses.

You can manually adjust a distorted image in-camera for both of these effects using the *Retouch Menu*. Or you can use software in-computer to do the same. If you are unsure, you have two courses of action:

- Don't worry about it because it's not usually a big problem. If you aren't seeing a lot of bowed lines that you know should be straight, then your lens is fine.
- Turn on *Auto distortion control* in your *Shooting Menu*.

Auto distortion control goes right along with the dual personality of this D5000 camera. Since you're clearly more interested in photography than many, having acquired a much more advanced DSLR camera, you may want to learn how to deal with lens distortions eventually. However, in the meantime, you can let your camera help you until you're ready to deal with it yourself.

If you turn *Auto distortion control* on, the D5000 will attempt to correct for lens distortions automatically. Just be aware of one important thing: When a lens distortion is corrected, the outside edges of the image might have to be removed by the camera during the correction process. It can make your images slightly smaller than their normal 4288x2848 pixel size because the camera compensates for the distortion effects by pushing or pulling the edges of the image in the opposite direction of the lens distortion. When a lens distortion correction takes place, the image might be slightly rounded or sunken in on the edges. The camera will crop off the edges to restore the image to its normal rectangular shape. According to how much cropping takes place, your image will get a little smaller. The more pronounced the distortion is, the more cropping must be done by the camera. Don't worry much about it; the camera is not going to turn your 12-megapixel images into 6-megapixel images. Just a small reduction usually does it.

Here are the steps for turning *Auto distortion control* on and off (see *figure 18*):

1. Press the MENU button and select the *Shooting Menu*.
2. Select *Auto distortion control*, and then scroll to the right.
3. Select *On* or *Off* from the list.
4. Press the *OK* button.

With *Auto distortion control* enabled, your D5000 is now lens distortion self-correcting. Cool stuff!

Experiment With *Auto Distortion Control*

Shoot some images of straight lines (for example, buildings). Zoom your lens in and out for different test pictures. Walk close and walk farther away. See if any of the lens positions cause lines to curve in one direction or the other. If not, don't worry about *Auto distortion control*. If you see curves where there should be straight lines, turn it on. Later, when you get more familiar with post-processing your images, you can correct the lens distortions yourself.

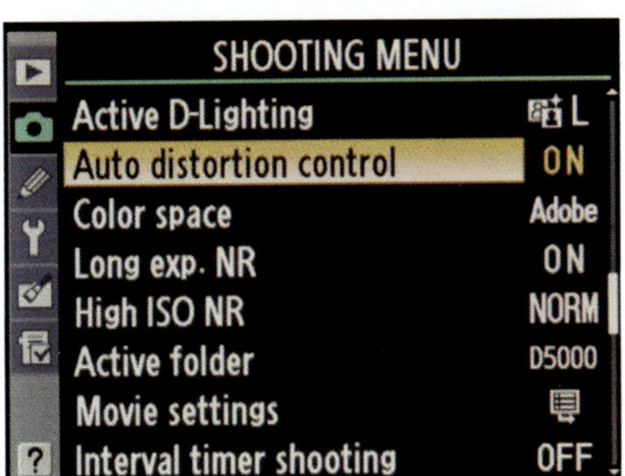

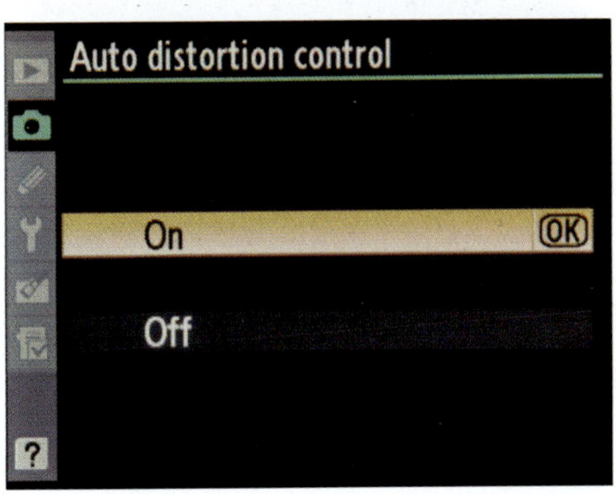

Figure 18 – Enabling *Auto distortion control*

Color Space

(User's Manual page 150)
Color spaces are an interesting and important part of digital photography. They help your images fit into a much broader range of imaging devices. Software, printers, monitors, and other devices recognize what color space is attached to your image and use it, along with other color profiles, to help balance the image to the correct output colors for the device in use. The two available color spaces each has a different *gamut*, or range, of color. Here's how to select your favorite color space (see *figure 19*):

1. Press the MENU button and select the *Shooting Menu*.
2. Select *Color space*, and then scroll right.
3. Select the color space that you want to use, keeping in mind that *Adobe RGB* has a larger color gamut.
4. Press the *OK* button.

The Nikon D5000 camera uses these two color space settings:

- *sRGB*
- *Adobe RGB*

Adobe RGB uses colors from a broader selection of the total color range. It has a wider gamut. If you are taking images that might later be printed, *Adobe RGB* is the best color space selection to use.

Adobe RGB Is for Me!

I personally always use *Adobe RGB* since I shoot a lot of nature with a wide range of color. I want as accurate color as my camera will give me. *Adobe RGB* has a wider range of colors, or gamut, so it can be more accurate when a wide range of colors is present in my image's subject.

There are some drawbacks to using *Adobe RGB*, though. The *sRGB* color space is widely used in printing and display devices. If you try to print directly to some inkjet printers using the *Adobe RGB* color space, the colors may not be as brilliant as with *sRGB*. If you aren't going to modify your images out-of-camera but just take them directly to print, you may want to use *sRGB*. If you shoot JPEGs only for computer display, it might be better to stay with *sRGB* for everyday shooting.

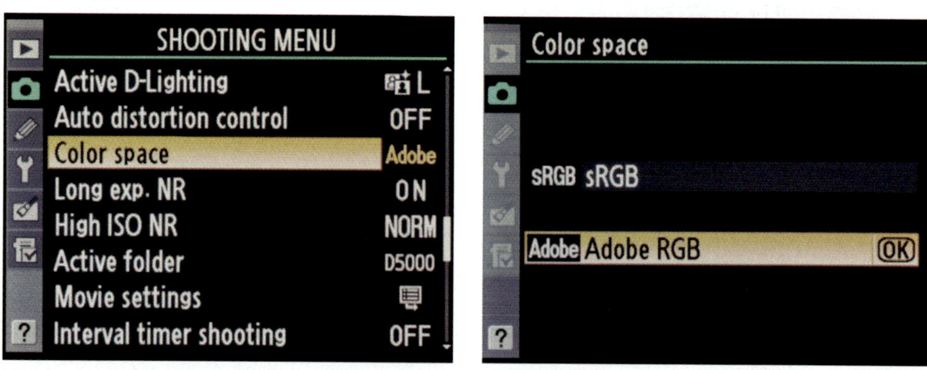

Figure 19 – *Color space* screens

To get technical for a moment, *Adobe RGB* contains about 50 percent of the CIELAB color space, while sRGB only has 35 percent. CIELAB color space is designed to approximate the color range of human vision. *Adobe RGB* gives your images access to significantly higher levels of cyans (bluish) and greens. That's what "wider gamut" means.

If you are a RAW shooter and regularly post-process your images, you should use *Adobe RGB*. You will then have a wider gamut of colors to work with and can make your images the best they can be. Later, you can convert your carefully crafted images to print with a good color profile and get great results from inkjet printers and other printing devices.

So, here's a rough guide:

- Many JPEG shooters use *sRGB*.
- Many RAW shooters use *Adobe RGB*.

This is not a hard-and-fast rule, but many people use these settings according to their style of shooting. I shoot RAW, so I use *Adobe RGB*. If you are shooting for money (such as for stock imaging), most clients expect that you'll be using *Adobe RGB*. It has more colors, so it's the quality standard.

Long Exposure NR

(User's Manual page 151)

Nikon knows its sensors well and feels that images taken at exposures longer than 8 seconds may exhibit more noise than is acceptable for normal use. Two settings are provided for *Long exp. NR* (long exposure noise reduction), as shown in *figure 20*. Here's how to turn it on and off:

1. Press the MENU button and select the *Shooting Menu*.
2. Select *Long exp. NR*, and then scroll right.
3. Select *On* or *Off*.
4. Press the *OK* button.

The two choices are as follows:

- *On*
- *Off*

On: When you select *On* and your exposure goes over 8 seconds, the D5000 will take two exposures with the exact same time for each. The first exposure is the normal picture-taking exposure. The second is a *black frame subtraction* exposure, in which an image is made for the same length of time as the first one but

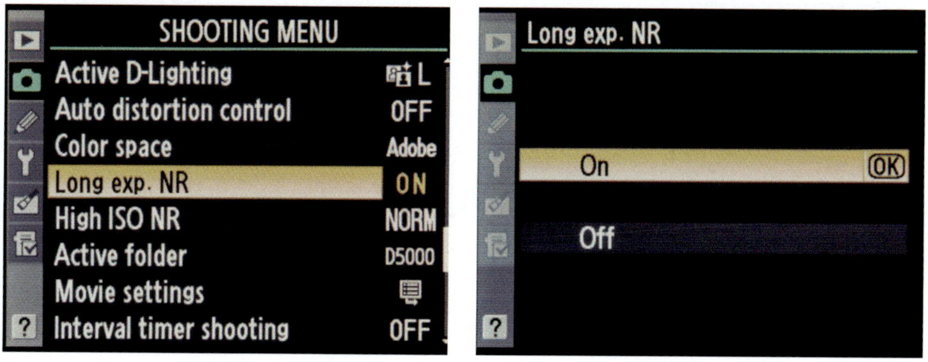

Figure 20 – *Long exposure NR* screens

with the shutter closed. The noise in the second, black frame, image is examined and subtracted from the original image. It's really quite effective and beats having to blur the image to get rid of noise. I've taken exposures of around 30 seconds and had perfectly usable results. The only drawback is that the exposure time is doubled because two exposures are taken, one right after the other.

When the second black frame exposure is being taken, the words *Job nr* will blink in the viewfinder. During this second exposure while *Job nr* is flashing, you cannot use the camera. If you turn it off while *Job nr* is flashing, the camera still keeps the first image; it just does not do any noise reduction on it.

If long exposure noise reduction is on, the frame advance rate may slow down and the capacity of the in-camera memory buffer will drop.

Off: If you select *Off*, then of course you will have no noise reduction with long exposures.

Recommendation

I always leave long exposure noise reduction turned on. I've found that the black frame subtraction method it uses gives me much higher-quality images with long exposures. *Figure 21* an example image of a lightning shot taken with the shutter open for 30 seconds to give time for a lightning flash. It has no appreciable noise.

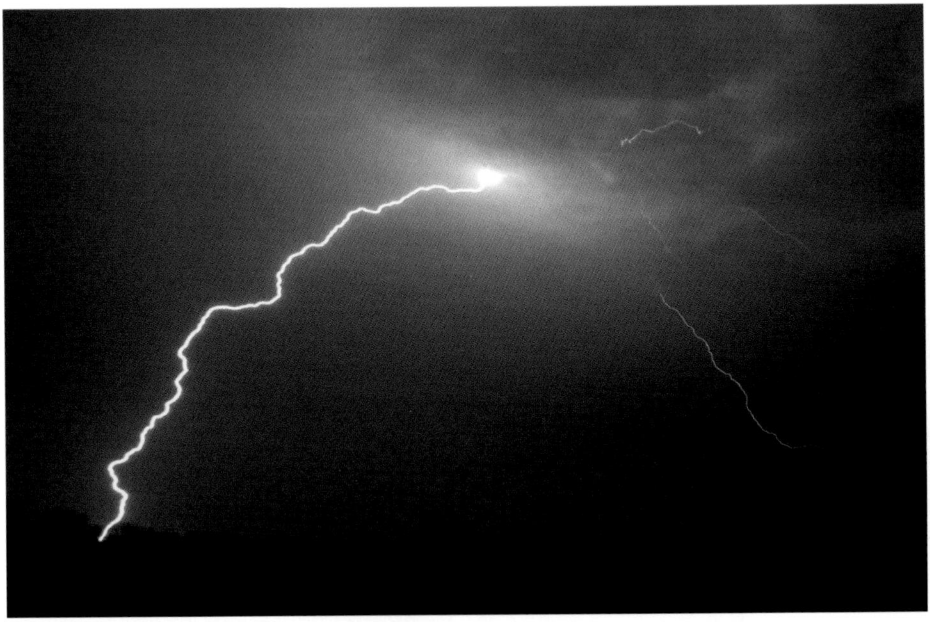

Figure 21 – Lightning shot with shutter open for 30 seconds

High ISO Noise Reduction

(User's Manual page 151)

The D5000 has better noise control than most cameras, so it is able to shoot up to ISO 800 with little noise. However, no digital camera is completely without noise, so it's a good idea to use some noise reduction above a certain level of exposure gain. With the D5000, the ISO can go up to 800 without reduction. After that, you should choose to allow or disallow high ISO noise reduction (NR). Here are the steps to enable the *High ISO NR* setting (see *figure 22*):

1. Press the MENU button and select the *Shooting Menu*.
2. Select *High ISO NR*, and then scroll right.
3. Select one of the noise reduction levels.
4. Press the *OK* button.

Here are the selections:

- *High*
- *Normal*
- *Low*
- *Off*

For any of these settings except *Off*, high ISO noise reduction will be performed starting at ISO 800. You'll need to shoot some high ISO exposures and decide for yourself whether you are comfortable with *High*, *Normal*, *Low*, or

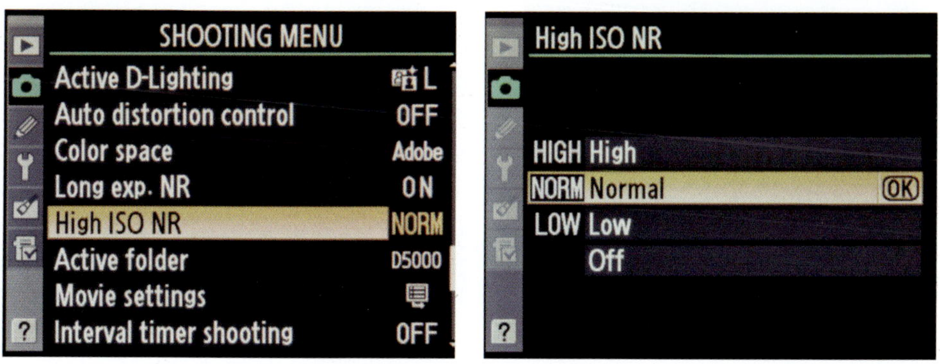

Figure 22 – *High ISO NR* selection

even *Off*. In *figure 23* is an image taken at a worst-case 3200 ISO with NR set to *Off*. The same image is then shown at *Low*, *Normal*, and *High* settings.

Even if you turn *High ISO NR* off, the D5000 will still apply NR when you exceed 3200 ISO. The official starting point for forced high ISO noise reduction is Hi 0.3, which is 1/3 step above 3200 ISO. There are two other 1/3 stop levels above Hi 0.3, namely Hi 0.7, and Hi 1.0. Hi 1 is approximately the same as ISO 6400.

Note on *High ISO NR*

If you have *High ISO NR* turned on, your in-camera memory buffer for images shot rapidly will be reduced by one image.

Recommendation

I leave *High ISO NR* set to *Low*. I do want some noise reduction at any level above 800 ISO. However, since any form of noise reduction blurs the image, I don't go too far with it. Why not test a few images at high ISO settings with NR turned on. You may like the output of *High*, or you might prefer *Normal* or *Low*.

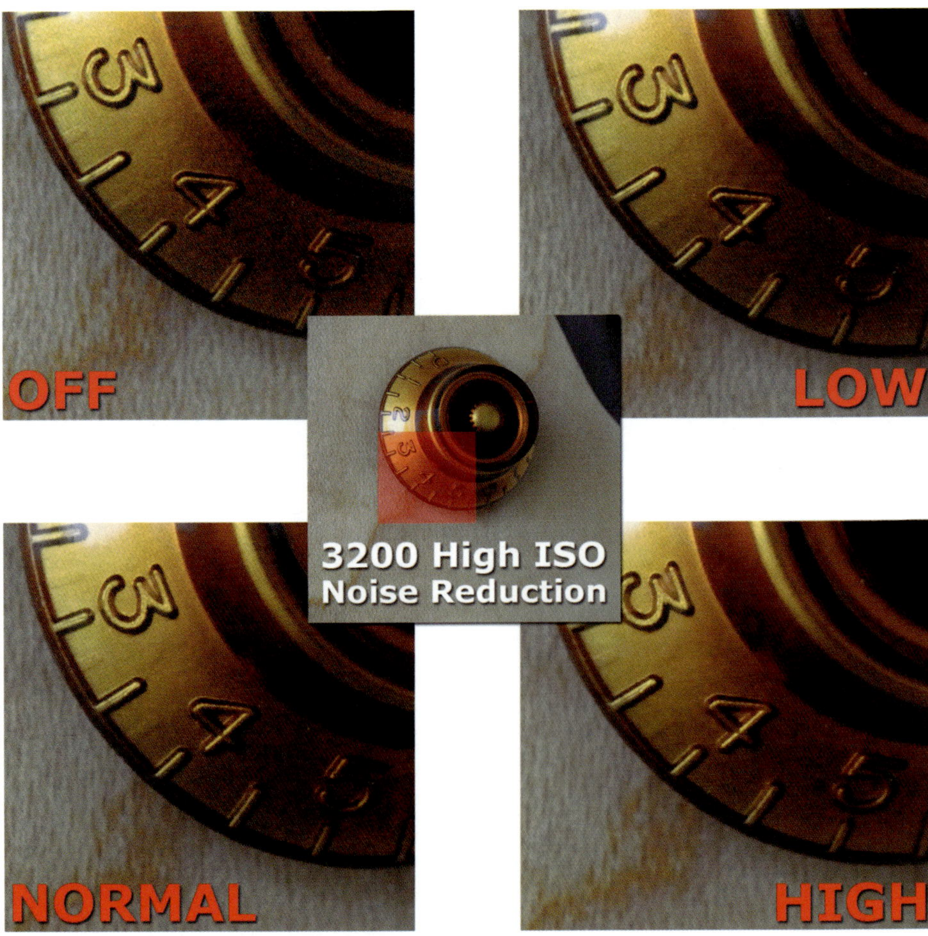

Figure 23 – A 3200 ISO image on all four settings

Active Folder

(User's Manual page 169)

The camera creates a folder named D5000 on your memory card. This folder can contain up to 999 images. If you feel that you might shoot more than 999 images on the current memory card, you might want to create a new folder, such as DRY01 (my initials plus 01) or FLDR9. Whatever name you can think of that uses only five of the characters available in the naming screen will work. Folder names are limited to five characters within the camera but show up as eight-digit names on the SD memory card.

On the memory card, you'll notice that the folder names are preceded by a three-digit number. So the name of your D5000 folder will look like this: 100D5000. If your folder ever contains 999 images, the camera will create a new folder with the same name except it will increment the digits it added to the front of the name. So, exceeding 999 images in a folder named 100D5000 will cause the camera to automatically create a new folder named 101D5000. Interestingly, the D5000 treats any new folders it creates as an extension of the first folder. This allows you to continue shooting a certain style of images and have them stay in the correct folder. If you create and select a new folder name, the D5000 will do the same with it.

This is a good way to isolate certain types of images on a long photographic outing. Maybe you'll put landscapes in a folder called *LAND1* and people shots in *PPL 1*. The D5000 will then create folders called 100LAND1, and 100PPL_1. Notice how the people folder name has an underscore between the *L* and 1? If you do not use all five characters, leaving a space, the camera will add an underscore to the blank character location. If you exceed 999 images in any of the folders, it will create the next one automatically (101LAND1 and 101PPL_1).

To you, the one using the camera, the folder names won't seem to increment because you'll see only the last five characters. The camera will not tell you that you've exceeded 999 images and that new images are going into a new folder. To you it will just seem as if there is one folder. The camera uses the numbers it adds to the beginning of the folder name to track the "series" of extra folders it creates when you exceed 999 images in each folder.

Select an Existing Folder: *Figure 24* shows the screens you'll use to select a folder.

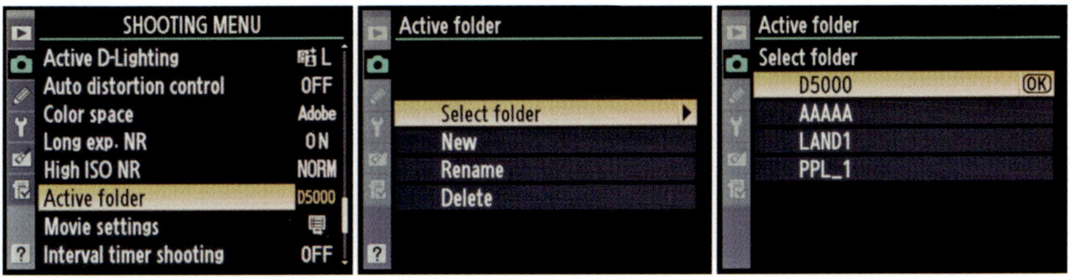

Figure 24 – Selecting an existing folder

Here are the steps to select an existing folder:

1. Press the MENU button and select the *Shooting Menu*.
2. Choose *Active folder*, and then scroll right.
3. Choose *Select folder*, and then scroll right.
4. You'll see the available folders displayed in a list that looks like this:

    D5000
    AAAA
    LAND1
    PPL_1

    Choose one of the folders to make it active. The currently active one will be at the top of the list.
5. Press the *OK* button.

All images will now be saved to the latest folder selected until you change it to another. You can tell at a glance which folder is active by looking at the *Shooting Menu*'s *Active folder* line. To the right of the words *Active folder*, you'll see the five-character name of the current folder (see the screen on the left in *figure 24*).

Notice how you don't see the three numeric characters in your list of folders (the screen on the right in *figure 24*). The camera keeps track of the numeric progression of folders that exceed 999 images and considers all folders with names in which the last five digits match as a single folder, even though there might actually be several camera-created folders in the series.

Create a New Folder: Now let's consider how you might create new folder names. As shown in *figure 25*, to create a new folder, do the following:

1. Press the MENU button and select the *Shooting Menu*.
2. Select *Active folder*, then scroll to the right.
3. Now scroll down and select *New*, then scroll to the right. You'll now see a screen that allows you to name the new folder. To insert a new character, position the yellow cursor in the character list above using the Multi Selector, and then press the playback zoom in button to add the character to the name. Whatever character is under the yellow cursor will appear on the name line below, at the position of the gray cursor. If a character is already under the gray cursor, it will be pushed to the right. If it's at the end of the line and you try to overwrite it, the new character will replace the old. Use the command dial to scroll back and forth within the old name. When you have the small gray cursor positioned over a character, you

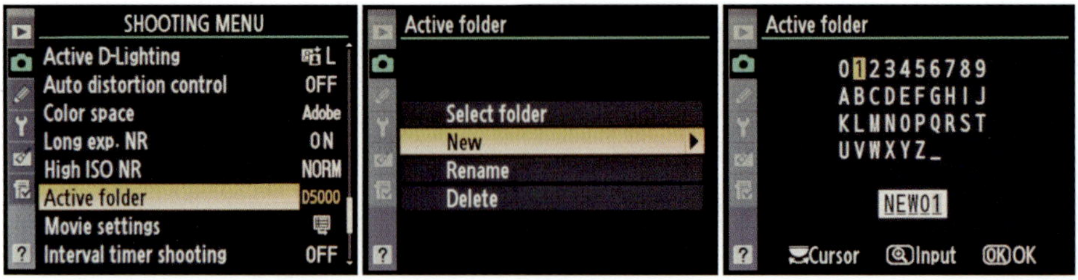

Figure 25 – Creating a new folder

can delete it with the trash can delete button. The name is limited to five characters. (See *figure 1* for the locations of the camera controls.)

4. Press the *OK* button when you've completed the new name. I named mine *NEW01*.

Once you have created a new folder it will automatically become the current folder.

Change a Folder Name: You can also change the name of an existing folder. To rename a folder, follow these steps (see *figure 26*):

1. Press the MENU button and select the *Shooting Menu*.
2. Select *Active folder*, then scroll to the right.
3. Scroll down and select *Rename*, then scroll to the right.
4. Select a folder name to modify, and then scroll right.
5. Use the command dial to scroll back and forth within the existing name. When you have the small gray cursor positioned over an existing character, you can delete it with the trash can delete button. To insert a new character, position the yellow cursor in the character list above and press the playback zoom in button. Whatever character is under the yellow cursor will appear on the name line below, at the position of the gray cursor. If a character is already under the gray cursor, it will be pushed to the right. If it's at the end of the line and you try to overwrite it, the new

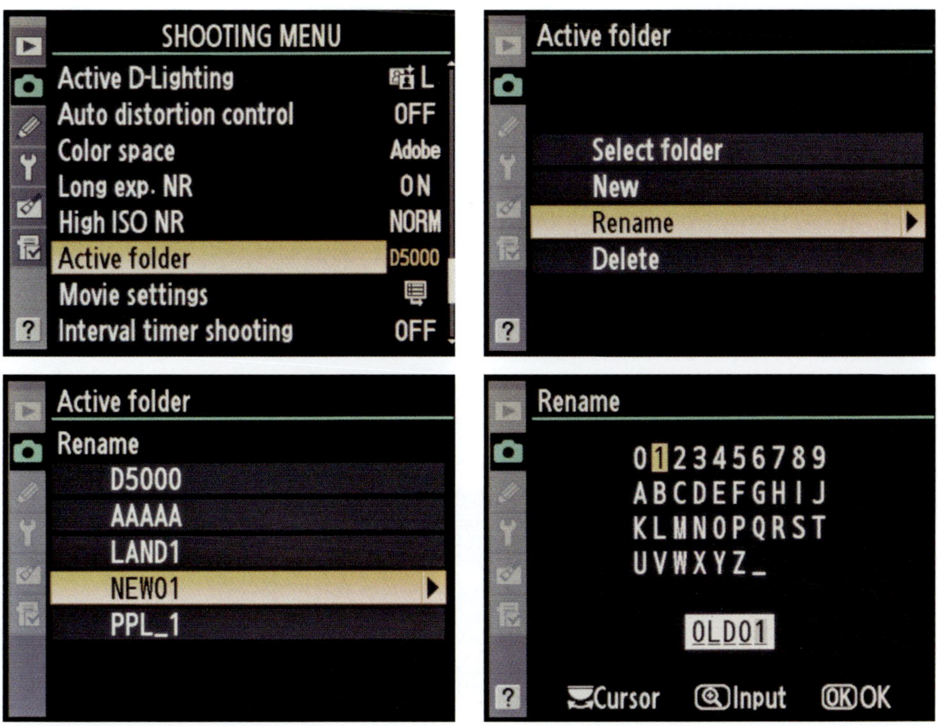

Figure 26 – Renaming an existing folder

character will replace the old. The name is limited to a maximum of five characters. I renamed mine *OLD01*. (See *figure 1* for the location of the camera control.)
6. Press the *OK* button when you've completed the new name.

If you rename a folder, the camera will look at your memory card and see if there are any other folders in the series (100D5000, 101D5000, 102D5000, etc.). If it finds other folders with names in which the last five digits match, it will rename those using new name you created in the preceding steps. Remember, the D5000 considers these camera-created folders one folder.

If you try to rename a folder with the name of a folder that already exists, the D5000 will flash up a warning when you press the *OK* button to save the name. The warning will inform you, *Folder with selected name already exists. Choose another name.*

Delete all Empty Folders: Now, let see how to delete all empty folders from the memory card. Use the following steps to delete the empty folders (see *figure 27*):

1. Press the MENU button and select the *Shooting Menu*.
2. Select *Active folder*, then scroll to the right.
3. Scroll down and select *Delete*, then scroll to the right.
4. You'll be presented with the *Delete* screen and the following message: *Empty folders will be deleted. OK?*
5. Scroll up to *Yes* and press the *OK* button.
6. You'll see a message flash up briefly saying *Folder(s) deleted.*

Remember, when you do a delete operation, all empty folders will be removed. Be careful not to use this function if you have a series of folders you use regularly and want them to stay in place. There is no way that I've found to delete just one folder. It's all "empty" folders or none. If there are no empty folders, nothing happens.

Movie Settings

(User's Manual pages 49–52)
Since the Nikon D5000 also has video capability, we need to look at the movie settings, which include the level of quality and sound.

In this chapter, we will just consider a few basics. Chapter 12, "D-Movie Mode: Video on Demand", goes into more detail about creating movies with the D5000.

There are three menu screens to set the quality of the video in the D5000. They're shown in *figure 28*. The three levels of quality are as follows:

- *1280x720 (16:9)*
- *640x424 (3:2)*
- *320x216 (3:2)*

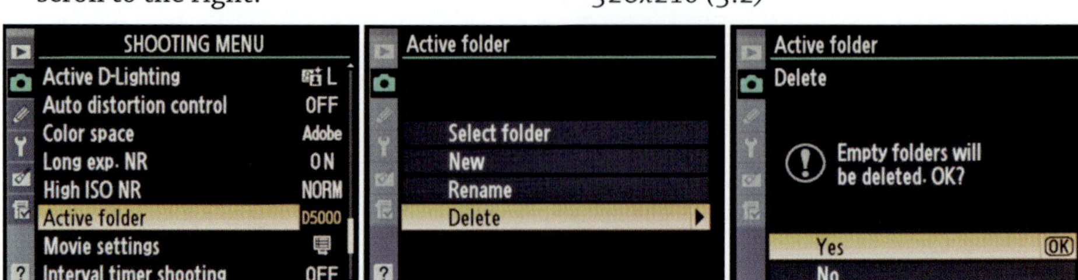

Figure 27 – Deleting an existing folder

The camera records video at 24 frames per second (fps), which is considered a "cinematic" frame rate. The file size of the finished video will be affected by how high the quality is set. The numbers in the preceding list mean the number of pixels in the video image. For instance, 1280x720 = 921600, or almost 1 megapixel per frame. That's high-definition (HD) quality on a normal monitor and can even be fed into an HDTV with an optional HDMI cable. It provides a 16x9 image ratio, which is the long narrow image we've grown accustomed to on HDTVs. The other two ratios are smaller and more square, like a normal TV or CRT computer monitor.

Recommendation on Video Format

I often shoot in *1280 x 720* mode because I like the HD format. It is nice and wide! The fact that I am using a zoom lens on my D5000 allows me to take advantage of the wide view I can later show on my wide LCD computer monitor or HDTV. However, if you are displaying your videos on a PDA or a regular computer monitor or TV, you might want to use the smaller settings. Remember, the larger the setting, the bigger the resulting video file size.

To select the video quality you'd like to use, refer to *figure 28*, and do the following:

1. Press the MENU button and select the *Shooting Menu*.
2. Select *Movie settings*, and then scroll right.
3. Select *Quality*, and then scroll right.
4. Choose from one of the *Quality* settings, and press the *OK* button.

Finally, let's examine how to turn the sound on and off while making movies.

There are only two simple selections (see *figure 29*):

- *On*
- *Off*

Select *On* and you'll hear surprisingly high-quality sound with each of your

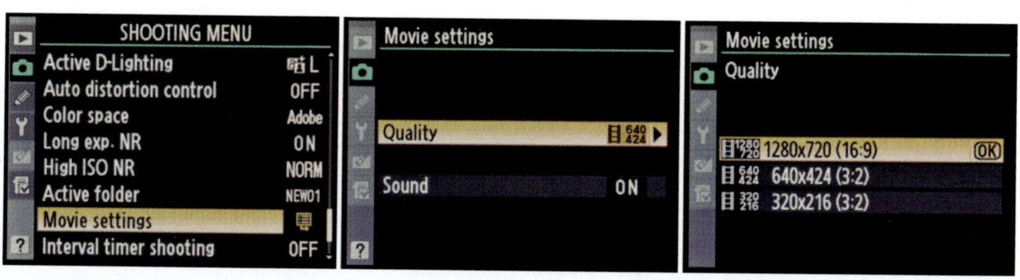

Figure 28 – *Movie settings – Quality*

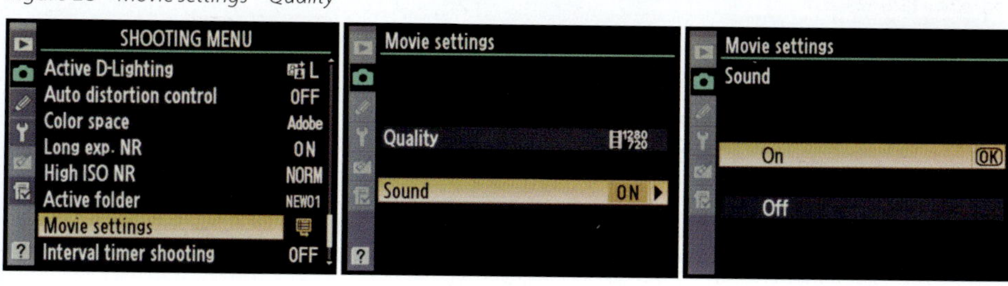

Figure 29 – *Movie settings – Sound*

movies. Or, if you want to, switch your camera to B&W mode, turn off the sound, and do some silent movies. Use a few props and a movie editing program and you'll be able to produce films of much higher quality than the original black and white movies of yesteryear.

There's Lots More to Learn on Video Mode

Please read chapter 12 thoroughly before using your video mode extensively. There are some important things you need to know, including some limitations, before you make D-Movies with your D5000.

Interval Timer Shooting

(User's Manual pages 76–77)

The *Interval timer shooting* setting allows you to set your D5000 up to shoot a series of images over a period of time. This is also referred to as *time-lapse photography*. Make sure you have a full battery or, for images taken over long periods of time, your camera should be connected to a full-time power source.

The first step in using *Interval timer shooting* is to make sure *World time* (for your particular location) and the time and date are set correctly in the *Setup Menu* of your D5000. If you don't have *World time* set on the D5000, your *Interval timer* menu will be grayed out and you won't be able to use it.

Figure 30 shows the *Shooting Menu* screens used to set Interval timer shooting.

The screens look a little daunting, but it might help you to understand that the lower half of screens 2 through 6 in *figure 30* is informational in nature. It shows the settings you have created with the top half of the screen.

There are three steps to setting your camera for *Interval timer shooting*:

1. Choose a *Start time*
2. Choose an *Interval*
3. Choose the *Number of intervals*

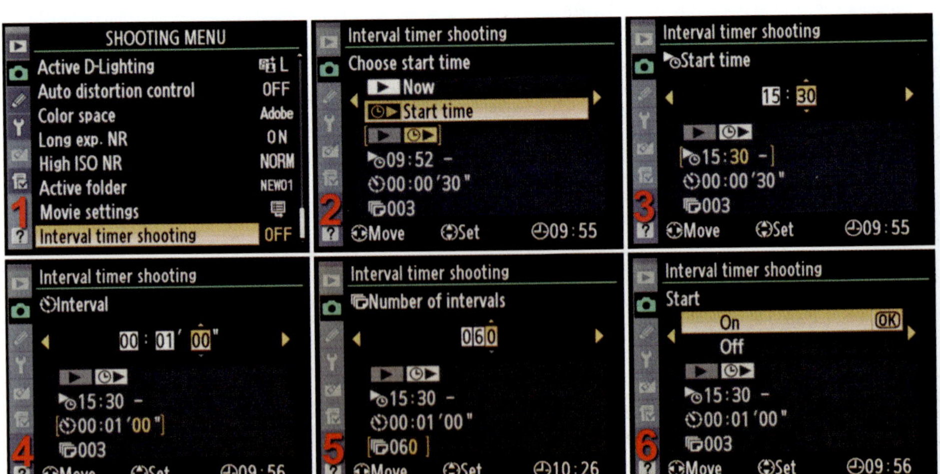

Figure 30 – *Interval timer shooting* setup

For example, I could take a series of images starting *Now,* or at a specified time (*Start time*), and shoot 1 image every minute (*Interval*), doing it 60 times (*Number of intervals*). This means I'll be taking one picture every minute over a one-hour period, starting *Now* or at a specific future *Start time* (60 pictures total).

Get your D5000 and try these steps yourself so that it will make sense to you:

1. On the screen numbered 2 in *figure 30*, you could select *Now* under *Choose start time*, and the timer will start about 3 seconds after you complete the rest of the steps (3 and 4). If you would rather start at a specific future time instead of immediately, simply select *Start time* instead of *Now* from screen 2, then scroll right and set a beginning time. If you select *Now*, skip step 2 and go directly to step 3. (Nikon calls the *Now* or *Start time* settings the starting trigger; see page 76, step 2 in the User's Manual.)
2. If you didn't choose *Now,* you'll see a *Start time* screen (screen 3 in *figure 30*) with the time in military 24-hour format looking like this:
   00:00
   If I wanted to start at 3:30 p.m., I would insert the following in the fields:
   15:30
   This is in 24-hour military time instead of the normal 12-hour time we're used to as civilians. There is no concept of a.m. or p.m. in 24-hour time.

24 Hour Time Equivalents

For your convenience, here is a 24-hour time equivalents chart:

A.M. Settings:

12:00 a.m. = 00:00 (midnight)
01:00 a.m. = 01:00
02:00 a.m. = 02:00
03:00 a.m. = 03:00
04:00 a.m. = 04:00
05:00 a.m. = 05:00
06:00 a.m. = 06:00
07:00 a.m. = 07:00
08:00 a.m. = 08:00
09:00 a.m. = 09:00
10:00 a.m. = 10:00
11:00 a.m. = 11:00

P.M. Settings:

12:00 p.m. = 12:00 (noon)
01:00 p.m. = 13:00
02:00 p.m. = 14:00
03:00 p.m. = 15:00
04:00 p.m. = 16:00
05:00 p.m. = 17:00
06:00 p.m. = 18:00
07:00 p.m. = 19:00
08:00 p.m. = 20:00
09:00 p.m. = 21:00
10:00 p.m. = 22:00
11:00 p.m. = 23:00

There is no 24:00. After 23:59, it becomes 00:00 instead (midnight).

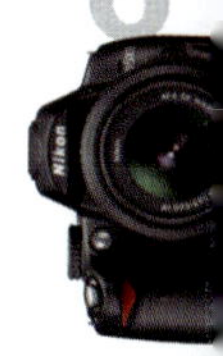

3. You will now see the *Interval* screen (see screen 4 in *figure 30*) with hours, minutes, and seconds" in the following format:
   00 : 00' 00"
   Since we want to start out with an interval of 1 minute, let's set the screen to look like this instead:
   00 : 01' 00"
   The first two sets of zeros represent the hours, the second set represents minutes, and the third set seconds. Since we have chosen an interval of 1 minute, the number in the second set of zeros should be 01, representing 1 minute. Scroll to the right.
4. Now we'll select the number of Intervals, using the screen numbered 5 in *figure 30*.
   This screen will say *Number of intervals* and will have this basic format, allowing up to 999 intervals.
   000
   Set *Number of intervals* so that it looks like this:
   060
   This means that there will be 60 intervals of 1 minute each (set in step 3) and that the camera will take a picture at each interval, for a total of 60 pictures. In other words, 1 picture will be taken every 1 minute over a period of 60 intervals (60 minutes in this case) for a total of 60 images. Now scroll to the right to the next screen.
5. Using the screen numbered 6 in *figure 30*, select *On* and press the *OK* button. A *Timer Active* message appears on your LCD for a few seconds. The small green memory card access lamp will blink every couple of seconds while the timer is running. Other than the light blinking. The camera will appear to shut down if the interval sequence is long. However, it wakes up right on time, takes a picture, then goes back to sleep until the next interval expires.

Interval Timer Operational Notes: Be sure that you are using a freshly charged battery before starting a long interval shooting session. Otherwise, the timer will fail when the battery is discharged. You can also acquire an EH-5a AC adapter and an EP-5 power connector and then connect the camera to an AC power source. This should allow you to do really long time-lapse photography sequences. If I figured it right, the maximum time-lapse sequence you could shoot is 1 image about every 100 hours up to 999 times. That's a picture about every 4 days over a time period of 3,996 days (4-day intervals x 999 intervals). So, you could take one picture every 4 days for about 11 years. That's a long timer sequence!

During the timer operation, you cannot use the camera. You can't access the menus or manually snap off a shot. About all I could get the D5000 to do when it was in timer mode was to display the information screen. The easiest way I've found to stop a timer operation is to turn the camera off. You can also rotate the mode dial to another position to stop the operation.

It may be a good idea to turn off *Image review* under the *Playback Menu* while using an extended timer operation.

Otherwise, the camera will happily display an image after each interval. Unless you are there to review the images, this is just a waste of battery life. Or, since you have a cool LCD screen, just put it in the closed position and the problem goes away.

If you are shooting this timed interval in daylight hours, be sure to use the little eye-piece cap (DK-5) supplied with your D5000. Otherwise, changes in the light from behind the camera could cause the exposure to be inaccurate. The camera refocuses and rechecks the meter for every picture taken during the sequence.

If you are shooting wildlife or any other noise-sensitive subjects, you had best turn the camera's "beep" off using *Custom Setting d1*. It may also be a good idea to use the *Information edit* screen's *Release mode* setting to select Q, or Quiet shutter-release mode. Q mode automatically turns off the autofocus confirmation beep and reduces the shutter release sound significantly.

Oh, and use a tripod!

My Conclusions

Using the D5000's *Shooting Menus* allows you a great deal of flexibility in how your camera operates. Learn to use each of these settings by adjusting them often. Your D5000 is a still frame and video camera all in one. Take full advantage of that power!

Congratulations! Now that you've fully configured your D5000's *Shooting Menus*, let's move on to the *Custom Settings* in the next chapter. These settings—like the *Shooting Menu* settings—give you a lot of control over how your camera works. Learn them well.

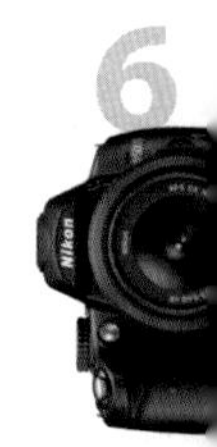

Custom Setting Menu

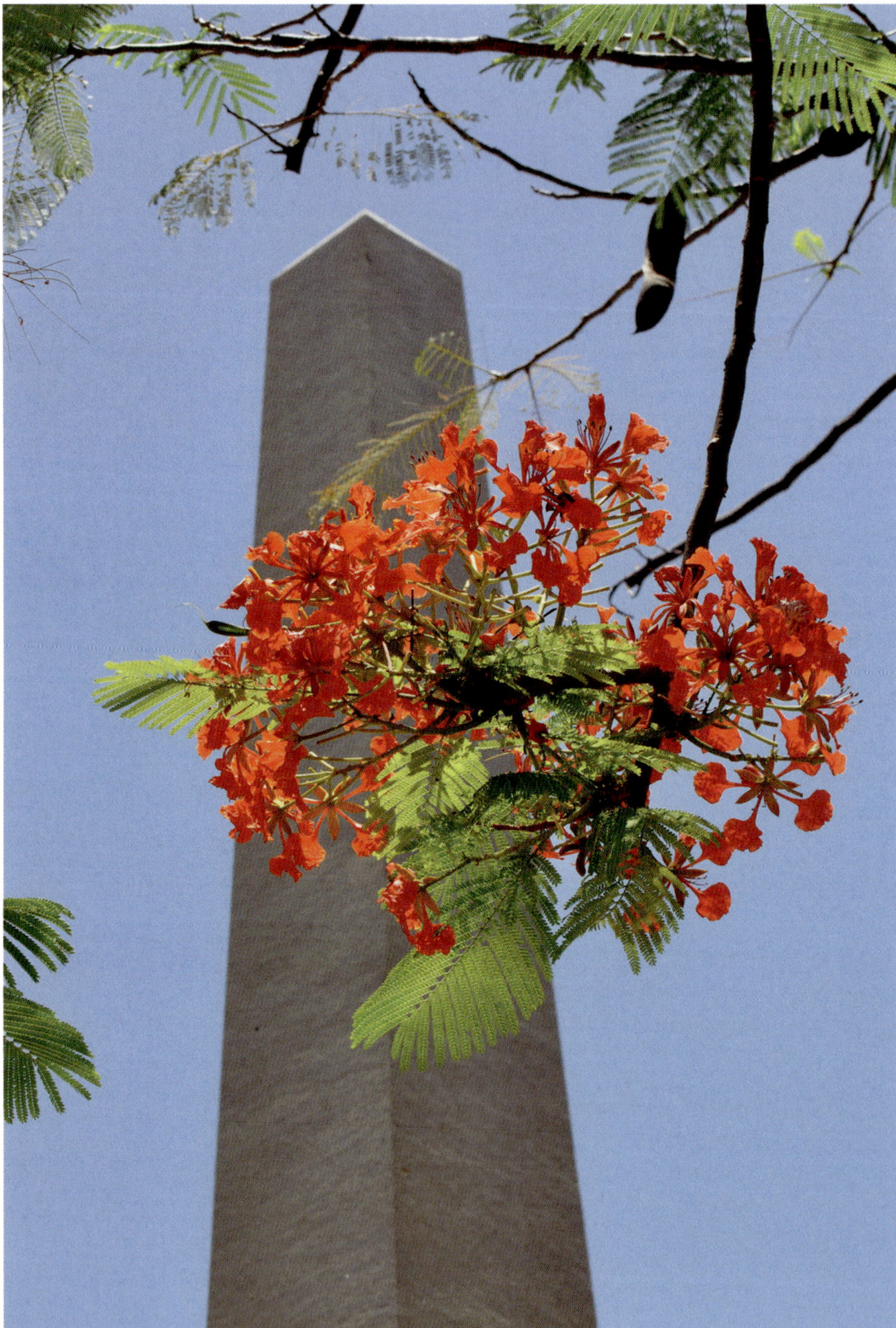

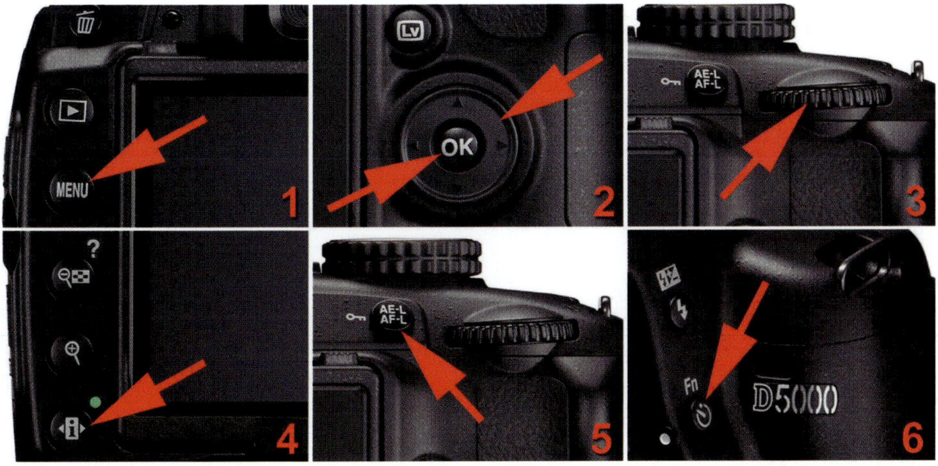

Figure 1 – The external camera controls

The D5000 has 23 separate Custom Settings, a1 through f5. They're designed to allow personalized configuration of the camera. This will be an extensive chapter because we have so many settings to cover in detail.

Combining these custom menu settings with the *Shooting Menu* functions covered in the previous chapter helps make your D5000 a very personal device that is customizable to your particular style of shooting. Few cameras have this level of complexity or power, and for many users the default settings will suffice. However, all this is available for your own personal customization based on your needs, so let's explore these settings step-by-step.

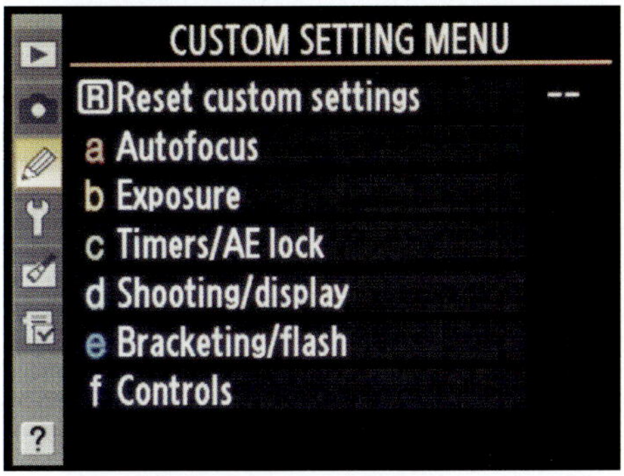

Figure 1A – The *Custom Setting Menu*

Keep this book in your camera bag so that you'll have a reference point for future adjustments to the D5000. You'll need it!

We'll be using the external camera controls to set various functions as we proceed through this chapter (see *figure 1*).

Referring to the numbers on the screens in *figure 1*, here is a list of the control names:

- MENU button
- Multi Selector and OK button
- Command dial
- Information edit button
- AE-L/AF-L button
- Fn button

You might want to place a bookmark at this position so that you can easily refer back to *figure 1* as you experiment with each Custom Setting. Let's examine each of the 23 items and discover the best settings for your methods of making pictures.

Figure 1A shows the *Custom Setting Menu* we'll be using in this chapter.

Now, let's get to configuring!

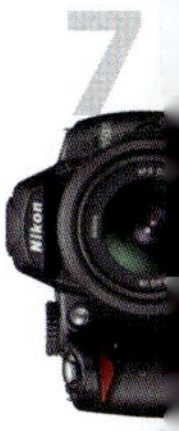

Configuring the Custom Settings

(User's Manual pages 153–164)

Let's start by looking at the *Reset Custom settings* menu. This is used in case you want to start fresh in configuring the camera.

Reset Custom Settings

Be careful with this selection because it resets the *Custom Setting Menu* back to the factory default settings. Here are the steps to reset the custom settings (see *figure 1B*):

1. Press the MENU button and scroll to the *Custom Setting Menu* (pencil icon).
2. Select *Reset custom settings* and then scroll to the right.
3. Select *Yes* from the menu.
4. Press the *OK* button.

All custom settings will return to their factory defaults when you press *OK*.

Recommendation

If you purchased your D5000 as a pre-owned camera, you may want to use the *Reset custom settings* function immediately. We'll be examining each of the Custom Settings so that you can make a decision as to how *you* want the camera configured. If your camera is brand-new, you don't need to use the *Reset Custom settings* feature right now.

Autofocus - Custom Settings a1 to a4

(User's Manual pages 155–156)

Custom Setting a1 *(AF-area mode)*

(User's Manual page 155)

This custom setting controls how the autofocus (AF) system selects a focus point. You can cause the camera to use just one AF point, a movable AF pattern, or all 11 points at once. I have devoted an entire chapter to understanding the AF system.

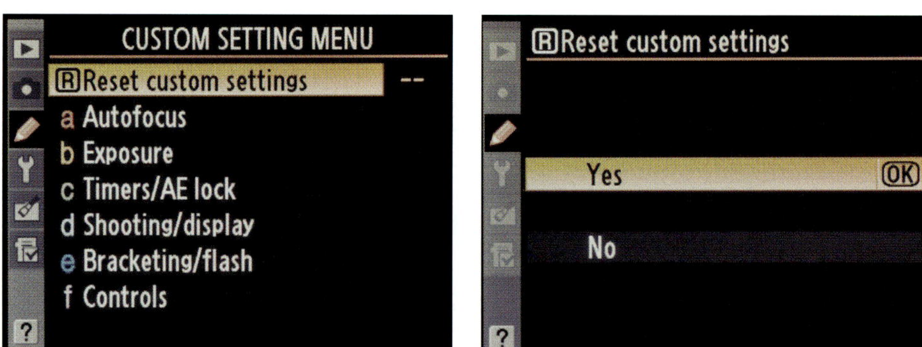

Figure 1B – Reset custom settings

See chapter 10, "Multi-CAM 1000 Autofocus," for detailed information on how to use the D5000's powerful autofocus feature. I'll list only configuration choices in the current chapter, with the understanding that chapter 10 is devoted to full understanding of autofocus issues.

Figure 2 shows the menu screens used to configure *Custom Setting a1*.

Notice that there are four *AF-area mode* settings to choose from:

- *Single point*
- *Dynamic area*
- *Auto-area*
- *3D-tracking (11 points)*

Here's how to select an *AF-area mode*:

1. Press the MENU button and scroll to the *Custom Setting Menu*.
2. Select *a Autofocus*, and then scroll to the right.
3. Select *a1 AF-area mode* from the menu, and then scroll to the right.
4. Select one of the *AF-area mode* choices from the four available.
5. Press the *OK* button to choose the mode.

These are discussed in great detail in chapter 10, so I won't do more than cover some basics and configuration here (User's Manual pages 56–57).

- ***Single point* AF** – This mode is for subjects that are stationary or are moving very slowly. You can select a single AF point out of the 11 available points and move it around the viewfinder to focus on whatever part of your subject you'd like. You'll use the Multi Selector to scroll among the 11 AF points and select the single point you choose for autofocus accuracy.
- ***Dynamic area* AF** – This mode works a lot like Single point AF except that you are moving an invisible cross-shaped pattern of 4 or 5 AF points around the 11 available sensor points. The AF points immediately surrounding the one you have selected are also active and seeking focus. These extra AF points are active in case the subject moves unexpectedly and you lose focus with the primary AF point.
- ***Auto-area* AF** – Your camera decides where and what the subject is and does the autofocus operation without input from you. It uses face-recognition technology to identify humans in your picture and give them preferential focus. Generally, the camera will select the closest and brightest objects for nonhuman subjects. You'll see multiple AF points focusing on various parts of the camera's chosen subject. This is an

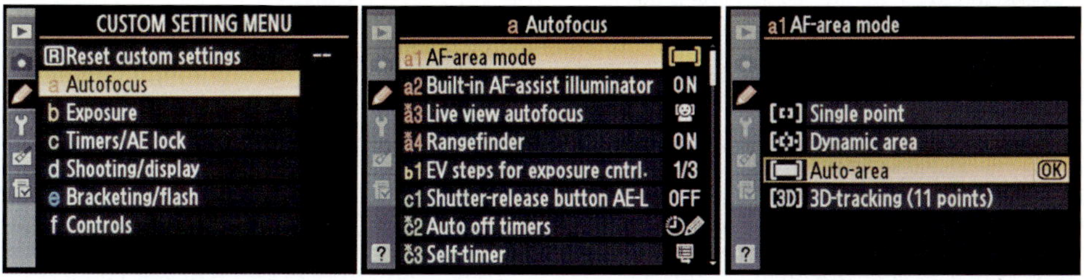

Figure 2 – Custom Setting a1 *(AF-area mode)*

automatic mode for those times when you just want to take pictures and not think about the camera.

- ***3D-tracking (11 points)*** – This is a mode for action shooters. The camera uses all 11 of its AF points to keep the subject in focus in case it moves. You select a single AF point to initiate autofocus and the camera does its best to keep the focus on your subject. If the initial AF point loses the subject, the rest of the AF points continue tracking the subject. This mode is also sensitive to the brightness and color of the subject and uses those two things to help maintain a tracked focus. If you're shooting quickly moving subjects like animals, races, or sports, this is your mode. In some cases, since all 11 of the sensors are active, this mode may be somewhat slower to get active initially. The camera's microprocessor is working considerably harder because it is processing a lot more information. If your subject is the same color as the background, you may not want to use this mode.

Recommendation

Until you have read chapter 10 and have time to experiment a bit, why not set the camera to *Auto-area*? This mode allows the camera to make appropriate focus choices without you worrying about it and it uses facial recognition technology to automatically find and focus on people as subjects. If you would rather exercise some control, switch to *Single point* and use the Multi Selector to move the AF point around the viewfinder so that one of the 11 focus points falls on your subject.

Custom Setting a2
(Built-in AF-assist illuminator)

(User's Manual pages 55 and 155)
You've seen the little autofocus assist light on the front of the D5000 (near the grip). Custom Setting a2 allows you to control when that little light comes on. Nikon calls this the *Built-in AF-assist illuminator* and it lights up under low-light conditions and under certain *Autofocus* and *AF-area* modes (not all) to help with autofocus.

Figure 3 shows the menu screens used to configure Custom Setting a2.

To select either on or off from the menu, follow these steps:

1. Press the MENU button and scroll to the *Custom Setting Menu*.
2. Select *a Autofocus*, and then scroll to the right.
3. Select *a2 Built-in AF-assist illuminator* from the menu, and then scroll to the right.
4. Select either *On* or *Off*.
5. Press the *OK* button.

Here's how the settings work:

1. ***On*** (default) – If the light level is low, the AF-assist illuminator sometimes lights up to help illuminate the subject enough for autofocus. It only works in certain modes though. When I was first writing this paragraph, I found myself experimenting with all the different modes. I was listing combinations of *Autofocus* and *AF-area* modes that would work in a long boring list that no one would ever find useful. After I wrote it, even I had a hard time using it. So, here is all I will tell you about

Nikon's choices of when the AF-assist light will and won't work:

a. If you are using any form of continuous-servo autofocus mode (AF-C), forget having an assist light. I could never get it to work in AF-C under any circumstances.

b. In most other autofocus modes, and AF-area modes, it will work as long as you are using only the center AF point. None of the other AF points will let the light shine. I guess they figure that your subject must be out of reach of the light if you're not using the center AF point.

The point is simply this: If the light doesn't come on, your camera is in a mode that it doesn't support. It isn't broken or flaky. It's just engineered in a way that is tedious to describe. Don't try to understand this setting from reading the paragraph in the User's Manual on page 155 in the Option *On* description. In the history of user's manuals, that is the most complicated sentence I've ever read. If the light *does* come on when you need it, consider yourself fortunate and make use of it.

2. ***Off*** – The *Built-in AF-assist illuminator* does not light up to help you in low-light autofocus situations. The D5000 may not be able to autofocus in very low light.

The *Built-in AF-assist illuminator* has a limited range of about 10 feet (3 meters). Anything closer than about 2 feet (0.5 meters) will be only partially lit by the light because it is off axis with the center of the lens (parallax failure and/or lens blockage).

Tip on Use of AF-Assist Illuminator

To use the *Built-in AF-assist illuminator*, stay out of continuous-servo autofocus mode (AF-C) and use the center AF focus point of the 11 available. Also, when I am trying to be sneaky and shoot pictures of people or animals without drawing attention to myself, I'll turn this feature off. Nothing grabs the attention of a living creature faster than shining a light within its sight range.

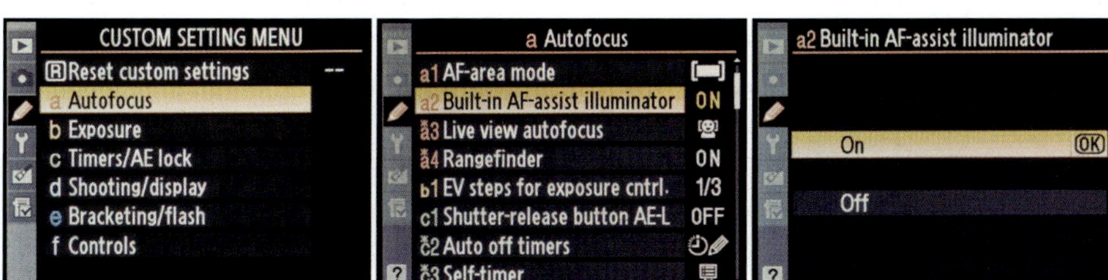

Figure 3 – Custom Setting a2 *(Built-in AF-assist illuminator)*

Custom Setting a3 *(Live view autofocus)*
(User's Manual pages 43 and 155)

Live view autofocus allows you to use the LCD on the back of your D5000 instead of the viewfinder. The AF method is contrast detection, which is slower than normal autofocus. (See chapter 10, where *Live View autofocus* is discussed in detail.)

Live view autofocus gives you four methods to select a subject (see *figure 4*).

Here are the menu selections available under Custom Setting a3:

- *Face priority*
- *Wide area*
- *Normal area*
- *Subject tracking*

Face priority – This allows the D5000 to seek human faces by looking for the relationship between the eyes and nose area. The faces must be turned directly into the camera to be found. When a face is found, the LCD screen will show a jumpy yellow square centered on the nose of the human subject. When autofocus is initiated, the yellow square will turn green. If there are no human subjects (or if faces are available but in profile only), the D5000 is still in face priority mode, but it acts more like wide area mode.

Wide area – This mode presents the user with a rather large red square that can be moved to any location in the viewfinder. Once the red square is focused on a subject, it turns green.

Normal area – This mode presents the user with a small red square that can be moved to any location in the viewfinder. Once the red square is focused on a subject, the square turns green. This mode is more exact because the smaller square makes you focus on a much smaller area of your subject. You might want to think of this mode as a "tripod mode" because it is best used on a tripod for very accurate focusing.

Subject tracking – The user sees a small white square in the middle of the screen. This little square works similarly to *Normal area* mode except that you cannot move the little square. If you use the shutter release button to start autofocus, the white square will turn green and the camera seems to find a good focus even more quickly than in other modes. However, using the shutter release button to start autofocus limits this mode seriously. Pay careful attention to the next sentence! To use subject tracking, you must initiate autofocus by pressing up on the multi selector switch. Only then does the camera enter into *Subject tracking* mode. This works a lot like *Face priority* mode except that it tracks any subject, not just a face. It is quite fun to use!

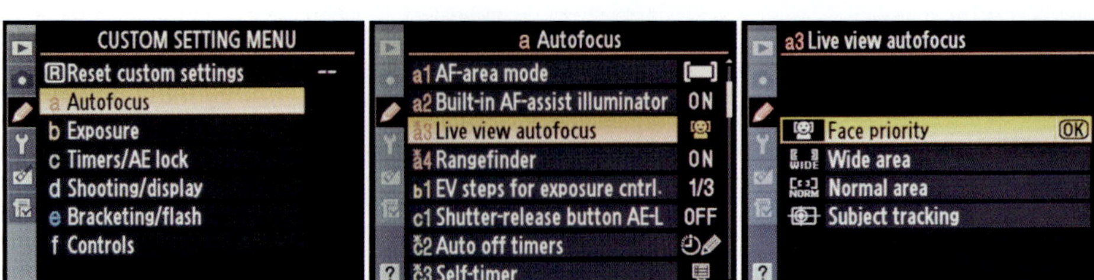

Figure 4 – Custom Setting a3 *(Live view autofocus)*

Here's how to select one of the focus modes (see *figure 4*):

1. Press the MENU button and scroll to the *Custom Setting Menu*.
2. Select *a Autofocus*, and then scroll to the right.
3. Select *a3 Live view autofocus* from the menu, and then scroll to the right.
4. Select one of the autofocus functions listed in the menu.
5. Press the *OK* button to select it.

My Own Use of Live View Autofocus

When I use *Live view autofocus* handheld, I usually leave it set to *Face priority*. This mode works well whether I have a human subject or not, and I can move the focus square around the screen to select off-center subjects. Only when I am using a tripod and trying to be very precise do I switch to the *Normal area* setting. I like to use *Live view Normal area* mode for macro/closeup shots because it reduces the strain I feel from leaning over the viewfinder. When I'm using *Live view mode* to track moving subjects, I'll use the *Subject tracking* setting. It has limitations since it takes time to acquire focus and can track only slow- to medium-speed subjects. If you want to track a racecar from up close, don't use live view. However, the *Subject tracking* setting works well when I am walking around the yard tracking people or pets. Please read more detailed information in chapter 10.

Custom Setting a4 *(Rangefinder)*

(User's Manual page 156)

This is an unusual little function that helps those who want to manually focus their lenses.

Follow these steps to set the *Rangefinder* to *On* or *Off* (see *figure 5*):

1. Press the MENU button and scroll to the *Custom Setting Menu*.
2. Select *a Autofocus*, and then scroll to the right.
3. Select *a4 Rangefinder* from the menu, and then scroll to the right.
4. Select *On* or *Off* from the list.
5. Press the *OK* button to select it.

What is this function designed to do? Provide you with an old-fashioned rangefinder in a more modern form. Manual focus assist!

Most AF lenses have an A/M switch on the side. If you leave it in A (*Autofocus* mode), the lens works like a normal autofocus lens. However, if you switch it to M (*Manual focus* mode), the autofocus motor disengages and you can manually focus the lens—if you can find the focus ring on today's lenses.

What the *Rangefinder* function does is provide an additional autofocus indicator so that you can see if the lens is in focus and, if not, just how far out of

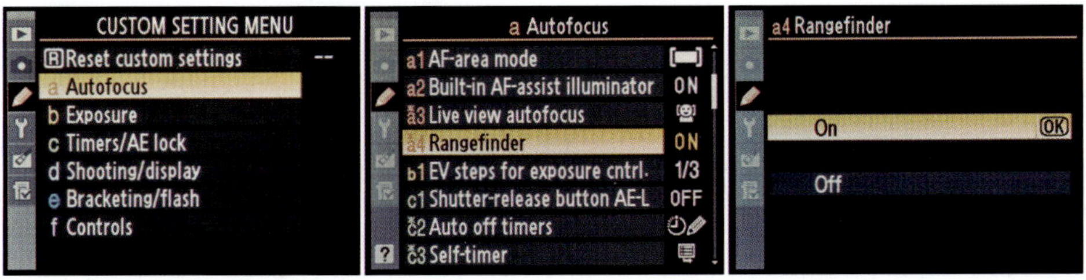

Figure 5 – Custom Setting a4 *(Rangefinder)*

focus it is. You may have noticed the little round green indicator on the lower left of your camera's viewfinder. It is a "good focus" indicator and comes on when your subject is in focus. In addition, with *Custom Setting a4* set to *On*, you will have a sliding scale in the lower middle of the viewfinder. It looks a little like the +/- exposure indicator when you are using M (or manual) on the mode dial. In *figure 5A*, you'll see six viewfinder screens that show the range of indications shown on the *Rangefinder* indicator. I've taken the bottom part of a D5000 viewfinder and made a closeup of the focus indicator area with each of its six indications.

1. ***In focus*** (*figure 5A, image 1*) – You'll see double lines just below the 0 in the middle of the viewfinder. This signifies that the image is in focus. You'll also see the round green focus indicator on the lower-left corner. This is the one you want to see before taking the picture. If you don't want to memorize what the patterns below mean—at least memorize this one. Make sure you have the double lines below the 0 and the little green light (see the red arrows) and your images should be in focus.
2. ***Focus point slightly behind subject*** (*figure 5A, image 2*) – You'll see three lines and an arrow pointing to the right of the 0. The D5000 is focused just behind the subject. The round green in focus indicator on the lower-left corner will be flickering or off.
3. ***Focus point slightly in front of subject*** (*figure 5A, image 3*) – You'll see three lines and an arrow pointing to the left of the 0. The D5000 is focused just in front of the subject. The round green good focus indicator on the lower-left corner will be flickering or off.
4. ***Focus point well behind subject*** (*figure 5A, image 4*) – You'll see six lines and an arrow pointing to the right of the 0. The D5000 is focused far behind the subject. The round green in focus indicator on the lower-left corner will be off.

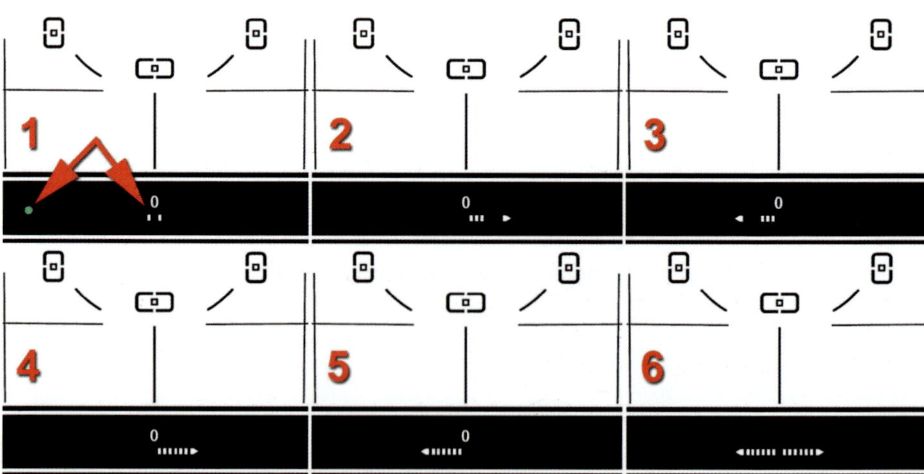

Figure 5A – Rangefinder indications

5. ***Focus point well in front of subject*** (*figure 5A, image 5*) – You'll see six lines and an arrow pointing to the left of the o. The D5000 is focused far in front of the subject. The round green good focus indicator on the lower-left corner will also be off.
6. ***Camera cannot autofocus on the subject*** (*figure 5A, image 6*) – You'll see six lines and an arrow on both the left and right, with no o. The subject contrast is not sufficient for the autofocus system to find and focus on the subject. The round green good focus indicator on the lower-left corner will be off.

My Own Use of the Rangefinder Setting

I sometimes like to manually focus the lens, such as when I'm shooting a group portrait and want to focus on the middle row instead of the front or back row. I leave Custom Setting a4 set to *On* all the time since it does nothing until you put the lens into M (manual focus) mode. I tried this out with an old manual focus Nikkor lens and the rangefinder seemed to work. However, the D5000 was very unhappy with the old "non-CPU" lens mounted on the camera and kept a blinking *F--* error in the viewfinder—even when I had the lens stopped down to its smallest aperture. It seems clear that Nikon does not want us using manual focus lenses on the D5000. However, we can switch our autofocus lenses to manual focus mode and focus manually as much as we like.

Exposure - Custom Setting b1

(User's Manual page 156)

Custom Setting b1
(EV steps for exposure cntrl.)

(User's Manual page 156)

What is an EV? As explained briefly in Chapter 2, EV simply means exposure value, which is an internationally agreed-upon incremental value of exposure metering. It is spoken of in full or partial EV steps, like 1/3, 1/2, and 1. It simply serves as a common denominator for various combinations of shutter speed, aperture, compensation, and bracketing that give similar exposures. An EV step corresponds to a standard logarithmic "power-of-2" exposure step, commonly referred to as a *stop*. So, instead of saying "1 EV," you could say "1 stop." EV 0 (zero) corresponds to an exposure time of 1 second at an aperture of f/1.0, or 15 seconds at f/4. EV can be positive or negative. EV -6 equals 60 seconds at f/1.0. EV 10 equals 1/1000 at f/1.0 or 1/60 at f/4. The EV step system was invented in Germany back in the 1950s. Interesting, huh?

Nikon chose to lump shutter speed, aperture, exposure and flash compensation, and bracketing EV increments under this one custom setting. If you set this custom setting to 1/3, it will affect all of the above. The factory default value for setting *b1* is *1/3 step*.

The menu screens used to configure Custom Setting b1 are shown in *figure* 6).

Exposure control (or *exposure cntrl.*) refers to the number of the steps in your shutter speed and aperture since those are your main exposure controls. It also encompasses the exposure compensation and bracketing system.

Here are the two settings available under the *EV steps for exposure contrl.* menu:

- *1/3 step*
- *1/2 step*

Here are the steps to configure Custom Setting b1 (see *Figure* 6):

1. Press the MENU button and scroll to the *Custom Setting Menu*.
2. Select *b Exposure*, and then scroll to the right.
3. Select *b1 EV steps for exposure cntrl.* from the menu, and then scroll to the right.
4. Select either *1/3 step* or *1/2 step* from the menu.
5. Press the *OK* button.

All this really means is that when you are making exposure adjustments, they will work incrementally in the following steps:

Shutter and exposure

(starting at a random shutter speed or aperture)

1/3 EV step:

- Shutter: 1/100, 1/125, 1/160, 1/200, 1/250, 1/320, etc.
- Aperture: f/5.6, f/6.3, f/7.1, f/8, f/9, f/10, etc.

1/2 EV step:

- Shutter: 1/90, 1/125, 1/180, 1/250, 1/350, 1/500, etc.
- Aperture: f/5.6, f/6.7, f/8, f/9.5, f/11, f/13, etc.

Compensation

(add a +/- sign according to direction)

1/3 EV step: (0.3 to 5.0)

- 0.3EV, 0.7EV, 1.0EV, 1.3EV, 1.7EV, 2.0 EV, 2.3EV, etc.

1/2 EV step: (0.5 to 5.0)

- 0.5EV, 1.0EV, 1.5EV, 2.0EV, 2.5EV, 3.0EV, 3.5EV, etc.

Bracketing

1/3 EV step: (0.3 to 2.0)

- Bracket: 0.3, 0.7, 1.0, 2.0 (or 1/3, 2/3, 1, 2.0 EV steps)

1/2 EV step: (0.5 to 2.0)

- Bracket: 0.5, 1.0 (or 1/2 and 1 EV steps)

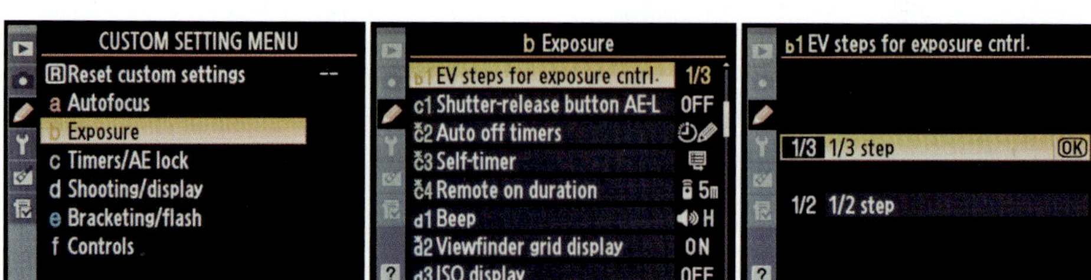

Figure 6 – Custom Setting b1 *(EV steps for exposure cntrl.)*

This is much more complex looking than it really is. Just remember that when you are making adjustments in shutter speed, aperture, compensation, or bracketing, you'll be using 1/3 or 1/2 steps (stops) EV.

My Personal EV Step Selection

I leave my camera set to the default of 1/3 EV step most of the time. This gives me finer control over my exposures. The only time I might consider using 1/2 EV steps is when I am bracketing for high dynamic range (HDR) photography. Often, I'll want to take fewer images than would be required were I to leave it set to 1/3 steps EV since the steps are finer. HDR does better with larger steps of exposure value difference.

How I Use Custom Setting c1

I leave Custom Setting c1 set to *On*. Since I am a nature shooter, I often have to deal with a wide range of exposure. Sometimes I want to try to average the exposures a little on my own. I might expose a beautiful sunset according to the best colors to the right or left of the setting sun disc. I simply focus my lens where I want it, hold the shutter button halfway down to get and lock the exposure, then recompose for the final image. If you would prefer to use only the AE-L/AF-L button for this purpose, then leave *c1* set to *Off*.

Timers/AE Lock - Custom Settings c1 to c4

(User's Manual pages 156–157)

Custom Setting c1 *(Shutter-release button AE-L)*

(User's Manual page 156)

Normally, to lock the exposure you must press the AE-L/AF-L button. However, Nikon has provided another way to lock exposure for those who want to take an exposure reading from one area of the scene and then recompose to take the picture.

If you set Custom Setting c1 to *On*, the exposure will lock each time you press the shutter release down halfway. With it set like this, you can easily take a reading and then move the camera to a new composition for the final exposure. The only settings available in Custom Setting c1 are *On* and *Off*.

In *Figure 7* are the screens used to set Custom Setting c1.

Here are the steps to configure Custom Setting c1:

1. Press the MENU button and scroll to the *Custom Setting Menu*.
2. Select *c Timers/AE lock*, and then scroll to the right.
3. Select *c1 Shutter-release button AE-L* from the menu, and then scroll to the right.
4. Select either *On* or *Off* from the menu.
5. Press the *OK* button.

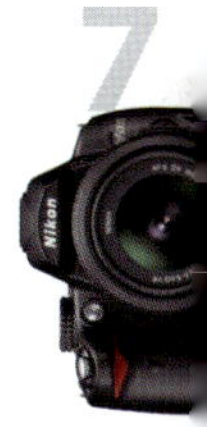

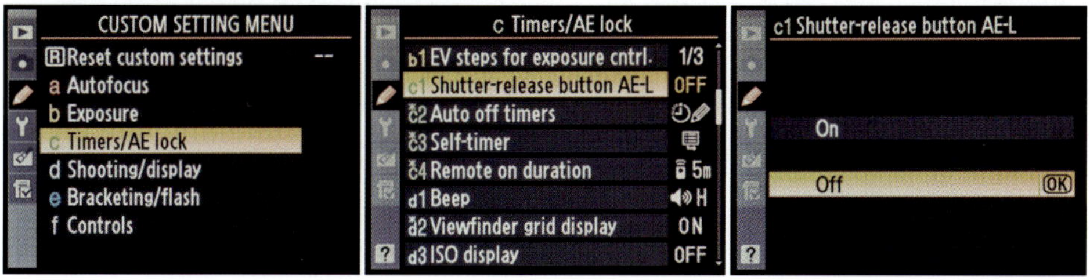

Figure 7 – Custom Setting c1 *(Shutter-release button AE-L)*

Custom Setting c2 *(Auto off timers)*

(User's Manual page 157)

Nikon has combined three separate timed functions under one custom setting. Here is a list of the three things that must be timed:

- *Playback/menus*
- *Image review*
- *Auto meter-off*

You can set these timed functions to one of four different settings.

Timed Functions

1. *SHORT* – Short
- *Playback/menus* get 8 seconds delay.
- *Image review* gets 4 seconds delay.
- *Auto meter-off* gets 4 seconds delay.

2. *NORM* – Normal
- *Playback/menus* get 12 seconds delay.
- *Image review* gets 4 seconds delay.
- *Auto meter-off* get 8 seconds delay.

3. *LONG* – Long
- *Playback/menus* get 20 seconds delay.
- *Image review* gets 20 seconds delay.
- *Auto meter-off* gets 1 minute delay.

4. *Custom*
- *Playback/menus* can be delayed from 8 seconds to 10 minutes.
- *Image review* can be delayed from 4 seconds to 10 minutes.
- *Auto meter-off* can be delayed from 4 seconds to 30 minutes.

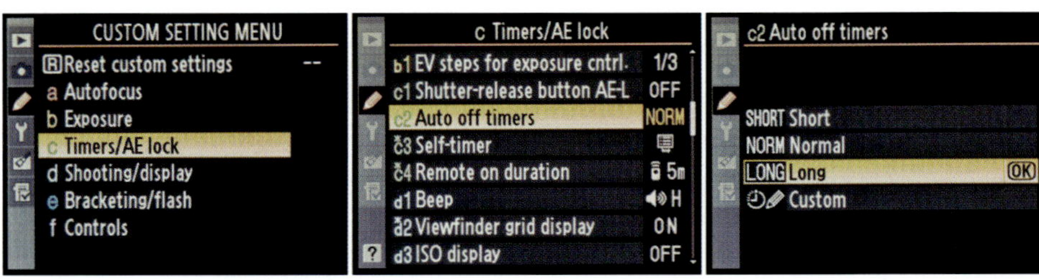

Figure 8 – *Custom Setting c2 (Auto off timers)*

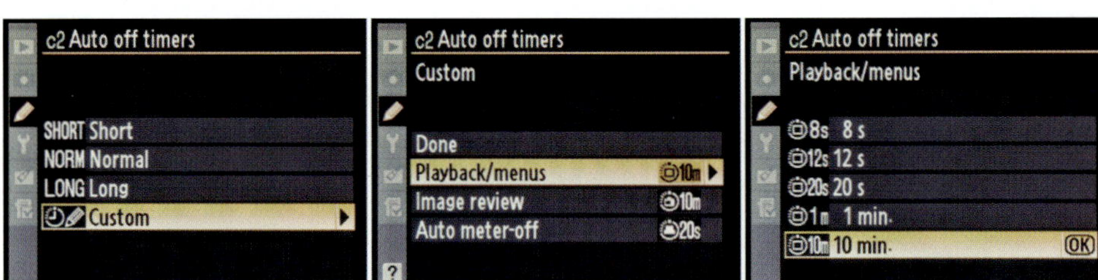

Figure 8A – *Playback/menus* time-out settings

Figure 8 shows the screens to configure the auto off timers to *SHORT*, *NORM*, or *LONG*. The menu screens used to configure the *Custom* option are shown in *figure 8A*, *figure 8B*, and *figure 8C*.

Here are the steps to set the auto off timers:

1. Press the MENU button and scroll to the *Custom Setting Menu*.
2. Select *c Timers/AE lock*, and then scroll to the right.
3. Select *c2 Auto off timers* from the menu, and then scroll to the right.
4. Select the time-out delay period. Please refer to the Timed Functions chart earlier in this section and *figures 8A, 8B, and 8C* for potential settings.
5. Press the *OK* button for *SHORT*, *NORMAL* or *LONG*, or if you're using the *Custom* selection, scroll up to *Done* and press *OK*.

My Own Use of Time Out Settings

This is a highly personal series of settings. I tend to like the longer time-out settings since I want to view my images or set configurations on menus without constantly having to wake up the camera. I do not worry about battery life with this camera since it will last all day, easily. A battery isn't cheap, but having a spare is a good way to remove worries about long time-outs. I use the custom timers and generally have time-outs set to minutes, not seconds.

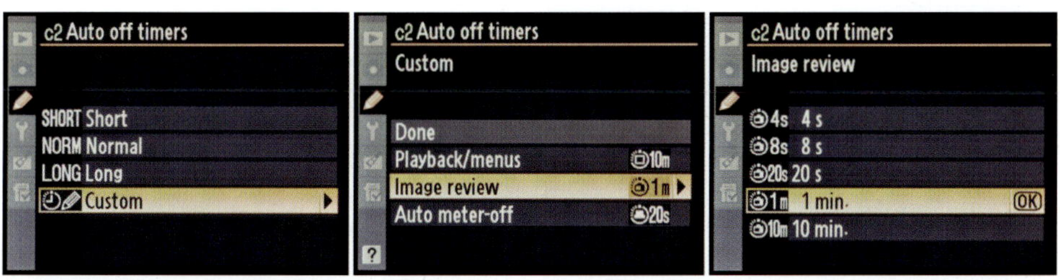

Figure 8B – *Image review* time-out settings

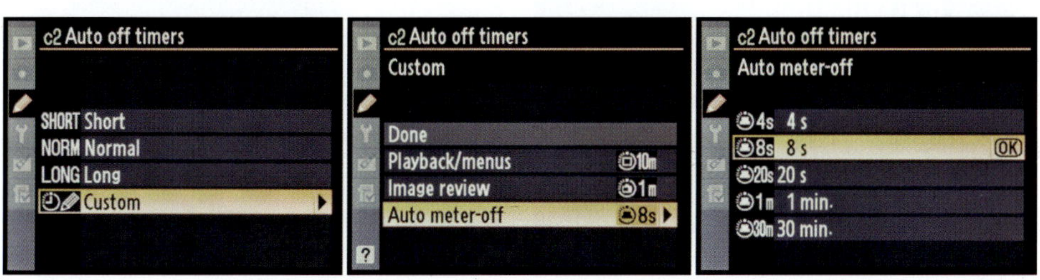

Figure 8C – *Auto meter-off* time-out settings

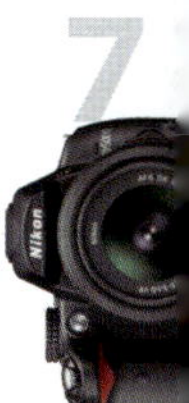

Custom Setting c3 *(Self-timer)*
(User's Manual page 157)
When you set your self-timer for group shots or self-portraits, do you find yourself running like a wild person trying to get in position before the camera fires? Have you ever knocked anyone or anything down or tripped and made a fool of yourself in the process?

Well, those problems are solved with the D5000's adjustable self-timer delay. Whether you are shooting a group shot or just using the self-timer as a cheap remote release, it's good to be able to adjust it up to 20 seconds or down to 2. At the maximum 20 seconds, you have enough time to calmly walk at least 40 or 50 feet from the camera, position yourself, and smile.

Figure 9 shows the menu screens used to configure Custom Setting c3.

One new feature that the D5000 provides is the ability to take multiple pictures each time the self-timer makes the camera fire (see *figure 9A*). You are not limited to just one picture. The D5000 will allow you to take up to nine images with each self-timer cycle. You can set the self-timer delay to these time values:

- *2s* – 2 seconds
- *5s* – 5 seconds
- *10s* – 10 seconds (default)
- *20s* – 20 seconds

Each time the self-timer fires, it will take from one to nine images. Here's how to set your camera to take three pictures

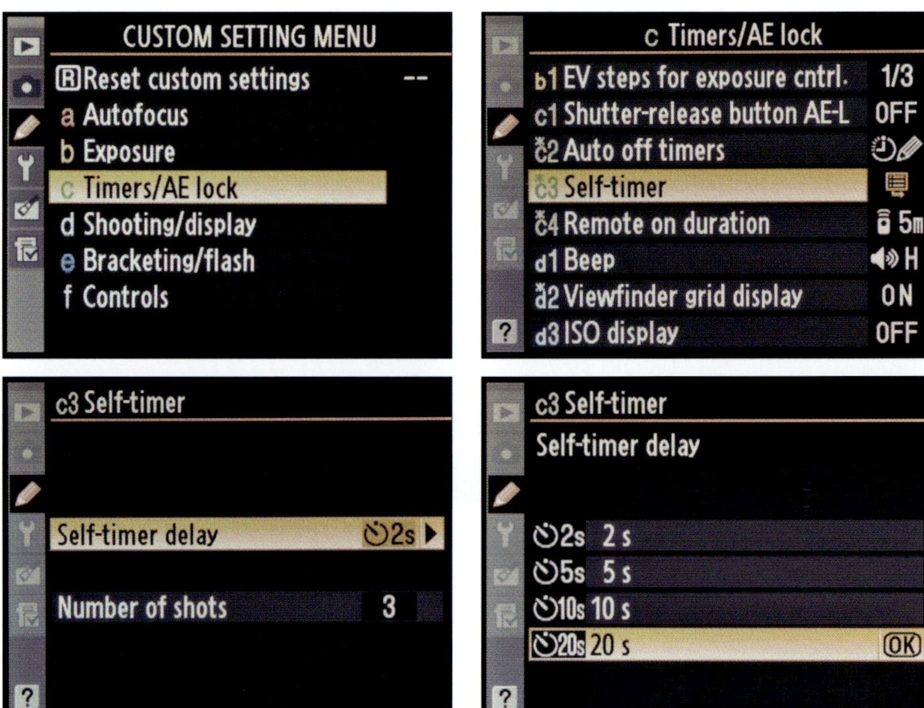

Figure 9 – Custom Setting c3 *(Self-timer)*

after a 20-second delay—for some extra shots in case someone blinks:

1. Press the MENU button and scroll to the *Custom Setting Menu.*
2. Select *c Timers/AE lock*, and then scroll to the right.
3. Select *c3 Self-timer* from the menu, and then scroll to the right.
4. Select *Self-timer delay* from the menu, and then scroll to the right.
5. Select a time value from 2 to 20 seconds from the menu, and then press the *OK* button.
6. Select *Number of shots* from the menu, and then scroll to the right.
7. Using the Multi Selector, scroll up and down until you have set the number of shots you want in this self-timer cycle, then press the *OK* button. (As you can see in *figure 9A*, I selected 3 for this example.)
8. Now you'll need to set the camera for self-timer mode. Press the <**i**> Information edit button twice to open the *Information edit* screen (on the left in *figure 9B*).
9. Select the *Release mode* setting about halfway down on the right. Press *OK* and the camera will switch to the second release mode screen.
10. Scroll down to the third selection from the top in the list (as shown on the right in *figure 9B*). You'll see the self-timer symbol with a number representing seconds to the right (*2s, 5s, 10s, or 20s*, according to what you selected in step 5.)

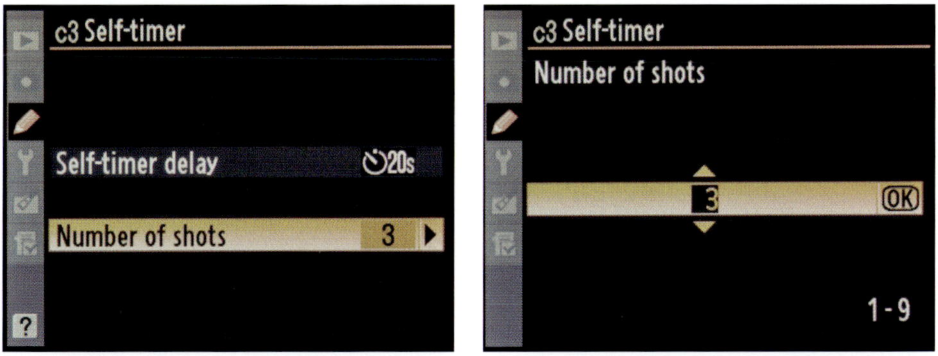

Figure 9A – Number of shots (1-9)

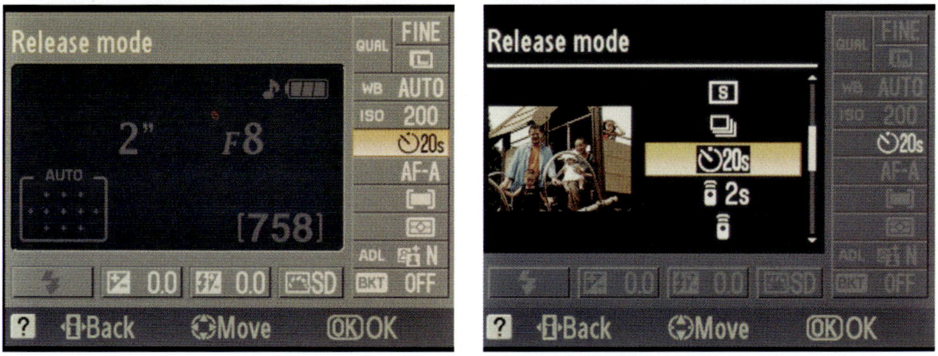

Figure 9B – Setting the self-timer mode with the information edit screens

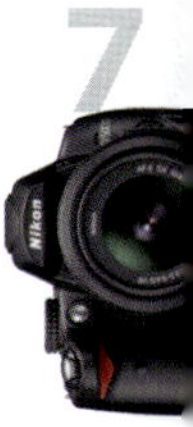

11. Now that you've set the camera to take three pictures after a 20-second delay, you're ready to shoot. At this point, you would set the camera up on a tripod, press the shutter release, and run (or walk) to your assigned spot in the group image.

As the self-timer counts down, it flashes the AF-assist light in a slow pulse and the camera beeps. During the last couple of seconds of countdown, the light stays on continuously and the beep doubles in speed.

When the self-timer delay is finished the D5000 will take however many pictures you've set under Custom Setting c3's *Number of shots* setting (see *figure 9A*). If more than one—as in the example of 3 shots—the camera will fire the shutter with the selected time-out delay between each shot. It might be good to set a short delay when you shoot more than one image in the self-timer cycle.

Special Note On Pop-Up Flash

If you've set your camera to take multiple pictures after a self-timer cycle and then you open the pop-up flash, the camera will ignore the number of images you've set and take only one image. *The pop-up flash cannot recycle fast enough to take more than one image at a time, so the camera will not attempt to take multiple flash shots.*

I used a Nikon SB-400 hot-shoe-mounted flash, instead of the pop-up and the D5000 happily fired the multiple frames. The bigger flash unit was powerful enough to handle the rapid frame rate, so the camera complied. If you do not use flash, the camera will fire however many shots you've selected with no complaint.

Custom Setting c4 *(Remote on duration)*

(User's Manual page 157)

This is an interesting function that controls how long the camera will wait for you to press the button on your self-timer infrared remote. If you set the camera to a self-timer remote mode, either delayed remote or quick-response remote, the D5000 will hold the camera in a ready state for the time delay set in Custom Setting c4. This means that the camera stays prepared for taking a picture, leaving the exposure meter active, until *Remote on duration* times out (User's Manual pages 65–69).

In *figure 10* are the self-timer remote displays in the *Information edit* screens. The screen in the middle shows delayed remote, which caused the camera to fire 2 seconds after you press the infrared remote's button. The screen on the right is the normal quick-response remote,

My Wish for Remote On Duration

At first, I was leaving my *Remote on duration* delay time set to 1 minute. However, recently I have been leaving it on 5 minutes. I wish there was a 2-minute setting because 1 minute is not quite enough time in some instances, especially when there is a large group involved, and 5 minutes is too long.

which causes the camera to fires instantly when you press the infrared remote's button.

Here are the *Remote on duration* delay times:

- *1 min* – 1 minute
- *5 min* – 5 minutes
- *10 min* – 10 minutes
- *15 min* - 15 minutes

Here are the steps to configure Custom Setting c4 (see *figure 10A*):

1. Press the MENU button and scroll to the *Custom Setting Menu.*
2. Select *c Timers/AE lock*, and then scroll to the right.
3. Select *c4 Remote on duration* from the menu, and then scroll to the right.
4. Select a time-out delay period from 1 to 15 minutes.
5. Press the *OK* button.

Shooting/Display - Custom Settings d1 to d7

(User's Manual pages 158–161)

Custom Setting d1 *(Beep)*

(User's Manual page 158)

I don't like my camera beeping at me. The D5000's beeping sound is quite audible. In fact, it sets up a harmonic resonance with the bones in my skull and causes my eyeballs to vibrate. However, you may like it.

The D5000's self-timer *Beep* function is used in a couple of ways. One is to let you know when the self-timer is about to fire. It counts down the seconds with a beep or two per second; then at the last moment, it doubles the beeping frantically to say "Hurry up!" The other is when you are using autofocus in some of its modes, like AF-S and AF-A.

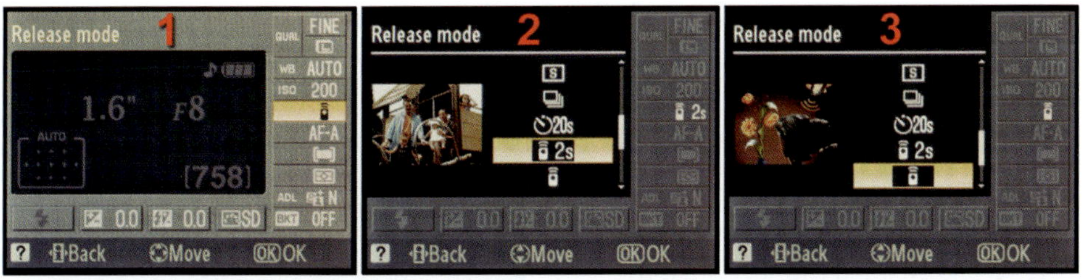

Figure 10 – Self-timer remote displays in the information edit screens

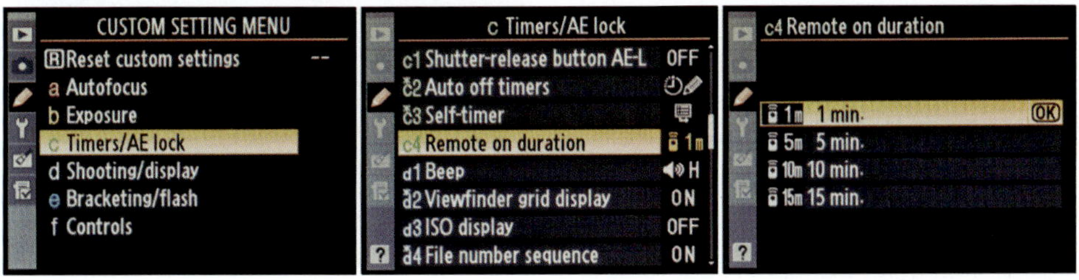

Figure 10A – Custom Setting c5 *(Remote on duration)*

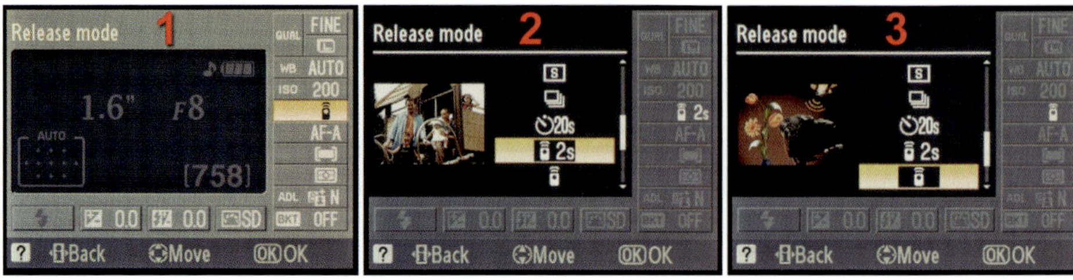

Figure 11 – Custom Setting d1 *(Beep)*

Figure 11 shows the menu screens used to configure Custom Setting d1.

There are three selections for Custom Setting d1:

- *H* –high-pitched beep
- *L* –low-pitched beep
- *Off* – no beep (ah, blessed silence!)

Here are the steps to configure Custom Setting d1:

1. Press the MENU button and scroll to the *Custom Setting Menu*.
2. Select *d Shooting/display*, and then scroll to the right.
3. Select *d1 Beep* from the menu, and then scroll to the right.
4. Select *High*, *Low*, or *Off* from the menu.
5. Press the *OK* button.

If *Beep* is enabled (high or low), the D5000 will beep to let you know the following:

1. When you have focused successfully in single-servo Autofocus (AF-S)
2. When you have focused successfully on a stationary subject in auto-servo autofocus (AF-A)
3. When the release timer is counting down in self-timer and delayed remote modes

Even if *Beep* is enabled, the D5000 will *not* beep under these circumstances:

1. In continuous-servo autofocus (AF-C), since it would be beeping constantly as the focus adjusts to the subject's movement
2. When you're using the Q, or quiet shutter-release, mode (User's Manual page 65)

When the beep is active, you'll see a little musical note displayed on the upper-right side of information screen (see *figure 11A*).

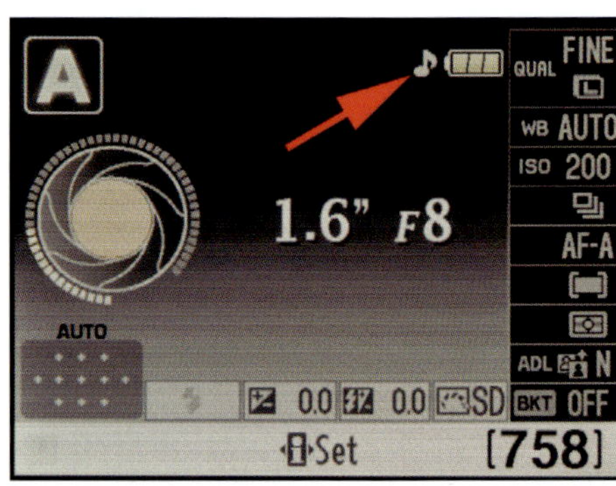

Figure 11A –The symbol in the information screen showing that *Beep* is enabled

I Turn the Beep Off

I turn it off, but you may choose to keep the default setting of on. The fact that the D5000 is set to beep as a default belies the advanced level of the camera. If I were using my camera in a quiet area, why would I want it beeping at me, disturbing those around me? I can just imagine me zooming in on that big grizzly bear, pressing the shutter, and listening to the grizzly roar his displeasure at my camera's beep and focus assist light. I want to live a while longer, so I turn off *Beep*. I wish the default for beeping were *Off*. You may not agree.

Custom Setting d2
(Viewfinder grid display)
(User's Manual page 158)

Several years ago, the Nikon D80 (F80) 35mm film camera was released with a viewfinder grid display and I immediately was hooked. Through the years, as I bought more professional cameras, I was often chagrined to find that they didn't have the "on-demand" gridlines that I had grown to love. With the D5000, we have the viewfinder gridlines!

I use the gridlines to avoid weird and tilted horizons. If you turn the on-demand gridlines on, I doubt you'll turn them back off. The nice thing is that you can turn them on and off at will.

Figure 12 shows the menu screens used to configure *Custom Setting d2*:

Custom Setting d2 has two selections:

- ***On*** – On-demand gridlines are displayed in the viewfinder.
- ***Off*** (default) – No gridlines are displayed.

Here are the steps to configure on-demand gridlines:

1. Press the MENU button and scroll to the *Custom Setting Menu*.
2. Select *d Shooting/display*, and then scroll to the right.
3. Select *d2 Viewfinder grid display* from the menu, and then scroll to the right.
4. Select *On* or *Off* from the menu.
5. Press the *OK* button.

I Love Those Gridlines!

The gridlines help me keep horizons level, and they help me pay attention to the overall level of all my images. I use them to line up with edges when I shoot buildings, trees, or other tall objects. They're a very useful feature. Try them yourself and see if you agree.

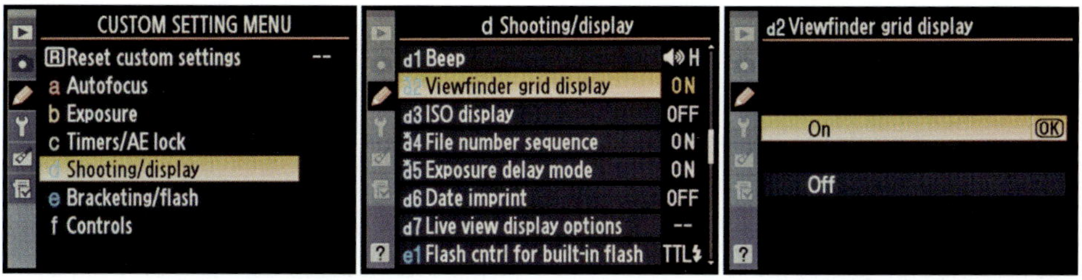

Figure 12 – Custom Setting d2 *(Viewfinder grid display)*

Custom Setting d3 *(ISO display)*

(User's Manual page 158)

This setting allows you to toggle between the frame count (the number of images left on the memory card) and the ISO sensitivity setting in the lower-right corner of the viewfinder.

The camera's information screen shows both the frame count and the ISO, so you always have that to view them both. However, you may prefer to have one of them show up in the viewfinder when you have the camera up to your eye. Use this setting to toggle between them. It won't affect the information display, only the viewfinder.

The screens used to configure the *ISO display* are shown in *figure 13*.

How Many Images Are Left?

I like being able to see how many images I have left. I rarely change the ISO. If I do desire to see or change the ISO sensitivity, I find it quite simple to press the <**i**> info button and load up the information screens. However, if I were more concerned with knowing my ISO on a constant basis, I suppose this would be a convenient feature. Use it if you feel that constant monitoring of your ISO status is more important than a quick reminder of how many frames you have left. I plan on ignoring it, therefore I leave my D5000 set to view the frame count.

Here are the two items that you can select for Custom Setting d3:

- *On*
- *Off*

On –Selecting this setting causes the D5000 to display the current camera ISO sensitivity where it normally would display the frame count.

Off – This is the viewfinder display that you expect to see when you want to know "How many images I can take before the card is full?"

Here are the steps used to configure Custom Setting d3:

1. Press the MENU button and scroll to the *Custom Setting Menu*.
2. Select *d Shooting/display*, and then scroll to the right.
3. Select *d3 ISO display* from the menu, and then scroll to the right.
4. Select *On* or *Off* from the menu.
5. Press the *OK* button.

Custom Setting d4 *(File number sequence)*

(User's Manual page 159)

This setting allows your camera to keep count of the image numbers in a running sequence from 0001 to 9999. After 9999, it rolls back over to 0001. Or, you can cause it to reset the image number to 0001 when you format or insert a new memory card.

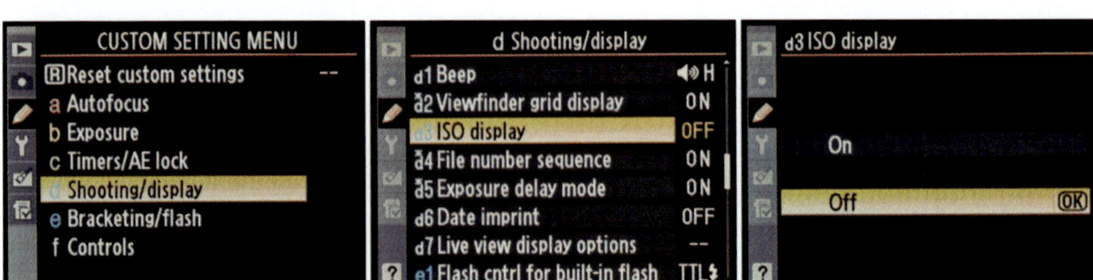

Figure 13 – Custom Setting d3 *(ISO display)*

Figure 14 shows the menu screens used to configure *Custom Setting d4*.

Here are the available selections:

- ***On*** – Image filename numbers start at 0001 and continue running in a series until you exceed 9999, at which time the numbers roll over to 0001 again. If you exceed 9999 images during a shoot, the camera will create a brand-new folder on the same memory card and start writing the new images in order starting from 0001 into the new folder.
- ***Off*** – Whenever you format or insert a new memory card, the number sequence starts over at 0001. If you exceed 999 images in a single folder, the D5000 creates a new folder and starts counting images at 0001 again.
- ***Reset*** – This is similar to the *On* setting. However, it is not a true solution to the running total limit of 9999 since the image number is dependent on the folder in use. The camera simply takes the last number it finds in the current folder and adds 1 to it, up to 999. If you switch to an empty folder, the numbering starts over at 0001.

Here's how to modify the settings under Custom Setting d4:

1. Press the MENU button and scroll to the *Custom Setting Menu*.
2. Select *d Shooting/display*, and then scroll to the right.
3. Select *d4 File number sequence* from the menu, and then scroll to the right.
4. Select *On*, *Off*, or *Reset* from the menu.
5. Press the *OK* button.

Note on Image and Folder Numbering

The D5000 User's Manual on page 182 describes an unusual situation that few of us will ever encounter, unless we manually create folders in a certain way. Each time you exceed 999 images on a memory card, the D5000 will create a new folder. If you ever exceed 999 folders (with 999 images in each) on a memory card (what a large card that would have to be) and your current folder (#999) has 999 images, or an image is numbered 9999, your D5000 will stop responding to shutter button presses.

If this situation occurs, set Custom Setting d4 to *Reset*, and format or insert a new memory card. What I think Nikon means by this warning is clearly that you should never let a folder number go as high as 999 and then shoot over 999 images or let the camera's running total of images exceed 9999 in a folder numbered 999. Basically, just keep your folder numbers lower than 999 if you are going to shoot more than 999 images in a day or your number sequence is about to exceed 9999.

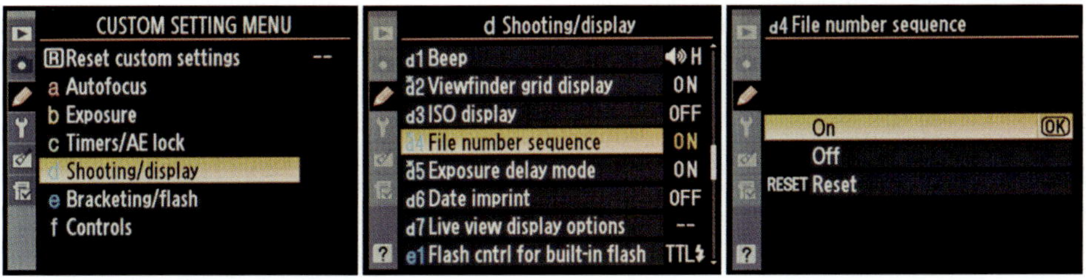

Figure 14 – *Custom Setting d4 (File number sequence)*

Custom Setting d5 ***(Exposure delay mode)***
(User's Manual page 159)

This setting is *very* important to me. As a nature shooter, I use it frequently. When I am shooting handheld (or even on a tripod), I want a really sharp image. The image you see in your viewfinder is provided with the help of a mirror placed in front of the sensor. When you take the picture, the mirror quickly flips out of the way and that sudden motion can cause a very small amount of vibration that you can easily feel each time you trip the shutter. This small vibration is not critical in most average shooting situations, but if you want to eliminate all possible vibration sources for the ultimate in camera stability, the exposure delay mode can help you.

Figure 15 shows the menu screens used to configure Custom Setting d5.

Here are the settings in *d5*:

- *On*
- *Off* (default)

On - The D5000 first raises the mirror and then waits about 1 second before firing the shutter. This allows the vibrations from the mirror to dissipate before the shutter fires. Of course, this won't be useful at all for anyone shooting moving subjects or any type of action shots. But for slow shots of static scenes, this is great to get the sharpest pictures possible.

Off – Shutter has no delay when this setting is turned off.

Here are the steps to configure *Custom Setting d5*:

1. Press the MENU button and scroll to the *Custom Setting Menu*.
2. Select *d Shooting/display*, and then scroll to the right.
3. Select *d5 Exposure delay mode* from the menu, and then scroll to the right.
4. Select *On* or *Off* from the menu.
5. Press the *OK* button.

Use Exposure Delay Mode for Steady Shots

If you handhold your camera, shoot mostly static subjects, and want sharp pictures, this mode will help. If you are using a tripod, this is an excellent setting to use in addition to the camera's self-timer. If you don't have an electronic release cable, just set this delay and shoot with the self-timer. When you press the shutter release, the self-timer will count down however many seconds you've selected in *Custom Setting c3*. Then it will fire the shutter, but the exposure delay mode will be active and make the camera wait a full second with the mirror raised. This action will allow vibrations to die down and provide sharper scenic images. This is one of the settings I always place on *My Menu* for quick access (see chapter 9).

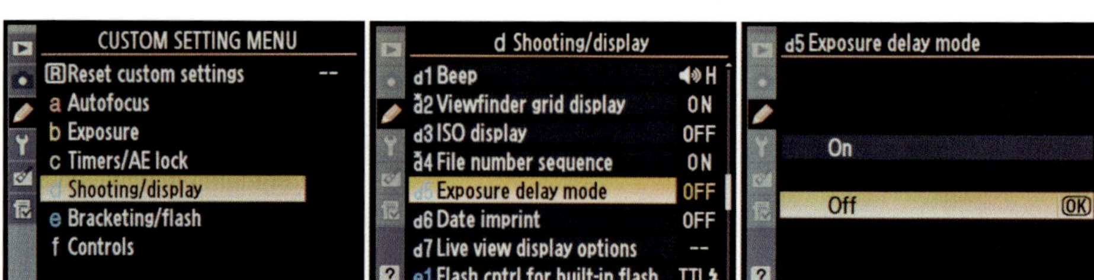

Figure 15 – Custom Setting d5 *(Exposure delay mode)*

Custom Setting d6 *(Date Imprint)*

(User's Manual pages 160 and 161)
Remember how we could set our cameras to imprint a little red date in the lower-right corner of our prints? Well, the D5000 does that too, and in a big way. Not only can you put a date visibly on your images, you can also imprint the date and time or the number of days between the date the image was taken and another chosen date. Here are the four menu choices, along with the formats you can use when you insert date information on your images—*permanently*—and in bright red:

Date Imprint Formatting:

- Off – Nothing is imprinted on the image.
- Date - looks like 7.25.2010
- Date and time – looks like 7.30.2011 08:05
- Date counter - has several formats:
  - Number of days/date: **564/07.18.2012**
  - Years and days/date: **001.198/07.18.2012**
  - Years, months, and days: **001.06.17/07.18.2012**

I understood the date/time well enough, but I had trouble understanding why there's a date counter. Finally, I started to see a reason for recording the number of years, months, and days between the date an image was taken and another chosen date.

An example might be a graduation party. Let's say my daughter graduated from high school on May 20, 2010, and I took a picture of her with some friends. Several years later, on July 30, 2015, I take a reunion picture of her and the same friends. Of course, they all want to see how much they've changed since the first picture 5 years and 10 days earlier, so I put the two images side-by-side. Since they are young and haven't changed much, the newest image needs a date counter. Here are the formats the counter will imprint on the second picture for the this scenario **May 20, 2010 to July 30, 2015:**

- Number of days: **1897/07.30.2015** (days/date)
- Years and days: **005.71/07.30.2015** (years.days/date)
- Years, months, and days: **005.02.10/07.30.2015** (years.months.days/date)

Now, I must admit, this is truly an unusual function to me, and I've been taking pictures since I was a kid back in the late 1960s. However, some segment of society must want this exact feature—and now has it. Maybe police forensic departments or private detectives really need this capability; after all, the information that is recorded is permanently added to the image. The "selected date" for comparison to the shooting date can be a past or future date.

Note on Date Formats

The date format I presented is based on the American MM/DD/YYYY format. However, the camera allows you to adjust the date readout to your favorite format under the *Setup Menu Time zone and date* function. Whatever format you choose under the *Setup Menu* will be shown in the date section of the date imprint. (See chapter 6 and page 169 in the User's Manual for more date format information.)

Figure 16 shows the menu screens to set up the date imprint system.

The screens used to choose an imprint format are shown in *figure 16A*.

Let's look at the steps to set up the entire function:

1. Press the MENU button and scroll to the *Custom Setting Menu*.
2. Select *d Shooting/display*, and then scroll to the right.
3. Select *d6 Date imprint* from the menu, and then scroll to the right.

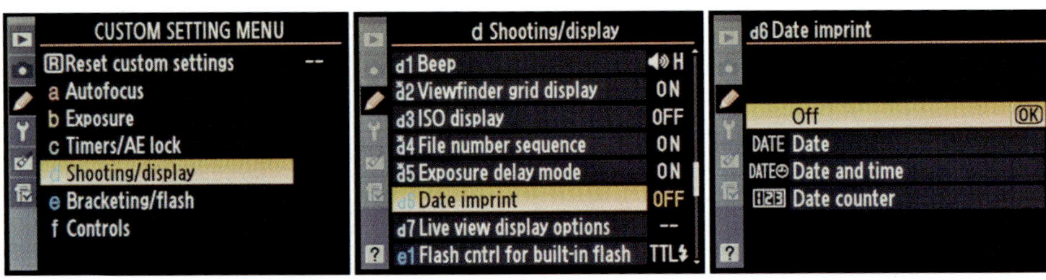

Figure 16 – Custom Setting d6 *(Date imprint)*

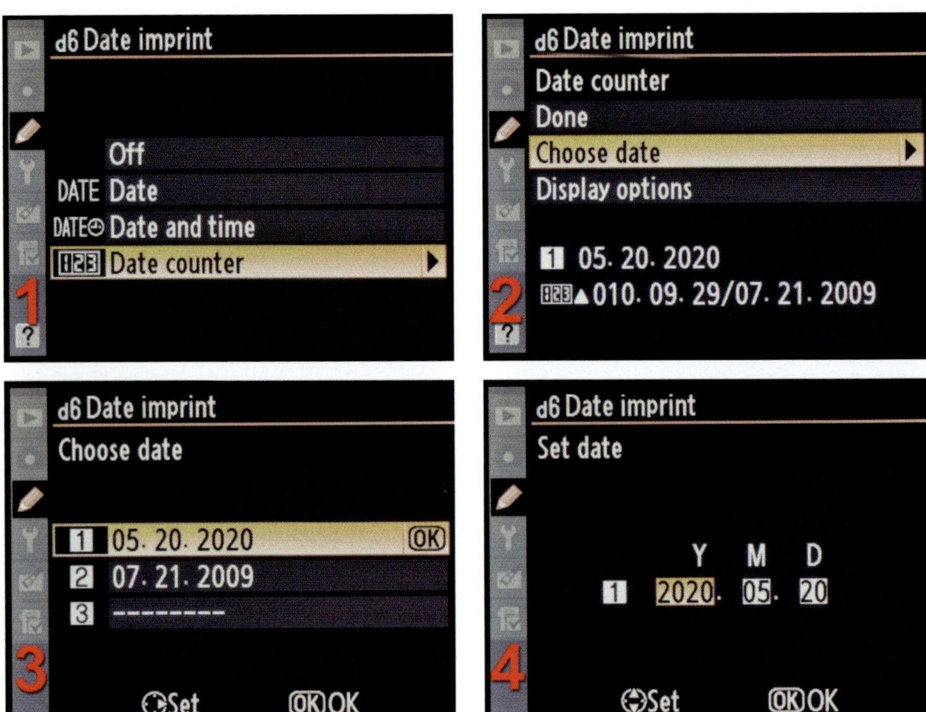

Figure 16A – Choosing the comparison date

4. Choose one of the four choices (*Off*, *Date*, *Date and time*, or *Date counter*). The first three are simple. If you choose *Off*, *Date*, or *Date and time*, just press the *OK* button and skip the rest of these steps. However, if you choose *Date counter*, you'll have to choose a comparison date and a final display format. The next step starts that process.
5. You've chosen *Date counter*, so scroll to the right to set the date and format.
6. On the *Date counter* screen, you'll need to choose the comparison date first. Scroll down to *Choose date*, and then scroll to the right (see *figure 16A, image 2*).
7. You'll find a list that contains either a previously entered date or just a line of dashes (see *figure 16A, image 3*). Choose one of the date positions and scroll to the right to change or set the date. (If an acceptable date is already there from doing this previously, just choose it and press the *OK* button).
8. You'll now see the *Set date* screen for the date position you chose on the previous screen (*1*, *2*, or *3*). Modify this date so that it matches the date you want to compare with your shooting date (see *figure 16A, image 4*). It can be a past or future date. Press the *OK* button, and the camera will return to the *Choose date* screen.
9. Press OK on the date you just modified, and the camera will return to the *Date counter* screen. Next you'll select a display option.
10. Scroll down to the *Display option* line and then scroll to the right (see the screen on the left in *figure 16B*).
11. You'll now see the *Display options* screen (on the right in *figure16b*). Your choices are *Number of days*, *Years and days*, and *Years, months, and days*. Choose one and press the *OK* button.
12. At the bottom of the *Date counter* screen, you'll see the chosen comparison date and below that the format in which the date will be written on the image (see the bottom half of the screen on the left in *figure 16B*). The format shows after the "*123*" icon and the small white triangle and looks like one of the formats in the date imprint format chart shown previously.
13. Take your picture.

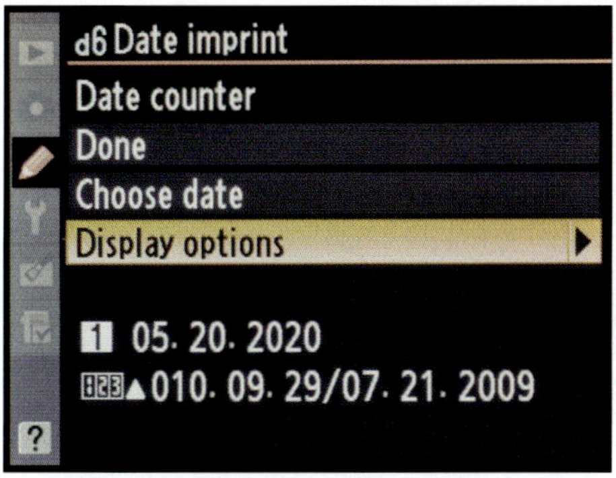

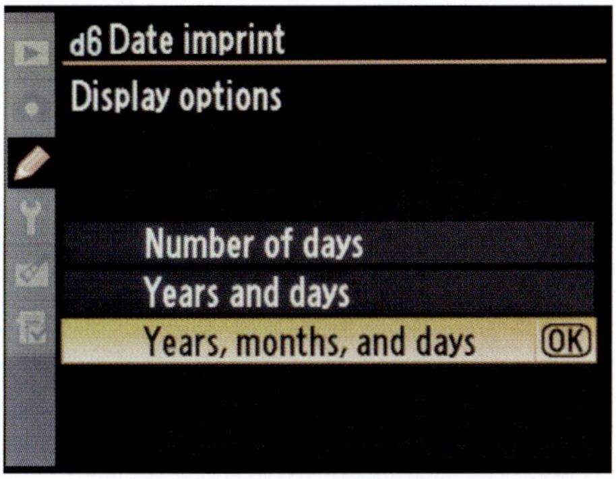

Figure 16B – Choosing a display option (format)

I realize that this is a somewhat complex-looking function. However, if you will study how the date counter formats work and use this function regularly, it will become easy to understand

Recommendation

I normally don't use this functionality myself since I don't want bright red characters written permanently on my images. The EXIF data inside the digital image contains dates and times in case I need to know that information. However, you may love having a date imprinted on your images—a lot of people do. Or, you might have a scientific, forensic, or surveillance purpose for some of these functions. They work easily and well. Nikon gives us a lot of choices with this little camera.

Custom Setting d7
(Live view display options)

(User's Manual pages 161 and 45)

This custom setting is designed to let you set up how the camera's display screen acts in live view and D-Movie modes. The setting is a bit confusing, to say the least, with mutually exclusive menu items that can be selected at the same time. This causes selected items you expect to see showing not to display at all. Normally, I am not all that critical of Nikon's superior software design, but in my opinion, this custom setting needs some attention.

Also, I've found what appears to be a label display bug in the D5000's firmware. It just shows a malformed label, not affecting functionality. I'm sure that this will be fixed in the first available firmware update, but I thought I should mention it in case you've purchased a new or used D5000 with firmware version A: 1.00, B: 1.00, and L: 1.001. You can look at the bottom of the *Setup Menu* under *Firmware version* to see what firmware your camera is using. If you have a newer firmware, you may not see the bug at all.

I'll show you the bug later, but first let's look at how this setting is configured. The menu screens you'll use to set the live view display options are shown in *figure 17*.

Here are the steps you'll use to configure Custom Setting d7:

1. Press the MENU button and scroll to the *Custom Setting Menu*.
2. Select *d Shooting/display*, and then scroll to the right.
3. Select *d7 Live view display options* from the menu, and then scroll to the right.
4. You'll now see the various check boxes you can select/deselect by scrolling to the right with the Multi Selector. Each of these changes how the camera dis-

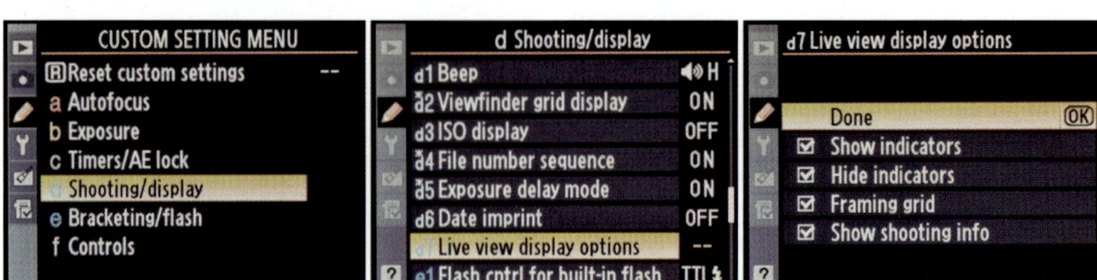

Figure 17 – Custom Setting d7 *(Live view display options)*

plays things on the live view screen. Choose your favorite selections.

5. Scroll up to the *Done* line, and press the *OK* button.

Here are the selections you can make and the live view screens that result. I shot the live view screens—on the right side—against a gray background to emphasize the appearance of the screen (otherwise an image would appear there).

- ***Show indicators*** –The image on the right in *figure 17A* shows how the live view screen looks when *Show indicators* is selected. This selection will override the next selection, *Hide indicators*. You can have both of them checked, even though you can't have it both ways. The indicators will still be displayed when you have both *Show indicators* and *Hide indicators* checked.
- ***Hide indicators*** –*Figure 17B* shows how the live view screen looks when *Hide indicators* is selected. There are no indicators showing as you saw in *figure 17A*. You must select *Hide indicators* only to actually hide the indicators. If you check both *Hide indicators* and *Show indicators*, they will show. It's a little unusual to have mutually exclusive items of this type that can both be selected at the same time. Maybe Nikon will improve on this setup in the next firmware update.
- ***Framing grid*** – See *figure 17C*. This lays out a very nice grid to allow you to

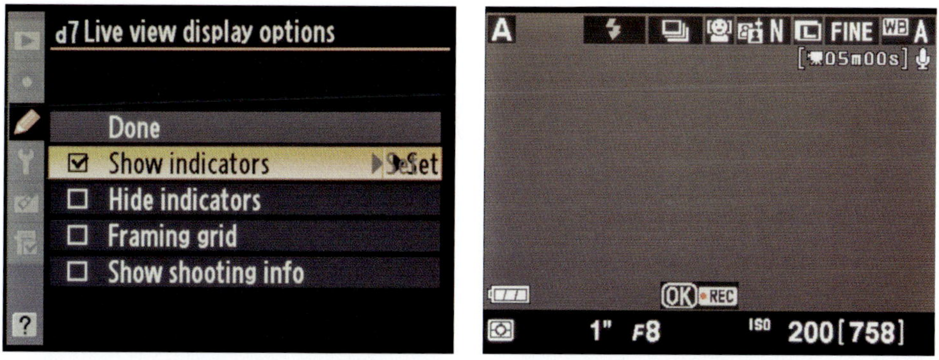

Figure 17A – *Show indicators* selected

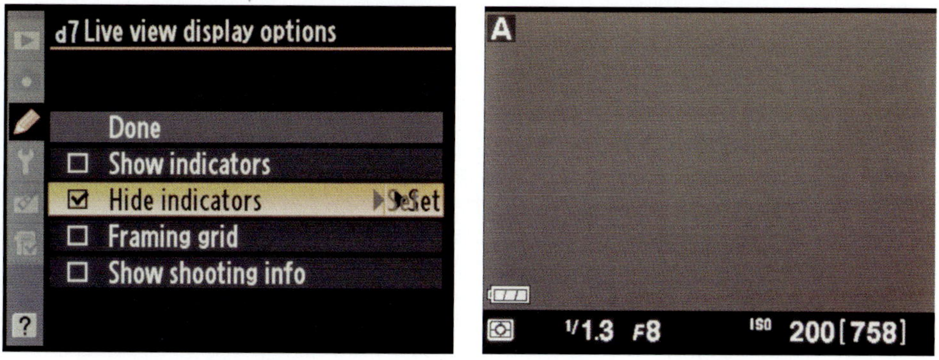

Figure 17B – *Hide indicators* selected

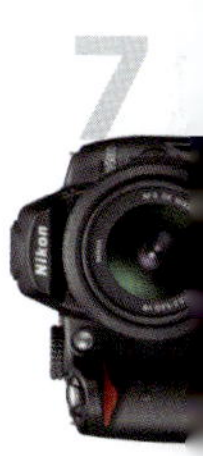

keep things straight and level when using the live view and D-Movie screens. *Framing grid* will not display if you have either *Show indicators* or *Hide indicators* checked. *Framing grid* overrides the next selection *Show shooting info*. If you select both *Framing grid* and *Show shooting info*, only *Framing grid* will be enabled.

- ***Show shooting info*** – See *figure 17D*. This selection causes the live view display to include a screen similar to the *Information edit* screen. You will see the basic shooting information for the current image or movie displayed on the right and bottom of the live view screen. If you have checked any of the first three menu selections, they will override this setting completely.

Consider each of these settings to be mutually exclusive, which means that you should expect only one of them to work at a time. Priority seems to be top to bottom in this list, with the top items overriding the bottom items, even if they are all checked as active. It would be good if Nikon fixes the firmware to make this clearer. Selecting an item that overrides an already selected item should cause the overridden item to uncheck by itself. You must always have at least one of the four display types checked. You cannot uncheck them all at the same time.

Recommendation

I normally use the *Show indicators* or *Framing grid* selection, according to what

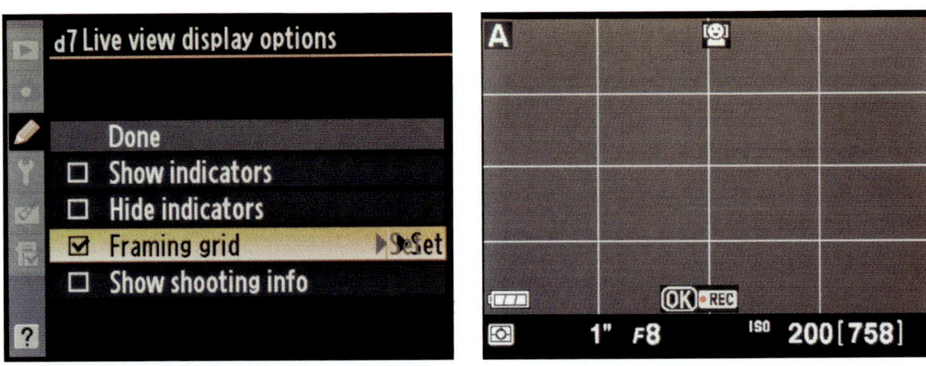

Figure 17C – *Framing grid* selected

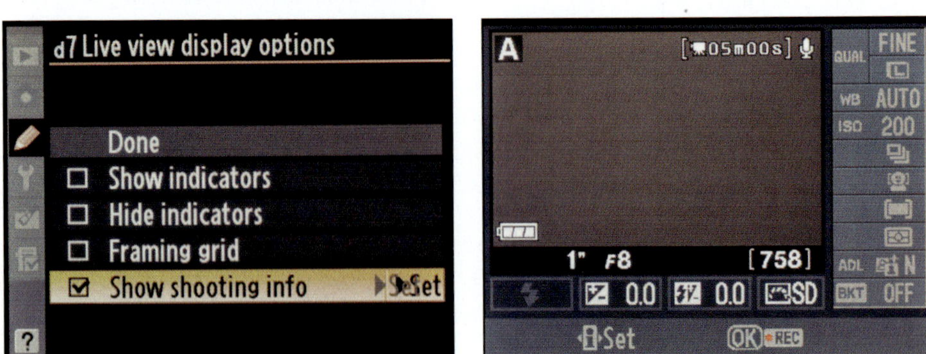

Figure 17D – *Show shooting info* selected

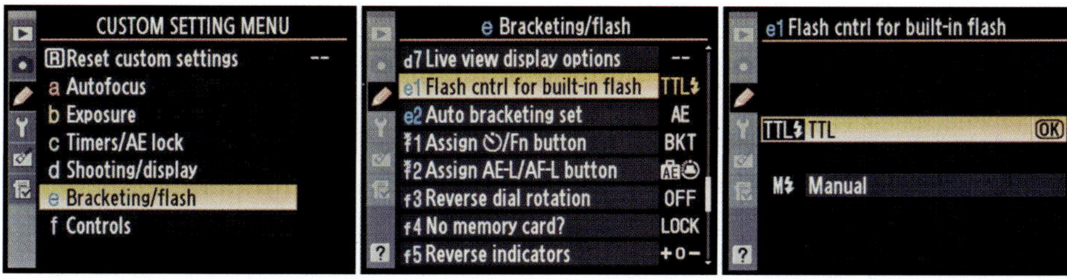

Figure 18 – Custom Setting e1 *(Flash cntrl for built-in flash)*

I'm shooting. Some may prefer the *Hide indicators* screen due to its simplicity or the *Show shooting info* screen to see and easily adjust the current aperture, shutter, and mode dial settings.

Note on Label Bug

You can clearly see the garbled label in any of the screens in *figures 17A* through *17D*, at the end of each line with a check box. As I mentioned earlier, if you have a newer version of the firmware, your camera may not display this bug. You'll see a garbled label only when you've unchecked all the items except for one. Once you check another of the selections, the labels look normal again. However, when you check more than one, just remember that selections at the top have priority and override selections lower in the list.

Note on D-Movie Mode

Please be aware that if you're using *Show shooting info* in the D-Movie mode, the information listed does not really apply. Even though you can adjust certain functions on this screen during the recording of a movie, the changed settings are *not* applied to the movie. This is discussed in greater detail in chapter 12, "D-Movie Mode: Video on Demand." You actually have very little control over the camera's settings when you are shooting a video.

Bracketing/Flash - Custom Settings e1 and e2

(User's Manual page 162)

Custom Setting e1 *(Flash cntrl for built-in flash)*

(User's Manual pages 70, 162, and 198)

If you are a frequent user of flash, Custom Setting e1 may be important to you. It allows you to configure your camera to use the built-in flash unit as a fully automatic unit or let's you take over and shoot manual flash.

Figure 18 shows the menu screens used to configure Custom Setting e1.

As you can see, the D5000 has two distinct ways to control flash output. First, we'll look at the most popular mode, TTL (see *figure 18A*):

TTL – Also known as iTTL, this mode is the standard mode for taking flash

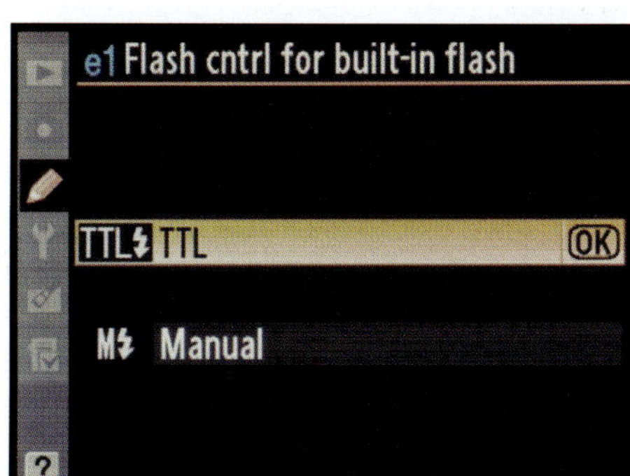

Figure 18A – TTL flash mode selected

pictures with the D5000. *TTL* stands for *through the lens*, and it allows very accurate and balanced flash output using a preflash method to determine correct exposure before the main flash burst fires. This is a completely automatic mode and will adjust to distances along with the various shutter speeds and apertures your camera is using.

Here are the steps to set the camera to *TTL* mode:

1. Press the MENU button and scroll to the *Custom Setting Menu*.
2. Select *e Bracketing/flash*, and then scroll to the right.
3. Select *e1 Flash cntrl for built-in flash* from the menu, and then scroll to the right.
4. Select *TTL* from the menu.
5. Press the *OK* button and go take your pictures.

M – ***Manual*** (see *figure 18B*) – This mode allows you to manually control the output of your flash. The range of settings can go from full power to 1/128 power,.

Here are the steps to set the camera to manual mode:

1. Press the MENU button and scroll to the *Custom Setting Menu*.
2. Select *e Bracketing/flash*, and then scroll to the right.
3. Select *e1 Flash cntrl for built-in flash* from the menu, and then scroll to the right.
4. Choose *Manual* from the menu and then scroll to the right.
5. You'll be presented with a list that allows you to select different levels of flash power output. Choose one of the selections from full to 1/32 power.
6. Press the *OK* button. You now have full manual control over the flash.

Recommendation

Unless you are using the flash unit in a very precise way in a controlled studio environment, it may be best to just leave it in *TTL* mode. The pop-up unit is powerful enough to light up your subjects out to between 10 and 15 feet, according to ISO sensitivity. It has a guide number of 59 (in feet) at 200 ISO (18 in meters). If you need more range, check out the cool little SB-400 flash. It mounts in the D5000's hot-shoe on top and will light up even further away.

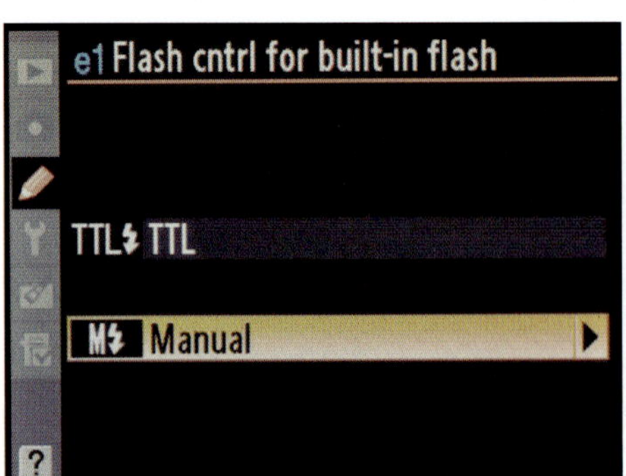

Figure 18B – Manual flash mode selected

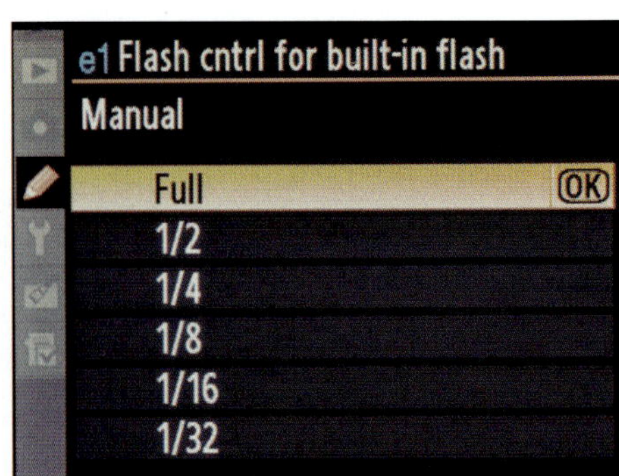

Creative Lighting System (CLS)

While the D5000 is not a commander unit for Nikon's powerful CLS flash system, you can mount the SU-800 Wireless Commander Unit on the D5000 to control up to three banks of an unlimited number of SB-600, SB-800, or SB-900 flash units. Or, you can use the commander mode built into the SB-800 or SB-900 flash units to control up to two banks. The SB-400 flash does not have a place in the CLS system.

Custom Setting e2 *(Auto bracketing set)*
(User's Manual pages 103-105 and 162)
This setting allows you to control how bracketing works within your D5000. There are three different functions that allow bracketing, which I'll discuss later. This setting is designed to work in exposure modes P, S, A, and M but none of the scene modes.

The menu screens used to configure Custom Setting e2 are shown in *Figure 19*.

Here are the settings within Custom Setting e2:

- *AE bracketing*
- *WB bracketing*
- *ADL bracketing*

AE bracketing – Your bracketing settings will affect only the exposure system and not the flash. It varies the exposure by a specific amount over three separate images. Bracketing is described in the next section.

WB bracketing – White balance bracketing is described in detail in chapter 4. It's similar to exposure and flash bracketing except it is designed for bracketing color in "mired" values instead of light in EV step values.

ADL bracketing – Active D-Lighting bracketing provides two images, one not D-Lighted and the second with your current D-Lighting selection in the *Shooting Menu > Active D-Lighting* section.

Here is how to configure Custom Setting e2 (see *figure 19*):

1. Press the MENU button and scroll to the *Custom Setting Menu*.
2. Select *e Bracketing/flash*, and then scroll to the right.
3. Select *e2 Auto bracketing set* from the menu, and then scroll to the right.
4. Select one of the three types of bracketing from the menu.
5. Press the *OK* button.

Now let's consider how to use the bracketing systems. We'll use the *Information edit* screen to select our bracketing parameters. However, it is necessary to first set the *type* of bracketing by using Custom Setting e2.

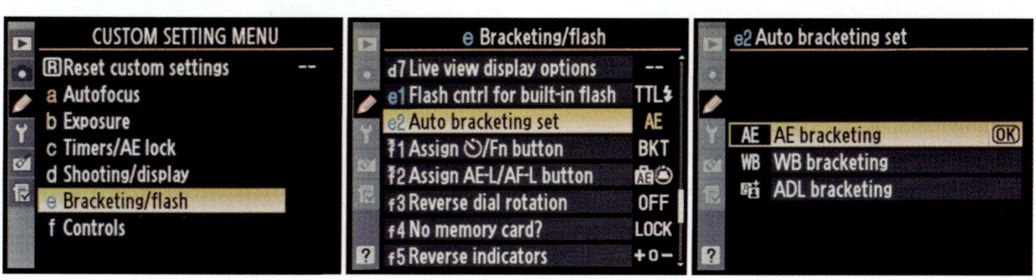

Figure 19 – Custom Setting e2 *(Auto bracketing set)*

How to Use AE Bracketing

You can select from several levels of bracketing. According to how you have Custom Setting b1, set you can bracket an image in .3 or .5 EV steps (see Custom Setting b1 *EV steps for exposure contrl* earlier in this chapter). There are two ways to implement bracketing:

- ***Using the Information edit screen:*** You can select the level of bracketing from the *Information edit* screen. This is the easiest and more visual of the methods.
- ***Using the Fn button/command dial:*** If you assign the Fn button to *Auto bracketing* (BKT) in Custom Setting f1, you can bracket images by holding down the Fn button and rotating the command dial to select a bracket level. Custom Setting f1 will be explained later in this chapter.

Let's discuss how to use both of these methods, and you choose your favorite:

- ***Using the Information edit screen:*** First, you'll need to set your camera to continuous release mode if you are using AE or ADL bracketing (see *figure 19A*).

When you set the camera to continuously take pictures when you hold down the shutter release button, your D5000 will fire off a three-image burst when you are in *AE bracketing* mode. The burst of three images will contain one underexposed by the EV level selected, one normally exposed, and one overexposed.

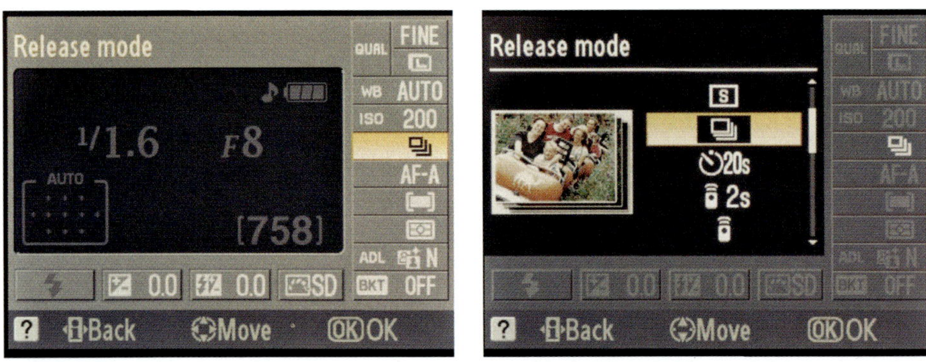

Figure 19A – Selecting continuous release mode

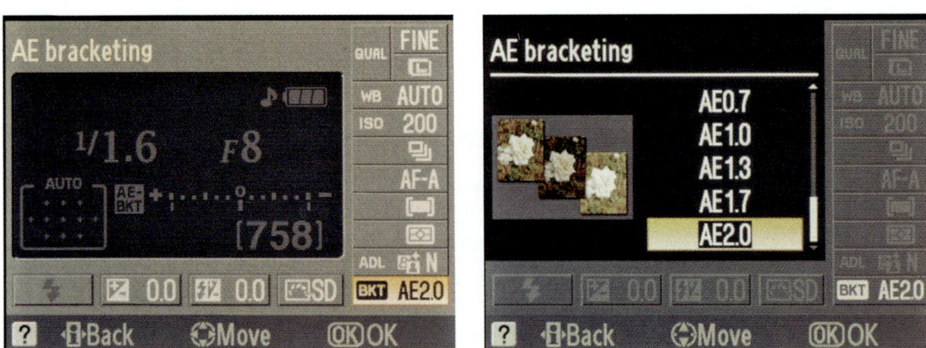

Figure 19B – *AE bracketing* set by using the information edit screens.

Then the camera will stop shooting. Normally, in continuous release mode the D5000 would shoot up to 4 frames per second until its memory buffer was full. However, while using *AE bracketing* and continuous release, the camera will fire only the three frames in the bracket. If you are shooting an ADL bracket, instead of AE, there will be only two images in the bracket. So continuous release will stop after the second image is taken. You do not need to set the camera to continuous release when you are shooting *WB bracketing* since the camera only takes one image and modifies it with three different white balance values (see chapter 4).

It isn't absolutely necessary that you use continuous release mode—you can just shoot the three pictures in the bracket individually. However, I've found that using continuous release often makes sharper pictures since you're only pressing and holding the shutter release once for the entire burst of images.

Next, you'll need to select an exposure level to use on the over- and underexposed images. This *level* will vary according to the type of bracketing. I'll discuss this in the step-by-step instructions.

Here are the specific steps used to make your series of bracketed images:

1. Press the <**i**> information edit button twice to open the *Information edit* screen. (See *figure 1* for the locations of the camera controls.)

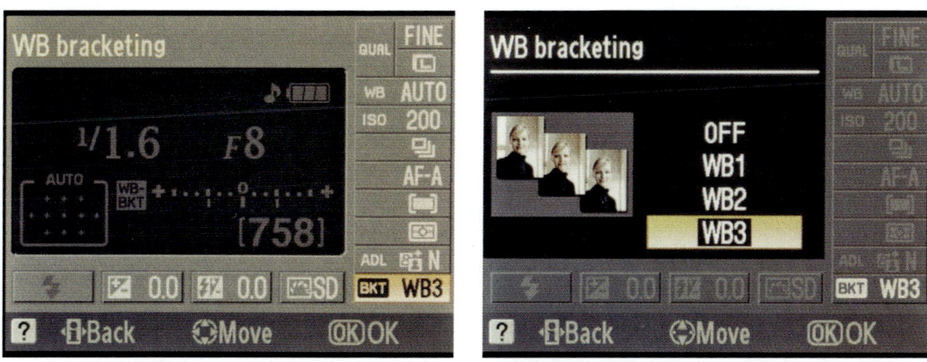

Figure 19C – *WB bracketing* set by using the information edit screens.

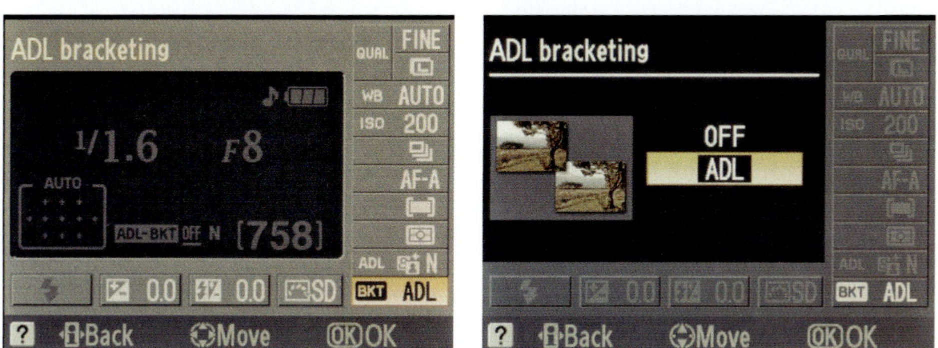

Figure 19D – *ADL bracketing* set by using the information edit screens.

2. Scroll down to the *Release mode* setting and press the *OK* button (see the screen on the left in *figure 19A*).
3. The camera will now switch to the second *Release mode* screen, with a list of release modes. Scroll down to the second one from the top (it looks like a series of three overlapping rectangles, as shown in the screen on the right in *figure 19A*).
4. Press the *OK* button to select continuous release mode. The camera will switch back to the main *Information edit* screen.
5. Now, scroll down to the bottom-right bracketing setting. The name will vary according to the type of bracketing you have selected in Custom Setting e2. It can be *AE bracketing*, *WB bracketing*, or *ADL bracketing*. Each will give you a different series of choices:
   - For *AE bracketing* your choices will be *AE0.3* (or *AE0.5*) to *AE2.0*.
   - For *WB bracketing* your choices will be *WB1* to *WB3* (see chapter 4).
   - For *ADL bracketing* your choice will be *ADL*.
6. Choose one of the bracketing levels that fits what you are shooting. The levels will work in this way:
   - ***AE bracketing*** uses three exposures. The first exposure is normal, the second is underexposed by the level value you've selected (0.3 [or 0.5] to 2.0 EV), and the third is overexposed by the same level. (See *figure 19B*.)
   - ***WB bracketing*** uses one exposure, creates two duplicates with different WB values, and saves them under new filenames. The first is the normal selected WB value; the second is 5,10, or 15 mode amber, according to what level you've selected (*WB1, WB2, WB3*); the third has additional blue added according to the same level. (See *figure 19C*.)
   - ***ADL bracketing*** uses two exposures. The first is a normal exposure with Active D-Lighting off, and the second is an exposure using the Active D-Lighting setting you've made in the *Shooting Menu* (low to extra high). (See *figure 19D*.)
7. Once you've selected the type of bracketing and the *level* of the various exposures, go shoot your images.

Now, let's examine how to set the bracketing type and levels using the *Fn* button (see *figure 1* for the locations of the camera control.) You'll have to set Custom Setting f1 to *Auto bracketing* (BKT) or these steps won't work—see the next section for how to configure *f1*.

Using the Fn button/command dial: There is little difference in this method other than how you select the level of the bracket. Once you've set Custom Setting f1 to *BKT*, or *Auto bracketing*, you'll have the ability to initiate your bracket levels by holding down the Fn button and rotating the command dial. Here are the steps to accomplish that:

1. Press and hold the Fn button next to the D5000 logo on the camera's front.
2. An information screen opens with the type of bracketing showing in a label in the upper-right corner. You'll see *AE bracketing*, *WB bracketing*, or *ADL bracketing*.

3. Rotate the command dial and select the level you want to use. Here's what happens when you hold down the Fn button and rotate the command dial for each type of bracketing:
   - ***AE bracketing*** shows in the upper-left corner of the information screen (see *figure 19E*). When you rotate the command dial, you'll see small lines appear below a 2-stop indicator. These lines hanging down below the indicator represent the level of exposure bracketing between 0.3 or 0.5 and 2.0 EV. Next to the *BKT* icon, in the lower-right corner of the screen, you'll see a setting from *AE0.3* to *AE2.0* appear as you turn the command dial. This number after *AE* (0.3 to 2.0) is a numerical representation of the 2-stop indicator's current value. The spread of these lines represents how wide the exposure variation is in the bracket. In *figure 19E*, I have selected a 1-stop variation (*AE1.0*). Each image you take will have 1 step EV difference (see chapter 2 for information on EV steps or stops). The first image will be a normal exposure, the second is an underexposure, and the third is an overexposure. Each of the exposure variations will be based on the level value you've selected. You'll need to take three exposures to get the complete bracket.
   - ***WB bracketing*** shows in the upper-left corner of the information screen (See *figure 19F*). It too has an indicator, but it does not represent EV steps. When you see the indicator change as you hold the Fn button and turn the command dial, each hanging line represents color differences in *mired* amounts (*WB1* = 5 mired, *WB2* = 10 mired, *WB3* = 15 mired). Each of those mired values adds either amber or blue—in increasing amounts—to the normal image according to which one you select. I've selected *WB3* in *figure*

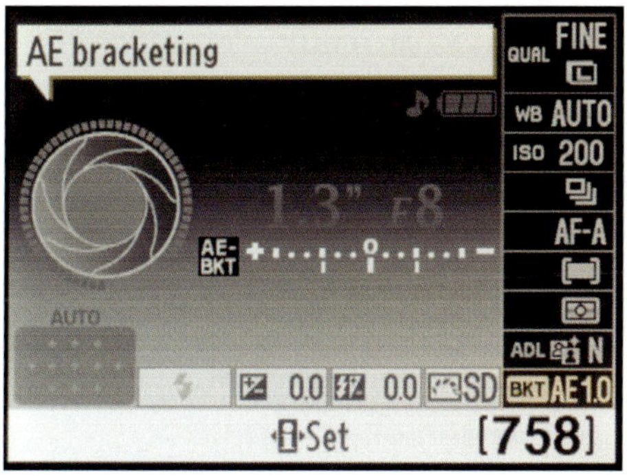

Figure 19E – *AE bracketing* set by using the Fn button

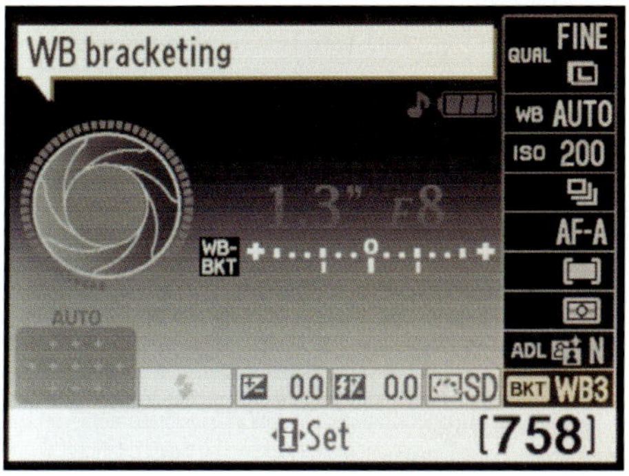

Figure 19F – *WB bracketing* set by using the Fn button

19F for 15 mired bracketing in the amber and blue directions. See chapter 4 for more detailed information. The first image will have the current camera white balance, the second will have more amber, the third more blue. You will only need to take one image and the camera will create the other two automatically under new filenames.

- ***ADL bracketing*** shows in the upper-left corner of the information screen (see *figure 19G*). There is no indicator shown with *ADL bracketing* because it only has two choices, no Active D-Lighting (ADL) and whatever the currently selected *Shooting Menu's* Active D-Lighting setting happens to be. When you hold the Fn button and turn the command dial, you'll simply see the BKT line change from *Off* to *ADL*. You'll need to take two images in the ADL bracket. The first will have no ADL, and the second will have the current camera ADL setting applied.

4. Once you've selected your type of bracketing and the level of exposure variation, go take your pictures.

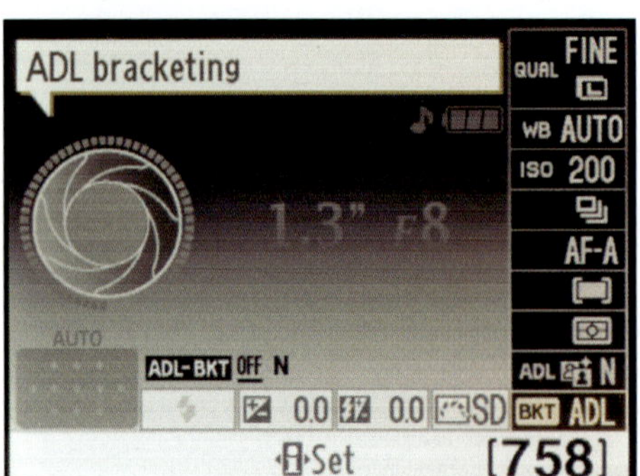

Figure 19G – *ADL bracketing* set by using the Fn button

Recommendation

I like to use the Fn button/command dial method simply because the information screen responds as soon as I press the Fn button and I can use the command dial instead of having to scroll through multiple screens to change the levels. However, the *Information edit* screen method is very simple to use and easy to understand. Maybe you'll learn to use it first and then learn the Fn button/command dial method when you've mastered the first.

Controls - Custom Settings f1 to f5

(User's Manual pages 163-164)

Custom Setting f1 *(Assign FN button)*

(User's Manual page 163)

The function, or Fn, button—also known as the FUNC. button in much Nikon literature—is a multipurpose programmable button for your use. There are eight specific functions from which you can select. The Fn button will then assume the particular function you've chosen, until you decide to change it. It's a shortcut to your favorite camera adjustments and may save you time because you won't have to scroll through several screens to set a frequently used function from the eight available.

The Fn button is located next to the D5000 label on the front of the camera (see *figure 1*). The screens used to configure Custom Setting f1 are shown in *figure 20*.

Here are the steps to configure Custom Setting f1:

1. Press the MENU button and scroll to the *Custom Setting Menu*.

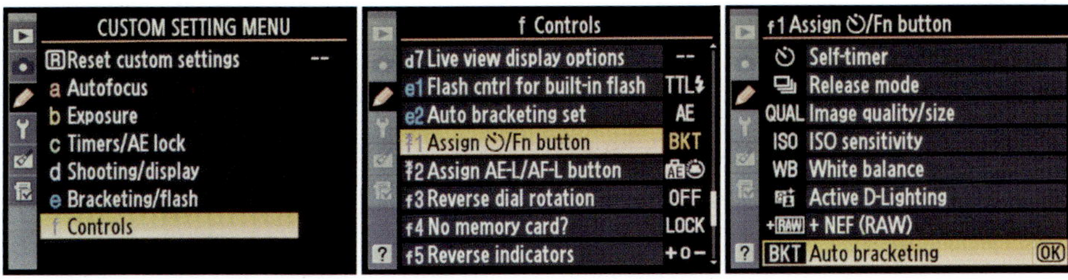

Figure 20 – Custom Setting f1 *(Assign Fn button)*

2. Select *f Controls*, and then scroll to the right.
3. Select *f3 Assign Fn button* from the menu, and then scroll to the right.
4. Select one of the eight choices from the menu.
5. Press the *OK* button.

Here is the list of the eight Fn button functions and how to use them:

- ***Self-timer:*** Press the Fn button to toggle the self-timer on and off. Whatever value you have set in Custom Setting c3 will be the amount of time delay used by the self-timer. When you press the button, you'll see the *Release mode* field of the information screen toggle between whatever mode you started with and the self-timer (User's Manual pages 69 and 157).
- ***Release mode:*** Press and hold the Fn button while rotating the command dial. You'll see the release modes scroll by on the information screen. You can select any of them, including single, continuous, self-timer, delayed and quick-response remote, and quiet shutter-release (User's Manual page 65).
- ***Image quality/size:*** Press and hold the Fn button while rotating the command dial. Each click-turn of the dial will present you with different image quality and size settings. You can scroll through all the qualities, like RAW, JPEG or RAW+JPEG, and each of the Basic, Fine, and Normal sizes. (User's Manual page 62).
- ***ISO sensitivity:*** Press and hold the Fn button while rotating the command dial. Each click-turn of the dial will present you with different ISO sensitivities between Lo 1.0 (100 ISO) and Hi 1.0 (6400 ISO). You'll see the ISO value changing in the information screen's ISO field. The normal range of ISO sensitivity is 200 to 3200. Be careful of ISO sensitivities above 800 ISO because extra noise may make your images look grainy (User's Manual page 74).
- ***White balance:*** Press and hold the Fn button while rotating the command dial. Each click-turn of the dial will present you with different white balance symbols. You'll see the value changing in the information screen's WB field. You'll need to familiarize yourself with each of the symbols shown in the *White balance* screen. Chapter 4 discusses these symbols, as does page 96 in the User's Manual. Remember, each *WB* symbol represents a preset color temperature (image tint), with the final

one called *PRE* containing the last ambient light *WB* reading you've made with a white or gray card.

- ***Active D-Lighting:*** Press and hold the Fn button while rotating the command dial. Each click-turn of the dial will present you with different ADL settings, such as *Off*, *L* (Low), *N* (Normal), *H* (High) *H** (Extra high), and *A* (Auto). Each setting will lower the image contrast so that more detail is found in darker areas. Be careful of ADL values above N because extra noise may make the darker areas of your images look grainy and the lack of shadows may make the image look unnatural (User's Manual pages 94 and 95).
- ***+ NEF (RAW):*** If the camera is set to any of the JPEG modes (fine, basic, or normal) and you press the Fn button, the next picture will add an additional NEF (RAW) image when you take the shot. In other words, for that one shot, the camera leaves JPEG mode and switches to RAW+F mode. That means you'll have both a NEF (RAW) and a JPEG file stored on your memory card for that image. The camera will act as though there's just one image when it displays it on your playback screen. It will not increment the image counter by the extra image. When you display the image on your computer using Nikon View or Nikon Transfer, the software will not acknowledge that there are two images, one RAW and one JPEG. However, when you finally transfer the images to your computer, you'll indeed find one NEF file and one JPEG file with the same file number but a different filename extension (i.e., _DSC1234.NEF and _DSC1234.JPG).
- ***Auto bracketing:*** I described this particular functionality in detail in the explanation of Custom Setting e2 *(Auto bracketing set)* when I covered the Fn button/command dial method of setting bracketing. This function under Custom Setting f1 works exactly the same way (User's Manual page 104).

Recommendation

Personally, I choose the *Auto bracketing* selection from Custom Setting f1. I bracket images using the AE bracketing function often so that I can combine them later for high dynamic range (HDR) imagery. To me, this is a shortcut way to quickly enable bracketing. However, if you don't bracket often, you may like a shortcut to functions like the *Release mode*, *Image quality/size*, and *ISO sensitivity*. Once again, Nikon has given us a flexible choice.

Custom Setting f2 *(Assign AE-L/AF-L button)* (User's Manual page 164)

This is another somewhat programmable button on your D5000, with the exception that the available functions all have something to do with either exposure or autofocus. The AE-L/AF-L button is just to the right of the viewfinder's eyepiece on the D5000.

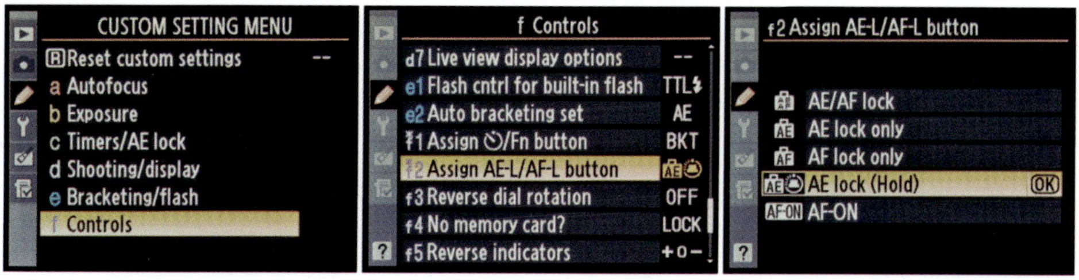

Figure 21 – Custom Setting f2 *(Assign AE-L/AF-L button)*

Figure 21 shows the screens used to configure Custom Setting f2.

Here are the steps to configure Custom Setting f2:

1. Press the MENU button and scroll to the *Custom Setting Menu*.
2. Select *f Controls*, and then scroll to the right.
3. Select *f2 Assign AE-L/AF-button* from the menu, and then scroll to the right.
4. Select one of the five choices from the menu. I chose *AE lock (Hold)*.
5. Press the *OK* button.

Here is a list of the functions you can select from, and what each does:

- ***AE/AF lock*** – Enabling this function causes AE (exposure) and AF (focus) to lock on the last meter and AF system reading while the AE-L/AF-L button is held down.
- ***AE lock only*** – This allows you to lock AE (exposure) on the last meter reading when you hold down the AE-L/AF-L button.
- ***AF lock only*** – When set, this function locks the AF system (focus) on the last autofocus reading while you hold down the AE-L/AF-L button.
- ***AE lock (Hold)*** – This allows you to lock AE (exposure) on the last meter reading when you press the AE-L/AF-L button once. To release the lock hold, press it again. If the meter goes off, it will also release the lock hold on the exposure. This works in normal still image mode and also the D-Movie mode.
- ***AF-ON*** – Some people don't want to use the shutter release for autofocus. They'd rather the shutter release button *only* release the shutter. This function is for those individuals. You can separate the autofocus and shutter release by assigning autofocus to the *AE-L/AF-L button*. Once this is set, the AE-L/AF-L button must be pressed to make the camera autofocus. The shutter release will only release the shutter. Either one of the buttons will cause the meter to become active.

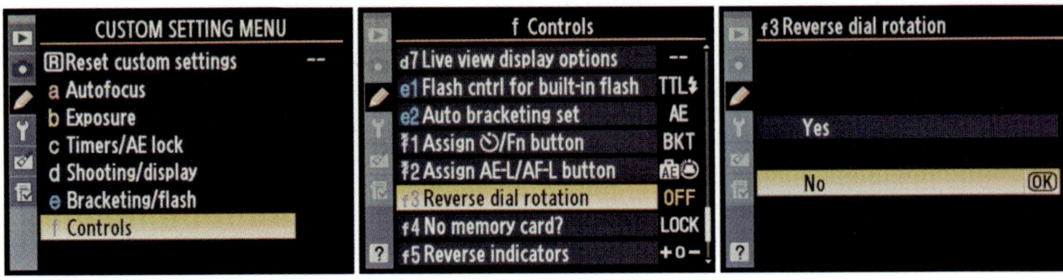

Figure 22 – Custom Setting f3 *(Reverse dial rotation)*

Recommendation

Personally, I choose the *AE lock only* selection from *Custom Setting Menu f4*. I want to be able to lock my exposure but leave AF active so that I can meter from one area of the subject and then recompose for the picture. I also use this when I start videoing in D-Movie mode, especially if there are windows with bright light outside. You know how a video camera will turn down the brightness whenever you pan past a bright window and your subjects in the room go dark? Well, using *AE lock only* prevents this. Whatever's outside the window might overexpose, but that's not my subject anyway. I want my subjects in the room to have consistent exposure. Of course, you may be interested in one of the other four functions. Play with this a bit—using this book and the User's Manual pages listed—until you feel comfortable with this setting. If you will do that, you'll be rewarded with a camera that works the way you want it to work.

Custom Setting f3 ***(Reverse dial rotation)***

(User's Manual page 164)

This is a very simple setting. All it does is let you reverse the direction of the command dial. If you do that, you'll be adjusting functions backwards, but they'll still work.

Figure 22 shows the screens used to configure Custom Setting f3.

Here are the steps to configure *Reverse rotation*:

1. Press the MENU button and scroll to the *Custom Setting Menu*.
2. Select *f Controls*, and then scroll to the right.
3. Select *f3 Reverse dial rotation* from the menu, and then scroll to the right.
4. Select *Yes* or *No* from the menu.
5. Press the *OK* button.

Recommendation

Unless you have a need for a reversed rotation command dial, it is fine to ignore this setting. I haven't needed to reverse my command dial yet.

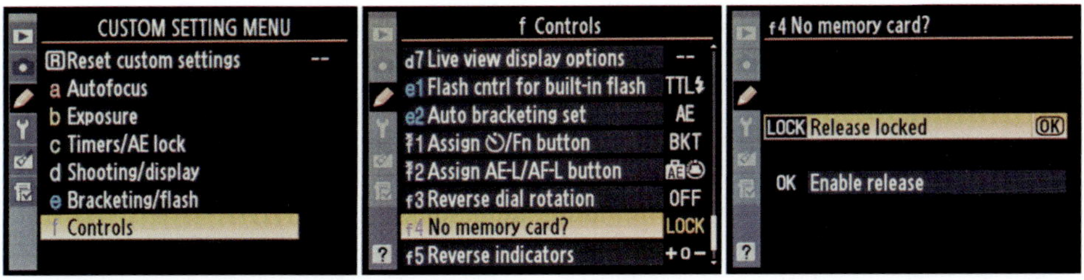

Figure 23 – Custom Setting f4 (No memory card?)

Custom Setting f4 *(No memory card?)*
(User's Manual page 164)
This setting defaults to locking the shutter when you try to take an image without a memory card inserted in the camera. By enabling it, you can take pictures without a memory card, but you can't save them anywhere unless you're using Nikon Camera Control Pro 2 software to send pictures directly to your computer. The software is not included with the D5000.

The screens used to configure Custom Setting f4 are shown in *figure* 23.

Here are the selections in *Custom Setting f4*:

- ***LOCK – Release locked*** – When you choose this default setting, your camera will refuse to release the shutter when there is no memory card present.
- ***OK – Enable release*** – Use this setting if you want to use the optional Nikon Camera Control Pro 2 software to send images from the camera directly to the computer.

Here are the steps to configure Custom Setting f6:

1. Press the MENU button and scroll to the *Custom Setting Menu*.
2. Select *f Controls*, and then scroll to the right.
3. Select *f4 No memory card?* from the menu, and then scroll to the right.
4. Select *Release locked* or *Enable release* from the menu.
5. Press the *OK* button.

Recommendation
There's no point in setting anything but *Released locked* unless you are using Nikon Camera Control Pro 2 software to control the camera. In that case, the camera feeds pictures to your computer, not a memory card. With it enabled, you can shoot pictures but can't save them.

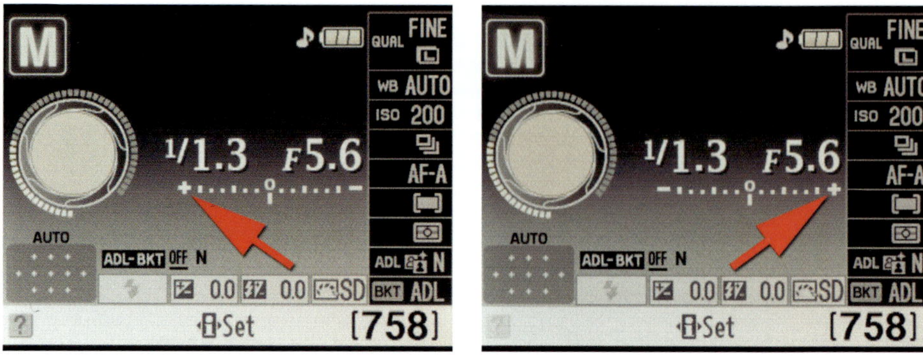

Figure 24 – Exposure indicator in M-manual mode both normal and reversed

Custom Setting f5 *(Reverse indicators)*
(User's Manual page 164)
Normally, anytime you see the exposure indicators in your D5000's viewfinder or information screen, the + is on the left, and the – is on the right. See the image on the left in *figure 24*; it shows the info screen and exposure indicator with the normal +/- configuration.

If you want, you can reverse this indicator so that the – is on the left and the + is on the right. Notice how the second screen of *figure 24* shows the exposure indicator in reversed mode with a -/+ configuration. The + is on the opposite end (see the red arrows).

Figure 24A shows the screens used to configure Custom Setting f5.

Here are the selections available for Custom Setting f5:

+o– is the normal polarity (+/–) of the exposure indicator.

–o+ is the reversed polarity (–/+) of the exposure indicator.

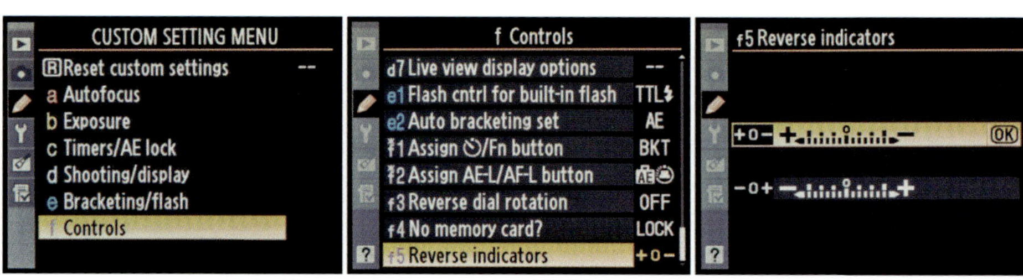

Figure 24A – Custom Setting f5 – Reverse indicators

Here are the steps to configure Custom Setting f5:

1. Press the MENU button and scroll to the *Custom Setting Menu*.
2. Select *f Controls*, and then scroll to the right.
3. Select *f5 Reverse indicators* from the menu, and then scroll to the right.
4. Select the polarity of the positive and negative indicators from the menu.
5. Press the *OK* button.

Recommendation

Select your favorite indicator direction for maximum camera comfort. I leave mine set at the normal factory default setting.

My Conclusions

Now that you've configured all the Custom Settings, your camera is customized just for you. There were 23 detailed settings to cover in this chapter, so just making it through is an accomplishment. Congratulations!

In the next chapter, we'll consider the *Setup Menu* and all the non-picture-related functions in your camera that you need to understand.

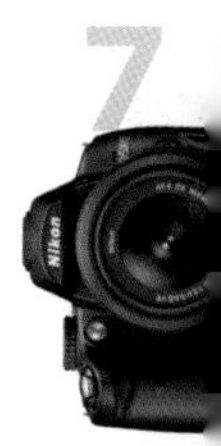

Setup Menu

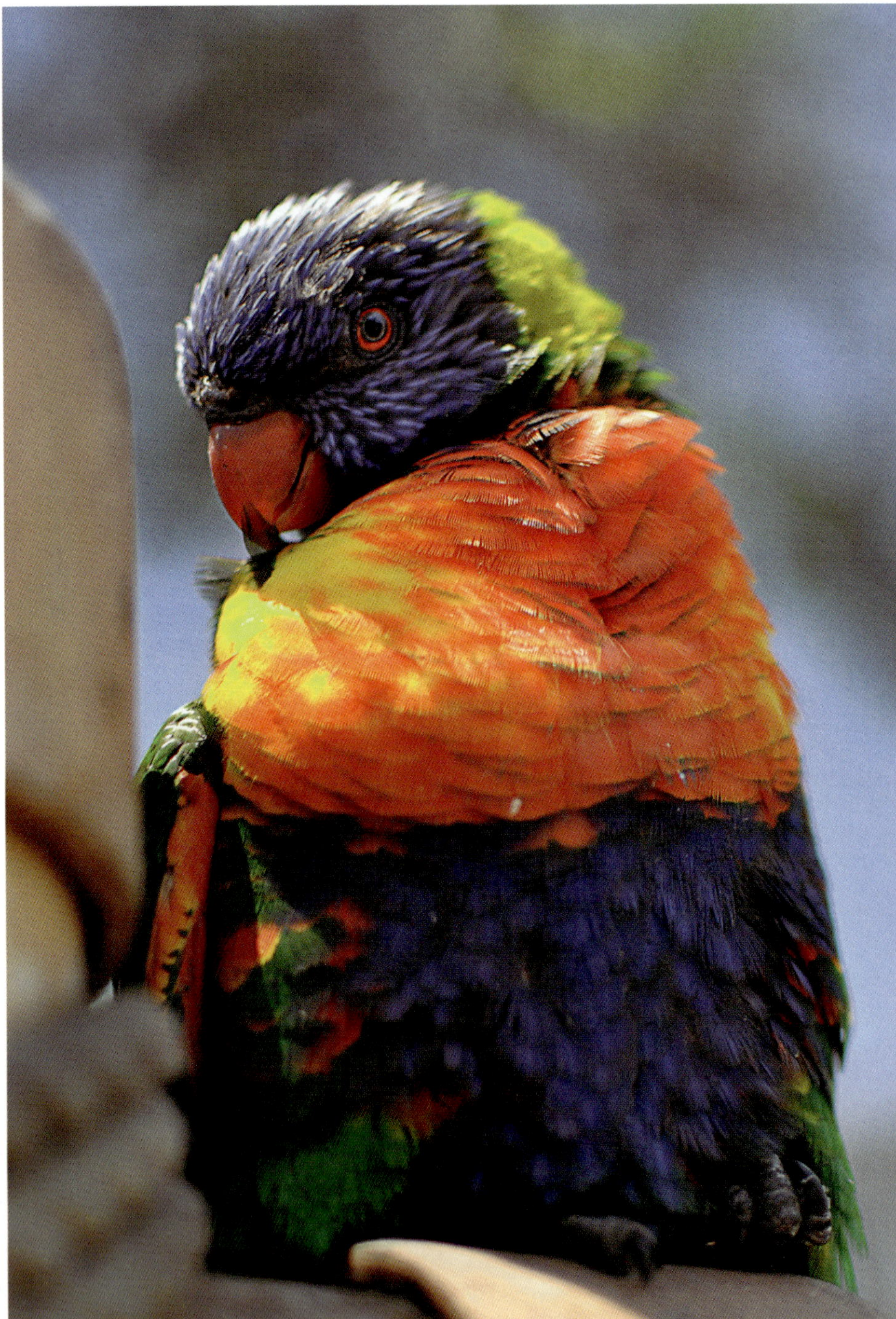

The *Setup Menu* on the Nikon D5000 consists of a series of basic camera settings not generally related to taking pictures. They cover things like how bright you'd like the LCD, firmware version, the default language, and image sensor cleaning.

These options are most likely the first you'll use when you prepare your new D5000. You'll have to set your camera's time zone and date right away, format a memory card, and set your LCD brightness.

The icon for the *Setup Menu* looks like a wrench (e.g., wrench icon). It is about midway down the menu tree, on the left. See *figure 1* for a look at the *Setup Menu* location.

In this chapter, we'll examine each setting in detail.

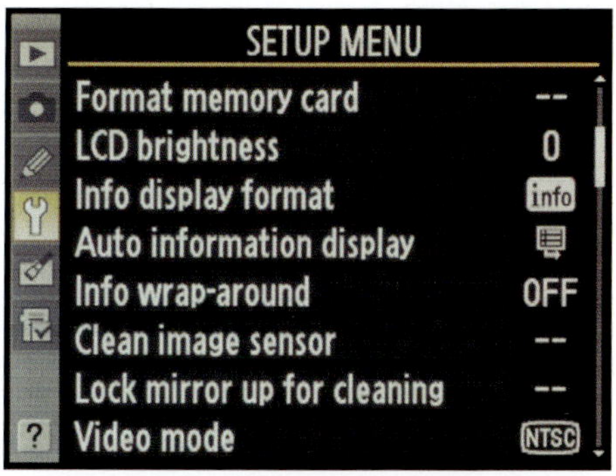

Figure 1 – The *Setup Menu*

Format Memory Card

(User's Manual pages 23 and 24)

You'll need to learn the location of this particular function on the *Setup Menu* since you'll be using it frequently. It is a good idea to use your camera—not your computer—to format the memory card that holds your pictures. That way, the card's format is customized to the camera. It's a relatively simple process to format the card. *Figure 2* shows the screens involved in the process.

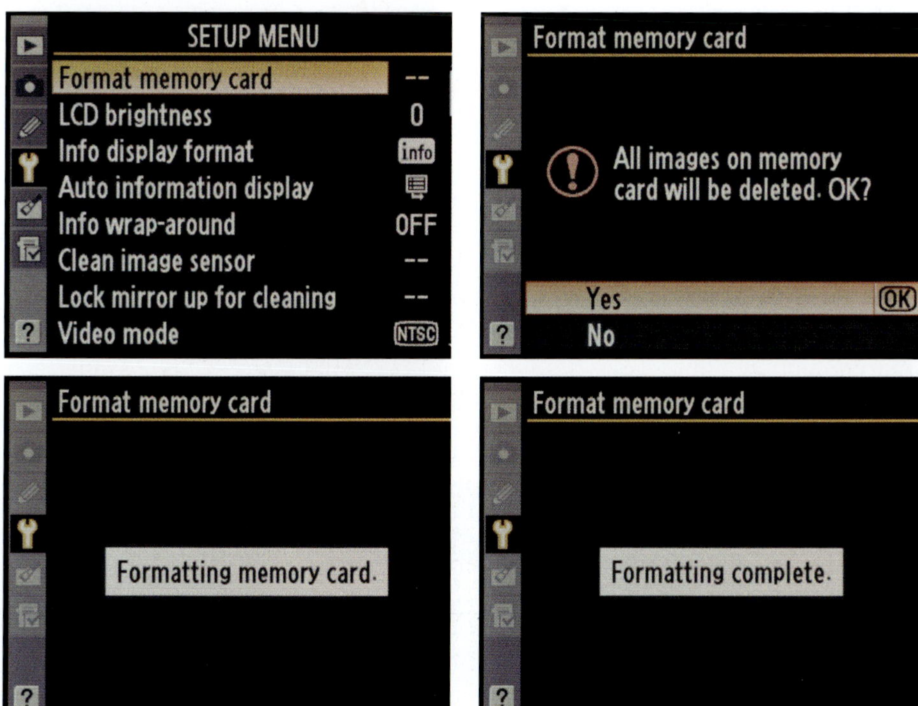

Figure 2 – Formatting a memory card

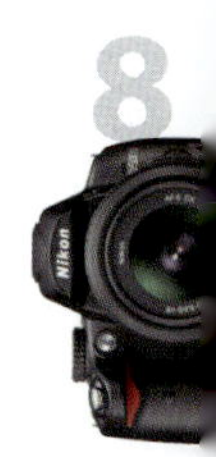

There are four screens you'll see when formatting an SD/SDHC memory card. You'll make selections from only two of them. Here are the steps:

1. Press the MENU button and scroll to the *Setup Menu*.
2. Select *Format memory card*, and then scroll to the right.
3. Select *Yes* from the screen with the big red exclamation point and the words *All images on memory card will be deleted. OK?*
4. Press the *OK* button.

Once you press the OK button, you'll see the next two screens in quick succession. One says *Formatting memory card* and the next says *Formatting complete*. Then the camera switches back to the *Setup Menu's* first screen. The card is now formatted, and you are ready take lots of pictures.

LCD Brightness

(User's Manual page 166)

The *LCD brightness* selection is more important than many people realize. If you set the LCD too dim, you'll have trouble seeing your images in bright light. If you set it too bright, you might allow some images to be underexposed, thinking that they look fine on the LCD unless you check the histogram. If the LCD is too bright, even a seriously underexposed image may look okay.

There are two settings available within the LCD brightness menu :

- *LCD brightness*
- *Auto dim*

LCD brightness

You can select from seven levels of brightness, from -3 to +3, as shown in *Figure 3*. Here are the available values:

-3, -2, -1, 0, +1, +2, +3

Here are the steps to adjust the brightness:

1. Press the MENU button and scroll to the *Setup Menu* (wrench icon).
2. Select *LCD brightness*, and then scroll to the right.
3. Once you've selected *LCD brightness* from the *Setup Menu*, you'll see a screen like the one on the right in *figure 3*. Use the Multi Selector button to scroll up or down through the values listed above (-3 to +3).
4. Press the *OK* button once you've found the value you like best.

Recommendation

The camera defaults to 0 (zero), which is right in the middle, yet the resulting LCD screen is quite bright. I feel that 0 is

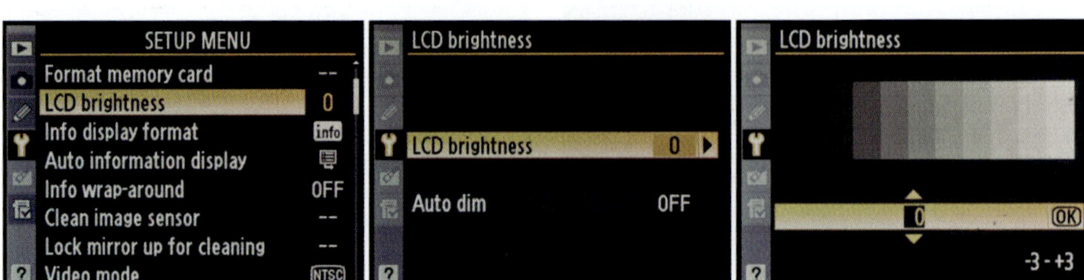

Figure 3 – *LCD brightness* settings

a little too bright and makes my images look like they are exposed more brightly than they are when I see them later in the computer. Recently, I've been using -1 on my D5000; that seems bright enough for outdoor use but doesn't make my images appear overly bright.

Using the bars with varying levels of brightness, as shown on the screen on the right in *figure 3*, adjust the brightness until you can barely make out a distinction between the last two dark bars on the left. That may be the best setting for your camera. Mine is best at -1 in normal outdoor light. Decide for yourself what looks best for you.

If you choose to set your camera to a level higher than about 0, just be sure you check the histogram frequently to validate your exposures. Otherwise, you may find that you are allowing the camera to slightly underexpose your images. The D5000 has an excellent exposure meter, but it is not perfect and needs your help sometimes. Letting your LCD run too brightly might mask those times that it needs help. Use your histogram!

Auto dim

This is a battery-saving feature that gradually dims the LCD monitor. You won't notice it unless you're watching for it. The easiest way to see it is to press the info or information edit button once and view the information screen. As you watch, the monitor will dim over a period of a few seconds to a lower light level. It cuts the brightness down by only a few percentage points, so it is not highly apparent. If you use a control, such as the *OK* button or the Multi Selector, the screen will revert to full brightness.

The screens used to enable or disable *Auto dim* are shown in *figure 3A*.

These steps are useful for configuring *Auto dim*:

1. Press the MENU button and scroll to the *Setup Menu*.
2. Select *LCD brightness*, and then scroll to the right.
3. Select *Auto dim*, and scroll to the right.
4. Select *On* or *Off* from the list.
5. Press the OK button.

Recommendation

Honestly, I don't worry much about the battery running down on my D5000. I have a spare battery. The camera seems to use little power, and a battery will last all day long. I leave this setting set to Off. However, if you don't have a spare battery, you might want to leave it set to On until you get one.

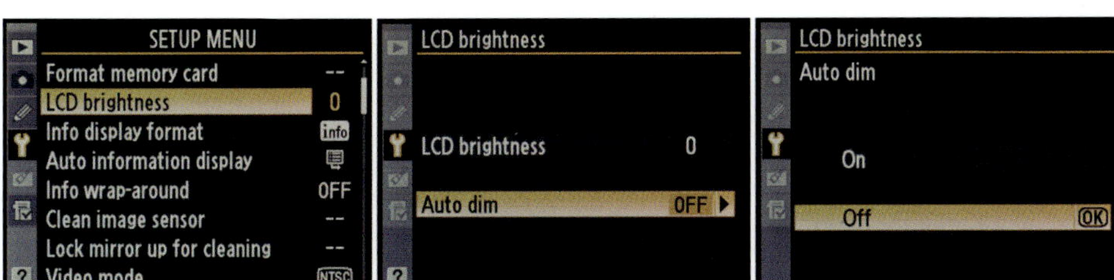

Figure 3A – *Auto dim* setting

Info Display Format

(User's Manual pages 166–167)

The D5000 is all about customizable variety. You can change the information display screen between the very graphical *Graphic* default setting to the somewhat less graphical *Classic* setting. The *Classic* format makes the information screen look more like the *Information edit* screen. See *figure 4* for a look at the two formats side-by-side.

You can also change the look of your display based on whether you are using the *P*, *S*, *A*, and *M* exposure modes or the auto/scene modes. These are found on the mode dial on top of the camera. Each has a Setup Menu setting to choose between Graphic or Classic.

Interestingly, you can also choose between several different color schemes. *Figure 4A* shows the choices for the Graphic format, which are green, black, and brown.

For the Classic format, you can choose blue, black, or orange (see *figure 4B*).

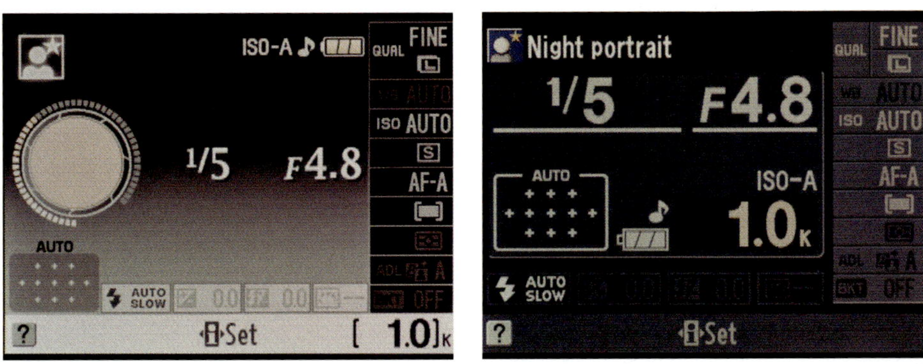

Figure 4 – *Graphic* vs. *Classic* black info screen

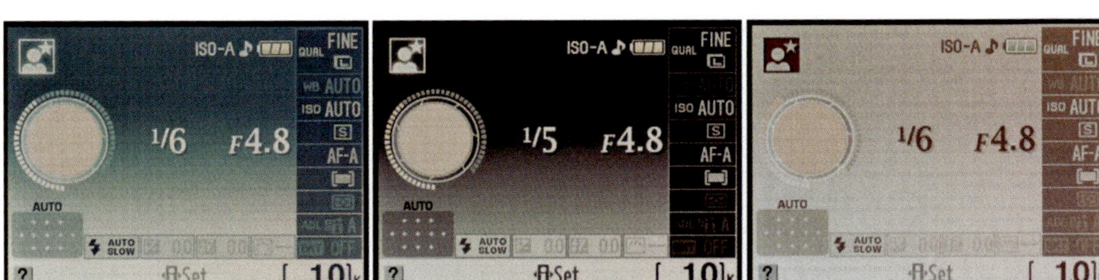

Figure 4A – *Graphic* info screen color schemes

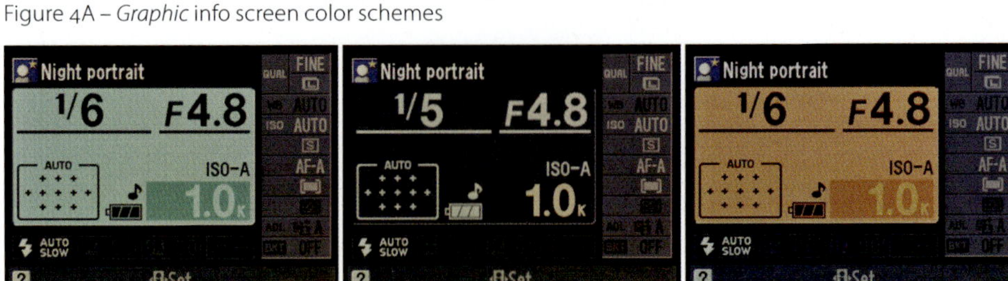

Figure 4B – *Classic* info screen color schemes

Figure 4C and *figure 4D* show the screens and steps used to change between the two formats.

Here are the steps used to change the format:

1. Press the MENU button and scroll to the *Setup Menu*.
2. Select *Info display format*, and then scroll to the right.
3. Select *Auto/scene modes* or *P, S, A, and M modes*, and then scroll to the right.
4. Select *Classic* or *Graphic* from the list, then scroll to the right.
5. Choose one of the color schemes from the list of three colors.
6. Press the *OK* button.

Recommendation

The default *Graphic>Black* scheme looks best to me. However, if I get tired of that scheme, the D5000 offers others. Use the settings to experiment with the colors and graphic styles and see which you prefer. You can always change it to a different scheme later.

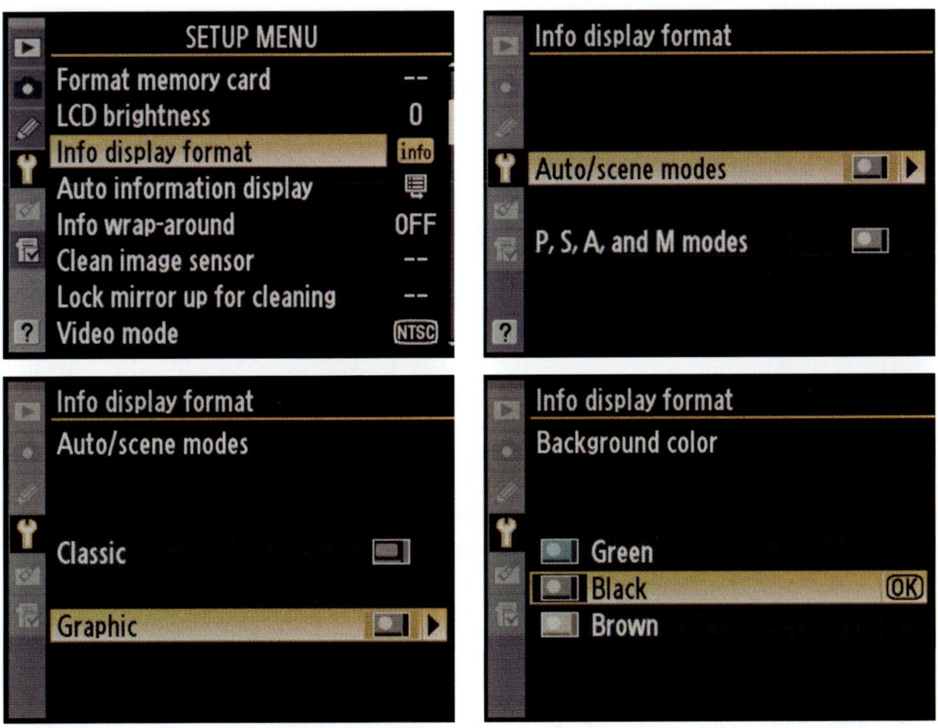

Figure 4C – Setting a color scheme for the display modes *Auto/scenes modes>Graphic>Black* background color format

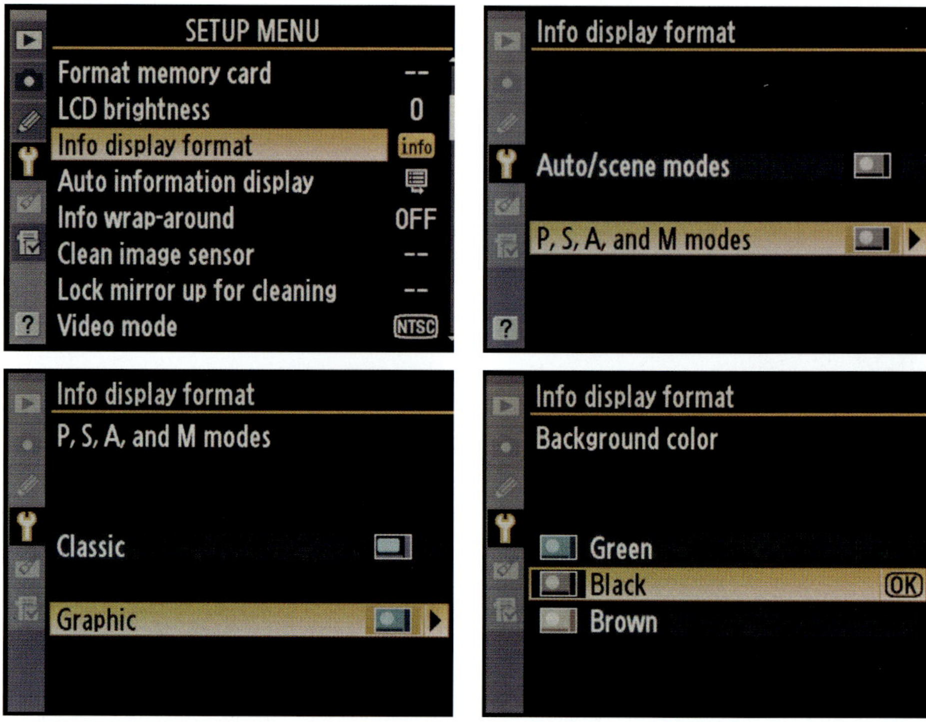

Figure 4D – Setting a color scheme for the *P,S,A, and M modes>Graphic>Black* background color format

Auto Information Display

(User's Manual page 168)

This function allows you to view the information screen when you press the shutter release button halfway down. It displays the screen that would appear if you pressed the info button. Many like to refer to camera settings without having to press the info or <i> information edit buttons.

This may be a good idea since the D5000 has no top control panel LCD like the larger DSLR cameras in Nikon's lineup. The control panel LCD added to the width of the camera significantly because the mode dial had to be placed somewhere else. On the D5000, the mode dial is where the control Panel LCD is placed on the Nikon D90 or D300, for instance. Since it has no control panel LCD, the D5000 can be significantly smaller in size. However, it is useful to look down at something like the control panel LCD when you want to change the camera settings. On the D5000, the rear LCD monitor is all we have, so it must do the work of a normal LCD by displaying images and menus plus allow us to view and change camera settings like the control panel on a larger camera would. The "smallness" of the D5000 has its advantages and disadvantages.

This Auto information display option on the Setup Menu allows you change when the information screen displays. With Auto information display turned

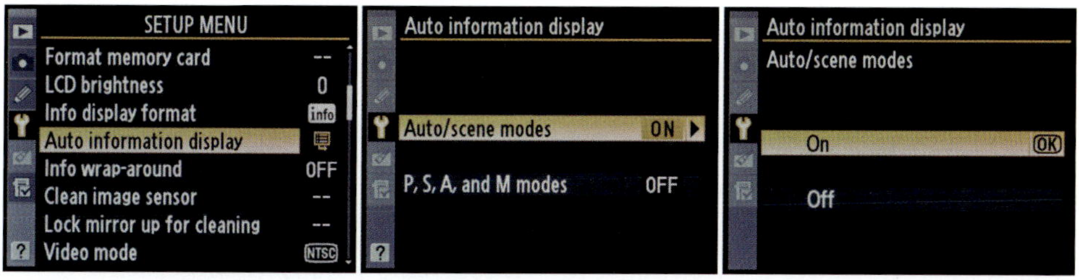

Figure 5 – *Auto information display – Auto/scene modes*

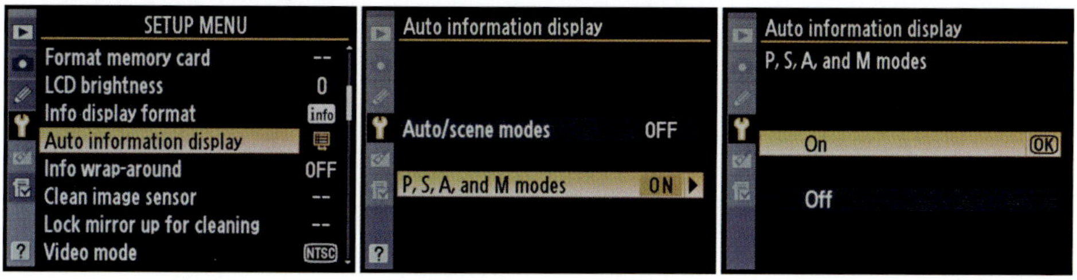

Figure 5A – *Auto information display – P, S, A, and M modes*

on, the information screen will be there whenever you press the shutter release button halfway down. You can also get to the screen at any time by pressing the info or <**i**>information edit buttons. The factory default is On.

This setting can also be configured to display the information screen differently in auto/scene modes and P, S, A, and M modes (see *figure* 5 and *figure* 5A).

Now let's look at the steps to configure this setting:

1. Press the MENU button and scroll to the *Setup Menu*.
2. Select *Auto information display*, and then scroll to the right.
3. Select *Auto/scene modes* or *P, S, A, and M modes*, and then scroll to the right.
4. Select *On* or *Off* from the list.
5. Press the *OK* button.

Recommendation

In the User's Manual on page 168, Nikon recommends this: "Choose On if you find yourself frequently referring to the information display during shooting." For many users, I agree for this setting. However, I personally keep it set to Off. Why? Well, as I've used Nikon DSLRs over the years, I've learned to tap the shutter button slightly to turn off the rear LCD monitor. It is unnerving to me to have the information screen appear. I tend to shut off the camera unnecessarily just to get the screen to go off. You see, I use long display time-outs on all the LCD screen displays. I don't think long display time-out settings and enabling this setting is a good idea because batteries don't stay charged forever. The D5000 has a very long battery life, but I don't want to drain it unnecessarily. I can get to the info screen by pressing the info button. However, many new DSLR users may indeed want the information screen to pop up often. If that describes you, then leave this set to *On*.

Info Wrap-Around

(User's Manual page 168)

I was confused about this setting when I first read about it. You see, in other Nikon DSLR cameras, it's possible to cause the active autofocus (AF) point to wrap around from one side of the viewfinder to the other when you scroll it off one side. But that is not what this function does.

What the camera "wraps around" is the *Information edit* screen's yellow "cursor." The cursor is what you use to select settings, and it looks like a yellow rectangle. The *Information edit* screen has various settings you can change along the right side and bottom. Setting Info wrap-around to On allows you to scroll the yellow cursor off of the left side of the bottom setting area, and then it will reappear on the top right, or vice versa. If you scroll down and left, and keep scrolling, the cursor will then reappear on the top right (in *figure 6*, where the red arrow points).

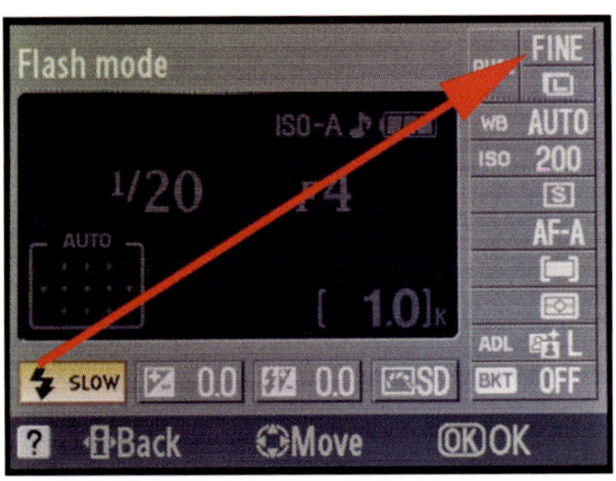

Figure 6 – The information edit screen cursor

If Info wrap-around is set to *Off*, the cursor simply stops when it reaches the boundaries of the *Information edit* screen's menu selections.

Use these steps to configure the wrap-around effect (see *figure 6A*):

1. Press the MENU button and scroll to the *Setup Menu*.
2. Select *Info wrap-around*, and then scroll to the right.
3. Select *On* or *Off* from the list.
4. Press the *OK* button.

Wrap-Around is Not for Me

I tend to lose sight of the cursor and wonder where it went. It could save me some time since it will allow the cursor to scroll to the other end of the menu instead of just stopping at the end. However, old habits die hard. Scrolling from one end to the other, or "wrapping around," is how all the main menus work—like the *Setup Menu*. If you scroll past the end, the cursor reappears at the top. Try it and see if you like it. You can always change it back if you don't.

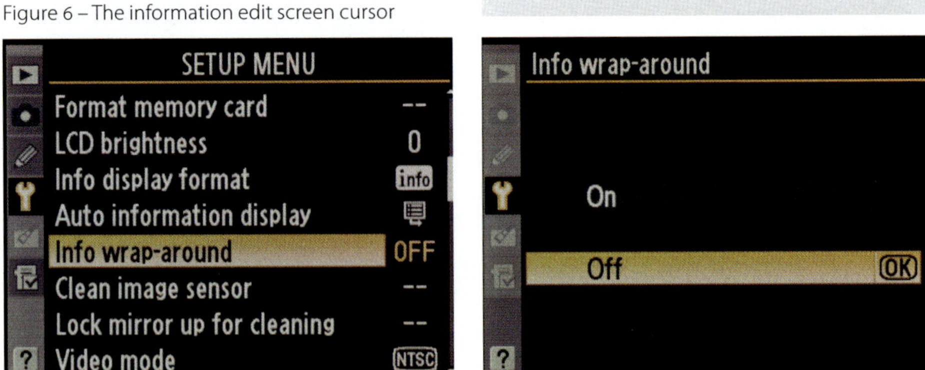

Figure 6A – Info-wrap around

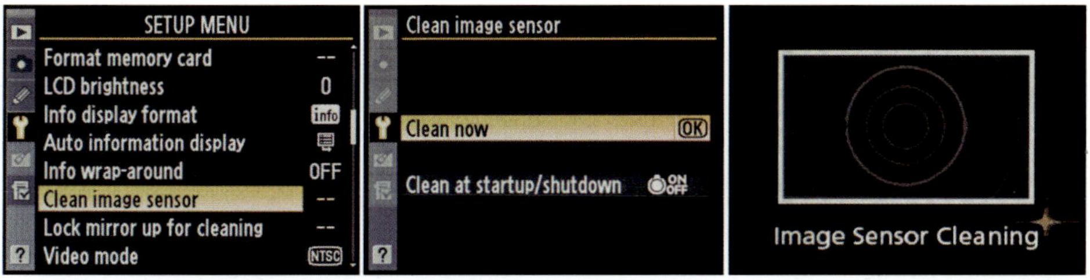

Figure 7 – The *Clean now* screens

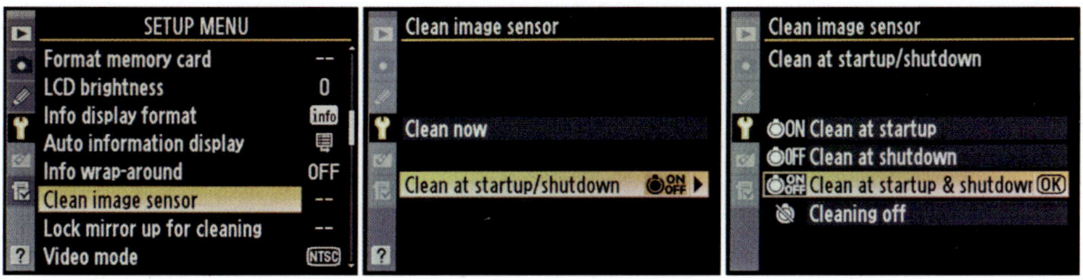

Figure 7A – *Clean sensor at startup/shutdown*

Clean Image Sensor

(User's Manual pages 206 and 207)
Dust is everywhere, and eventually it will get on your camera's imaging sensor. Fortunately, the D5000 provides sensor cleaning by vibrating the low-pass filter in front of the sensor. These high-frequency vibrations will dislodge most dust and make it fall off the filter so you won't see it as spots on your pictures.

The low-pass filter is directly in front of the imaging sensor, so dust should never really get on the sensor itself. However, if you go to the beach, where sand is blowing in the wind, and change your lenses a few times, you might develop a dust problem.

Here are the options for cleaning the camera's sensor (see *figure 7*):

- *Clean now*
- *Clean at startup/shutdown*

Clean now

This option allows you to clean the sensor anytime you choose. If you detect a dust spot, or just get nervous because you are in a dusty environment with your D5000, you can simply select Clean now and the camera will execute a cleaning cycle. Here are the steps:

1. Press the MENU button and scroll to the *Setup Menu*.
2. Select *Clean image sensor*, and then scroll to the right.
3. To execute the cleaning function, select *Clean now*, as shown in the middle screen in *figure 7*.
4. Press the *OK* button. The graphical *Image Sensor Cleaning* screen will display for a couple of seconds and then the cleaning is complete (see *figure 7B*).

Clean at startup/shutdown

For preventive dust control, many users will set their cameras to clean the sensor at startup, shutdown, or both. There are four selections for startup/shutdown cleaning (see *figure 7A*):

- *Clean at startup*
- *Clean at shutdown*
- *Clean at startup & shutdown*
- *Cleaning off*

These settings are all self-explanatory. I find it interesting that I do not detect any serious startup or shutdown delay because of the cleaning cycle. I can turn my camera on and immediately take a picture, even though it's in the middle of about a 2-second cleaning cycle. Taking a picture or pressing any button seems to interrupt the cycle.

Let's select Clean at startup & shutdown as an example. This is the mode I recommend. If you prefer a different one, just use the following steps and substitute your choice:

1. Press the MENU button and scroll to the *Setup Menu*.
2. Select *Clean image sensor*, and then scroll to the right.
3. Select *Clean at startup/shutdown*, and scroll to the right.
4. Select one of the choices (startup, shutdown, startup & shutdown, or Off).
5. Press the *OK* button.

Figure 7B shows a picture of the graphical *Image Sensor Cleaning* screen that appears during a cleaning cycle. You'll see it when you turn the camera on or off if you have Clean at startup & shutdown selected.

Nikon suggests that you have the camera base down when you use these modes to clean the sensor. Checking with Nikon technical support, I found the reason for that guidance. Those high-frequency vibrations will indeed dislodge most dust particles, but if the camera is not positioned with the base down, you may end up only shaking the dust from one part of the sensor to another. It's a lot like putting a grain of salt in your palm and shaking your palm left and right while it's facing the ceiling. The grain of salt may just move from one side of your palm to another. If you turn your palm 90 degrees—like shaking someone's hand—and then vibrate it, the grain of salt has a better chance of falling off your palm.

Recommendation

As mentioned previously, I use the Clean at startup & shutdown setting on my D5000. In the months I've been using the D5000, I have yet to see a dust spot. It's important to keep dust off of your camera as much as possible, especially when changing lenses, and this camera's extra cleaning method seems to make a big difference compared to older digital Nikons I've used. When I'm really concerned about cleaning the sensor, I use the Clean now method.

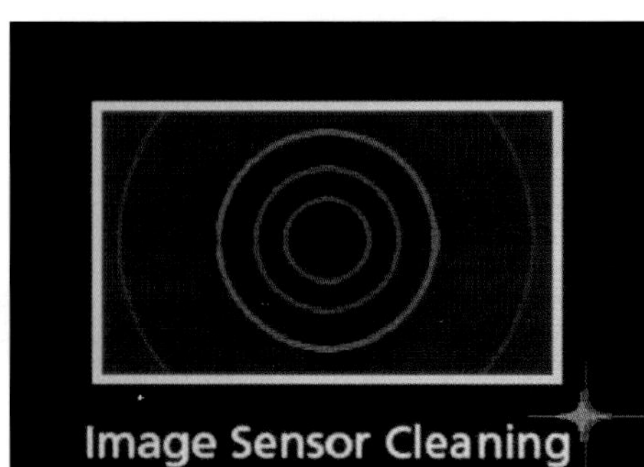

Figure 7B – *Image Sensor Cleaning* screen

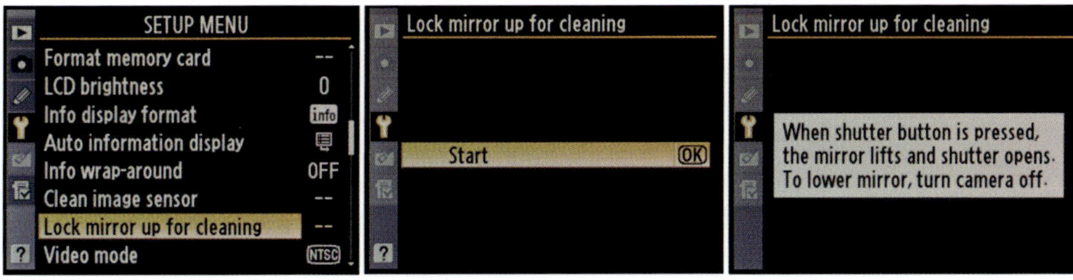

Figure 8 – *Lock mirror up for cleaning* screens

Lock Mirror Up for Cleaning

(User's Manual pages 208 and 209)
If the high-frequency vibration method of cleaning your D5000's sensor does not dislodge some stickier-than-normal dust, you may have to clean your sensor more aggressively.

In many cases all that's needed is a dust blower to remove the dust with a puff of air. I remember having to do this with my Nikon D100 in 2002, and I was always afraid I might ruin the shutter if I did it incorrectly. With the D100, I had to hold the shutter open in bulb mode with one hand while I blew off the sensor with the other.

The D5000 helps out by providing this Lock mirror up for cleaning mode so that you can more safely blow a stubborn piece of dust off the low-pass filter. Using this function, it is much safer to blow off the sensor, and you can use both hands.

Figure 8 shows the three screens you'll use to select this mode for manual sensor cleaning.

Here are the steps to move the mirror and shutter out of the way for cleaning:

1. Press the MENU button and scroll to the *Setup Menu*.
2. Select *Lock mirror up for cleaning*, and then scroll to the right.
3. Next, select *Start*.
4. Press the *OK* button.
5. When the camera has locked the mirror and shutter in an open position and exposed the low-pass filter in front of the sensor, you'll see the screen on the right in *figure 8* with the following message: *When shutter button is pressed, the mirror lifts and shutter opens. To lower the mirror, turn camera off.*
6. Remove the lens, if you haven't already done so.
7. Press the shutter release button fully, as you would if you were taking a picture.
8. The camera now raises the mirror and retracts the shutter. When you look inside the front of the camera, you'll see the bluish-looking low-pass filter in front of the sensor. Carefully insert the tip of a blower, without touching the sensor, and blow off the dust with a few puffs of air.
9. To close the shutter and lower the mirror, turn the D5000 off.

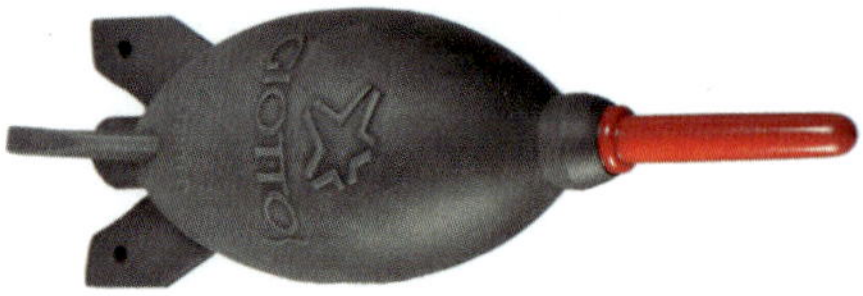

Figure 8A – Giottos Rocket-Air blower

You'll need a good quality, professional sensor-cleaning blower such as my favorite, the Giottos Rocket-Air blower with its long red tip for easy insertion (see *figure 8A*). I bought mine from the Nikonians Pro Shop (www.PhotoProShop.com).

Make sure you have a fresh battery in the camera because that's what holds the shutter open for cleaning. It must be above a 60% charge or the camera will gray out the menu selection, refusing to allow you to start the process.

Special Note On Sensor Cleaning

If even an air blower fails to remove stubborn dust or pollen, you will have to either have your sensor professionally cleaned or do it yourself. Nikon states that you will void your warranty if you touch the low-pass filter. However, many people still wet or brush-clean their D5000's sensor. I've done it to various Nikons in the past, although I'll never admit it!

Critical Information on Wet Cleaning Your Sensor

The Nikon D5000 has a special tin-oxide coating on the low-pass filter that is designed to make it harder for dust to stick to its surface. Unfortunately, the fluids that have been used for several years to clean sensors may adversely affect this coating. You must purchase the correct cleaning fluid to wet-clean the low-pass filter. It is called Eclipse E2, and it is said to be safe for cleaning the filter without damaging the tin-oxide coating.

If all of this makes you nervous, send your camera off to Nikon for approved cleaning or use a professional service. Fortunately, a few puffs of air will often remove dust too stubborn for the high-frequency vibration methods to remove.

Recommendation

It helps to have the proper tools, such as the Giottos Rocket-Air blower from the Nikonians PhotoProShop.com. I've used other blower types, but this one is the best and doesn't cost too much. It has a special check valve that allows air to blow out of the nozzle but not suck back in because that might draw dust into the blower's squeeze bulb and you'd later blow it right back onto the sensor. It pulls air back into the bulb from the opposite end, not through the nozzle. It's an excellent design, with a strong air blast.

Video Mode

(User's Manual page 168)

If you plan on connecting your D5000 to a video device, you'll need to be sure you use the correct video mode for communication with the device.

There are two video modes available in the D5000:

- *NTSC*
- *PAL*

Here are the steps used to set the mode (see *figure 9*):

1. Press the MENU button and scroll to the *Setup Menu*.
2. Select *Video mode*, and then scroll to the right.
3. Select *NTSC* or *PAL* (probably *NTSC*) from the menu.
4. Press the *OK* button to set the mode and return to the *Setup Menu*.

You'll need to refer to the manual of your television, VCR, or other device to determine what video input it uses. Select the mode you want to use with the A/V out port under the flap on the side of the D5000.

Figure 9A shows a picture of the A/V out port on under the flap on the side of the D5000. There is a cable included with the camera that plugs into this port. The other ends, two RCA jacks, are for plugging into the audio (white) and video (yellow) ports on your video device. We'll discuss this in more detail in chapter 12, "D-Movie Mode: Video on Demand."

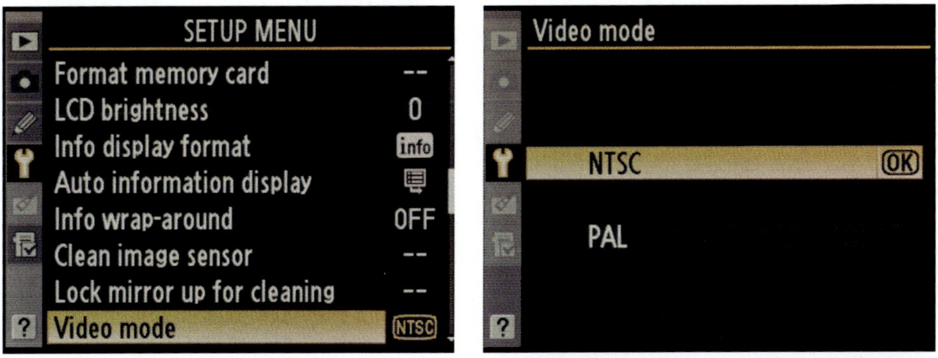

Figure 9 – *Video mode* selection screens

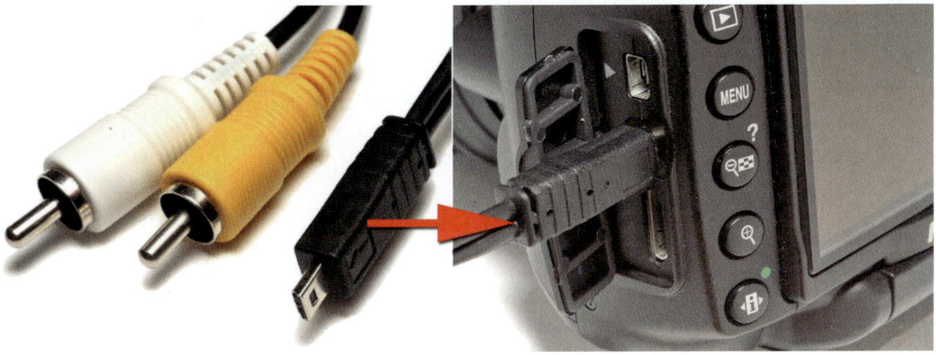

Figure 9A – A/V Out Cable and Camera Port

High-Definition Multimedia Interface (HDMI)

(User's Manual page 168)

If you would like to display your images on a high-definition monitor or television, your D5000 has the modes and connector you need. You'll need an HDMI Type C mini to Type A standard cable, which is not included with the camera but is available from many electronic stores. We'll talk more about this in chapter 12. The formats that the D5000 supports are shown in *figure 10*.

Before you connect the camera to your HDMI display, you'll need to set one of these HDMI formats:

- ***Auto*** – Allows the camera to select the most appropriate format for displaying on the currently connected device
- ***480p*** *(progressive)* – 640x480 progressive format
- ***576p*** *(progressive)* – 720x576 progressive format
- ***720p*** *(progressive)* – 1280x720 progressive format
- ***1080i*** *(interlaced)* – 1920x1080 interlaced format

Here are the steps to choose a setting:

1. Press the MENU button and scroll to the *Setup Menu*.
2. Select *HDMI*, and then scroll to the right.
3. Select your choice of modes. (Not sure? Select *Auto*.)
4. Press the *OK* button.

Clearly, the D5000 can interface with both progressive and interlaced devices. The HDMI display will take the place of the small LCD video monitor on the back of your D5000. The camera monitor will turn off as soon as you connect an HDMI device.

Recommendation

Unless you are heavily into HDMI and understand the various formats, I would just leave the camera set to Auto. That allows the D5000 to determine the proper format as soon as it is plugged into the display device. Chapter 12 covers the use of your camera in D-Movie mode and talks quite a bit about cabling and connectivity.

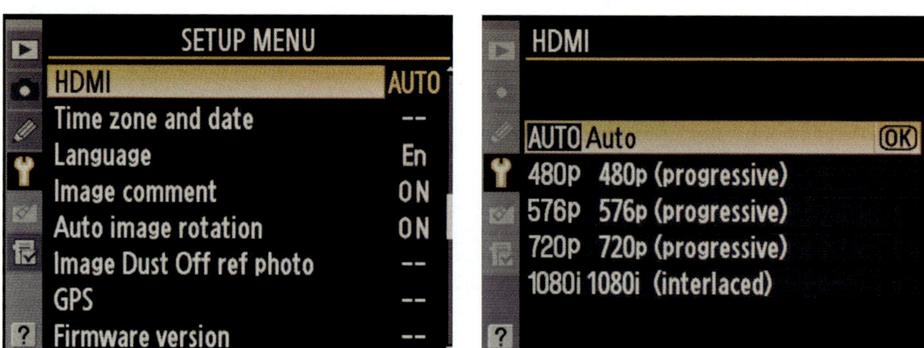

Figure 10 – HDMI format selection

Time Zone and Date

(User's Manual page 169)

There are several functions to set under the *Time zone and date* section of the *Setup Menus*:

- *Time zone*
- *Date and time*
- *Date format*
- *Daylight saving time*

Time zone

Figure 11 shows the Time zone configuration screens. You'll use a familiar world map interface to select the area of the world in which you are using the camera. Since I live in the eastern half of the United States, I selected New York (Eastern) time zone.

To set the time zone, follow these steps (see *figure 11*):

1. Press the MENU button and scroll to the *Setup Menu*.
2. Select *Time zone and date*, and then scroll to the right.
3. Select *Time zone*, and then scroll to the right.
4. Use the multi selector thumb switch to scroll left or right until your time zone is under the yellow vertical bar in the center of the world map screen.
5. Once you have your time zone selected, press the *OK* button to save the setting.

Date and time

Figure 11A shows the three Date and time configuration screens. The final screen in the series allows you to select the year, month, and day (*Y, M, D*) and the hour, minute, and second (*H, M, S*):

1. Press the MENU button and scroll to the *Setup Menu*.
2. Select *Time zone and date*, and then scroll to the right.
3. Select *Date and time*, and then scroll to the right.
4. Using the multi selector button, scroll left or right until you have selected the

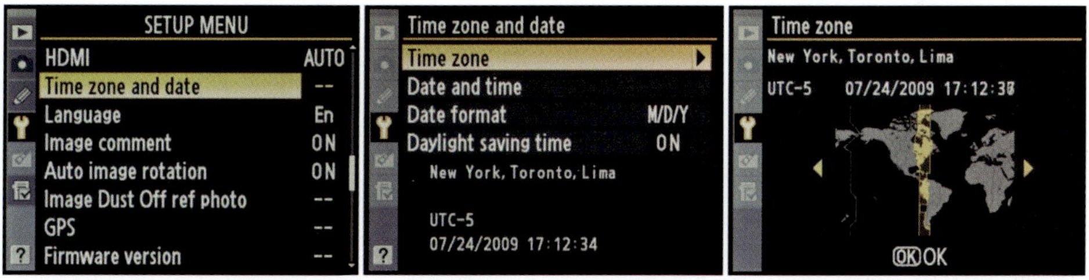

Figure 11 – *Time zone* setup

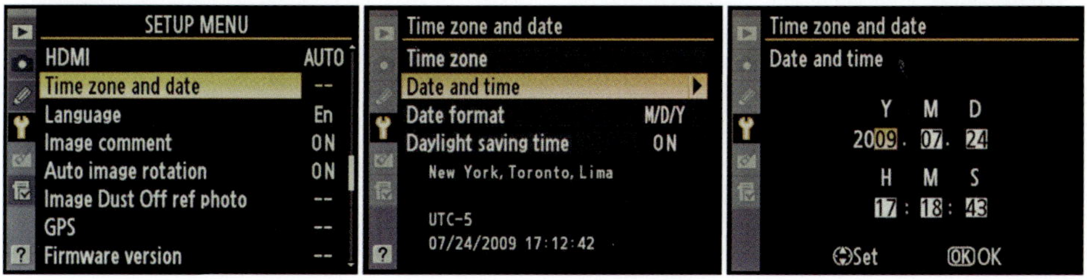

Figure 11A – *Date and time* setup

value you want to change. Then scroll up or down to actually change the value.

5. When you have set the correct date and time, press the OK button to save the settings. Please note that the time setting uses the 24-hour military-style clock. To set 3 p.m., for example, you would set *H* and *M* to 15:00.

24 Hour Time Equivalents

For your convenience, here is a 24-hour time equivalents chart:

A.M. Settings:

12:00 a.m. = 00:00 (midnight)
01:00 a.m. = 01:00
02:00 a.m. = 02:00
03:00 a.m. = 03:00
04:00 a.m. = 04:00
05:00 a.m. = 05:00
06:00 a.m. = 06:00
07:00 a.m. = 07:00
08:00 a.m. = 08:00
09:00 a.m. = 09:00
10:00 a.m. = 10:00
11:00 a.m. = 11:00

P.M. Settings:

12:00 p.m. = 12:00 (noon)
01:00 p.m. = 13:00
02:00 p.m. = 14:00
03:00 p.m. = 15:00
04:00 p.m. = 16:00
05:00 p.m. = 17:00
06:00 p.m. = 18:00
07:00 p.m. = 19:00
08:00 p.m. = 20:00
09:00 p.m. = 21:00
10:00 p.m. = 22:00
11:00 p.m. = 23:00

Note: There is no 24:00 time (midnight). After 23:59 comes 00:00.

Date format

The D5000 gives you three different ways to format the date (see *figure 11B*):

1. *Y/M/D* = Year/Month/Day (2010/12/31)
2. *M/D/Y* = Month/Day/Year (12/31/2010)
3. *D/M/Y* = Day/Month/Year (31/12/2010)

United States D5000 owners will probably use the *M/D/Y* setting, which matches the *MM/DD/YYYY* format so familiar to Americans. People in other areas of the world can select their favorite date format.

To select the date format of your choice, do the following:

1. Press the button and scroll to the *Setup Menu*.
2. Select *Time zone and date*, and then scroll to the right.
3. Select *Date format*, and then scroll to the right.
4. Choose the format you like best from the three available formats.
5. Press the *OK* button.

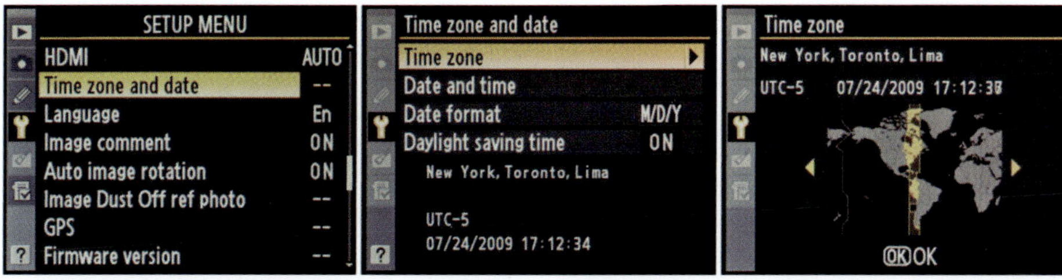

Figure 11B – *Date format* setup

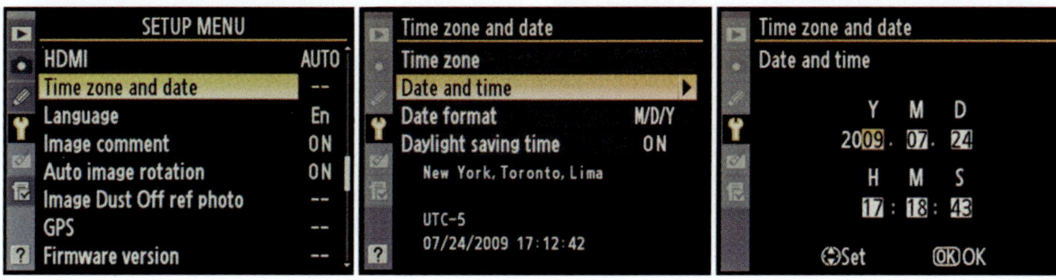

Figure 11C – *Daylight saving time* screens

Daylight saving time

Many areas of the United States observe daylight saving time. In the spring, many American residents set their clocks forward by one hour on a specified day each year. Then in the fall they set it back, leading to the clever saying, "spring forward, fall back."

To enable automatic Daylight saving time, do the following steps (see *figure 11C*):

1. Press the MENU button and scroll to the *Setup Menu*.
2. Select *Time zone and date*, and then scroll to the right.
3. Select *Daylight saving time*, and then scroll to the right.
4. Select *On* or *Off* from the menu.
5. Press the *OK* button.

If you selected *On*, your D5000 will now automatically "spring forward and fall back," adjusting your time forward by one hour in the spring and back one hour in the fall.

Recommendation

I always leave mine set to *On* because I want my camera to record an accurate time on each image. Anything that keeps me from having to remember an annual adjustment is appreciated. My computer adjusts its own time, and now my camera can do the same.

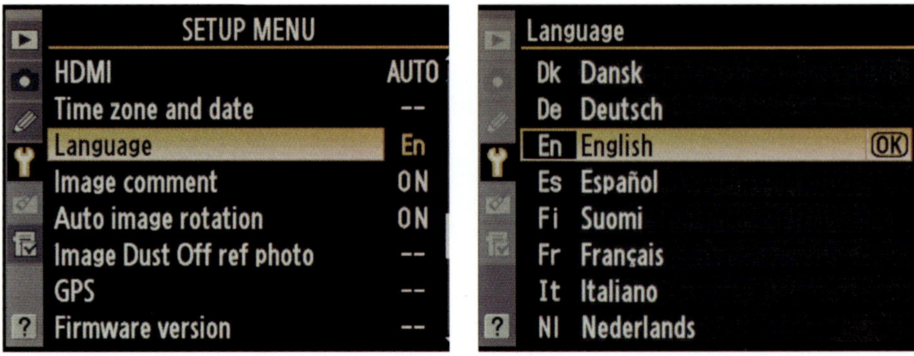

Figure 12 – *Language* selection screens

Language

(User's Manual page 169)

Nikon is a company that sells cameras and lenses around the world. For that reason, your D5000 can display in up to 17 languages. *Figure 12* shows the screens you can use to select the display language for your camera.

The following languages are included with the D5000 using firmware version 1.0:

- Danish
- German
- English
- Spanish
- Finnish
- French
- Italian
- Dutch
- Norwegian
- Polish
- Portuguese
- Russian
- Swedish
- Traditional Chinese
- Simplified Chinese
- Japanese
- Korean

Your D5000 should default to the language of the area in which you purchased it. However, you may choose to use a different language from your multilingual camera.

Here are the steps to select a language (see *figure 12*):

1. Press the MENU button and scroll to the *Setup Menu*.
2. Select *Language*, and then scroll to the right.
3. Choose your favorite language from the list of 17 languages. (You might have to scroll up or down in the menu to find yours.)
4. Press the *OK* button.

Image Comment

(User's Manual page 169)

This is a useful setting that you can use to attach a comment to each image you shoot. I attach the words *Copyright Darrell Young* to my images. Unfortunately, Nikon does not include the copyright symbol © in the list of numbers and letters or I would include that in my copyright notice.

The screens shown in figure 13 are used to add a comment to your image.

Here are the steps to create an image comment that attaches to each of your images:

1. Press the MENU button and scroll to the *Setup Menu*.
2. Select *Image comment*, and then scroll to the right.
3. From the second screen shown in *figure 13*, you'll select the *Input comment* line and scroll to the right with the Multi Selector.
4. In screen 3, you'll see a series of symbols, numbers, and letters on top and a line of tiny dashes at the bottom.
5. To create a new comment, scroll back and forth within the new comment with the command dial. When you have the small gray cursor positioned over a character, you can delete it with the garbage can delete button. To insert a new character, position the yellow cursor in the character list above and press the playback zoom in button. Whatever character is under the yellow cursor will appear on the name line below, at the position of the gray cursor. If a character is already under the gray cursor, it will be pushed to the right. Limit your comment to 36 characters.
6. Press the *OK* button when you have completed the new comment, and the camera will return to the previous menu.
7. Scroll down to the *Attach comment* selection.
8. Scroll to the right one time to "Set" the check box. You'll see the little check box receive a check on the left of the line (see the red arrows in *figure 13, images 4 and 5*).
9. Finally, scroll up to the *Done* menu selection, and then press the *OK* button (see *figure 13, image 6*).

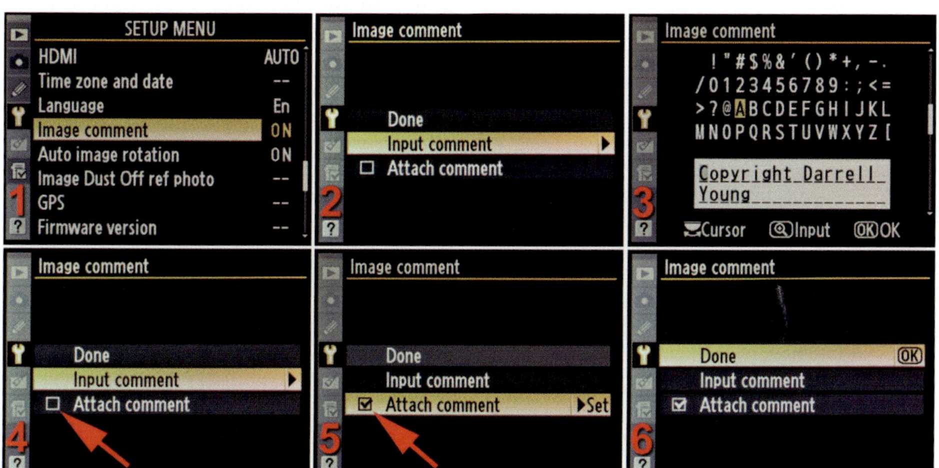

Figure 13 – *Image comment* setup screens

I keep forgetting to finish the process with the *Done* selection and usually lose my comment. Make sure you complete the process, or any comment you arduously entered will simply disappear! Your comment will be added internally to the metadata of new images. It will not show on the image itself.

Auto Image Rotation

(User's Manual page 170)

This function is concerned with how a vertical image displays on the back of your camera, and later in software. Horizontal images are not affected by this setting. The D5000 has a direction-sensing device so that it knows how a picture is oriented.

According to how you have Auto image rotation set and how you hold your D5000's handgrip, the camera will display vertical images as upright portrait images with the top of the image at the top of the LCD monitor or in a horizontal direction with the top to the left or right.

Figure 14 shows the two screens used to set the *Auto image rotation* function.

There are two selections:

- *On*
- *Off*

On - With *Auto image rotation* set to On, the D5000 will automatically record the direction or orientation of an image within the image itself. In other words, it records, as part of the image's metadata, whether you were holding your camera horizontally or vertically (handgrip down) and even upside-down vertically (handgrip up). It saves the orientation information with the image so that it will display correctly in computer software. It will display in the correct orientation on your camera's LCD monitor only if you have the *Playback Menu's Rotate tall* function set to *On*. Many people do not fully understand that *Auto image rotation* and *Rotate tall* work together in how the image displays on the D5000's monitor. *Auto image rotation* lets the image "speak" for itself as to orientation, while *Rotate tall* lets the camera "listen" to the image and display it in the proper orientation.

Off - If *Auto image rotation* is turned off, the camera does not record orientation information with the image. The vertical image will be displayed as a horizontal image lying on its side in computer software and on the camera's LCD monitor. The top of the image will be on the

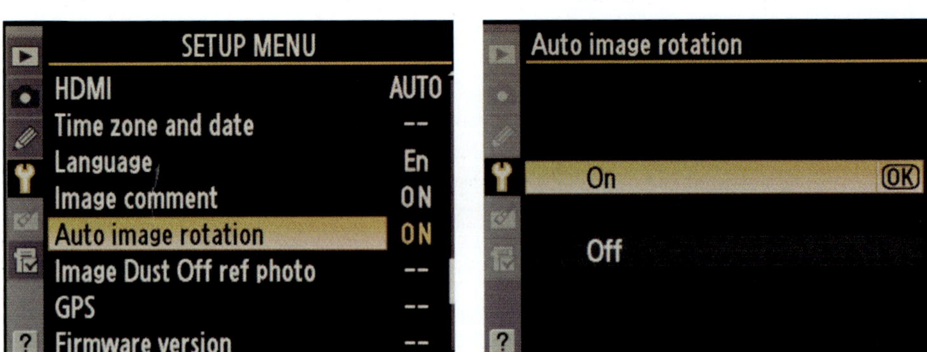

Figure 14 – *Auto image rotation* setup screens

left or right according to how you held the handgrip, up or down.

Here are the steps to enable Auto image rotation (see *figure 14*):

1. Press the MENU button and scroll to the *Setup Menu*.
2. Select *Auto image rotation*, and then scroll to the right.
3. Select *On* or *Off* from the menu.
4. Press the *OK* button.

If you are shooting in continuous release mode, the way you're holding the camera for the first shot sets the direction the images are displayed, even if you change direction while shooting.

Remember, if you have *Auto image rotation* set to *Off*, the camera does not record orientation information for the image, so no matter how you have the *Playback Menu's Rotate tall* option set, the image still will be displayed in a horizontal direction.

Recommendation

The manual states that you might want to choose *Off*, if you are "taking photographs with the lens pointing up or down." However, I have tested it carefully, and the D5000 seems quite good at determining when you have the camera held horizontally or vertically, even when you do have the lens pointed up or down. Test this for yourself and determine which you would prefer. I want all my images to have orientation information stored within them so I won't have to manually rotate dozens of images after an extensive shoot. I leave mine set to *On* and I've had no problems.

Image Dust Off Ref Photo

(User's Manual pages 171 and 172)

You may go out and do an expensive shoot only to return and find that some dust spots have appeared in the worst possible place in your images. If you then create an image dust off reference photo, you can use it to remove the dust spots from your images and afterward go clean the sensor for the next shooting session. Here's how it works.

When you use the instructions that follow to create the dust off reference photo, you will be shooting a blank unfocused picture of a pure white or gray background. The dust spots in the image will then be readily apparent to Nikon Capture NX2 software. When you load the image to be cleaned into Capture NX2 along with the dust-off image, it will use the image to remove the spots in your production image.

Remember that you take the dust-off reference photo after you've taken your other images. It needs to identify the dust spots so that it can remove them from your real images.

The position and amount of dust on the low-pass filter may change. It is recommended that you take reference images regularly and use a reference image that was taken within one day of the photograph you wish to clean up.

Finding a Subject for the Dust Off Reference Photo

First, select a "featureless" subject to photograph for the reference photo. The key here is to use a material that has no graininess, such as bright white, slick plastic or a white card. I tried using plain white sheets of paper held up to a bright window, but the resulting reference photo was unsatisfactory to Capture NX2. It gave me a message that my reference photo was "too dusty" when I tried to use it.

After some experimentation, I finally settled on three different subjects that seem to work well:

- A slide-viewing light table with the light turned on
- A computer monitor screen with a blank white word processor document displayed
- A plain white card in the same bright light in which the subject resides

All of these provided enough light and "featurelessness" to satisfy both my camera and Capture NX2. The key is to photograph something fairly bright, but not too bright. You may need to experiment with different subjects if you have no light table or computer.

Now, let's prepare the camera for the actual reference photo (see figure 15):

1. Press the MENU button on the back of your D5000.
2. Select the *Setup Menu* and scroll down until you find the *Image Dust Off ref photo* menu selection.
3. Once there, scroll to the right and you will find the *Start > OK* selection. There is also a *Clean sensor and then start* selection. Since we're removing dust on current pictures, we won't use this setting. (It might remove the dust bunny that is imprinted on the last 500 images I just shot! I'll clean my sensor *after* I get a good dust off reference photo.)
4. After you have selected *Start > OK*, your camera is ready to take the reference image. You will find the word *rEF* in the viewfinder and upper control panel LCD. This simply means that we are ready to create the image.
5. Once the camera is ready, hold the lens about 4 inches (10 cm) away from the blank subject. The camera will not try to autofocus during the process, which is good because you want the lens at infinity. We are not trying to take a viewable picture; we're just creating an image that shows where the dust is on the sensor. Focus is not important, and neither is minor camera shake. If you try to take the picture and the subject is not bright enough, or if it's too bright, you will see the screen in *figure 15A*.
6. If you are having problems with too much brightness, use a gray surface

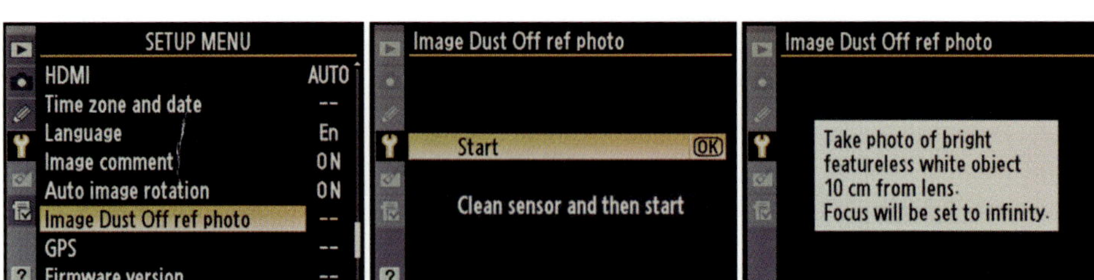

Figure 15 – Dust off reference photo preparation

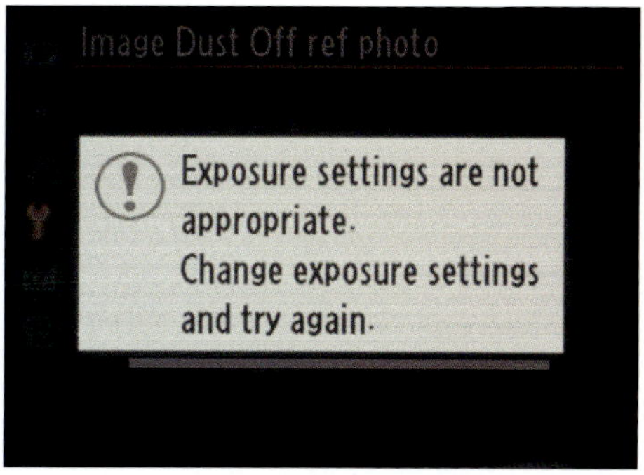

Figure 15A – *Exposure settings are not appropriate* warning

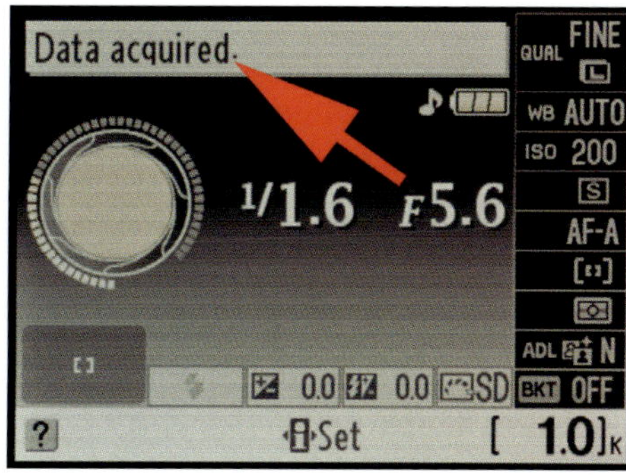

Figure 15B – Successful dust off reference photo notice

instead of white. Most of the time this error is caused by insufficient light, though.

7. If you don't see the screen in *figure 15A* and the shutter fires, you have successfully created a dust off reference photo. The information screen will now appear with a label in the top left announcing *Data acquired* (see *figure 15B*). A 2-megabyte file is created on your camera's image card with a filename ending in .ndf instead of the normal .nef or .jpg (for example, DSC_1234.ndf). This NDF file is basically a small database of the millions of clean pixels in your imaging sensor, and a few dirty ones.

You cannot display the NDF file on your computer. It will not open in Capture NX2 or any other graphics program that I tried.

Where to Store the Reference Photo

Copy the NDF file from your camera's memory card to the computer folder containing the NEF (RAW) images that have dust spots on them and for which you created this dust off reference photo. Later, when you are ready to post-process your NEF (RAW) images for dust spot removal, you'll have a reference photo with a picture of the dust only so that a program like Nikon Capture NX2 can automatically remove it for you.

GPS

(User's Manual page 114)

Nikon has wisely included the ability to GEO-tag your images with GPS location data if you purchase an optional GPS unit, such as Nikon's new GP-1 GPS. If a GPS is connected when you shoot a spectacular travel image, you can rest assured that you'll be able to find that exact spot next year. The D5000 will record the following GPS information about your location in the metadata of each image:

- *Latitude*
- *Longitude*
- *Altitude*
- *UTC time*

The Nikon GP-1 GPS Unit

Nikon recently released a very small, hotshoe-mounted GPS unit called the GP-1. This unit attaches to the D5000 using its hot shoe and the GPS port on the lower-left side of the camera. If you purchase the GP-1 GPS unit, you will get with it two accessory cables. One cable plugs into the GP-1 and then into your D5000's GPS port. The second included cable plugs into any other Nikon camera with a round 10-pin port (D200, D300, D700, D2x, D2h, D3, D3x, etc.), so you can still use your GP-1 when you save up enough money to buy that D3x you've been wanting.

See *figure 16* for a look at the GP-1 GPS unit mounted on a Nikon D5000.

The GP-1 GPS unit is powered by the camera, so you don't have to buy any extra batteries. It will have an effect on camera battery life, so if you're shooting all day, make sure you have at least one extra camera battery with you.

There are several screens used in setting up the D5000 for GPS use. First, a decision should be made about the exposure meter when a GPS unit is plugged into the D5000. While the GPS is plugged in, your exposure meter must be active to record the GPS data to the image. You'll have to do one of two things:

1. Set the exposure meter to stay on for the entire time that a GPS is plugged in, which, of course, will increase battery drain.

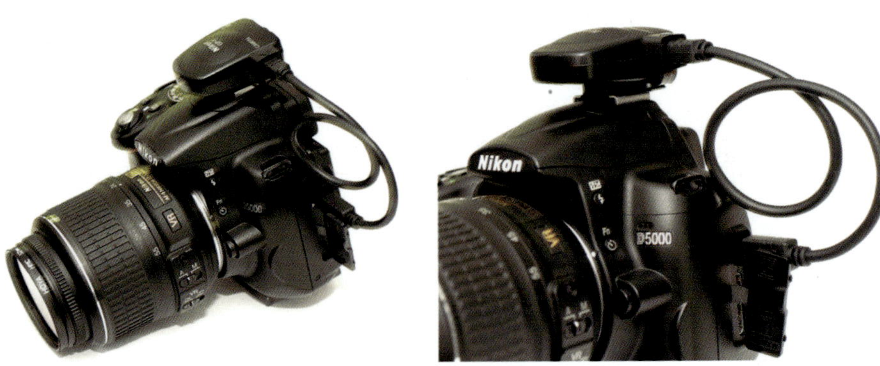

Figure 16 – D5000 with GP-1 GPS unit in hot shoe

2. Press the shutter down halfway to activate the exposure meter before finishing the exposure. If you just push the shutter button down quickly and the meter is not active, you may not record GPS data to the image. The meter must be on before GPS data will be added.

Figure 16A shows the screens to set the meter to stay on all the time the GPS is connected or to act normally and shut down after the auto meter-off delay expires (see Custom Setting c2 in chapter 7 and page 157 in the User's Manual).

You can select either:

- *Enable*
- *Disable*

Enable – The meter turns off at the end of the auto meter-off delay time, as set in Custom Setting c2. GPS data will be recorded only when the exposure meter is active, so take your time.

Disable – The exposure meter stays on all the time a GPS unit is connected. As long as you have a good GPS signal, you will be able to record GPS data at any time.

There is also a *Position* setting, as shown in Figure 16B, middle screen. If your GPS unit isn't attached or isn't reading satellite positions, the *Position* selection is grayed out (can't be selected). Once a GPS is actively feeding data to the camera, you can select and scroll to

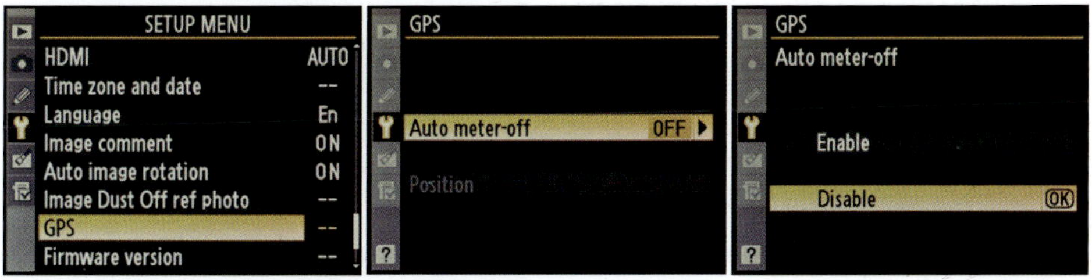

Figure 16A – GPS *Auto meter-ff* enable/disable screens

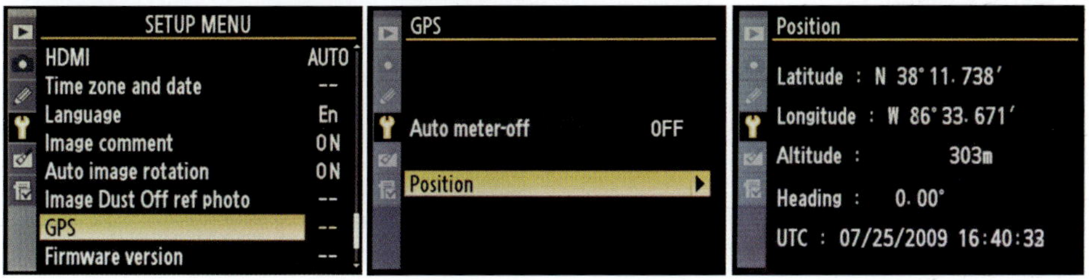

Figure 16B – GPS Position information screen

the right on the *Position* selection. You'll then see a screen that shows the actual GPS location data being detected by the D5000 (see the image on the right in figure 16B).

When the D5000 establishes communication with your GPS, it does two things:

1. A small *GPS* icon will be displayed in the upper-left corner of the information screen (*figure 16C*).
2. Position information shows on the *GPS* menu screen (*figure16B* and *figure 16D*).

An additional GPS information page may be displayed when you're reviewing the captured images (*figure 16E*). (See page 114 of the user's manual.) To get to this screen, press the Playback button to display an image, then scroll up until you see the GPS information screen. You will see this screen only if there is GPS information attached. Also, you must have the Playback Menu > Display mode option set to include the data screens (see chapter 5 "Playback Menu").

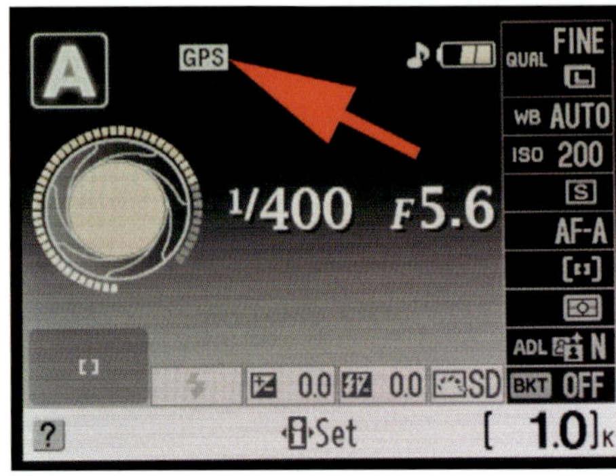

Figure 16C – *GPS* icon on information screen

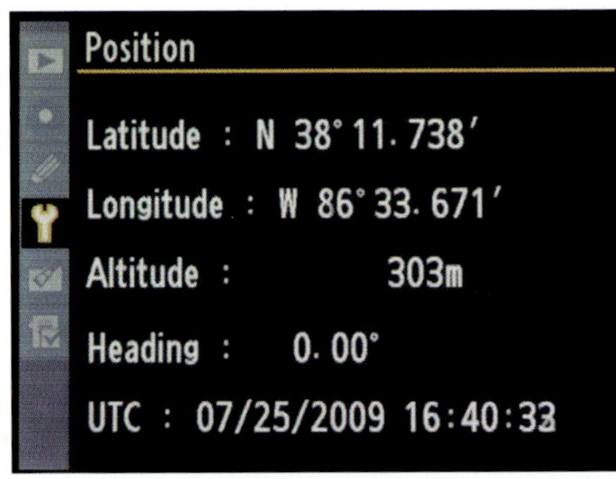

Figure 16D – Position information

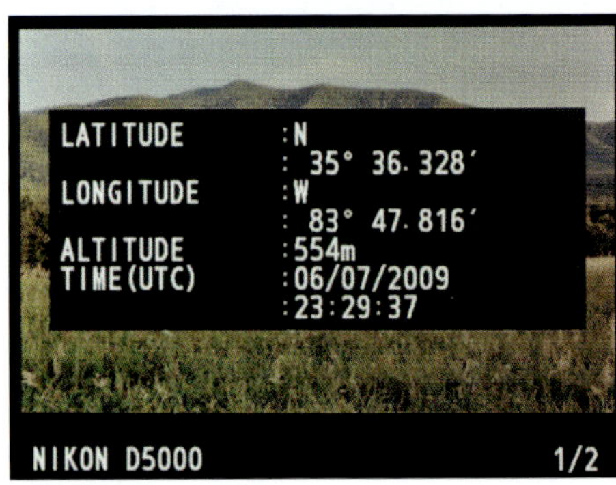

Figure 16E – GPS information playback screen

Understanding the Nikon GP-1 GPS Unit

Once you've mounted your GP-1 GPS unit in the hot shoe of your D5000 and plugged the cable into the GPS port, here's what to expect:

If the *GPS* icon is blinking on the information screen, it means that the GPS is searching for a signal. You'll also notice that the little LED light on the back of the GP-1 is blinking in red. If you take a picture with the *GPS* icon or GP-1 LED blinking red, no GPS data will be recorded.

If the *GPS* icon is not flashing, and the GP-1 LED is green, it means that the D5000 is receiving good GPS data and is ready to record data to a picture. Here is a list of what the LED light on the back of the GP-1 GPS unit can communicate to you:

- ***Blinking red*** – No satellites being tracked. Searching for satellites.
- ***Blinking green*** – Only three satellites being tracked, minimal accuracy.
- ***Solid green*** – At least four satellites being tracked for best accuracy. (Maximum 18 tracking channels.)

Tips on Using GPS

When you first start using the GP-1 GPS unit, it may take a few minutes to acquire the first satellite tracking lock. I was in a moving car on a cloudy day the first time I powered mine up. It took so long to find the satellites that I thought the unit was broken. Of course, it had probably just arrived from Japan, so it took a bit of time to figure out where it was. You may want to go outside and stand in your yard when you first turn the GP-1 GPS unit on. Make sure it has an unbroken view of the sky. After it acquires satellites the first time, it gets a satellite lock within a minute. When the GPS has been active recently and you haven't moved too far, it will usually acquire a satellite lock in a few seconds.

If the D5000 loses communication with the GPS unit for over 2 seconds, the *GPS* icon on information screen will disappear.

The Nikon GP-1 GPS unit does not provide compass (direction) information. It tracks longitude, latitude, altitude, and UTC (Coordinated Universal Time).

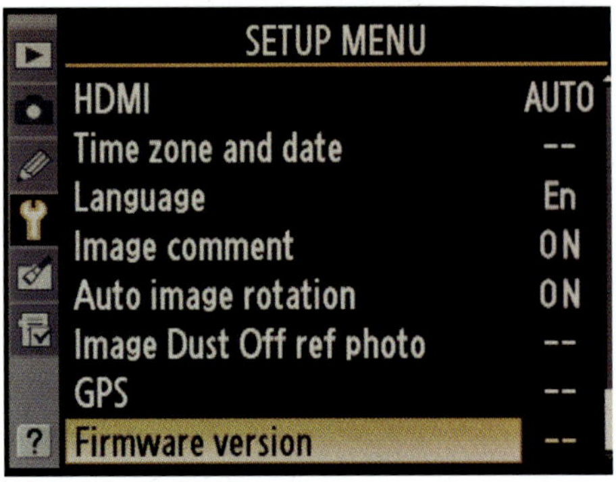

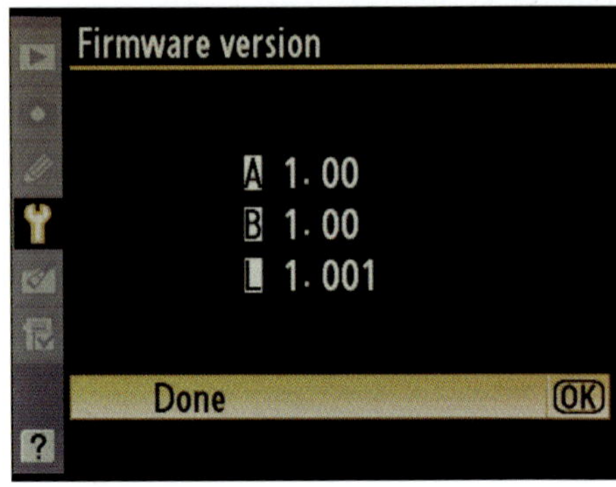

Figure 17 – Firmware version selection screens

Firmware Version

(User's Manual page 173)
This is a simple informational screen that informs you of which version of the Nikon D5000's internal software (firmware) your camera is running. My D5000 has the firmware included with the D5000 from the factory because a firmware update was not yet available at the time this book was published. The two screens to see the firmware version are shown in *figure 17*.

Follow these steps to see your camera's firmware version:

1. Press the MENU button and scroll to the *Setup Menu*.
2. Select *Firmware version*, and then scroll to the right.
3. View the *Firmware version* screen.

When a firmware update becomes available and you install it, this is the screen you'll use to validate that the firmware update was successful.

Firmware Updates

If you want to check for a firmware update on any Nikon digital camera, you can go to this web page on the NikonTech website. It lists virtually all the camera firmware updates that are available from Nikon:

http://support.nikontech.com/app/answers/detail/a_id/13783

If by the time this book is published that Internet address has changed, you can always go to the Nikon website in your part of the globe and start a search under technical support for "firmware updates."

My Conclusions

Now that you have your D5000 fully set up, you're ready to take a large number of premium images.

The next chapter is about the Retouch Menu and the last two menus in the D5000, *Recent Settings* and *My Menu*. The *Retouch Menu* is designed to help you adjust images you've already taken, in-camera, without having to resort to using your computer. The *Recent Settings* menu displays items you've changed recently.

We'll also examine a special menu that is specific to you alone, *My Menu*. This menu is a place to store all your most-used settings for immediate use so you won't have to search through the dozens of settings in the D5000.

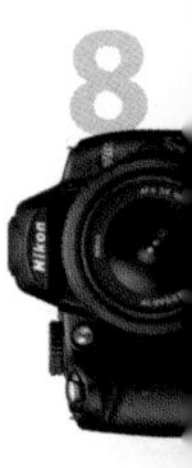

Retouch Menu, Recent Settings/My Menu

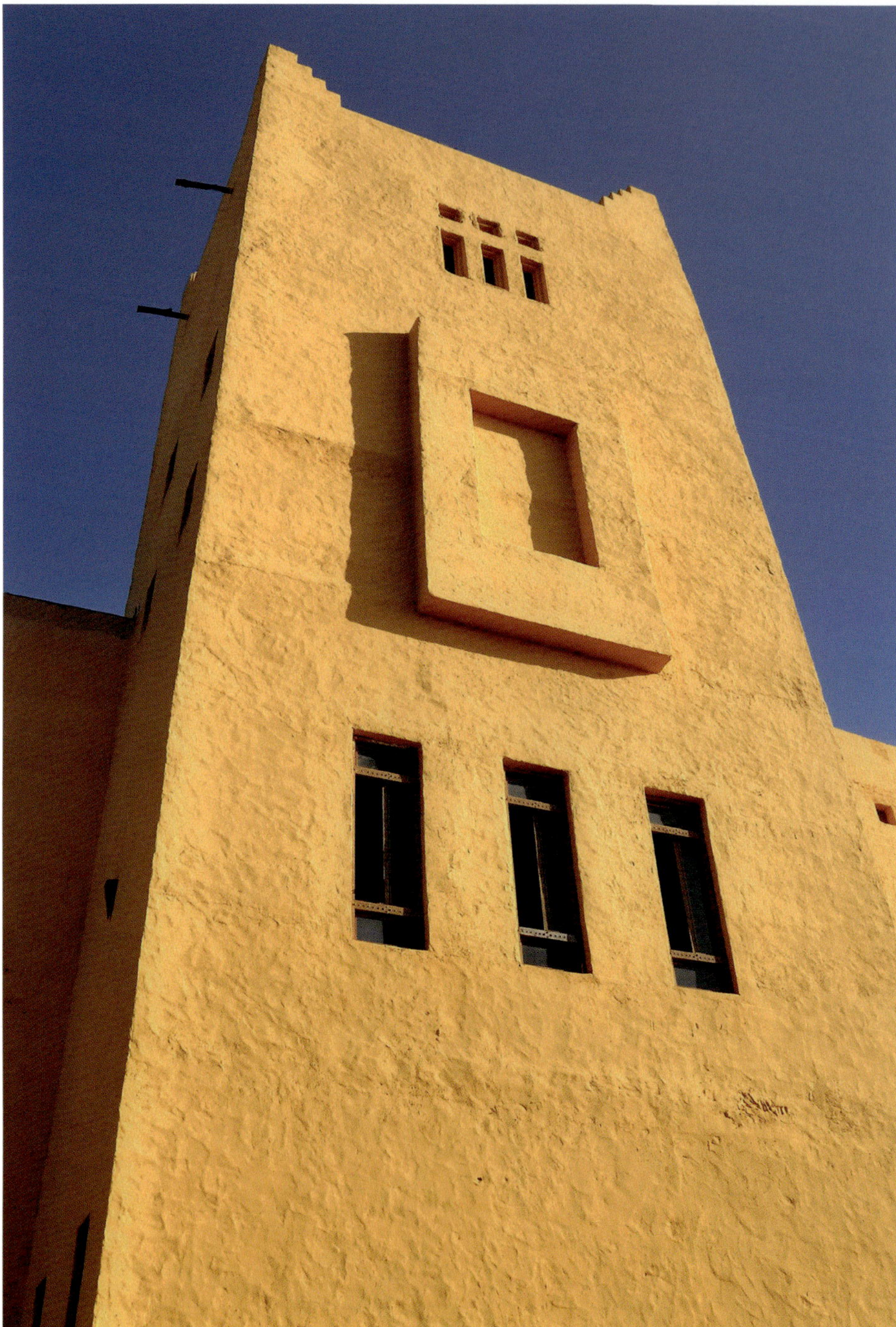

9

This chapter covers the last three menu systems in the Nikon D5000: the *Retouch Menu*, *Recent Settings*, and *My Menu*.

There are two sections.

- **Section 1** – The *Retouch Menu* consists of 17 in-camera image adjustments allowing you to do things to the image that normally would be done in a graphics program on your computer. If you don't particularly like using a computer and you're not very good with Photoshop but you still want to shoot RAW images, the *Retouch Menu* will be of great help to you.
- **Section 2** – *Recent Settings* is a list of the 20 menu items you've changed most recently from the *Playback*, *Shooting*, *Custom Setting*, and *Setup Menus*. If you've made a recent camera adjustment, it will appear here.

My Menu is whatever you want it to be. If you use certain menus or settings in the camera on a regular basis, you can add them to *My Menu* and then use them without searching through dozens of other menus.

To make it easier for you to make modifications to your images with the *Retouch Menu*, the external camera controls you'll use are shown in *figure 1*. The numbers in the list match the numbers in the figure:

1. MENU button
2. Multi Selector and OK button
3. Thumbnail/playback zoom out button
4. Playback zoom in button
5. Command dial
6. Playback button

Retouch Menu

(User's Manual pages 174–189)

There are two ways to access the *Retouch Menu*:

1. Press the MENU button and select the fifth menu down from the top, the *Retouch Menu*.
2. Use the Playback button to review an image, and then press the OK button while the image is showing on the LCD monitor.

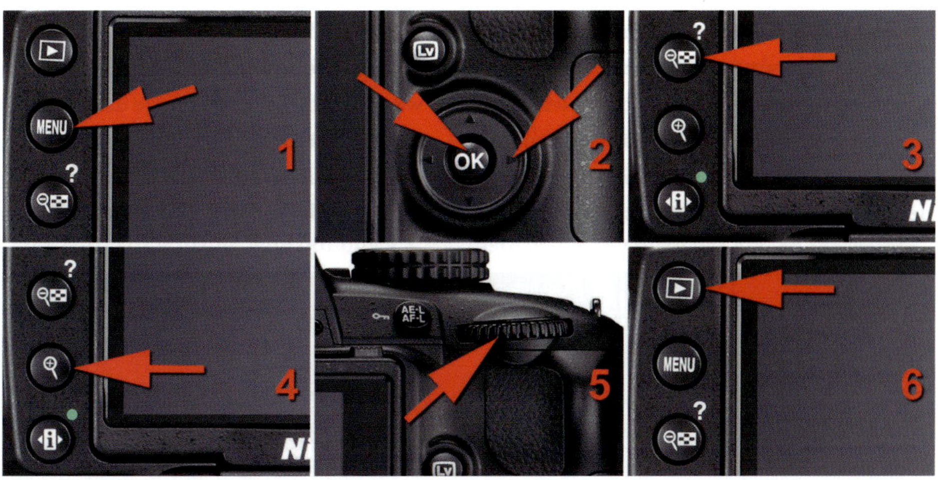

Figure 1 – Controls used to configure the *Shooting Menus*

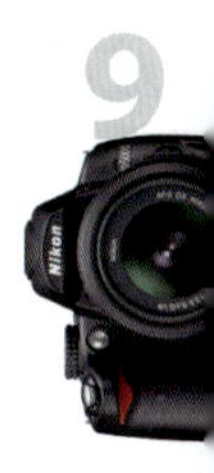

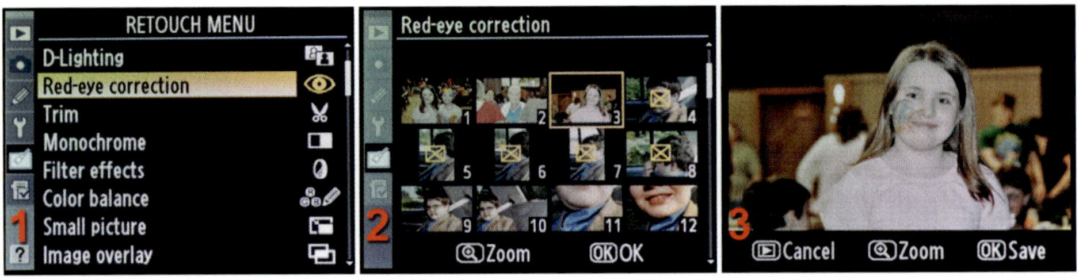

Figure 3 – *Red-eye correction* screens

still try to select it, the D5000 will tersely inform you, *Cannot select this file.*

The steps to execute the *Red-eye correction* function on an image are as follows:

1. Press the MENU button and select the *Retouch Menu.*
2. Select *Red-eye correction* from the *Retouch Menu,* and then scroll right (see *figure 3, image 1*).
3. Select the image you want to modify with the Multi Selector. You can't select images that have little yellow x-boxes on them since they were taken without flash right (see *figure 3, image 2*).
4. Press the OK button and the *Red-eye correction* routines will execute. You'll see an hourglass on your screen for several seconds.
5. After *Red-eye correction* is done, you can zoom in on the image and see how well it worked (see *figure 3, image 3*).
6. Press OK to save the file under a new file number.

I really like this *Red-eye correction* function! If I'm shooting flash pictures at an event, I'll invariably get a few images with red-eye in the series. Since red-eye can make a person look angry or evil, I tend to want to remove it. This function makes it easy.

Trim

(User's Manual page 177)

The *Trim* function allows you to crop an image in-camera and/or change the aspect ratio of the trimmed section and then save the file out to a new image. Your original image is not modified. *Trim* is merely another word for cropping the image.

You can trim up to six crop levels deep, the smallest of which crops a 640x424-pixel section out of the 4288x2848-pixel image (in the 3:2 aspect ratio). You can crop a section from anywhere in the image by moving the yellow trim frame around with the Multi Selector. Here are the six crop-levels for a D5000 default 3:2 aspect ratio image:

- *3424 x 2280*
- *2560 x 1704*
- *1920 x 1280*
- *1280 x 856*
- *960 x 640*
- *640 x 424*

Also, here are the aspect ratios you can select:

- *3:2*
- *4:3*
- *5:4*
- *1:1* (square)
- *16:9* (fits an HD screen)

These aspect ratios are controlled by the command dial. When you have the image and the yellow crop rectangle showing, just turn the command dial.

Here are the steps to trim an image in the D5000:

1. Press the MENU button and select the *Retouch Menu*.
2. Select the *Trim* function from the *Retouch Menu* and then scroll right (see *figure 4, image 1*).
3. Select the image you want to modify and press the OK button (see *figure 4, image 2*).
4. You'll be presented with a screen that has a crop outlined in yellow. Using the normal zoom buttons (thumbnail/playback zoom out and playback zoom in), you can zoom in for a deeper crop or zoom out for a lesser crop. Zoom until you find your best crop position. Move the yellow trim frame with the Multi Selector until it is exactly positioned in the image. (See *figure 1* earlier in this chapter for the locations of the camera control.)
5. Select the aspect ratio of the crop by rotating the command dial. See where the red arrows point in *figure 4, image 3* and *image 4*. They show that I changed from 3:2 to 1:1 ratio with the command dial. Notice how the yellow frame changed size to the new ratio between the images. I then increased the crop with the thumbnail/playback zoom out button until I had just a close-up of the young lad's face as my subject.
6. Once you have the aspect ratio set and the crop correctly sized, press the OK button to save the trimmed image under a new file number. You can see the final cropped file in the last image of *figure 4*. Notice the little retouch symbol on the top left of the image.

I haven't found a way to turn the yellow box upright so that I can make a vertical crop out of the center of a horizontal image. However, for a basic crop, it does a sufficient job. The closest I can come to a

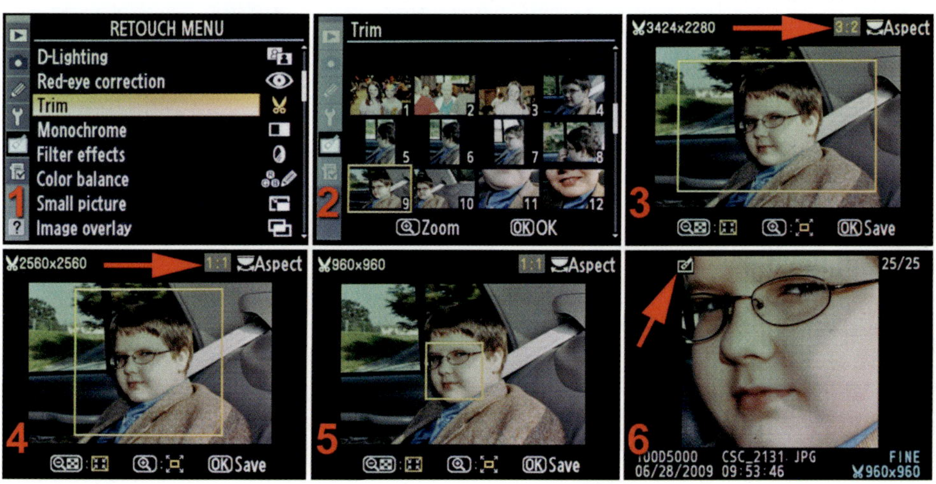

Figure 4 – *Trim* screens

vertical crop is the 1:1 ratio, which makes a square image.

Remember that these functions are for convenience and quick "in-the-field" use. If you are serious about post-processing—or have many images to modify—it's much easier to accomplish this type of work in-computer with a good graphics package.

Monochrome

(User's Manual page 178)

The *Monochrome* functions in the D5000 are fun to play with and can make some interesting images. You can convert a normal color image into a normal black andwhite, or you can create a monochrome with two types of tones: warm and cool.

You can choose from three different types of monochrome (see *figure* 5, *image* 4, *image* 5, and *image* 6):

- *Black-and-white*
- *Sepia*
- *Cyanotype*

Here are the steps to create a monochrome image from one of your existing color images on the camera's memory card:

1. Press the MENU button and select the *Retouch Menu*.
2. Select *Monochrome* from the *Retouch Menu*, and then scroll right (see *figure* 5, *image* 1).
3. Select a monochrome tone (*Black-and-white*, *Sepia*, or *Cyanotype*), and then scroll to the right (see *figure* 5, *image* 2).
4. Select the image you want to modify with the Multi Selector, and then press the OK button (see *figure* 5, *image* 3).
5. You'll be presented with an image converted and toned to the tint you selected. I've included a sample of each in *figure* 5 (*image* 4, *image* 5, and *image* 6).
6. Press the *OK* button to save the new image under a new file number or the *Playback* button to cancel. You'll see the retouch symbol in the upper-left corner of the new image.

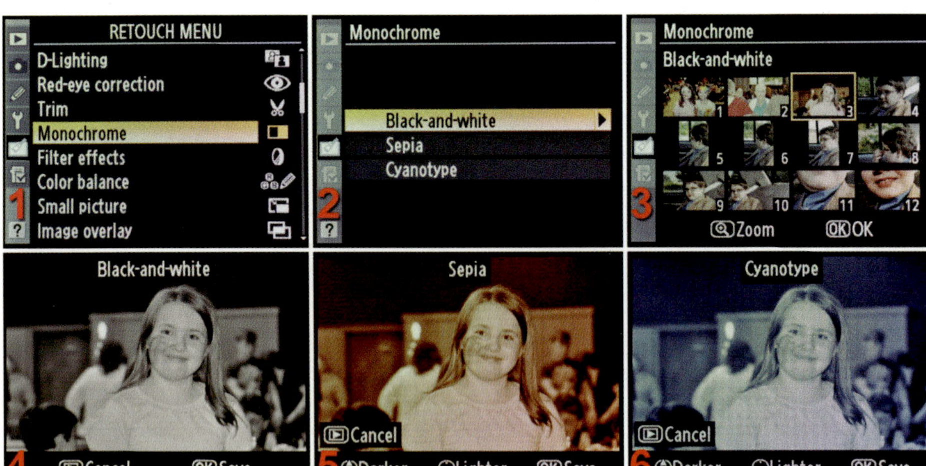

Figure 5 – *Monochrome* selection screens

Recommendation

If you're serious about making black-and-white images with the D5000, why not use the *MC–Monochrome* setting under *Shooting Menu > Set Picture Control* (see chapter 6). *MC-Monochrome* allows you to shoot initially with various levels of tinting, far exceeding the basic conversion and three tints of the *Retouch Menu*'s version. Use the *Retouch Menu*'s *Monochrome* function to convert a color picture to one of three types of monochrome. It's easy and effective.

Filter Effects

(User's Manual pages 178 and 179)

The D5000 allows you to add six filter effects to any previously taken image. You can intensify the image colors in various ways and add starburst effects to points of light. In addition to changing colors and adding starbursts, you can soften an image for a pleasing "soft-filter" portrait effect (three levels).

Here is a list of the effects that are available:

- *Skylight*
- *Warm filter*
- *Red intensifier*
- *Green intensifier*
- *Blue intensifier*
- *Cross screen* (starburst filter)
- *Soft*

Skylight – This effect is rather mild and removes the blue effect caused by atmospheric diffraction in distant scenes. Basically, by using this you will make the image slightly less blue. It is rather hard to see any difference. Here's how to set the *Skylight* effect (see *figure 6A*):

1. Select *Filter effects* from the *Retouch Menu*, and scroll right.
2. Select *Skylight*, and scroll to the right.
3. Choose an image with the Multi Selector and press the OK button.
4. The image appears with the *Skylight* effect added.

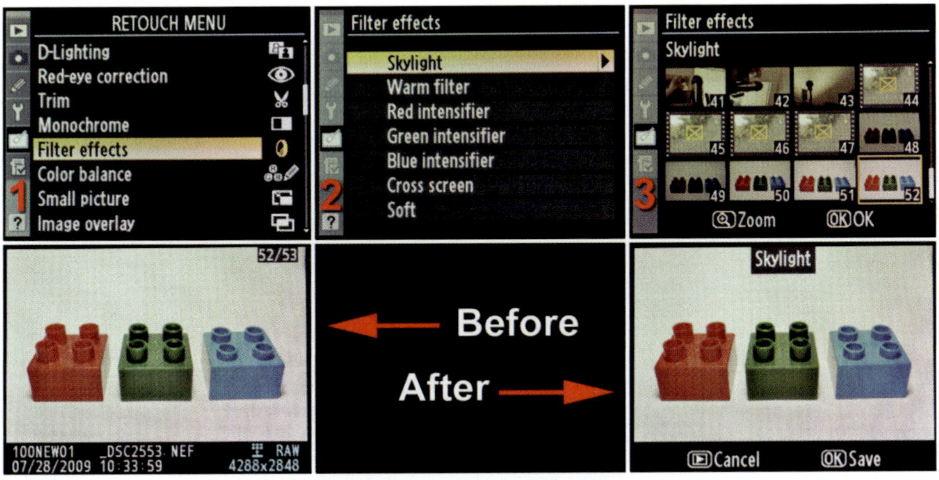

Figure 6A – The screens for the *Skylight* effect

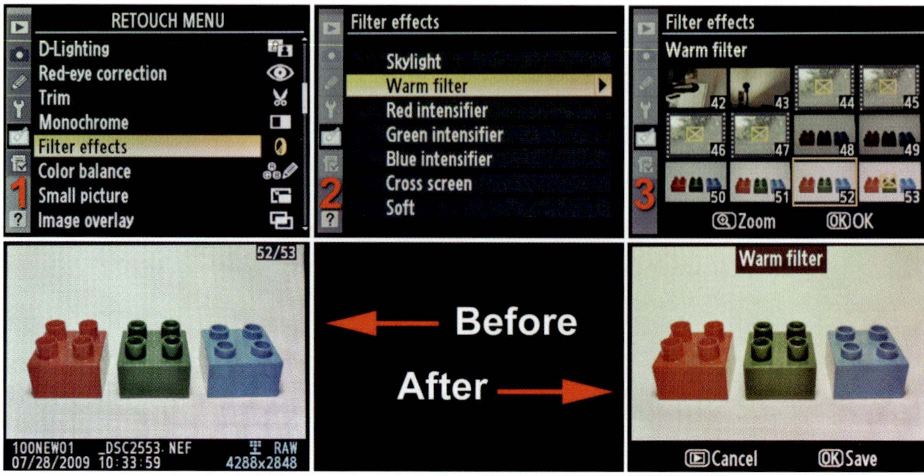

Figure 6B – The screens for the *Warm filter* effect

5. Press the OK button to save the image under a new filename, or press the Playback button to cancel.

Warm filter – This effect adds red to the image to make it appear a little warmer. In fact, it adds a mild red cast to the image. Here's how to set the *Warm filter* effect (see *figure 6B*):

1. Select *Filter effects* from the *Retouch Menu*, and scroll right.
2. Select *Warm filter*, and scroll to the right.
3. Choose an image with the Multi Selector and press the OK button.
4. The image appears with the *Warm filter* effect added.
5. Press the OK button to save the image under a new filename, or press the Playback button to cancel.

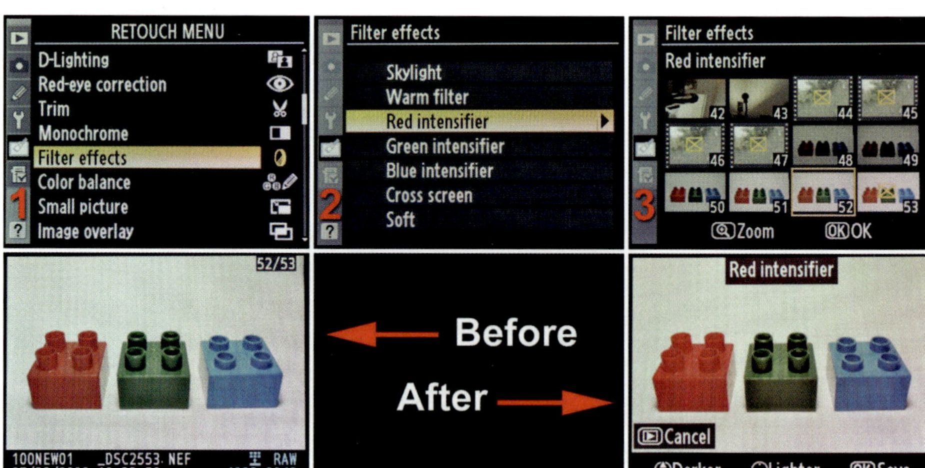

Figure 6C – The screens for the *Red intensifier* effect

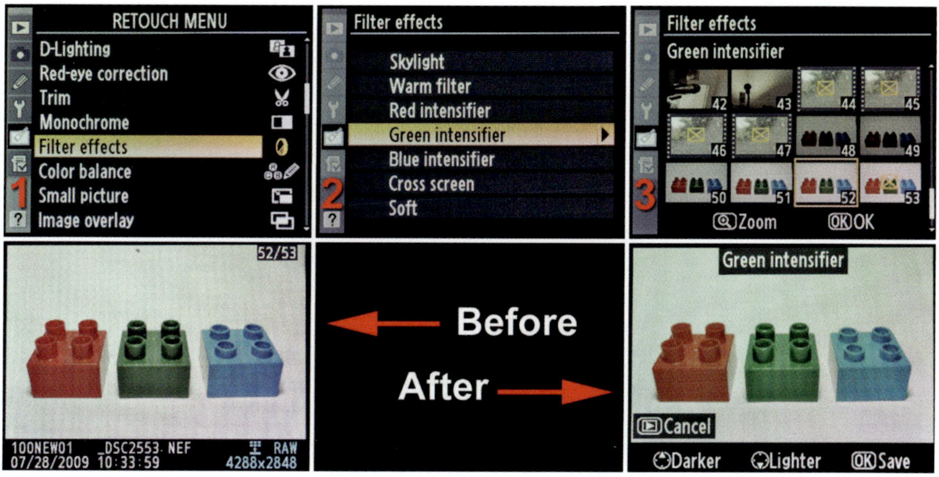

Figure 6D – The screens for the Green intensifier effect

Red intensifier – This effect intensifies the reds in an image and also adds a red cast. It can be controlled by making an initial selection, and then when the image is onscreen, increasing or reducing the effect by using the Multi Selector to scroll up or down. Even though it doesn't tell you, there are three levels of intensity. Scroll up for maximum effect, and down for minimum effect. Here's how to set the *Red intensifier* effect (see *figure 6C*):

1. Select *Filter effects* from the *Retouch Menu*, and scroll right.
2. Select *Red intensifier*, and scroll to the right.
3. Choose an image with the Multi Selector and press the OK button.
4. The image appears with the *Red intensifier* effect added.
5. Scroll up or down with the Multi Selector to intensify or reduce the effect.
6. Press the OK button to save the image under a new filename, or press the Playback button to cancel.

Green intensifier - This effect intensifies the greens in an image and also adds a green cast. It can be controlled by making an initial selection, and then when the image is onscreen, increasing or reducing the effect by using the Multi Selector to scroll up or down. There are three levels of intensity. Scroll up for maximum effect and down for minimum effect. Here's how to set the *Green intensifier* effect (see *figure 6D*):

1. Select *Filter effects* from the *Retouch Menu*, and scroll right.
2. Select *Green intensifier*, and scroll to the right.
3. Choose an image with the Multi Selector and press the OK button.
4. The image appears with the *Green intensifier* effect added.
5. Scroll up or down with the Multi Selector to intensify or reduce the effect.
6. Press the OK button to save the image under a new filename, or press the Playback button to cancel.

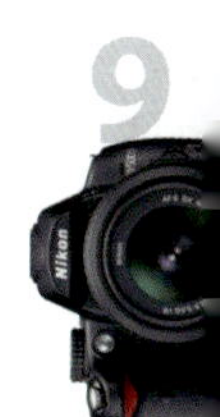

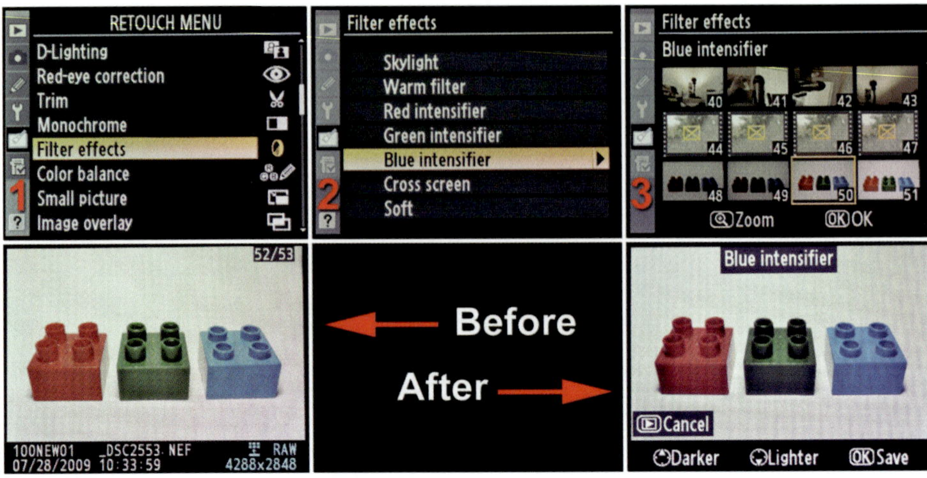

Figure 6E – The screens for the *Blue intensifier* effect

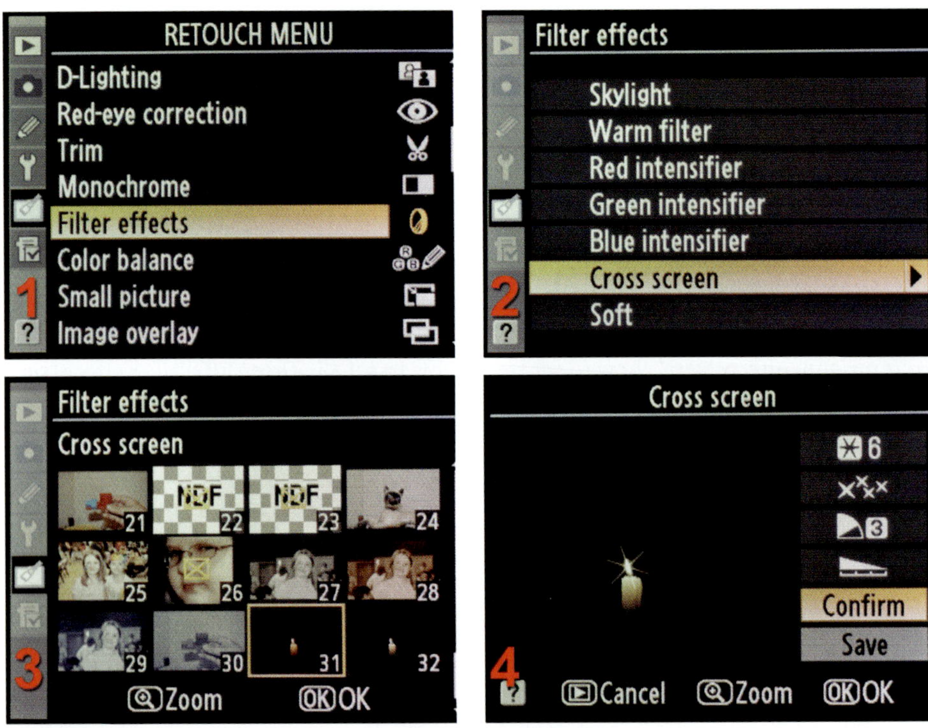

Figure 6F – The screens for the *Cross screen* effect

Blue intensifier - This effect intensifies the blues in an image and also adds a blue cast. It can be controlled by making an initial selection, and then when the image is onscreen, increasing or reducing the effect by using the Multi Selector to scroll up or down. There are three levels of intensity. Scroll up for maximum effect and down for minimum effect. Here's how to set the *Blue intensifier* effect (see *figure 6E*):

1. Select *Filter effects* from the *Retouch Menu*, and scroll right.
2. Select *Blue intensifier*, and scroll to the right.
3. Choose an image with the Multi Selector and press the OK button.
4. The image appears with the *Blue intensifier* effect added.
5. Scroll up or down with the Multi Selector to intensify or reduce the effect.
6. Press the OK button to save the image under a new filename, or press the Playback button to cancel.

Cross screen – This effect is designed to work like a cross-screen filter and adds a starburst (rays) effect to any points of light (see *figure 6F*). There are four different adjustments to this effect, along with *Confirm* and *Save* options. To create the starburst rays effect, do the following:

1. Select *Filter effects* from the *Retouch Menu*, and scroll right.
2. Select *Cross screen*, and scroll to the right.
3. Choose an image with the Multi Selector and press the OK button.
4. Select the number of points (4, 6, or 8) in the star effect's rays using the two screens in *figure 6G*.
5. Select the filter amount with the two screens in *figure 6H*. This affects the brightness of the light sources.
6. Select the filter angle (ray clockwise rotation) with the two screens in *figure 6I*.

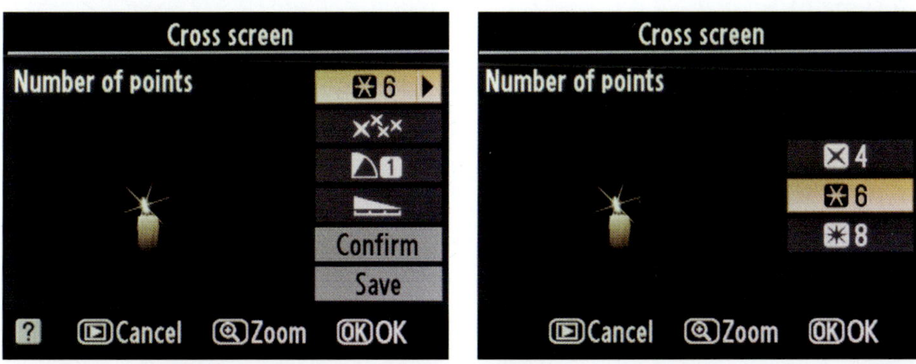

Figure 6G –The *Number of points* screens for the *Cross screen* effect

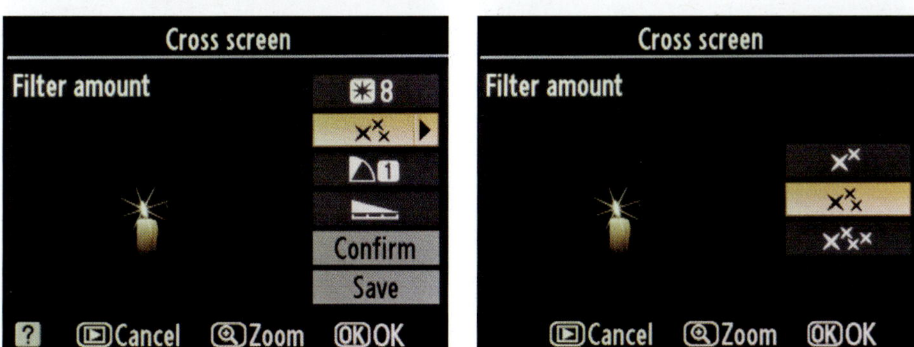

Figure 6H –The *Filter amount* screens for the *Cross screen* effect

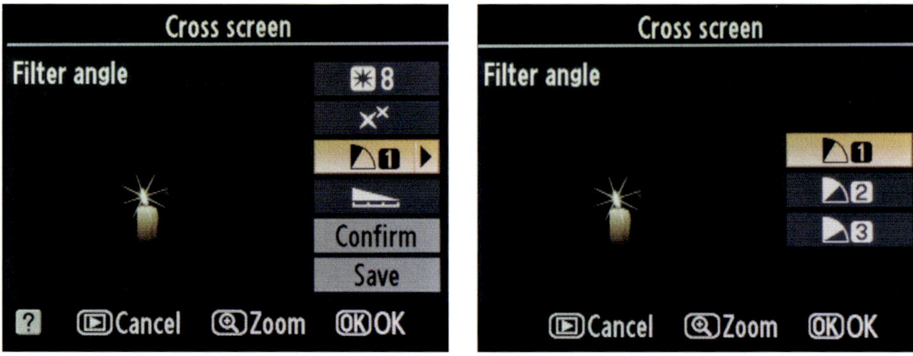

) Figure 6I – The *Filter angle* screens for the *Cross screen* effect

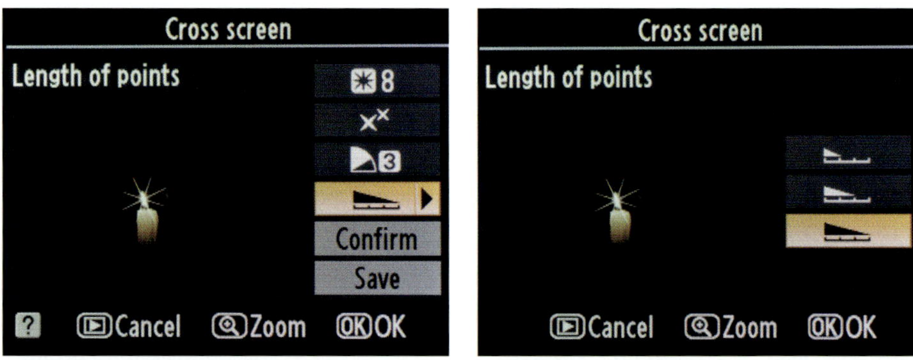

Figure 6J – Cross Screen - The *Length of points* screens for the *Cross screen* effect

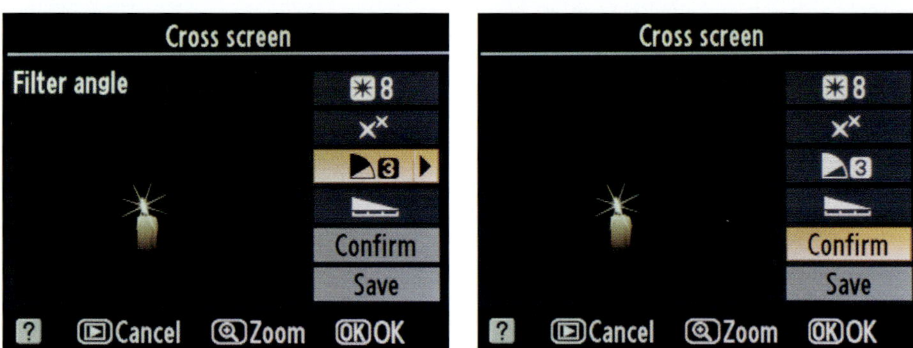

Figure 6K – The *Confirm* screen for the *Cross screen* effect

7. Select the length of the points (longer rays) with the two screens in *figure 6J*.
8. Press the *Confirm* button to see the effect. This is like an update button. You can repeat the confirm step multiple times, confirming/updating each time, until you have the effect just the way you want it to look. In this example, I set *Filter angle* to 3, and then I confirmed the effect (*figure 6K*).
9. Select the *Save* menu item and then press the OK button. The full-sized image appears in normal playback mode (*figure 6L*).

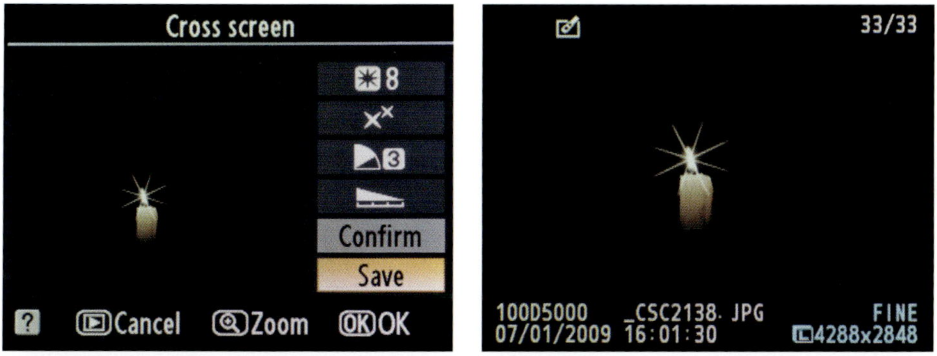

Figure 6L –The save and playback screens for the *Cross screen* effect

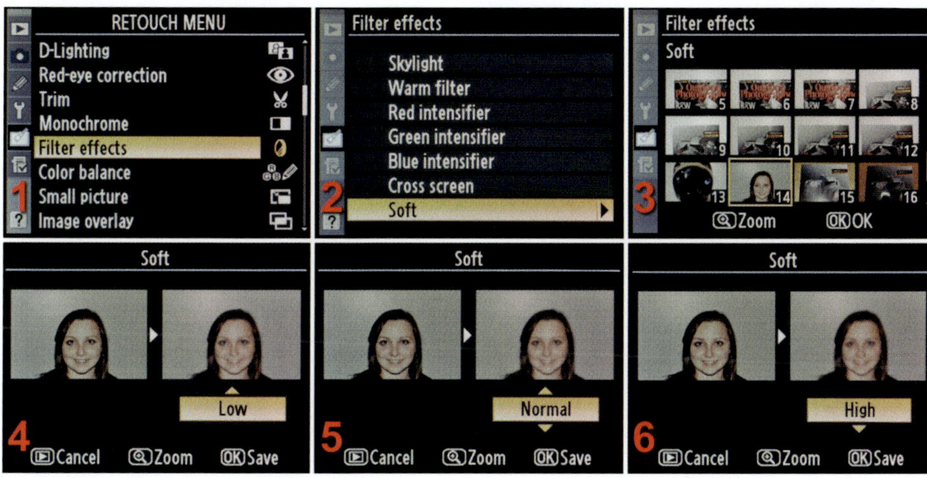

Figure 6M – The screens for the *Soft* effect

Soft – If you've ever wanted to make one of those "dreamy" effect shots of a lovely lady, as they used to do in the old 1960s *Star Trek* shows, the D5000 has the filter for you.

The *Soft* effect filter softens the image and adds a misty effect. If you are doing portraits of an older individual, or someone with skin problems, this filter will provide a nicer portrait effect. There are three levels to the softening effect. *Figure 6M* shows all three, but the dreamy, misty look will be easier to see when you have the camera in your hand.

Here are the steps to select the *Soft* filter effect (see *figure 6M*):

1. Select *Filter effects* from the *Retouch Menu*, and scroll right.
2. Select *Soft*, and scroll to the right.
3. Choose an image with the Multi Selector and press the OK *button* (see *figure 6M, image 3*).
4. A side-by-side comparison of the image appears with the *Normal* setting applied. Scroll down to set *Low* and up to set *High* (see *figure 6M, images 4, 5*, and *6*).
5. Press the OK button to save the image under a new filename, or press the Playback button to cancel.

9

Figure 6N shows four larger images that will hopefully allow you to see the soft effect a little better. The Soft effect isn't applied to the first image, and the next three are set to *Low*, *Normal*, and *High*.

Recommendation

The *Low* setting provides a nice effect. However, the dreaminess increases with each level. I think that *High* is too blurry, but it may work well for high-contrast subjects. These levels will be very much a personal decision and may vary based on the subject.

Color Balance

(User's Manual page 179)

The *Color balance* function allows you to change the color of your image after the fact. You might just want to warm things up a bit by adding a touch of red or cool things down with a touch of blue. Or, you could get creative and easily add various color casts to the image for special effects. You'll see what I mean when you try it.

The *Color balance* menu screens are shown in *figure 7*.

To modify the color balance of an image, follow these steps:

1. Press the MENU button and select the *Retouch Menu*.
2. Select *Color balance* from the *Retouch menu*, and then scroll right.
3. Select the image you want to modify with the Multi Selector, and then press the *OK* button. You'll see a screen with a series of histograms on the right and a small color selection box on the bottom left (see where the red arrow is

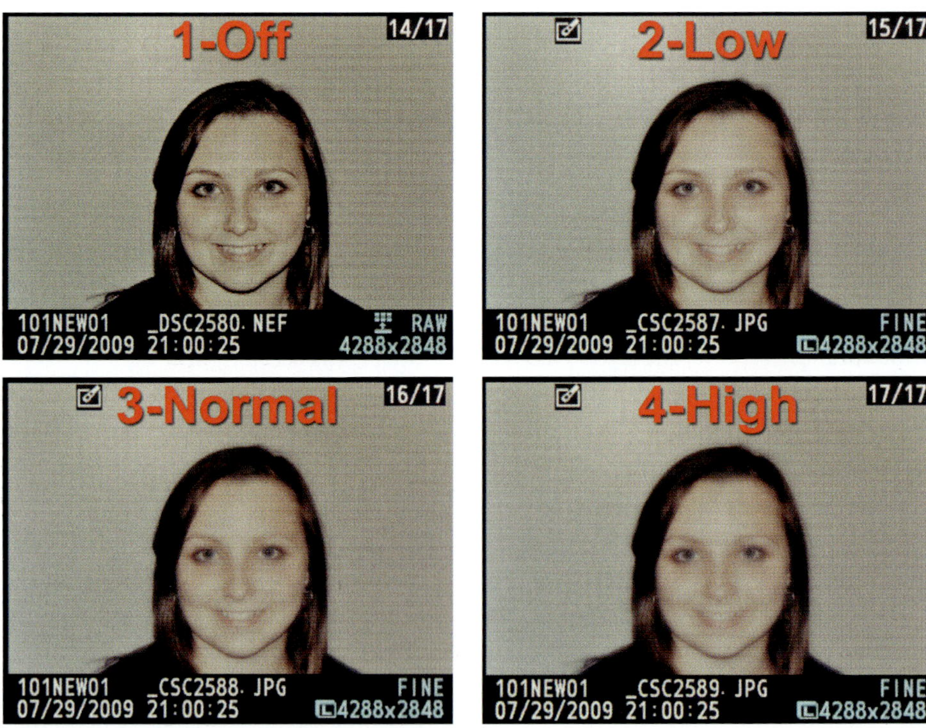

Figure 6N – The Soft effect – *Off* to *High*

pointing in the screen on the right in *figure 7*).

4. Use the Multi Selector to move the tiny black indicator square in the center of the color box toward whatever color tint you'd like to use. Watch the histograms as they display the changing color relationships between the red, green, and blue color channels. You can see the color changes as they are applied to the small version of your image in the upper-left corner of the screen (*figure 7A*).
5. Press the OK button to save the new image under a new file number or the Playback button to cancel.

Small Picture

(User's Manual pages 180 and 181)

If you want to convert an existing image on your camera's memory card to a smaller-than-normal size, you can use this

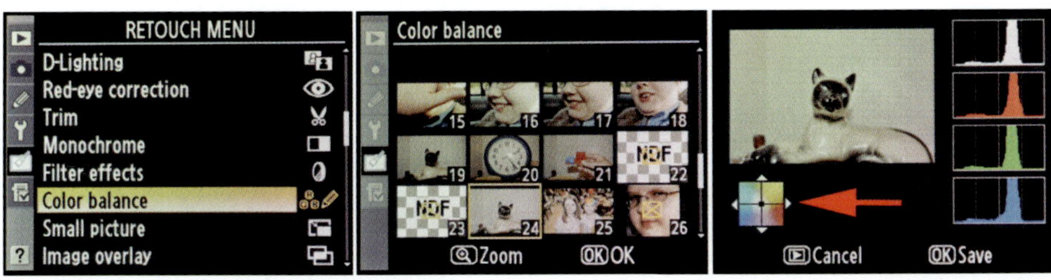

Figure 7 – The *Color balance* retouch screens

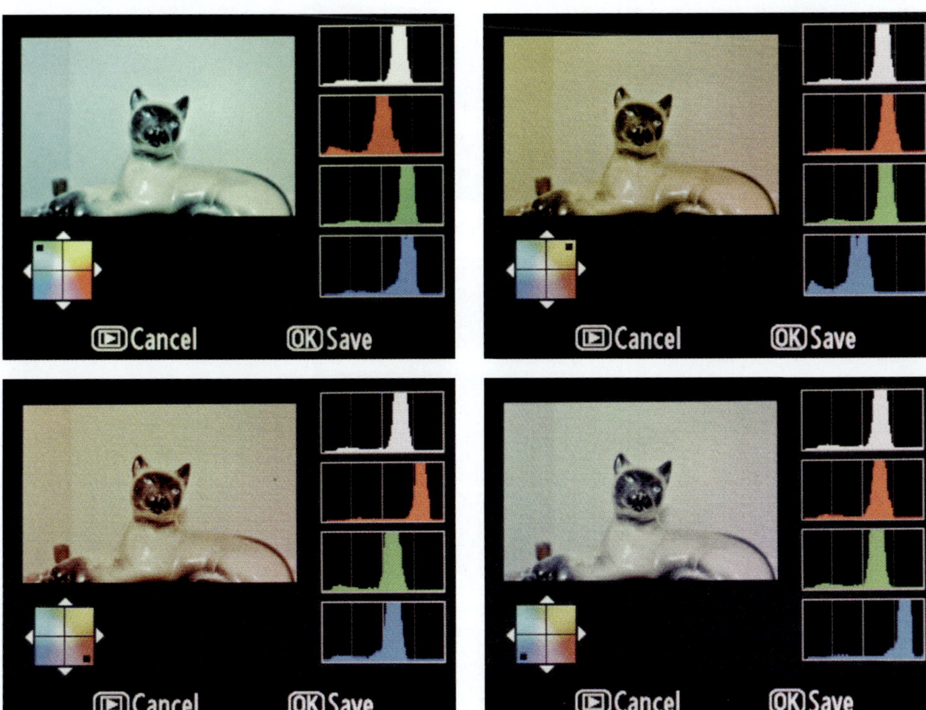

Figure 7A – Four *Color balance* tint variations

function. This is handy when you want to send someone an image over the Internet, display it on a TV or web page, or give someone a small version that can't be easily enlarged and printed.

There are three levels of "smallness" available in the *Small picture* setting (in pixels):

- *640x480*
- *320x240*
- *160x120*

Here are the steps to make use of the small picture reduction function:

1. Press the MENU button and select the *Retouch Menu*.
2. Select *Small picture* from the *Retouch Menu*, then scroll right (see *figure 8*).
3. Select *Choose size*, and scroll right.
4. Select one of the three sizes, and press the OK button.
5. The camera returns to the *Small picture* screen.
6. Now choose *Select image*, and scroll to the right (see *figure 8A*).
7. Use the thumbnail/playback zoom out button and the Multi Selector to select one or more images to convert to a smaller size. You'll see a tiny resize box appear in the upper-top corner of the selected images (see where the red arrow is pointing in *figure 8A, image 3*).
8. When you have selected all the images you want to resize, press the *OK* button.
9. A screen with the question *Create small picture?* appears and gives you a Yes/No

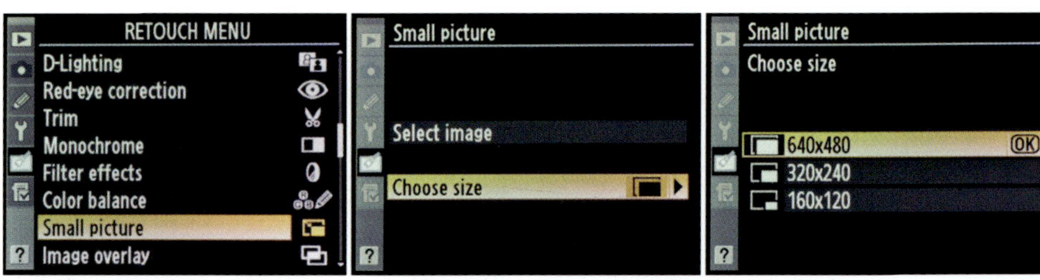

Figure 8 – The *Choose size* selection screens for the *Small picture* option

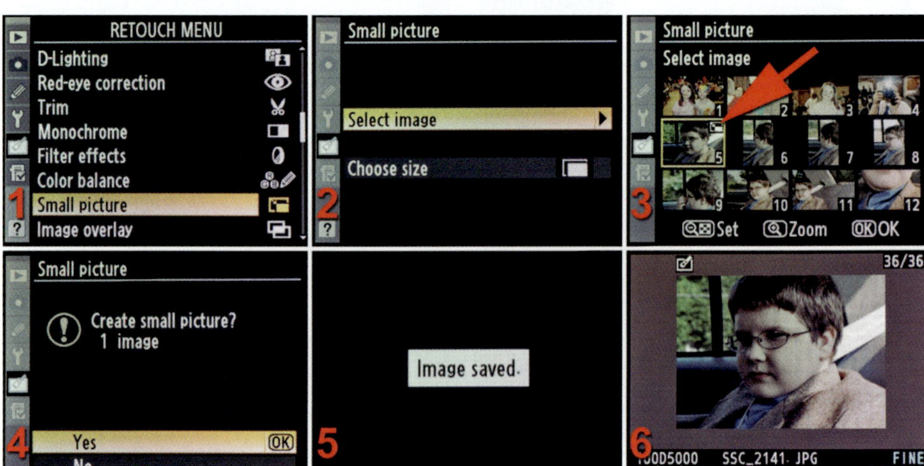

Figure 8A – The *Select image* screens for the *Small picture* option

choice. Choose *Yes* and press the OK button (see *figure 8A, image 4*).

10. You'll see an hourglass for a few seconds, and then *Image saved* appears on the screen.
11. Next, the newly converted images display in normal playback mode. If you selected multiple images to convert, the playback screen will be showing the last image in the series. Scroll backwards to see all of them. You'll be able to identify the images converted to small size by the large gray border, the retouch symbol in the upper-left corner, and the small size (e.g., 640x480) listing in the lower-right corner (see *figure 8A, image 6*).

You cannot zoom into the smaller files the way you can the normal sized ones. Now that you have made the small size conversion, you can plug your memory card into a computer and transfer the smaller files for whatever use you have for them.

Image Overlay

(User's Manual pages 182 and 183)
This particular function only works with NEF (RAW) files. You won't even be able to see JPEGs in the image selection screen.

Image overlay allows you to overlay two existing images from your camera's memory card and then save the overlaid image as a brand-new image with a different image number. Your original images are protected. You can also vary the lightness/darkness (gain) on each image before overlaying them. According to Nikon, images overlaid in this way are "noticeably better than overlays created in an imaging application."

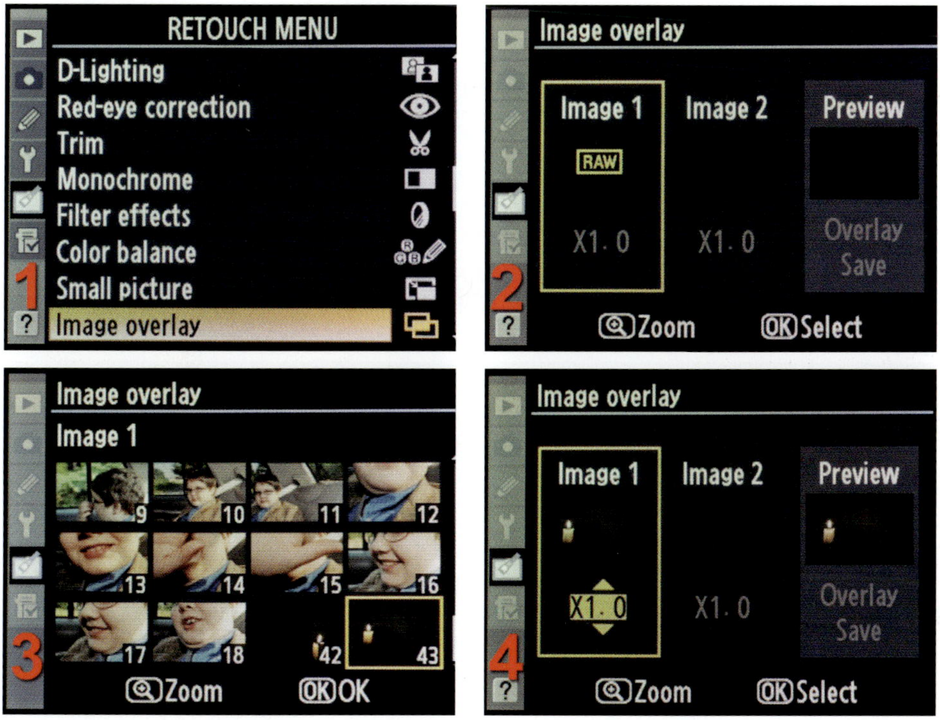

Figure 9 – Overlaying two images – selecting the first image

You'll need to use multiple screens to overlay the two images. Here's the procedure (see *figure 9*):

1. Press the MENU button and select the *Retouch Menu*.
2. Select *Image overlay*, and then scroll to the right (see *figure 9, image 1*).
3. You'll now see the screen that allows you to select the two images you'll be overlaying. The yellow selection box should be surrounding the *Image 1* area, with the word *RAW* in a small box (see *figure 9, image 2*).
4. Press the *OK* button and you will be presented with any NEF (RAW) images on your camera's memory card (see *figure 9, image 3)*. If none are there, the camera won't display anything.
5. Scroll through the available NEF (RAW) images and then press the OK button to select the first image. The image selection screen will display again. Your selected image will display in the *Image 1* position (see *figure 9, image 4*).
6. Move the yellow selection box to the *Image 2* area with the Multi Selector (see *figure 9A*).
7. Press the OK button, and you'll be presented with a display of any NEF (RAW) images on the memory card.
8. Select a different image this time unless you want to overlay the same image. Press the OK button to select your second image. The image you select will become the second image in the overlay.
9. You now have the two images you are going to overlay in their respective *Image 1* and *Image 2* boxes (see *figure 9B*).
10. Now you'll need to select and change the gain on each image (if you want to add this step). Notice the X1.0 characters below each image (see where the red arrows are pointing in *figure 9B*)? Use your Multi Selector to scroll up or down

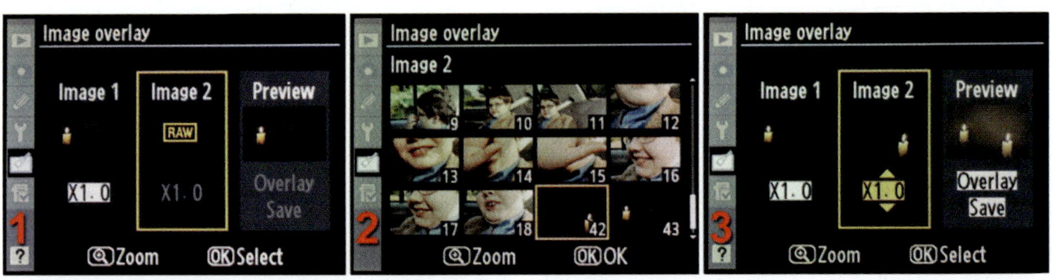

Figure 9A – Overlaying two images – selecting the second image

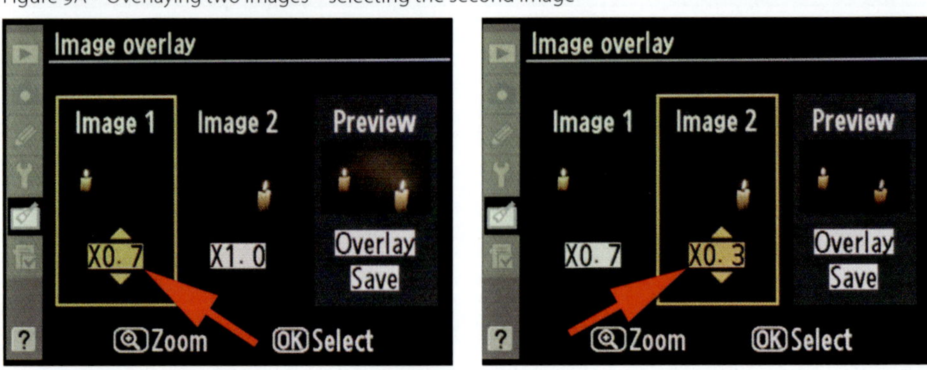

Figure 9B – Overlaying two images – changing image gain

on these X1.0 (gain) settings. You'll see that you can scroll up to X2.0, or down to X0.1. While you are scrolling the X-gain numbers, pay attention to what is happening in the preview box to the far right. As you increase the gain in one of the images, it gets darker in the preview box. If you decrease the gain, that image in the preview box gets lighter. Use the X-gain function on both images 1 and 2 until you have the previewed image looking just the way you want it to look.

11. Scroll the yellow selection box to the preview area. You have two selections available, *Overlay* and *Save* (see *figure 9C, image 1*).

Using *figure 9C* as a guide, if you select *Overlay* and press the OK button, the camera will overlay the image and show you a larger version of it. You can preview before selecting *Overlay* by pressing the playback zoom in button. If you don't like the looks of the image and want to readjust the gain, simply press the thumbnail/playback zoom out button and the main overlay configuration screen will reappear. The word *Preview* will have been replaced with *Overlay*. If you press *OK* on the screen in image 2 of *figure 9C*, please skip step 12 (next) since the save will take place immediately. (See *figure 1* earlier in this chapter for the locations of the camera controls.)

12. Once you are happy with the overlaid image, simply scroll to the *Save* menu item in the new *Overlay* section and press the OK button. The final image will now be created with a new image number and will be displayed in normal playback mode (see *figure 9D*). This is the second way to save an overlaid image, only this one does it without an *overlay preview*.

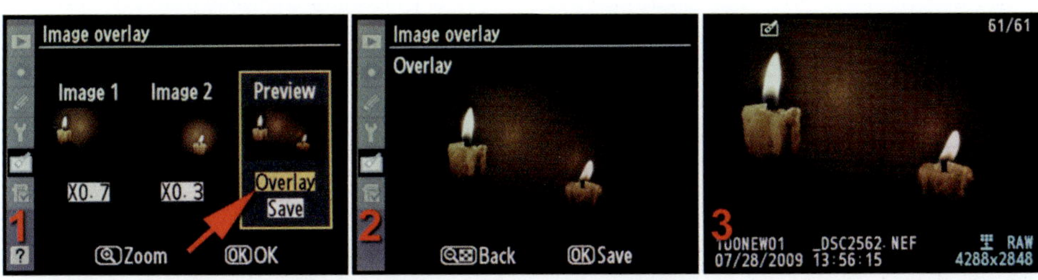

Figure 9C – Overlaying two images – previewing and saving the overlay

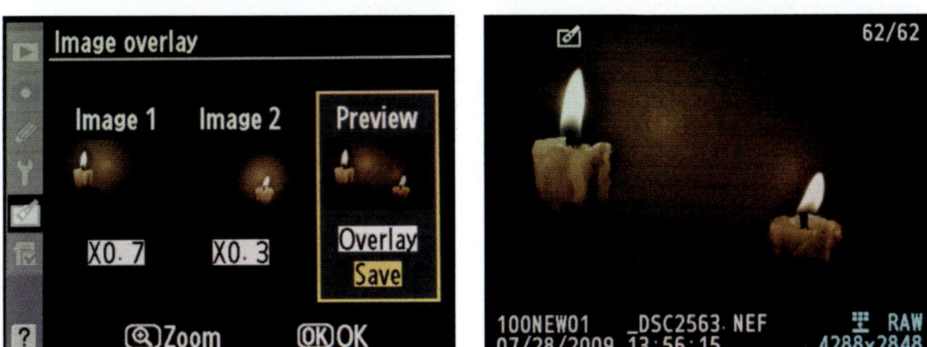

Figure 9D – Overlaying two images – saving the overlay

NEF (RAW) Processing

(User's Manual page 184)

Without using your computer, you can process a RAW file into a JPEG, right in the camera. Why is this different from just shooting an NEF (RAW) + JPEG fine at the same time? (See the section on the *Shooting Menu*'s *Image quality* setting in chapter 6.)

Well, when you shoot a JPEG, all settings are applied to the image immediately—and irreversibly. *NEF (RAW) processing* gives you an opportunity to take an existing NEF (RAW) file, which has no permanent settings applied, and use it to create whatever type of JPEG you want. It's an after-the-fact, or post-processing method, that Nikon has given us. Conversion from NEF to JPEG with *your* settings!

You can apply the following settings to your new JPEG:

- *Image quality*
- *Image size*
- *White balance*
- *Exposure compensation*
- *Picture Control*

Let's look at the screens and steps involved with converting from NEF (RAW) to JPEG in-camera (*figure 10*):

1. Press the MENU button and select the *Retouch Menu*.
2. Select *NEF (RAW) processing*, and then scroll to the right.
3. Select a RAW image from the list with the camera's Multi Selector, and then press the OK button.
4. Select one of the *Image quality* settings—*Fine*, *Norm*, or *Basic*—from the *Image quality* menu (see *figure 10A*). *Fine* gives you the best possible quality

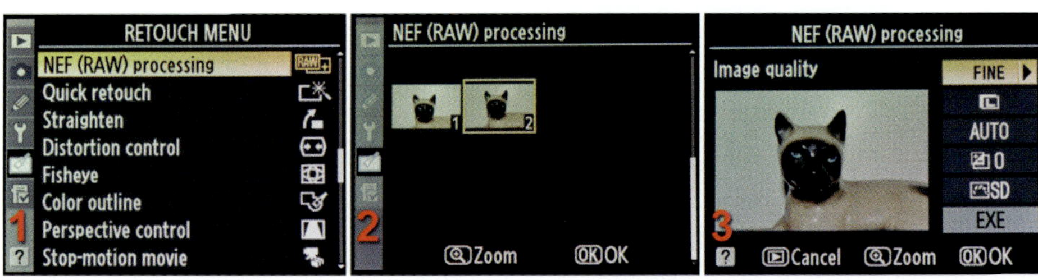

Figure 10 – The *NEF (RAW) processing* screens

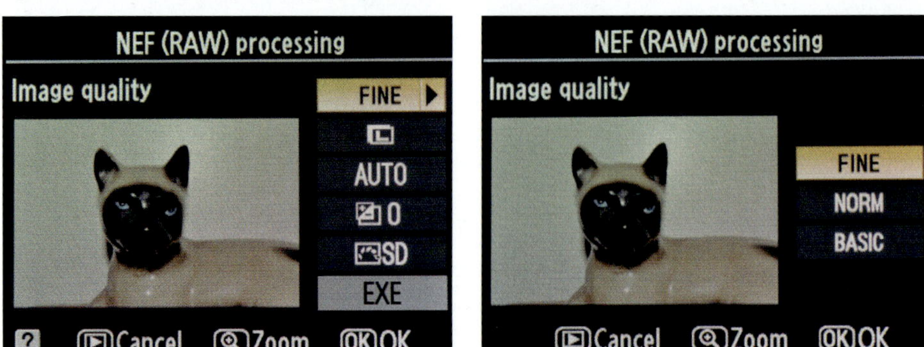

Figure 10A – The *Image quality* screens

in a JPEG image. Select the setting you want to use, and then press the OK button to return to the main *NEF (RAW) processing* configuration screen.

5. Select one of the *Image size* settings—*L* (large, 4288x2848), *M* (medium, 3126x2136), or *S* (small, 2144x1424)—from the *Image size* menu (see *figure 10B*). Large gives you the biggest possible size in a JPEG image. Select the setting you want to use, and then press the OK button to return to the main *NEF (RAW) processing* configuration screen.
6. Select one of the *White balance* settings for your new JPEG (see *figure 10C*). You can choose from *Auto*, *Incandescent*, *Fluorescent*, *Direct sunlight*, *Flash*, *Cloudy*, *Shade*, *Choose a color temp.*, or *PRE* (preset manual from a previous ambient light white balance reading). Please review chapter 4 for detailed information on each of these selections. As you scroll through the list of settings, you'll be able to see the color temperature of the image change. Select the setting you want to use, and then press the OK button to return to the main *NEF (RAW) processing* configuration screen. You can modify the colors of the individual white balance settings for this image by scrolling to the right and changing the value in the color adjustment box. You'll see your fine-tuning adjustment change the color temperature of image.
7. Now you have an opportunity to lighten or darken the image by selecting an *Exposure compensation* value of +/- 3 stops in either direction (see *figure 10D*). When the image looks just right, press the OK button to return to the main *NEF (RAW) processing* configuration screen.
8. Now you can apply a Nikon Picture Control or one of your own custom

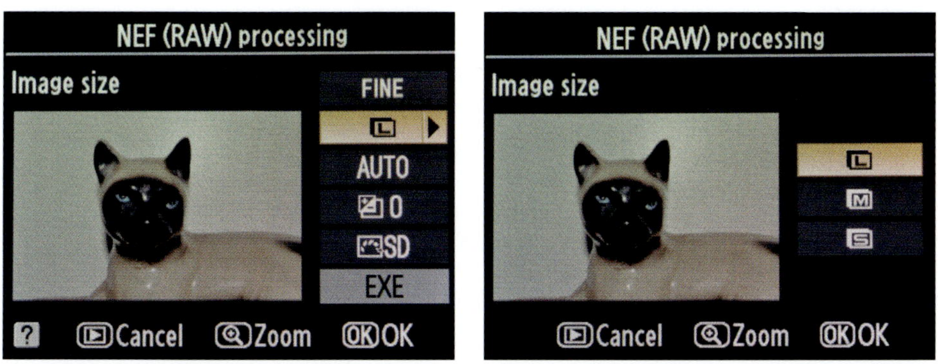

Figure 10B – The *Image size* screens

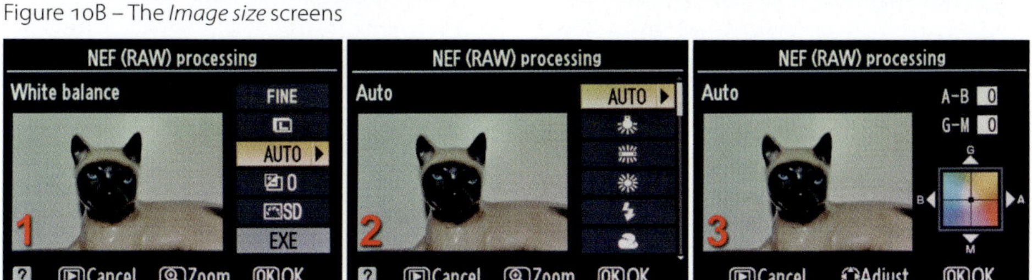

Figure 10C – The *White balance* screens

Picture Controls, if you've created any, from the list shown (see chapter 6, "Shooting Menu"). These controls make changes to how the image looks. You can make it more contrasty, give it greater or lesser color saturation, or even change it to monochrome. Choose from *SD-Standard*, *NL-Neutral*, *VI-Vivid*, *MC-Monochrome*, *PT-Portrait*, *LS-Landscape*, or any of your custom controls that appear on the list (see *figure 10E*). When the image looks just right, press the OK button to return to the main *NEF (RAW) processing* configuration screen.

9. Now, scroll down to the EXE menu selection and press the OK button. The hourglass will show for a few seconds while the new JPEG is being created with your carefully crafted settings, an

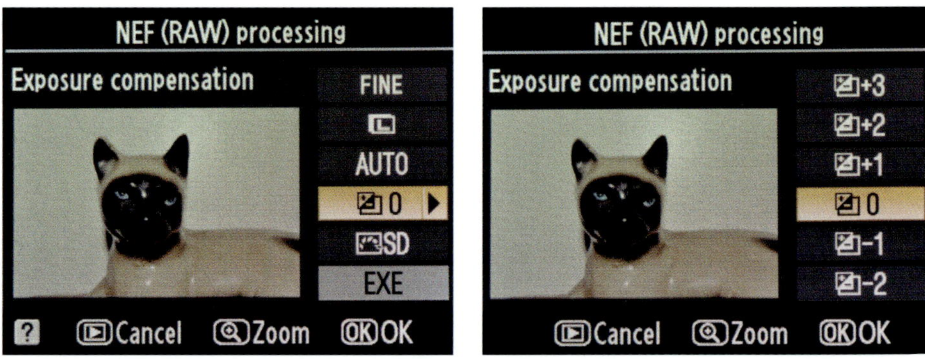

Figure 10D – The *Exposure compensation* screens

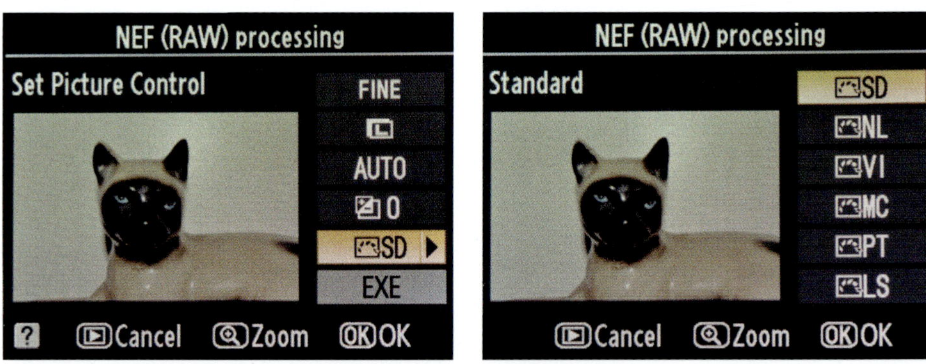

Figure 10E – The *Set Picture Control* screens

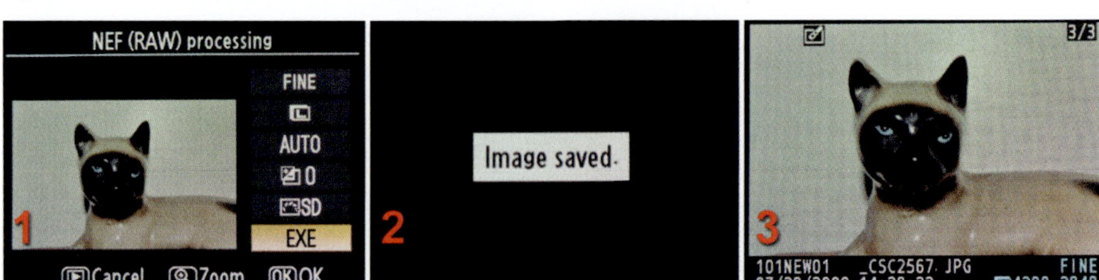

Figure 10F – Saving the new JPEG

Image saved screen will show briefly, and the new JPEG will be shown in a normal playback screen (see *figure 10F*).

This is a convenient way to create specialized JPEG images from NEF (RAW) files without using a computer. How much longer will it be until our cameras come with a keyboard, monitor, and mouse ports? They are computerized after all!

Quick Retouch

(User's Manual page 185)

If you want to simply adjust an image so that all parameters are within viewable range, that's the purpose of this *Quick retouch* function. It creates a new copy of an existing image with "enhanced saturation and contrast." D-Lighting is automatically applied to your old image and the new image is supposed to look better. You can scroll up and down in the preview screen to see the range of enhancements that can be applied when the new image is created. Here are the steps:

1. Press the MENU button and select the *Retouch Menu*.
2. Select *Quick retouch*, and scroll to the right.
3. You'll be presented with the images on your SD memory card that are eligible for a quick retouch.
4. Scroll to an image you want to retouch with your Multi Selector, and press the OK button to select it.
5. Use your Multi Selector to scroll up or down, selecting *High*, *Normal*, or *Low*. You can preview the effect of your changes on the image by looking at the before and after images (see *figure 11*).
6. Press the OK button when you're satisfied with the look. The new image will be created and shown to you in the playback window.

Straighten

(User's Manual page 185)

This is another really cool function that I'm glad to see and use. Often, I'll be shooting a landscape or ocean view handheld, and in my excitement I'll forget to level the horizon. Now, without using my computer, I can adjust the image to level before anyone else sees it.

You can rotate an image up to 5 degrees clockwise or counterclockwise. You use the Multi Selector to scroll right or left through a graduated scale line. Each increment is equal to about 1/4 degree (0.25). As you rotate the image, the camera will automatically trim the edges so that the picture looks normal. Of course, this means you are throwing away some of the edges of the image and

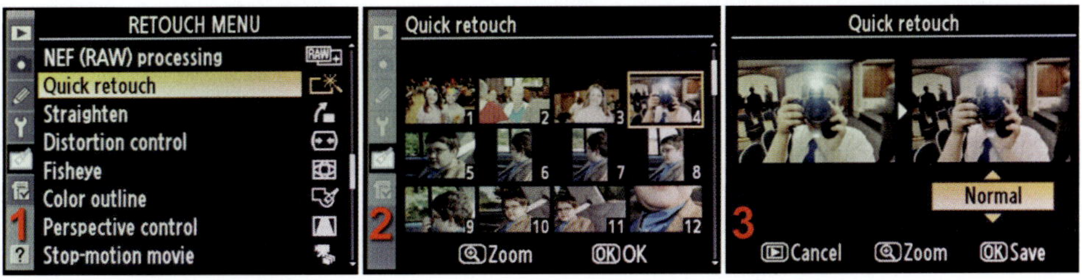

Figure 11 – The *Quick retouch* screens

making it smaller. However, it's better for the image to be a little smaller and have a nice level horizon, don't you think?

Here are the steps to straighten or level an image (see *figure12*):

1. Press the MENU button and select the *Retouch Menu*.
2. Select *Straighten*, and scroll to the right (see *figure 12*, *image 1*).
3. The images on your SD memory card appear. Select the one you want to straighten with the Multi Selector, and press the *OK* button to select it (see *figure 12*, *image 2*).
4. Now, rotate the image to the right (clockwise) or the left (counterclockwise) in 0.25 degree increments with the Multi Selector. You'll notice a little yellow pointer under an indicator scale (see where the red arrow is pointing in *figure 12*, *image 3*). Move this yellow pointer back and forth along the scale to change the angle of the image.
5. When you are happy with the straightness of the new image, press the OK button to save it, or press the Playback button to cancel. *Image 3* and *image 4* in *figure 12* show the pointer moved to the limits of its indicator scale. See how the kitty is leaning one way or another as the pointer is moved?
6. The newly saved image appears in a normal playback window. Notice in *figure 12*, *image 3* that my cat is leaning to the left but the background wall corner is straight. Then, at the end of the *Straighten* process in *figure 12*, *image 6*, the cat is straight while the wall is angled. I wanted my subject—the strange cat— to be straightened.

The degree of tilt I added to the image in *figure 12* (*image 4* and *image 5*) shows how much you can adjust the level of any image. Notice the little yellow selection pointer where the red arrow is pointing in *image 3*. This will move as you use the Multi Selector. You'll see the image tilt, and the gridlines will help line things up well.

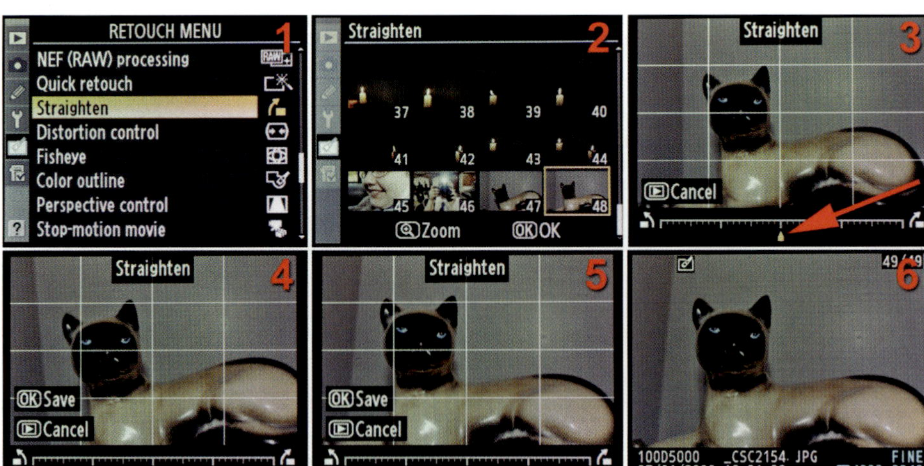

Figure 12 – Straightening an image

Distortion Control

(User's Manual page 185)

This *Distortion control* function is a companion to the *Straighten* function. While the *Straighten* function is concerned with leveling the image left to right, the *Distortion control* function is concerned with barrel and pincushion distortion. Barrel distortion causes the edges of a subject to bow outward, like a barrel. Pincushion distortion is the opposite; the edges bow inward, like an hourglass. Using this control will remove some of the edge of the image as distortion compensation takes place.

There are two settings in the *Distortion control* function:

- *Auto*
- *Manual*

Auto is usable only if you have a D or G type lens on your D5000. You select *Auto* when you want the camera to make its best adjustments, and then you can make more yourself if you think the new image needs it.

Manual is entirely your operation. You can adjust the image until you feel like it looks best, without interference from the camera.

Here are the steps to let the camera make an *Auto* distortion adjustment:

1. Press the MENU button and select the *Retouch Menu*.
2. Select *Distortion control*, and scroll to the right (see *figure 13, image 1*).
3. Choose *Auto* from the menu, and scroll to the right (see *figure 13, image 2*).
4. You'll be presented with the images on the camera's memory card. Select the one you want to fix with the Multi Selector, and press the OK button to select it (see *figure 13, image 3*).
5. The camera will automatically make its best adjustment and will then present you with the adjusted image (see *figure 13, image 4*).
6. If you are not satisfied with the camera's *Auto* adjustment, move the yellow pointer along the scale to the left, with the Multi Selector, to remove pincushion distortion (add barrel) or to the right to remove barrel distortion (add pincushion). I slid the pointer all the

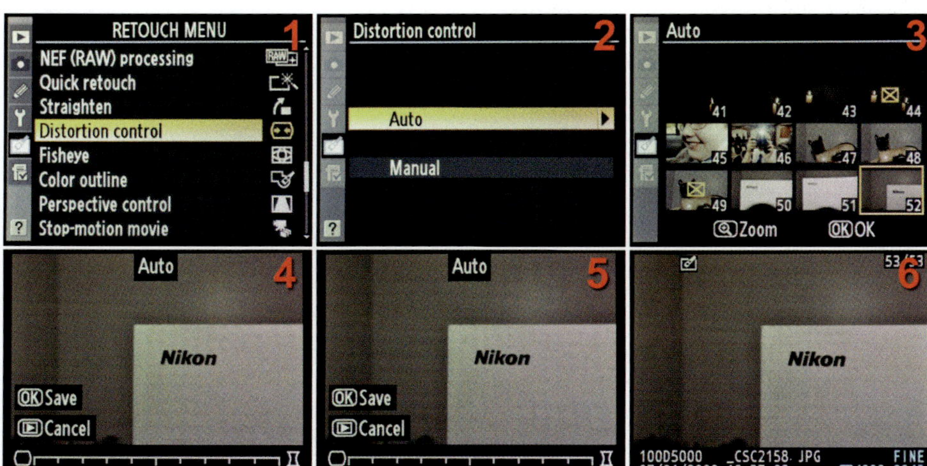

Figure 13 – *Distortion control - Auto*

way to the right (see *figure 13, image 5*). It is rather difficult to see the distortion adjustment in the small images in this book. It will be more apparent when you are making the adjustment yourself.

7. When you are happy with the appearance of the image, press the OK button to save it or the Playback button to cancel. The new adjusted image appears in a normal playback window (see *figure 13, image 6*).

It works the same way for the *Manual* distortion adjustments, presented next, except that the camera does not make an *Auto* adjustment before presenting you with an image to manually adjust.

Here are the steps to let the camera make an *Auto* distortion adjustment:

1. Press the MENU button and select the *Retouch Menu*.
2. Select *Distortion control*, and scroll to the right (see *figure 13A, image 1*).
3. Choose *Manual* from the menu and then scroll to the right (see *figure 13A, image 2*).
4. You'll be presented with the images on your camera's memory card. Select the one you want to fix with the Multi Selector, and press the OK button to select it (see *figure 13A, image 3*).
5. Now the camera presents you with an image to examine for problems (see *figure 13A, image 4*).
6. Move the yellow pointer along the scale to the left to remove pincushion distortion (add barrel) or to the right to remove barrel distortion (add pincushion). I slid the pointer all the way to the left into barrel distortion territory (see *figure 13A, image 5*). You can see the slight curvature in the left edge of the Nikon manual and the wall corner.
7. When you are happy with the appearance of the image, press the OK button to save it or the Playback button to cancel. The new adjusted image appears in a normal playback window (see *figure 13A, image 6*).

Once again, as with the *Auto* distortion adjustment, the effect is rather hard to see.

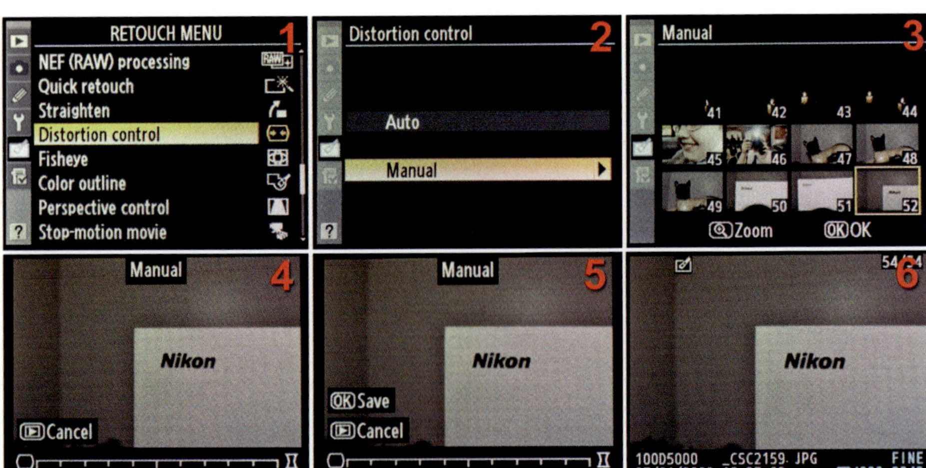

Figure 13A – *Distortion control - Manual*

If you look closely at *figure 13A, image 4*, and then compare it to *Figure 13A, image 6*, you'll see that the lines in the image are slightly bowed. In *figure 13A, image 5*, I introduced barrel distortion by pushing the slider all the way to the left, toward the barrel distortion symbol. Of course, this control is normally used to remove distortion, not add it.

Fisheye

(User's Manual page 185)

This function is quite fun! You can "fish-eye" your friends and make hilarious distortions that will make everyone laugh. While the results are not true circular fisheye images, they do have a similar distorted appearance. *Figure 14* shows three images. The first is normal, the second somewhat distorted, and the third fully "fisheyed"! What do you think?

Here are the steps to select and distort one of your images:

1. Press the MENU button and select the *Retouch Menu*.
2. Select *Fisheye*, and scroll to the right (see *figure 14, image 1*).
3. The images on your camera's memory card appear. Select the one you want to "fisheye" with the Multi Selector, and press the OK button to select it (see *figure 14, image 2*).
4. Now press the Multi Selector to the right and watch the yellow pointer move and the distortion grow (see where the red arrow is pointing in *figure 14, image 3*).
5. Once you've found the perfect distortion amount—like to the max—simply press the OK button to save or the Playback button to cancel. In *figure 14*, I have introduced an increasing amount of distortion in *image 4* and *image 5* until it is at maximum in *image 6*.
6. Press the OK button to save or the Playback button to cancel. If you save, you'll be presented with your fisheye creation in a normal playback window.

Just be careful with this one! If you publish pictures of your friends with this effect, I'm afraid that they'll start running when they see you with your camera.

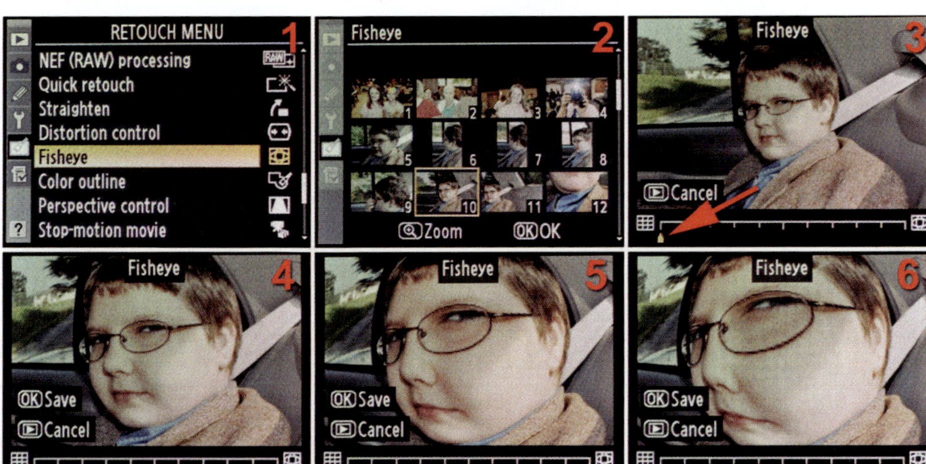

Figure 14 – *Fisheye* effect screens

Color Outline

(User's Manual page 186)

Have you ever wanted to convert one of your images to a cartoon or a line drawing? This retouch setting is fun to use, providing an interesting outline effect on the distinct lines or color changes in your image. *Figure 15* shows an original image and the image after *Color outline* was applied.

You can convert the image to a color outline, open it in Photoshop, and use the fill functions to add cartoon colors between the lines. Or you can post-process it into a fine-art line tracing. This is an unusual functionality, and shows

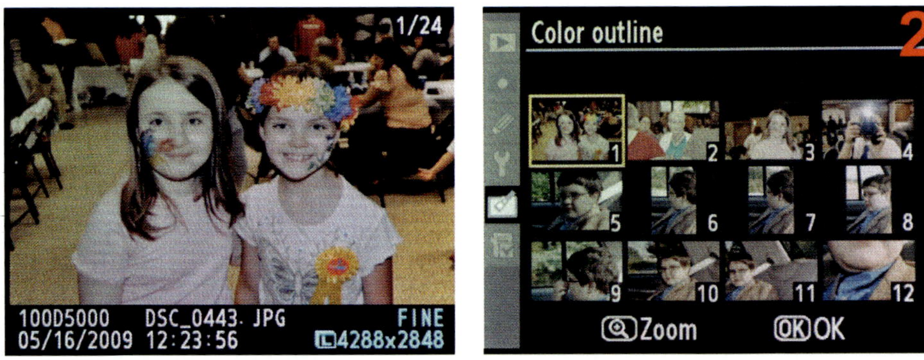

Figure 15 – *Color outline* – original and conversion

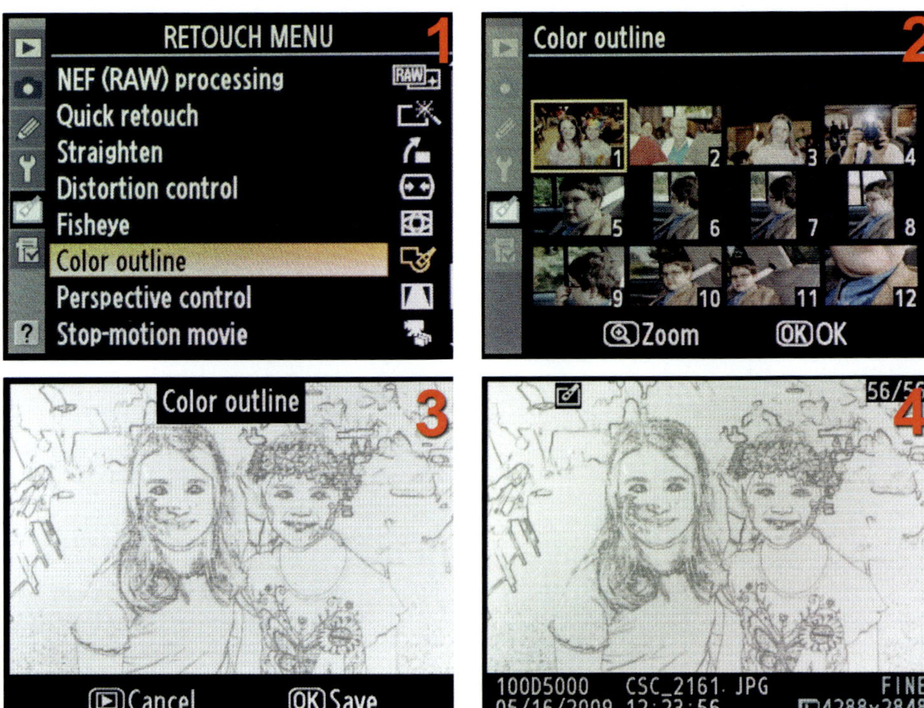

Figure 15A – *Color outline* setup

the direction that our highly computerized cameras are going. They have computer power built in, so why not make use of that power in new and fun ways?

The screens used to set *Color outline* are shown in *figure 15A*.

Here are the steps used to implement the conversions:

1. Press the MENU button and select the *Retouch Menu*.
2. Select *Color outline*, and scroll to the right.
3. Choose an image from the list of thumbnails.
4. Press the OK button and the conversion to outline form will take place.
5. Press the OK button again to save or the Playback button to cancel.

This setting givea us the opportunity to be creative and have some fun with our images. I'm going to use *Color outline* often!

Perspective Control

(User's Manual page 186)

When you take a picture from the base of a tall object like a building with a wide-angle lens, the building looks like it's falling over backwards. You can correct the problem with a certain type of camera controls. That's the reason "view" cameras exist with their rise, fall, shift, tilt, and swing controls. Nikon makes perspective control lenses that will do some of the functions of a view camera, namely tilt and shift. However, view cameras and perspective lenses cost *significantly* more than the D5000 camera.

Nikon has given D5000 users some image correction capability with the *Straighten*, *Distortion control*, and *Perspective control* functions. We discussed the first two earlier in this chapter. Now let's see how to use *Perspective control*.

Perspective control allows you to stretch the left, right, top, or bottom of an image in a way that tends to twist objects that are leaning so that they appear straighter in the corrected image. *Figure 16*, *image 3*, shows yellow pointers and their indicators (identified by the red arrows). You can move these pointers to change the perspective of the image by tilting the top toward or away from you or rotating the image to the left or right. This is a powerful control because it can help give certain images a much better perspective.

The screens used to set *Perspective control* are shown in *figure 16*.

These steps will help you do the actual configuration:

1. Press the MENU button and select the *Retouch Menu*.
2. Select *Perspective control*, and scroll to the right.

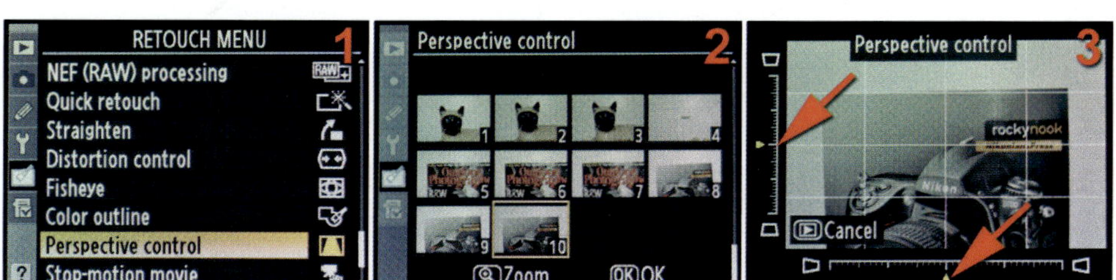

Figure 16 – Adjusting an image with *Perspective control*

3. Choose an image from the list of thumbnails.
4. Press the OK button and you'll be presented with grid lines for edge comparison and two slider controls operated by the Multi Selector (*figure 16, image 3*). Move the yellow pointer on the left up or down to tilt the top of image toward or away from you. Slide the yellow pointer on the bottom of the screen to the left or right, which turns the image's left or right edge toward or away from you.

In *figure 16A* is a view of what moving these sliders do to the image. Pay careful attention to the position of the yellow pointers and how they each change the image.

The first image in *figure 16A* shows what happens to the subject when you use the left-hand slider (see red arrows). See how the top of the subject leans either toward or away from you according to how the slider is positioned?

Can you see how powerful this functionality is to control perspective? You could use this camera without Photoshop and still make great post-processed images.

5. The camera automatically crops off the top and bottom of the stretched ends to keep the image looking like a normal rectangle. The final image will be smaller since some edges are removed.
6. Once you have the image looking the way you want, press the OK button again to save or the Playback button to cancel. In

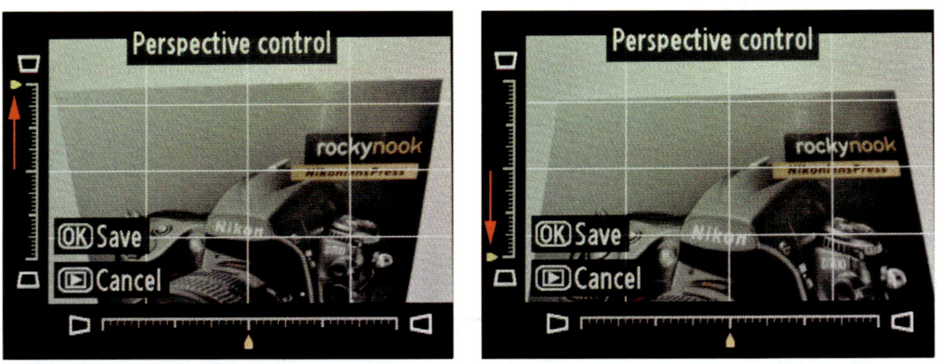

Figure 16A – Tilting the top of the image

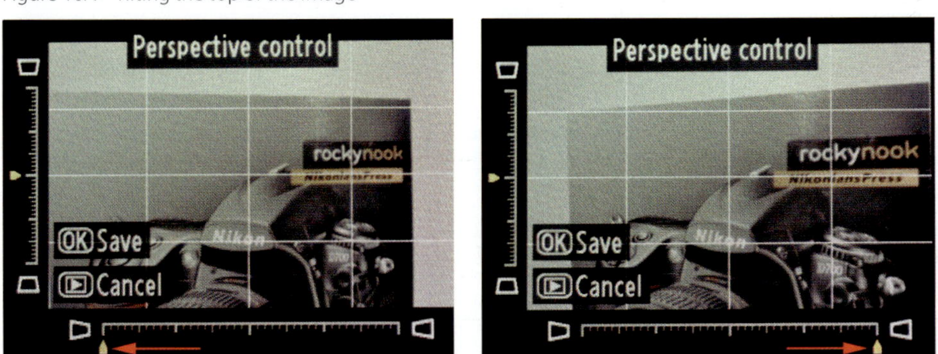

Figure 16B – Rotating the sides of the image

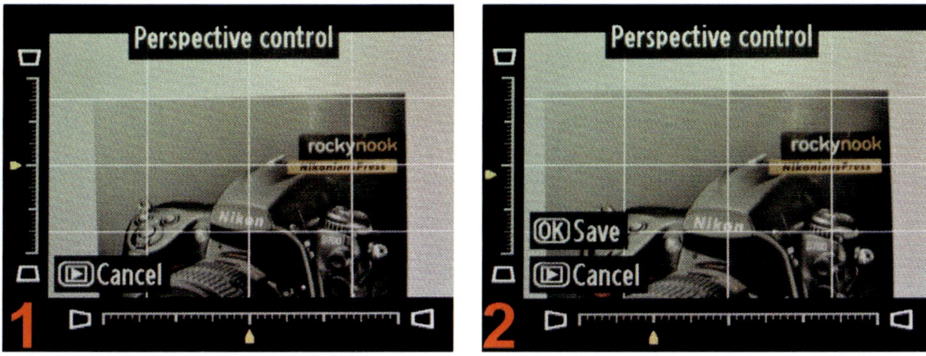

Figure 16C – Original vs. corrected image

figure 16C, image 1, is the original, which I deliberately photographed at an angle. *Image 2* shows the adjusted image.

You now have excellent perspective control, with no additional lens purchases! Add *Straighten* for rotating the image toward horizontal and vertical, then *Distortion control* for removing barrel and pincushion distortion, and you have the basics of a graphics software program built right into the camera. Then, remember that you can convert NEF (RAW) files to JPEG in-camera and create DPOF print orders for printing directly to a PictBridge printer. Why do we need a computer? What an amazing camera!

Stop-Motion Movie

(User's Manual page 187–188)

You might wonder why Nikon gave us the ability to do stop-motion movies when we also have an impressive *D-Movie* mode that makes real video movies. Maybe it's because stop-motion movies are a great deal of fun.

Stop-motion is an animation technique used for moving inanimate objects a short distance between frames so that when all the frames are replayed, the object seems to move by itself. It works in a similar way to a normal movie except the frame rate is a lot slower. Where a D-Movie records and is played back at 24 frames per second, a stop-motion movie can be

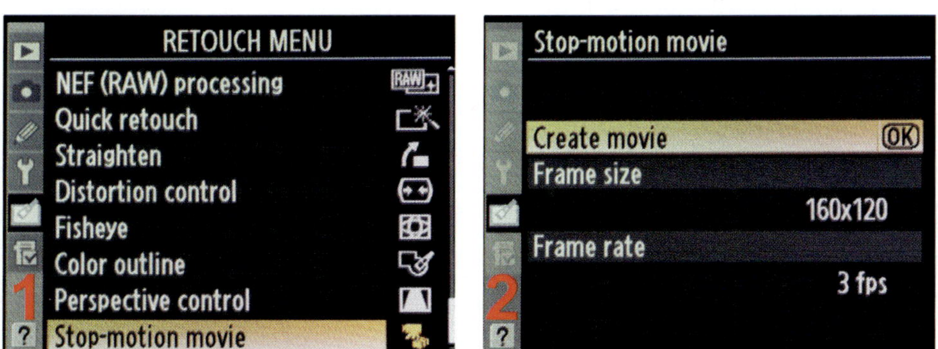

Figure 17 – Assembling a stop-motion movie

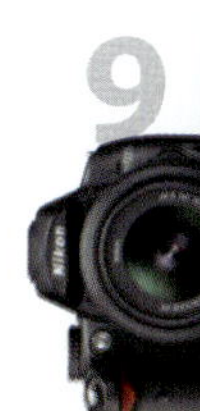

created at frame rates between 3 and 15 frames per second with a limitation of 100 frames in a segment. I suppose you could make a full-length animation movie by assembling 100 frame segments into a larger group. However, stop-motion movies use the camera's normal shutter instead of its electronic rolling shutter, so you'd wear out the camera pretty quickly by making a long movie this way.

Figure 17 shows the screens you use to assemble the stop-motion frames into a short movie. Here are the steps:

1. Shoot a series of controlled images in sequence. You can shoot up to 100 images to include in the movie. Make sure they are still on the camera's memory card.
2. Press the MENU button and select the *Retouch Menu*.
3. Select *Stop-motion movie*, and scroll to the right.
4. Select *Frame size* from the menu and scroll to the right. Choose one of the Frame sizes (640x480, 320x240, or 160x120) and press the *OK* button (see *figure 17A*).
5. Select *Frame rate* from the menu and scroll to the right. Choose a frame rate from one of the available rates (3, 6, 10, or 15 fps) and press the *OK* button (see *figure 17B*).
6. Select *Create movie* to select the first and last frame in the stop-motion movie. If you choose the last image first and the first image last, the movie will play

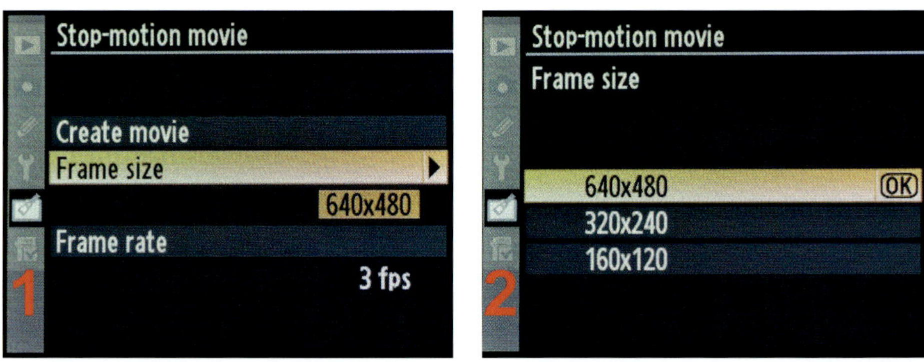

Figure 17A – Selecting a frame size

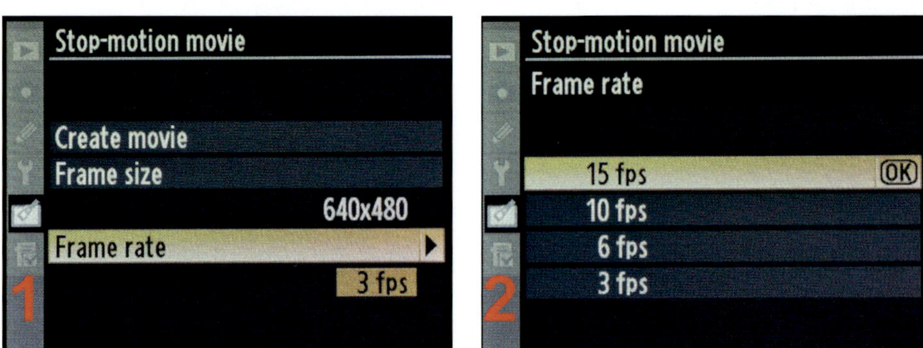

Figure 17B – Selecting a frame rate

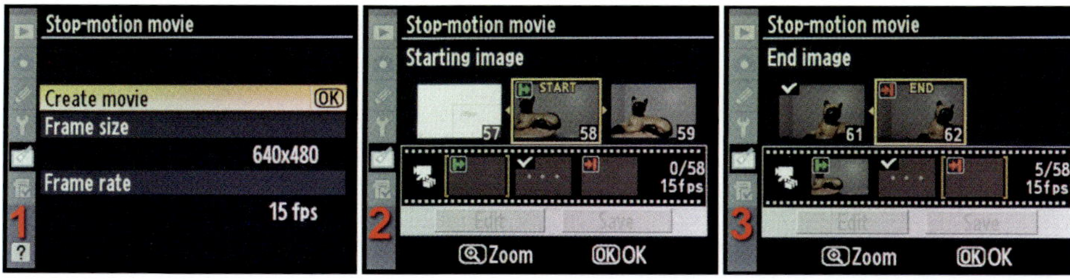

Figure 17C – Selecting the first and last frames

backwards. You can see the *Starting image* screen in *Figure 17C, image 2*, and the *End image* screen in *image 3*.

7. Edit and/or save the selected image order. If you choose *Edit*, when you're done, select *Save* and press the OK button (see *figure 17D*).
8. You'll now see the *Create movie* menu from which you can choose *Save*, *Preview*, *Frame rate*, or *Edit*.
   - ***Save*** - If you select *Save*, you'll see a screen that says *Creating stop-motion movie*. Once it has finished, your new movie will be displayed in a playback screen. Press the OK button to view the movie.
   - ***Preview*** – If you select *Preview*, you'll see a different screen with the words *Creating preview* as the movie is assembled. Then the movie will play. Afterward, the *Create movie* screen reappears.
   - ***Frame rate*** – If you choose *Frame rate*, you can change the number of frames per second that will display in your stop-motion movie. Your choices are 3, 6, 10, or 15 frames per second.
   - ***Edit*** – Choosing *Edit* takes you to the *Edit* screen (see *figure 17E*). You can choose to edit the starting, middle, or end image. Editing the starting image allows you to change which image begins the series. Editing middle images allows you to deselect any of the images in the middle with the Multi Selector, thereby removing them from the movie. Editing the ending image allows you to select a different final image for the movie. Everything between the first and last image that has not been deselected will play when you press Preview or save it for later playing.

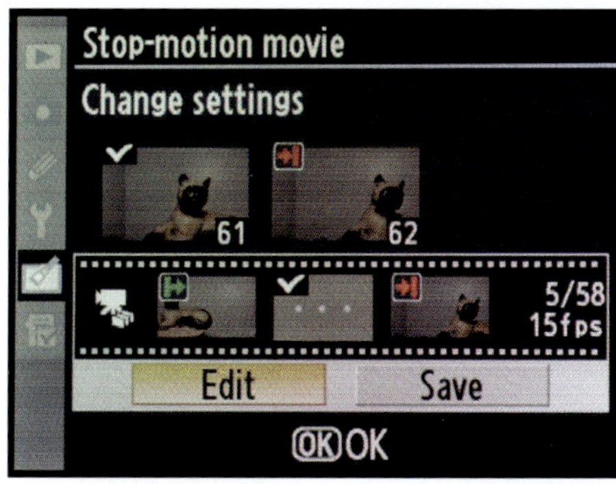

Figure 17D – Editing or saving the movie

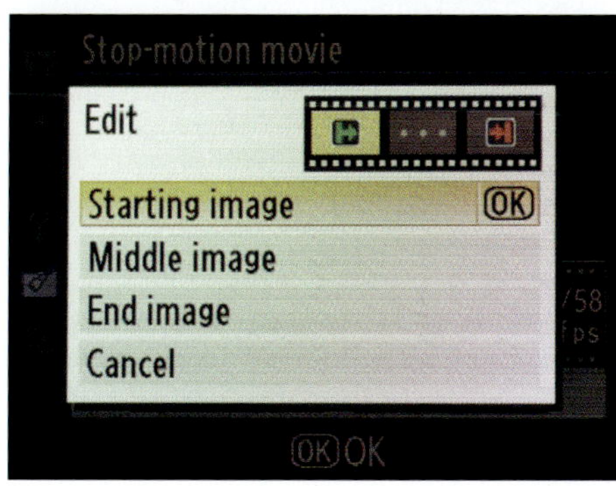

Figure 17E – Edit menu functions

The screen shown in *figure 17E* appears if you select *Edit* in the screen shown in *figure 17D*. This is a screen that allows you to modify things during the creation of the movie. Nikon also gives you a final chance to save and preview your image if you select *Save*, as shown in *figure 17F*, *image 1*, while *image 2* shows the final *Create movie Save/Edit* screen. You can use this screen to make last-minute tweaks and changes to the format of the movie, and then preview and do the final save.

9. Now, select *Save* and press the OK button. You'll see two final screens, one of which is the movie being created and then the actual movie itself, ready to be played (see *figure 17G*).
10. Once you've saved your movie you can play it at any time on your camera or your TV via the A/V out cable, or you can transfer it to your computer for playing there. At 3 fps, it can resemble a really fast slide show, while at 15 fps it is almost full movie quality.

Not only is your camera an extremely high-quality still image-maker, it also has two types of movie capability: stop-motion and D-Movies. I just love this camera!

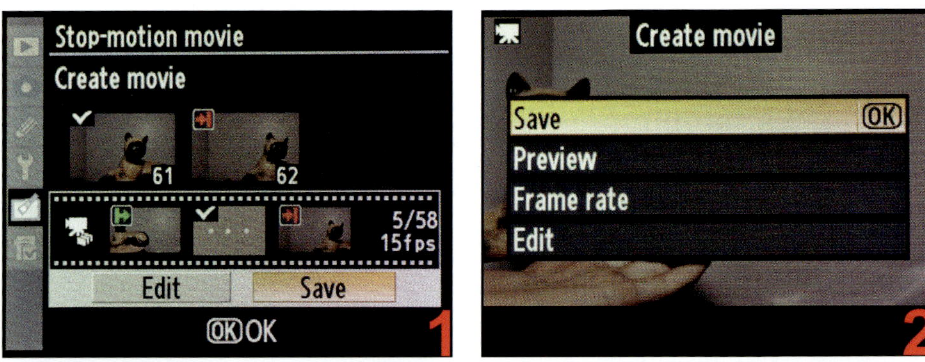

Figure 17F – Final *Save/Edit* screen

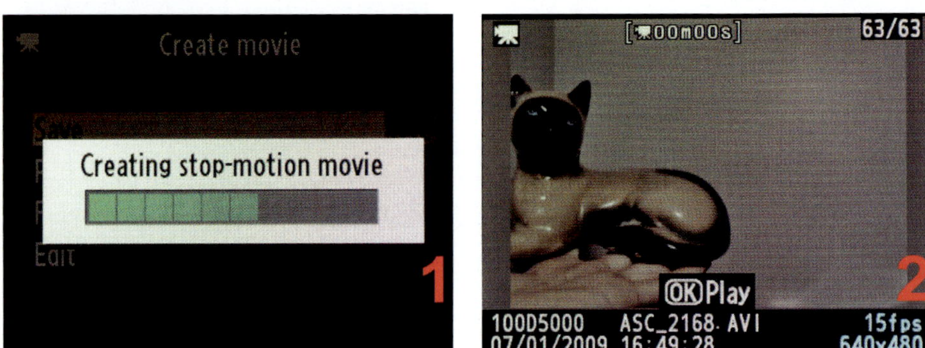

Figure 17G – Movie being created and ready to be played

Side-by-Side Comparison

(User's Manual page 189)

Now that you've learned to use all these new tools for image adjustment, you may find yourself wanting to view the original image and the retouched image side by side. You can enjoy a before and after view of the two images.

This particular *Side-by-side comparison* function is not available on the *Retouch Menu* by selecting it directly. The only way to get to it is to view a "retouched" image in the normal playback window and then press the OK button. One of the menu selections you'll find is *Side-by-side comparison*. It's down at the bottom of the available selections (see *figure 18*, middle image).

Let's look at what the *Side-by-side comparison* function does for us. Here are the steps:

1. Using the normal image playback system, find an image that has been retouched. You can tell when you've found one because it will have a small square in the upper-left corner with a brush and pallet.
2. Press the OK button to open up the special retouch image menu.
3. Scroll down until you find the *Side-by-side comparison* selection, and then press the OK button.
4. You'll be presented with an informational side-by-side view of the original and retouched image so that you can compare them.

If you happen to be looking at an image that was created from an overlay, then it has two source files. It will show one of the originals along with the retouched version. You can select the first original and then scroll up or down with the Multi Selector to see the other original. The side-by-side comparison will not work if the original has been deleted from the memory card.

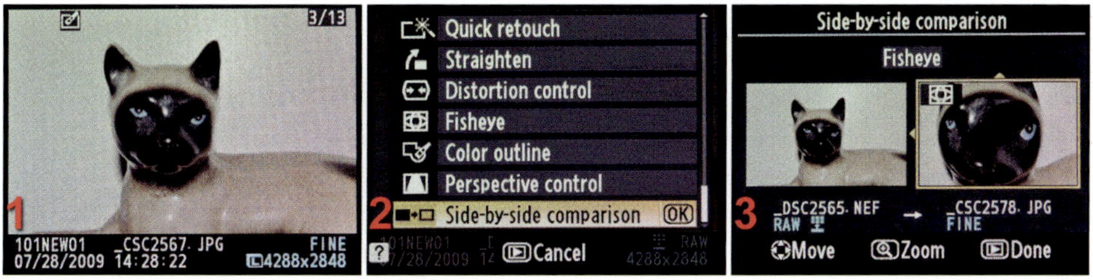

Figure 18 – *Side-by-side comparison* screens

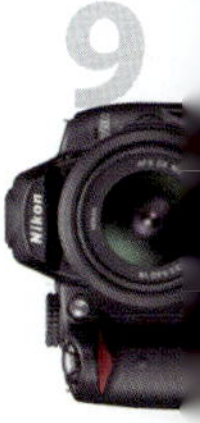

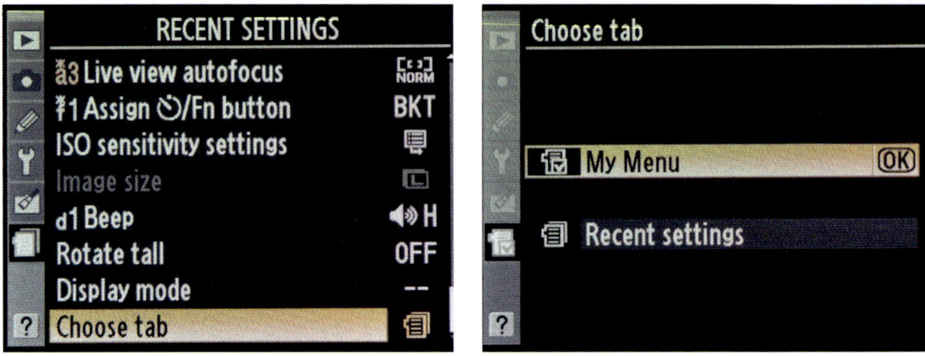

Figure 19 – *Recent settings* and *My Menu*

Recent Settings/My Menu

(User's Manual pages 190–192)

My Menu is not on the left with the other menus like *Shooting* and *Custom Settings,* as a factory default.

It is available via a selection called *Choose tab* at the bottom of the *Recent Settings* menu (see *figure 19*).

Using the *Choose tab* selection, I found that I could toggle one of two menus to live on my main menu tab system bar on the left. As *figure 19* shows, *Choose tab* (the one at the bottom left) lets me select either *Recent Settings* or *My Menu* for the last menu slot Basically, Nikon didn't want to put an extra menu on the menu tab, so it made one optional, the *My Menu* system. *Recent Settings* is the factory default. I like *My Menu* better!

Let's consider both of these menus. You can then choose which one you want to live on your menu tab bar.

Recent Settings

Recent Settings is very simple. It is a menu that remembers the last 20 distinct changes you've made to your D5000 camera. Each setting you changed is stored in a temporary menu called *Recent Settings*.

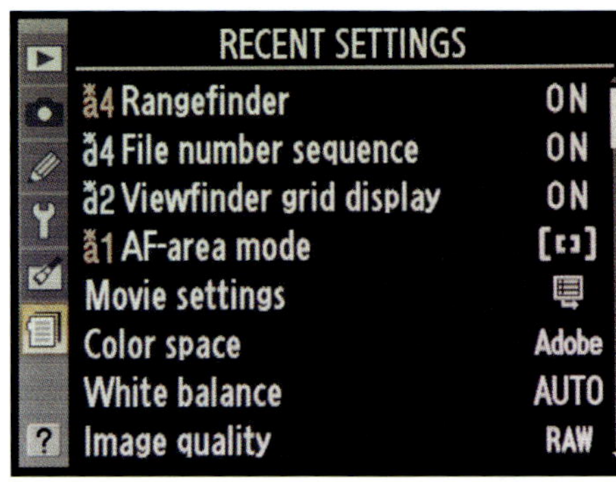

Figure 20 – *Recent Settings* menu

If you change something in your camera that is not already on the *Recent Settings* menu, it will be added to the menu; if there is no room left, it will replace the oldest (or least recent) change. This can be a convenient way to find something you've changed recently but have trouble remembering where it is on the main menu systems.

Recommendation

If you want a more permanent menu for your "favorite" changes to the D5000, you should enable the *My Menu* system instead of the *Recent Settings* menu. *Recent Settings* is fine, but I want to directly control what menus I have quick access to without searching. *My Menu* really is "my" menu!

My Menu

The D5000 is quite a complex camera. There are key functions and settings that each of us use frequently. For instance, I often turn *Exposure delay mode* (*Custom Setting d5*) on and off. Instead of having to search through all those Custom Settings and trying to remember which is *Exposure delay mode*, I simply added that custom setting to *My Menu*. Then, whenever I want to add a delay to my exposure so that mirror vibrations can settle down, I just go to *My Menu* and enable *Exposure delay mode*.

There are several other functions and settings I keep in *My Menu* along with *Exposure delay mode*. I'm sure you'll have a few you use often too. Let's examine the menu screens we'll use to add and remove items from *My Menu*.

When you first open *My Menu*, you'll find only four menu choices, as shown in *figure 21*:

- *Add items*
- *Remove items*
- *Rank items*
- *Choose tab*

Let's examine each of these menu choices in detail.

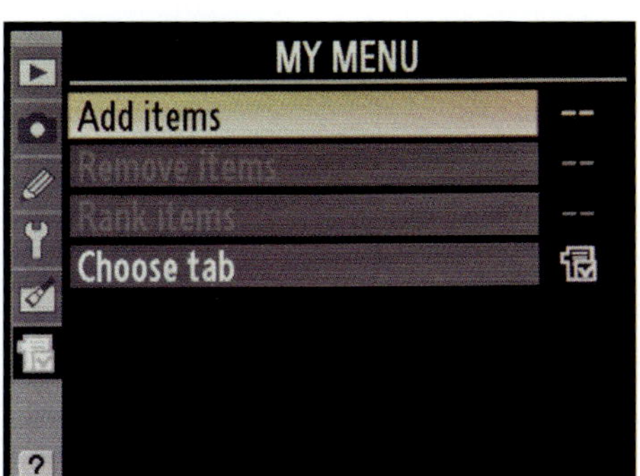

Figure 21 – Blank *My Menu* screen

Add Items

To add an item to *My Menu*, you'll need to locate the item first. Search through the menus until you find the item you want to add and then make note of where it is located. You could do this from within the *Add item* screen, but I find that it is harder to find what I am looking for if I've not already confirmed in my mind where it lives. Is it under the *Custom Settings* or the *Shooting Menu*, for instance?

Once I have found the item I want to add and made note of its location I do the following:

1. Select *Add items* from the *My Menu* screen. You'll notice in *figure 21A* that I already have *Set Picture Control* and *Active D-Lighting* added to *My Menu*. Let's add something else.

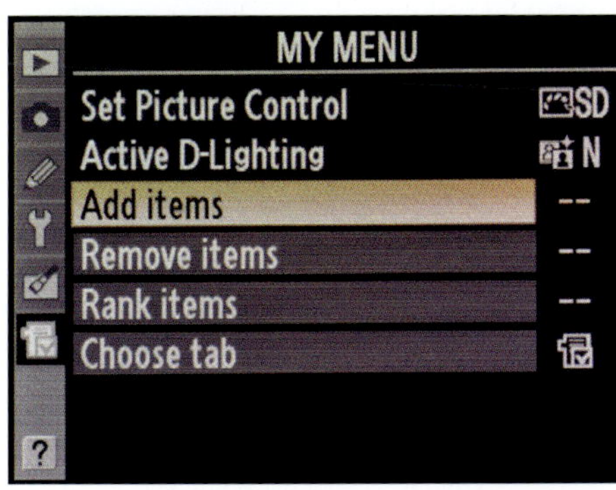

Figure 21A – *My Menu* screen with *Add items* selected

2. Use the Multi Selector to scroll right and you'll find a list of menus from which to choose (see *figure 21B*). These menus are all the menus available in the D5000 except for *My Menu*.
3. I will add *Custom Setting d5 (Exposure delay mode)* to *My Menu* as an example. I already looked and know that *Exposure delay mode* is under the *Custom Setting Menu*, so let's scroll down to it. After selecting it, I'll scroll to the right (see *figure 21C, image 1*).

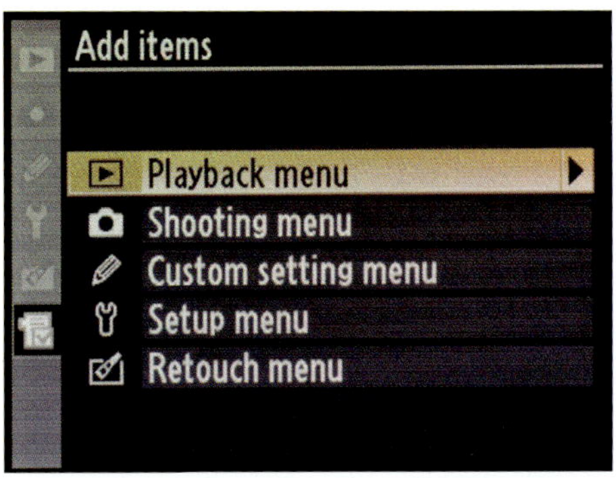

Figure 21B – *Add items* screen with *Playback menu* selected

4. The custom setting bank and *Custom Settings a-f* appear (see *figure 21C, image 2*). I scroll down to *d – Shooting/display*. Then I scroll right again so that I can select the actual custom setting I want.
5. Now that I have found *Custom Setting d5*, all I have to do is highlight it and press the OK button (see *figure 21C, image 3*). Once I've done that, the D5000 switches to the *Choose position* screen.
6. Since I already had a couple of other items added to *My Menu*, I now have to decide in which order I want them to be presented. The *d5 Exposure delay mode* setting is on top because it is the newest entry. I think I'll move it down to the bottom and let *Set Picture Control* have the top position. To move the position of the selected item, I simply scroll down two rows. *D5 Exposure delay mode* stays highlighted with a yellow box surrounding it. As I scroll down

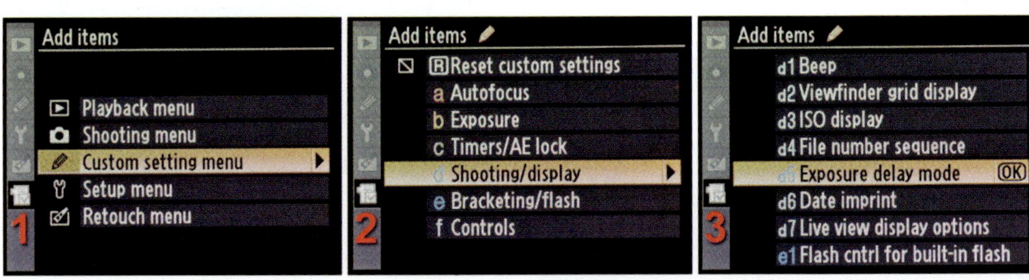

Figure 21C – Adding *Custom Setting d10* to *My Menu*

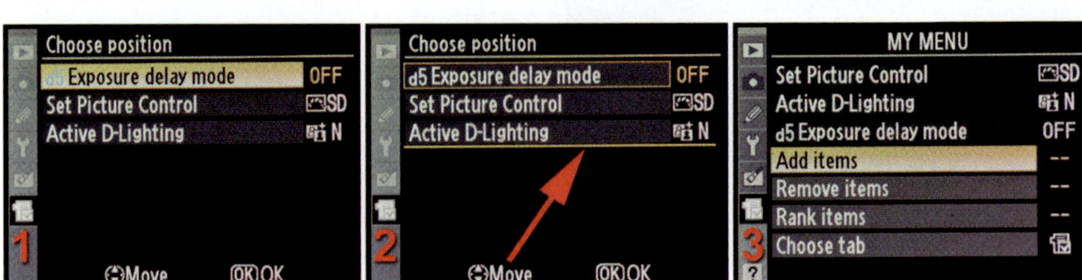

Figure 21D – Choosing a bottom position for *Custom Setting d5 (Exposure delay mode)*

two rows, a yellow underline moves to the bottom position (see the red arrow in *Figure 21D, image 2*). This yellow underline represents the place to which I will finally move *d5 Exposure delay mode*. Once I have decided the position and have the yellow underline in place, I just press the *OK* button. *Custom Setting d5 (Exposure delay mode)* moves to the bottom position. The screen pops back to the beginning *My Menu* screen, with everything arranged the way I desired (see *figure 21D, image 3*).

Remove Items

Now that I've shown you how to add items, let's examine how *Remove items* works. I've decided that one of my items, *Active D-Lighting*, is not used often enough to waste a spot on *My Menu*, so I'll remove it. Here's how:

1. Select *Remove items* from *My Menu* and scroll to the right (see *figure 21E, image 1*).
2. The *Remove items* screen presents a series of check boxes. Whatever items I check will be deleted when I select *Done*. You can check the boxes by highlighting the line item and pressing the OK button, or you can scroll right on each item you want to check. I like to use the OK button method because trying to uncheck a selection by scrolling left doesn't work; it instead takes you back to the *My Menu* screen. The OK button acts like a toggle and pressing it will check or uncheck a line item (see *figure 21E, image 2*).

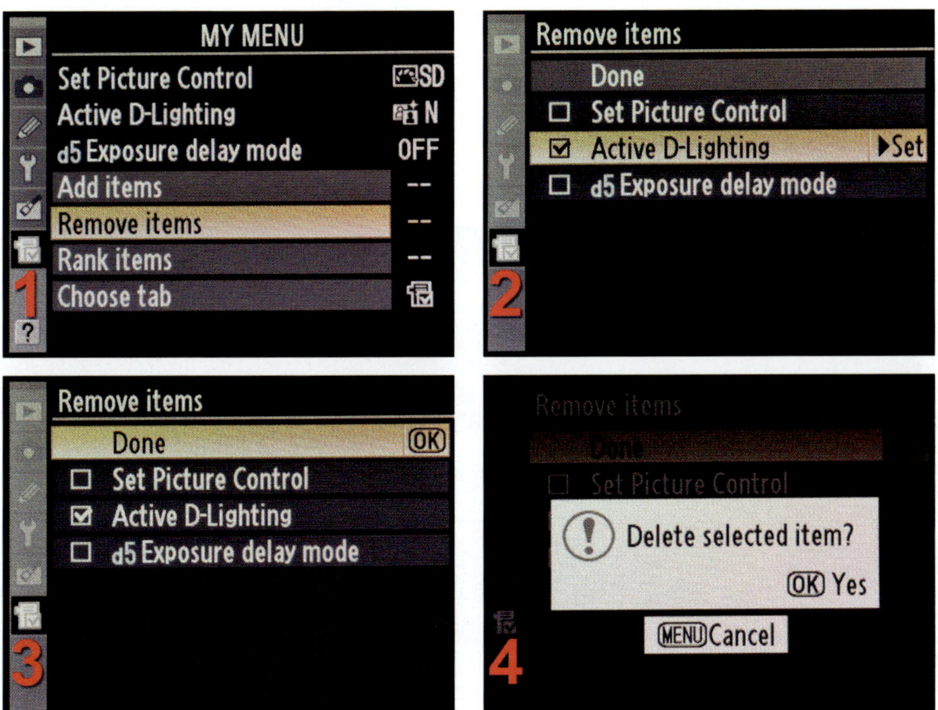

Figure 21E – Removing *Active D-Lighting* from *My Menu*

3. Once I have the items I want to delete checked, I'll simply scroll back up to the *Done* selection and press the OK button (see *figure 21E, image 3*).
4. A small white box pops up and asks, *Delete selected item?* Press the *OK* button again and the item is removed from *My Menu* (see *figure 21E, image 4*). A box pops up informing you that the item has been deleted, and then the D5000 switches to *My Menu*'s main screen.

Rank Items

Ranking items is similar to positioning new additions in *My Menu*. All the *Rank items* selection does is move the item up or down in *My Menu*. You can switch your most-used *My Menu* items to the top of the list. Here's how:

1. Select *Rank items* from *My Menu* and scroll to the right (see *figure 21F, image 1*).
2. The *Rank items* screen and all the current *My Menu* items appear. I have decided that *d5 Exposure delay mode* is used more than *Set Picture Control*, so I'll move it to the top. I move my yellow highlight down to *d5 Exposure delay mode* and press the OK button to select it (where the red arrow is pointing in *figure 21F, image 2*). Now the screen changes so that I have a *Move* selection at the bottom (where the red arrow is pointing in *figure 21F, image 3*).
3. A yellow underline can now be moved around with the thumb switch. I moved the yellow underline up to the top to represent where I am finally going to position *d5 Exposure delay mode*. *Exposure delay mode* is still highlighted with a surrounding yellow box (see *figure 21F, image 4*).
4. Once my yellow underline is at the position I want, I press the OK button and *d5 Exposure delay mode* moves to the top (see *figure 21F, image 5*).
5. After pressing OK in step 4, I'm back at *My Menu*'s main screen (see *figure 21F, image 6*).

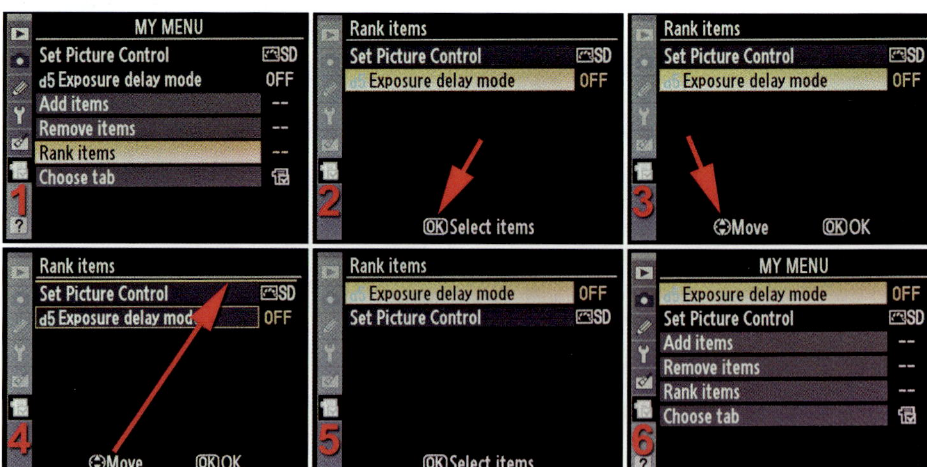

Figure 21F – Moving, *Custom Setting d10 (Exposure delay mode)* to the top, or "ranking" it

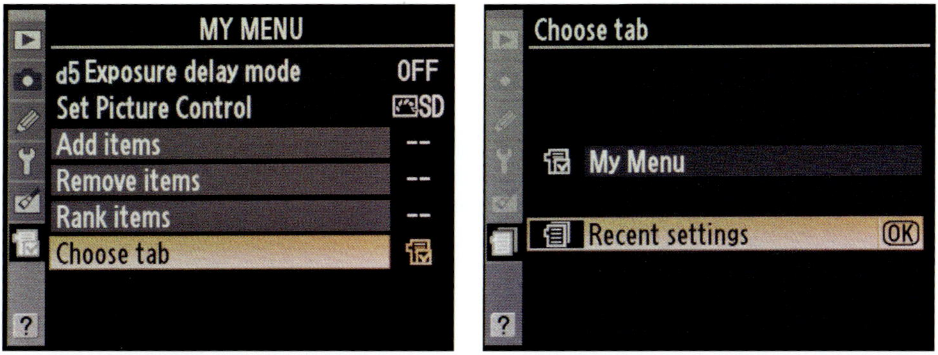

Figure 22 – Switching from *My Menu* to the *Recent Settings* menu

Choose Tab

As you discovered earlier, this selection lets us switch between *Recent Settings* and *My Menu*. To change from *My Menu* back to *Recent Settings*, simply select *Recent settings* from *Choose tab* menu (see *figure* 22).

My Conclusions

Whew! The D5000 is surely a complicated little beast. I guess that's the price of putting advanced functionality in a small DSLR body. Complex as it is though, I'm certainly delighted with the camera. In fact, it's one of my favorite "carry-with-me-everywhere" cameras.

Now, let's spend some time working through the autofocus system. In the next chapter, we'll consider the Multi-CAM 1000 autofocus module and its functionality. Plus, we'll consider information that supports accurate autofocus, like tracking, frame rate, and other functions. I've tried to pull everything related to or supporting autofocus into one chapter so that you can get an overview of the system in a way that will help you understand it well. Next, chapter 10, "Multi-CAM 1000 Autofocus."

10

Multi-CAM 1000 Autofocus

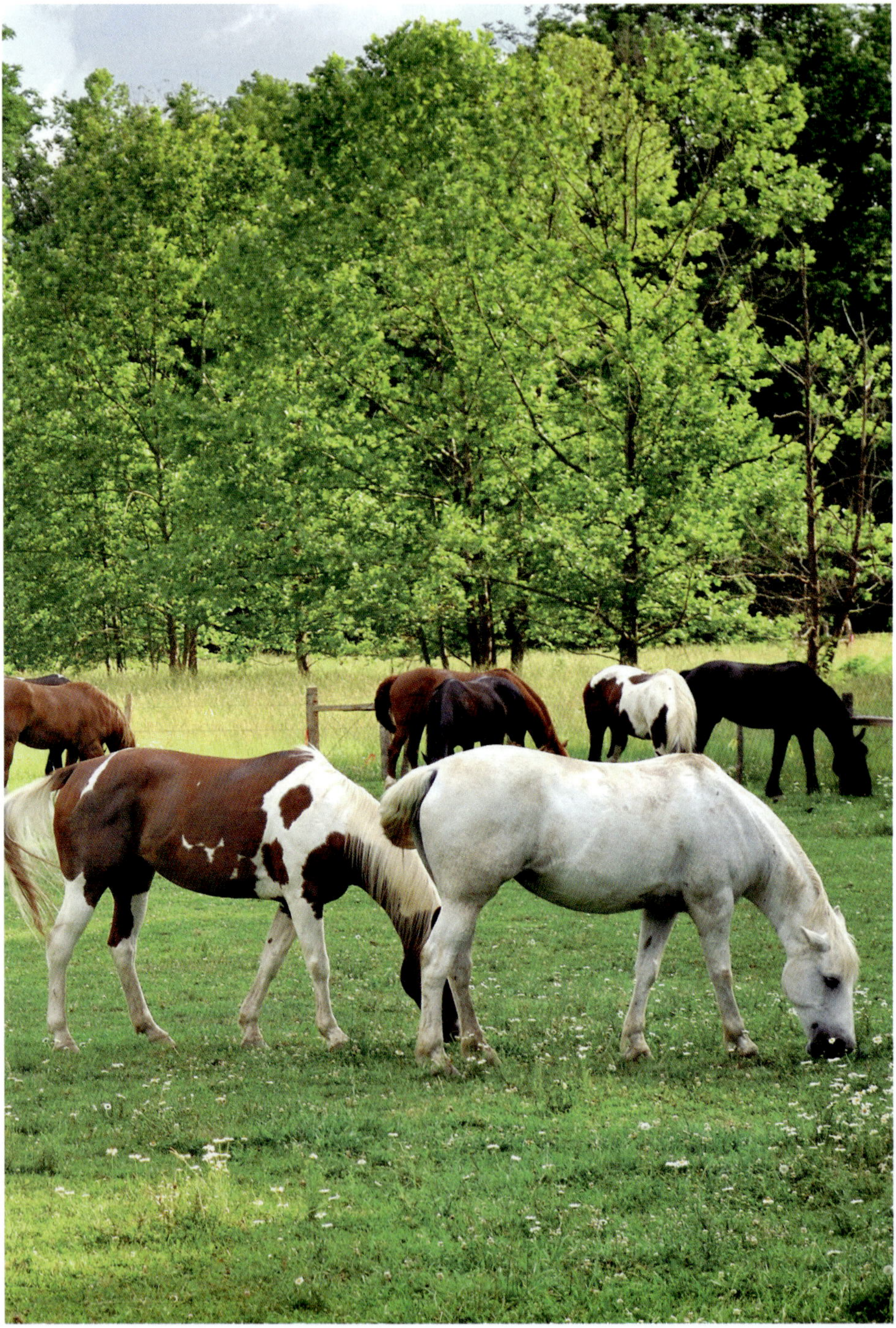

The first autofocus camera I owned was a "pro-level" film SLR back in the late 1980s. I remember shooting a football game and trying to get the autofocus (AF) to stay locked on my chosen subject. Often it would lose the subject and the lens would rack back and forth very slowly as it tried to recover. Then, when it found the subject, it was probably the wrong one. And that was on a pro-level camera!

I'm not complaining, just remembering. Back then autofocus was almost a novelty. There were few AF lenses and even fewer cameras with AF. The majority of my lenses were lovely, single focal length manual-focus primes. Those times are gone.

The autofocus in the Nikon D5000 is so far advanced in comparison to those early days of AF that it's like comparing one of today's cars with a car from the 1940s. Most American cars from the '40s were big, heavy, slow, and not extremely safe or comfortable. Today's cars are smaller, lighter, and faster and are computer controlled for comfort and safety. The AF system in the Nikon D5000 is, likewise, very advanced and feature rich.

I wrote this chapter to help you get the most use out of a somewhat complex but powerful system. Let's examine each aspect of the AF system in detail.

What Is the Multi-CAM 1000 Autofocus Module?

Inside your Nikon D5000 is a Multi-CAM 1000 autofocus module. It has the ability to handle autofocus with the normal viewfinder, but it also works with Live View.

Basically, this module examines the scene under your selected AF focus point and uses advanced technology to obtain a correct focus.

There are several ways to autofocus a camera:

- **Active AF** – Either ultrasonic sound waves or an infrared beam is sent out to find the subject. When the return reflection is detected, the time lapse is measured and autofocus distance is calculated from that delay. This is sort of like the old submarine movies where the sub is pinging the surroundings looking for a subject in the water.
- **Passive AF** – The autofocus system simply does an analysis of whatever it sees in its view. It can then use phase detection or contrast detection to find the subject and focus on it. If it's too dark, sometimes a passive system will get a little more active and shine a nice infrared beam on the subject to help in its analysis (camera dependant).
- **Contrast detection AF** – The autofocus system detects intensity differences between pixels next to each other on the camera's sensor. This is a very slow but accurate method of autofocus. It doesn't work very well in dim light when contrast is quite low.
- **Phase detection AF** (D5000 default) – Remember how you used to use a split-prism viewfinder screen in your film camera back in the "old days"? Well, that is rather similar to how phase detection AF works. The incoming image is split into two beams with a beam splitter and they are compared. In a sense, the camera is doing what you

used to do with your own eye, bringing two split images together in the split-prism circle. Few of today's cameras have a split-prism viewfinder for human use because AF is handled automatically by the camera.

The Nikon D5000 uses the third and fourth methods: contrast detection AF and phase detection AF. TTL (through the lens) phase detection AF is the primary autofocus method used for day-to-day shooting. Contrast detection AF is used when in Live View mode. We'll talk more about them later in the chapter.

The D5000's Multi-CAM 1000 has a 420-pixel RGB sensor. With so many contrast-sensing elements in the AF system, it will autofocus in low to high light levels and at high speeds. So, the Multi-CAM 1000 AF module is basically a flexible multimode autofocus system designed to assist or replace your eye in getting a good focus on your lenses' subject.

As we proceed through this chapter, I'm going to call the Multi-CAM 1000 autofocus module by the simpler name: AF module.

The AF module has four AF-area modes (User's Manual pages 56–61):

- *Single-point AF*
- *Dynamic-area AF*
- *Auto-area AF*
- *3D-tracking (11 points)*

It also has four focus modes (User's Manual pages 54–55):

- AF-A, *or auto select*
- *AF-S, or single-servo*
- *AF-C, or continuous-servo*
- *MF, or manual focus*

What's the difference? Basically, think of the AF-area modes as *where* the AF module focuses, and the autofocus modes as *how* it focuses.

In addition, the D5000 allows you to control how fast and how often a picture is taken. We'll look at how the image frame rate works in relation to the AF system. The frame rate used to be controlled by the "motor-drive" speed in days gone by. Tied in closely with the AF system are the release modes (single frame and continuous). This determines how the camera takes the picture, one at a time or in continuous bursts.

With the controls built into the D5000's body, you'll be able to select whether the AF module uses one or several of the 11 AF sensors to find your subject. You'll also select whether the camera grabs the focus and "locks" on a static subject or whether it continuously seeks new focus if your subject is moving and how fast, in frames-per-second (FPS), it takes to capture the images.

You can turn AF off completely with the MF selection in the *Focus* mode section of the *Information edit* screen and simply use manual focus. This may be useful when you are taking an extreme close-up picture with a macro lens. There

AF System Override With Lens Setting

If you'd like, you can use the A-M switch found on most AF Nikkors to set the lens to manual focus (MF), and override the AF system completely. If the AF Nikkor lens supports autofocus with manual priority, you can use the AF module to obtain primary focus and then fine-tune it manually.

is so little depth of field in a close-up that it is often easier to manually focus the lens. You can then select the exact area that you want in focus. This may only be a few millimeters at macro ranges.

You can look through the viewfinder to compose, or use the Live View (LV) mode. Live View enables the 2.7-inch (6.86 cm) LCD monitor on the back of the D5000 to be used as a viewfinder instead of the normal viewfinder, as with a Nikon COOLPIX point-and-shoot camera.

The AF module has four custom settings, a1 to a4. We examined each in detail in chapter 7, but we will review their use in this chapter.

Let's consider the various features of the Multi-CAM 1000 AF module in detail.

Understanding the Autofocus, AF-Area, and Release Modes

The D5000 has distinct modes for *how* and *when* to focus. We'll examine each of those modes as a starting point for understanding of autofocus with the Multi-CAM 1000 AF module. We'll tie together information about the *Focus*, *AF-area*, and *Release* modes since they work together to acquire and maintain good focus on your subject.

In fact, this chapter encompasses information found in the D5000 User's Manual chapters on focus (pages 54–61), and release modes (pages 65–66). It goes deeper than merely looking at the AF module alone, since other related camera functions such as the release modes directly affect how the AF system performs.

All this information is available in the user's manual, but it is spread out in various places in a way that makes it hard to connect it all together. This chapter is designed to help you bring the information together in a way that will assist you in remembering how to use it.

To get started in our examination of the autofocus system, let's examine a

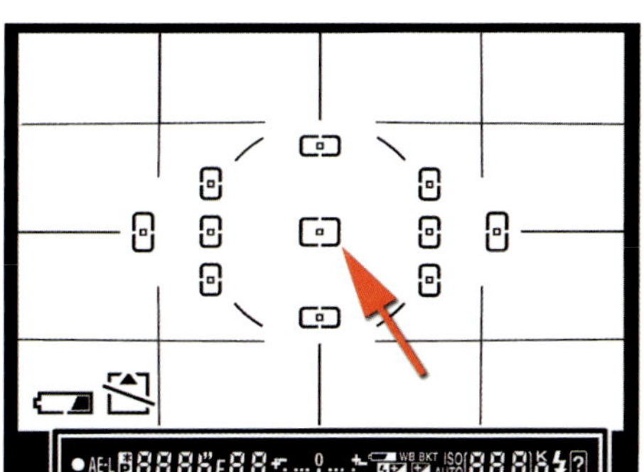

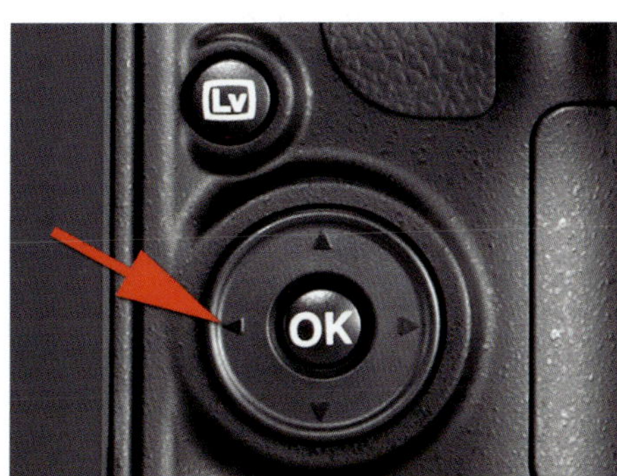

Figure 1 – Select AF points with the Multi Selector

basic control you will use to select combinations of the 11 AF points in the D5000 viewfinder. In the image on the left in *figure 1*, the red arrow points at one of the 11 available AF points.

In three of the focus modes, you'll move the AF sensor point around the viewfinder with the Multi Selector (see the image on the right in *figure 1*). You can select which of the 11 AF points are best used to focus on your subject. You can do this in three of the four focus modes: *single-point, dynamic-area,* and *3D-tracking*. In *Auto-area* mode, the camera completely controls all 11 AF sensors and decides which to use on its own (see *Custom Setting a1, AF-area mode,* in chapter 7). If you want to use the D5000 like a point-and-shoot camera, select *Auto-area* mode.

If you look at the camera's viewfinder, you'll notice the 11 tiny squares that represent the AF sensors. Surrounding one of them (except in auto-area mode), you'll see a larger bracket that represents your "selected" AF focus point. You can move this large bracket around with the Multi Selector in all AF-area modes except auto-area.

One of the 11 AF sensors on the D5000 is a cross-type sensor, which means that it will initiate focus in a horizontal or vertical direction. The center AF sensor point is the only cross-type sensor. All other AF points are sensitive only in a horizontal direction.

Now, let's start examining how autofocus works in the D5000.

Focus Modes in Detail

(User's Manual pages 54–55)

The focus modes allow you to control how the autofocus works with static and moving subjects. They allow your camera to "lock" focus on a subject that is not moving or is moving very slowly. They also allow your camera to "follow" focus on an actively moving subject.

Here are the four focus modes in the D5000:

- *AF-A*, or Auto-servo AF
- *AF-S*, or Single-servo AF
- *AF-C*, or Continuous-servo AF
- *MF*, or Manual focus

Let's consider each of the focus modes to see when and how you might use them best.

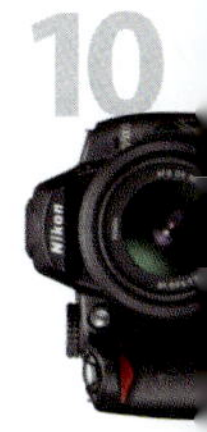

Auto-servo AF mode *(AF-A)*

This mode is best for a less-experienced user or someone who doesn't want to be bothered with selecting AF modes (see *figure 2A*).

Subject is not moving: The camera sees a static subject so it uses single-servo AF (*AF-S*) mode automatically. Focus is static on the subject and does not continue updating. However, in my experience it is not really "locked" as when you are using normal *AF-S* mode.

Subject is moving: The D5000 uses continuous-servo AF (*AF-C*), and as long as the subject is moving, the camera keeps seeking the best focus.

I have done some tests in this mode and here is what I found. When I focus on a static subject, the focus seems to lock. However, if I move the camera to a different subject, the D5000 will often clearly go into *AF-C* mode and start autofocusing again. So, the focus only appears to be locked. It is not really locked, as in *AF-S* mode where you have to tap the shutter release to get a refocus. If the subject, or your camera, moves and a different focus plane is required (near to far), the camera will refocus.

When I focus on a moving subject, the camera will often hesitate to fire the shutter while there is no clear focus, but it sometimes seems to be a bit unsure and will fire anyway. Maybe it is switching rapidly between *AF-S* and *AF-C* modes as it detects movement from a previously static subject? I think the point of *AF-A* mode it that the camera detects subject movement, or the lack thereof, when you first press the shutter release to focus. However, the camera seems to be able to detect movement in a subject that was previously static and then switch to *AF-C* mode. I can't find any verification of this, but my own observations seem to bear it out. Try it yourself and see what you think.

My Observations

The camera automatically selects single-servo autofocus (*AF-S*) when the subject is stationary and continuous-servo autofocus (*AF-C*) when the subject is moving. The shutter can only be released if the camera is able to focus.

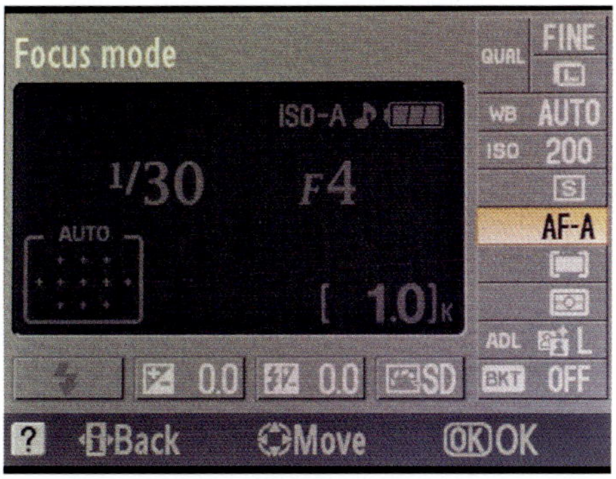

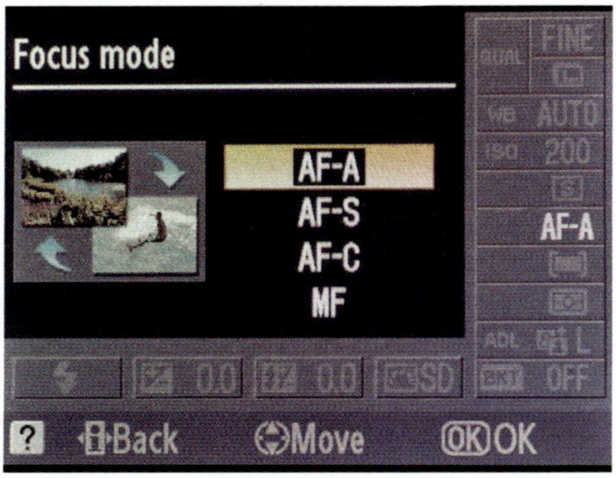

Figure 2A – *AF-A* focus mode

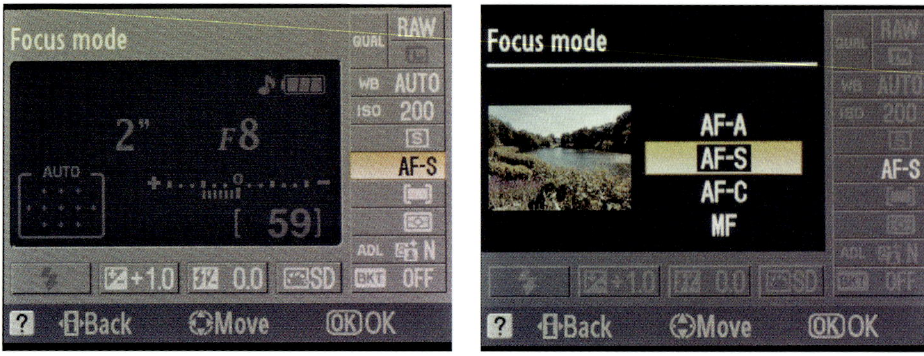

Figure 2B – *AF-S* focus mode

Single-servo AF mode *(AF-S)*

Subject is not moving: When you press the shutter release button halfway down, the AF module quickly locks the focus on your subject and waits for you to fire the shutter. If you don't release pressure on the shutter button and refocus and your subject starts moving, the focus will be obsolete and useless. Once you have focus lock, take the picture quickly. This is perfect for stationary subjects or in some cases even very slowly moving subjects. The shutter will not release unless the little green dot "in-focus indicator" is on in the viewfinder.

Subject is regularly moving: This will require a little more work on your part. Since the AF system locks the focus on your subject, if it moves even slightly, the focus is no longer good. You'll have to lift your finger off of the shutter release and reapply pressure halfway down to refocus. If the subject continues moving, you'll need to press the shutter release button halfway down, over and over, to keep the focus accurate. If your subject never stops moving, is moving erratically, or only stops briefly, single-servo AF (*AF-S*) is probably not the best mode to use. Continuous-servo AF (*AF-C*) is better because it never locks focus and you can better follow movement. You could also use auto select (*AF-A*) since it will automatically switch to continuous-servo AF (*AF-C*) if the subject moves.

It is best to use *AF-S* mode only with static subjects such as beautiful mountains scenes. Mountains don't move very fast!

Continuous-servo AF mode *(AF-C)*

Subject is not moving: When the subject is standing still, continuous-servo AF acts a lot like single-servo AF, with the exception that the focus never locks. If you have camera movement, you may hear your lens chattering a little as the autofocus motor makes minute adjustments in the focus position. Since it never locks in this mode, you'll need to be careful that you don't accidentally move the AF sensor off of the subject or it may focus on something in the background instead.

Subject is moving across the viewfinder: If your subject moves from left to right or up and down in the viewfinder, you will need to keep your AF sensor on

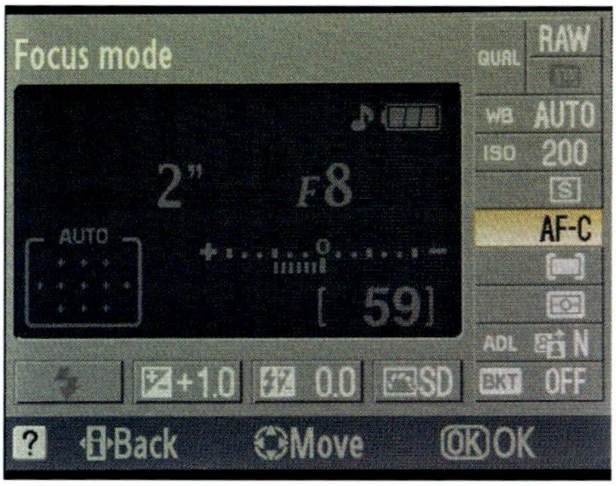

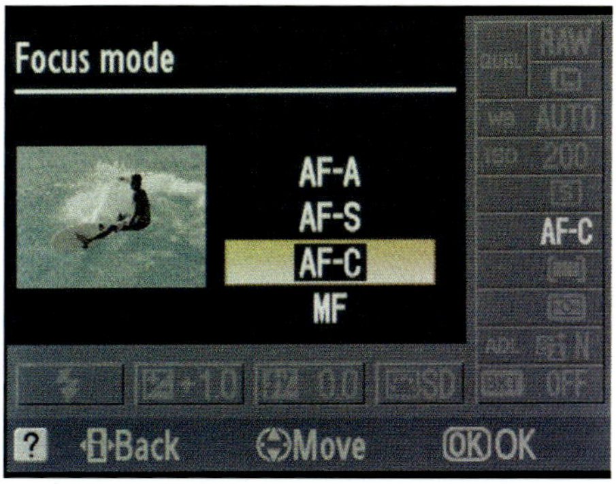

Figure 2C – *AF-C* focus Mode

the subject if you are using *single-point* AF mode. If you are using *dynamic-area* AF, auto-area AF, or *3D-tracking*, your camera will have the ability to track the subject across a few, or all of the 11 AF sensors. We'll cover this in more detail in the upcoming section "AF-Area Modes in Detail."

Subject is moving toward or away from the camera: If your subject is coming toward you, another automatic function of the camera kicks in. It is called predictive focus tracking, and it figures out how far the subject will move before the shutter fires. Once you've pressed the shutter button all the way down, predictive focus tracking moves the lens elements slightly to correspond to where the subject should be when the shutter fires a few milliseconds later. In other words, if the subject is moving toward you, it focuses slightly in front of your subject so that the camera has time to move the mirror and get the shutter blades out of the way. It takes just under 1 second (85 milliseconds, or 0.85 sec) for the camera to respond to the shutter release being pressed when it is focused on a subject.

Example of Use

If you are shooting an air show, for instance, in 85 milliseconds a fast-moving airplane can move enough to slightly change the focus area by the time the shutter opens. If you press the shutter release while the camera is focused on a moving aircraft, the mirror moves up and the shutter starts opening. That takes about 85 milliseconds in the D5000. In the time it takes for the camera to respond to your shutter release press, the airplane has moved slightly, which just barely throws the autofocus off. The camera's computer predicts where the airplane will be when the image is actually exposed and adjusts the focus accordingly.

Additional Example of Use

Let's say you are playing in a ball game and you through the ball to a running player. You would have to throw the ball slightly in front of the receiving player so that he and the ball arrive in the same place at the same time. Predictive focus tracking does something like that for you so that you don't have to focus your camera in front of your subject and wait 85 milliseconds for it to arrive. That would be a bit hard to time!

Predictive Focus Tracking Tips

Lens movement, especially with long lenses, can be misinterpreted by the camera as subject movement. Predictive focus tracking, in that case, is tracking your camera movement while simultaneously trying to track your subject. You can drive your camera crazy by attempting to handhold a long lens. Use a vibration reduction (VR) lens or a tripod for best results. Nikon says that there are special algorithms in predictive focus tracking that notice sideways or up and down movement and shuts this process down. So, predictive focus tracking is not activated by the D5000 for sideways or up and down subject movement or panning.

Manual focus *(MF)*

Sometimes it is better to manually focus a camera (see *figure 2D*). Manual focus works better when extra accuracy is needed, such as with macro shots. Some lenses have an A/M switch that lets you switch the lens to MF (M) without using the manual focus (*MF*) mode setting in the camera. If you have the 18-55mm kit lens, it has the A/M switch (A=autofocus, M=manual focus).

With Manual focus, you are completely responsible for focusing the camera. Autofocus is turned off. Some older AF Nikkor lenses will still work on the D5000 but will require you to focus manually because the camera body does not have a focus motor and requires lenses that have one built in.

I've tried using older "non-CPU" AI and AI-S manual focus lenses on my D5000, but the shutter refuses to release with one mounted. Stick with AF and *AF-S* lenses for best results. The camera will assist you in manually focusing with lenses that have a CPU built in. It uses the round, green "good focus" indicator when you have correctly focused the lens. That's important since it is harder to do fine manual focus on a viewfinder screen with no split prism, like the D5000's viewfinder.

Recommendation

Personally, I use *AF-S* most of the time because I most often shoot static nature subjects. If you're shooting active events with moving subjects, *AF-S* will probably not work well for you and you should use *AF-C* mode. *AF-A* mode is an in-between mode that tries its best to deal with difficult subjects, often static but sometimes moving. If I were a newer photographer, I

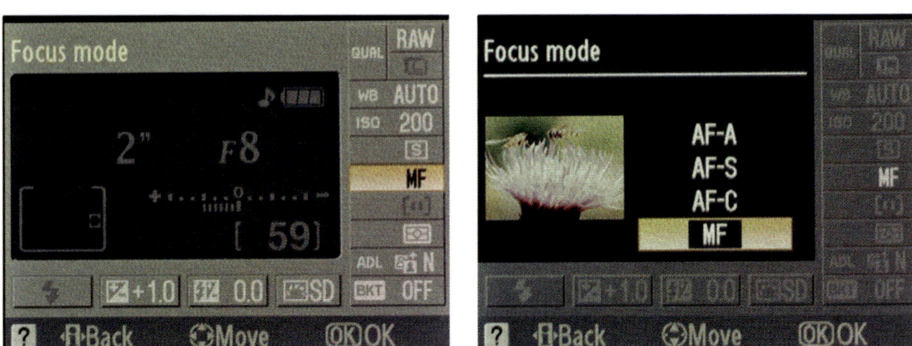

Figure 2D – *MF* focus mode

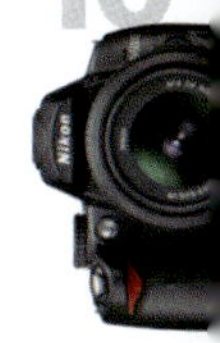

would leave my camera set to *AF*-A mode. It works well enough to keep one out of trouble most of the time. I look at *AF-A* as I do any of the automatic camera functions. It is convenient, but I use it only when I need convenience. If I am doing critical work, I want full control and will generally turn off any automatic modes.

AF-Area Modes in Detail

(User's Manual pages 56–61)

The *AF-area* modes are designed to give you control over how many AF sensors are in use at one time and offer various ways to track subject movement. Let's carefully examine each of the focus "area" modes. (See *Custom Setting a1* in chapter 7 and pages 56 and 155 in the User's Manual.)

Here are the four *AF-area* modes in the Nikon D5000:

- *Single-point*
- *Dynamic-area*
- *Auto-area*
- *3D-tracking* (11 points)

Each of the AF-area modes has both an *Information edit* screen and a Custom Setting a1 menu. You can use either to change modes. The *Information edit* screens are simpler to use, in most cases, since there are fewer steps. We'll look at both types of screens, plus how each *AF-area* mode works. In figure 3A and figure 3B are the *Single-point* area AF selection screens.

Single-Point Autofocus

This mode uses a single AF focus sensor point out of the array of 11 points to acquire a good focus. Usually, the center AF sensor point is the one that provides focus information. You can control which sensor provides focus information with the Multi Selector. Move the AF point around the viewfinder if a secondary AF point better fits your image composition.

Here is a common problem with *Single-point* AF. If two people are standing next to each other, with a gap in the middle, the single center AF point will be examining the space between the two subjects. That will lead to a nice sharp picture of the background, with your friends out of focus. You can do one of three things to overcome this problem:

- **One:** You could get the focus first by pointing the center sensor at the face of one of the subjects, pressing the

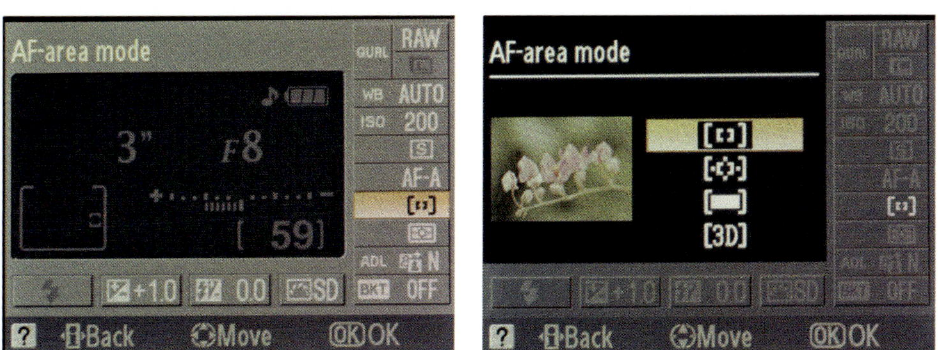

Figure 3A – *Single-point* area mode – information edit screens

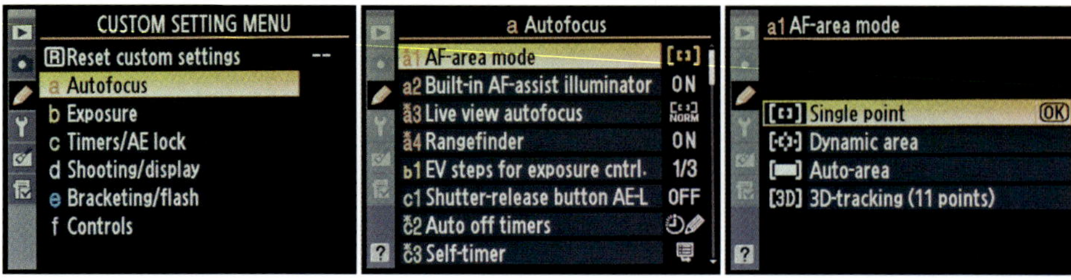

Figure 3B – *Single-point* area mode – *Custom Setting a1*

shutter release button halfway to get a focus, then holding it down while recomposing the image. When you have recomposed the shot, you'll finish pressing the shutter release the rest of the way and take the picture. This is called the "focus and recompose" method.

- **Two:** Using the Multi Selector, you can move the AF sensor point selector bracket around the viewfinder. You can compose the picture first by centering it however you'd like, then using the Multi Selector to move the single AF sensor until it rests on the face of one of the subjects. Then you'll press the shutter button halfway down to get good focus and the rest of the way down to take the picture.
- **Three:** You can use auto-area AF with its ability to find the nearest subject, especially a human face, and focus on it.

Any of these methods will solve the problem of having a perfectly focused background with out-of-focus subjects caused by a center AF sensor concentrating on the background between them.

Many of us will use *Single-point* AF mode. It works particularly well for static or slowly moving subjects. When I'm out shooting beautiful nature images or at an event like a wedding, I'll often use *Single-point area* mode, *Single-servo* focus mode (*AF-S*), and *Single frame release* mode (*S*).

Example of Use

If a subject is not moving (like a tree or a standing person), then *Single-point* area mode and *Single frame release* mode will allow you to acquire focus. Once the focus is acquired, the AF module will "lock" focus on the subject, and it will not change. If the subject moves, your chosen focus point may no longer be perfect and you'll need to recompose while releasing and then pressing the shutter release button halfway again. Often, if the subject is moving very slowly or sporadically, I'll not even use continuous release mode but will leave it in *Single frame release mode*. I'll tap the shutter button halfway to acquire focus when the subject moves and tap it again as needed. When I'm ready, I simply press the shutter release the rest of the way down and I've got the shot.

When I'm shooting a stationary or slowly moving simple subject, I'll often use *Single-point* area mode along with single frame or continuous release mode.

Now, let's move on to *Dynamic-area* AF and see what benefits it brings us.

Dynamic-Area Autofocus

This mode is best used when your subject is moving. Instead of a single AF sensor used alone for autofocus, several sensors surrounding the one you have selected with the Multi Selector are also active. *Figure 4A* and *figure 4B* show the *Dynamic-area* AF selection screens.

Once you've selected *Dynamic-area* AF, your camera has the capability to do some basic subject tracking. When you look into the viewfinder, you won't see anything that helps you know you are in that mode. The viewfinder screen looks just as it does when the camera is in *Single-point* AF mode. You still just see the one big bracket surrounding a small square AF point, and you can move it around among the 11 points with the Multi Selector. However, there is a difference that is not visible.

In *Single-point* AF mode, you are truly using a *single* AF focus point to get autofocus. Even though *Dynamic-area* AF looks the same, there are, in fact, up to five AF focus points being used in this mode. Imagine a cross-shaped pattern of AF sensors, with the big-bracketed one in the center. You are still selecting a single AF point to start the autofocus in this mode. However, if the subject moves a bit and the selected AF sensor is no longer on the subject, the AF focus points surrounding the selected focus point will

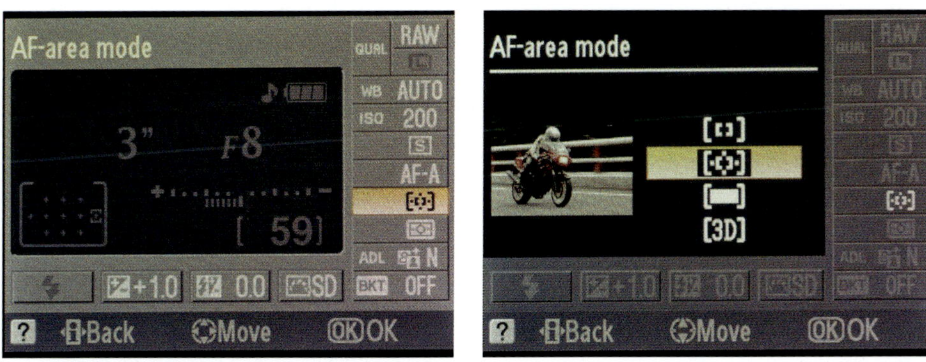

Figure 4A – *Dynamic-area* mode – information edit screens

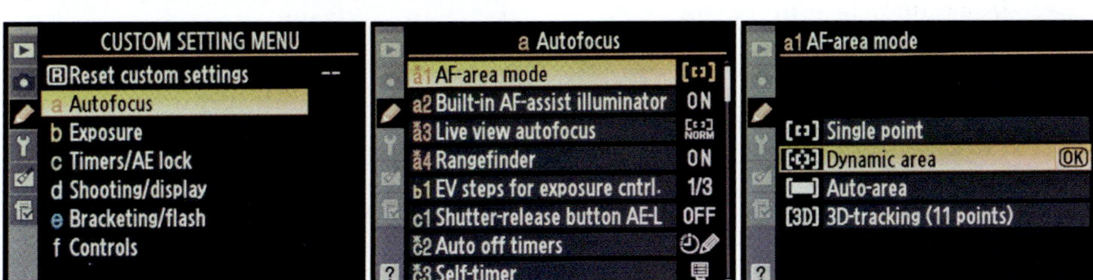

Figure 4B – *Dynamic-area* mode – *Custom Setting a1*

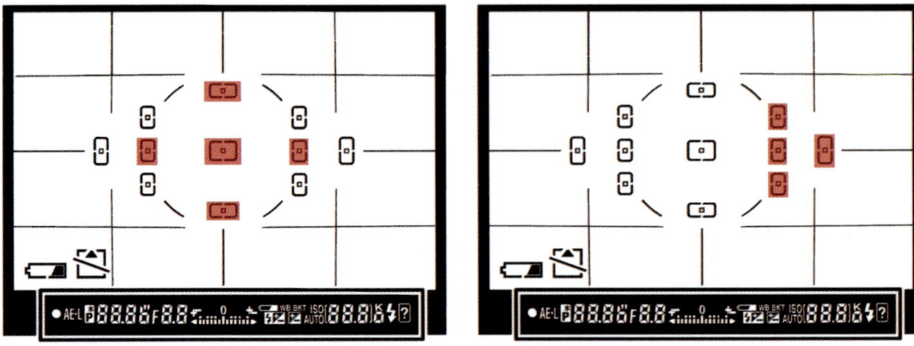

Figure 4C – AF sensor point patterns in *Dynamic-area* AF

start providing autofocus services. They will take over when needed to keep the focus accurate. *Figure 4C* provides a look at the otherwise invisible cross-shaped pattern that can be moved around the viewfinder with the Multi Selector.

Notice how you lose one AF sensor in the pattern when you move to the edge of the viewfinder in any direction. The only time you'll have five active sensors seeking a subject is when the selected AF sensor point is directly in the middle of the viewfinder. On the edges, only four sensors are active. The image on the left in *figure 4C* shows the center pattern, while the image on the right shows the right edge pattern.

Can you see how flexible the *Dynamic-area* AF mode is? Maybe you're doing some macro shots of a bee on a flower and it is moving around the blossom. The extra AF points allow you to track the bee around the small area without moving the camera. Or, you might be panning with a running person during a football game and using the extra AF points to stay with the subject without losing the focus, even if your main AF point leaves the subject briefly.

11 Point Focus Tracking

We'll talk more about focus tracking with all 11 points later in this chapter by considering another pattern called 11 points (*3D-tracking*). This mode allows your D5000 to use all its AF points for tracking and to pay attention to the color and brightness of the subject to improve tracking accuracy with some subjects.

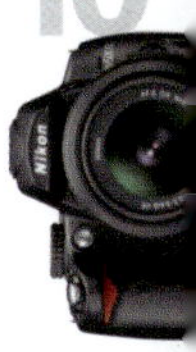

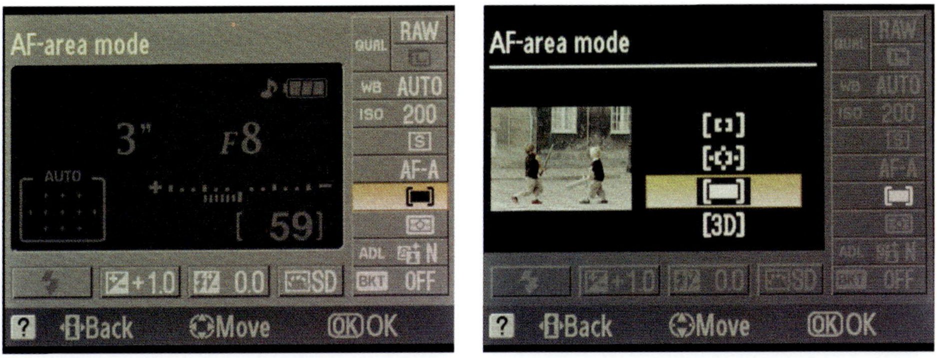

Figure 5A – *Auto-area mode* – information edit screens

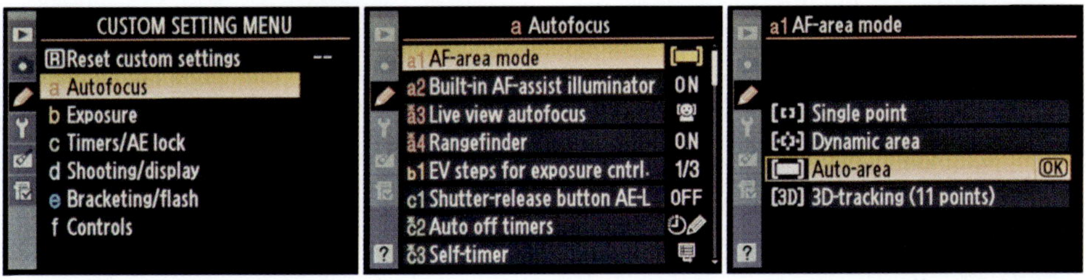

Figure 5B – *Auto-area mode – Custom Setting a1*

Auto-Area Autofocus

Auto-area autofocus mode turns the D5000 into an expensive point-and-shoot camera. Use this mode when you simply have little time to adjust your camera but would still like to get great images. The AF module decides what the subject is and selects the AF sensors it thinks work best. *Figure 5A* and *figure 5B* show the *Auto-area* AF selection screens.

When you use this mode, you'll notice how the camera itself selects various AF points as it examines the entire view its lens finds. Usually, it will select the closest and brightest subject, with special emphasis on human faces.

According to Nikon, if you are using a D or G lens, there is "human recognition technology" built into this mode. Since most of us will be using *Auto-area* AF only when we want to shoot for fun—at a party for example—a human subject that is closest to the camera is the most likely subject anyway. Your D5000 can usually detect a human and not focus on the background instead. Face recognition technology has come a long way in the last few years. Nikon has given you a great tool for taking sharp pictures of people when you use *Auto-area* AF mode.

If you are shooting nonhuman subjects, just pay careful attention to what the camera considers to be the subject. Usually, it will select what you want it to select. However, if you are focusing on an object in the middle distance and the camera notices a brighter and closer object between you and your subject, it may very well choose the closer object. Using this mode means that you must keep watch on what the camera thinks the subject is and move slightly if it won't focus where you want it to focus.

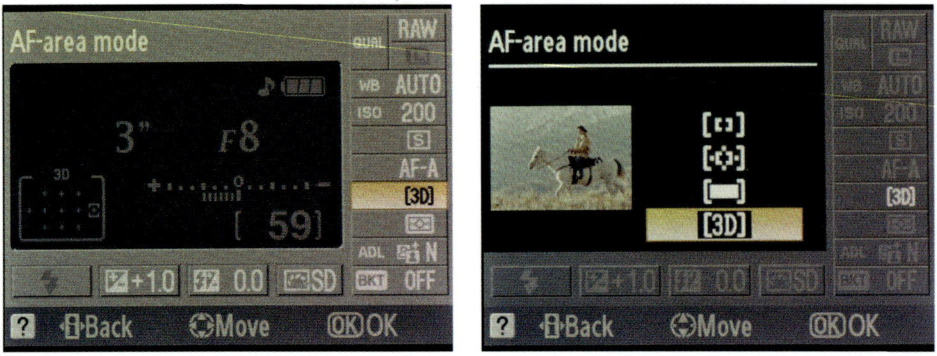

Figure 6A – *AF-area mode* – information edit screens

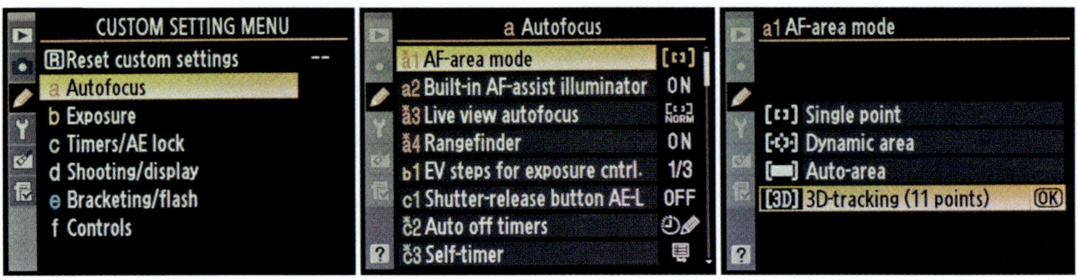

Figure 6B – *AF-area mode – 3D-tracking (11 points)*

3D-Tracking (11 Points) Autofocus

This mode is designed for action shooters. Images of action sports, moving animals, auto races, and air shows will all benefit from the camera's ability to track a subject. You'll select your subject by using one of the AF sensor points. If the subject moves, the camera will hand off the AF responsibility to other sensors. As the subject travels across the viewfinder, the adjacent sensor will take over. You can see this progression because the D5000 displays which AF sensor point is active at any given moment. *Figure 6A* and *figure 6B* shown the *Dynamic-area* AF selection screens.

An easy way to see how this works is to select *3D-tracking (11 points)*, either through the *Information edit* screen or from the *Custom Setting Menu* screens. This mode is available only if you have *AF-A* or *AF-C* focus mode active. If you have *AF-S* selected, *3D-trackin (11 points) g* will be grayed out on the *Custom Setting a1* menu and completely disappear from the *Information edit* screens. When I had *3D tracking* selected and changed the focus mode to *AF-S*, the camera automatically switched to *Dynamic-area* mode.

Select *3D-Tracking (11 points)* and then focus on a static subject. Slowly move your camera away from the subject. You'll be able to see the tracking happen as the AF sensor in use changes to a different one. It is quite fascinating to see how this happens when you are focusing on a moving subject.

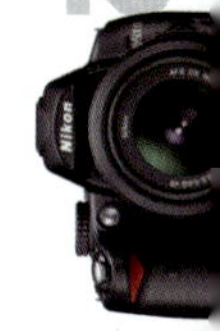

Example of Use

Let's imagine that you are photographing a bird perched in a tree but you want some shots of it in flight. You are patiently waiting for it to fly. You have 3D-Tracking selected with all its 11 AF points active so that the camera will track the bird instantly when it starts flying. You've already established focus with the sensor you selected using the Multi Selector and are holding the shutter release halfway down to maintain focus. You've also previously set the release mode to continuous so that you can fire off rapid bursts of images (up to four per second). Suddenly, and faster than you can react, the bird takes flight. By the time you can get the camera moving, the bird has moved to the left in the viewfinder, and the focus tracking system has reacted by instantly switching away from the primary sensor you established focus with and is now using other AF sensors within the 11 to maintain focus on the bird. You press the shutter release button all the way down, and the images start pouring into your camera's memory card. You are panning with the bird, firing bursts, until it moves out of range. You've got the shot, yet again!

In shooting a bird flying across the sky while I panned with the D5000, it was gratifying to see the AF focus points jumping around on the viewfinder as my aim varied. The focus stayed right with the bird, and I was able to capture several sharp images.

Nikon states that the camera uses color and brightness information to track your moving subject when you use *3D-tracking (11 points)*. Here is a direct quote from a Nikon website: "When using *3D-tracking (11 points)* mode, the camera uses your subject's color and brightness information to keep it in sharp focus as you change the composition."

Recommendation

I normally use *Single-point* AF most of the time since my static subjects call for it. However, when I am shooting images of things like moving wildlife, I'll switch immediately to *3D-tracking (11 points)*. I use *Dynamic-area* AF when I'm shooting macro shots, primarily. I even use *Auto-area* AF at parties and events. I recommend that you use all these AF-area modes as your needs vary. Don't be afraid to learn them well. It will definitely improve your photography if you learn when to switch between them. Another thing to test for yourself is whether or not any particular mode is fast enough for you. Anytime the camera has to process more data, or "think" deeper thoughts, it will take a little more time to obtain a good focus. This is especially true in the *Auto-area mode* because all the AF sensors are active.

We've covered the focus and AF-area modes pretty well, so now let's move on to the *Release* modes.

Release Modes in Detail

(User's Manual pages 65–69)

The D5000 has several release modes, which determine how many and how quickly images can be taken. The D5000 has six release modes (we're concerned with only the first two in this chapter on autofocus):

- *Single frame*
- *Continuous*
- *Self-timer*
- *Delayed remote*
- *Quick-response remote*
- *Quiet shutter-release*

In the good-old-film-days, the first two release modes would have been called "motor-drive" settings because they are concerned with how fast the camera is allowed to take pictures. I've already talked about these modes to some degree earlier in this chapter in the discussion of the AF-area modes. However, let's look at each of the release modes in greater detail now. We are primarily concerned with single frame and continuous modes, since this chapter is on autofocus.

Single Frame Mode

Figure 7A shows the screens for single frame mode. This is the simplest frame rate because it takes a single picture each time you fully depress the shutter release button. No speed here! This is for those shooting a few frames at a time. Nature shooters will often use this mode since they are more concerned with correct depth of field and excellent composition.

Continuous Mode

Figure 7B shows the screens for continuous mode. This high-speed mode is designed for when you want to take a lot of images in a short period of time. The camera will attempt to capture up to 4 frames per second every time you hold the shutter release button down. This is a great mode for action shooters who want to get as many frames as possible so they can select the best ones for later use. Think about it: in about 10 seconds you can fire off up to 40 frames, if the camera's shutter speed allows it. If you like to hold down the shutter release and get lots of pictures, your camera is happy to oblige!

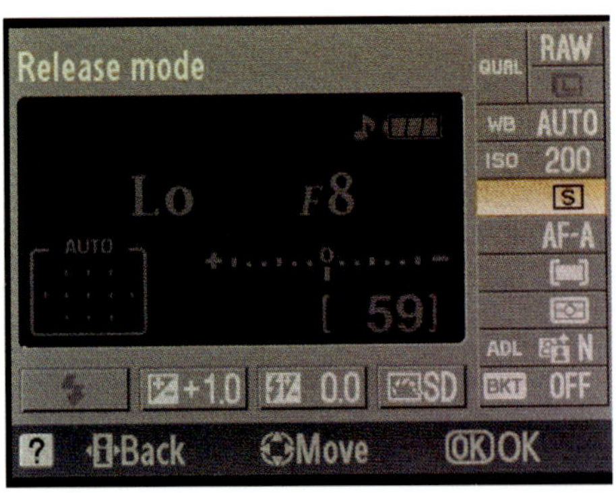

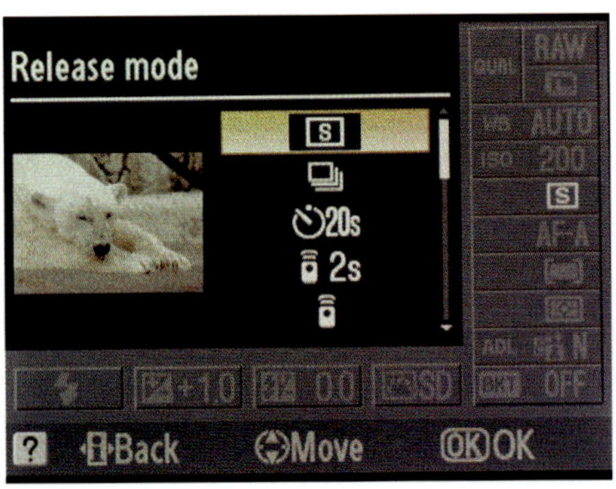

Figure 7A – Single frame mode

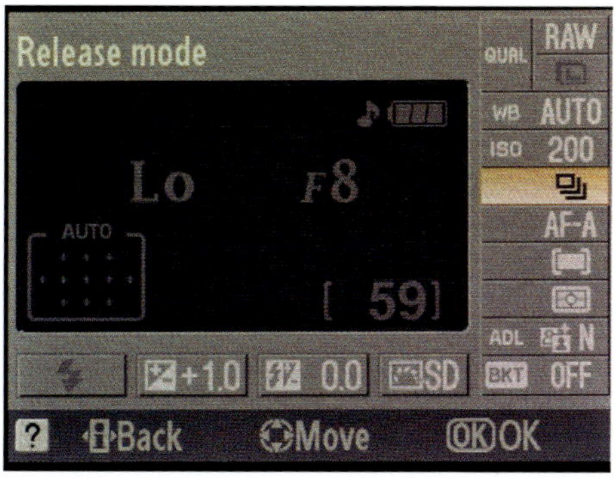

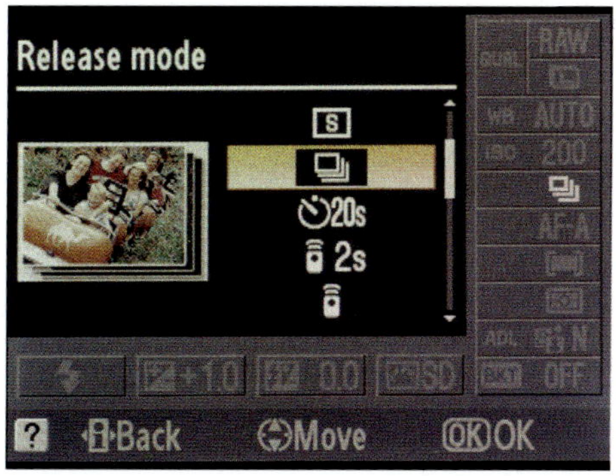

Figure 7B – Continuous mode

Four Other Release Modes

There are four more release modes available. However, this is a special chapter to bring together information related to effectively using the Multi-CAM 1000 autofocus system. We will not cover self-timer, Delayed remote, Quick-response remote, or Quiet shutter-release in this chapter. These are covered thoroughly in other sections of this book.

Recommendation

You may be required to use both of these modes at one time or the other. I usually have my camera set to single frame mode since trees and mountains are not known to move around quickly. However, sometimes I'm shooting an event that requires mashing the shutter release and hoping for some great shots. I like to shoot birds in flight and even bigger birds at air shows. In those situations, I'll set my camera to continuous mode and fire away. Learn to use both modes for best camera control.

Custom Setting f1 Reminder

As a reminder, you can also set *Custom Setting f1* to *Release mode*. This allows you to hold down the Fn button and rotate the command dial, which causes the camera to scroll through all six release modes on the *Information edit* screen. This is covered in chapter 7, "Custom Settings."

Live View Autofocus

(User's Manual pages 42–47)

Normally, one would not use the LCD monitor to compose an important image because it's not as stable as holding the camera close to your body while looking through the viewfinder, and could result in shaky images.

However, in some instances a live view on the monitor is quite useful. For instance, what if you want to take an image of a small flower that is growing very close to the ground? You could just lie down on the ground and get your clothes dirty, or you could use *Live view autofocus* mode with the cool tilt-and-swivel screen instead. Or what if you need to shoot over the heads of a crowd to get the arrival of the dignitary? *Live view autofocus* mode and the swivel screen allows you to see what your camera's lens sees, without using the viewfinder.

While the viewfinder shows only around 95 or 96 percent of what the lens sees, *Live view autofocus* mode shows 100 percent.

Anytime you need to take pictures high or low, or even on a tripod, the D5000 will happily give you that power with its *Live view autofocus* mode. How hard is it to get the camera into LV mode? Simply turn on the camera and press the Live view button on back of the D5000 (see *figure 8*).

There are four *Live view autofocus* modes that we need to consider:

- *Face priority*
- *Wide area*
- *Normal area*
- *Subject tracking*

Now, let's take a look at *Custom Setting a3*, which we'll use to select one of the four modes. *Figure 8A* shows the *Custom Setting a3* menus for configuring Live View AF.

Following is a detailed look at each of the *Live view autofocus* selections.

Face Priority Mode

If you take a lot of *Live view* pictures of people, *Face priority* is your mode. The D5000 has face recognition technology. In fact, *it* probably smiles when *you* pick it up!

If you use this mode, your D5000 will search for faces and focus on them automatically. You'll see a little yellow double-framed square surrounding the face. (First frame is solid, second frame is broken, see *figure 8B* and *figure 8C*). The camera will follow a face if you move it slowly. Try it! Through experimentation, I have found that the D5000 can recognize a face if it's in full profile, directly facing the camera or even when tilted. It's an amazing camera, in that respect, since many other cameras cannot recognize a face unless it is directly facing the camera.

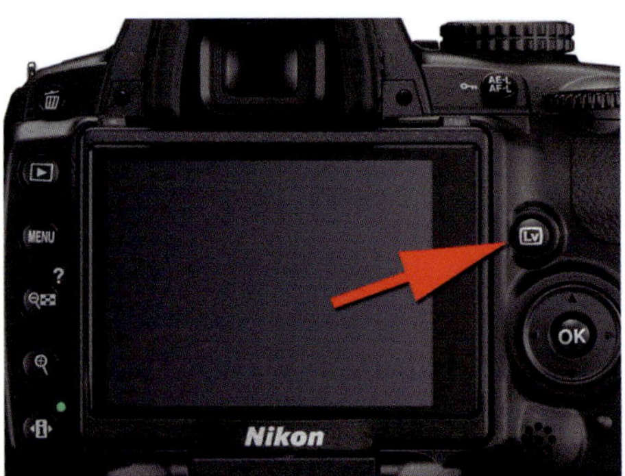

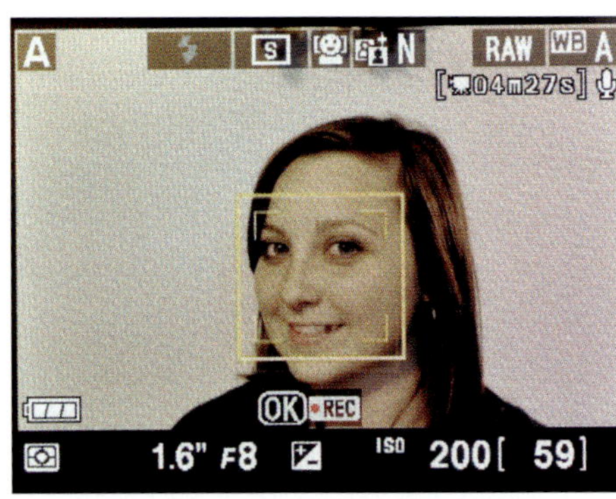

Figure 8 – *Live view* (LV) mode

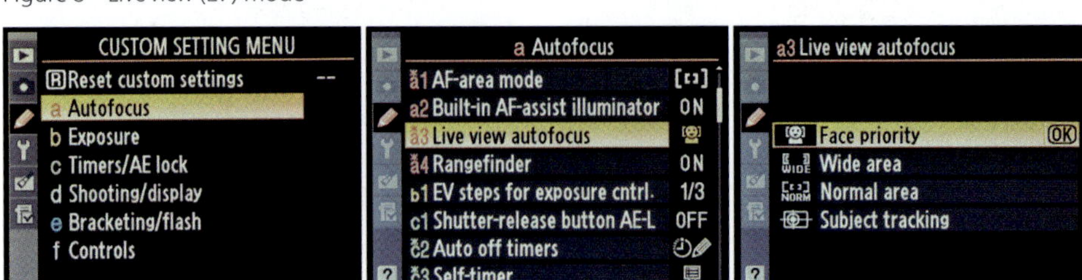

Figure 8A – *Custom Setting a3* screens to select *Live view* AF mode

Figure 8C shows the frame that you'll see if your D5000's *Face priority* mode detects a face. While you are preparing to take the shot, the little yellow frame is tracking the person's face. If the person or your camera moves, the yellow frame will jump around a bit.

Let's look at the *Wide area* mode next.

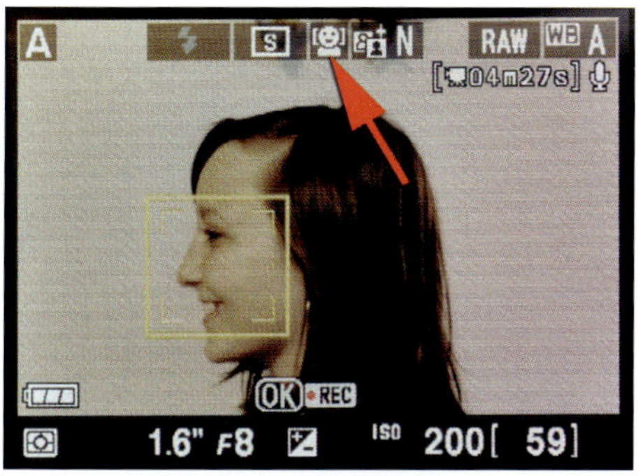

Figure 8B – *Face priority* LV autofocus

Wide Area Mode

The *Wide area* mode is used mostly for shooting landscapes or other subjects needing a broad autofocus area (see *figure 8D*). The little autofocus square is larger than it is for *Normal area* mode, by at least twice the size. It considers a broader area for contrast detection. You can move the AF square around the screen to any point in the frame. This gives you autofocus flexibility, although the slow speed of contrast detection AF will hold you back from using it with anything but the slowest moving subjects.

At first the AF square will be red because the camera is probably in an unfocused state. When you press the shutter release halfway down, the camera will attempt to focus and the AF square

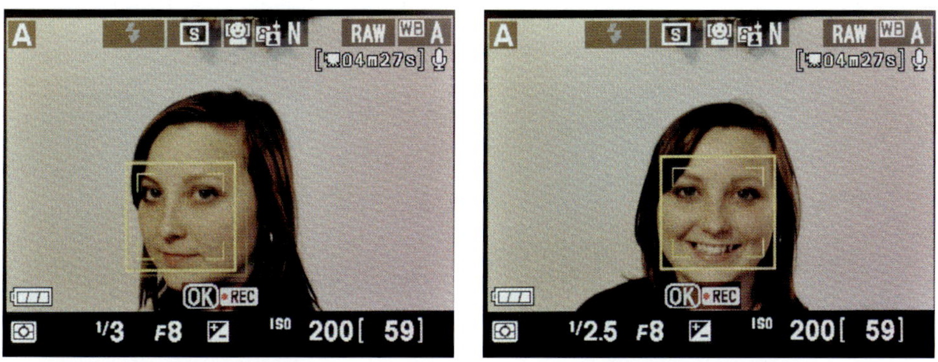

Figure 8C – *Face priority* sees a face

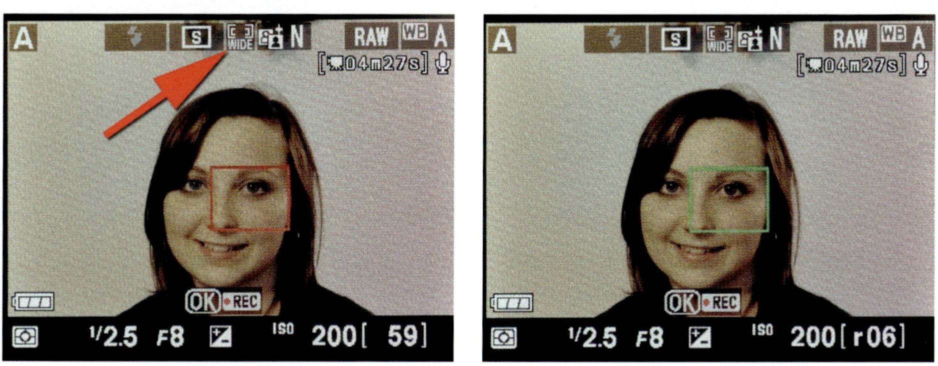

Figure 8D – *Wide area* LV autofocus

will flash green. The AF square will stop flashing and will simply turn green if focus is good. When it gets focus, you'll hear a beep. If it can't focus, it will flash red, but be careful because you can still press the shutter and get an unfocused picture.

***Normal Area* Mode**

Normal area mode is for more precise tripod work, such as close-ups and images in which a small area provides the focus point of interest. The AF square gets rather small, but you can still move it to any part of the screen and focus where you'd like. *Figure 8E* shows the screens for this mode.

It works just like *Wide area* mode otherwise, with the same flashing green while the camera is focusing, solid green and a beep when AF has been successful, and flashing red if the camera can't get good autofocus.

Autofocus During Video Recording

Since you can go into video recording mode while in *Live view* merely by pressing the *OK* button, you should be aware that autofocus does not work at all during video recording. You should obtain your autofocus before you press OK to start recording videos. If you zoom your lens during a video, you may have to refocus manually. Feel free to zoom in and out, refocus, and have fun capturing videos from *Live view autofocus* mode. See chapter 12, "D-Movie Mode: Video on Demand," for detailed information on recording videos.

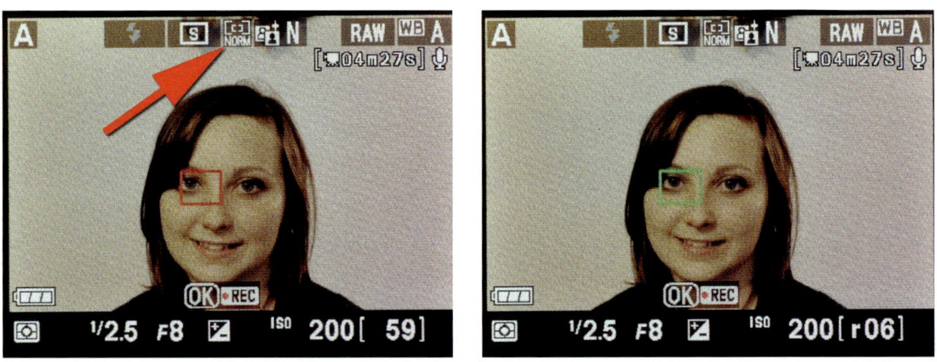

Figure 8E – *Normal area* mode LV autofocus

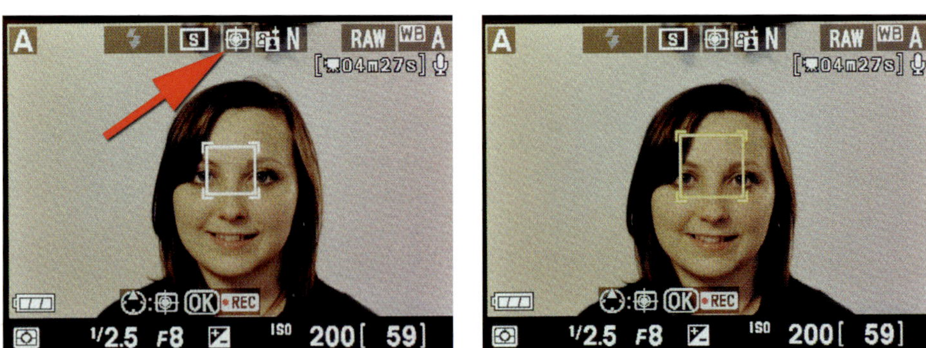

Figure 8F – *Subject tracking* mode *Live view autofocus*

Subject Tracking

When in *Subject tracking* mode, the user sees a small white square in the middle of the screen (see *figure 8F*). This little square works similarly to how it works in *Normal area* mode except that you cannot move it. If you use the shutter release button to start *Autofocus*, the white square will turn green and the camera seems to find a good focus even more quickly than it does in other modes. However, using the shutter release button to start *Autofocus* seriously limits this mode.

To use subject tracking, you *must* initiate autofocus by pressing up on the Multi Selector. Only then does the camera enter *Subject tracking* mode. This works a lot like *Face priority* mode except that it tracks any subject, not just a face. I like this mode a lot.

Recommendation

Of the four available modes, I most often use the *Normal mode*. I use *Live view* mode mostly for macro and close-up work. It can cause neck or back strain to bend over a camera for periods of time while doing some types of macro work. It is much easier to use *Live view autofocus* mode and the swivel screen to focus on my subject. I find *Live view autofocus* mode to be quite easy to use for macro work, and I recommend it. The contrast detection is somewhat slow, but I can zoom in with the playback zoom in button for very accurate views of my subject while autofocusing. Try it! You can use the zoom in and out buttons to get accurate autofocus on very specific areas of your subject (see *figure 9*).

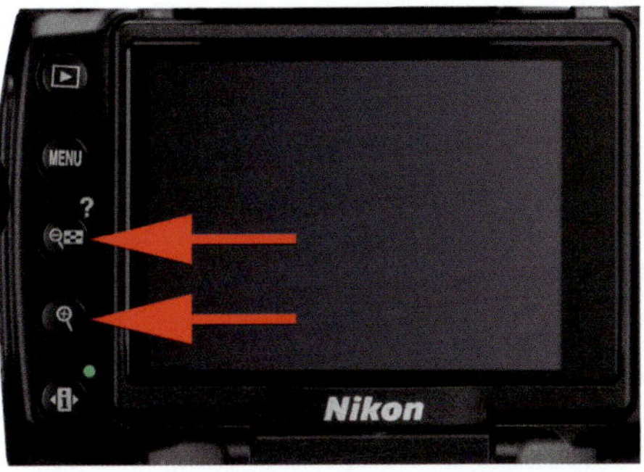

Figure 9 – LV mode zoom in and out buttons

My Conclusions

I've followed the development of the Nikon autofocus systems since back in the late 1980s. My first camera with autofocus was the Nikon F4 professional film SLR. Through 21 years I've experienced each new level of autofocus released by Nikon. It's gotten better and better with each new generation.

The current generation with the D5000 is a real pleasure. Nikon has really learned how to make excellent technology. The D5000 has a more powerful AF system than many enthusiast cameras before it, and yet somewhat it's simplified in its operation. I'm particularly impressed with the superior face recognition and subject tracking capabilities in this fine camera. Great job, Nikon!

The AF system is still necessarily complex, though. If you'll spend some time with this chapter and chapter 7 on *Custom Settings a1 to a4*, you should come away with a much greater understanding of the D5000's AF module. You'll better understand how you can adapt your camera to work best for your style of photography.

Enjoy your D5000's excellent Multi-CAM 1000 autofocus system.

Speedlight Flash Photography

11

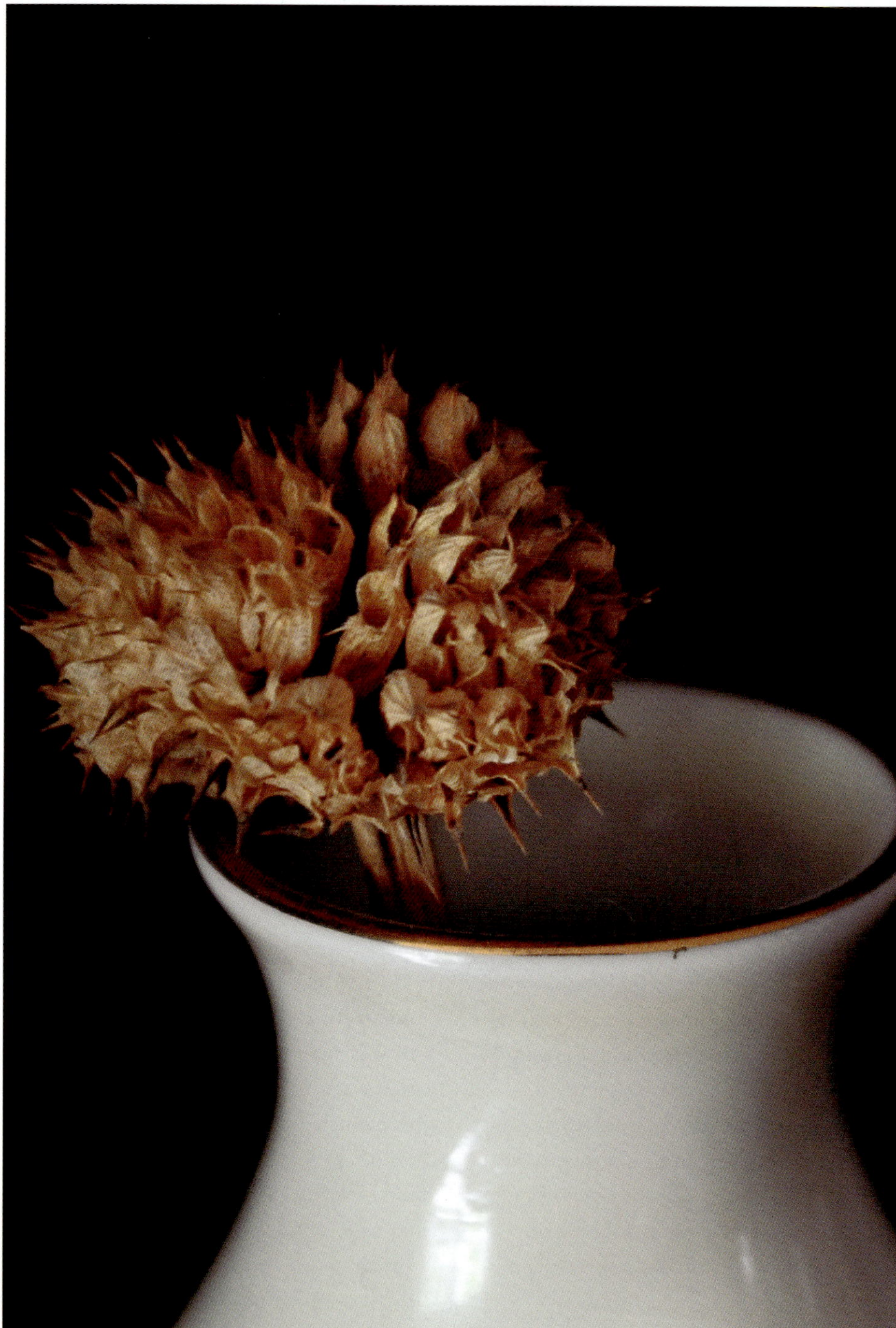

Light is the photographer's friend.

Knowing how to control light is the primary thing that separates excellent from not-so-excellent photographers. On beautiful balmy summer evenings, the light wraps around the land and gives us that so-called "golden hour" look that we so crave.

However, some days are rainy, some are dark and gloomy. As photographers, we want to take pictures. We don't want to stop just because the sun won't cooperate. We need light that we can take with us. We need it to be available quickly. We need a Speedlight!

Your D5000 has a built-in Speedlight. The little pop-up unit that's always with the camera is the Nikon Speedlight flash. That's Nikon's name for its flash units, large and small. From the tiny pop-up to the SB-400—excellent for the D5000—and on up to the flagship SB-900 flash, you have several choices. You can even create a wireless array of flashes using your camera, a commander unit, and several Speedlight flash units. These types of setups are called the Nikon Creative Lighting System, abbreviated CLS. We'll look at this later in the chapter. First let's examine some general flash information and how the D5000 uses flash.

How can you determine just which flash will work best for your style of shooting? Will the pop-up flash be enough with its limitations in range, or do you need more power to reach out and light up more distant subjects? How does one rate the power output of a flash unit?

This chapter contains information that will help you make a good choice in flash units. First, we'll look at how to rate the power output of a flash by examining the guide number.

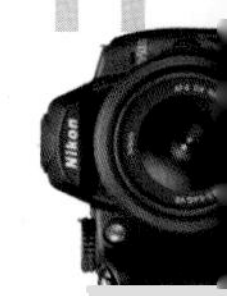

What Is a Guide Number?

The guide number (GN) for a flash unit measures how well your flash unit can light a subject at a specific ISO sensitivity and with a precise angle of view (wide angle vs. telephoto lens). To put it simply, a higher guide number means the flash is more powerful, all other things being equal.

Be careful when you are deciding on an external flash unit to use, whether it is a genuine Nikon Speedlight or an aftermarket unit. Simply comparing the GN is not enough. You must understand the settings the GN is based upon. Many flash units have zoom capability and will be able to light up subjects farther away when zoomed out. However, imagine buying a flash unit from a manufacturer who publishes the GN based on a longer zoom position and then comparing it to a different flash unit based on a shorter non-zoom position. The GN rating on the flash that is zoomed out would seem to be higher than the same unit when not zoomed out. However, unless you are comparing flash unit guide numbers with exactly the same settings, it is truly like comparing apples and oranges.

For instance, to get an exact comparison of guide numbers, you'd have to know the following:

- Distance from flash head to the subject
- Aperture f/number in use on the camera
- ISO sensitivity of your camera's image sensor
- Angle-of-view setting on the flash's zoom head
- Actual angle of view your lens provides (must match flash head)
- Temperature of ambient air

In reality, the camera has little to do with figuring the GN other than providing an aperture f/number and ISO sensitivity. So, how can you decide what GN is best without whipping out a scientific calculator? Just look at the flash unit advertisement to see what the GN is based on:

- Flash "zoom" angle of view setting (e.g., 18 mm or 105 mm, etc.)
- ISO sensitivity

If you see a unit advertised as GN 98, just realize that this is *not* enough information to make a decision. The number 98 in this instance *is* the GN, but it represents the *number of feet from flash head to subject* (98 feet). In countries that use the metric system, an equivalent GN is 18, and that represents the number of meters from flash head to subject (18 meters). That number by itself is simply incomplete. Don't buy a flash unit based solely on a GN like 98 or 100 or 111. Here's why.

Let's think about this for a second. Let's say I was a manufacturer who was desperate to sell you a flash unit. I might stretch things a little bit. I might say my "Super-Duper" flash unit has a GN of 98 (feet) or 18 (meters), hoping you'll not ask about the settings I used to figure the number. Here is a comparison of two flash units with a "comparable" guide number:

Super-Duper Flash Unit GN Information

- GN 98 (18)
- 80 mm zoom-head setting
- ISO 200 sensitivity

Nikon SB-400 Flash Unit GN Information (real values)

- GN of 98 (18)
- 35 mm zoom-head setting
- ISO 100 sensitivity

Both of these flash units have the same GN listed. Which is really more powerful? The Nikon SB-400 will literally blow away the Super-Duper unit. Yet the Super-Duper manufacturer lists the same GN! The Super-Duper unit must have its zoom head set to 80 mm, a much narrower beam, and have twice the camera ISO sensitivity to equal the Nikon SB-400 unit. Mr. Super-Duper is hoping you'll not check the fine print at the bottom of the advertisement so you'll think that his much less powerful unit equals the Nikon SB-400. Surprisingly, there are flash unit manufacturers who will do exactly what I am describing.

What can you learn from this? The actual GN itself is not enough to make a decision on which flash unit to use. You must know what the GN is based upon in order to make an informed decision.

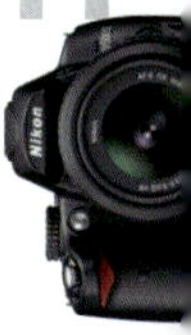

Take your time when buying a flash unit. You're safe in sticking with Nikon's Speedlights because the ratings are well known and they're designed to support all the features of your D5000. There are excellent "aftermarket" flash units available from manufacturers like Vivitar, Sigma, Sunpak, Metz, Braun/Leitz, and others. Examine the underlying settings and not just the guide number itself. What the GN is based on is as important as the actual number.

The GN of the D5000's pop-up Speedlight is 56 (feet) at ISO 200 or 17 (meters) at ISO 200. The SB-400 Speedlight is 98 (feet) at ISO 100 or 18 (meters) at ISO 100.

Technical Information

For the technically inclined among us, the GN is based on a specific formula: GN = distance × f/number. It is based on the inverse-square law, which states that doubling the GN requires four times more flash power. So, a flash with a GN of 100 is four times more powerful than a flash with a GN of 50. The guide number represents an exposure constant for a flash unit. For example, a GN of 80 feet at ISO 100 means that a subject 20 feet away can be completely illuminated with an aperture of f/4 (80 = 20 × 4) using a sensitivity of ISO 100. For the same guide number and an aperture of f/8, the light source should be 10 feet from the subject (80 = 10 × 8). Fortunately, your camera and flash combination are capable of figuring the correct values for you when you use TTL mode.

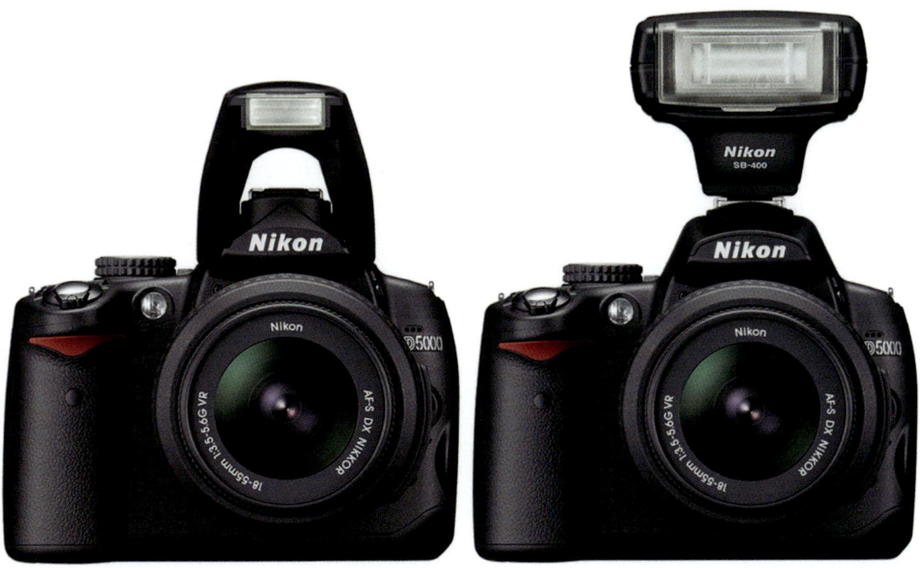

Figure 1 – Pop-up flash unit and the Nikon SB-400

Using the D5000's Flash Settings

(User's Manual pages 71–73)

The Nikon D5000 has a total of 11 different flash modes:

- Fill flash (front-curtain sync)
- Rear-curtain sync
- Slow sync
- Red-eye reduction
- Slow sync + red-eye reduction
- Rear curtain + slow sync
- Auto
- Auto + red-eye reduction
- Auto + slow sync
- Auto + slow sync + red-eye reduction
- Off

This is a bit complicated—but don't worry about it—we'll discuss how they work and list how you can get to each mode. All the different versions of flash are not available in all exposure or scene modes. Each mode has particular flash settings that work and others that don't. I'll list those in sequence after I discuss what each flash setting does. First, though, I need to cover some important information about the Nikon D5000's shutter and how it relates to using flash.

Shutter Curtain Information

Before we go into a deeper discussion about the flash modes, let me interject some related information that may help you understand flash better. To fully know what's happening when the flash fires, you must understand a little bit about the shutter curtains in your camera.

Your D5000 exposes the sensor to light for specific periods of time. This is your shutter speed. The exposure is handled by two moving objects called "curtains". The D5000 has two shutter curtains. One gets out of the way of the sensor to start the exposure and the other replaces it to stop the exposure. The first one is called the *front curtain* and the second one is known as the *rear curtain*. The "front" and "rear" are not important as indicators of position, in this context, as much as they indicators of which moves first and which moves second.

The flash must fire when the first, or front, curtain is fully open and before the second, or rear, curtain starts closing. The time between the front curtain opening and the rear curtain closing is the actual shutter speed.

The flash must fire sometime between the time the front curtain opens and the rear curtain closes. The whole sensor must be uncovered when the flash fires. If the shutter speed is too fast, the rear curtain will closely follow the front curtain and partially block the sensor when the flash fires. That's why the shutter speed is limited to a maximum of 1/200 of a second on the D5000. Faster than that and the sensor is always partially covered by one of the shutter curtains. If the flash fires while one of the curtains covers part of the sensor, then that part of the sensor would not get a proper exposure from the flash and there would be an underexposed black band in your image.

The whole point of all these flash modes is at what point during shutter curtain movement the flash fires and whether it's the main source of light or some ambient light is mixed in. Keep this information in mind as we discuss the flash modes.

Understanding the Flash Modes

Here is a list of the flash modes mentioned previously, along with what each does:

1. **Fill flash (front-curtain sync)** – Available only in *Exposure modes* P, S, A, M and *food scene* mode (see *figure 2A*). In front-curtain sync (fill flash), the camera tries its best to balance the light if you are using a lens that has a CPU in it. Older non-CPU lenses cause the camera to ignore the ambient light completely and only the flash is used to expose the subject. With a CPU lens, like a Nikkor AF-S G or D lens, it holds ambient light and light from the flash equally and works to make the light look very natural. If you use this correctly outdoors, it will be hard to tell that you were using flash, except for the catch light in your subject's eyes and the lack of damaging shadows. The flash simply "fills" in some extra light without overpowering the ambient light. In a situation where there is very little ambient light, the camera will use only the flash to get a correct exposure. It balances with ambient light only if there is enough ambient light to balance with in the first place. Pretty smart little camera, I say! There is a side effect to using this mode with slow shutter speeds. Fill flash simply causes the flash to fire as soon as the front shutter curtain is out of the way and before the rear shutter curtain starts closing. If there is some ambient light and the shutter speed is long—like 1/2 second—and the subject is moving, you'll see a well-exposed subject with a blurry trail in front of it. The flash correctly exposes the subject as soon as the front curtain gets out of the way, but the ambient light continues exposing the subject before the rear curtain closes, and since it is moving, you may see a ghostlike blur *before* or *in front of* the well-exposed moving subject in the picture. This can be seen at shutter speeds as fast as 1/60 of a second if ambient light is strong enough and the subject is moving.
2. **Rear-curtain sync** – Available only in *Exposure modes* S and M (see *figure 2B*). This is the reverse of front-curtain sync. The flash waits to fire just before

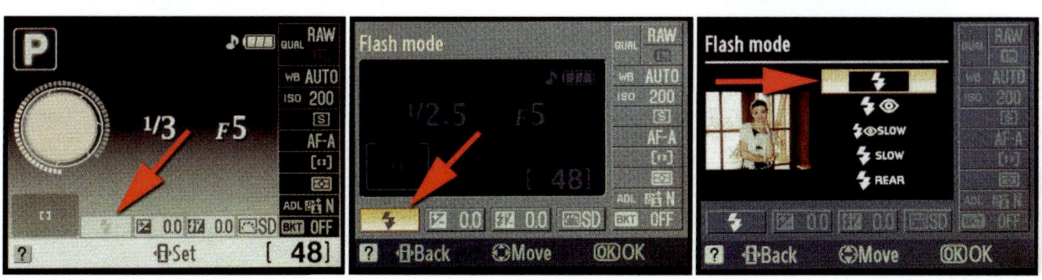

Figure 2A – Selecting fill flash (front-curtain sync)

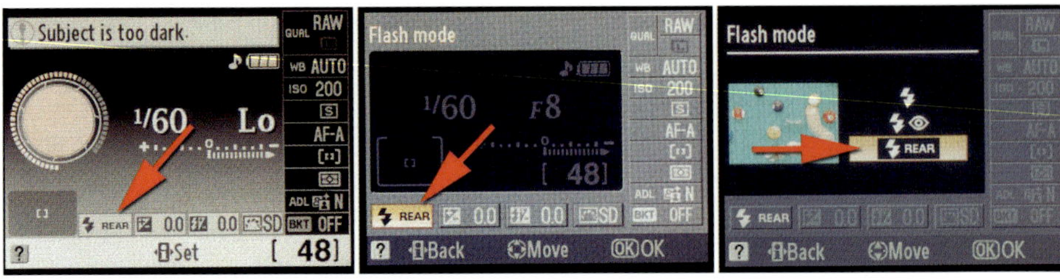

Figure 2B – Selecting rear-curtain sync

the rear curtain starts to close. The entire shutter speed time is just ending when the flash fires. This causes a ghosting effect for moving subjects in higher ambient light with slow shutter speeds. You press the shutter, the front curtain opens, ambient light starts hitting the sensor, and the subject starts being recorded. As the shutter is about to close, the flash fires, exposing the subject at its current position. The subject was fully exposed by the flash at the end of the shutter speed time, so the ambient light had time to register the subject before the flash fired, thereby making a blurred ghost *behind* or *after* the well-exposed subject.

3. **Slow sync** – Available only in *Exposure modes* P and A (see *figure 2C*). The flash unit lets the camera use ambient light to make a good exposure, then fires the flash to add some extra light, rounding out the shadows or better exposing a foreground subject. Use this mode in people shots outdoors or where you want ambient light to provide the primary exposure and the flash to provide more exposure in one area. This is

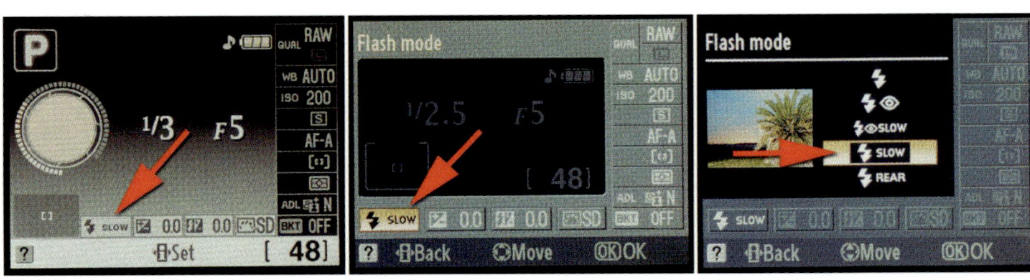

Figure 2C – Selecting slow sync

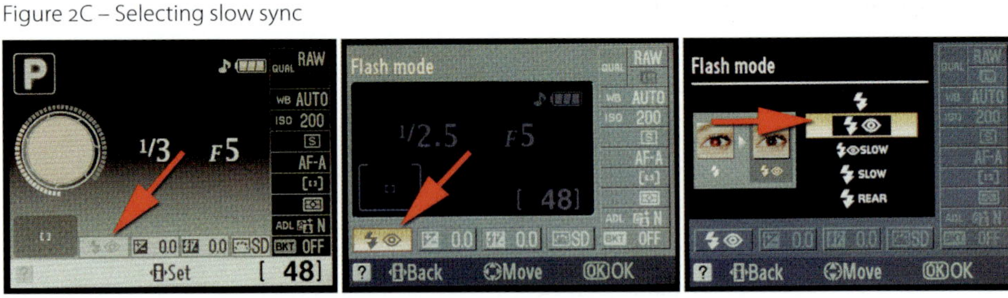

Figure 2D – Selecting red-eye reduction

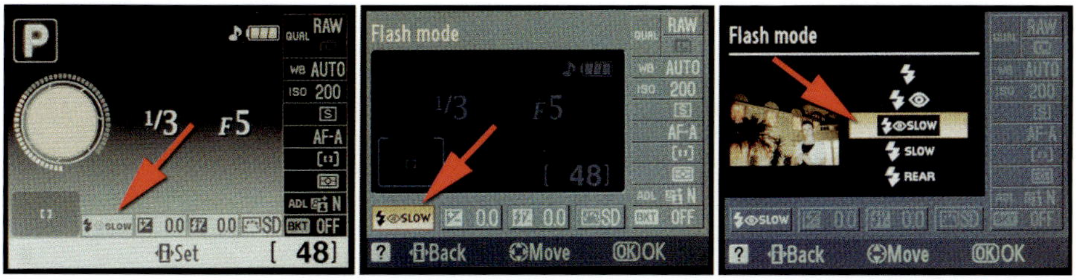

Figure 2E – Selecting slow sync + red-eye reduction

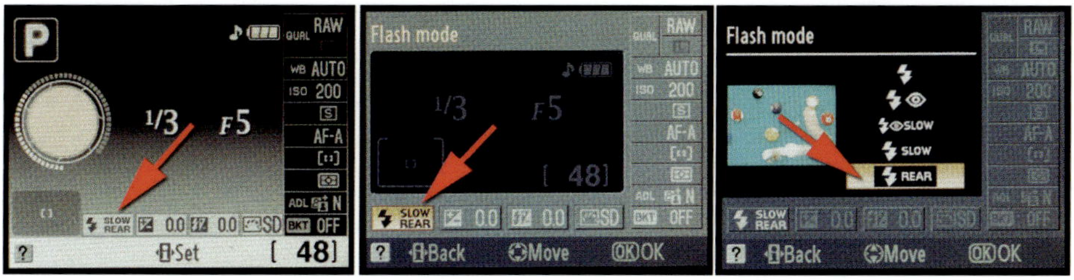

Figure 2F – Selecting rear-curtain + slow sync

closely related to fill flash, except that the ambient light is more important to the camera than the light from the flash. Be careful when using this mode indoors since it will expose for ambient light and only assist with some flash light. You can get some terrible ghosting and blurred handheld shots when using slow sync indoors. Ambient light rules in this mode!

4. **Red-eye reduction** – Available only in *Exposure modes* P, S, A, and M (see *figure 2D*). This is not really a flash mode. It simply means that the focus assist light shines brightly in the face of your subject before the flash fires using fill flash mode. It is hoped that the bright focus assist light will cause your subject's pupils to close somewhat and reduce the red-eye effect. It acts like you are using fill flash (front-curtain sync) mode otherwise.
5. **Slow sync + red-eye reduction** – Available only in *Exposure modes* P, S, A, and M (see *figure 2E*). This works the same way as slow sync except that the focus assist light shines before the flash fires. This let's you take pictures with an emphasis on ambient light while preventing the extra flash exposure from causing red-eye.
6. **Rear-curtain + slow sync** – Available only in *Exposure modes* P and A (see *figure 2F*). This is a combination of modes 2 and 4 in this mode list. Please refer to those list items for detail. This mode is good to use for ambient light exposures where you still need a bit of flash to expose a close-up subject. The icon for this mode looks like a lightning bolt and the word *Slow*. However, the information screen will display *Slow* and *Rear* when this mode is selected (see *figure 2F*).

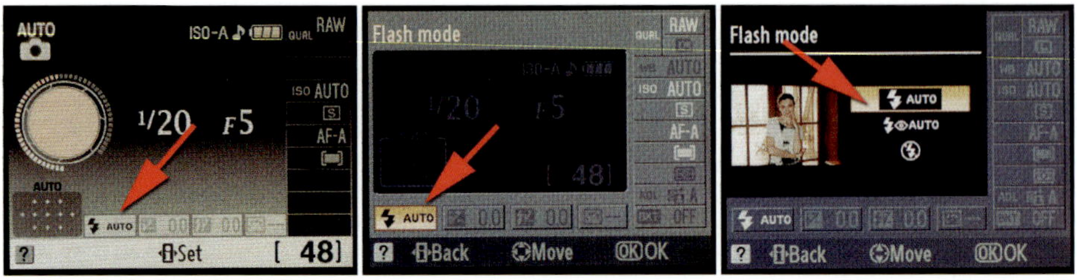

Figure 2G – Selecting auto

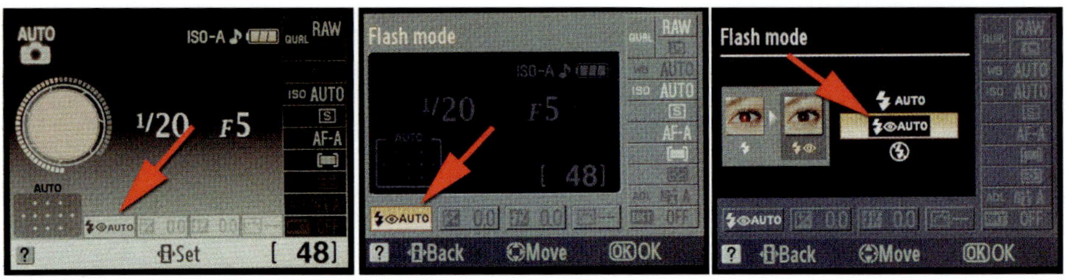

Figure 2H – Selecting auto + red-eye reduction

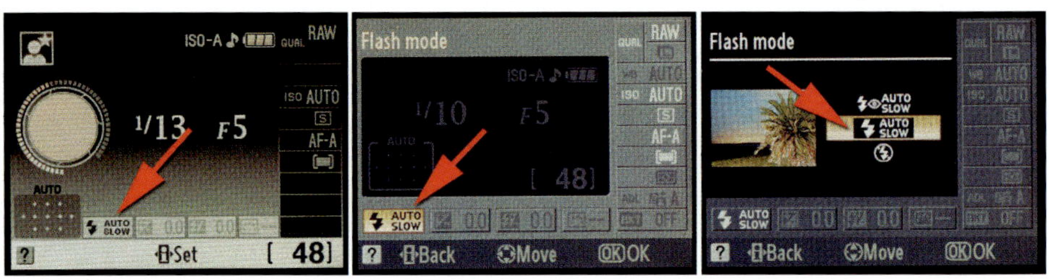

Figure 2I – Selecting auto + slow sync

7. ***Auto*** – Available only in SCENE modes AUTO, *portrait*, *child*, *close-up*, *party/indoor*, and *pet* (see *figure 2G*). This mode simply lets the camera decide when you need to use flash instead of you pressing the flash button. Otherwise, it uses fill flash mode to make the exposure.
8. ***Auto + red-eye reduction*** –Available only in SCENE modes AUTO, *portrait*, *child*, *close-up*, *party/indoor*, and *pet* (see *figure 2H*). This mode simply lets the camera decide when you need to use flash instead of you pressing the flash button. It also shines the focus assist light into your subject's eyes to reduce red-eye. Otherwise, it uses fill flash mode to make the exposure.
9. ***Auto + Slow sync*** – Available only in *night portrait* SCENE mode (see *figure 2I*). This mode lets your camera decide when the light is low enough that it needs to use some flash to light a close-up subject while a night portrait is being made. Otherwise, it uses slow sync to get background details exposed by ambient light (see mode list items 3 and 7).
10. ***Auto + slow sync + red-eye reduction*** – Available only in *night portrait* SCENE mode (see *figure 2J*). This mode lets your camera decide when the light is

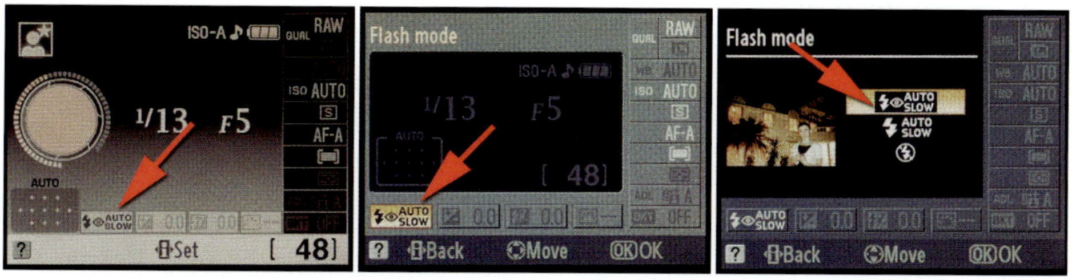

Figure 2J – Selecting auto + slow sync + red-eye reduction

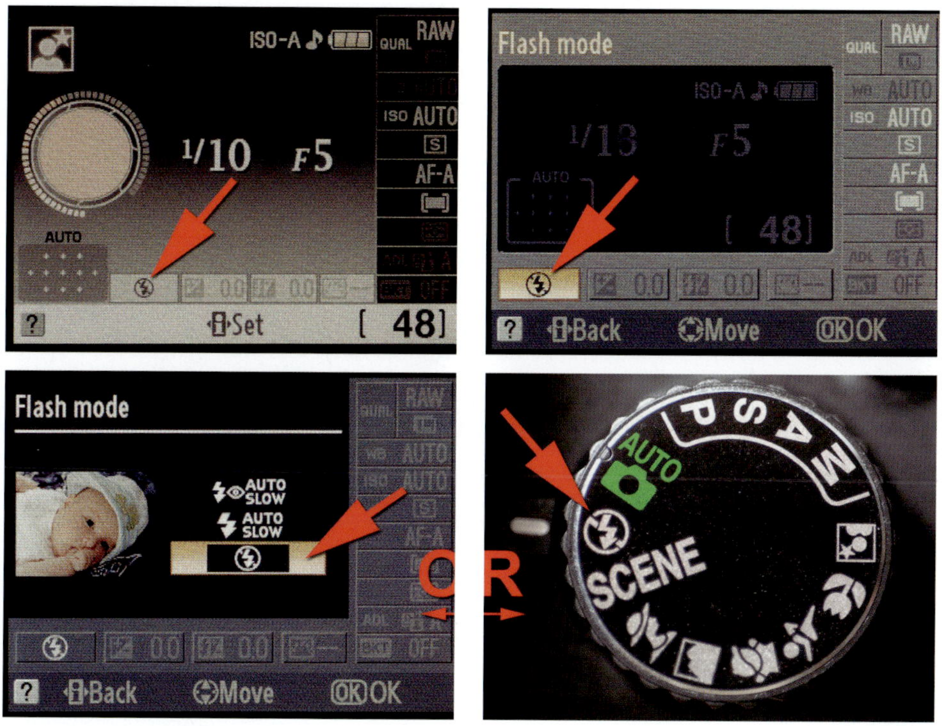

Figure 2K – Selecting flash off

low enough that it needs to use some flash to light a close-up subject while a night portrait is being made. It also shines the focus assist light into your subject's eyes to reduce red-eye. Otherwise, it uses slow sync to get background details exposed by ambient light (see mode list items 3, 4, and 7).

11. ***Off*** – Available only in SCENE modes AUTO, *portrait, child, close-up, party/indoor, pet*, and *night portrait* (see *figure 2K*). For this mode, you turn the flash off by using the *Information edit* screen. You can also use the off selection on the mode dial to turn the flash off completely (see where the red arrow is pointing in the lower-right image in *figure 2K*).

Primarily, you should select the exposure or SCENE mode in which you plan to take pictures and only then select a flash mode. It is hard to keep up with what's actually available at which time. After choosing the exposure or scene mode, check the *Information edit* screen to see what flash modes are available.

Recommendation

I mostly use the fill flash and slow sync flash modes. My normal flash is fill flash, and the slow sync is what I use when I want ambient to rule. In a sense, I tend to use slow sync as a way to add fill flash instead of using the fill flash (front-curtain sync) mode. I think calling the front-curtain sync mode by the name *fill flash* is not a great idea, but it used to be called balanced fill flash mode, so I suspect that's where *fill flash* comes from.

Now, let's look at a very powerful flash method you might want to experiment with called Nikon Creative Lighting System, or CLS for short. This is a professional lighting system that your D5000 can use.

What Is the Nikon Creative Lighting System (CLS)?

CLS is an advanced wireless lighting technology that allows you to use your imagination in designing "creative" lighting arrangements. No wires are used, and the remote flash units are controlled by a central "commander." You can use the commander mode built into a hot-shoe-mounted commander device such as the SB-800 and SB-900 Speedlights or the dedicated SU-800 Commander Unit.

You can easily experiment with setups and flash output. There is no need to figure complex lighting ratios when you can control your flash banks right from the commander unit and see the results immediately. CLS simplifies the use of multiple flash unit setups for portraiture, interiors, nature, or any situation where several Speedlights need to work in unison.

You can simply position the flash units where you'd like them to be and let CLS automatically figure the "correct" exposure, or you can change the lighting ratios

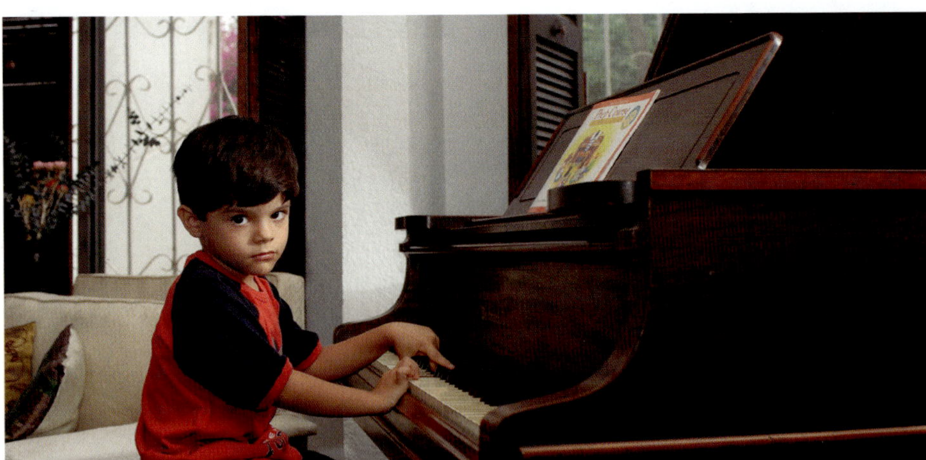

Sample image taken by J. Ramon Palacios of Nikonians.org using Nikon CLS

directly from the commander mode menu of the hot-shoe-mounted commander unit.

Nikon's Creative Lighting System is world class in power and not too difficult to use. The Nikon D5000, a commander unit, and extra Speedlight flashes are all you need to create a simple CLS setup.

How Does the D5000 Fit into the CLS Scheme?

The Nikon D5000 camera *requires* the separate purchase of a hot-shoe-mounted "commander unit" in order to control a CLS layout. *Figure* 3 shows the most powerful wireless infrared commander unit for the D5000, the SU-800.

You can use the SU-800 commander unit, or an SB-800 or SB-900 Speedlight flash in commander mode, to control up to several banks of an unlimited number of external Nikon Speedlight flash units. With the SU-800 commander unit, you can control up to three banks of flashes. With the SB-800 or SB-900 flash units, you can control up to two banks of flashes.

Nikon makes the powerful SB-900 and SB-800 flash units, along with its slightly less-powerful SB-600 brother, and several other smaller Speedlight units, such as the SB-400 or SB-R200. Only the SB-400 cannot be used in the CLS layout. It is a stand-alone, low-cost flash for personal use only.

The Nikon D5000 is happy to let you arrange professional lighting setups using these relatively inexpensive and

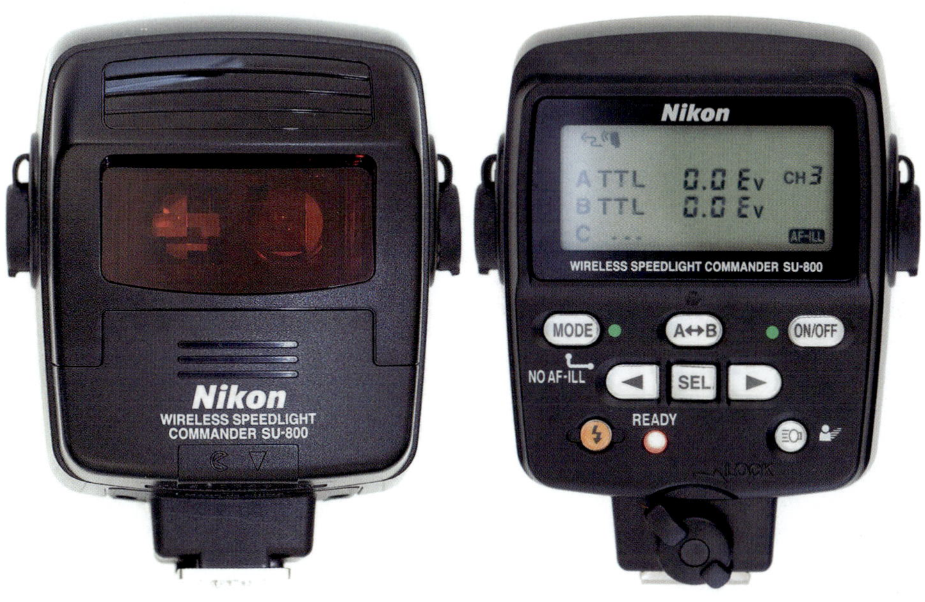

Figure 3 – SU-800 wireless Speedlight commander unit

very portable Speedlights as commanders and slaves in the Creative Lighting System. How CLS works is beyond the scope of this book, but I wanted to give you a preview of a powerful Nikon lighting system that you can use to make a small studio in your home. Many of us use the D5000 to create images for sale on stock image websites. You might want to do the same!

Selecting a Nikon Speedlight Flash Unit

Nikon makes several Speedlight units that work very well with the Nikon D5000. I personally have used the SB-400, SB-600, SB-800, and SB-900 units with the D5000. There are also the R1C1 flash units (SB-R200), which are designed to be used in small groups, such as for a ring-light arrangement.

SB-900 – Nikon's Flagship Flash and Commander Unit

I really enjoy using the Nikon SB-900 Speedlight unit (see *figure 4*). It's very powerful and easy to use in the CLS arrangement because it has external controls for setting remote mode. It can also be used as a CLS commander when needed.

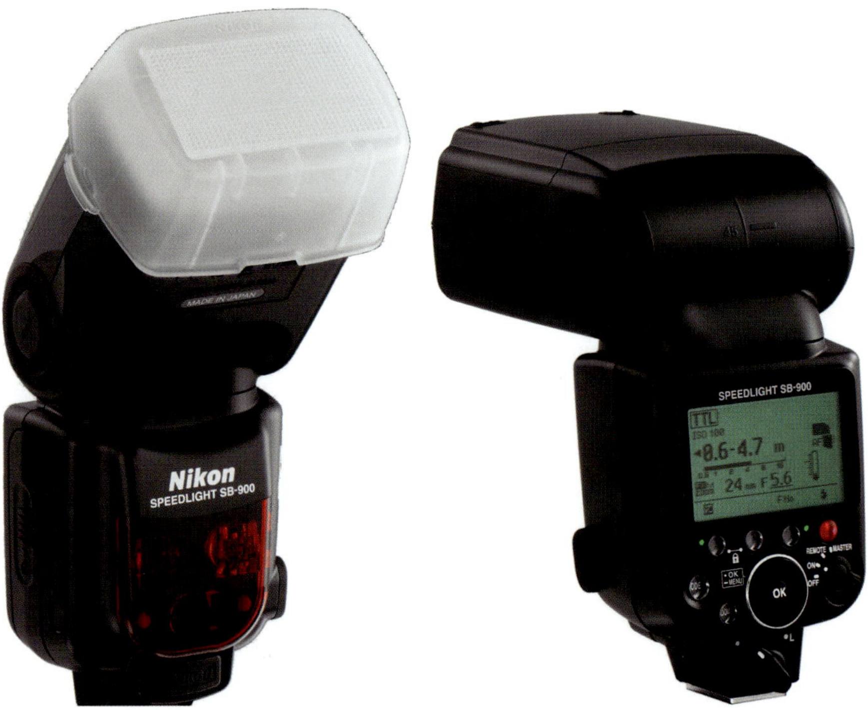

Figure 4 – SB-900 Speedlight

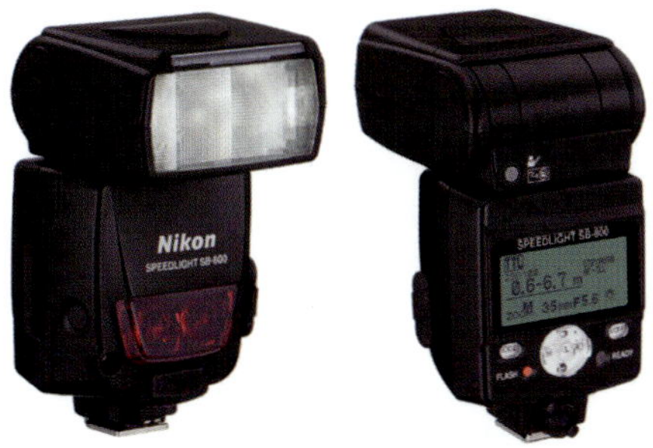

Figure 5 – SB-800 Speedlight

SB-800 – Flash and Commander Unit

The SB-800 Speedlight unit (see *figure* 5) is close to the power of the SB-900 and has the ability to be a CLS commander too. The controls are less easy to use than the SB-900, but the cost is less for almost the same level of power. I've used these successfully for several years.

SB-600 – Flash and CLS Slave Unit

The Nikon SB-600 Speedlight unit is the low-cost flash for users on a budget (see *figure* 6). It's about one stop less powerful than the SB-800 unit and costs considerably less. Buying several of these won't set you back much and will allow you to set up a great CLS system with your D5000 if you purchase the SU-800, SB-800, or SB-900 to use as a commander unit. The SB-600 can only work as a slave in a CLS layout.

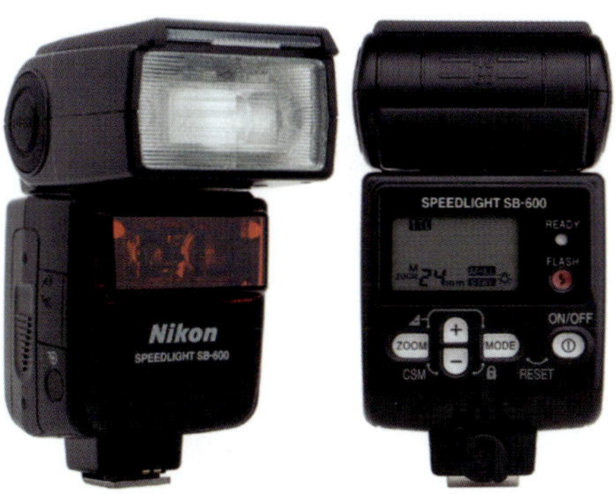

Figure 6 – SB-600 Speedlight

If you are just getting started in CLS, these might be your best investments for your flash banks.

SB-R200 – CLS Slave Unit

Then there are the SB-R200 Speedlight units (see *figure* 7). These are primarily designed to use in special arrangements on brackets that Nikon created for them. You'll see these Speedlights in use if you watch many crime dramas on TV since the investigators often use them for close-up flashes of crime scene evidence. They are also just CLS slave units with no commander capability.

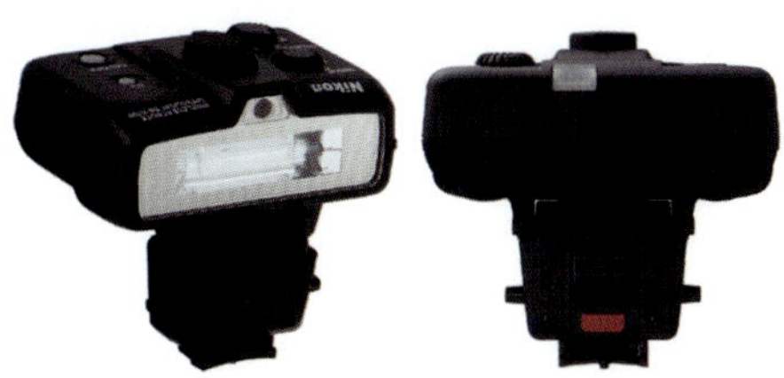

Figure 7 – SB-R200 Speedlight

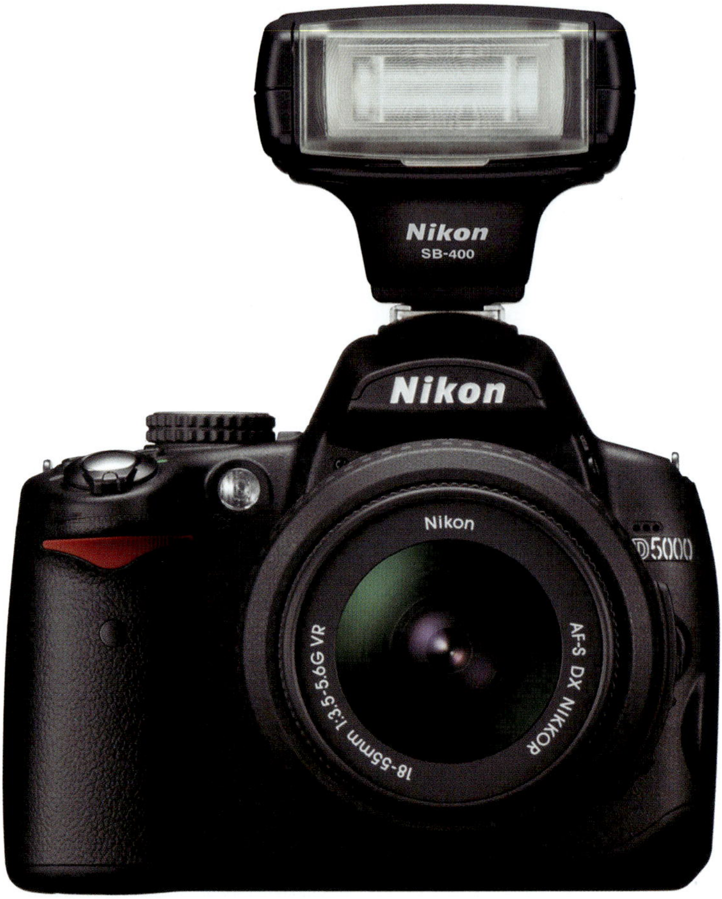

Figure 8 – SB-400 Speedlight in the D5000's hot shoe

SB-400 – Personal Flash Unit (Not CLS Compatible)

Finally, there is the humble little SB-400 flash unit (see *figure 8*). It can be used only as a personal unit because it will not work with Nikon CLS. However, I always have one of these little low-cost units with me. They make a perfect companion to the D5000 for general flash shooting.

My Conclusions

Nikon has given D5000 users an amazing number of flash mode choices. You can do things with your camera that people only dreamed of a few years ago. Experiment with these flash modes and see which ones you will use most often.

The Nikon D5000 and a separate commander unit gives you control over the world-class Nikon Creative Lighting System. It is the envy of many other camera brand manufacturers and users. Rocky Nook's Nikonians Press has an excellent book dedicated to this subject. Check Amazon.com and book stores for the title (see *figure 9*).

The book is called *The Nikon Creative Lighting System: Using the SB-600, SB-800, SB-900, and R1C1 Flashes*, and it was written by fellow Nikonian Mike Hagen. Mike's book is an excellent resource for increasing your knowledge of the Nikon CLS system. My book covers CLS only in relation to the Nikon D5000 camera. Mike's book goes into great detail on using Nikon cameras to control all the major flash units that Nikon currently makes. With these two books, and some practice, you can become a Nikon Creative Lighting System expert!

I also suggest that you find a good book on lighting techniques and study it well. You'll have to learn how to control shadows and reflections. Plus, you'll have to understand something about lighting ratios so that you can recognize a good image when you see one.

Buy a couple of light stands and some cheap white flash umbrellas and set up some portrait sessions of your family, or even some product shots. With the Nikon D5000 and even one extra Speedlight, you can create some very impressive images with much less work than ever before.

The really nice thing is that the Nikon Creative Lighting System, executed by your Nikon D5000 and a commander unit along with external Speedlight flashes, will allow you to shoot without worrying about detailed exposure issues. Instead, you can concentrate on creating a great-looking image.

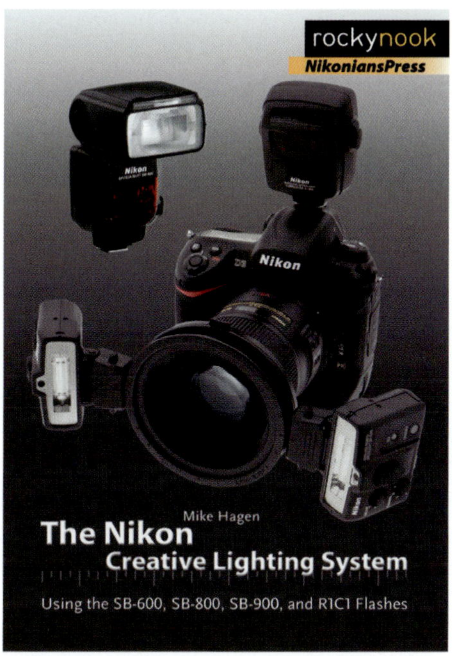

Figure 9 – *The Nikon Creative Lighting System* by Mike Hagen

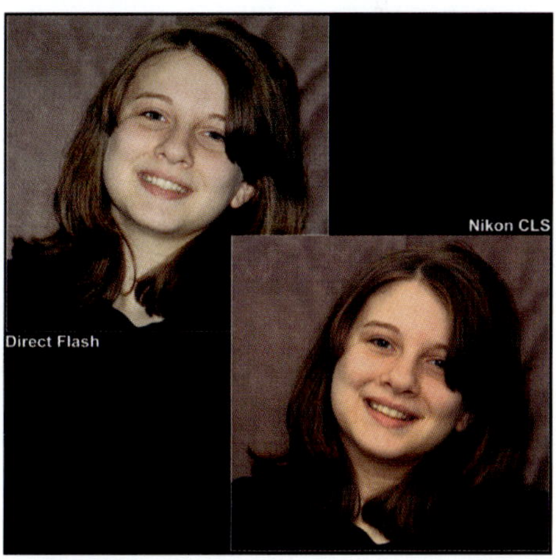

Figure 10 – Single Flash Nikon CLS Compared to Direct Flash

12

D-Movie Mode: Video on Demand

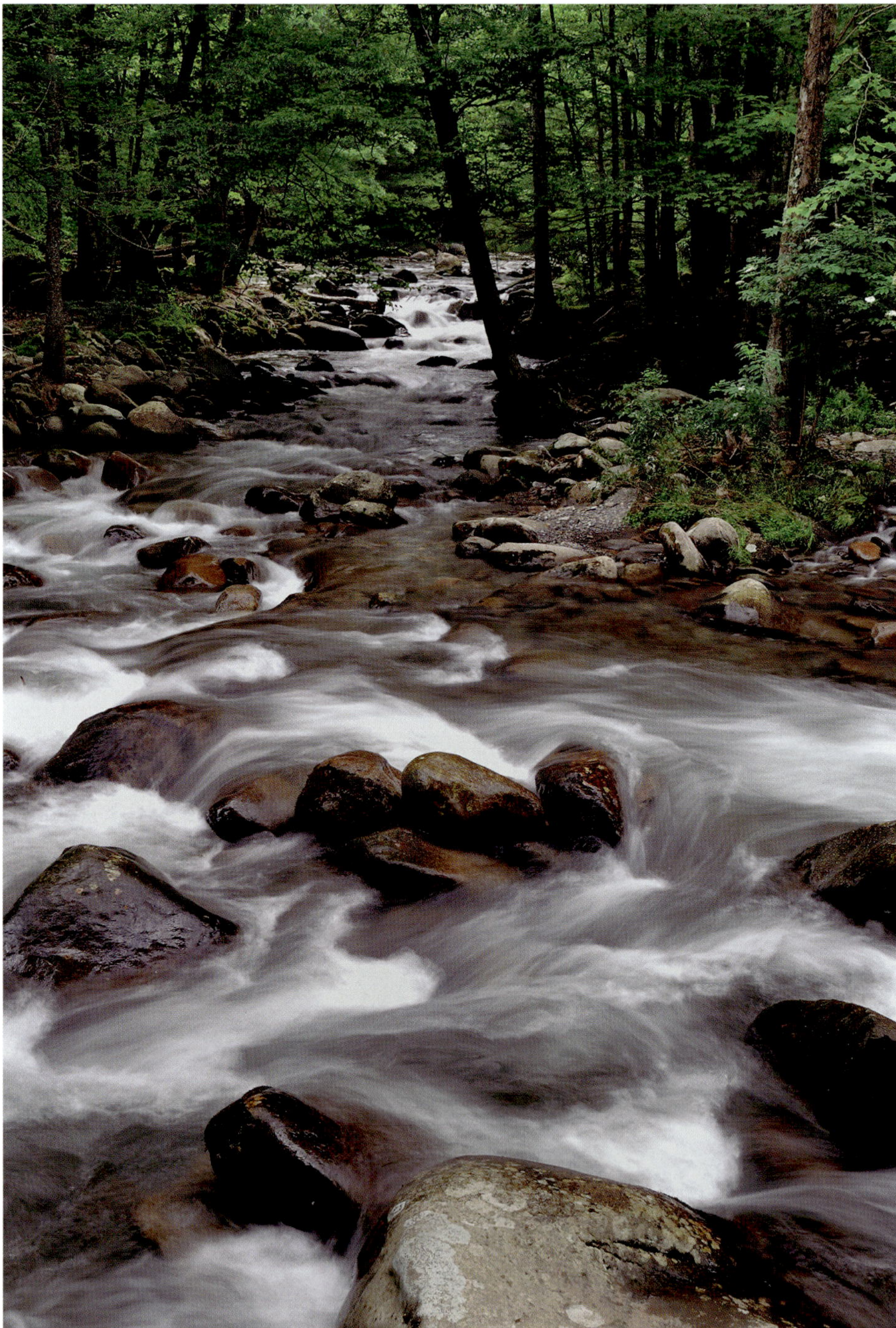

I went to the Great Smoky Mountains in Tennessee to test my new D5000's capabilities. A trip to the "Smokies" is always refreshing and provides an opportunity to shoot a variety of picture styles.

My trip to the mountains was different than other times because I had an added dimension to my photography—video capture. I was shooting in the Tremont and Greenbrier areas of the Smokies where there are many waterfalls and streams. After I shot several excellent still image scenics, I turned on the D-Movie mode in the High-definition (HD) setting and captured some 3-minute segments of the Little Pigeon River flowing down from the ancient mountains.

It was a simple matter of walking upstream, searching for some scenic spots, and making a short movie of each place. Later, at home, it was time to look at my still images and watch my videos. I turned the sound up on my computer and eagerly began viewing the show. The rushing sound of a river filled the room. It was simply marvelous. I've always enjoyed photography and bringing home the pictures, but this was different. I felt more like I was bringing home a piece of the mountains when I saw the HD video and heard the sound. It was almost like being there. This winter, I'll be sitting at my computer watching all my D-Movies, waiting for the spring thaw to start all over again.

I've been investigating various movie-editing software for my own use. At the end of this chapter, I list some of my favorites. I am looking forward to making some nicely edited videos of the mountains, with music. Maybe I'll post them on YouTube and become world famous!

Have you used your camera's D-Movie mode yet? The D5000 can produce

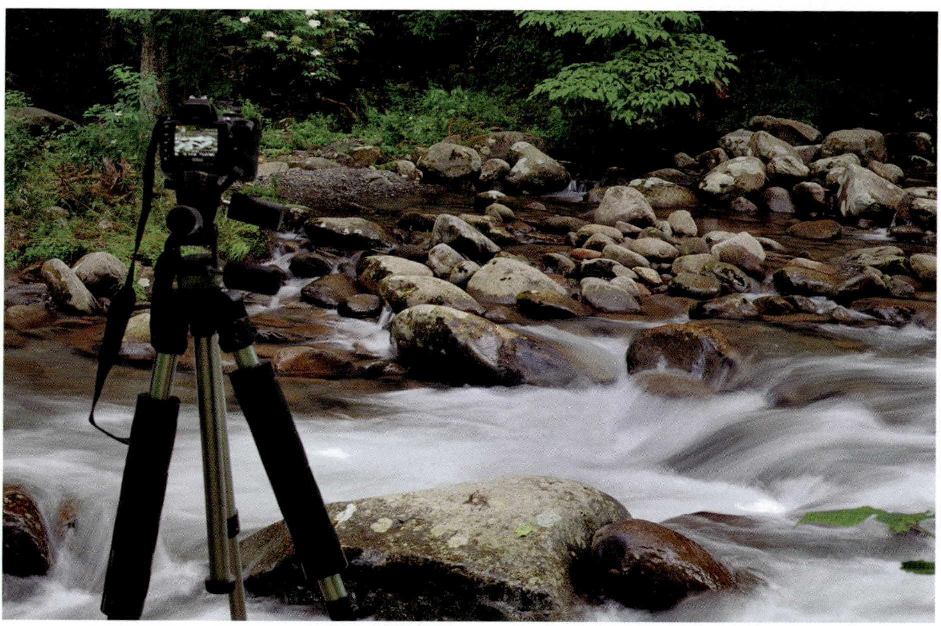

Videoing in Greenbrier, in the Great Smoky Mountains

excellent videos when the camera is handled properly. Let's see how you might use D-Movie mode to gain extra enjoyment from your chosen photography subjects.

Basic Video Standards Information

I don't want to get too deep into theory in this chapter, because most people are not really interested in reading a technical manual. However, since the Nikon D5000 is also capable of video camera functions, it's beneficial to understand some basics.

High-Definition (HD) Video

Before shooting your first D-Movie, you'll need to configure the camera for the correct video frame size; that is, the number of pixels that are in each frame. We'll look into the actual configuration in a later section. For now, let's just discuss some basics.

Here are the available D-Movie frame sizes in your D5000 (User's Manual page 51):

- *1280x720* pixels (720p - 16:9 format HD) – 24 fps
- *640x424* pixels (3:2 format SD) – 24 fps (default)
- *320x216* pixels (3:2 format SD) – 24 fps

A video frame is much smaller pixelwise than a normal still image frame. While your D5000 can create beautiful 12-megapixel still images, its best high-definition video image is just below 1 megapixel, at 921,600 pixels, or 0.9 megapixels.

Whoa! How can less than 1 megapixel be considered high-definition (HD)? Simply because it matches one of the broadcast resolutions high-definition television (HDTV). In the good old days of standard-definition television (SDTV) that we all grew up watching, there was even less resolution. Would you believe that the old TV you have stored in the garage displays only 345,600 pixels, or 0.3 megapixels?

I've been talking about the number of megapixels, but that's not normally how HD devices are rated. Instead of the number of pixels, most HD information refers to the number of "lines" of resolution. There are several HD standards for lines of resolution. The standards that are probably the most used are 720p, 1080i, and 1080p. The *p* and *i* after the numbers refer to *progressive* and *interlaced*. I'll talk about what that means in the next section.

The D5000's best D-Movie mode captures in 720p, which is a broadcast-quality HDTV standard. The 720 simply means that your camera captures and displays HD images with 720 lines of vertical resolution. Each of those lines can be 1280 pixels long, which allows the D5000 to match the 16:9 aspect ratio expected in HDTV. An older SDTV usually has an aspect ratio of 4:3, which is taller and narrower than the HDTV 16:9 aspect ratio.

If you're interested in more extensive information on this topic, there's a huge amount of technical detail available on the Internet. We'll cover the high points in this chapter.

Progressive vs. Interlaced

What's the difference between progressive and interlaced? Technically speaking, *progressive* video output displays the video frame starting with the top line and then draws the other lines until the entire frame is shown. In 720p mode, the D5000 displays 720 lines progressively from top to bottom of what the imaging sensor captured (lines 1,2,3,4...720, etc.).

Interlaced displays every even line from top to bottom, then comes back to the top and displays every odd line (lines 2,4,6,8...720, then 1,3,5,7...719, etc.).

Usually, progressive output provides a better-quality image with less "flicker" and a more cinematic look. I'm sure that's why Nikon chose to make our cameras shoot progressive video.

Now, let's set up the camera and make some D-Movies!

Camera Setup for Making D-Movies

We discussed this subject briefly in chapter 1, "Nikon D5000 Initial Configuration." We'll now go into much more detail. Later in this chapter, we'll also examine some D-Movie mode limitations about which you should be aware.

First, let's take a look at the external camera controls we'll be using to change settings and use the D-Movie system (see figure 1). The list that follows and the screen numbers in the figure match for easy reference:

Here are the external camera controls:

- Playback and MENU buttons
- Live view (Lv) button
- OK button and Multi Selector
- Thumbnail/playback zoom out button
- Playback zoom in button
- Command dial

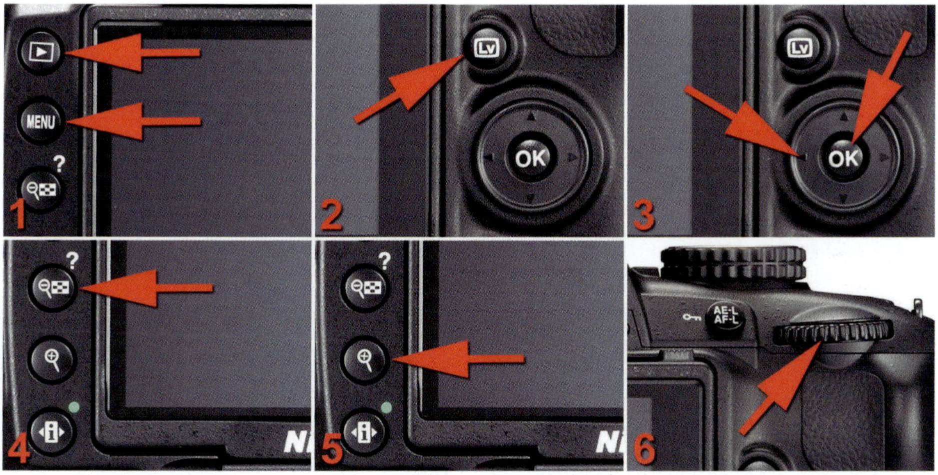

Figure 1 – External camera controls used for D-Movies

Now, let's get right into working with the D-Movie mode. Before you make your movie, you need to set three separate things on your D5000.

- *Setup Menu – Video mode* – Encoding method (*NTSC* or *PAL*)
- *Shooting Menu – Movie settings – Quality*
- *Shooting Menu – Movie settings – Sound*

Which Video Encoding Method?

(User's Manual page 168)

The D5000 allows you to record using either the NTSC or PAL encoding method. These are two different video encoding systems. NTSC is the standard in North America, Japan, some of South America, and a few other areas. PAL is the standard in most of Europe, Asia, and Australia. There is very little quality difference between the two.

Figure 1A shows the *Setup Menu* screens used to select the encoding mode.

Here are the steps used to set the encoding mode:

1. Press the MENU button and scroll to the *Setup Menu* (wrench icon).
2. Select *Video mode*, and then scroll to the right.
3. Select *NTSC* or *PAL* from the menu. You'll need to refer to the manual of your display device to determine what video encoding type it uses.
4. Press the OK button to set the mode and return to the *Setup Menu*.

Recommendation

If you live in the United States, you'll probably use NTSC. If you live in Europe, you'll probably use PAL. Check your display device manuals and guides.

Selecting a D-Movie Video Quality

(User's Manual page 51)

There are three basic D-Movie *Quality* settings available in the D5000. The first, 1280x720, is for when you want to shoot high-definition video for display on HD devices. The other two settings, 640x424 and 320x216, are standard-definition modes for display on SD devices.

The screens used to select the movie *Quality* settings are shown in *figure 2*.

As mentioned in the previous section, there are three available D-Movie frame sizes in your D5000:

- *1280 x 720* pixels (720p - 16:9 format HD) – 24 fps

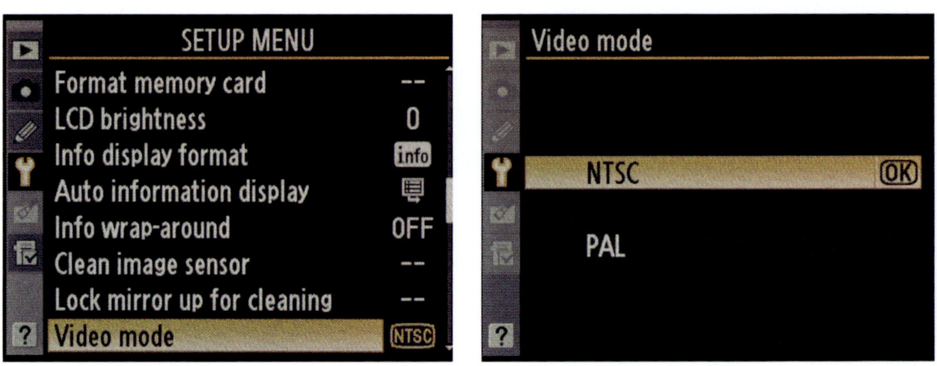

Figure 1A – Video encoding mode

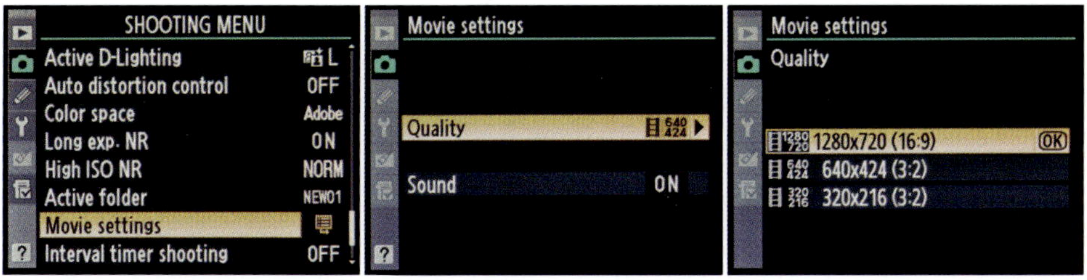

Figure 2 – D-Movie *Quality* settings

- *640 x 424* pixels (3:2 format SD) – 24 fps (default)
- *320 x 216* pixels (3:2 format SD) – 24 fps

To select one of the *Quality* settings, do the following:

1. Press the MENU button and scroll to the *Shooting Menu*.
2. Select *Movie settings*, and then scroll to the right.
3. Select *Quality*, and then scroll to the right.
4. Select one of the three available *Quality* settings.
5. Press the OK button to select a setting.

The *Quality* setting also changes the size of the resulting video movie file. It has been my experience that the D5000 uses the following amounts of storage memory when recording videos. These are approximations and will vary with the subject matter's detail:

- ***1280 x 720:*** 585 MB for a 5-minute video, 1950 KB per second. Full-length movie fits on a DVD or CD (for storage and later copying to a computer).
- ***640 x 424:*** 248 MB for a 5-minute video, 992 MB for 20 minutes, 826KB per second. *Full-length movie can be stored on a DVD only*.
- ***320 x 216:*** 119 MB for a 5-minute video, 447 MB for 20 minutes, 398KB per second. Full-length movie fits on a DVD or CD for storage.

Remember, these values may vary *greatly* according to how complex the scene and how much motion is in the video. These are just base values I found by videoing a subject with medium complexity and little movement. Your storage experience will vary.

The D5000's factory default video mode is set to 640x424 pixels (3:2 aspect ratio), which is good for keeping the video file sizes down somewhat. However, it is not an HD mode. If you want to make even smaller videos, you can choose the 320x216 pixels (3:2 aspect ratio) mode. Each of these two SD modes allows you to shoot up to 20-minute video clips. That is a generally sufficient length for many uses.

The video clips are limited in length to 5 minutes for high-res 1280x720 (16:9 aspect ratio), and the video is of sufficient resolution to be displayed on an HD device, such as an HDTV.

The file format used by the D5000's video is the popular AVI format. This is played by virtually all computer movie players and is the default format for Microsoft Windows Media Player. AVI stands for Audio Video Interleave.

Note on Video Formats

The actual video frames recorded inside the AVI file are in OpenDML JPEG video, or Motion JPEG (M-JPEG) format.

A computer should display any of the video formats, as will a standard TV (SDTV). Any of the video modes, including the HD 1280x720, will play on your SDTV through the "included in the box" AV cable. The HD mode displays in the *wide-screen*, or *letterbox*, format with a black space at the top and bottom of the picture. Using an HDMI mini (type C) to HDMI standard (type A) cable, you can play full HD videos on an HDTV. This HDMI cable is not included with the camera. It's easily available online and in many electronics stores. There will be more about how to display video in a later section, including pictures of the cables.

Recommendation

I like to shoot longer videos, so I often use the 640x424 mode. It has enough resolution that I can display it on my computer monitor, and it easily works on a standard television (SD) for grandma and grandpa to see. If their TV doesn't have RCA jacks to plug in the AV cable, their VCR usually does. The 20-minute length of 640x424 is usually sufficient for what I am shooting and displays full screen on an SDTV. If I know I can get by with a 5-minute length, I may switch to HD mode (1280x720), especially if I am shooting a video of some spectacular place. HD video will display in wide-screen format on an SDTV directly from the camera.

CD Storage Recommendation

Since the segment length is limited to 5 minutes in the HD 1280x720 mode, the file size is not a big concern. It should fit on a standard CD. If you want to use 640x424 mode to send files to friends on a CD, just remember to limit your video length to about 12 minutes, 10 to be absolutely safe. A full-length 20-minute segment at 640x424 will *not* fit on a CD. A 20-minute segment in 320x216 mode *will* fit on a CD.

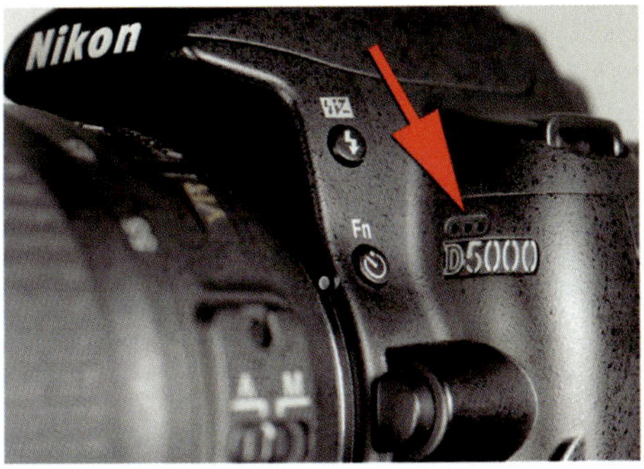

Figure 3 – Sound recording microphone

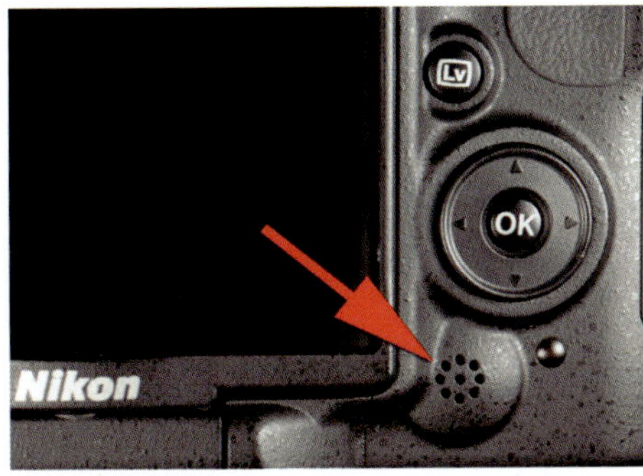

Figure 4 – Small speaker on camera handgrip

Dealing with Sound on D-Movies

Sound recording on the D5000 is accomplished with a little monaural (as opposed to stereo) microphone that is located just above the D5000 logo on the front of the camera. It looks like a three tiny holes in a line (see *figure 3*).

Be careful about accidentally covering the pickup microphone with a finger or you will have very muted sound. Also, be careful about letting wind blow directly on the microphone when recording. The wind might cause a rushing sound that interferes with the sound you are trying to record.

The sound is output during playback through a small speaker on the bottom rear of the camera just below the *OK* button and multi selector (see *figure 4*). You'll see nine small holes in a circle. This little speaker can output an amazing amount of volume. You can raise and lower the playback sound volume using the thumbnail/playback zoom out and playback zoom in buttons (see *figure 1* for button locations).

In order to record sound in sync with your video, you'll need to make sure *Sound* is enabled on the D5000, using the *Shooting Menu* screens shown in *figure 5* (User's Manual page 51).

You can select either *On* or *Off*. Here are the steps:

1. Press the MENU button and scroll to the *Shooting Menu*.
2. Select *Movie settings*, and then scroll to the right.
3. Select *Sound*, and then scroll to the right.
4. Select either *On* or *Off*.
5. Press the OK button.

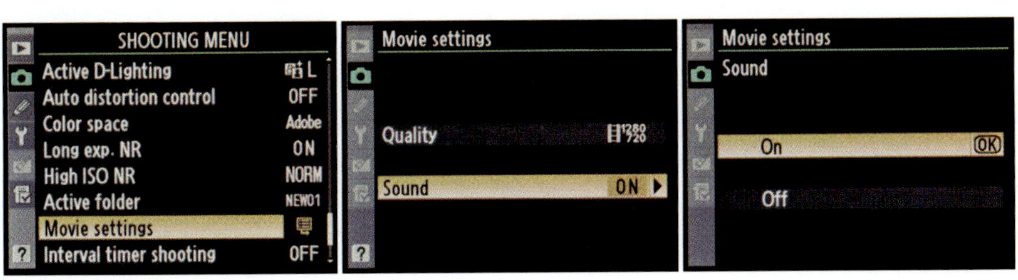

Figure 5 – D-Movie *Sound* setting

The D5000 only shoots mono (monaural) sound, and there are no external connectors to record in stereo. This is a limitation of a primarily still camera that shoots video. There's not a lot to say about the sound except that it is reasonably good and does the job well enough. If you are a sound fanatic, why not carry a quality stereo digital sound recorder with you. Record the video with the mono sound turned on, as a reference, and then replace the mono with your stereo sound recording in a computer video editing program (see later in this chapter for software suggestions).

Of course, if you are willing to go that far for quality, you probably have a high-end video camera with stereo sound already. The D5000 is simply a still camera that also captures video with sound. Use it to the best of its abilities.

Recording a Video with Your D5000

Now, let's look at the process of recording a video. It is rather simple! There are approximately five steps.

To start recording a video, simply follow these steps:

1. Turn the camera on, and remove the lens cap.
2. Press the Lv button on the D5000's back (*figure 6, image 1*).
3. Prefocus the camera on your subject by pressing the shutter release button halfway down until the little green square stops flashing (*figure 6, image 2*).
4. Press the OK button to start the video recording (*figure 6, image 3*).
5. When you are finished, press the OK button again to stop recording.

Amazingly that's all there is to it. You have a cool video camera built into your still camera. It's available with the press of two buttons: Lv and OK.

The actual recording of video is an automated process. Your camera does not give you much control over exposure. In a sense, the video system is like the auto exposure mode. What you see is what you get. The camera decides how to deal with changes in exposure, motion, and so on.

In most cases, unless you really want to try to control the camera, just shoot your video and enjoy what you captured. The camera will make a good exposure in most all circumstances.

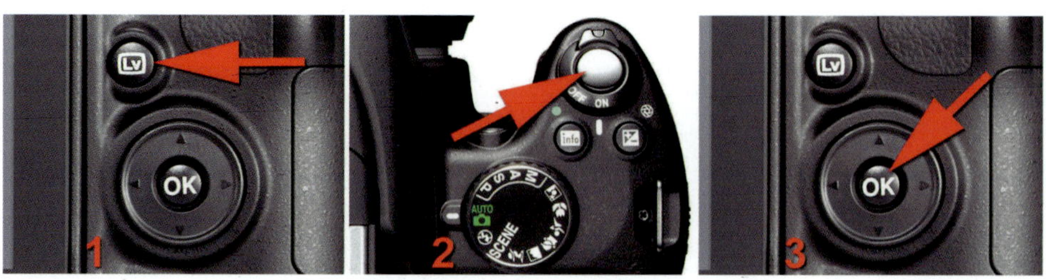

Figure 6 – D-Movie External Camera Controls

Dealing with Lack of Autofocus in D-Movie Mode

The autofocus (AF) system does not work once you press the OK button to start recording a video. You can consider this to be an aggravation or an asset, according to how you create video.

Primarily, be sure that you've prefocused on your subject before you start the video. If you zoom your lens or change to a closer or more distant subject, you'll probably need to refocus the lens.

For those of us who can remember a time before autofocus cameras, this is not a big deal. However, if you've always used autofocus, it might be a good idea to use Live View mode and learn where the focus ring is on your favorite lenses. In LV mode, don't use the shutter button to autofocus; set the lens' A/M switch to M and just do it yourself. It works just like taking a video.

Learn how it looks to see an out-of-focus (OOF) image. Learn how to bring the image into focus quickly—or slowly for special effects. Controlling the focus yourself may not be as convenient as using AF, but it gives you greater control over what you are videoing. When you combine manual focus with the information on aperture and depth of field control in the next section, you can create some cool cinematic effects, like deliberately starting the video on your subject with the lens completely out of focus and then turning the focus ring until your subject's face is in focus. It can be quite dramatic.

Or you can focus on one person in the foreground and then change the focus to another person in the background. Limited depth of field can be fun to experiment with, and it's not available in many standard video cameras. Some perceived limitations could be benefits, after all. When you find lemons, make lemonade!

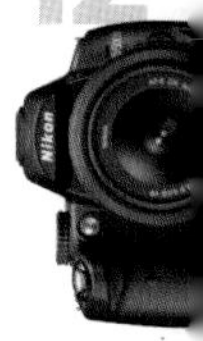

Controlling the Aperture and Exposure During Video Capture

This section is for people who love to experiment with the edges of what their camera is capable of doing and try to wring out as much control as possible. If you are content to just take nice videos, you may not need to read this section. The camera is perfectly capable of controlling itself during D-Movie creation. However, if you like manually controlling your camera in still image mode, you'll probably like this section.

You do have some control over the aperture, and the exposure too. It is not intuitive or well-documented, and it's a bit inflexible, but you do have a bit of control over the important depth of field (DOF) and exposure. (For a review of depth of field, see chapter 2 "Aperture and Shutter Speed").

Here is what I found through direct experimentation:

1. **How does exposure control work?** Once you have started taking a video, the aperture doesn't change. Nor have I seen any indication of a shutter speed change. The only way the shutter could change is by speeding up or slowing down how fast it captures a

video frame (scan rate), and since that is locked at 24 frames per second, the shutter speed is inflexible. How does the camera control the exposure? It appears that the camera simply varies the sensitivity of the complementary metal-oxide semiconductor CMOS image sensor to match the current need for light. You can prove this to yourself by videoing in a darker area and noticing how grainy the video looks. It is apparent that the ISO of the camera is being varied according to how much light the scene needs to expose correctly.

2. **How can I override the camera's choice of exposure settings?**
   You can control the exposure, overriding the camera, in two ways:
   a. By holding down the exposure compensation button and turning the rear main command dial. The camera will then adjust the exposure using your new settings. It won't over- or underexpose the video when you add or subtract exposure compensation. It just adjusts the ISO from the new base level that you provided. You can force the camera to use a higher or lower ISO as a base by several stops (up to 5). Turn the compensation to the overexposure side and the camera will lower the base ISO used and vice versa. By adding compensation to the plus side, you are forcing the D5000 to let in more light by overexposing, so it must lower the ISO sensitivity to compensate, keeping the exposure correct.
   b. By setting *Custom Setting f2* (*Assign* AE-L/AF-L button) to *AE lock* (Hold). Then when you want to keep the same exposure for a time, you simply press and lock the exposure. When the AE-L/AF-L button is pressed, the camera locks the exposure until you press it again. It acts like a toggle, turning *AE lock* on and off with each press of the button. If you don't want to set *Custom setting f2* to *AE lock* (Hold), you can leave it set to *AE lock* only instead. Then you must hold the AE-L/AF-L button in to lock the exposure, and it unlocks as soon as you release the button. What this auto exposure lock does is force the camera to use whatever exposure level (or ISO) it initially selected and not vary from it. The exposure is locked. This is useful for when you are recording in a room with ambient light in addition to some bright windows here and there. If you don't lock the exposure, the D5000 will see the bright window as you scan the room videoing and will adjust the exposure for the outside light instead of room light. Anyone sitting in front of or near the window will be underexposed. Locking the exposure allows you to record right on past a bright window without the camera making an exposure adjustment. You can then capture a good exposure of your subject sitting in front of the bright window.

3. **How can I control depth of field?** This is a very important section for those who really want to control DOF in their videos. The D5000 *will* allow you to set the aperture *before* you start your movie. (See chapter 2 to review DOF.) Here's how it works.

Set your camera's mode dial to A (aperture priority, see *figure 7*).

Once you have the camera set to aperture priority, you have some initial control. *Whatever aperture you set the camera to use will be the aperture the camera utilizes for the entire video recording.* Please understand the preceding sentence! You *can* control the aperture by choosing it before you start the video if you are using aperture priority exposure mode.

The aperture will not vary during the entire video clip, no matter how the light changes. The camera will keep right on using the ISO sensitivity of the sensor to control exposure, only it uses your chosen aperture the entire time. No matter how much you crank the command dial 'round and 'round, it will not vary the aperture once the video has begun. I tested this over and over by starting my video in dark places and then walking out into the light. I even went so far as to start the video in a dark closet and then shine an intense flashlight beam into the lens. The aperture blades never moved—even when I tried to move them with the command dial! (Even in auto exposure mode, it starts with a wide open aperture and never moves it.)

What does this mean for you? Do you want to shoot a dreamy, shallow-focused video, carefully isolating your subject and blurring the background? Set your mode dial to A, use a lens with a big aperture like f/1.4 to f/3.5, and select the wide open aperture *before* you start the video. Your entire video clip will be shot at the selected wide aperture, and depth of field will be minimized. If you want some depth of field, such as for a beautiful

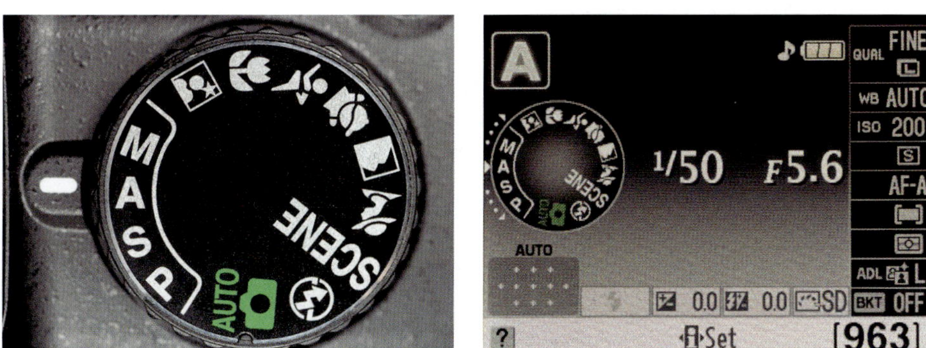

Figure 7 – Setting the D5000 to aperture priority mode

scenic waterfall or landscape video, just select an initial aperture of f/5.6 to f/22, according to how much ambient light is present. Now when you're shooting video, you can have the same deeper DOF benefits.

The fact that the D5000 has a nice large CMOS sensor compared to regular video cameras is a benefit to you. The larger the sensor, the less the DOF. With this new knowledge, and your "fast" lenses, you can now control the DOF in your videos in a way that you can with few other video camera types can.

You can also control certain aspects of the "look" of the video by using the various *Shooting Menu* Picture Controls, but that's about it. We'll discuss Picture Controls in the next section.

Using Picture Controls and Scene Modes

Another form of control you have over the "look" of your D-Movies is using the Nikon Picture Controls included with the camera or even your own custom Picture Controls. I'm not going to go into a great deal of information here on using or modifying Picture Controls because this subject is covered thoroughly in chapter 6.

However, once you've understood Picture Controls (and even modified a couple), you will realize that your videos will benefit from selecting different ones before you start recording.

For instance, let's say you are shooting a video on an overcast, low-contrast day and you want to add some "snap" to your movie. You can simply stop the movie, select the *Vivid* control, which will saturate the colors and darken the shadows, and then start shooting again.

Or you might be shooting on a very high-contrast sunny day and want to tone down the contrast a bit. Simply select the *Neutral* control, which will open up the shadows and extend the dynamic range of the sensor for a lower-contrast look.

Maybe you are shooting a video of a lovely colorful autumn scenic and want to maximize the colorful look. Simply select the *Landscape* control and your video will be optimized for beautiful scenics.

Figure 8 shows the menu screens you use to select and adjust picture controls (see chapter 6, and pages 106 to 113 in the User's Manual).

At the bottom of the list in the middle image in *figure 8*, you'll see a custom Picture Control that I created by modifying and saving the tonal curves of a Nikon Picture Control. It's called STANDARD-03, which is my unimaginative name for a modified *Standard* Nikon Picture Control.

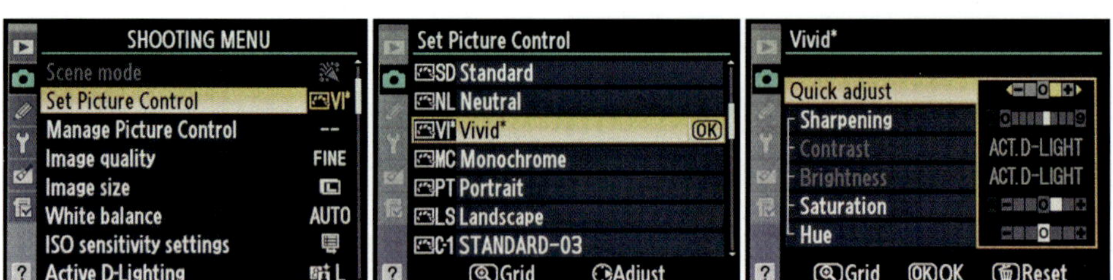

Figure 8 – Selecting a Picture Control

Here is a list of the available Nikon Picture Controls:

- *SD - Standard*
- *NL - Neutral*
- *VI - Vivid*
- *MC - Monochrome*
- *PT - Portrait*
- *LS - Landscape*

Here are the steps to select a Picture Control for your next video:

1. Press the MENU button and select the *Shooting Menu*.
2. Scroll to *Set Picture Control,* and then scroll to the right.
3. Select one of the Nikon Picture Controls from the menu. *Vivid* is selected in *figure 8*.
4. If you want to modify the control to have different sharpening, contrast, brightness, saturation, or hue, scroll to the right for the fine-tuning screen. (the screen on the right in *figure 8*), otherwise, just press the OK button and skip step 5.
5. Modify the control's settings and press the OK button to make the selected control active. The two-letter abbreviation for the control will show on the *Shooting Menu*. For example, in the image on the left in *figure 8*, you'll see *VI* for *Vivid* after *Set Picture Control*.

Scene modes on the mode dial are not very useful in D-Movie mode, or at least they have undocumented effects. These are the creative photography modes on the mode dial, like the Sports, Close up, and Portrait Scene modes. See the section "Full Auto and Scene Modes" in chapter 3, "Exposure Metering System, Exposure Modes, and Histogram," for more information.

When I am videoing, and turn the mode dial to a scene mode, I can see contrast changes in the video with scene modes like landscape. I assume that these modes use various Picture Controls, and I might be seeing them change the scene's contrast as I turn the mode dial.

Since Nikon has chosen to self-control the camera so deeply in D-Movie mode, the scene modes will probably have little effect. In still photography, they modify things like the aperture, shutter speed, and frame rate to obtain certain effects. It is highly unlikely that any of the normal scene mode effects will be applied to the video capture other than Picture Control changes within a mode.

If you would like to experiment, you might discover some useful information. If you do, please let me know, and after I validate it, it may appear in a future book.

Displaying D-Movies

(User's Manual pages 132 and133)

Now, the fun begins! The whole point of this chapter is to allow you to capture some great videos. After reading the previous information and learning about a few "gotchas" described later in this chapter, you'll soon have quite a collection of video clips.

There are three ways to play back one of your cool D-Movies from the camera itself:

- By playing it back on the LCD monitor on the camera's back
- By using the "included in the box" AV cable and connecting to a standard-definition TV (SDTV)
- By using an HDMI cable that you've purchased to connect to a high definition TV (HDTV)

Let's talk about each of these three display methods.

Displaying a D-Movie on the Camera LCD

The method to view a movie on the D5000's LCD screen is simplicity itself, just as capturing a video is. Here are the steps (see *figure 1* to identify the various external controls used):

1. Press the Playback button to start displaying images on the LCD. It's the same button you use to look at a series of your pictures.
2. Locate the video you want to replay by scrolling through your images and videos with the multi selector thumb switch.
3. When the video shows on the D5000's LCD screen, you'll be able to identify it by three signs. On top of the screen you'll see a small D-Movie icon and a minutes and seconds counter, and at the bottom of the screen you'll see the words *OK Play*. The image you see is the first frame of the video (see *figure 9*).
4. Press the OK button, and the video will start playing.

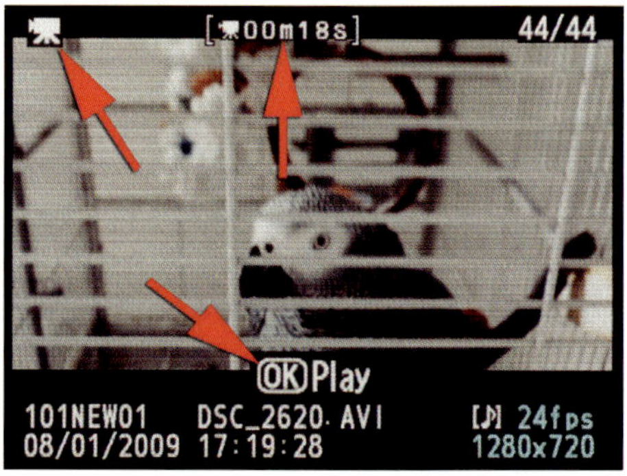

Figure 9 – Viewing a video on the camera screen

The LCD screen on the D5000 is big enough for a couple of people to enjoy one of your videos. Don't be afraid to show off a bit; your camera is one of the first Nikon DSLRs to offer video capture.

Displaying a D-Movie on a Standard-Definition TV (SDTV)

You can plug in the standard AV cable included in the box with your D5000 and display videos directly on your SDTV. The AV cable looks like the one shown in *figure 10*.

This AV cable has a mini USB-style plug that you'll insert into your D5000 and two RCA jacks, yellow and white. The yellow jack carries the video signal, and the white jack carries the mono sound. *Figure 11* shows the port on the side of

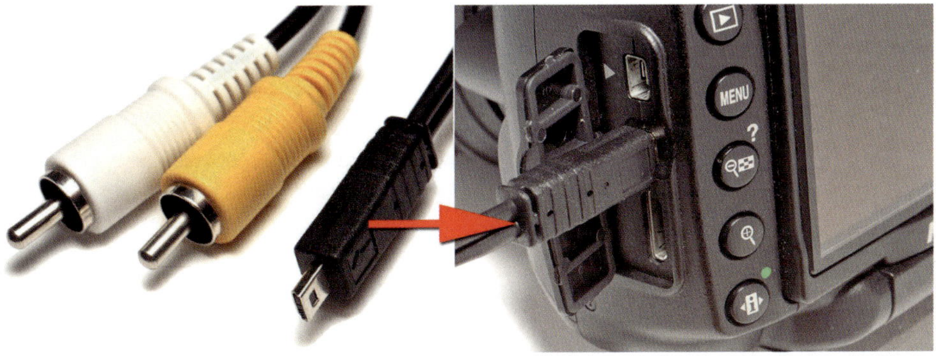

Figure 10 – AV cable for connecting to an SDTV

your D5000 where you'll insert the AV cable's black plug. (Open the plastic flap and find middle AV OUT port.).

Here are the steps to display a video on your SDTV or another device, like a VCR:

1. Turn your camera off temporarily. I never like plugging things into live devices. It may not hurt it, but why take a chance?
2. Open the plastic flap on the left side of your D5000, and insert the AV cable mini USB plug into the middle USB connector (AV OUT port). See *figure 11*.
3. Insert the RCA jacks into their respective ports on the display device. Be sure to match the colors. Yellow is video, white is sound. If your SDTV has no RCA jacks, you can often feed the signal through an attached VCR or DVD player.
4. Set your TV to channel 3, which seems to be the standard for displaying video. (If channel 3 doesn't work, try 4. Consult your TV's manual if those don't work. They should!)
5. Some TVs require you to press a button on the remote that puts it into "video" mode. This drove me crazy at first because I had everything hooked up and no video would show on my TV. I was about to give up when my sweet wife found the TV/Video button on the remote. After pressing that, it worked fine. Thank goodness for wives!
6. Turn on the camera, press the Playback button, and then locate the video you want to show off with the Multi Selector.
7. Press the OK button to play the video on your TV (or record it on your VCR or DVD burner).

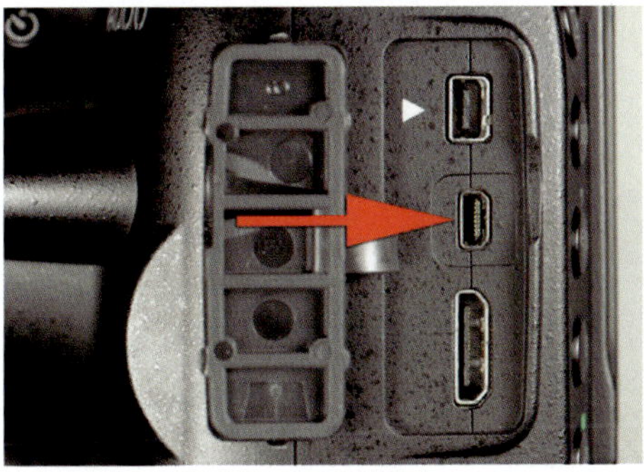

Figure 11 – USB A/V OUT port

I've found that any of the three available video quality modes will display just fine on my older SDTV. I was surprised when the 720p HD mode video played (1280x720). It used the wide-screen format with a black space at the top and bottom of the screen. That's often referred to by the term *letterboxed*. The 640x424 mode video filled the whole TV screen.

You'll enjoy playing video for your family and friends on their TVs. The screen is big enough to see things well, and the video quality is good too.

Displaying a D-Movie on a High-Definition TV (HDTV)

This mode works like the SDTV mode except that you will display your 720p HD videos in their native size and format full-screen on an HDTV. You'll need an HDMI cable with a mini HDMI (Type C) end to insert into your D5000, and the other end will have to match your HDTV's HDMI port, which is usually HDMI Standard (Type A). We'll talk more about the cable specs in a moment, but first let's discuss your camera's HDMI output frequencies.

Before you attempt to connect your Nikon D5000 to your HDTV, be sure that you've correctly configured your HDMI output to match what your HDTV needs or you won't get a picture. Use the *Setup Menu*'s HDMI setting to select a specific output type, or just select *Auto* so that the camera and HDTV can figure it out for you. Next I'll explain the formats and steps.

Select one of the following HDMI output formats in your D5000 (User's Manual page 168):

- ***Auto*** – Allows the camera to select the most appropriate format for displaying on the currently connected device
- ***480p*** *(progressive)* – 640x480 progressive format
- ***576p*** *(progressive)* – 720x576 progressive format
- ***720p*** *(progressive)* – 1280x720 progressive format
- ***1080i*** *(interlaced)* – 1920x1080 interlaced format

Here are the steps to choose a setting (see *figure 12*):

1. Press the MENU button and scroll to the *Setup Menu*.

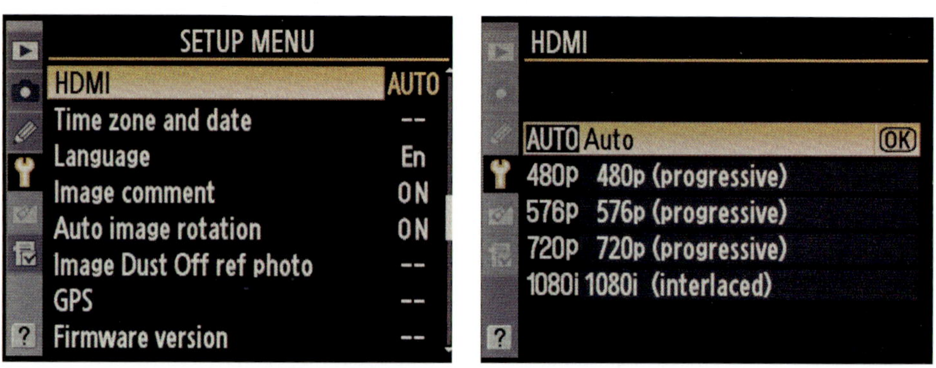

Figure 12 – HDMI formats

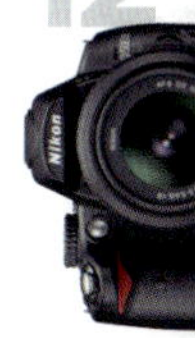

2. Select *HDMI*, and then scroll to the right.
3. Select your choice of modes. (Not sure? Select *Auto*.)
4. Press the OK button.

Now your camera is ready to output video on a compatible HDTV. *Figure 13* shows what a compatible HDMI cable's ends look like. Unfortunately, you'll have to purchase an HDMI cable because one is *not* included in the box with your D5000. The cable you'll need is an HDMI mini (Type C) to HDMI standard (Type A) cable. Adapter cables and plugs for HDMI are readily available at your local Radio Shack or through various online sources.

And, of course, you'll need to plug your HDMI cable into the correct port on the D5000. *Figure 14* provides a look at the port you'll need to use with your HDMI mini (Type C) connector.

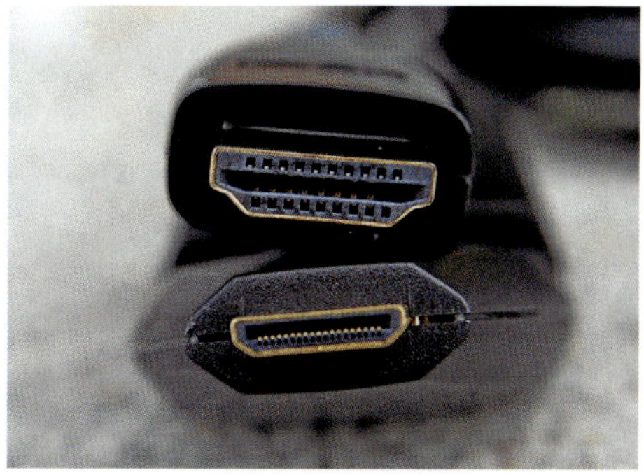

Figure 13 – HDMI standard and mini cable ends

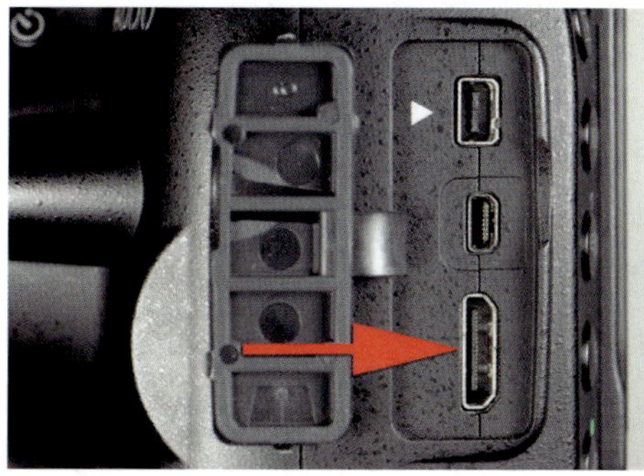

Figure 14 – HDMI mini port on D5000

Once the cable is connected, here are the steps to display a video on your HDTV:

1. Turn your camera off temporarily. Why take a chance on blowing up your camera from a static spark?
2. Open the plastic flap on the left side of your D5000, and insert the HDMI mini (Type C) cable end into the HDMI port (see where the red arrow is pointing in *figure 14*).
3. Insert the HDMI standard (Type A) cable end into one of your HDTV's HDMI ports. (Both video and sound are carried on this one cable.)
4. Your HDTV *may* have multiple HDMI ports, and you may have other devices connected, like a cable box or satellite receiver. If your HDTV has multiple input ports, be sure to select the proper port or you won't see the D5000's video output. You may have to select the input from your remote or use another method. If in doubt, check your HDTV's manual. (If your TV only has one HDMI port, please ignore this step.)
5. Turn on the camera, press the Playback button, and then locate the video you want to show off with the Multi Selector.
6. Press the OK button to play the video on your HDTV.

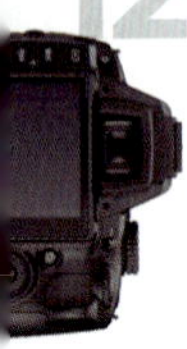

The HDMI display will take the place of the small LCD video monitor on the back of your D5000. The camera monitor will turn off as soon as you connect an HDMI device.

Sound Volume Control

You can raise and lower the playback sound volume using the thumbnail/playback zoom out and playback zoom in buttons (see *figure 1* for button locations). Or, you can turn the TV's volume up or down.

Recommendation

Unless you are heavily into HDMI and understand the various formats, I would just leave the camera set to Auto because that allows the D5000 to determine the proper format as soon as it's plugged into the display device and the HDMI input is selected (if the TV has multiple ports).

Limitations in D-Movie Mode Video Capture

Now let's look at a few limitations in the Nikon D5000's implementation of video capture. No multiuse device can have all the features of a dedicated device, consequently the D5000 has some limitations in how it captures video.

The D5000 uses a CMOS sensor to record video. This type of sensor uses a "rolling shutter" and has three potential issues that we need to discuss: skew, wobble, and partial exposure. We'll discuss each of these in some detail in the following sections.

How the Rolling Shutter Works in D-Movie Mode

Since video is captured at 24 frames per second (fps), the D5000 has an electronic shutter in addition to the normal mechanical shutter.

Have you ever used your D5000 in continuous release mode, where you are capturing up to four still images per second? The mechanical shutter activation combines with mirror movement to make this cool "chicka-chicka-chicka" machine-gun sound that causes passersby—with their little point-and-shoot cameras—to look at you in awe. However, you don't hear that sound when using the D-Movie mode, do you? That's because your D5000 does not use the mechanical shutter when it's shooting movies. If it did, you would wear the camera's shutter out with only an hour or two of video capture. Remember, the camera captures video at 24 fps. An hour of video requires 86,400 frames at that speed. You would quickly exceed the "tested" lifetime 100,000-image capacity of the mechanical shutter.

Instead, the camera uses its electronic shutter capability and turns the sensor's pixel rows on and off as needed in a scan from top to bottom. In other words, the camera records each video frame by scanning it—one line at a time—from top to bottom. Not all parts of the image are recorded at exactly the same time! This can produce a skewed and/or wobbly video with rapidly moving subjects like a race car or flying bird. This is called a *rolling shutter*.

Rolling shutters are used by video cameras that have CMOS sensors, like the Nikon D5000. Most dedicated video cameras have CCD sensors, with global shutters that do not scan the image. They are mostly immune to the effects we are about to discuss.

Here is a list of the effects that can be experienced in extreme circumstances when a CMOS sensor's rolling shutter is used:

- **Skew** – The image leans in one direction or another as the camera or subject moves. This is often seen in the edges of buildings and other static objects.
- **Wobble** – This effect is harder to describe. The whole image wobbles in a strange way. It looks like the top of the image is out of sync with the middle and bottom of the image. Since video is a moving picture, the whole video can wobble back and forth in a very unnatural and dizzying way.
- **Partial exposure** – If another camera's flash goes off in the shot, the burst of light may be present for only some of the rows of pixels in that frame of video. The flash may brightly light the top part of the frame, while the bottom part appears dark. The partial exposure appears as a bright band in one or a few frames, depending on how long the brighter light lasts. Some older forms of fluorescent light have slow ballasts and can cause the video to have a series of moving bands as the light flickers. Our eyes can't see it, but the fast video captures it well. If you are shooting images of an ambulance with its light flashing, it too can cause banding. Anything that has intense bursts of light for short periods may cause partially exposed bands to appear in the video.

To understand skew and wobble better, let's compare the camera to a copy machine or scanner. It works in a similar way. If you place a paper document on a scanner and press the scan button, you'll see the little row of light under the glass travel from the top to the bottom of the document as it records it one line at a time. At the end of the scan, you have a copy of the document in your computer's memory that can be saved to your computer's hard drive. You usually put the scanner's lid down on a paper document to hold it flat and keep it from moving.

Now, let me ask you to imagine something. What if you were scanning a paper document on your desktop scanner and halfway through the scan you moved the paper a little? The top part of the scan would look normal because it had already been captured by the scanner's sensor, but the bottom part of the scan would be at a different angle than the top part, or you could say that it is "skewed" away from the original angle. This is an example of the skew issue I mentioned earlier.

Or, what if you grabbed the paper and rotated it back and forth all the way through the entire scan? The final scanned document would be a series of zigzags, with some parts at one angle and other parts at a different angle. The end result would not be very clear, would it?

This is an example of the wobble issue I mentioned.

The D5000 records video in a similar manner, except much faster than a scanner. It records a frame of video in $1/24^{h}$ of a second, or 24 fps. Since the Nikon D5000 is scanning the image the lens sees at 24 fps, there isn't a problem in most cases. Most movement is too slow to be zigzagged (wobble) or off-angled (skew).

Skew and wobble becomes especially evident when a person is walking and videoing at the same time. The subject of the video is moving, and the person taking the video is moving too. These combined movements can be enough to cause the strange wobbly look to the video. I call this the "jellywobble effect." Your video looks as if it's wobbling like a bowl of Jello. What can you do?

Avoiding the Jellywobble Effect

Primarily, you have to be careful not to allow too much camera movement. It truly is best to use the D5000 on a good quality, fluid-head video tripod if you want great results. I've found that Nikon's vibration reduction (VR) lenses help when you don't want to use a tripod since they stabilize the camera a little. VR won't help much if you're walking while videoing because the camera movements are often too great for the VR system to overcome. If you're standing quietly and doing your best to hold the camera perfectly still, it will help overcome small movements caused by your heartbeat and breathing.

This is one of the main differences between a dedicated video camera and a hybrid like the D5000. Most dedicated video cameras use a CCD sensor instead of a CMOS sensor like the D5000 has. A CCD sensor does not have a rolling shutter but uses a global shutter instead. *Global shutter* simply means that a dedicated video camera is not scanning the image one line at a time. It's using the whole sensor at once to grab the image, not individual lines of the sensor. There are some newer low-cost video cameras on the market that use a rolling shutter, but the better video cameras use a global shutter.

This is probably the worst problem we'll discuss concerning D5000 video. True videophiles will turn up their noses at a rolling shutter. They'll buy a dedicated video camera with three separate CCD sensors—one for each basic RGB color—and efficient global shutters for no jellywobbles. And they'll pay several thousand dollars for the privilege of owning that equipment.

You, however, realize that the D5000 is primarily a very high-quality still camera with added video capabilities. Since video is combined with still image capability, you'll have both with you when carrying your camera. You'll probably be standing in a superstore parking lot one day when an alien spacecraft just happens to land. If that happens, you can get both still images and cool video from the same camera (and a few jellywobbles in your video won't matter). One of the rules for getting great video is having a video camera with you. With the D5000, you have one at all times—with no extra effort. You do keep your camera with you, just in case?

Avoid Jellywobble Effects

Try to hold your camera still and any jellywobble effects will be greatly reduced. Use a tripod when you can, or even a VR lens. Anything that helps stabilize the camera will give you much higher-quality video.

My Conclusions

At the beginning of the chapter I asked a series of questions and will answer them now (my opinion; yours may vary):

Q. How well does D-Movie mode work?

A. It works quite well, is easy to use, and is always with you when you have your Nikon D5000 in your bag.

Q. What are the pros and cons of using the D5000 compared to using a regular video camera?

A. Pros:

1. No need to carry another video camera and bag.
2. Good image quality.
3. Shallow depth of field for cinematic look.
4. Huge variety of lenses available for various effects.
5. Picture Controls give an interesting "look" to the video.
6. Video clips are immediately usable on your computer.
7. People don't know you are videoing when using the D5000.

Cons:

1. CMOS rolling shutter can cause skew, wobble, and partial exposure.
2. Lack of autofocus is difficult for some users.
3. Lack of detailed control over the camera's functions.
4. Short 5-minute video clips in HD mode.
5. Limited storage on memory cards.
6. Basic mono sound quality.

Q. Can the D5000's D-Movie mode replace a dedicated video camera?

A. Yes and no. The fact that it's always with you means that you have it to take video when you otherwise wouldn't. On the other hand, a dedicated video camera will record for hours and hours without stopping. And, since a normal video camera usually has a CCD sensor with a global shutter, you have no rolling shutter effects. The answer to this question will be based on your shooting needs.

Video Editing Software

If you've already been shooting videos and editing them on your computer, you probably won't need much advice. However, if you're new to digital computer movie shooting and editing, you need to know that there are several great programs out there (including some free ones) that allow you to create cool movies with intros and effects.

Here is a list of excellent editing software that you can purchase. Most sell for less than $100:

- Adobe Premier Elements
- Corel VideoStudio
- Roxio Creator
- CyberLink PowerDirector
- Nero

Then, my favorites, a list of freeware and shareware video editing software that you can download online:

- Microsoft Windows Movie Maker (Easiest to get since it is built into Microsoft Windows XP, Service Pack 3 and also available as a free download, and it is easy to use. Search for "Download Windows Movie Maker.")
- Apple iMovie (Free if you buy a new Mac.)
- Avid FreeDV (Available for both PC and Mac.)
- Wax
- Zwei-Stein

Recommendation

If you are using a PC, try Windows Movie Maker. It's the one you've seen advertised on TV where the 7-year-old is assembling movies and pictures into a presentation. If you use a Mac, buy a new one and get iMovie, or check to see if you already have it on your newer Mac. You can purchase it from Apple if you don't. Both programs are easy to use.

I am well pleased with my D5000's D-Movie mode. I have true "video on demand," and I use it often. Until I got the D5000, I had little interest in video, but now I am really enjoying it. You can even sell video clips these days at many stock image sites on the Internet.

When I go up into the ancient Great Smoky Mountains, or cruise the magnificent Blue Ridge Parkway, I now can take great still images as well as set my D5000 up on a tripod to capture some great, relaxing home videos. Later, I can assemble both types of images into a longer presentation combined with music for my family and friends to enjoy. Having HD video capability in our DSLR cameras will revolutionize photography as we know it.

Go make some great videos!

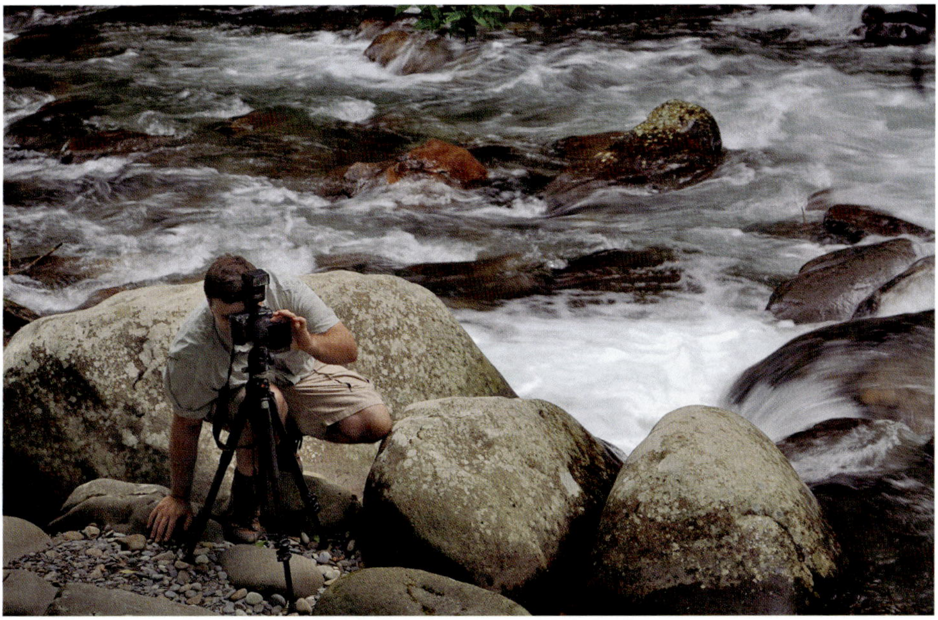

Photographing in Greenbrier in the Great Smoky Mountains

Credits for Chapter Opening Images

Chapter 1

Richerd Reynolds (slartybartfast)
Female Robin on the fence
D5000 and Sigma APO 70-300mm f/4-5.6 DG MACRO
Richerd's Description: Waterloo, ON Canada. I had been playing cat and mouse with this Robin and her mate all spring/summer. One day she actually stayed around long enough for me to grab my camera.
Taken hand held at a distance of approximately 5-6 meters (18-20 ft) at 300mm.

Chapter 2

Gratien Jonxis (gratienjonxis)
Bike Rider
D5000 and AF-S DX VR Zoom-NIKKOR 18-200mm f/3.5-5.6G IF-ED
Gratien's Description: My grandson Maxime (8) riding his brand new bike in my yard on a cloudy July afternoon.
Lens at 56mm – f/4.8 – 1/500 sec – ISO 1000 – AF dynamic.

Chapter 3

Gratien Jonxis (gratienjonxis)
Parachute
D5000 and AF-S DX VR Zoom-NIKKOR 18-200mm f/3.5-5.6G IF-ED
Gratien's Description: Parascending over the sea in Port El Kantaoui (Tunisia) on a sunny afternoon. Shot from the beach.
Lens at 90 mm – f/5.6 – 1/125 sec – ISO 200.

Chapter 4

Edward J. Larsen (el090719)
Key West Light House
AF-S DX NIKKOR 18-55mm f/3.5-5.6G VR
Ed's Description: This is an image of the Key West Lighthouse at Whiteheads Point in Key West, Florida. This picture was taken from the outside second floor veranda of Ernest Hemingway's Home which is located just north of the lighthouse.
1/320 sec – f/9.0 – ISO 200 – Lens at 55mm.

Chapter 5

Richerd Reynolds (slartybartfast)
The Flower and The Fly
D5000 and Sigma APO 70-300mm f/4-5.6 DG MACRO
Richerd's Description: This shot was taken in my back yard in Waterloo, Ontario. The camera was hand held and the lens was set to macro. I was taking some shots of the flowers in my back yard. When this green bottle fly landed a flower beside the one I was shooting, I took advantage of the situation. The D5000 really did a bang up job of handling the colors in this shot.
1/400s - f/8 - ISO 400.

Chapter 6

Gratien Jonxis (gratienjonxis)
Dishes
D5000 and AF-S DX VR Zoom-NIKKOR 18-200mm f/3.5-5.6G IF-ED
Gratien's Description: Typical colorful Tunisian dishes displayed in a store along the marina of Port El Kantaou, Tunisia.
Lens at 46 mm – f/8 – 1/200 sec – ISO 200

Chapter 7

Edward J. Larsen (el090719)

Of Royalty and Obelisks

D5000 and AF-S DX NIKKOR 18-55mm f/3.5-5.6G VR

Ed's Description: This is an image of the memorial obelisk located at the center of Clinton Place Park, Key West, Florida. I focused the camera upon the flowering Royal Poinciana tree branch in the foreground and used the obelisk to add a little depth and contrast to the shot.

1/320 sec - f/9.0 - ISO 200 - Lens at 55mm

Chapter 8

Jose Matutina (ImageHunter)

Yellow and Blue Parrot

D5000 and AF-S DX NIKKOR 35mm f/1.8G

Jose's Description: This is a Lorikeet taken at the Aquarium of the Pacific in Long Beach, CA. No flash or tripod was used since it was a bright sunny day and I was using a fast 35mm f/1.8 prime lens. f/1.8 at 1/160sec.

Chapter 9

Gratien Jonxis (gratienjonxis)

Yellow Building

D5000 and AF-S DX VR Zoom-NIKKOR 18-200mm f/3.5-5.6G IF-ED

Gratien's Description: Typical Berber building in Tunisia—about an hour before sunset in May.

Lens at 18 mm – f/11 – 1/400 sec – ISO 200.

Chapter 10

Ethan Young (DigitalEthan)

Horses at Cades Cove

D5000 and AF-S DX NIKKOR 18-55mm f/3.5-5.6G VR

Ethan's Description: I took this shot in Cades Cove of the Great Smoky Mountains National Park on a trip with my mom, dad, and sisters. It was our first trip of the year to the mountains, and my first time using the Nikon D5000 that Dad gave me. We all had our Nikons with us. The image started off as a horizontal, but I liked the horses so I had Dad crop the right side of the picture into a vertical.

Aperture was f/5.6, shutter speed 1/160 sec at ISO 200.

Chapter 11

Richerd Reynolds (slartybartfast)

Dried flower in Vase

D5000 and Sigma APO 70-300mm f/4-5.6 DG MACRO

Richerd's Description: This dried flower has been a fixture in our living room in Waterloo, Ontario, Canada for a number of years. The camera was hand held using ambient lighting. For this shot, I went manual focus, because the AF was just not hitting the spot where I wanted it (somewhere between the rim of the vase and the flower). I also wanted the image to be somewhat low key, and since this was one of my earliest experiences with the camera (and DSLRs in general), I chose to use one of the scene modes: Silhouette.

1/10s - f/5.6 - ISO 800.

Chapter 12

Darrell Young (DigitalDarrell)

Greenbrier in the Smokies

D5000 and AF-S DX NIKKOR 18-55mm f/3.5-5.6G VR

Darrell's Description: It was a very bright day, allowing for a 1/3 second exposure. To get the water flow correctly in many situations it often takes an exposure of three to four seconds.

Lens at 24mm, f/11, 1/3s, +0.7EV compensation, 100 ISO, Matrix meter, Aperture Priority. Tripod mounted.

Index

D

E

F

H

I

J

L

M

N

P

R

S

W